# Final Report

## of the

# School Board

# for London,

## 1870—1904.

FIVE SHILLINGS.

# FINAL REPORT

OF THE

# SCHOOL BOARD FOR LONDON

1870—1904.

# FINAL REPORT

OF THE

# SCHOOL BOARD FOR LONDON,

## 1870–1904.

WITH THE

## *VALEDICTORY ADDRESS*

OF

### *THE RIGHT HONOURABLE THE*

## LORD REAY, G.C.S.I., G.C.I.E.,

CHAIRMAN OF THE BOARD.

## SECOND EDITION: REVISED.

**London:**

P. S. KING & SON,

2 AND 4, GREAT SMITH STREET, VICTORIA STREET,
WESTMINSTER, S.W.

1904.

LONDON:

PRINTED BY ALEXANDER AND SHEPHEARD, LTD.,

NORWICH STREET, FETTER LANE, E.C.

A. & S.—C. 349—750—30.4.04.

# CONTENTS.

# VALEDICTORY ADDRESS

DELIVERED BY

*THE RIGHT HONOURABLE THE*

## LORD REAY, G.C.S.I., G.C.I.E.,

AT THE

## FINAL MEETING OF THE SCHOOL BOARD FOR LONDON,

ON

*THURSDAY, APRIL 28th, 1904.*

IT is an unusual occurrence in the history of English Institutions that a local authority should be called into existence without having any predecessor to whose duties it succeeded, and that its existence should be of short duration. The School Board was the creation of the Act of 1870, and its extinction is due to the Act of 1903. It has achieved its record within the short space of one generation, without any guidance from the operations of a preceding authority, whose experience might have been useful to it. It was compelled to break entirely new ground, and to solve a problem which had perplexed Parliament for the greater part of a century.

On the eve of resigning into other hands the powers and duties which the Board has exercised for 34 years, a retrospective review of the work which the Board has accomplished will, I think, prove interesting. Such a review is placed in your hands to-day. It has been prepared with great care, and it deals with the work of the Board in all its diversified aspects. It narrates the manifold difficulties which the Board has had to overcome, and the manner in which it has dealt with them. It sounds, I hope, no unduly triumphant note of praise, and it describes errors as well as successes. As a handbook for those who succeed us it should prove useful in showing where continuity of administration is essential, and where reform of methods is possible.

Some change in the form of administration of our educational system was probably inevitable, on account of the advances which have been made in Elementary and Secondary Education since 1870, and of the consequent external pressure which has been brought to bear upon the Board to extend the scope of its operations. Although the popular interest in education is not even now so strong as we could wish it to be, it must be admitted that it is far greater than it was in 1870, and that since that date its growth has been continuous. For many years the Board was the only organised authority upon which this pressure could make itself felt, and it has forced the Board into activities which have since been decided by the courts of law to be outside the legal scope of the Elementary Education Acts.

But it must be remembered that the authors of the Act of 1870 anticipated, and intended to provide for, some such progressive expansion. Mr. W. E. Forster, speaking on the First Reading of the Bill, said: " We are aware that by no Bill dealing with this matter can we hope to effect real good unless it be a Bill which does not merely meet present necessities, but is also capable of development so as to meet the necessities of the future. Indeed, no Bill would really meet the needs of to-day unless its provisions are likewise adapted to meet the needs of to-morrow." [1]

This was a statesmanlike policy, but one which of necessity, after the lapse of time, must lead to difficulties of interpretation. Such a policy involves a lack of definiteness in expression when formulated in an Act of Parliament, which, sooner or later, gives rise to doubt as to the limits of the powers to be exercised. It was in pursuance of this policy that the Act did not contain two definitions of prime importance: (1) A definition of "a child"; and (2) a definition of the scope of "Elementary Education."

With regard to the age of children attending school, Mr. Forster said, in the speech from which I have already quoted: "Look at the ages of the children with whom we have to deal. The great majority are probably under ten years of age; but some are over that age, and under twelve, and I fear that but comparatively few are over twelve and under fourteen." [2] It is to be noted also that the first draft of the Bill made twelve the maximum age for the permissive compulsion which it was proposed to enact. The age was raised to thirteen in Committee.

With regard to Elementary Education, the limits which then prevailed, and, indeed, were possible, were extremely narrow. The Code of the Education Department for 1870 recognised Reading, Writing and Arithmetic only for all standards, and one specific subject for children beyond Standard VI.

If, therefore, the current ideas as to the limits of age and the scope of Elementary Education had been embodied in the Act in the form of definitions, all natural progress might have been greatly hindered. The growing desire of parents to keep their children longer at school might have failed in its intent: the growing capacity of the children to receive a broader and more liberal education might have been artificially checked. To afford freedom for the operation of these forces, Acts of Parliament would have been necessary for the removal of the artificial impediments imposed by the Act, and the inevitable delay would have been disastrous. The indefiniteness of the Act of 1870 has been the foundation of much of our progress in Elementary Education.

Yet it was precisely this indefiniteness which caused the recent educational crisis, and rendered further legislation imperative. The Judges of the High Court, when they were called upon to decide certain questions recently in dispute, found no statutory definition of "a child." They were, therefore, compelled to infer one, which rendered illegal the greater part of the Board's work in Evening Schools and Pupil Teachers' centres. They also failed to find any complete definition of "Elementary Education," and they were compelled to infer one which affected the Board's work in Evening schools, Pupil Teachers' centres and Higher Grade schools. The permanent solution

---

[1] Hansard, Vol. 199, col. 439.          [2] *Ib.*, col. 457.

which Parliament has devised for these difficulties ‿ to be found in the Acts of 1902 and 1903.

Until the time of the legal decisions to which I have referred, the expansion of the Board's work proceeded without artificial interruption. This expansion has two aspects: it is due, on the one hand, to causes which may be termed natural, namely, the immense increase in the size and population of London. On the other hand, it is due to an impetus to which I have already slightly alluded, and is intellectual in its origin, namely, the increased receptivity and capacity of the children attending Public Elementary schools.

The expansion which is due to natural causes is amazing. Since 1871 the population of London has grown from 3,261,000 to 4,536,000 in 1901, a total increase of 1,275,000 persons. It is difficult to realise the full meaning of these figures. I may, perhaps, be allowed to illustrate it by the fact that the increase of the population of London during the period mentioned is greater than the combined populations of Manchester and Liverpool in 1901. It would be necessary to add to these the population of Darlington to establish an equilibrium. Or, to put it in another way, the number of inhabited houses in London has grown from 418,802 in 1871 to 574,346 in 1901, an increase of 155,544. The total number of inhabited houses in Liverpool in 1901 was only 123,469. Still more remarkable is the increase in the ratable value of the Metropolis. In 1872 it was nearly £20,000,000, in 1903 it was nearly £40,000,000. Thus, though the population has increased by 39 per cent., and inhabited houses have increased by 37 per cent., the ratable value has increased by 100 per cent.

The low average standard of capacity of the children in and about 1870 may best be illustrated from contemporary records. But it must not be forgotten that a large number of children never attended school at all: that a great proportion of those who attended schools were not in "efficient" schools, even according to the standard of efficiency then prevalent; and that before 1870 there were no compulsory Bye-laws.

This is what one of H.M. Inspectors said of "efficient" schools in 1869:—

"I have experienced one difficulty in connection with the examination of the children in several of these elementary schools. . . . *eg.* boys and girls attending school at the age of 9, 10 and 11 years, may be in school nearly two years before they are examined in the second standard,[1] and from this cause they will in all probability never rise to the upper standard at all. It is this hanging down at the bottom of the school, this lingering at doing almost nothing, which appears to me to be one of the great barriers to the advance of elementary education in our schools . . . As long as a period of two and a-half years is allowed for boys and girls who are over the age of

---

[1] The subjects of examination in Standard II. were :—

Reading.—One of the narratives next in order after monosyllables in an elementary reading-book used in the school.

Writing.—Copy in manuscript character a line of print.

Arithmetic.—A sum in simple addition or subtraction and the multiplication table.

The grant was withheld if the girls were not taught Plain Needlework.

infants on admission to arrive at Standard III., I see no hope of the great body of children ever being presented in the upper standards." [1]

It is worth while to refer to this definite statement upon the subject of the capacity of the children for the purpose of gauging the progress which has been made. In the Report which is before you the present relation of ages of children to standards is analysed and discussed. [2] It is not pretended that this relation is altogether satisfactory : it is shown that the actual average age of passing into the lower standards is considerably above the " ideal" age. But, when that is admitted, the facts nevertheless demonstrate what vast strides have been taken in the improvement of the intellectual capacity of the children since the gloomy report which I have quoted was submitted to the Education Department.

Nor was the condition of affairs much improved even after compulsion had been enforced for four years. Sir Charles Reed, in his annual address to the Board in 1874, said : "Of the school work and its results I do not say one word. It is too soon altogether to speak upon the question. Tens of thousands of children are in our schools who are, I regret to say, grossly ignorant and utterly uninstructed, and the only thing we can do is to look to their cleanliness and give them habits of order, and promote their regularity of attendance, and then leave the question of results ; quite certain that, with good schools and most efficient teachers—all schools being now full—the results are sure to follow. [3]

I will only call one more witness, and that one of the highest authority. Mr. Matthew Arnold in 1874 said, in regard to our system of Elementary Education : " The weakness is the unawakened and uninformed minds of the majority of our school children. even of those who can pass the examination in Reading, Writing, and Arithmetic, and sometimes in an extra subject or two besides. This exceeds, so far as my observation goes, anything of the kind to be found in the schools of other countries." [4]

Such was the material with which the Board had to deal when it first assumed the duties which had been imposed upon it. Its condition was the result of long years of neglect, and its improvement required long years of labour before any amelioration was observable. The task of providing sufficient school accommodation was one which necessarily absorbed much time, and until the schools were erected little progress could be made. The reports of H.M. Inspectors during the first ten years of the Board's work did not indicate any very definite improvement in the intellectual condition of the scholars, although hints of promise for the future were not lacking, and praise was given to the methods and energy of the teaching staff. [5] The social and moral influence of the schools was also strongly asserted [6] ; but even during the decade 1881-1890 little was said that showed more than a very slow improvement in intellectual capacity. The first definite recognition of such a result occurs in a report

[1] Education Department Report, 1869-70, pp. 243-4.
[2] See pp. 152-158.
[3] *School Board Chronicle*, October 3rd, 1874, p. 320.
[4] Education Department Report, 1874-5, p. 30.
[5] See *Ib.*, 1877-8, p. 401 ; 1878-9, p. 550 ; 1881-2, p. 445.
[6] *Ib.*, 1880-1, p. 238.

made in 1891, when H.M. Inspector wrote : " The large proportion of full grants obtained in London schools, both Board and Voluntary, shows conclusively that the full number of subjects [obligatory, class, and specific] is, as a rule, taught with great intelligence and success. The highest grant for elementary subjects cannot be paid in schools for older scholars unless a high degree of accuracy and intelligence has been reached in regard to all elementary subjects (a similarly high standard is required in the class and specific subjects)." [1]

The same note has been dominant ever since, and statistics confirm the conclusions of trained observation. In 1873 only 2·2 per cent. of the children in the Board's schools were in standards above the third; in 1903 the percentage stood at 30·0. In 1886 only 1·2 of the children were in the Seventh and ex-Seventh Standards; in 1903 the percentage had risen to 4·4. Further evidence on this question will be found in the chapter on Curriculum in the Report.

The slow rate of improvement was due not only to the low capacity of the children, but to the low standard of education which existed in 1870, and to the almost impossible conditions under which it was in many cases imparted. It is difficult to realise the educational destitution of London at that time. I will quote one illustration, out of several given in the Report, of the condition of a school existing so late as 1874, which was only tolerated because no sufficient supply of efficient school places existed. The words are those of an Inspector appointed by the Board in 1874 to examine into the condition of certain schools. " Some idea," he wrote, " of the inefficient state of this school may be formed from the fact that not one scholar out of fifty, ranging from eight to eleven years of age, could pass in the easy Arithmetic required—in other words, not one of them could go as far as simple short division. Further, one child out of fifteen ranging from six to eight years of age, could write the letters of the alphabet from dictation. As regards the accommodation provided, thirty-six young children were sitting in an upper room into which the rays of the sun, on a bright day in June, could not enter—twilight in midday. Coming to the question of teaching staff, one teacher, a master, was present on the day of inspection; one teacher for 128 children, and he an earnest, hardworking missionary." [2]

Such conditions as these were possible in London four years after the German schoolmaster had transformed the face of central Europe; after the great exhibitions in London had taught us the conditions of industrial and artistic development abroad; at a time when English Literature, Science and Art were conspicuous by the great leaders of the Victorian era.

Much of the progress that has been made is doubtless attributable to the wise policy adopted by the Board of leaving a large amount of discretion to the head teacher of each department in fixing the curriculum. This policy has encouraged experiment, has utilised the special knowledge of various teachers to the greatest extent, and has enabled them to adapt the curriculum to local requirements. Much of that progress is also due to the high ideal set before the Board and the public by the Committee appointed by

---

[1] Education Department Report, 1891-2, p. 424.    [2] See pp. 10, 11.

the first Board to consider curriculum, of which no less an expert than Professor Huxley was the Chairman. In the report of that Committee, which was doubtless inspired to a great extent by its Chairman, the following subjects were stated to be essential:—The Bible and the Principles of Religion and Morality, taught in accordance with the famous "compromise," which the Board had already adopted; Reading, Writing, Arithmetic, English Grammar and Composition, Book-keeping in the Senior schools, and Mensuration in Senior Boys' Schools, systematised Object Lessons, embracing in the six school years a course of Elementary instruction in Physical Science, and serving as an introduction to the Science examinations conducted by the Science and Art Department; the History of England, Elementary Geography, Elementary Social Economy, Elementary Drawing, Music and Drill, Plain Needlework and Cutting-out in Girls' departments. The discretionary subjects were:—Domestic Economy,[1] Algebra and Geometry.[2] The Report is an important document, as it shows the opinion prevailing at the time among educationists with regard to what was desirable. How far the scheme was from any approach to realisation may be measured by the fact that in the year ended December, 1873, the numbers of children who earned grant in specific subjects were as follows:—Geography, 150; Grammar, 70; History, 42; Algebra, 6; and Animal Physiology, 2. In 1876 the number of children earning grant in specific subjects had risen to 3,381, and in 1903 the number receiving instruction in "optional" subjects was 185,611. The history of the development of teaching in class and specific subjects is clearly set out in the tables and diagrams given in the section on "Curriculum."[3]

The next important changes in the curriculum were introduced in 1888 on the report of a Committee appointed in 1887 to consider the subjects and modes of instruction in the Board's schools. Its main object was to secure "that children leaving school should be more fitted than they now are to perform the duties and work of life before them." As a consequence, Manual Training, Slöjd, Mechanics, Practical Geometry, Hand and Eye Training, and Cookery for girls, were given a prominent place in the curriculum. Intelligence in reading was to be encouraged; and it was laid down that "reading-books should be for imparting a knowledge of Geography, History, Social Economy, and Facts of Common Life to all children who may not be able to take these subjects for examination."[4] The development of Manual Training for boys and of the teaching of Domestic Subjects to girls was to a great extent the result of the co-operation of the City and Guilds of London with the Board. Before these subjects were included in the Code the teaching was carried on by a Joint Committee of members of the Guilds and of the Board, the necessary funds being provided by the Drapers' Company and the City and Guilds of London Institute. This Joint Committee commenced their operations in 1887. The initiative of the Board and of the Joint Committee had an important influence upon the policy of the Education Department. The subjects taught were sooner or later included in the Code as grant-earning subjects.

---

[1] This subject was substituted by the Board for "Latin or a Modern Language" in the original scheme.

[2] See pp. 94, 95.
[3] See pp. 127-131.
[4] See pp. 96-98.

The institution of the "block" grant in 1900 was another important phase in the history of the curriculum. It was the result of a conviction in educational circles that a curriculum should constitute an organic whole, and that the time-table should be judged, not on its details, but as an harmonious entity. Overpressure can be avoided when subjects are properly co-ordinated.

One curious feature in the history of English education has been the slight value which has been attached to the teaching of English. Although the Code, before 1900, dealt in a meagre and spasmodic manner with this important subject, neither the Department nor the Board seem to have considered that a full command of their own language, such as is obtained in the Elementary schools of the United States, Germany, and France, ought to be acquired by all children before leaving school. The Code of 1900 has assigned to English its proper place in the curriculum, and I trust that we shall emulate the Americans in the attention that they bestow on this subject.

History shared in the neglect of English until the appearance of the Code of 1900. The Board has provided for its proper teaching, which is essential in countries which are self-governed, if the citizen is to discharge his public duties with a sense of the magnitude of the issues which are at stake.

From the beginning, the Board, under the guidance of Professor Huxley and Dr. Gladstone, have paid attention to the claims of Elementary Science, which in Boys' departments allies itself with the quantitative work and Mechanical Drawing in the Manual Training school, and in Girls' departments with the training which they receive in the Domestic Economy centres.

Drawing has always received much attention, and the success with which it has been taught has been publicly demonstrated at the annual exhibitions of the work of the scholars which have been held by the Board. The present system of teaching is largely experimental, and leaves the teachers a selection out of three syllabuses.

Vocal Music has from the first been taught in the schools. This is another of the few subjects with regard to which it is possible to submit results to the public judgment. Those who have heard the refined singing of school choirs at the Crystal Palace will hardly believe that, in 1873, the Singing Instructor reported that in the schools "the singing generally is fearfully coarse and noisy, the boys especially singing with all the force they can command." [1]

No subject has given rise to less difficulty in the schools than the teaching of the Scriptures, and we may feel a legitimate satisfaction that throughout the country the syllabus of the School Board for London has been quoted with approval. The excellent results of this teaching, due to the discrimination of the teachers, have been admitted by all impartial critics. Hundreds of thousands of children have reaped the benefit of the illuminating pages of Holy Writ, and in after life will have realised, amidst the vicissitudes of their existence, how much they owe to the teachers who, through this teaching, created an atmosphere which permeated the day's work.

The physical training of the children has from the first received attention, and the

---

[1] Board Minutes, Vol. II., p. 744.

methods of instruction have been carefully considered and developed. This training is of supreme importance for the youth of a crowded city, and it is supplemented in many schools by the organisation of outdoor sports and games, under the auspices of Managers and Teachers.

The merit certificate provides a good stimulus to effort, and will, it may be hoped, become an object of ambition to both parents and children. It has none of the defects which are inherent in competitive examinations, which do not take into account the previous teaching, and it is easily obtained by those who have made a fair use of the instruction which they have received.

One of the causes of the improvement in the education of the children has been the greater regularity of attendance. In 1871, when it may be assumed that only those children were in school whose parents were anxious to have them educated, the percentage stood at 78·3, but this percentage was not again reached until 1877. In 1881 the percentage of average attendance had risen to 79·7, but it was not until the year 1895 that so high a percentage was again reached. In the following year it was 80·4, and there was no very great improvement until 1899, when the percentage was 81·2. But in 1901 the percentage had risen to 82·4, and from that time each year has shown a very considerable improvement; the percentage for 1902-3 being 85·6. I am informed that the figures for 1903-4 will in all probability show a further improvement of 1·6 per cent., making a percentage of 87·2.

As a natural result of the development of the work in the lower standards, it became necessary to improve the higher standards, and this led to the organisation of Higher Grade schools. The character of these schools is undoubtedly elementary, not secondary. They provide for children who, though unable to go to Secondary schools, can give a longer time to education than the bulk of their comrades. The Board of Education, by their Minute on Higher Elementary schools, admitted the need for such schools; but they gave to them a less elastic character than the Board has given to the Higher Grade schools. I have no doubt that these schools will receive from the new Education Authority the attention they deserve as the coping stone of the structure of elementary education.

A further natural development of the teaching in the Day schools was the instruction in Evening schools, in order to prevent wastage in the results obtained by the Day schools. No stronger evidence of the transformation which has come over our system of education during the lifetime of the Board is to be found than in the history of these classes. In 1870 the Evening school was a place where the uneducated adult endeavoured to acquire some rudiments of education. As the work of the Day school began to tell upon the education of the people, such institutions became less and less necessary, and the desideratum was an Evening school which would carry on and expand the work of the Day school. The difficulty which was experienced in enabling the Evening school to adapt itself to altered circumstances is told in the Report.[1] In the absence of compulsion, and of all means of ensuring

---

[1] See pp. 284-290.

regularity of attendance, except by making the schools attractive, the results obtained by a carefully selected body of teachers, under circumstances of great difficulty, must be considered, on the whole, satisfactory. The great drawback undoubtedly is irregularity of attendance.

A third offshoot from the Day school must not be passed over. The establishment of centres for the training of physically and mentally defective children is a comparatively recent development under special statutory provisions. The admirable work which has been done for the blind, the deaf, the cripples, and the feeble-minded is, I believe, universally recognised.

Nor must I pass over the work of another department of the Board's activities which, as a rule, receives less public recognition than it deserves. The work of the Industrial Schools Committee is so complicated, is involved in so much detail, and requires so much tact and discretion in its administration, that it might well absorb the energies of a single authority. I believe that the work of reclamation which the Committee has carried on has met with singular success, and that the public are hardly aware of how much they have done for the well-being of those unfortunate children who are born into evil surroundings.

I have dealt thus fully with the school, and the adjuncts to the school, because they are, after all, the kernel of the Board's work. The other sections of that work, vast and important as they are, are ancillary to the main educational object. It appears to be undoubted that the number of children who needed educational provision when the Board commenced work in 1870 was at least a quarter of a million, although the Board did not at first recognise the full extent of the deficiency. From that time up to the present the Board have provided 559,667 places in permanent schools, and a large number of school places are projected. There are now 475 permanent schools. We are so used to the sight of the handsome school buildings which are such prominent features in most parts of London, that we are apt to think that the type has been long established. The fact is that, in 1870, a satisfactory plan for a school building was non-existent. The Board had to create it, and the process of evolution was lengthy. The story of it is told in the Report, and the genesis of the modern school-house is illustrated by plans.[1] It was inevitable that the earlier schools built by the Board should prove defective in the light of accumulated experience, and many of these have had to be altered so as to bring them into harmony with the present standard of efficiency. For many years past central halls have been provided in all new schools, and the class-rooms are not, as a rule, planned for such large numbers as was formerly the case. The Board of Education's new rules for planning require that, except in special circumstances, schools should not be of more than two storeys, and, if possible, of only one. Apart from the cost of site, the one-storey school is cheaper, and more convenient for teaching purposes. The architect in planning a school has to depend on the instructions he receives from educational experts with regard to the purposes for which accommodation is to be provided.

---

[1] See pp. 34-40 and 60-72.

The total expenditure which has been incurred, up to September 29th, 1903, upon the purchase of 531 sites, amounts to £3,832,818, together with a sum of £522,192 for costs. The total area of these sites is 493 acres. The expenditure upon Loan Account for building Day schools has been rather more than £14,000,000, and the total expenditure upon Loan Account has been £14,567,256. Of this sum, £3,695,957 has been repaid.

The cost of maintenance per child has steadily grown. In 1890 the average annual gross cost was £3 8s. 8d. per child, and the net cost £2 1s. 8d. In 1903 these figures stood at £4 2s. 9d. and £3 2s. respectively. The most serious item in this cost is the salaries of the teachers. This has grown from £2 10s. 6d. per child in 1890 to £3 14s. 8d. in 1903. The difficult question of the scale of teachers' salaries is one from which the Board has rarely been free. The history of it has been given in some detail in the Report,[1] not only because of the magnitude of the interests involved, but also because finality has not yet been reached.

As the Board has required a supply of about 1,000 teachers per annum, it has been very directly interested in the increase of facilities for their training. The training of pupil teachers has, therefore, engaged the attention of the Board continuously. The whole tendency of the Board's schemes has been to decrease the amount of time given by the pupil teacher to teaching in the Day school, and to increase the time devoted to instruction at the centre. That the work has been done well is proved by the fact that the Board of Education has relaxed its claim to examine the pupil teachers periodically, and has accepted in substitution the examinations of the Board. I have no doubt that the County Council will give to this subject of training teachers the attention that it deserves. The supply of trained teachers is very much below the demand, and great difficulty is experienced in filling vacancies.

To the individual relations of the Members of the Board with the schools under their charge, with the Managers, with the teachers, and with the parents of the children must be attributed much of the smooth working of the system of elementary education in London and of the progress which has been made. Being in close touch with the practical work of the schools, Members were able to speak from personal experience in committees, and at the meetings of the Board. Teachers were always able to state their views informally to the Member who was responsible for the schools in which they served. The Board was not merely a debating assembly for the purpose of discussing abstract educational problems, and leaving to executive officers the duty of carrying out its resolutions; it exercised the double function of laying down the principles which were to govern its activity, and of seeing how they were carried into effect and watching the results. To this mode of procedure, and to the constant exertions of individual Members of the Board, the success of the Board's work is largely due. Our proceedings would have been much more cumbrous if Members of the Board had relied only on official reports, and not also on their own supervision. Questions could be quickly settled in Committee, and at the Board, notwithstanding elaborate agenda, because members were fully acquainted with their merits.

---

[1] See pp. 161-177.

If the Bye-laws have been administered without undue friction, this must also be attributed, to a great extent, to the personal intervention of members of the Board. It is this personal interest of members of the central authority in the details of the work which has given to that work its humanising character, and has prevented it from degenerating into mere bureaucratic routine. The presence on the Board of men and women who were prepared to devote themselves, in the spirit which I have described, to the educational interests of the children committed to their care has infused vitality into the work. The ratepayers have been fortunate in being able to secure from the first the services of a succession of members of whom a large number have been able to make the work of education the chief occupation of their lives. In dealing with the moral and intellectual development of human beings, personal influence is a paramount condition of success.

The administration of schools differs from the administration of other undertakings which do not require constant personal attention, and admit of delegation on a more or less extended scale. The neglect of details in education might easily lead to inefficiency and failure. For this reason the School Board has not been able to delegate duties which were seemingly unimportant, but which, in the aggregate, determined the character of the education given in the schools. Delegation would have complicated, not simplified, the work by multiplying references. I am well aware that the American system is the exact opposite of ours : responsibility is concentrated in a superintendent. If any difficulty were experienced here in finding men and women who were prepared to undertake these arduous duties, we should most probably have to accept the American system ; but while their co-operation can be obtained, it is undoubtedly politic to utilise it. Of its beneficial influence upon our Day, Evening, Industrial, and Special schools since the Act of 1870 came into force, no one who has followed the course of events can have any doubt. The condition of the masses is still far from satisfactory ; but it is appalling to think what it would have been if School Boards had not performed their duties in the spirit which I have attempted to describe.

We transfer to the new Education Authority an administration which has grown to its present dimensions concurrently with the expansion of the Metropolis. We place at their disposal a staff of experienced officials, some of whom have grown grey in our service, all of whom have served us with zeal. We transfer a large staff of teachers, to whose exertions the efficiency of the schools is mainly due, and London has every reason to appreciate the devotion with which they discharge their duties, often under many discouragements and difficulties. The organisation of elementary education in London is very superior to that of secondary and higher education, for which much remains to be done. The rate of progress since the Act of 1870 came into operation has been very marked. The rate of progress during the next thirty years cannot be the same, but I have no doubt that we shall witness further progress, and that the children will leave school always better equipped for the battle of life.

I consider it a privilege to have been closely connected with all grades of education in London, and with the men and women who play a leading part in controlling them.

I have invariably met on this Board with the cordial co-operation of my colleagues, and I desire to tender them my sincere thanks for the confidence which they have placed in me, notwithstanding their knowledge of the very strong convictions that I hold with regard to the principles which should obtain in the development of a national system of education. I have never, I hope, had any difficulty in showing due regard for the convictions of others.

I desire to express on behalf of the Board sincere thanks to the Local Managers of schools, and to all other persons who have voluntarily given their services to the promotion of the work of the Board, to the encouragement of social undertakings, and to the administration of charitable relief in our schools. This work has been done so unostentatiously, and the workers have so little sought the meed of public praise, that it is in danger of being overlooked. I can only say that the value of such services to the cause of education is immeasurable.

I offer my sincere thanks to the officials of the Board and to the teaching staff. I have always found them able and willing to enlighten me on all questions relating to the Board's work.

No one who has not been associated with the management of schools in London can have any idea of the intricacy, and of the delicate nature, of the problems which are constantly arising, or of the magnitude of the task which now devolves upon the London County Council. Those who are engaged in this vast field of operations, in all parts of this great metropolis, are entitled to the support of all who desire that the schools of London should contribute to the greatness of the Empire. Our prosperity depends to a large extent on the training given to the children, who are the heirs of that vast inheritance transmitted to us by the energy of our ancestors, which will require all the sagacity of future generations to maintain and to develop, and upon which we invoke God's blessing.

# FINAL REPORT

OF THE

# SCHOOL BOARD FOR LONDON

---

## THE PROVISION OF ACCOMMODATION.

### I.—THE FIRST STATISTICS.

IN a record of the work accomplished by the London School Board it is advisable, at the very outset, to make it clear that the extent of the educational destitution of London, at the time of the passing of the Elementary Education Act of 1870, was not fully realised by the first Board. Indeed, there can be no doubt that the Board greatly under-estimated the deficiency of school places in the Metropolis. Had they adopted the theoretical basis, which had been approved by the Education Department prior to 1870, that one-sixth of the population required Elementary school provision, which experience had proved to be practically correct, a deficiency of over a quarter of a million of Elementary school places would have been shown at the time the first School Board made their inquiry into the school needs of London.

The reasons are not recorded which induced the Board to reject this method of ascertaining the number of school places necessary[1]; but, in all probability, the very magnitude of the deficiency which this basis of computation would have disclosed made the Board shrink from adopting it. The experience, however, of later years has shown the general accuracy of the method. In fact, the Board's own figures for the year 1887 showed a number of children needing Elementary school places equal to one-sixth of the whole population of London, and since that date the proportion has considerably increased.

Consequently, it must be assumed that the best means of ascertaining the amount of work before the School Board at its inception would have been that which, in practice, has proved trustworthy. Therefore, the estimates of the first Board which set out the deficiency as 103,863 must be considered as falling far short of the actual requirements at the time.

Section 67 of the Act of 1870 required that, within four months from the date of the election of the Chairman of the London School Board, a Return should be submitted to the Education Department containing such particulars with respect to Elementary schools and children requiring Elementary Education as the Department might

---

[1] An apology for it will be found in the Board Minutes, Vol. III., p. 1072.

B

demand; and Section 68 provided that the Department should draw up the necessary forms for this purpose. The Chairman of the first Board was elected on December 15th, 1870. On February 1st, 1871, the Board had officially before them a communication from the Department, dated December 23rd, 1870, which forwarded a copy of a circular letter addressed to all the School Boards which had been constituted. This letter was designated Circular 86, and it was the first intimation of the nature and extent of the Department's requirements under Section 67 of the Act. The following extracts from the Circular show how comprehensive were the demands of the Department :—

My Lords would be glad to receive from the Board . . . a Report showing :—1. The number of children . . . for whom means of Elementary Education should be provided—(a) between the ages of three and five, and (b) between the ages of five and thirteen. 2. The provision to meet the requirements of these children, which the Board considers to be—(a) already supplied by efficient schools, or (b) likely to be supplied by schools either contemplated or in course of erection. 3. The deficiency (if any) in the supply of efficient Elementary Education for the borough, as shown by comparing 1 and 2. 4. By means of what schools the Board would propose to supply this deficiency. 5. The precise localities in which such schools will be needed.

This Report should be supported by detailed information respecting the individual schools which the Board take into account, either as efficient or otherwise. Separate schedules should, therefore, be carefully prepared and appended to the Report, setting forth the name, description (whether for Boys, Girls, Mixed, or Infants), situation, superficial and cubical area (in school and class-rooms), and average attendance of each of the schools from which returns have been received, which the Board propose to classify, as :—

I.—*Supplying efficient Elementary Education.*—These schools should be arranged under the following heads :—(a) Schools now in receipt of annual grants from this Department; (b) schools not receiving such grants, but which will be conducted as public Elementary schools, and will seek annual aid; (c) schools which will not seek annual aid; (d) private adventure schools (to which no annual grants can be made).

II.—Not *supplying efficient education.*—Under this head, the Board should point out the schools or buildings which, with improvements, might be recognised as efficient, and the steps recommended to be taken for making them so.

III.—*Required to complete the school supply.* . . .

According to the Act, the whole of this information should have been supplied to the Department within four months from the date of the election of the Chairman of the Board. This was, of course, found to be absolutely impossible. Still, the Board evidently set to work upon this stupendous task in the hope of at least fulfilling some of the requirements of the Department by the specified time. Indeed, they had appointed, so early as January 5th, 1871, a Special Committee for making the Returns, and even before the Circular from the Department had been laid before the Board, this Committee had selected Agents to make the first part of the inquiry, and they had made the following arrangements for conducting the inquiry :—

Every Agent to be provided with—(1) A list of schools in each district known to the Education Department, the National Society, the British and Foreign School Society, the Wesleyan, and the Roman Catholic School Societies, and others; (2) a sufficient number of " Educational Returns," so that two copies could be filled up for every school, one copy for the Education Department, and another for the use of the Board.

The teachers to be requested to fill up the "Returns" in duplicate, but in case of any difficulty, then the Agent to do this himself. If any Sub-agents required, they could be employed with the sanction of the Members of the Board who nominated the principal Agents for each Division. To each Member so nominating shall be sent ten copies of the " Letter of Instructions," to be given to the Agents and Sub-agents by him.

Public notice to be given in each Division that "Educational Returns " are required by the Board, and all Managers and teachers of existing Elementary schools, whether public or private, and all promoters of projected schools, to be invited to make application for copies of ' Returns,' if they have not received them from the Agents for the Division, such application to be addressed to the Clerk of the Board, and marked outside with the words, ' Statistical Returns.' The Public Notices to be advertised in the various local newspapers, and posted at the doors of churches, chapels, or other conspicuous situations likely to attract public attention.

The following instructions were given to the Agents employed for collecting Returns for the London School Board : —

(1) It will be your duty to ascertain how many Elementary day schools, private as well as public, there are in your district.

N.B.—No return is to be made by any school in which the ordinary fee exceeds ninepence per week. In schools where some scholars pay more and some less than ninepence, all those paying ninepence and under are to be returned. Of course, all Free, Ragged, and Industrial schools are to be included in the inquiry.

(2) In order to find out where such schools exist, you will, in the first place, apply to the rate-making authorities for lists of all schools known to them, and then you will make inquiries from the ministers of religion, teachers, Scripture-readers, missionaries, and others who are likely to be acquainted with existing schools.

(3) You will, in the course of your inquiries, endeavour to ascertain from ministers of religion and others whether any new schools are projected, or are in course of erection in your Division, and will record all the information you can glean upon this point for the guidance of the Board.

(4) You will call personally upon the Managers, master, or mistress of each school, and request him or her to fill up two copies of the form now placed in your hands, and you will offer to give any explanations that may be required.

(5) At the end of a week you will call again, and will ascertain, before leaving the school, that the Returns have been duly signed, and the questions contained in them answered as clearly as possible ; and, if necessary, you will then assist in filling up the forms, so as to render them as complete and accurate as you can.

(6) When you get possession of the Returns thus completed you will tie them in bundles, with labels denoting the parishes and wards to which they respectively refer ; you will make an accurate list of the addresses of the schools from which you have obtained Returns, and you will then deposit the list and Returns, together with a list of projected schools, in the hands of the Clerk of the School Board.

These proposals met with the approval of the Board, and this part of the inquiry was carried out in accordance with these arrangements. This ended the work of the Returns Committee, and it was then merged in a standing committee, known as the Statistical Committee, which had been constituted on January 19th, 1871. This Committee, therefore, became responsible for securing the information for the Department.

The first Return for the Department was submitted to the Board on April 5th, 1871. It gave an analysis of the Returns from upwards of 3,000 schools claiming to give Elementary Education; and it set out, by Divisions, the estimated population of London. This estimate was based upon the Census figures for 1861, with an allowance for the assumed increase of population from that date, and it showed a total population of 3,258,469. In submitting these figures the Committee stated that they regretted that they were not in possession of data sufficiently trustworthy to enable them to advise the Board as to "the proportion of the population in each Division which is of the class whose children will attend Public Elementary schools."

Before leaving this part of the inquiry, emphasis should be laid upon the fact that the Board realised that many schools included in the Return were not efficient; and at the suggestion of the Board, the Department undertook to inquire into the *efficiency* of the schools on the condition that the Board should report upon the *suitability* and *sufficiency* of existing accommodation. It is worthy of notice that, even so early as August, 1871, a great many schools, which had been included in the Board's Return of April, had been condemned by the Department's Inspectors on account of inefficiency.

Having supplied the first part of the information, the Board immediately appointed the Members of each Division a Committee to obtain, so far as their own Division was concerned, information as to the number of children in London requiring Elementary Education, between the ages of three and five, and five and thirteen. These Divisional Committees were asked to inquire into the social and religious condition of their respective districts, and were recommended to avail themselves of the assistance of residents in the Division, it being understood that all responsibility for the inquiry rested upon the Statistical Committee, whose Chairman was appointed an *ex-officio* Member of each Divisional Committee.

The Board instructed the Statistical Committee to prepare a general plan of operation for the whole of London designed to secure uniformity combined with accuracy; but at the same time each Divisional Committee was empowered to adopt whatever additional means they might judge specially suitable in order to obtain the desired information for their locality and circumstances. It was on this basis that the Board completed their inquiry.

The Board had given the Statistical Committee power to obtain from the Registrar-General, at the cost of the Board, such statistics as might be necessary for the inquiry. A Deputation from the Board had interviewed the Registrar-General early in April, 1871, and he had given an estimate of the total number of children in London, and had promised to give the Board an estimate of the population of each Division of London. He explained to the Deputation that the staff of the Census Office had continuous work for the ensuing two and a half years, and he declined to allow any officer of the Board to have access to the Census papers. He, however, suggested that, if the Board should decide to employ Enumerators on their own account, the District Registrars might be willing to help the Board in securing the services of some of the men who had been engaged in distributing and collecting the Census papers.

In view of the fact that the Census had been taken on April 2nd, 1871, the Board were very desirous of obtaining further information from the Registrar-General. With this object, a Deputation of the Board waited upon the Home Secretary and urged that the Registrar-General should be authorised to furnish, at the cost of the Board, copies of the householders' schedules. The Home Secretary acceded to this request, and the information was supplied by the Registrar-General. This information formed the basis of the Board's inquiry into the number of children needing Elementary school places. The Board had decided that their Census Books should take the following form:—

| _____Parish._ | | | _____Ward (if any)._ | | | | _____Street._ | |
| --- | --- | --- | --- | --- | --- | --- | --- | --- |
| No. or Name of House. | Name of Head of Family. | Occupation. | Names of Children. | | Age. | If now attending School. Where ? | If not now attending School. Why not ? | Children. | |
| | | | Males. | Females. | | | | Whether earning full wages. | Whether Half-timers. |

The books were forwarded to the Census Office, and the staff in that office filled up the first six columns, the information being obtained from the householders' schedules.

Where a child had been returned as a scholar, i.e. as attending school or receiving instruction at home, an "S" was entered in the seventh column. The steps then taken are those detailed in the Report of the Board to the Education Department, dated March, 1872, of which the following is an extract:—

The ground having so far been secured, the Board now took measures for completing their inquiry. A staff of enumerators and a Superintendent were appointed, under the direction of the Divisional Committee in each of the ten divisions of the Metropolis, viz. the City of London, Chelsea, Finsbury, Greenwich, Hackney, Lambeth, Marylebone, Southwark, the Tower Hamlets, and Westminster. The duty of the Enumerator was, first, to distinguish between the children who did and those who did not require Elementary schools; and, secondly, with reference to the former class, to ascertain what school they were attending, or, if they were attending no school, the cause of their absence. As a general rule, the Enumerators made their inquiries verbally, as they called from house to house. But, to save trouble, wherever the head of the family was absent, or it was thought more desirable to do so, a schedule, printed for the purpose, was left to be filled up, and was called for a few days later. As it was a matter of importance that the statistics should refer to some precise point of time, the Enumerators were instructed to limit their inquiries to those houses in which children of the given age were returned as present on the night of the General Census.

Some weeks were necessarily spent in obtaining this information. But, in proportion as the books were transmitted to the Head Office, the work of tabulation was at once proceeded with. It appeared to the Board that, looking to the work before them, and the future establishment of schools, it would not be judicious to classify the children according to the old boundaries of parishes and wards, but that it would be preferable to sub-divide the different School Divisions into compact blocks, the boundaries of which should either be impassable barriers, or, at all events, great thoroughfares. Each of the Divisional Committees was accordingly requested to sub-divide its Division in accordance with this plan, and the result, as approved by the Board, is shown in the maps which accompany this Report.

The tabulation of the Census Books, in Divisions and Sub-divisions, was made in the following manner. The streets (or sides of a street) within a given Sub-division were arranged in due order, and the number of families noted. The children were then distributed in the first instance into three classes: (1) those belonging to the class who attend, or should attend, a school where the weekly fee exceeds ninepence; (2) those in institutions, i.e. in Asylums, Reformatories, Poor Law schools, Boarding-schools, etc.; and (3) those who attend, or should attend, an Elementary school.

This analysis enabled the Board to deduct the first two classes of children who were beyond the scope of their inquiry. The next step was to sift the children who require Elementary schools, distinguishing between those attending and those not attending school, arranging them according to age, and classifying the absentees according to the causes of their absence. The causes of absence were enumerated as follows: Working at home; ill; working for wages; disabled; (a) half-timers, too young; (b) whole-timers, neglect and other causes.

These terms require very little explanation. The information as to children at work is necessary, in order to illustrate the action of the Factory and Workshop Acts, in virtue of which no child is allowed to work before the age of eight, and from that age up to the age of thirteen must attend school for ten hours in each week. It is also necessary, for purposes of comparison, with reference to Bye-law IV. of the School Board, which altogether exempts a child of not less than ten years of age from attendance at school, provided he has reached a certain standard of education, and partially exempts him if he is shown to be beneficially and necessarily at work. It may be added that ' ill " was defined as implying an illness which had lasted more than three weeks, and that "too young" was ente ed where the parent pleaded that excuse, and where, in addition, the child was less than five years of age, at which age only do the compulsory powers of the Board come into operation. The column for 'neglect and other causes' naturally contains the bulk of the children for whom the Board hereafter will have to find provision.

The time occupied by the Enumerators in supplementing the Returns furnished by the Registrar-General was seven or eight weeks. Some of the children accordingly who slept in London the night of the Census were no longer to be found in the same houses, and, as the Enumerators had been instructed to confine themselves to the houses contained in their books, the particulars with reference to these children were not ascertained. They have been distributed *pro ratâ* amongst the other columns; but it is not likely that any considerable error has been introduced on that account

The results of the Board's inquiry are set out in the Report to the Education Department as follows :—

The population of London on April 2nd, 1871, was 3,265,005. The number of children between the ages of three and thirteen was 681,101; of whom 97,307 were being educated at home, or in schools where the weekly fee exceeds ninepence, and 9,101 were inmates of institutions. The number of children remaining and belonging to the class which requires Elementary schools was 574,693, of whom 398,679 were attending, and 176,014, for various causes, were not attending school.

With reference to age, the whole number of children requiring Elementary schools was found to be divisible as follows: Those between three and five were 139,095; those between five and thirteen were 435,598. The corresponding numbers for those attending were 70,440 and 328,239; and for those not attending 68,655 and 107,359 respectively.

The children who require, or would require, Elementary schools, but who do not attend, may be classified as follows: Ill, 14,829; Disabled, 2,673; Too young, 55,760; Working at Home, 9,816; Working Abroad, Half-timers 1,332, Whole-timers 27,045—28,377; absent from neglect or other causes, 64,559—total, 176,014.

The Board have now to decide how far the above excuses may be considered as valid. The pleas of illness, as already defined, and physical disability must be admitted at once. It is probable that, with reference to the whole population of children, the numbers above given will bear a tolerably constant ratio. The plea urged by a parent that a child under five years of age is too young to attend school must also be admitted, inasmuch as the Board has no power to compel him to send his child to school. With reference to children at work, the Board are of opinion that, for practical purposes, they may admit the plea in half the total number of cases. In the case of half-timers, who attend school only ten hours in the week, a little less than half the nominal amount of school accommodation would be necessary. In the case of children above the age of ten, many will, no doubt, claim whole or partial exemption under the fourth Bye-law, but, on the other hand, many will not be able to claim exemption at all. Having no positive means of estimating the ratio of these two classes of children, the Board suppose them to be equal. And, as a general rule, the Board have assumed that the whole number of children at work will correspond to half that number for whom school provisions should be made.

On the whole, it would appear that of the total number of children classed as not attending school, 95,975 may be considered to have valid excuses for non-attendance; and 80,039 to have no reasonable excuse at all.

The number of children attending Elementary schools was given above as 398,679. If to these we add the children who should undoubtedly be at school, we have as the gross total of children for whom Elementary schools should be provided the number of *478,718.*

Dealing with the available accommodation, the Board stated :—

It has been determined, then, that the total number of children, of between three and thirteen years of age, for whom means of Elementary Education should be provided, amounts to 478,718. The Board have now to ascertain, in the second place, what provision there is to meet the requirements of these children (a) already made by efficient schools, or (b) likely to be made by schools either con‐templated or in course of erection. The returns forwarded to the Department in April of last year have furnished the basis for this part of the inquiry.

These returns included (with a few exceptions) every Elementary school in the Metropolis, i.e every school or department of a school at which Elementary Education is the principal part of the education there given, and at which the ordinary payments in respect of the instruction for each scholar do not exceed ninepence a week. The total number of existing schools included in the Returns was 3,130. In addition to which it appeared that 145 new schools, or enlargements of schools, were projected. The former class already provided accommodation for 370,960 scholars, and the latter proposed to provide additional accommodation for 42,273 scholars. In other words, the existing and the projected accommodation together was sufficient for 413,233 scholars.

The Department, in asking for the original Returns, had distinguished Elementary schools as follows :—

(1) *Public Schools,* i.e. held in premises secured by deed for education, with Managers acting under that deed, who appoint and control the teachers.

(2) *Private Schools,* i.e. governed by private Managers, or a Committee, not acting under any deed.

(3) *Adventure Schools,* i.e. conducted by the teacher at his (or her) own risk, and on his (or her) own responsibility.

This classification was adopted in the Tabular Report based upon the original Returns, and is followed in the present Report. One exception, however, has been made in the case of private schools, which, if in receipt of a Government Grant, have been classed with the public schools.

The next step was to ascertain which of the existing schools were efficient and which were in‐efficient. It appeared to the Board that this investigation would be best conducted by Her Majesty's Inspectors, who had all the necessary experience for the task, whereas the Board had no staff imme‐diately available for the purpose. The Education Department concurred in the view taken by the Board, and accordingly, whilst the latter were engaged in obtaining the census of children, nine of Her Majesty's Inspectors, assisted in each case by an Inspector of Returns, were employed, in accord‐ance with the 71st Section of the Elementary Education Act, to separate the efficient from the in‐efficient schools.

With reference to those schools, or departments of schools, which were under inspection, no inquiry was necessary. But with reference to all other schools, it was obvious that a special investi‐gation must be undertaken. These latter schools were nearly all Private or Adventure schools, and the two points, to which the attention of the Inspectors was directed, were the nature of the build‐ings and the character of the instruction. Under the circumstances of the case, the Board submitted to the Department that it would not be advisable to interpret too literally the requirements of the Department as laid down in the New Code. Some latitude must be allowed, so that, if a school could pass in a certain standard in the first instance, time might be given for the attainment of a higher standard. As the Inspectors completed their examination of different districts, their conclusions were communicated to the Board. Some schools were passed both for buildings and instruction, and these are consequently classed with the efficient schools. Others were condemned in both respects, and have, therefore, not been taken into account as providing suitable accommodation. But an intermediate class of schools has been reported to be efficient either in buildings or instruction, but not in both; and, with reference to these, the Board have obtained the consent of the Department that a period of grace should be accorded to them. To the Managers of all the schools in this category a circular has been addressed, inviting them within three months to bring their schools up to the necessary standard of efficiency, and undertaking that, meantime, the accommodation they provide shall provisionally be taken into account.

At the present moment it appears that in the Metropolis there are 1,149 efficient schools, accommodating 312,925 scholars, and 250 schools, efficient in buildings or instruction alone, accommodating 37,995 scholars, i.e. on the whole 1,399 schools completely or partially efficient, with a total accommodation for *350,920* scholars.

Coming to the question of the amount of accommodation which the Board considered necessary, the Board's Report stated :—

It has now been shown (1) that the number of children for whom means of Elementary Education should be provided is 478,718; and (2) that the available school accommodation is only sufficient for 350,920 children. The Board have lastly to determine (3) what is the deficiency in the supply of efficient Elementary schools as shown by comparing (1) and (2); (4) what schools are required to meet the deficiency; (5) in what localities such schools should be provided.

The Board have explained the process by which they arrive at the number of children for whom Elementary school accommodation should be provided. From the total number of children they first deducted those requiring a higher class of schools, and those in Institutions. From the remainder, which were now limited to those who should attend Elementary schools, they then deducted the ill, the disabled, the children under five years of age whose parents pleaded they were too young to attend school, and half the children at work. The result gave 478,718 as the total number of children for whose regular absence from school no valid excuse could be alleged.

A further and final deduction, however, must now be made, in order to determine the school accommodation which will be necessary for the above number of children. This deduction is on account of merely temporary causes of absence. The Board procured a return from thirty of the largest schools in London, giving the absence, day by day, for a whole week, and assigning to each absence its proper cause. The result shows that, on the average, about 5.09 of the number on the rolls were absent day by day, owing to these temporary causes. No doubt the absence is greater in many schools; but this percentage is no more than needs to be the case in a well-conducted school. The Board entertain the hope that, with the Bye-laws in force, this percentage may be considerably reduced in the best schools, and that, on the whole, it will be sufficient to deduct 5 per cent. from the number of children who could attend school, in order to ascertain the number of places which will be necessary to receive them.

On this basis of calculation, the schools for 478,718 children should have accommodation for 454,783 children in average attendance. On the other hand, the number of available school places has been shown to be 350,920.

It follows that schools have still to be provided with accommodation for *103,863* children in average attendance.

In submitting these statistics to the Department, the Board expressed the conviction that the conclusions arrived at were as accurate as could reasonably be expected. They stated that they did not propose that the whole of the accommodation for 103,863 children should be provided at once, but they asked the Department to authorise the immediate provision of schools for 100,600 children. The Board also stated that even to provide accommodation for 100,000 children, would be a task not easily accomplished in eighteen months or two years; and that, during that time, they would be able to see the result of the operation of the Bye-laws, the Half-time Acts, and the extent to which schools condemned would be transferred to, and made efficient by, the Board.

This section of the Report concludes by calling attention to the fact that the original schedules on which the Census of children was founded, having been collected by the Registrar-General from parents whose answers were given under a penalty for inaccurate returns, are as trustworthy as can be obtained, but that the statistics both from schools and parents had to be collected from persons who were not compelled to act under the same sense of responsibility, and may contain some elements of error. The Board had, therefore, thought it wisest, on the whole, to leave a margin for any possible miscalculations, and to provide, in the first instance, for a number of children less than the absolute number which represents the total deficiency.

It is evident that any errors in the calculations must have been on the side of showing a smaller number of children requiring Elementary Education than actually existed. Notwithstanding this fact, the Board came to the conclusion that it would be the wisest course to provide, in the first instance, for a number of children less than the number which, even according to their own calculations, represented the deficiency, and so they decided to ask for authority to provide for only 100,600 children. Yet they had realised that, if they had adopted the Department's method of ascertaining the number of school places required, a deficiency of over a quarter of a million would have been the result. Nevertheless, the conclusion which they had arrived at to provide considerably less than half this number of places appears to have caused the Board at the time no uneasiness.

In the light of the knowledge subsequently obtained, the conclusion is inevitable that, for reasons of policy, the Board endeavoured to minimise to the greatest possible extent the appalling lack of school places. This, in all probability, was the Board's unexpressed reason for deducting from the number of children requiring accommodation the 14,829 who had not been at school for three or more weeks in consequence of illness; for considering that half of the 28,377 children between the ages of three and thirteen returned as being at work would not need provision; for making no provision for the 55,760 children between three and five simply because at the time of the inquiry the parents of these children stated that they did not desire to send the children to school; for making no allowance for the well-known growth of the population in London; and again, for accepting without question the statement of the parents that 97,307 children were being taught at home, or were attending schools with fees of over ninepence per week. There is still another deduction which was made by the Board which showed their great anxiety to show as small a deficiency of school places as possible, namely, a deduction of 5 per cent. on account of temporary absence in consequence of illness.

Moreover, there can be little doubt that the same policy led the Board to reckon that there were 350,920 available efficient school places, although the information they had obtained during even the first few months of their existence must have convinced them that a very great number of these places were inefficient. Indeed, in their Report of 1873, the number of efficient school places had been reduced by 37,359. Again, in the total number of available school places, the Board had reckoned the whole of the places which had been returned as projected, although they must have been well aware that many of these places would simply be in substitution for places already counted, and that in other cases the accommodation would never be provided.

From a Report called for by Parliament in 1876, at the instance of Lord Francis Hervey, it is shown conclusively that the number of efficient school places in London in 1871 was only 262,259, or 88,661 less places than those reckoned as available in the Board's Report of 1872. Therefore, 88,661 places must be added to the estimate of the Board that 103,863 places were needed, which at once brings up the deficiency of school places to 192,524; and when due allowance is made for the extraordinary deductions which were made by the Board, the statement that at the time the Board started their work upwards of a quarter of a million of school places were needed is practically proved by the Board's own figures.

It has already been stated that, if the Board had adopted the basis which has been recognised by the Education Department—viz. that one-sixth of the population required Elementary school provision, the result would have been a deficiency of over a quarter of a million school places. The following figures will prove the accuracy of this statement :—The population of London revealed by the Census of 1871 was 3,266,987, one-sixth of which would give 544,498. According to Lord Francis Hervey's Return there were, in 1871, 262,259 efficient school places in London, leaving a deficiency of 282,239.

Although sufficient evidence has been adduced to prove conclusively the deplorable educational destitution of London when the Board was called into existence, the following extracts from Reports of an Inspector appointed to examine certain schools which were included in the Board's original figures will present a vivid picture of the condition of many schools in existence, at any rate, so late as the year 1874 :—

1. ————— *School.*

This is a wretched place, a disgrace to the Metropolis. The "school" is held in an old dwelling-house in Clerkenwell. The house was at one time used as a stable. The approach is most unwelcome, and, on entering the schoolroom (upstairs), a most deplorable picture presented itself to the eye. Fifty children crowded together in a small, dingy, shapeless room with space for sixteen, and the window and door carefully closed—in fact, the latter and the doors downstairs carefully bolted. There were two women in charge of the children, but, of course, there was no attempt at teaching, and no registration of the children's attendance. The results of the examination were such as might be expected—out of twenty children examined, three had a notion of figures, and the writing was not much better.

The sooner this place is closed, the better.

2. ————— *School.*

Some idea of the inefficient state of this school may be formed from the fact that not one scholar out of fifty, ranging from eight to eleven years of age, could pass in the easy arithmetic required—in other words, not one of them could go as far as simple short division.

Further, one child out of fifteen ranging from six to eight years of age could write the letters of the alphabet from dictation.

As regards the accommodation provided, thirty-six young children were sitting in an upper room into which the rays of the sun on a bright day in June could not enter—twilight in mid-day.

Coming to the question of the teaching staff—one teacher, a master, was present on the day of inspection; one teacher for 128 children, and he an earnest, hard-working missionary, who had been labouring in —— for the last —— years.

·Such are the salient features of the —— School.

3. ———— *School.*

It would be impossible for words to describe the inefficient state of this so-called school. Eighty-two children of different ages—boys and girls—huddled together in a miserable, badly lighted, badly ventilated room, affording accommodation for twenty-three at the utmost.

No books, no apparatus, no seats—floor and bare walls: the "teacher," an aged man, standing in the midst of a crowd of children and wielding a cane to keep the "scholars" quiet—and thus the time goes on.

A few children read; writing is not and could not be taught; arithmetic is not thought of. Fifty per cent. of the children could not be examined—forty-two left the room in a batch at Mr. M——'s request, having been recently admitted. They left schools to waste their time here, and to get stifled in a sickening atmosphere.

4. ———— *School.*

This is not a school—it seems a baby-farm. Seventeen children in a small, filthy hovel. There were four infants a few months old; one lay on a small bed, another in a small cot, and the two others in positions which I cannot here describe. The little ones were quite naked. The woman who pretends to look after this "school," was engaged in a back yard, washing. From the woman down to the infant, all here seemed steeped in ignorance and wretchedness.

## II.—The First School Provision.

The detailed Report of the Board, which was the completion of their inquiry into the school needs of London, and in which they decided to apply for authority to provide 100,600 places, was not before the School Board until March 27th, 1872.

At a very early period of their existence the Board were, however, greatly impressed by the urgent needs of certain districts of London, and so early as May 3rd, 1871, they had decided to apply to the Education Department for authority to provide forthwith a limited number of schools in the districts where the deficiency of school places had been ascertained to be very great.

The Statistical Committee were instructed to select the localities for these schools; and after consultation with the Divisional Members, application was made to the Education Department for power to establish twenty schools in London, located as follows:—One in Chelsea, three in Finsbury, one in Greenwich, two in Hackney, one in Lambeth, four in Marylebone, three in Southwark, four in Tower Hamlets, and one in Westminster.

The application was made to the Education Department on July 6th, 1871, and so impressed were the Department with the urgent need for school provision, that they sanctioned the erection of these twenty schools on July 11th. They requested the

School Board to give the exact localities in which it was proposed to erect the schools, so that the Department might be able to frame the necessary requisition.

Four additional schools were sanctioned before the Board made their application for the 100,600 places. Therefore twenty-four schools in all had been sanctioned, and it was understood that the accommodation to be provided by these twenty-four schools should be considered as a part of the 100,600 school places.

It is evident that the Board had hoped that the greater number of these places would have been provided in about two years. The difficulties experienced by the Board, however, seem to have been much greater than they had at first anticipated; and even their earliest proposals for schools in districts where the deficiencies were the greatest, met, in many cases, with most strenuous opposition.

Still, by the end of 1872, the Board had opened two departments of the Berner-street School, with accommodation for nearly 400 children. In 1873, twenty-eight schools were provided, with accommodation for 22,218 children. In 1874, seventy new schools were provided, with accommodation for 64,961 children; and, by the end of 1875, a total of ninety-nine new schools had been provided, with accommodation for 88,913 children. The Board, in their General Report in 1872, had anticipated that they would have been able to provide about 100,000 school places in about two years; but it was, however, not until the year 1876 that the Board's permanent accommodation had reached that number. Meanwhile, the Elementary child population of London had been increasing at the rate of 10,000 per annum. Indeed, at this period the Board must have realised how greatly their predecessors had under-estimated the task before them; for, in spite of the fact that the Board had provided nearly 90,000 places by the end of 1875, and the accommodation in efficient Voluntary schools had increased by over 27,000, there were, in London, at the end of 1875, 89,097 children known to the School Board Visitors not to be attending any school, and 53,623 children in attendance at non-efficient Voluntary schools. The Board were, however, now providing school places at a very rapid rate. The report of the Statistical Committee, submitted in September, 1877, shows that the Board had then provided over 140,000 permanent school places.

### III.—TRANSFERRED SCHOOLS.

The Board had, however, a number of schools which had been transferred to them under the authority contained in Sections 19 and 23 of the Elementary Education Act, 1870, and the accommodation provided by these schools in 1876 amounted to 16,080.

In the first two years of the Board's existence, the transfer of schools was arranged by the Works Committee: subsequently this work was performed by the Statistical Committee and their successors, the School Accommodation and Attendance Committee.

At first, the Board were compelled to exercise extreme care before they accepted the transfer of schools, in order that they might not have left upon their hands a number of practically useless buildings.

The following Table sets out year by year the number of schools which have been transferred to the Board, together with a summary of all the schools transferred, distinguishing between those still open and those which have been closed:—

ANALYSIS OF EFFICIENT AND NON-EFFICIENT SCHOOLS TRANSFERRED YEAR BY YEAR TO THE BOARD.

[*There were no Schools transferred to the Board during the years* 1880, 1887, 1893, 1894, 1896, *and* 1897.]

| Denomination. | 1871. | | | | | | 1872. | | | | | | 1873. | | | | | |
|---|---|---|---|---|---|---|---|---|---|---|---|---|---|---|---|---|---|---|
| | Efficient. | | Non-Efficient. | | Total. | | Efficient. | | Non-Efficient. | | Total. | | Efficient. | | Non-Efficient. | | Total. | |
| | No. | Accom | No. | Accom | | | No. | Accom | No. | Accom | | | No | Accom | No. | Accom | | |
| Church ... | 1 | 165 | .. | ... | 1 | 165 | 1 | 326 | 1 | 93 | 2 | 419 | 3 | 816 | (a) | 90 | 3 | 906 |
| Church Ragged | 2 | 230 | 1 | 99 | 3 | 329 | 4 | 674 | (a) | 353 | 4 | 1,027 | ... | ... | ... | ... | ... | ... |
| British... ... | 1 | 212 | ... | ... | 1 | 212 | 8 | 2 397 | 4 | 785 | 12 | 3,182 | 9 | 2,942 | ... | ... | 9 | 2,942 |
| Wesleyan ... | ... | ... | ... | ... | | | ... | ... | ... | ... | | | 3 | 850 | ... | ... | 3 | 850 |
| Congregational | 1 | 225 | ... | ... | 1 | 225 | 1 | 135 | 1 | 591 | 2 | 726 | 1 | 360 | ... | ... | 1 | 360 |
| Ragged .. | 3 | 499 | 1 | 219 | 4 | 718 | 6 | 2,943 | 8 | 1,395 | 14 | 4,338 | 1 | 201 | 2 | 392 | 3 | 593 |
| Miscellaneous... | ... | ... | ... | ... | ... | | 5 | 1,093 | 5 | 1,073 | 10 | 2,166 | ... | ... | 1 | 189 | 1 | 189 |
| Total ... | 8 | 1,331 | 2 | 318 | 10 | 1,649 | 25 | 7,568 | 19 | 4,290 | 44 | 11858 | 17 | 5 169 | 3 | 671 | 20 | 5,840 |

| Denomination. | 1874. | | | | 1875. | | 1876. | | 1877. | | 1878. | | 1879. | | 1881. | | 1882. | |
|---|---|---|---|---|---|---|---|---|---|---|---|---|---|---|---|---|---|---|
| | Efficient. | | Non-Efficient. | | Efficient. | | Efficient. | | Efficient. | | Efficient | | Efficient. | | Efficient. | | Efficient. | |
| | No. | Accom | No. | Accom | No. | Accom | No. | Accom | No. | Accom | No. | Accom | No. | Accom | No. | Accom | No. | Accom. |
| Church | 7 | 2 171 | ... | ... | 4 | 1,125 | 5 | 2,195 | 7 | 2.893 | 9 | 4,835 | 3 | 1,274 | 3 | 1 469 | ... | ... |
| Church Ragged | ... | ... | ... | ... | ... | ... | ... | ... | ... | ... | ... | ... | ... | ... | ... | ... | ... | ... |
| British... ... | 2 | 1,277 | ... | ... | ... | ... | 2 | 337 | 2 | 411 | 2 | 802 | ... | ... | 1 | 469 | 2 | 799 |
| Wesleyan ... | 2 | 467 | ... | ... | ... | ... | ... | ... | ... | ... | ... | ... | ... | ... | ... | ... | ... | ... |
| Congregational | ... | ... | ... | ... | ... | ... | ... | ... | ... | ... | 2 | 1,918 | ... | ... | ... | ... | ... | ... |
| Ragged | 1 | 137 | 1 | 161 | ... | ... | ... | ... | ... | ... | ... | ... | ... | ... | ... | ... | ... | ... |
| Miscellaneous... | ... | ... | ... | ... | 1 | 460 | ... | ... | ... | ... | 1 | 423 | .. | ... | ... | ... | ... | ... |
| Total ... | 12 | 4,052 | 1 | 161 | 5 | 1,585 | 7 | 2,532 | 9 | 3,304 | 14 | 7,978 | 3 | 1,274 | 4 | 1,938 | 2 | 799 |

| Denomination. | 1883. | | 1884. | | 1885. | | 1886. | | 1888. | | 1889. | | 1890. | | 1891. | |
|---|---|---|---|---|---|---|---|---|---|---|---|---|---|---|---|---|
| | Efficient. | | Efficient. | | Efficient. | | Efficient. | | Efficient. | | Efficient. | | Efficient. | | Efficient. | |
| | No. | Accom. | No. | Accom. | No. | Accom. | No. | Accom. | No. | Accom. | No. | Accom. | No. | Accom. | No. | Accom. |
| Church ... | 1 | 202 | 4 | 1,382 | 1 | 339 | ... | ... | 2 | 790 | ... | ... | 1 | 369 | ... | ... |
| Church Ragged | ... | ... | ... | ... | ... | ... | ... | ... | ... | ... | ... | ... | ... | ... | ... | ... |
| British... ... | 2 | 992 | ... | ... | ... | ... | 2 | 404 | ... | ... | ... | ... | ... | ... | 2 | 1,369 |
| Wesleyan ... | ... | ... | ... | ... | ... | ... | ... | ... | 1 | 170 | ... | ... | ... | ... | ... | ... |
| Congregational | ... | ... | ... | ... | ... | ... | ... | ... | ... | ... | ... | ... | ... | ... | ... | ... |
| Ragged ... | ... | ... | ... | ... | ... | ... | ... | ... | ... | ... | ... | ... | ... | ... | ... | ... |
| Miscellaneous... | ... | ... | 1 | 198 | ... | ... | ... | ... | ... | ... | 1 | 258 | ... | ... | ... | ... |
| Total ... | 3 | 1,194 | 5 | 1,580 | 1 | 339 | 2 | 404 | 3 | 960 | 1 | 258 | 1 | 369 | 2 | 1,369 |

(a) In the case of certain schools part of the accommodation only was passed by H.M.I., in 1871, as efficient. In these cases the schools have been counted in the number of efficient schools.

| Denomination. | 1892. Efficient. No. | Accom. | 1895. Efficient. No. | Accom. | 1898. Efficient. No. | Accom. | 1899. Efficient. No. | Accom. | 1900. Efficient. No. | Accom. | 1901 Efficient. No. | Accom. | 1902. Efficient. No. | Accom. | 1903. Efficient. No. | Accom. |
|---|---|---|---|---|---|---|---|---|---|---|---|---|---|---|---|---|
| Church ... | ... | ... | 1 | 675 | .. | ... | ... | ... | ... | ... | 3 | 1,201 | 1 | 242 | ... | ... |
| Church Ragged | ... | ... | ... | ... | ... | ... | ... | ... | ... | ... | ... | ... | .. | ... | ... | ... |
| British... ... | ... | ... | 1 | 524 | 1 | 862 | 1 | 482 | 2 | 763 | ... | ... | .. | ... | 1 | 625 |
| Wesleyan ... | 1 | 366 | 1 | 393 | ... | ... | 1 | 528 | ... | ... | ... | ... | ... | ... | ... | ... |
| Congregational | 1 | 559 | ... | ... | ... | ... | ... | ... | ... | ... | ... | ... | ... | ... | ... | ... |
| Ragged ... | ... | ... | ... | ... | ... | ... | ... | ... | ... | ... | ... | ... | ... | ... | ... | ... |
| Miscellaneous... | ... | ... | ... | ... | ... | ... | ... | ... | ... | ... | ... | ... | . | ... | ... | ... |
| Total ... | 2 | 925 | 3 | 1,592 | 1 | 862 | 2 | 1,010 | 2 | 763 | 3 | 1,201 | 1 | 242 | 1 | 625 |

| Denomination. | Open. Efficient. No. | Accom. | Non-Efficient. No. | Accom. | Closed. Efficient. No. | Accom. | Non Efficient. No. | Accom. | Total No. Transferred. Efficient and Non-Efficient. No. | Accom. |
|---|---|---|---|---|---|---|---|---|---|---|
| Church ... | 8 | 4,208 | ... | ... | 49 | 18,261 | 1 | 183 | 58 | 22,652 |
| Church Ragged | ... | ... | ... | ... | 6 | 904 | 1 | 452 | 7 | 1,356 |
| British... ... | 7 | 3,894 | ... | ... | 34 | 11,773 | 4 | 785 | 45 | 16,452 |
| Wesleyan ... | 1 | 528 | ... | ... | 8 | 2,246 | ... | ... | 9 | 2,774 |
| Congregational | ... | ... | ... | ... | 6 | 3,197 | 1 | 591 | 7 | 3,788 |
| Ragged ... | ... | ... | ... | ... | 11 | 3,780 | 12 | 2,167 | 23 | 5,947 |
| Miscellaneous (a) | ... | ... | ... | ... | 9 | 2,432 | 6 | 1,262 | 15 | 3,694 |
| Total ... | 16 | 8,630 | ... | ... | 123 | 42,593 (b) | 25 | 5,440 | 164 | 56,663 (c) |

(a) Under Miscellaneous are included the following schools :—" Hope Schools for All " ; "Undenominational" "Southwark Sunday School Society " ; " Anerley and Penge Day School " ; one Presbyterian School ; " Nonconformist " "Poplar and Blackwall Free School " ; Mr. Spurgeon's School, Station-road, &c

(b) With eight exceptions (Brewer-street, Abbey-street, Benfield-street, All Saint's, Lyham-road (Boys), London-street, Darby-street, Crown-court, and Hart-street), the children in these schools were transferred to permanent schools of the Board.

(c) The accommodation has been reckoned as follows :—Schools closed ; at the time of closing : Schools still open : at the time of transfer to the Board.

## IV.—METHOD OF ASCERTAINING SCHOOL PROVISION REQUIRED.

Although the Board's officers had received instructions in 1874 to keep a record of the children in their respective districts, and to re-schedule each district at least once during the year, the Board relied for many years upon the figures obtained from the Census of 1871. In the report of the Bye-laws Committee for 1874, it is stated that it had been decided to omit the number of children requiring Elementary Education as returned by the Visitors' schedules, as the Committee had come to the conclusion that the figures derived from the schedules could not altogether be relied upon, in consequence of the Visitors obtaining their information, not at a single point of time, as in the case of the Enumerators of the Registrar-General, but in the course of visits which were some-times spread over several months ; and also because the Visitors obtained their information without the assistance of the penalty which is imposed at the time of the General Census. The Committee further reported that these circumstances combined rendered the figures obtained by the Visitors less authentic than those of the Registrar-General. In those districts, however, where the Board had reason to think that a great variation had taken place in the population, they caused a special scheduling to be made.

It was not until the year 1878 that a general and simultaneous scheduling was made by the Visitors. This scheduling did not produce very satisfactory results; for the number of children returned was 71,000 less than that estimated to exist on the basis of the Registrar-General Returns. It should be stated that, with the acquiescence of the Education Department, 10 per cent. was added to the number of children returned by the Visitors to account for children who escaped the scheduling, and from the number thus obtained a deduction of 23 per cent. was made for all causes of absence. This arrangement continued down to the year 1881. But even the Visitors' figures, with the 10 per cent. addition, fell 9,760 short of the estimated number based upon the Registrar-General's Returns.

The Board had no powers to compel the parents to give information, and in those early days the Visitors had to contend with the greatest difficulties. As, however, the officers became more accustomed to their work, and gained more information concerning their districts, the number of children returned by them in their simultaneous scheduling gradually approximated to the number estimated to exist according to the Registrar-General's Returns, until, in the year 1892, the Statistical Committee were able to report that the number of children scheduled by the Visitors was 10,545 more than the number arrived at upon the basis of the Registrar-General's figures; and in the Board's latest Return it is shown that the proportion of the population requiring Elementary provision is now nearly one-fifth, as against the original estimate of the Education Department of one-sixth of all classes.

The diagram on the following page shows the number of children estimated to require Elementary school accommodation on the basis of one-sixth of the population, and the total number of children returned by the Visitors.

Early in 1881, the following correspondence took place between the School Board and the Education Department :—

Letter addressed to the Education Department by the Board on March 8th, 1881 :—

Sir,—The Department are aware that it is the practice of the Board, in estimating the amount of school accommodation required in any given district, to deduct 23 per cent. from the total number of children on account of absenteeism.

Their Lordships' letter, dated April 24th, 1875, sets out the two rules used by the Department for the purpose of calculating the school requirements of a district. It will be found that the "one-sixth" rule allows a deduction of 16 per cent. for all causes of absence, and that the "one-fifth" rule allows a deduction of only 13 per cent.

The Board have always been aware that the deduction made by them, as compared with the deduction made by the Department, is very large, and that, as a consequence, their calculations as to the number of school places required are understated. More especially is this the case when it is

*Diagram showing the estimated number of children requiring Elementary school provision on the basis of one-sixth of the population, and the total number returned by the Visitors :—*

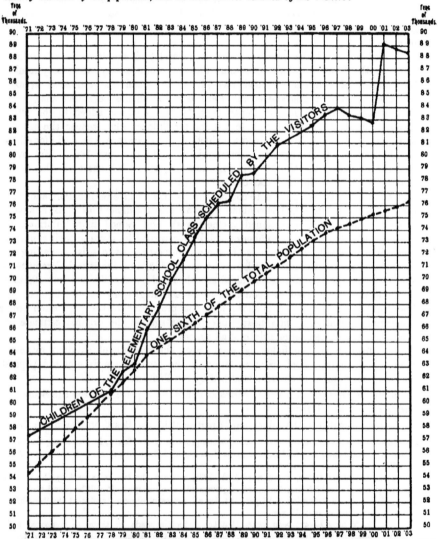

There was no return of the children of the Elementary School Class in the years 1872 to 1877 inclusive, and no simultaneous scheduling by the Visitors in the years 1891, 1893, and 1894.

The Elementary Education Act of 1900 raised the superior limit of age for compulsory attendance from 13 to 14 years of age, and all children from 13 to 14 years of age were scheduled for the first time in May, 1901.

remembered that children over thirteen years of age attend school. The last Report of the Committee of Council on Education shows that in the public Elementary schools of England and Wales the number over thirteen who were attending school amounted to 4.45 per cent. of the children on the rolls. Since Lord Sandon's Act has come into operation some other children over thirteen years of age who do not comply with certain statutory requirements can be compelled to attend school. The Board, therefore, think that these two classes of children should no longer be left out of their calculations, but that some allowance should be made on their account when they are estimating the number of school places required. After careful consideration, they are of opinion that the result may be attained by deducting for the future 20 per cent. on account of absenteeism instead of 23 per cent. as heretofore.

Reply of the Education Department, April 9th, 1881 :—

With reference to your statement that the deduction made by your Board on account of absenteeism is very large as compared with the deduction made by this Department in other cases, my Lords would observe that they understand your Board's deduction of 23 per cent. has been made, not from the number of children actually enumerated, but from a hypothetical total obtained by adding 10 per cent. to the number enumerated.

It is probable that in the earlier years of your Board's existence, when the Attendance Officers were new to the work of enumerating, such an allowance may have been necessary. But after so many years' experience, it must surely be possible for the Attendance Officers to make enumerations more nearly approaching correctness; and my Lords think that this addition of 10 per cent. (which is not generally made by other School Boards) is likely to swell unduly the number of children for whom school accommodation is provided.

I am, therefore, directed to suggest that, in future, your Board should take the number enumerated to be the total number of children, and, from this total, should deduct 12½ per cent., according to the rule adopted by this Department, after full consideration of all the circumstances, including the fact that a certain percentage of children (smaller in London than in the country generally) attend after thirteen years of age.

The practical result of this rule would be almost the same as that of the method proposed in your letter, while it would agree with the rule adopted by this Department without causing complaint in dealing with other districts.

The School Board agreed to adopt the suggestion of the Education Department.

This method of calculation, with certain modifications, has continued ever since its adoption, but the following Report of the Statistical Committee of February 29th, 1888, recommending that instead of the 12½ per cent. deduction for all causes of absence the deduction should be increased to 20 per cent., was approved by the Board, and an application was accordingly made to the Education Department for permission to reckon the school needs of London by this method :—

The Committee have from time to time had before them the question of the present method of estimating the number of school places required. They are of opinion, now that the Visitors have become so thoroughly acquainted with their districts as to succeed in scheduling all but a small percentage of the children, that the deduction of 12½ per cent. from the number of children enumerated for all causes of absence, is insufficient. They think that the matter should be brought before the Education Department with a view to an alteration in the present method of calculation being made in the direction of increasing the deduction on account of absentees. They submit the following draft letter, which they suggest should be forwarded to the Education Department : —

"Sir,—I am requested by the School Board for London to state that the issue of their first Annual Report, of which I enclose a copy, offers a favourable opportunity of reviewing the method

C

according to which the necessity for additional school accommodation is ascertained.   It appears, from the figures set out upon p. 3 of this Report, that the number of children enumerated by the School Board Visitors, instead of being, as at first, 10 per cent. below the estimated figures of the Registrar-General, are now only 3.6 per cent. below that estimate.

It will be remembered by their Lordships that at the period when 10 per cent. of the children of school age escaped enumeration, 10 per cent. was added on that account to the number of children enumerated, and 23 per cent. was deducted from the total so obtained for all causes of absence.   This complicated method of calculation was equivalent to a net deduction of 15.3 per cent. from the number of children scheduled by the Visitors.

At a later period, namely in 1881, when the number of children enumerated by the Visitors was within 8.21 per cent. of the Registrar-General's estimate, the then School Board applied to the Education Department to reduce the deduction from 23 per cent. to 20 per cent.   (See Appendix No. I.) This method of calculation would have been equivalent to a net deduction of 12 per cent.   The Education Department, however, suggested that instead of the previous method of adding one percentage and deducting another, it would be preferable if the Board adopted a deduction of 12½ per cent., which was the rule adopted by the Education Department for the country generally.   The Board adopted this suggestion, the immediate effect of which was to increase the number of children for whom school accommodation was apparently required by 18,477 above the number which would have required school accommodation upon the old calculation.

Since that date, however, the enumeration of children by the Visitors of the School Board for London has been so carefully performed as to bring the number of children enumerated to within 3.6 per cent. of the estimated figures of the Registrar-General.   This improvement has increased the number of children by 35,932 above the number which would have been obtained if the calculation was based upon those of six years ago.   The Board, therefore, submit that the percentage of deduction for all cases of absence should now be increased at least by an addition corresponding to the increased accuracy of the Scheduling by the School Board Visitors.

The Board would also observe that the percentage of average attendance upon the number on the roll has remained at practically 80 per cent. in both Board and non-Board schools for years past, notwithstanding the utmost endeavours of the Board to increase it—a fact which points to some permanent causes of absence which are not amenable to the Board's control.   It must also be remembered that on the school roll 29,313 children over thirteen years of age, who are not enumerated by the Visitors, are reckoned.

In addition to this fact the Board would also direct the attention of the Education Department to the number of children under five years of age who can neither be compelled nor induced to attend school, but who are reckoned in the number of those for whom school accommodation is said to be required.   This number amounts to 106,386, and is alone more than equal to a deduction of 14 per cent. from the number of children enumerated by the Visitors. It is evident that an additional deduction ought to be allowed on account of the children of this age, for notwithstanding the utmost endeavours of the Board to attract these children to the schools, the proportion of those who actually attend remains practically stationary.

That the present system of deducting only 12½ per cent. from the gross number of children enumerated is unsuitable to the present condition of school accommodation in the Metropolis is evident from the fact that, although upon gross figures school accommodation is required for 761,963 children, yet the moment the figures are examined it is found that, after making allowance for Standard I. children in the Infant schools, there exists 226,962 school places for 216,755 boys enumerated; 225,408 places for 216,756 girls enumerated, and 205,017 places for 328,452 infants enumerated.   When, however, 12½ per cent. is deducted from the gross number of these several classes of children, the result is an excess of accommodation upon the figures, as seen in the Table given in the Appendix No. II., of 37,301 boys, 35,746 girls, and a deficiency of accommodation for infants under Standard I. of 82,378.   To meet this apparent deficiency of infants' accommodation the Education Department have already approved of a further supply of accommodation for 14,209 boys, and 14,209 girls who are not infants, and 17,173 children who are infants.

The Education Department will, therefore, observe that whilst the stated deficiency is one for infant children only under Standard I., the method now adopted compels the Board in supplying that deficiency to increase the provision for boys and girls above Standard I., for whom there is already a large excess of school accommodation. In Appendix No. II. a Table is given showing what has been the result of this method of procedure since the year 1884. In that year there was an apparent deficiency of school accommodation for infant children of 94,917 school places, and an excess of 30,445 school places for boys, and 25,099 for girls. In providing for the stated deficiency of infant school children by making provision, in the proportion of six boys and girls to four infants, according to the present method approved by the Education Department of dealing with the figures in totals without reference to their constituent parts, the Board, with the sanction of the Education Department, have actually increased in three years the excess of accommodation for boys by 6,856 school places, for girls by 10,647 school places, whilst they have only diminished the apparent deficiency of accommodation for infants by 12,539 school places.

In Appendix No. III. the Department will find some detailed information from the Chairman of the Statistical Committee on the subject.

The School Board for London trust that it is only necessary to bring these facts under the notice of the Education Department in order to convince their Lordships that an end should immediately be put to a method of ascertaining and supplying school provision which is not only useless for the purpose for which it is designed, but which also results in compelling the Board to incur a costly and needless expenditure of the public money.

The School Board are of opinion that a deduction *equivalent* to a uniform deduction of at least 20 per cent. will be necessary in order to ascertain from the number of children scheduled the amount of school provision which is really required.

In conclusion I am directed to ask that their Lordships will be good enough to receive a Deputation from the Board to discuss the question." [1]

The Education Department did not make any direct answer to the application, but, from time to time, as the School Board submitted proposals for additional accommodation, they declined to consider any applications based upon figures calculated upon a deduction of 20 per cent. from the number of children scheduled by the Visitors, and desired the School Board to furnish figures in connection with these applications calculated upon the basis of a deduction of 12½ per cent. The result was that on May 3rd, 1889, the Board rescinded their resolution to alter the method of computation which had been in use since 1881.

The first modification of this system was made early in 1899. In consequence of the number of children attending school over the age of thirteen having increased to a very great extent, the Board, in December, 1898, addressed the following communication to the Education Department:—

In 1881, the Board agreed to a suggestion of the Education Department that in estimating the number of school places required the Board should take the number enumerated to be the total number of children, and that from this total they should deduct 12½ per cent., according to the rule adopted by the Department, after full consideration of all the circumstances, including the fact that a certain percentage of children (smaller in London than in the country generally) attend after thirteen years of age.

----

[1] The Appendixes may be found in the Report of the Statistical Committee for March 8th, 1888.

In 1883, when the Board first obtained Returns of the number of children over thirteen and not exempt, or exempt and attending school, it was found that the number of such children was 16,644, or 2.8 per cent. of the total number of children enumerated between the ages of three and thirteen.

This number has continuously increased to the present time, and at Lady-day, 1898, it reached the total of 52,717, or 6.8 per cent. of the total number of children enumerated between the ages of three and thirteen.

In view of the general advance of public opinion in the appreciation of the value of education, the Board believe that the number of children over thirteen years of age who will voluntarily attend school will continue to grow.

An examination of the statistics, however, has revealed the fact that the increase is not uniform throughout London. In the poorer districts, parents generally are still anxious to send their children to work as soon as they have reached the age of thirteen; but in other districts the better paid artisans and others who set a higher value on education for their children keep them at school as long as possible in larger numbers than heretofore.

Inasmuch as the increase in the number of children over thirteen upon the rolls since 1883 has been 4 per cent. of the number of children between three and thirteen scheduled, the Board are now of opinion that, for the future, in submitting statistics with regard to additional school provision, the method should be adopted of adding to the present estimate of the number of school places required the number of children over thirteen years of age and not exempt (or exempt and attending school), in excess of 2½ per cent. of the total number of such children scheduled by the Visitors.

The Board will be glad if their Lordships will give this proposal their favourable consideration.

### The Department replied on January 10th, 1899:—

Adverting to your letter dated the 9th ultimo, I am directed to state that, while in view of the different character of different localities, my Lords are not prepared to accept such a general rule as the Board suggest, they would be willing to consider, when schools are proposed for erection in districts which the Board regard as likely to supply a number of scholars between thirteen and fourteen, whether any addition can be made to the number of children to be provided for; and I am to point out that it is not necessary for the Board to provide for children over fourteen who are exempt from attendance at school.

### On February 17th, 1899, the Board sent the following letter to the Department:—

I beg leave to acknowledge the receipt of their Lordships' letter, dated January 10th, 1899, with reference to the basis of deduction from the gross number of children scheduled, upon which is ascertained the estimated number of school places needed for children requiring Elementary Education.

In reply, I am directed to state that the Board propose to submit applications based not on the number of children over thirteen who may be expected to attend school in the particular locality, but on the number of such children actually found to be attending school.

The number over fourteen attending school in any particular locality is always small, but the Board do not consider it their duty to turn such children out of school, nor do the Board suppose that the Department desire them to do so. It is obvious, however, that such children if in school are occupying school places, and must be taken into consideration.

### And in a letter dated February 27th, 1899, the Department wrote:—

Adverting to your letter dated the 17th instant, I am directed to state that my Lords will be prepared to entertain applications based as proposed in your letter.

The result of this correspondence was that, from this date until 1901, the Board added the number of children attending Elementary schools over the age of thirteen to the estimated number of children needing accommodation.

The only other modification of the method agreed to in 1881 of estimating the number of school places required was made in the year 1901, when the superior age for exemption was raised to fourteen. The Board then caused all children between three and fourteen of the Elementary school class to be scheduled, and from the number returned deducted 12½ per cent., and then added the number of children over the age of fourteen actually in attendance at school.

This system continued in operation up to the end of the year 1903.

On December 4th, 1903, however, the Board of Education, when declining to sanction the provision of additional accommodation in Hoxton (in which district, upon this basis of calculation, a large deficiency of school places was shown to exist) stated that they were unable to find that they had ever agreed to the above-mentioned method of calculation. The School Board pointed out, in reply, that the alteration in method was consequent upon the raising of the superior limit of age in London for exemption from school attendance from thirteen to fourteen under the Bye-Laws sanctioned by the Board of Education in 1901; and that their attention was called to this alteration of method in the first applications for additional accommodation made to them upon this basis.

The School Board, however, informed the Board of Education that, while they were of opinion that the basis they adopted in 1901 as a result of the alteration of the Bye-Laws was the correct one, they would, nevertheless, not object, if the Board of Education preferred to adhere to the arrangement assented to by them on February 27th, 1899, to revert to the method of estimating places required by deducting 12½ per cent. from children scheduled three to thirteen, and adding to the result thus obtained the number of children over thirteen years of age in attendance at school.

The Board of Education, in a letter dated January 28th, 1904, stated that they would be prepared to consider applications upon this basis of calculation, but that they would reserve to themselves liberty to treat each case on its individual merits, and to apply such tests as they might consider applicable to the particular circumstances.

In reply to this communication the School Board informed the Board of Education, in a letter dated March 4th, 1904, that they would revert to the method set out above, and added that they assumed that this system would be definitely accepted by the Board of Education as the specific rule for determining the need of school provision.

From that date all applications for additional school accommodation have been based upon the method of deducting 12½ per cent. from the number of children scheduled between the ages of 3 and 13, and adding to the result the number over 13 in attendance at school.

It may be added that the Board of Education, in a letter dated March 11th, 1904, stated that they were of opinion that this method would furnish a better guide for discovering the actual needs of a district than the system adopted in 1901; but that they could not accept any purely statistical system as a specific rule for determining the need of school provision, and must adhere to the reservation mentioned above in their letter of January 28th, 1904.

## V.—BASIS OF CALCULATING ACCOMMODATION.

The Commissioners appointed to inquire into the Elementary Education Acts, in their final Report in 1888, came to the following conclusions with reference to the basis for estimating the accommodation of existing schools :—[1]

[1] In our previous chapter we have shown that, roughly speaking, school provision is needed throughout England and Wales, for one-sixth of the population, though in certain districts, such as Lancashire or the West Riding, the requirements amount to nearly a fifth; and if we take the total school accommodation of the whole country, as it appears in the Returns of the Education Department, this proportion of the population is adequately provided for. But in estimating the sufficiency of school accommodation we have, as yet, taken no account of its quality or of the difference which exists in different classes of schools in the scale of allowance of space for each child in average attendance. The suitability also of the actual space provided for the purposes of Elementary Education must obviously affect the conclusion we have drawn, that, on the whole, the demand for school accommodation has been fairly met. Since the provision of school buildings has been going on without intermission for half a century, great differences exist in the suitability of school premises for the purposes for which they have been erected. The standard of what is required in the way of buildings and appliances has during that period been very properly raised, though uniformity has of necessity not been insisted upon. And many groups of schools, which, at the time they were built, conformed to the requirements of the Education Department, or to the most advanced public opinion of the time, would now be deemed unsuited for educational purposes, were it not that from time to time they have been improved to meet the demands made by Her Majesty's Inspectors. These improvements have very frequently taken the form of the addition of classrooms, which would seem to be going forward in many directions, and would, we are informed, be still more largely carried out but for the badness of the times, a limitation which specially affects agricultural districts. Some schools have been built primarily for purposes other than day school instruction, and have been subsequently adapted for the latter purpose. These, as will be seen in the answers to our Circular B, are in many cases over large, far too wide as regards the main room, while the classrooms are insufficient in number, and unsuitable owing to the want of proper height and width.

One broad line of demarcation, however, exists between the accommodation provided by voluntary effort and that which has been created by School Boards out of loans sanctioned by the Education Department. Whereas a minimum of eight square feet is insisted on by the Department as a provision for each child in average attendance in the former class of schools, in the latter ten square feet has been the established minimum for some years. There can be no doubt that the latter calculation more nearly represents the indispensable requirements that have to be met, and many of the Inspectors urge that there should be a review of the accommodation, so as to bring it up to the higher standard of capacity. In the earlier years after the passing of the Act of 1870 the deficiency to be supplied in the matter of school accommodation was so great that it was not expedient for the Education Department to examine too closely into the quality of the school provision then available. A very great strain was thrown on the resources of the populous and growing districts where school provision was mostly needed. But the time has now come when the chief stress of school provision is past, and when the State may well be more exacting in requiring for all children a proper amount of air and space, suitable premises, airiness and lightness of site, and reasonable extent of playground. We may note that in the Scotch Code it is stated that ten square feet or area for each child in average attendance is to be considered as the normal scale in an efficient school. In his general report for the year 1886, Mr. Blakiston, Chief Inspector of the Northern Division, who has reported more fully on school buildings and equipment than any of his colleagues in the last Report of the Committee of Council (1886-7), while recognising the general improvement in regard to the state of school build-

---

[1] Final Report, pp. 61-4.

ings and premises, and the greater attention paid to cleanliness, repairs, and the supply of apparatus, recommends, with the unanimous concurrence of his colleagues in the district, that the minimum of accommodation in all schools should be raised to ten square feet for each child in average attendance.

It must be borne in mind, however, that superficial area is but a rough approximation to the actual accommodation of a school, and that the truer criterion, especially in schools for older children, is to be found in the amount of seat-room provided. Measured by this standard, it may often be found that overcrowding may exist under the more liberal scale of measurement, equally as under the more restricted measurement of eight square feet for each child. In all schools, indeed, there must be some elbow-room, some surplus accommodation, which is not vacant or unused in any reasonable sense of the term. The more elbow-room there is the better, so long as the children are not withdrawn thereby out of the reach of the eye and voice of their teacher. But we think that the demand for increased accommodation for each child in those buildings in which it has been hitherto calculated at eight square feet per child should be measured rather by the need of more seat-room than by the simple calculation of superficial area. The proper measure of a school's accommodation should be the seat supply, and that measure might well be acted on by the Department, in accordance with the ground plans of the school submitted to them in any review of the sufficiency of the accommodation.

o　　o　　o　　o　　o

It would, indeed, be a hardship were any sudden demand for more space for each child to be made on the schools built by aid of a building grant from the Committee of Council, since they frequently owe their restricted area not so much to the views of their promoters, as to the limits put by the Department on the dimensions of school buildings, especially in regard to breadth, in which direction it was strongly maintained for many years by the Department that any increase on a minimum, which would now be held to be insufficient, was money thrown away, and, therefore, was not to be encouraged by a grant. It is a matter of congratulation that a more liberal scale of estimating accommodation now prevails, and it is a most important rule of the Department that ten square feet should be the minimum accommodation for each child in average attendance in all school buildings in future to be erected.

Some of the above observations as to area apply also to the cubical contents of schoolrooms, which are required to be on a minimum scale of 80 cubic feet for each child in attendance, except in the case of Board schools and of new Voluntary schools, in which the present rules of the Department would exact a minimum of at least 100 cubic feet. Here, again, the amount of air secured by these regulations for each child in attendance is no criterion of the healthiness of such rooms, unless account be further taken of the means provided for changing the air as soon as it becomes vitiated —in other words, for good ventilation. Merely raising the scale of the cubical contents by no means of itself secures the sanitary ends in view; while a remedy for the closeness of those school buildings which have been constructed originally on a low scale of cubical contents may often be best applied by improving the system of ventilation rather than any increase of space. Mr. Blakiston tells us that a gradual amelioration is going on in the sanitary condition of the schools in his district through the substitution of shafts and wall openings for roof ventilation, which latter is found in practice to be attended with so much draught that it is rarely used by the teachers. The system of warming, we are told by the same authority, is now better understood, and fresh air is often admitted in the close neighbourhood of the stove, so as to secure that it shall be warmed before it circulates in the school. We draw attention, at the same time, to a practical suggestion of the same Inspector, which is said largely to improve the attendance in bad weather—viz. the provision of arrangements for drying wet clothes, parents hesitating much less to send their children to school in doubtful weather when they know that they will not have to sit all day in their wet things.

We are of opinion that existing schools should gradually, but within reasonable limits of time, be brought up to the higher estimate of the space required for school accommodation. But we think that this would be more advantageously brought about, in cases where it is required, by pressure exerted on Managers through Her Majesty's Inspectors at the time of their visits than by a hard and fast rule of the Department, which might have the effect of requiring a sudden increase of 25 per cent. in the accommodation in a considerable number of schools throughout the country. The peremptory enforcement of such a requirement would, in our opinion, at the present moment press hardly upon many districts, whether it had to be met by voluntary contribution or out of the rates, and would not, we believe, be consistent with the best interests of the public or the advancement of Elementary Education. Whilst recommending that ten square feet should be provided for each child, it must be borne in mind that such accommodation is needed for the number of children in average attendance, and not for those whose names are on the school books. We find from the Returns for 1886 that, whilst there was room in the schools for 5,145,292 children, the average attendance was only 3,438,425, and the number present on the day of inspection was 4,064,463. To require, therefore, an addition to the accommodation to bring it up to a theoretical standard would produce unnecessary hardship, and it should only be demanded when the average attendance shows that the eixsting schools are insufficient for the number of children that are being educated in them. In these cases a liberal allowance of time ought to be given to the Managers to make the necessary alterations. If, therefore, eight square feet were provided for all children on the rolls, it may be safely assumed that the cases would be comparatively few where the accommodation would not exceed ten square feet for those actually present at any given moment.

In May, 1889, the Managers of the National School, Luton, Bedfordshire, addressed the following communication to the Education Department :—

We, the undersigned Managers of the Luton National Schools, beg to call the attention of their Lordships to the following facts bearing upon the proposed extension of Board schools in the borough.

In a letter from the Department to the Luton School Board received a short time back, we find it stated that there is a deficiency on the north side of the railway only of thirty-two older children. We would respectfully submit, therefore, that to build there for 250 boys, 160 girls, and 150 infants, in addition to the accommodation already existing there, would be a wanton and needless expenditure of public money, and that the only effect will be to draw off children from other schools in which they are at present being taught.

We learn also upon inquiry that there are already fifty vacant spaces in the Hitchin Road Board school, and that if the new schools are sanctioned they will draw away fifty of the children now at school there, thus leaving 100 vacant spaces in that school alone.

Further, we beg to point out that as children in that neighbourhood cannot be found to fill the proposed new schools, the intention of the Board to draft children from the Waller Street school into them, if carried out, would be both undesirable and unjust to the parents of those children, inasmuch as it would compel them in many cases to send their children from one extremity of the town to the other.

Having regard to the school accommodation in the town, as recognised both by the Department and the School Board, we would express our conviction that there is an ample supply both for boys and girls. We forward herewith the School Board Report for 1883 to 1886, from which it will be seen that on the north side of the railway there was accommodation for 887, to which have been added 103 more at St. Matthew's Schools, giving a total of 990; whereas we believe, after making the usual deductions and allowing two-sevenths for boys, two-sevenths for girls, and three-sevenths for infants, accommodation for 968 only is required; and on the south side of the railway there is accommodation for 2,607, to which additions have been made at New Town, raising it to 2,747, whereas, making a like reduction, spaces only for 1,972 are required. We may add that the figures in the School Board Report here are based on the published Schedule of the Department in 1872, on the Report made by Her Majesty's Inspector, Mr. Johnstone, in 1877, and on re-measurement by the School Board in 1886. With such an excess of school places, as School Managers, we feel the only effect of new schools will be needlessly to draw away children from our schools, and to make it more difficult to carry them on, and as ratepayers (we represent a large body) who feel aggrieved by a proposal to spend so large a sum of money as that which will be required without any adequate demand for the outlay.

Adverting to statements made by the School Board, as a plea for new schools, that the Board schools are full, and that it is only in Voluntary schools vacant spaces are to be found, we believe that the use made of rates, in paying fees for 500 children previous to the last election, together with the fact that the Board of Guardians paid only 1s. for the children of indigent parents last year in Voluntary schools, sufficiently accounts for the above difference, and constitutes a hardship, for which we shall be thankful to know what remedy my Lords suggest.

Adverting also to the proposal to convert Waller Street School into a Higher Grade school, we venture to express grave doubt as to the expediency of it.

Waller Street and two other schools in the town are now giving substantially the instruction which would be given in such a school with its new name; but should the change which is sought for take place, many children of the poorer classes will be driven from that school, towards which they have to pay rates, and the school then made one for wealthier classes who can well pay for the education of their children elsewhere.

Probably as a result of the conclusions of the Royal Commission, which have already been set out, the Education Department, on June 17th, 1889, made the following reply to the Managers of the Luton National School :—

In reply to the letter addressed by you and other Managers of Luton National School to the Education Department on the 18th ultimo, I am to state that the whole question therein referred to was very fully considered, as will appear from the correspondence which has passed between this Department and the Luton School Board. My Lords cannot agree with the opinion that the only effect of the completion of the Old Bedford Road Schools will be to draw off children from other schools in which they are at present being taught. They consider that for the purpose of determining whether the application of a School Board for a loan under Section 10 of the Elementary Education Act of 1873 should be granted, the existing accommodation for older children should not be taken at eight square feet per child, which is the minimum allowance under the Code for the purposes of annual grants, but should be calculated at ten square feet.

Her Majesty's Inspector reported as follows, on March 30th last :—

" I find that if ten square feet per child is taken as the basis of calculation, Luton National Boys' School is now fairly full (300 with accommodation for 308) and that St. Mary's Hall is the same, for if 89 places be subtracted from the accommodation for girls, there remain 214 places, with 230 girls on the books; that, taking Christ Church Boys' and Girls', St. Matthew's Boys' and Girls', Chapel Street Boys' and Girls', Langley Street Girls', Waller Street Boys', and Hitchin Road Girls' Schools, these schools are overfull to the extent, in the aggregate, of 321 boys and 298 girls on the books; that, if the ascertained excess of 150 places for elder children on the south side of the railway were devoted to relieving the overflow of children at Chapel Street and Langley Street, there would yet remain in Christ Church Boys' and Girls', St. Matthew's Boys' and Girls', Waller Street Boys', and Hitchin Road Girls', an excess of 251 boys and 149 girls, over the recognised accommodation, who could be conveniently accommodated at Old Bedford Road."

My Lords, upon a review of all the circumstances, saw no sufficient reason for treating the accommodation in the Bedford Street School as practically restricted to children living on the same side of the railway.

They also felt that the enlargement of that school would best be made on such a scale as would render it unnecessary to interrupt the school work, and to increase the aggregate expense, by further additions hereafter, for the purpose of completing the organisation.

This correspondence was considered of such great importance that it was published as a Parliamentary Paper.

In March, 1898, a deputation from the Burton Latimer School Board waited upon the Vice-President of the Committee of Council on Education, and were informed that, in estimating the needs of the parish, they were entitled to base their application at ten square feet per child.[1] It was probably in consequence of this public declaration, that the Board's attention was called to the matter. In 1899, the following correspondence took place between the London School Board and the Education Department:—

On February 3rd, 1899, the Board forwarded to the Department a letter in the following terms:—

The attention of the Board has been called to a Return, ordered by the House of Lords in 1889, for the "Recent correspondence between the Managers of the National School, Luton, Beds, and the Education Department, in reference to a proposed loan to be raised by the Luton School Board upon the security of the rates."

This correspondence consists of two letters, one from the Managers of the Luton National School, dated May 18th, 1889, and the reply from the Education Department, dated June 17th, 1889. In the course of this reply their Lordships state that "they consider that for the purpose of determining whether the application of a School Board for a loan under Section 10 of the Elementary Education Act of 1873 should be granted, the existing accommodation for older children should not be taken at eight square feet per child, which is the minimum allowance under the Code for the purposes of annual grants, but should be calculated at ten square feet.'

A public confirmation of this rule was made by the Secretary to the Education Department on March 24th, 1898, upon the occasion of a deputation waiting upon the Vice-President of the Council with regard to the question of school provision at Burton Latimer. Sir George Kekewich then pointed out to the deputation that, in estimating the needs of the parish, they were entitled to base their application at ten square feet per child.

The Board are aware that, in their statistics of existing school accommodation contained in the reports of the School Accommodation and Attendance Committee, whilst the accommodation of the senior departments of the Board schools is, as a rule, reckoned upon the ten square feet basis, the accommodation of the senior departments of the Voluntary schools is, as a rule, reckoned upon the eight square feet basis. It has now, for a considerable time, been generally recognised that eight square feet of superficial area is quite inadequate for the accommodation in boys' and girls' schools, and, as a matter of fact, in the case of many Voluntary schools, although they are reckoned in the Board's statistics upon the eight square feet basis, in practice the admissions are restricted to the number which can be accommodated upon the ten square feet basis.

In these circumstances, the Board have decided that the rule laid down by the Education Department in 1889, as quoted above, and confirmed on March 24th, 1898, should be acted upon with regard to the statistics of Voluntary school accommodation in all future applications of the Board for the provision of additional school places, and they have now directed me to inform the Education Department of this decision.

In reply to the foregoing letter, the Education Department, on February 17th, 1899, wrote as follows:—

Adverting to your letter dated the 3rd inst., their Lordships note that your Board intends in future, in compiling statistics of school accommodation, to reckon the accommodation provided for elder children in Voluntary schools on the basis of ten square feet per head of average attendance.

---

[1] *School Board Chronicle*, April 2nd, 1898.

I am, however, to inform you that their Lordships will preserve their liberty of action, and decide each case submitted to them by the Board in accordance with the particular circumstances which affect the case.

Consequently, the accommodation of the Senior departments of all Voluntary schools was reckoned for the purposes of school provision from 1899 onwards at ten square feet per child, and it is this alteration which caused the apparent reduction, for the year 1899, in the accommodation of Voluntary schools in the accompanying tables. This alteration did not affect the actual enrolment at Voluntary schools, which still depends upon the figures recognised by the Board of Education.

The accommodation of Infants' departments in the older Board schools was reckoned at eight square feet per child. The Education Department, on February 23rd, 1897, sanctioned the accommodation, at nine square feet per child, of all Infants' departments of Board schools, plans of which had been submitted to their Lordships since March 7th, 1895, and also of all Infants' departments to be planned in the future. In some of the later plans of these departments which have been submitted sanction has, however, been given for ten square feet per child.

Early in the year 1900 the Board experienced considerable difficulty with the Education Department in obtaining sanction to their applications for additional accommodation, and in a letter dated March 6th, 1900, the Education Department stated that the average attendance in the schools in question showed a considerable number of vacant places. Despite this fact, the recognised method of calculating the number of school places required showed a large deficiency. As the Board had a very considerable number of applications outstanding, they decided, early in March, 1900, to forward a communication to the Education Department dealing with the whole question, and the following is an extract from the letter:—

### CALCULATING ACCOMMODATION ON THE AVERAGE ATTENDANCE.

The School Board for London must call serious attention to the method of *calculating vacant places by deducting average attendance from accommodation.*

The following words occur in the Department's letter of January 24th, 1900:—

"The average attendance in both the schools in question shows a considerable number of vacant places."

From this, it is evident that, in the case under review (Tower Hamlets C), one of the Department's officials had been calculating the vacant places by deducting the average attendance from the accommodation instead of comparing the latter with the roll.

It is difficult for the Board to believe that this action has received the formal sanction of the Department, as it is totally inconsistent with the official declarations upon this subject. Upon this point, it is only necessary to call attention to the following extracts:—

Extract from the Report of the Committee of Council on Education for the year 1871, p. xvi. :—

"We assume that in England and Wales, with a population of upwards of twenty-two millions, the average daily attendance at efficient Elementary schools ought to amount to about three millions. The accommodation for this number of scholars ought to be considerably in excess of the average daily attendance, and provide for a maximum attendance of not much less than four millions.

Extract from a letter from the Education Department, dated January 14th, 1893, to the Stockport School Board :—

" I am to explain that the number of vacant places in a school must be measured by the excess of the number of children for whom the accommodation is provided over the number of children on the books (*not the number in average attendance*)."

At a public inquiry held at the Crawford Street Board School by the Rev. C. D. Du Port, H.M. Inspector, on March 27th, 1899, respecting the proposal of the Board to erect a new school for 1,200 children in Sub-divisions W and X of East Lambeth, he made the following statement :—

" I can lay this down and say officially—we will not accept average attendance as a governing factor relating to the supply of schools. We have never ruled questions of supply by average attendance. The regularity of attendance would be interfered with."

The Board would point out that the principle laid down in the Stockport letter above-mentioned was acted upon by the Department in all their communications to the Board respecting the provision of free school places in London, this basis of calculating accommodation having been adopted by their Lordships in no fewer than fifteen letters, ranging from October 27th, 1893, to December 30th, 1893, particulars of which can be furnished.

The statements quoted above show that it cannot be in the interests of education that schools should be allowed, as a matter of principle, to be crowded up to an average attendance equal to their accommodation upon the eight square feet basis. Such a regulation would prevent all possibility of improvement in the attendance of a school so worked. The only possibility of change would have to be in the direction of further irregularity of attendance, as the slightest improvement would cause the grant to be forfeited.

### The Accommodation in Voluntary Schools.

The Board consider it their duty again to call the attention of the Department to the fact that the number of school places, given by the Education Department as representing the accommodation of the Voluntary schools, is, in their opinion, often exaggerated. During the past year the Department have forwarded to the Board the recognised accommodation of sixty-four schools, amounting in all to 38,707 school places, and it would have been a great convenience to the Board if they had felt justified in substituting these figures for those given in their Tables, as such a course would have led to the recognition of 5,540 additional school places in London

The Board made such inquiries as lay in their power to ascertain whether the figures sent to them by the Department were correct, but the Board not only failed to substantiate the figures forwarded to them by the Department, but in some cases the Managers of the schools declared that their schools could not possibly accommodate the number of children with which the Department would have the Board credit them. For instance, at the Jews' Free School, Whitechapel, it was ascertained that the Department based their figures upon the total area of the school, including drill and examination halls, workshop, cookery room, etc., and that as these were not available as classrooms they should not have been reckoned in the accommodation. In the case of the Wesleyan School, Westminster, it should be pointed out that the accommodation, even upon the eight square feet basis, would not, according to the dimensions furnished by the Managers, amount to the number given by the Education Department. It should also be stated that this school, which is a practising school in connection with a Training College, and charges high fees, had on March 25th, 1899, the names of only 540 children upon the rolls, whereas the Education Department state that the school is recognised for 1,261 children. The Board consider that, so far from proceeding upon the assumption of the Department that it is possible to send another 721 children to the school, it is far safer to assume that this type of school would only continue to accommodate the number actually upon the roll.

It should further be pointed out that when it is proposed to transfer a Voluntary school to the Board the Education Department have required the Board to incur considerable expenditure upon the building before consenting even to recognise the premises as a temporary Board school ; and that, upon the school being taken over by the Board, it has invariably resulted in the accommodation being greatly reduced. As instances of this, the following cases may be cited :—

| Name of School. | Accom. as a Voluntary School at 8 sq. ft. | E.D. Blue Book. | Accom. as a Board School. |
|---|---|---|---|
| Allen Street British, Chelsea ... ... ... | 783 | 822 | 483 |
| British, Frogmore Lane, Wandsworth ... ... ... | 524 | 523 | 435 |
| St. Jude's (N), Commercial Street, Whitechapel ... | 675 | 675 | 618 |
| Portland British, Little Titchfield Street, W. ... | 862 | 865 | 738 |
| Tidey Street Wesleyan School, Bow Common, E. ... | 610 | 637 | 522 |
| Kentish Town British School ... ... ... ... | 598 | 598 | 504 |

Although the Board feel convinced that, in all cases of error, the Department would at once correct their figures, unfortunately it is quite beyond the power of the Board to obtain accurate information of Voluntary schools except in those cases where it has been willingly tendered by the Managers themselves, or where the facts are disclosed by the transfer of the schools to the Board.

The Board noticed with satisfaction that the President of the Council at the opening of the English Education Exhibition this year, stated, in the presence of the Prince of Wales, that he hoped the exhibition would 'incite us one and all to spare no pains in the endeavour to fulfil each one his own due part in the great national duty of providing, not for our own sons and daughters only, but for all the sons and daughters of the country, the noblest education, the best training, and the finest discipline that the wit of man and the love of God can together produce and inspire."

The School Board for London, in view of this declaration, trust they will be encouraged by the Education Department in their efforts to secure necessary conditions of health and educational efficiency for the children of the Metropolis."

Further correspondence ensued, and the School Board, in their final communication on July 20th, 1900, stated that, in view of the expressed declarations to which they had called attention, they relied on the Board of Education not to recede from the reasonable position which the Education Department took up for so many years in acting upon the methods of estimating the need of school provision by reckoning the accommodation of senior departments of all schools upon the ten square feet basis, and by ascertaining the number of vacant places in a school by comparing the recognised accommodation with the number on the roll, and not with the average attendance. All applications to the Board of Education since this date have been based upon the above-mentioned methods.

## VI. Provision of School Accommodation.

The Table on the following pages comprehensively deals with the progress made in the provision of school accommodation year by year from the commencement of the Board's work.

The following expressions of opinion by the last two Senior Chief Inspectors of Elementary schools, which are contained in their official Reports to the Board of Education, adequately deal with the question of the apparent excess of school places which is shown by the figures. The Rev. T. W. Sharp, C.B., in 1897, said :—

As I have stated in previous Reports, this excess is entirely fictitious; these 20,469 places are not only unavailable for the distant new and growing districts, but useless also in their own immediate neighbourhoods. A large number of school places should be "written off '; the vacant places in Westminster and the City have not been occupied for many years; in Southwark, where the population is nearly stationary, the substitution of workshops for dwelling-houses at the City end of the district tends to empty the schools at that end, while the erection of workmen's dwellings in the distant parts requires the erection of fresh schools at the other end. Among the many causes requiring fresh schools we may note the annual increase of the child population, the transference of working people from the centre to the suburbs, the gratifying, though small, increase in the average attendance, the presence in the school of more than 40,000 scholars over fourteen years of age who are under no legal obligation to attend school. The Board has, therefore, decided to provide 52,438 addi-

| Year. | Permanent Existing Accommodation. | | | Increase or *Decrease* on the Preceding Year. | | | Estimated Number of School Places Required. |
|---|---|---|---|---|---|---|---|
| | Board. | Non-Board. | Total. | Board. | Non-Board. | Total. | |
| 1871 | 1,101° | 261,158 | 262,259 | ... | ... | ... | ... |
| 1872 | 28,227° | 249,705 | 277,932 | 27,126 | *11,453* | 15,673 | 454,783 |
| 1873 | 58,581° | 282,936 | 341,517 | 30,354 | 33,231 | 63,585 | 452,836 |
| 1874 | 99,042° | 283,451 | 382,493 | 40,461 | 515 | 40,976 | † |
| 1875 | 123 557° | 288,702 | 412,259 | 24,515 | 5,251 | 29,766 | † |
| 1876 | 146,074° | 287,116 | 433,190 | 22,517 | *1,586* | 20,931 | † |
| 1877 | 141,693 | 282,626 | 424,319 | *4,381* | *4,490* | *8,871* | † |
| 1878 | 175,882 | 274,451 | 450,333 | 34,189 | *8,175* | 26,014 | 517,846 |
| 1879 | 199,788 | 271,314 | 471,102 | 23,906 | *3,137* | 20,769 | 531,063 |
| 1880 | 210 057 | 267,989 | 478,046 | 10,269 | *3,325* | 6,944 | 535,869 |
| 1881 | 238 163 | 262,878 | 501,041 | 28,106 | *5,111* | 22,995 | 577,303 |
| 1882 | 264,647 | 263,617 | 528,264 | 26,484 | 739 | 27,223 | 593,666 |
| 1883 | 290,632 | 260,906 | 551,538 | 25,985 | *2,711* | 23,274 | 613,282 |
| 1884 | 317,418 | 262,075 | 579,493 | 26,786 | 1,169 | 27,955 | 627,236 |
| 1885 | 337,865 | 260 597 | 598,462 | 20,447 | *1,478* | 18,969 | 642,862 |
| 1886 | 358,929 | 260,158 | 619,087 | 21,064 | *439* | 20,625 | 655,976 |
| 1887 | 385,171 | 260,270 | 645,441 | 26,242 | 112 | 26,354 | 666,718 |
| 1888 | 396,703 | 262 022 | 658,725 | 11 532 | 1,752 | 13,284 | 668,220‡ |
| 1889 | 404,462 | 262,270 | 666,732 | 7,759 | 248 | 8,007 | 686,620 |
| 1890 | 407,985 | 260,449 | 668,434 | 3,523 | *1,821* | 1,702 | 688,057 |
| 1891 | 415,719 | 258,329 | 674,048 | 7,734 | *2,120* | 5,614 | † |
| 1892 | 422,648 | 256,266 | 678,914 | 6,929 | *2,063* | 4,866 | 707,342 |
| 1893 | 436,193 | 258,604 | 694,797 | 13,545 | *2,338* | 15,883 | † |
| 1894 | 458,143 | 257,652 | 715,795 | 21,950 | *952* | 20,998 | † |
| 1895 | 473,053 | 255,721 | 728,774 | 14,910 | *1,931* | 12,979 | 723,074 |
| 1896 | 483,077 | 256,863 | 739,940 | 10,024 | 1,142 | 11,166 | 728,845 |
| 1897 | 494,555 | 257,527 | 752,082 | 11,478 | 664 | 12,142 | 734,770 |
| 1898 | 510,388 | 257,124 | 767,512 | 15,833 | *403* | 15,430 | 728,882 |
| 1899 | 521,826 | 224,360 | 746,186 | 11.438 | *32,764*§ | *21,326* | 784,590 |
| 1900 | 531,494 | 221,387 | 752,881 | 9,668 | *2,973* | 6,695 | 781,553 |
| 1901 | 538,342 | 221,121 | 759,463 | 6,848 | *266* | 6,582 | 791,053¶ |
| 1902 | 549,482 | 218,376 | 767,858 | 11,140 | *2,745* | 8,395 | 787,678 |
| 1903 | 554,198 | 217,088 | 771,286 | 4,716 | *1,288* | 3,428 | 784,355 |

\* As the permanent accommodation in Board schools cannot be determined for the years 1871-6, all accommodation, whether permanent or temporary, is given for the years 1871 to 1876. This will account for the apparent decrease in 1877.

† No simultaneous scheduling in the years 1874 to 1877 and 1891, 1893 and 1894.

‡ In the Report for 1888, the estimated number of school places required was obtained by deducting 20 per cent. from the number of children scheduled. For the purpose of comparison, however, the usual practice of deducting 12½ per cent. has been adopted in this Table.

§ Of the above number, only 2,269 places were actually closed, the apparent reduction being mainly due to the fact that the accommodation of the Senior

tional school places, and has projected twenty-three other schools, the sites of some of which are already secured. Nor should this large provision be considered in any sense extravagant or unnecessary; it is almost impossible that any part of .t should have been made without sufficient forethought. Any addition to the provision of schools is open to the criticism of the more economical members in Committee, and in the meetings of the School Board, and has subsequently to undergo the challenge of the expert Inspectors of the Department. There can be very little doubt that every one of these contemplated places will be filled as soon as the schools are completed, or after a short interval.

| Year. | Permanent Existing Accommodation. | | | Projected School Places. | Existing and Projected Accommodation. | | |
|---|---|---|---|---|---|---|---|
| | Number of School Places. | Excess of School Places. | Deficiency of School Places. | | Number of School Places. | Excess of School Places. | Deficiency of School Places. |
| 1871 | 262 259° | ... | ... | ... | ... | ... | ... |
| 1872 | 277,932° | ... | 176,851 | 100,600 | 378,532 | ... | 76,251 |
| 1873 | 341,517° | ... | 111,319 | 85,427 | 426,944 | ... | 25,892 |
| 1874 | 382,493° | ... | ... | 62,635 | 445,128 | ... | ... |
| 1875 | 412,259° | ... | ... | 70,264 | 482,523 | ... | ... |
| 1876 | 433,190° | ... | ... | 70,267 | 503,457 | ... | ... |
| 1877 | 424,319 | ... | ... | 81,364 | 505,683 | ... | ... |
| 1878 | 450,333 | ... | 67,513 | 96 497 | 546,830 | 28,984 | ... |
| 1879 | 471,102 | ... | 59,961 | 78 271 | 549,373 | 18,310 | ... |
| 1880 | 478,046 | ... | 57,823 | 86,209 | 564,255 | 28,386 | ... |
| 1881 | 501,041 | ... | 76,262 | 99,597 | 600,638 | 23,335 | ... |
| 1882 | 528,264 | ... | 65,402 | 90 569 | 618,833 | 25,167 | ... |
| 1883 | 551,538 | ... | 61,744 | 96 770 | 648,308 | 35,026 | ... |
| 1884 | 579,493 | ... | 47,743 | 89,005 | 668,498 | 41,262 | ... |
| 1885 | 598,462 | ... | 44,400 | 69,144 | 667,606 | 24,744 | ... |
| 1886 | 619,087 | ... | 36 889 | 67.728 | 686,815 | 30,839 | ... |
| 1887 | 645,441 | ... | 21,277 | 46.813 | 692,254 | 25,536 | ... |
| 1888 | 658,725 | ... | 9,495 | 48 872 | 707,597 | 39,377 | ... |
| 1889 | 666,732 | ... | 19,888 | 41,772 | 708,504 | 21 884 | ... |
| 1890 | 668,434 | ... | 19,623 | 59,945 | 728,379 | 40,322 | ... |
| 1891 | 674,048 | ... | ... | 57,983 | 732,031 | ... | ... |
| 1892 | 678,914 | ... | 28,428 | 57,028 | 735,942 | 28 600 | ... |
| 1893 | 694,797 | ... | ... | 54,301 | 749,098 | ... | ... |
| 1894 | 715,795 | ... | ... | 47,167 | 762,962 | ... | ... |
| 1895 | 728,774 | 5,700 | ... | 58 692 | 787,466 | 64,392 | ... |
| 1896 | 739,940 | 11,095 | ... | 63,827 | 803,767 | 74,922 | ... |
| 1897 | 752,082 | 17,312 | ... | 54,762 | 806,844 | 72,074 | ... |
| 1898 | 767,512 | 38,630 | ... | 52,867 | 820,379 | 91,497 | ... |
| 1899 | 746,186 | ... | 38,404 | 47,837 | 794 023 | 9,433 | ... |
| 1900 | 752,881 | ... | 28,672 | 51,619 | 804,500 | 22,947 | ... |
| 1901 | 759,463 | ... | 31,590 | 50,241 | 809,704 | 18,651 | ... |
| 1902 | 767,858 | ... | 19,820 | 51,762 | 819,620 | 31,942 | ... |
| 1903 | 771,286 | ... | 13,069 | 59,780 | 831,066 | 46,711 | ... |

Departments, which had hitherto been reckoned generally at 8 square feet per child, was this year, for the first time, reckoned at 10 square feet per child.

‖ This increase is accounted for by the fact that, in estimating the number of school places required, the number of children over 13 years of age in attendance at Public Elementary schools was this year, for the first time (with the concurrence of the Board of Education), added to the number scheduled between 3 and 13, less 12½ per cent.

¶ In this year the superior age limit for the attendance of children at school was raised from 13 to 14, and consequently all the children of the Elementary school class between those years have since been scheduled. This accounts for the increase shown in 1901 in the number of school places estimated to be required.

The late Mr. T. King said in his Report of 1901 :—

In estimating the excess or deficiency of school places within any of the sub-divisions of London the Board calculated for "projected" school places. A few of these projected schools appear to be near completion, but apparently no considerable addition to the supply of schools will be actually made during the next two years. If then the existing supply of school places be compared with the estimated number of places required, a startling result is obtained. Instead of an excess of more than 18,000 school places, as the Board estimate, there is a deficiency of more than 30,000 places. The discrepancy is due, as has already been stated, to the omission of "projected" places which may become available at some future time, but certainly are not now. To some extent this deficiency is reduced by the use of temporary buildings which supply more than 24,000 [14,000] places; still, even taking these into account, the urgent need of additional accommodation is undeniable. This need, too, is greater than the summary indicates, for an examination of the condition of the different divisions of London, or of different portions of the same division, will show a large extent of unused accommodation in the City, Westminster, and Southwark, and a large deficiency in Chelsea, Greenwich, West Lambeth, Tower Hamlets, which is little, if at all, relieved by the vacant places in the first-mentioned group of districts. (A few children from West Lambeth attend schools in Westminster.)

The fact must be taken into account that, even in parts of the same districts, there may be an excess of accommodation which is not available to relieve deficiencies in other parts; and this is especially true of districts like Chelsea, which has been growing rapidly on its western border. Here numerous streets of houses have been recently erected which will probably provide a large number of scholars who require Elementary instruction. Again, in Tower Hamlets, there is a temporary superabundance of school places towards the east which cannot relieve the overcrowded schools in Whitechapel. The migration of the working class population from the central part of London to the outskirts and over the border further complicates the problem of providing school accommodation. The conclusion is stated in the Report of the School Attendance and Accommodation Committee of the Board that, "even if there were a large net decrease in the number of children, the Board might still be compelled to provide for many thousands whose parents had removed from districts · where there was ample accommodation to districts inadequately provided with schools." Probably the local authorities of districts which are now outside the Administrative County of London will have to undertake some share of the work, but much will be left for the School Board of London; and their proposal to add 50,000 school places during the next few years, although it shows some excess of accommodation above the total number of children for whom provision is required, will probably be justified by the necessity of the case.

It will, of course, still be necessary, from time to time, to provide for certain districts of London as vacant land is covered with houses, and where better class property is replaced by smaller houses, and to meet such changes as are at present being experienced in Whitechapel and Stepney by the population becoming much denser. Moreover, the whole tendency of latter-day legislation is to extend the school-life of the children. Even apart from legislation, there is undoubtedly a growing feeling of appreciation of the value of the education given in Elementary schools, as is proved by the fact that prior to the establishment of the School Board, one-seventh of the population belonged to the class above that which uses Public Elementary schools; at the present time that class is only one-tenth.

It is evident, for these and other reasons, that further school accommodation will

**Chelsea.**
1. Ashburnham.
2. Cook's Ground.
3. Marlborough Road.
4. Park Walk.
5. Walton Street.

**Fulham.**
6. Ackmar Road.
7. Beaufort House.
8. Everington Street.
9. Fulham Palace Road.
10. Halford Road.
11. Harwood Road.
12. Hugon Road.
13. Kingwood Road.
14. Langford Road.
15. Lillie Road.
16. Mac Murdo Road.
17. Munster Road.
18. North End Road.
19. Peterborough.
20. St. Dunstan's Road.
21. Sherbrooke Road.
22. Star Lane.
23. Townmead Road.
24. William Street.

**Hammersmith.**
25. Addison Gardens.
26. Brackenbury Road.
27. Cobbald Road.
28. Elbrick Road.
29. Flora Gardens.
30. Kenmont Gardens.
31. Latimer Road.
32. Lannlers Road.
33. Victoria Road.
34. Waterloo Street.
35. Westville Road.

**Hampstead.**
36. Fleet Road.
37. Heath Street.
38. Kingsgate Road.
39. Netherwood Street.
40. Rosslyn Hill.
41. Worsley Road.

**Kensington.**
42. Allen Street.
43. Buckingham Terrace.
44. Edinburgh Road.
45. Fox.
46. Gloucester Grove East.
47. Middle Row.
48. Oxford Gardens.
49. Portobello Road.
50. Sirdar Road.
51. Wornington Road.

**Paddington.**
52. Amberley Road.
53. Beethoven Street.
54. Campbell Street.
55. Droop Street.
56. Essendine Road.
57. Kilburn Lane.
58. Moberly.

**Marylebone.**
59. Barrett Street.
60. Barrow Hill Road.
61. Bell Street.
62. Capland Street.
63. Capland Street, Junior.
64. Portland Street.
65. Stephen Street.

**St. Pancras.**
66. Aldenham Street.
67. Arlington Road.
68. Brecknock.
69. Burghley Road.
70. Carlton Road.
71. Camden Street.
72. Fortess Road.
73. Great College Street.
74. Hawkstock Hill.
75. Harmay Crescent.
76. Holmes Road.
77. Kentish Town Road.
78. Mansfield Road.
79. Netherden Street.
80. Nutley Street.
81. Princes Road.
82. Rhyl Street.
83. Stanhope Street.
84. White Street.

**Westminster.**
85. Buckingham Gate.
86. Charing Cross Road.
87. Horseferry Road.
88. Millbank.
89. Millbank Road.
90. Pulteney.
91. St. George's Row.

**Bermondsey.**
1. Albion Street.
2. East Lane.
3. Fair Street.
4. Farncombe Street.
5. Keetons Road.
6. Lawes Street.
7. Magdalen Street.
8. Neckinger Road.
9. Riley Street.
10. Snowsfields.
11. Webb Street.

**Bethnal Green.**
12. Beaver Street.
13. Chisenhale Road.
14. Columbia Road.
15. Cranbrook Road.
16. Daniel Street.
17. Globe Terrace.
18. Hague Street.
19. Mansford Street.
20. Mowlem Street.
21. Olga Street.
22. Portman Place.
23. Pritchard's Road.
24. Rochelle Street.
25. Summerford Street.
26. Teesdale Street.
27. Turin Street.
28. Virginia Road.
29. Wilmot Street.
30. Wolverley Street.
31. Wood Close.

**Finsbury.**
32. Ann Street.
33. Baltic Street.
34. Bath Street.
35. Central Street.
36. Chequer Street.
37. Compton Street.
38. Hugh Myddelton.
39. Hugh Myddelton, Junr.
40. Martyrs Memorial.
41. Moreland Street.
42. Risinghill Street.
43. St. John's Lane.
44. White Lion Street.
45. Winchester Street.

**Hackney.**
46. Bailey's Lane.
47. Benthall Road.
48. Berger Road.
49. Cass and Road.
50. Daubeney Road.
51. Detmold Road.
52. Eleanor Road.
53. Enfield Road.
54. Gainsborough Road.
55. Gayhurst Road.
56. Glyn Road.
57. High Street, Stoke Newington.
58. Hindle Street.
59. Homerton Row.
60. Lauriston Road.
61. London Fields.
62. Mandeville Street.
63. Millfields Road.
64. Morning Lane.
65. Northwold Road.
66. Orchard Street.
67. Queen's Road.
68. Rushmore Road and Chatsworth Road.
69. Sigdon Road.
70. Sydney Road.
71. Tottenham Road.
72. Wilton Road.
73. Windsor Road.

**Holborn.**
74. Great Wild Street.
75. Princeton Street.
76. Rosebery Avenue.
77. Saffron Hill.
78. Tower Street.

**Islington.**
79. Ambler Road.
80. Arlington Road.
81. Blackstock Road.
82. Blundell Street.
83. Buckingham Street.
84. Caledonian Road.
85. Canonbury Road.
86. Cottenham Road.
87. Duncombe Road.
88. Ecclesbourne Road.
89. Elthorne Road.
90. Fowler.
91. Gifford Street.
92. Gillespie Road.
93. Grafton Road.
94. Hanover Street.
95. Hargrave Park.
96. Harvist Road.
97. Hungerford Road.
98. Montem Street.
99. Newington Green.
100. Offord Road.
101. Pakeman Street.
102. Pooles Park.
103. Popham Road.
104. Queen's Head Street.
105. Richard Street.
106. Rotherfield Street.
107. St. Bartholomew.
108. Shepperton Road.
109. Station Road.
110. Thornhill Road.
111. Upper Hornsey Road.
112. Victoria Place.
113. Westbourne Road.
114. Whittington.
115. Yerbury Road.
116. York Road.

**Lambeth.**
117. Addington Street.
118. Johanna Street.
119. Waterloo Road.

**City of London.**
120. Gravel Lane, Houndsditch.
121. Graystoke Place, Fetter Lane.
122. Swan Street, Minories.

**Poplar.**
123. All Hallow's.
124. Alton Street.
125. Atley Road.
126. Bow Creek.
127. Bromley Hall Road.
128. Byron and Bright Street.
129. Culloden Street.
130. Fairfield Road.
131. Glaucus Street.
132. Gougal Road.
133. High Street, Bromley.
134. Knapp Road.
135. Malmesbury Road.
136. Marner Street.
137. Midwall.
138. Monteith Road.
139. Oban Street.
140. Old Palace.
141. Ricardo Street.
142. Roman Road.
143. St. Leonard's Road.
144. Speed Road.
145. Tidey Street.
146. Upper North Street.
147. Wedmore Street.

**St. Pancras.**
148. Manchester Street.
149. Prospect Terrace.

**Shoreditch.**
150. Canal Road.
151. Catherine Street.
152. Chatham Gardens.
153. Curtain Road.
154. Fellows Street.
155. Gopsall Street.
156. Haggerston Road.
157. Hamond Square.
158. Maidstone Street.
159. Napier Street.
160. Redvers Street.
161. St. John's Road.
162. Scawfell Street.
163. Stratton Street.
164. Stap Street.
165. Trinity Place.
166. Wenlock Road.

**Southwark.**
167. Belvedere Place.
168. Chaucer.
169. Harfield Street.
170. Holland Street.
171. Lant Street.
172. Marlborough Street.
173. Orange Street.
174. Pocock Street.
175. Rockingham Street.
176. Westminster Bridge Road.

**Stepney.**
177. Baker Street.
178. Ben Jonson.
179. Berner Street.
180. Little Street.
181. Brewhouse Lane.
182. Broad Street.
183. Bucks Row.
184. Coble Street.
185. Cayley Street.
186. Clicksand Street.
187. Christian Street.
188. Collingwood Street.
189. Commercial Street.
190. Dalgleish Street.
191. Deal Street.
192. Dempsey Street.
193. Essex Street.
194. Ferrance Street.
195. Garden Street.
196. Gill Street.
197. Globe Street.
198. Hanbury Street.
199. Highway.
200. Lower Chapman Street.
201. Northey Street.
202. Old Castle Street.
203. Old Montague Street.
204. Philpot Street.
205. Raisind Street.
206. St. John's, Halley Street.
207. St. Paul's Road.
208. Settles Street.
209. Single Street.
210. Smith Street.
211. South Grove.
212. Thomas Street.
213. Trafalgar Square.
214. Vallance Road.

**Stoke Newington.**
215. Church Street.
216. Oldfield Road.
217. Princess May Road.
218. Wordsworth Road.

**INDUSTRIAL SCHOOLS.**
**Hackney.**
1. Upton House Truant.
**Holborn.**
2. Drury Lane.
**Islington.**
3. Highbury Truant.
**Poplar.**
4. Brunswick Road.

**Battersea.**
1. Basnett Road.
2. Battersea Park Road.
3. Boileville Road.
4. Bolingbroke Road.
5. Ethelburga Street.
6. Gideon Road.
7. Holden Street.
8. Honeywell Road.
9. Latchmere
10. Lavender Hill.
11. Mantua Street.
12. Plough Road.
13. Ponton Road.
14. Raywood Street.
15. Shillington Street.
16. Seaford Street.
17. Surrey Lane.
18. Tennyson Street.
19. Winstanley Road.
20. Wix's Lane.

**Bermondsey.**
21. Alexis Street.
22. Alma.
23. Galleywall Road.
24. Monnow Road.
25. Page's Walk.
26. Southwark Park.

**Camberwell.**
27. Adys Road.
28. Arthur Street.
29. Bellenden Road.
30. Boundary Lane.
31. Cator Street.
32. Choumert Road.
33. Cobourg Road.
34. Colls Road.
35. Crawford Road.
36. Credon Road.
37. Dulwich Hamlet.
38. Edgecombe Road.
39. Friern
40. George Street.
41. Gloucester Road.
42. Goodrich Road.
43. Grove Vale.
44. Heber Road.
45. Ilderton Road.
46. Leipsic Road.
47. Leo Street.
48. Lyndhurst Grove.
49. Mawbey Road.
50. Nunhead Passage.
51. Oliver Goldsmith.
52. Peckham Park.
53. Reddins Road.
54. Rolls Road.
55. Ruby Street.
56. Scarsdale Road.
57. Southampton Street.
58. Sumner Road.
59. Vestry Road.
60. Woods Road.

**Lambeth.**
61. Church Street.
62. Cormont Road.
63. Effra Parade.
64. Gipsy Road.
65. Hackford Road.
66. Jessop Road.
67. Kennington Road.
68. Lollard Street.
69. Lyham Road.
70. Priory Grove.
71. Rosendale Road.
72. Salter's Hill.
73. Santley Street.
74. South Lambeth Road.
75. Springfield
76. Stockwell Road.
77. Sussex Road.
78. Upper Kennington Lane.
79. Vauxhall Street.
80. Walnut Tree Walk.
81. Woodland Road.

**Southwark.**
82. Beresford Street.
83. Crampton Street.
84. Faunce Street.
85. Flint Street.
86. Harper Street.
87. John Ruskin.
88. King and Queen Street.
89. Michael Faraday.
90. Mina Road.
91. Paragon.
92. Penrose Street.
93. Sandford Row.
94. Sayer Street.
95. Surrey Square.
96. Townsend Street.
97. Victory Place.
98. West Square.
99. Westmoreland Road.
100. Weston Street.

**Wandsworth.**
101. Aristotle Road.
102. Bonneville Road.
103. Brandlehow Road.
104. Broadwater Road.
105. Cavendish Road.
106. Deodar Road.
107. Eardley Road.
108. Earlsfield.
109. Eltringham Street.
110. Ensham Street.
111. Fircroft Road.
112. Frogmore.
113. Garrett Lane.
114. Haselrigge Road.
115. Hitherfield Road.
116. Larkhall Lane.
117. Merton Road.
118. Mitcham Lane.
119. New Park Road.
120. New Road.
121. Oldridge Road.
122. St. Andrew Street.
123. Smallwood Road.
124. Sunnyhill Road.
125. Swaffield Road.
126. Telferscot Road.
127. Tooting Graveney.
128. Waldron Road.
129. Warple Way.
130. West Hill.
131. Wirtemberg Street.

**INDUSTRIAL SCHOOLS.**
**Battersea.**
1. Ponton Road.
**Wandsworth.**
2. Clapham Park.

George Philip & Son Ltd.

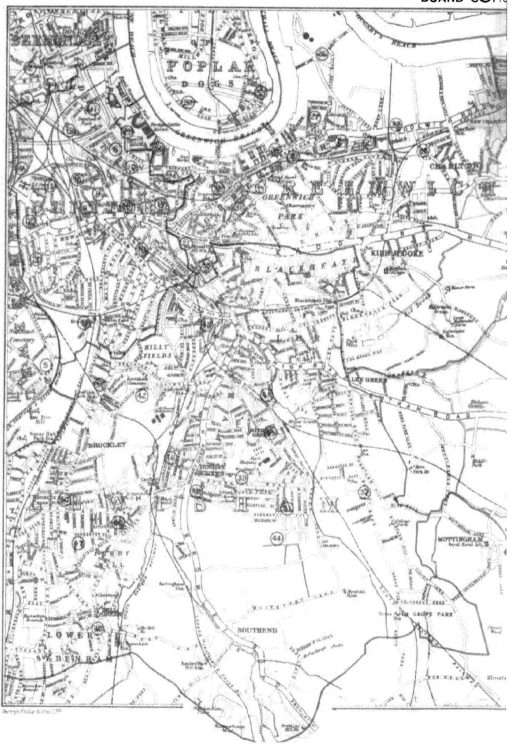

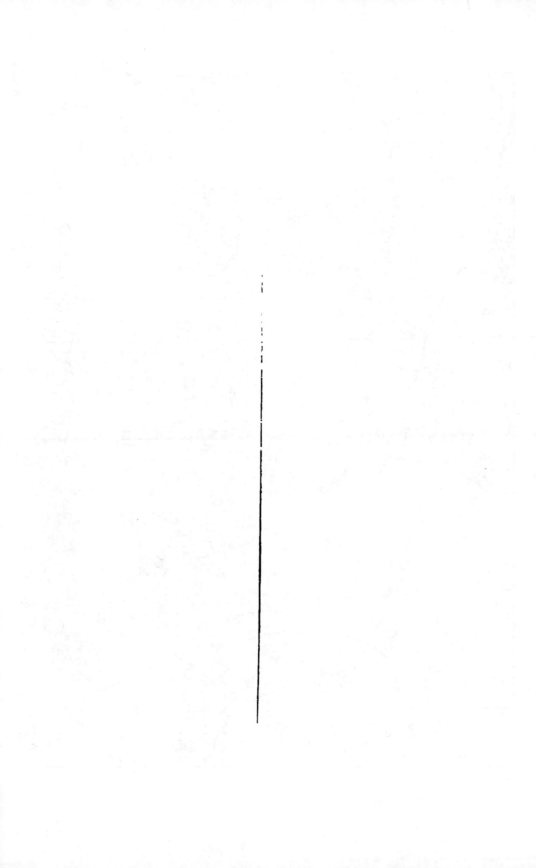

**City of London.**
1. Aldersgate Ward.
2. Aldgate Ward.
3. Bilingsgate & Tower.
4. Bishopsgate.
5. Coleman street.
6. Cripplegate.
7. St. Ann's.
8. St. Bartholomew the Great.
9. St. Botolph's.
10. St. Bride's.
11. St. Dunstan's, Fleet Street
12. St. Dunstan's, Fetter Lane.
13. Sir John Cass's Foundation
14. St. Sepulchre.

**Bermondsey.**
15. All Saints' (R.C.)
16. Bacon's.
17. Christ Church, Paradise Street.
18. Christ Church, Prospect Place.
19. Dockhead (R.C.)
20. Holy Trinity.
21. Roman Catholic.
22. Rotherhithe Amicable Society's.
23. Rotherhithe National.
24. St. Andrew's.
25. St. James'.
26. St. Joseph's (R.C.)
27. St. Mary Magdalene's.
28. St. Mary, Rotherhithe.
29. St. Olaves Charity.
30. St. Paul's.
31. Stephen the Yeoman's

**Bethnal Green.**
32. Roman Catholic.
33. St. Barnabas'.
34. St. Bartholomew's.
35. St. James the Less.
36. St. John's.
37. St. Jude's.
38. St. Matthias'.
39. St. Peter's.
40. St. Philip's.
41. Wesleyan.

**Finsbury.**
42. National, Amwell Street
43. St. Barnabas.
44. St. Joseph's (R.C.)
45. St. Jude's.
46. St. Mark's, Brewer Street.
47. St. Mark's, Old Street.
48. St. Peter & St. Paul.
49. St. Thomas', Charterhouse (Girls)
50. St. Thomas', Charterhouse (Boys)

**Hackney.**
51. Hackney Free.
52. Holy Trinity.
53. Miss Munro.
54. Miss Smith.
55. Parochial.
56. Rams.
57. St. James'.
58. St. John Baptist
59. St. Joseph's (R.C.) Clapton.
60. St. Joseph's (R.C.) Clapton.
61. St. Mary of the Immaculate Heart (R.C.)
62. St. Matthew's.
63. St. Michael & All Angels.
64. St. Paul's
65. Upper Clapton & Stamford Hill.
66. Wesleyan.
67. West Hackney.

**Holborn.**
68. Christchurch.
69. Holy Family (R.C.)
70. Macklin Street.
71. St. Alban's.
72. St. Andrew's.
73. St. George the Martyr.
74. St. George's.
75. St. Giles'.
76. St. John the Evangelist.
77. St. Mary's (R.C.)
78. St. Peter's (R.C.)

**Islington.**
79. All Saints'.
80. Eden Grove (K.C.)
81. German School.
82. Highbury Vale.
83. Highbury Wesleyan.
84. Holy Trinity.
85. St. Clement's.
86. St. James'.
87. St. John the Evangelist (R.C.)
88. St. John's.
89. St. Joseph's (R.C.)
90. St. Jude's, King Henry's Walk.
91. St. Jude's, Mildmay Park.
92. St. Mark's.
93. St. Mary Magdalene.
94. St. Mary's.
95. St. Matthew's.
96. St. Paul's.
97. St. Thomas'.

**Lambeth.**
98. Holy Trinity.
99. St. Andrew's.
100. St. John's & All Saints'.
101. St. Patrick's Charity.
102. St. Patrick's (R.C.)

**Poplar.**
103. All Saints', Bow Lane.
104. All Saints', High Street.
105. All Saints', Newby Place
106. Bromley National, Priory Street.
107. Bromley National, St. Leonard's Road.
108. Mrs. Hill.
109. St. Agnes (R.C.)
110. St. Gabriel's.
111. St. John's.
112. St. Luke's.
113. St. Matthias'.
114. St. Saviour's.
115. St. Stephen's.
116. Wade Street.
117. Wesleyan, Bow.
118. Wesleyan, Poplar.

**St Pancras.**
119. St. Jude's.

**Shoreditch.**
120. Christchurch.
121. St. Columba's.
122. St. John's.
123. St. Mary's.
124. St. Monica's (R.C.)
125. St. Paul's.
126. St. Saviour's.

**Southwark.**
127. Mrs. Newcome's.
128. National and Parochial
129. Roman Catholic, Mint.
130. St. George's (R.C.)
131. St. George the Martyr.
132. St. Jude's.
133. St. Peter's, Emerson Street
134. St. Peter's, Sumner Street
135. St. Saviour's.
136. Trinity.

**Stepney.**
137. All Saints'.
138. Barnado's Free.
139. Christ Church.
140. Colet.
141. Crispin Street (R.C.).
142. Davenant.
143. George Yard Free.
144. Good Shepherd (R.C.)
145. Gower's Walk Free.
146. Guardian Angels (R.C.)
147. Hamlet of Ratcliff.
148. Holy Name (R.C.)
149. Jews' Free.
150. Jews' (Infants) Spitalfields.
151. Jews' (Infants) Whitechapel.
152. Mile End Old Town.
153. Our Lady (R.C.)
154. Poi Street (R.C.)
155. Raines Foundation.
156. Redman's Road.
157. Sacred Heart (R.C.)
158. St. Anne's.
159. St. Anne's (R.C.)
160. St. Boniface's (R.C.)
161. St. George's.
162. St. John's Charity.
163. St. Joseph's (R.C.)
164. St. Luke's.
165. St. Marks.
166. St. Mary's.
167. St. Patrick's (R.C.)
168. St. Patrick and St. Augustine's (R.C.)
169. St. Paul's, Burdett Road.
170. St. Paul's, Shadwell.
171. St. Paul's, Whitechapel.
172. St. Peter's, Mile End Old Town.
173. St. Peter's Pearl Street.
174. St. Peter's, Red Lion Street.
175. St. Stephen's.
176. Spanish and Portuguese Jews.
177. Stepney.
178. Tower Hill.
179. Trinity.

**Stoke Newington.**
180. Miss Bright.
181. Miss Whitcher.
182. St. Mary's.
183. St. Matthias'.

**Westminster.**
184. Chapel Royal Savoy.
185. St. Clement Dane's Charity.
186. St. Martin's Northern.

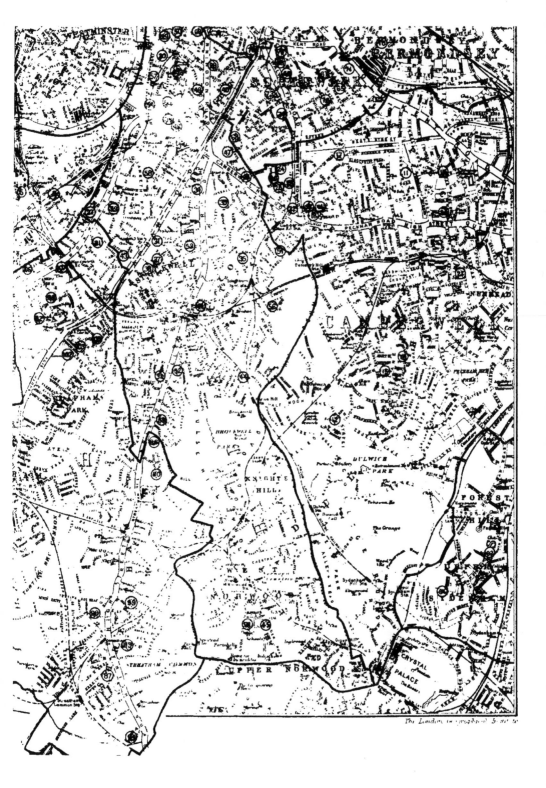

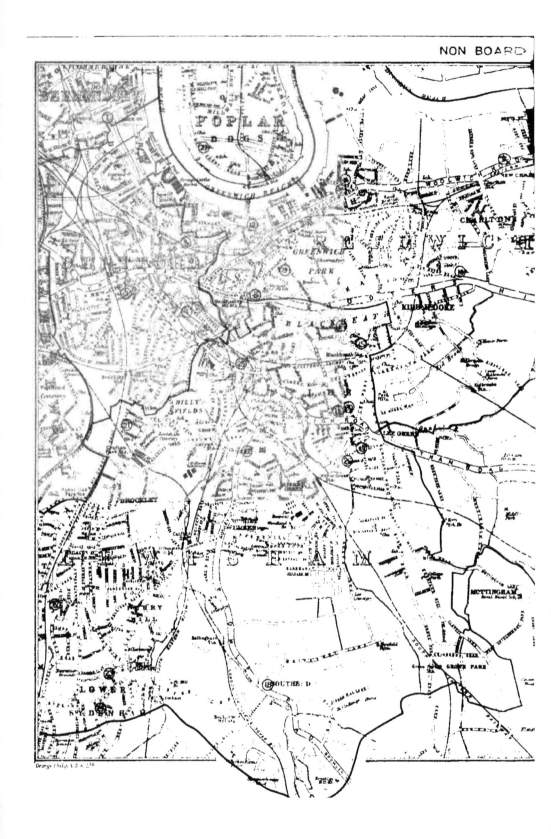

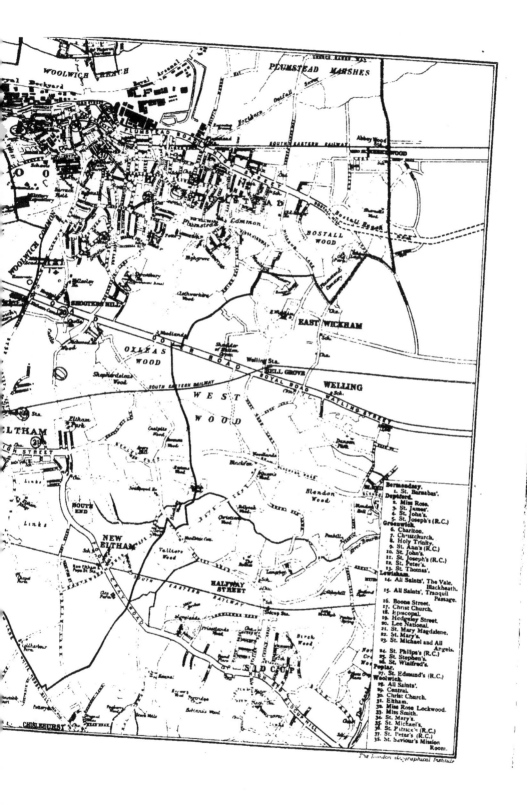

Bermondsey.
1. St. Barnabas'.
Deptford.
2. Miss Rose.
3. St. James'.
4. St. John's.
5. St. Joseph's (R.C.).
Greenwich.
6. Charlton.
7. Christchurch.
8. Holy Trinity.
9. St. Ann's (R.C.).
10. St. John's.
11. St. Joseph's (R.C.).
12. St. Peter's.
13. St. Thomas'.
Lewisham.
14. All Saints', The Vale, Blackheath.
15. All Saints', Tranquil Passage.
16. Boone Street.
17. Christ Church.
18. Episcopal.
19. Hedgeley Street.
20. Lee National.
21. St. Mary Magdalene.
22. St. Mary's.
23. St. Michael and All Angels.
24. St. Philip's (R.C.).
25. St. Stephen's.
26. St. Winifred's.
Poplar.
27. St. Edmund's (R.C.).
Woolwich.
28. All Saints'.
29. Central.
30. Christ Church.
31. Eltham.
32. Miss Rose Lockwood.
33. Miss Smith.
34. St. Mary's.
35. St. Michael's.
36. St. Patrick's (R.C.).
37. St. Peter's (R.C.).
38. St. Saviour's Mission Room.

The London Geographical Institute.

have to be provided by the new Local Education Authority; but the School Board for London will hand over to that authority an inheritance of which they may well be proud. In 1871 the Board were face to face with a deficiency of over a quarter of a million places. Not only have they provided for this, and for subsequent deficiences caused by the growth of the great City, but they have also anticipated the future requirements of growing localities by the projected provision of many thousands of school places, and by securing or projecting a large number of sites, which will be available for the erection of schools when the local needs require them.

# WORKS.

THE chief duties of the Works Committee are (*a*) the purchase of sites; (*b*) the planning and erection of new schools, of enlargements of schools, of centres for various purposes, and the various Offices of the Board; (*c*) the improvement of existing schools; (*d*) the repair and maintenance, including the periodical painting, of the buildings; (*e*) the supply and repair of furniture; (*f*) the supply of fuel, lighting, and water; (*g*) the nomination and control of schoolkeepers and cleaners; (*h*) the letting of the schools out of school hours; (*i*) the provision of temporary accommodation, when required, by the hire of buildings, or by the erection of iron or brick structures; and (*j*) the general care of all the properties of the Board.

## I.—SITES.

Originally the selection and scheduling of sites was done by the Works Committee. In 1891 these duties were transferred to the School Accommodation and Attendance Committee, and since that date the position of new sites to be acquired has been determined by the latter Committee, who have also taken the necessary steps for the scheduling of the sites to be acquired under compulsory powers. The actual purchase of the sites (including the service of the notices to treat in the cases of scheduled sites) is effected by the Works Committee. The half-yearly statement prepared by the Finance Committee shows that the total expenditure which has been incurred up to September 29th, 1903, upon the purchase of 531 sites for permanent day schools amounts to £3,832,818, together with the sum of £522,192 for costs; and that the total area of these sites is about 21,502,562 square feet, or about 493 acres, giving an average area of 40,494 square feet for each school. These figures are exclusive of the sites of transferred schools, residential schools, &c.

In the early part of the existence of the Board, very small sites were acquired. Some of them were exceptionally small, such as those in Buck's-row and Chicksand-street, in the densely crowded district of Whitechapel; the area of the former site, as originally scheduled in 1872-3, being 3,325 square feet, and that of the latter 3,040 square feet. Later on, however, the Board enlarged these sites at considerable expense so as to bring the playgrounds more into conformity with what was felt to be requisite.

In the year 1894, the Works Committee decided " that in the outskirts of London, if vacant land can be obtained at a reasonable price, the Land Surveyor be instructed to secure two acres or thereabouts for a site." As an illustration of the areas now acquired, it may be mentioned that the average area of all the sites for new schools which it was originally proposed to schedule in the Session 1902-3, including some sites which were necessarily comparatively small, was about one acre and a quarter.

## II.—PLANNING OF SCHOOLS.

When the London School Board began their building work, and before they appointed an architect of their own for the purpose, in consequence of the urgent need of school accommodation, the planning and erection of the first thirty schools was entrusted to various architects. These schools, although in some cases built by architects of considerable reputation, and though sometimes handsome in elevation, were ill-adapted to teaching, partly because of the fact that there was very little professional knowledge of the requirements of a good school, and partly because there was a very meagre code of the then Education Department, the building rules being of a most elementary description, and such rules and illustrations as existed tending rather to encourage defects than to stimulate improvement. The staircases were long, steep, narrow, and ill-lighted. Cloakrooms were either insufficient or altogether absent. The classrooms were of unsuitable sizes; the lighting was bad, being chiefly from the backs of the scholars. Most of the rooms were passages, and, in addition, the sites were so small that the playgrounds were very insufficient. A great many of these earlier schools have since been improved, halls added, new staircases of a modern type built, and the schools properly equipped with cloakrooms, lavatories, teachers rooms, &c. After the Board appointed their own architect, the earlier schools built by him showed no marked departure in planning from the previous type, but gradually a certain improvement was effected. But the dominant idea was still that of a schoolroom holding several classes, supplemented by a moderate number of classrooms. Corridors for reaching the end rooms were introduced, but these were made also to serve the purpose of cloakrooms; they were far too narrow, and the hanging of cloaks in them was inconvenient and dangerous.

But even at the beginning the Board built one or two schools which lent themselves to the typical arrangement of separate classrooms and a central hall. Of these, " Ben Jonson " (Tower Hamlets N)[1] and Haverstock Hill (Marylebone U),[2] opened in 1873 and 1874, might be cited as instances. At the same time, the Board recognised the importance of Drawing, and the necessity of securing proper facilities for it, by providing in the " Rules for the Planning and Fitting-up of Schools," which were approved by the Board on April 24th, 1872, that Drawing classrooms should be provided in the schools. These, however, were as a rule not very convenient, and some of them, as at Hawley-crescent (Marylebone L),[3] were subsequently absorbed, owing to the pressure for school places in the ordinary accommodation of the school.

Soon the need for enabling each classroom to dismiss its scholars without passing through other rooms suggested the planning of such schools as Northey-street (Tower Hamlets P),[4] with a small central area, but the anxiety to be economical in the purchase of land led to the acquisition of such small and badly shaped and lighted sites as prevented the adoption of any general pattern of school.

The latest type of the old-fashioned school, before important modifications set in, may be found in Hatfield-street (Southwark A),[5] where 6 rooms were calculated at 9 square feet per child to provide for 352 scholars in a department, and all but one opened on to corridors with a central area. This school was opened in January, 1878.

---

[1] Plan No. 1, p. 60.
[2] Plan No. 3, p. 60.
[3] Plan No. 4, p. 60.
[4] Plan No. 2, p. 60.
[5] Plan No. 6, p. 60.

D 2

| 2 |. At about this time, the Board adopted the policy of planning their schools with separate classrooms with the unit of 60 scholars, the Code then allowing 80 to a certificated teacher; and the earliest schools built on this plan were opened in 1879. Among these may be mentioned Gillespie-road (Finsbury AZ²)[1]; Grafton road (Finsbury BB²)[2]; Church-street, Kennington (West Lambeth O)[3]; Haggerston-road (Hackney H)[4]; and Berger-road (Hackney L¹)[5]. At this time, also, the Education Department, which had previously acquiesced in the reckoning of the accommodation in Senior departments at 9 sq. ft. per child, insisted on 10 ft., and after a protracted correspondence, the School Board gave way on some allowances being made to them in respect of the loans; for the Education Department were at the same time pressing for a reduction of cost.

Among the last schools in which the Senior departments were reckoned at 9 ft. may be mentioned Berger-road (Hackney L¹), opened in September, 1879, where the classrooms reckoned for 60 will only hold 50 at 10 ft. per scholar; and Fleet-road (Marylebone AB)[6], opened in January, 1879; where, when the plans were submitted showing rooms 20 ft. wide, the Board were required to make them 22 ft. wide; but each classroom was reckoned for 72.

From this time classrooms for 60, with a minimum superficial area of 10 sq. ft. per scholar in the Senior departments, became the rule in school planning. The experience, however, of the Board, in their few schools with halls, made them desire more room outside the classrooms, and the attempts to accomplish this object may be seen in some of the schools already mentioned.

Thus Church-street, Kennington (West Lambeth O), opened September, 1879, has four classrooms, two on each side of a central corridor about 9 ft. 9 in. wide. This type was further adopted in Bath-street (Finsbury X)[7] (corridor 19 ft. wide) opened August, 1880, where, nevertheless, the corridor was spoilt by being half the height of the classrooms, the mezzanine being utilised for cloakrooms; and a similar plan was adopted in Cator-street (East Lambeth R)[8] (corridor 19 ft. wide) opened in 1881. In these cases the mezzanine floors have been, or are about to be removed, and external cloakrooms built, the corridor giving a fair substitute for a central hall. Another attempt was made to get a hall on the ground floor by an expansion of the Hatfield-street (Southwark A)[9] type. This led to such schools as Haggerston-road (Hackney H)[10], opened August, 1879, Brackenbury-road (Chelsea V²)[11], opened December, 1879, both of which were planned for future enlargement, and Somerford-street (Hackney T¹)[11], opened in January, 1881. A somewhat improved type of this school may be found in Sidney-road (Hackney L²)[12], opened November, 1882, Credon-road (East Lambeth N)[14], opened October, 1882, Crampton-street (East Lambeth D)[15], opened April, 1883, and Heber-road (East Lambeth AE)[16], opened April, 1883. But these schools, also, were not satisfactory.

---

| | | |
|---|---|---|
| [1] Plan No. 10, p. 61. | [7] Plan No. 19, p. 62. | [13] Plan No. 21, p. 64. |
| [2] Plan No. 13, p. 63. | [8] Plan No. 18, p. 62. | [14] Plan No. 22, p. 63. |
| [3] Plan No. 14, p. 63. | [9] Plan No. 6, p. 60. | [15] Plan No. 23, p. 64. |
| [4] Plan No. 12, p. 61. | [10] Plan No. 12, p. 61. | [16] Plan No. 24, p. 64. |
| [5] Plan No. 11, p. 62. | [11] Plan No. 15, p. 63. | |
| [6] Plan No. 9, p. 61. | [12] Plan No. 17, p. 62. | |

About this time there was a slight departure from the unit of 60 for a classroom, and one or two larger rooms were provided to each department, as at Compton-street (Finsbury S)[1], opened November, 1881, where in a school of the Bath-street type two classrooms were built for 90 each. A classroom for 90 was also provided in the enlargement of Gifford-street (Finsbury T),[2] opened September, 1879.

In order to combine teaching with the occasional use of a large room for collective purposes, two types were now tried; one the Mansford-street (Hackney S)[3] and Mina-road (East Lambeth K)[4] type, of which four schools were built. Here there were large halls available for infants and for boys, but each of them were occupied permanently by two classes and the corresponding rooms for the girls were supplied on a separate floor over the hall. This type, though providing two handsome rooms, was not serviceable for teaching or for assembling the children. These schools are being improved by the halls being freed from the classes and used for their special purpose. The other type was that of King and Queen-street (East Lambeth B)[5] of which six schools were built. In these the wide corridor which grew out of the Bath-street type was retained, but two classrooms were placed across one end, and in the top floor these rooms, about 30 ft. wide, extended over the staircases of the lower floor.

Still, these expedients did not solve the difficulty, and the next two schools to be mentioned are St. John's-road (Hackney Y[1])[6], and " Latchmere " School (West Lambeth BI)[7] opened October, 1883. In the former case there is an inner hall for the infants, and one over it for the girls; but the boys have a corridor running round the upper part of the girls' hall. These halls were much too dark on the lower floor, and there was the further inconvenience that one department had no hall. In the case of the " Latchmere " School, the halls of the infants and the boys were well lighted, and the girls communicated by a corridor; but this also was inconvenient. The first three-storey school planned with halls for all three departments was Betts-street (Tower Hamlets E)[8], opened in September, 1884. In the same year the Carlton-road School (Marylebone U)[9] was opened in February, with three halls; but, in that case, to save expense, each hall was reckoned for a class.

In 1885, 32 schools were opened, and nearly all of them had halls, or were so planned that halls could be easily added with the enlargement. In one case, at the " Alma " School (Southwark V)[10] a class was put in the halls to enable the cost of the school to be covered by the loan, as in the case of Carlton-road School, mentioned above.

It was not until the year 1891 that the Education Department so far acknowledged the desirableness of a hall in a school as to grant a special loan for the purpose for every school. Previously to this date the hall, when provided, had to be included within the loan limit of £10 per child accommodated, unless an allowance was specially made. Consequently the cost was nearly always prohibitive, unless the hall was

---

[1] Plan No. 20, p. 62.
[2] Plan No. 16, p. 62.
[3] Plan. No. 26, p. 63.
[4] Plan No. 25, p. 63.

[5] Plan No. 27, p. 64.
[6] Plan No. 29, p. 63.
[7] Plan No. 28, p. 63.
[8] Plan No. 33, p. 66.

[9] Plan No. 30, p. 65.
[10] Plan No. 34, p. 66.

reckoned in the accommodation, or planned of such restricted dimensions as to be more of a corridor than a hall. Since the Department allowed a loan of £1 per foot floor space for the halls, the Board have been able to provide them in every new school.

In 1883 the Board began to be more careful of left lighting, and to secure this object, planned square classrooms for 60 children with five rows of dual desks, arranged six deep, as an improvement on the former sized classroom – viz., 29 ft. 4 in. by 22 ft. This arrangement was objected to by the Education Department, on the ground that desks should not be more than five deep; but the Board adhered to their plans, which were tacitly and continuously accepted. Among the earlier schools having square rooms for 60 may be mentioned Deptford Park (Greenwich A²),[1] and Lombard-wall (Greenwich F),[2] both of which were opened in October, 1884. From this time the progress of school planning has been continuous, and with no very important changes. The Board found that the square room for 60 children was hardly sufficiently lighted at the point furthest from the windows; they therefore introduced rooms for 56 children seated seven rows deep, with eight in a row. These rooms were first introduced in the enlargement of Westville-road (Chelsea AF),[3] opened 1890-1. The Board of Education raised some objection to this arrangement, on the score of the seats being seven deep, but on its being shown that it worked well, their objections were withdrawn.

In 1891, the Board, which had for several years neglected the Resolution as to the provision of Drawing classrooms, determined to give effect to it, and many spacious and convenient rooms have been built for this purpose over the halls. Lately the Board of Education have objected to the size of these rooms, and they are now divided—half for drawing, half for practical science: the new code limiting their area to 600 superficial feet in each case.

On July 4th, 1901, the Board determined that, in order that no class should exceed 50 usually present, or 60 on the roll, in new schools, the rooms be, as a rule, planned for 40, 48, 50; and that not more than one or two rooms be planned for 56 or 60.

The new rules of planning recently issued by the Board of Education limiting the size of departments have hampered the action of the School Board, especially in cases where their existing schools were planned for enlargement, where the glazed bricks for future staircases were already built into the walls, and where, as in some cases, the foundations of the new rooms had been put in up to the damp course. In all cases school planning must follow and be dependent upon school organisation. Questions as to the provision of Mixed schools, or separate schools for boys and girls, and as to the size of schools, are pre-eminently questions of school management.

The new rules of planning requiring schools, as a rule, to be of not more than two storeys and, preferably, all of one storey, compelled the Board to examine carefully their system of planning, which, owing to most of the schools being built in the heart of London, has been predominantly one of three-storey buildings. Careful examination of the relative cost establishes the fact that two-storey and one-storey buildings are cheaper to build, *cæteris paribus*, than three-storey schools; and, as undoubtedly the former are

---

[1] Plan No. 32, p. 65.   [2] Plan No. 31, p. 66.   [3] Plan No. 35, p. 65.

more convenient for teaching purposes, schools in the future should be placed, as far as possible, on the ground floor, except where the smallness of the site compels the erection of three-storey buildings.

Another item in the cost of schools is the amount of decorative detail put into them. The policy of the School Board has almost always been to give these buildings, as public buildings, some dignity of appearance, and make them ornaments rather than disfigurements to the neighbourhoods in which they are erected. Where, in a few cases, striving after the sternest economy has led to very plain buildings being erected, as in the case of Trundley's-road (Greenwich A³) (*see elevation and plan post*, p. 67), Enfield-road (Hackney G) Ellerslie-road (Chelsea AE) and others, the resentment of those who contrasted the appearance of these with other schools in the neighbourhood has led to a reversion to the more dignified type. It was found that the difference of cost between bare utilitarianism and buildings designed in some sort of style and with regard for materials and colour, was rather less than 5 per cent. At the same time, this ornamental appearance may be secured either by richness of detail or by a dignified grouping of masses; and sometimes the Board have put into their buildings a greater amount of decorative work than they were prepared to continue after fuller experience of the cost. Thus, in the earlier history of the Board, in the case of such schools as Blackheath-road (Greenwich M), Gillespie-road (Finsbury AZ³), Barrett-street (Marylebone E), Whitfield street (Marylebone D), with no halls, and narrow corridors, and but little real convenience for teaching, the character of the elevation led to a considerable cost. The Board therefore fell back upon simpler elevations, and sought to obtain a good result by the treatment of mass rather than by ornamentation of detail. In some cases, no doubt, where a school has been built in a prominent position, the Board indulged more freely in ornament, such as in the "Oliver Goldsmith" School (East Lambeth Q), in which case the Camberwell Vestry (now the Borough Council of Camberwell) appealed to the Board to put up a building in harmony with the importance of the thoroughfare; and a considerable number of schools about this period—e.g. Fulham Palace-road (Chelsea T¹) (*see elevation and plan post*, pp. 70, 71), Northwold-road (Hackney B¹) and Mansfield-road (Marylebone AB) were erected, the effect of which was undoubtedly very handsome, but the cost of the material used, especially where a considerable amount of terra-cotta was provided, proved too great an addition to the necessary cost of the school for the Board to pursue this type further.

The later schools of the Board, therefore, have been designed more cheaply, and yet, as the Board consider, not without reasonable attractiveness (*see elevation and plan of* "*Peterborough*" *School, post*, pp. 68, 69).

Undoubtedly, with the building of ground-floor schools (*see plan post*, p. 72), there will be less opportunity for elaborate treatment and architectural effect than in the case of buildings which tower in the poorer parts of London. It is the policy, however, of the Board, while studying, in the first instance, suitable arrangements for teaching, not to set aside the dignity and attractiveness of buildings, which the Board have always felt should be a contrast to their poor surroundings.

The particulars of the cost, &c., of the schools mentioned above are given on pages 58 and 59.

In 1892, the Board were desirous of ascertaining whether it would be possible to obtain any fresh ideas in the planning of their schools from outside architects, and empowered the Committee to invite architects to compete, in accordance with the rules of the Royal Institute of British Architects, for the planning of a school for 1,200 children, capable of being erected on any ordinary site purchased by the Board. The President of the Institute was appointed as assessor to advise the Committee, and to draw up the terms and conditions of the competition. The Board further decided that three premiums of £150, £100, and £50 respectively, should be awarded, in the discretion of the assessor, to the architects whose plans were most successful.

The site finally selected was a vacant piece of ground in Fulham Palace-road, and the competition, besides being advertised in the daily and trade journals, was specially brought to the notice of a large number of architects by an intimation sent through the post. One hundred and twelve architects applied for the instructions, 61 of whom sent in designs which were afterwards publicly exhibited in the upper hall of the Hugh Myddelton School, Clerkenwell.

The result of the competition was that the assessor, Mr. MacVicar Anderson, reported that it had not produced a novel treatment in respect of plan that had been deemed worthy of approval; and on April 26th, 1894, a report was submitted by the Committee to the Board stating that it was gratifying, as a result, to find that the schools of the Board had not only been erected upon what may be fairly considered the most approved plans, but that the cost appeared to be as moderate as seemed possible, judging from the estimates forwarded by the various competitors of the probable cost of the schools if erected according to their designs.

The table on the opposite page shows the number of new schools opened each year; and also the number of those which have been materially improved. In some cases this improvement has been effected in connection with an enlargement of the school; in other cases, the accommodation of the existing school has been reduced as a consequence of the improvement.

The original "Rules for the Planning and Fitting-up of Schools" which were approved by the Board on April 24th, 1872, and which were in operation when the earlier schools of the Board were built, will be found on pages 73 to 77. It should be stated, however, that these rules were not steadily acted upon, and that many of them speedily fell into desuetude.

TABLE SHOWING THE NUMBER OF NEW SCHOOLS OPENED DURING EACH YEAR

| Year in which Schools were opened. | (a) Number of Schools opened. | (b) Number of Schools included in Column (a) which have since been materially improved. | (c) Number of Schools included in Column (a) where halls have also been added. | (d) Number of Schools in Column (a) not needing Halls. |
|---|---|---|---|---|
| 1873 | 16 | 5 | 3 | 1 |
| 1874 | 49 | 36 | 31 | 1 |
| 1875 | 28 | 13 | 12 | .. |
| 1876 | 30 | 10 | 10 | 1 |
| 1877 | 35 | 15 | 15 | .. |
| 1878 | 13 | 3 | 2 | .. |
| 1879 | 20 | 6 | 5 | 3 |
| 1880 | 12 | 2 | 2 | .. |
| 1881 | 25 | 11 | 11 | 3 |
| 1882 | 17 | 3 | 3 | .. |
| 1883 | 15 | 2 | 2 | .. |
| 1884 | 19 | 9 | 8 | 6 |
| °1885 | 32 | | | |
| °1886 | 15 | 115 | 104 | 15 |
| 1887 | 15 | | | |
| 1888 | 6 | | | |
| 1889 | 3 | | | |
| 1890 | 4 | | | |
| 1891 | 4 | | | |
| 1892 | 6 | | | |
| 1893 | 17 | | | |
| 1894 | 10 | | | |
| 1895 | 2 | | | |
| 1896 | 10 | | | |
| 1897 | 9 | | | |
| 1898 | 10 | | | |
| 1899 | 9 | | | |
| 1900 | 9 | | | |
| 1901 | 10 | | | |
| 1902 | 6 | | | |
| 1903 | 13 | | | |
| | 469 | | | |

° Of the schools opened in 1885, four are in need of improvement and also one of those opened in 1886.

### III.—SCHOOL ACCOMMODATION IN THE COURSE OF PROVISION.

The following statement shows the accommodation which was in course of provision on March 25th, 1904 :—

27 New Schools were in course of erection, or tenders had been accepted, providing accommodation for 24,863 children.

16 Enlargements were in course of erection, providing accommodation for 4,720 children.

29 Additional sites for new schools had been or were being purchased. The schools to be erected on 20 of these sites will provide accommodation for 15,950 children.

In the case of the remaining 9 sites the accommodation to be provided has not yet been determined.

10 Sites for new schools had been scheduled in the Session 1903-4. The schools to be erected on 5 of these sites will provide accommodation for 3,900 children.

In the case of the remaining 5 sites the accommodation to be provided has not yet been determined.

13 Enlargements of schools had been sanctioned by the Board, or the Board of Education, for which tenders had not been accepted, providing accomodation for 3,785 children.

The Board, or the Board of Education, had also sanctioned the provision of sites in 10 districts, but no steps have yet been taken in regard to purchase. The schools to be erected on 6 of these sites will provide accommodation for 4,100 children.

In the case of the remaining 4 sites the accommodation to be provided has not yet been determined.

## IV.—SPECIAL ROOMS.

In addition to Drawing classrooms, the Board have, of late years, provided a large number of additional rooms to supplement the ordinary instruction given in the classrooms of a school.

*Cookery Centres.*—The first Cookery centre was built by the Board at Stephen-street, Lisson-grove, and was opened on November 11th, 1878. The earlier Cookery centres were built comparatively cheaply, and were so small that the Board have since had to reduce the number taught in them, a course which entails greater cost in teaching than is saved in the first cost of erection.

There are now 183 Cookery centres in operation.

*Laundry Centres.*—The introduction of Laundry teaching led to the erection of the first Laundry centre at William-street, Hammersmith, in 1890. There are now 142 Laundry centres in operation.

*Housewifery Centres.*—When Housewifery teaching was first introduced, it was in the nature of an experiment carried on by the aid of the City Guilds. In connection with the school in William-street, Hammersmith, a house was adapted for the purpose, and was opened on February 4th, 1901. Since then, additional Housewifery centres have been provided, either by the erection of new premises or by the adaptation of existing premises; and there are now 31 such centres in operation.

Plans of the Domestic Economy School which has been erected in connection with the "Paragon" School, New Kent-road, containing Cookery centre, Laundry centre, and also a Housewifery centre, are given on page 65.

*Manual Training Centres.*—In 1885 the Board, being desirous of making an experiment in some school in the instruction of boys in the use of tools, commenced a class in the Beethoven-street School, Queen's Park Estate, a shed being erected for that purpose in a corner of the playground. The subject of Manual Instruction was recognised by the Education Department in the Code of 1890. At one time considerable pressure was brought to bear upon the Board to build these centres cheaply, the Education Department of the time being of opinion that they should be erected as "workshops." It was found, however, that the centres were so cold and the inconvenience of working in them was so great that it was necessary to improve them at some expense to the Board; and they are now built more as classrooms for the purpose of teaching. There are, at the present time, 187 Manual Training centres in operation.

*Metalwork Centres.*—The first Metalwork centre was provided at Thomas-street, Limehouse, in 1895, and there are now eight such centres in operation.

*Laboratories.*—The first laboratory provided was that in connection with the Plumstead-road School, in 1885. This laboratory was of a very imperfect kind, and was erected in the playground. The Board subsequently found it convenient to incorporate these rooms in the plans of the schools.

### V.—PUPIL TEACHERS' SCHOOLS.

When it was first determined, in 1880, that Pupil Teachers should be instructed in the day-time at suitable centres, the Board, after opening some centres in temporary premises, proceeded to provide permanent buildings in some of the districts. The earliest of these centres, viz. the "Stepney" Centre, erected on the Trafalgar-square site, Stepney, was provided on the fourth storey of the school building, and was opened in 1885.

The "Deptford" Centre, in Clyde-street, was opened in 1886, being provided on the second floor of the building; the "Chelsea" Centre, in William-street, Hammersmith, was opened in 1887, being built over the Infants' school; and the "Mile End" Centre, in Essex-street, Mile End Old Town, in 1888, the Board adapting the Junior Mixed school for this purpose.

The Board, however, found these buildings inadequate, and proceeded to build centres of a better type. The "Hackney" Centre, in Tottenham-road, was opened in 1887, and the "Stockwell" Centre, in Hackford-road, in 1888; the "Peckham" Centre, in Summer-avenue, in 1888; the "Battersea" Centre, in Amies-street, Lavender-hill, in 1892; the "Southwark" Centre, at the "Alma" School, and the "Woolwich" Centre, at the Maxey-road School, in 1894; and the "Marylebone" Centre, at the Burghley-road School in 1895.

The last completed Pupil Teachers' school erected by the Board was that in Offord-road, Barnsbury, a plan of which is given on page 64 (No. 41). The Board then proceeded to build the Hilldrop-road Centre, Camden-road, on similar lines, when, to their surprise, although the Board of Education had from time to time sanctioned the scheduling of various sites for Pupil Teachers' centres, and had co operated with the School Board in the provision of the schools, it was discovered that the instruction of Pupil Teachers, whom the Board were required to teach, was an illegal act.

### VI.—COST OF SCHOOLS.

The schools erected by the Board during the first few years of their existence were, for various reasons, built at much less cost than those erected in later years. The accommodation of the Boys' and Girls' departments was then calculated on the 9 square feet basis, and that of the Infants' department on the 8 square feet basis; a Drawing classroom was usually provided, but no other special rooms; with one or two exceptions there were no halls; the rooms were not sub-divided to the same extent as at present, and were to a large extent used as passages; the staircases, judged by present requirements, were very insufficient; the cloaks were hung in narrow passages, which were neither properly lighted, ventilated, nor warmed; the drainage and sanitation were much below the standard at present required; and the entire equipment of the schools was inferior to that now insisted upon. Gradually the Board became aware of the necessity of improving these conditions; a larger superficial area was allowed to each child; smaller classrooms were provided; and also rooms for head and assistant teachers; more and better staircase accommodation; more liberal provision of cloakrooms and lavatories; improved drainage and sanitation; and better provision for the warming and ventilating of the schools.

At first many of these improvements were required to be included within the ordinary limits of the loan allowed by the Education Department. As, however, the cost of the schools was thereby considerably increased, the Education Department consented to make special allowances in the loan to cover the cost of the halls and the special rooms provided.

In the year 1889, as the result of the deliberations of a Special Committee on the Works Department, more stringent regulations with regard to the character of the building-work were introduced; a wages clause was inserted in the form of contract; building-work was largely done in cement, instead of mortar; artificial warming apparatus, instead of open fires, was generally adopted; and the partial use of glazed bricks in the rooms and on the staircases was introduced. These alterations considerably increased the cost of the schools. But the recent regulation of the Board of Education that schools should be built preferably on one floor, and that it is desirable that a school building should not be on more than two floors, has tended to reduce somewhat the cost of the schools, rendering unnecessary expensive staircases, fire-resisting floors, iron girders, and thicker walls.

### VII.—IMPROVEMENT OF OLD SCHOOLS.

On March 17th, 1898, the School Management Committee submitted to the Board a memorandum, which had been prepared by the Vice-Chairman of the Board, proposing a scheme for the gradual improvement of the older schools of the Board by the addition of halls, &c., where these had not been provided in the first instance.

In this memorandum it was suggested that a sum of £100,000 should be set apart each year for the improvement of these schools, and that lists should be prepared in which the schools should be classed according to the urgency of the need for improvement. The memorandum further stated that there were in all 175 schools without halls, which should sooner or later be dealt with, and that under this scheme they could be taken in hand gradually, and probably all, or nearly all of them could be improved in about a dozen years.

The following resolutions were then passed by the Board:—

1. That the sum of £100,000 in the coming year be set apart on loan for the purpose of improving old schools, and that the Finance Committee be instructed accordingly.

2. That the School Management Committee after consulting the School Accommodation and Attendance Committee and the Works Committee, shall determine what schools shall be improved, and, after determining the list and the order in which the schools shall be taken, shall report the list to the Board for information, as a preliminary to asking specific sanction of the Board, before any individual school is undertaken.

3. That the School Management Committee shall bear in mind (*a*) any sanctioned enlargement of a school ; (*b*) the cost of the improvement of the school ; and (*c*) the urgent need of improving the school from the point of view of teaching.

After consulting with the above-mentioned Committees, and also with the Divisional Members, the School Management Committee reported to the Board on the 23rd June, 1898, the names of ten schools which they had selected for improvement.

On July 17th, 1898, and subsequent dates, the Board decided to carry out similar improvements to a second list of 26 schools, and on the December 14th, 1899, to a third list of 40 additional schools. On other dates, by various special votes of the Board, it was agreed to add 27 other schools to the lists, making a total of 103 schools to be thus improved.

Since 1898, a provision has been included each year in the annual loan estimate of such a sum as was considered sufficient to meet the cost of improvements likely to be carried out during the year.

The following table shows the progress which has been made in carrying out these improvements since the inception of the scheme, and the total amount of the expenditure to which the Board was committed for this purpose by the acceptance of tenders during each year since March, 1898.

It need hardly be pointed out, however, that these figures do not represent the actual amount of the payments made during each of the specified years :—

| Division and Name of School. | Date of acceptance of Tender. | Amount of Tender accepted. | Division and Name of School. | Date of acceptance of Tender. | Amount of Tender accepted. |
|---|---|---|---|---|---|
| *Hackney.* | | £ | *Hackney.* | | |
| Cranbrook-road ... | 23.2.99 | 5,189 | Globe-terrace ... | 11.5.99 | 1,694 |
| Nichol-street ... | 9.2.99 | 6,185 | | | |
| Olga-street ... ... | 15.12.98 | 18,245 | *East Lambeth.* | | |
| | | | Harper-street ... | 19.10.99 | 11,665 |
| *East Lambeth.* | | | Penrose-street ... | 16.11.99 | 5,513 |
| Westmoreland-road | 22.12.98 | 7,579 | Rockingham-street ... | 11.5.99 | 4,054 |
| | | | Scarsdale-road ... | 19.10.99 | 3,555 |
| *West Lambeth.* | | | | | |
| Tennyson-street ... | 23.3.99 | 15,987 | *West Lambeth.* | | |
| | | | Gipsy-road ... ... | 27.7.99 | 11,629 |
| *Marylebone.* | | | Holden-street ... | 14.12.99 | 11,930 |
| " The Stanley " ... | 14.7.98 | 15,636 | | | |
| | | | *Southwark.* | | |
| *Southwark.* | | | Lant-street ... ... | 7.12.99 | 12,847 |
| Farncombe-street ... | 20.10.98 | 3,290 | | | |
| Year ended March | 25th, 1899. | £72,111 | Year ended March | 25th, 1900, | £62,887 |

| Division and Name of School. | Date of acceptance of Tender. | Amount of Tender accepted. |
|---|---|---|
| *Chelsea.* | | £ |
| Portobello-road ... | 26.7.00 | 4,832 |
| *Hackney.* | | |
| Canal-road ... ... | 31.5.00 | 13,756 |
| *East Lambeth.* | | |
| Canterbury road ... | 7.3.01 | 5,778 |
| *West Lambeth.* | | |
| Winstanley-road ... | 15.11.00 | 9,888 |
| *Southwark.* | | |
| Galleywall-road ... | 12.7.00 | 12,201 |
| *Tower Hamlets.* | | |
| Collingwood-street ... | 24.5.00 | 3,072 |
| **Year ended March** | **25th, 1901,** | **£49,527** |
| *Chelsea.* | | |
| Edinburgh-road ... | 28.3.01 | 7,984 |
| Park-walk .. ... | 31.10.01 | 11,329 |
| Saunders-road ... | 9.5.01 | 13,222 |
| *Greenwich.* | | |
| Lucas-street ... ... | 20.2.02 | 12,400 |
| *East Lambeth.* | | |
| Woods-road ... ... | 4.7.01 | 13,120 |
| *West Lambeth.* | | |
| Stockwell-road ... | 25.7.01 | 12,229 |
| Winstanley-road ... | 19.12.01 | 2,388 |
| *Marylebone.* | | |
| Princess-road ... | 6.2.02 | 1,814 |

| Division and Name of School. | Date of acceptance of Tender. | Amount of Tender accepted. |
|---|---|---|
| *Southwark.* | | £ |
| Alexis-street... ... | 14.11.01 | 12,188 |
| Weston-street ... | 4.7.01 | 3,958 |
| **Year ended March** | **25th, 1902,** | **£90,632** |
| *Finsbury.* | | |
| Popham-road ... | 24.7.02 | 6,633 |
| *Hackney.* | | |
| Bonner-street ... | 16.10.02 | 2,494 |
| *East Lambeth.* | | |
| Boundary-lane ... | 10.7.02 | 14,287 |
| *Marylebone.* | | |
| Netley-street ... | 5.3.03 | 3,760 |
| *Tower Hamlets.* | | |
| Northey-street ... | 30.10.02 | 8,757 |
| **Year ended March** | **25th, 1903,** | **£35,931** |
| *Greenwich.* | | |
| Calvert-road... ... | 1.10.03 | 1,649 |
| Creek-road ... ... | 1.10.03 | 2,617 |
| *Hackney.* | | |
| Turin-street ... ... | 15.10.03 | 1,246 |
| *East Lambeth.* | | |
| Flint-street ... ... | 29.10.03 | 11,770 |
| Mina-road ... ... | 12.11.03 | †3,149 |
| *West Lambeth.* | | |
| Salter's Hill ... ... | 1.10.03 | ‡3,352 |
| *Tower Hamlets.* | | |
| Dalgleish-street ... | 2.4.03 | 6,379 |
| **From 26.3.03** | **to 31.12.03,** | **£29,811** |

† Approximate cost only as supplied by Architect. The improvements were included in the Tender amounting to £15,739 for building new Higher Grade School and Manual Training Centre.

‡ Approximate cost only as supplied by Architect. The improvements were included in the Tender amounting to £12,988 for Enlargement of School by 372 places.

It will be seen from the above table that up to December 31st, 1903, tenders had been accepted for improving 43 schools. In 35 of these cases, the work has already been completed.

It should be added that this table includes three schools (viz., those in Olga-street

Tennyson-street, and Medburn-street, now known as " The Stanley " school) the improvement of which had been sanctioned by the Board before the above-mentioned general scheme was adopted.

In the following cases it has been necessary to abandon the proposed improvements, owing to objections which have been raised by the Education Department generally on the ground of cost:—

Chelsea.—Middle-row; Star-lane; Everington-street.

Finsbury.—Gillespie-road; Pooles-park; Shepperton-road; Vittoria-place.

Greenwich.—Nynehead-street; " Slade "; Union-street; Vicarage-road.

Hackney.—Pritchards-road; Tottenham-road.

West Lambeth.—" Springfield "; Gideon-road.

Marylebone.—" The Stanley," late Medburn-street, Junior Girls.

Tower Hamlets.—Dempsey-street; Cayley-street.

Westminster.—" Pulteney."

In addition to the above schools, improvements have been carried out at a number of other schools in connection with an enlargement of the school which has been sanctioned by the Board of Education.

Apart from the more extensive improvement of schools, the rooms in a very large number of schools have been sub-divided, with a view to reducing the size of classrooms, but much work yet remains to be done in this respect.

## VIII.—DRAINAGE OF SCHOOLS.

On January 30th, 1890, the Committee submitted the following report to the Board:—

The Committee have found it necessary, from time to time, to call the attention of the Board to the defective drainage of a number of the schools of the Board, and the experience they have obtained leads them to the conclusion that it is desirable that they should be authorised to thoroughly examine the whole of the drainage of any school where they may think it necessary, and to put the sanitary arrangements of the school into proper condition.

The Board then passed the following resolution:—

That the Committee be authorised to thoroughly examine the whole of the drainage of any school of the Board where they may think it necessary, to report to the Board each case, and obtain the sanction of the Board to make the necessary alterations in the sanitary arrangements of the school.

The drainage of all the schools of the Board was subsequently examined, and the schools were classified into lists as follow:—

List I. consisted of schools where tenders for providing new drainage were to be obtained as soon as possible;

List II. consisted of schools where the requirements were of a less urgent character and where tenders were to be obtained for carrying out the work in due course;

List III. consisted of schools where sanitary work had been carried out, but where the drainage system had not been overhauled;

List IV. consisted of new schools where drainage had been provided of a more modern character and where no alteration was required, or of schools where no improvements were proposed.

292 schools have been placed upon List I., for which re-drainage is required. Of these, re-drainage has been completed in 264 cases; in twelve other cases the work is in progress; and plans and specifications are being, or will be, prepared in the remaining sixteen cases.

At the present time there are six schools on List II., eighteen schools on List III., and 181 schools on List IV.

Arrangements for the periodical cleansing of the drains of all the schools of the Board by workmen employed direct by the Board are in operation, a staff of eight workmen being engaged in this work at the present time; and the Board, on March 17th, 1904, agreed to increase this staff to sixteen workmen in order that each school might be visited once in every three months in accordance with the original intention of the Board.

### IX.—Repairs and Maintenance of School Buildings.

The schools of the Board are, for the purposes of repairs, divided into 22 districts, each district being under the superintendence of a local Clerk of Works for Repairs, and containing about 25 schools. In 14 of these districts, the Board employ their own workmen to carry out repairs up to £15 in value. Work from £15 to £50 in estimated value in these districts, and all work up to £50 in value in the remaining districts, is done by contractors on a printed schedule of prices for repairs, with an additional percentage on these prices, the amount of which was determined by competitive tendering. For structural alterations and other work exceeding £50 in value, competitive tenders are obtained from a selected list of contractors.

The work of painting and cleaning the schools is one of some difficulty, owing to the large number of schools and the limited amount of time during which the work can be done. It has been found inadvisable to carry out painting work during the Christmas holidays, as, owing to the dampness of the weather, the paint and varnish cannot properly dry, and, save in exceptional cases, therefore, only distempering and cleaning are done at this period. Again, as the Easter holidays are short, and it is inadvisable to disturb the Evening classes held at this time of the year, by far the greater part of this class of work must necessarily be done during the summer holidays. The Committee have decided that, as a general rule, the exterior of a school shall be painted every five years, and the interior every eight years, the school being cleaned, the ceilings whitened, and the walls distempered midway between the interior paintings. This rule is varied to some extent to suit the local circumstances of the school.

### X.—Supply of, and Repairs to, Furniture.

Previous to the year 1889, furniture required by the schools of the Board was supplied direct from the contractor. The Board then opened a temporary store, at first in the House of Detention, Clerkenwell Close, and afterwards in the old transferred school at

High-street, Shadwell. In 1897, the Board erected a new store for this purpose in Clerkenwell Close. All articles of furniture now supplied to the schools, with the exception of desks, clocks, and a few articles which cannot conveniently be stored, are obtained wholesale from the contractors whose tenders have been accepted for the supply of these articles, are sent to and examined at the store, and, if passed, are then ready to be sent to the schools as required.

The repairs to furniture are now done by the Board's own workmen, in connection with the repairs to buildings.

### XI.—Supply of Fuel, Light, and Water.

The Board obtain annually contracts for the supply of coals, coke and fire-wood. Advertisements are issued in various journals inviting contractors to tender, the yearly contract terminating on June 30th. The consumption of fuel during the twelve months ended on June 30th, 1903, was as follows :—

29,857 tons of coal and coke ...       ...       Total cost, £28,929
Firewood      ...       ...       ...       ...       „       „       £2,505

The cost of the gas and electric light consumed during the year ended June 24th, 1903, was £29,206, and of the water, £9,118.

### XII.—Schoolkeepers and Cleaners.

Schoolkeepers and cleaners were originally appointed by the School Management Committee, but in the year 1874 the appointment and supervision of these officers was transferred to the Works Committee. There are now 474 schoolkeepers of permanent schools, and 53 cleaners of temporary schools under the control of the Committee.

The "Code of Regulations for the Guidance of Schoolkeepers" is revised annually. This Code contains a list of the duties of schoolkeepers and cleaners, the scale of salary which varies with the accommodation of the school, and the extra payments which are allowed.

### XIII.—Letting of Schools.

On March 11th, 1874, the Board passed the following resolution :—

"That it is important to utilise the Board Schools at certain hours of week-day evenings and of Sundays."

Regulations for the letting of schools for this purpose were then passed, and have been amended from time to time as experience suggested.

*Sunday Tenancies.*—At the present time 199 schools are occupied wholly or partly for Sunday-school purposes, some occupations being for the morning only, some for the afternoon, and some for both. The amount charged for rent was calculated to cover the cost of the necessary warming, lighting, &c. The total rents receivable from the tenants amount to £4,090 5s. 3d. per annum. Of this sum, £1,835 5s. 10d. is for rent, and £2,254 19s. 5d. for cleaning, the latter amount being paid over to the school-keepers, who are responsible for doing this work.

E

*Week-Evening Tenancies.*—The-week evening tenancies may be divided into paying tenancies and free tenancies. The former (of which there are 152) consist largely of Bands of Hope, temperance and friendly societies, clubs for boys or girls, classes for violin and band practice, &c. The amounts receivable for these tenancies is approximately about £1,542 per annum (£840 being for rent and £702 for cleaning), but this amount is variable, as in some cases the rental is calculated on the number of times the rooms are occupied during the quarter, and also on the amount of accommodation required.

There are 169 free week-evening tenancies; in fifty-three of these cases the rooms being let to the Children's Happy Evenings Association, who pay only a fixed charge to the schoolkeepers for cleaning. The majority of the other free evening tenancies, which consist chiefly of guilds and associations in connection with the past or present scholars of the schools, are allowed on the understanding that the respective tenants remunerate the schoolkeepers.

*Occasional Lettings.*—In addition to the above running tenancies, the Board also let their schools for occasional meetings at fixed charges, the chief kinds of occupation being (a) for political, social, and other meetings, and (b) for committee meetings of various kinds. For the former meetings special regulations have been passed, and 292 schools have been placed upon the list of schools containing halls or rooms available for this purpose. These schools are, as a rule, supplied with from 100 to 300 chairs each, according to their storage capacity, &c. The rental charge is low, the use of a hall being allowed for a public meeting for the sum of 5s. where no charge is made by the hirer for admission, with 2s. 6d. to the schoolkeeper for cleaning; or 5s. for cleaning if desks or other furniture have to be moved.

On March 28th, 1895, the Board resolved to allow teachers, visitors and schoolkeepers, to hold business and social meetings at a charge sufficient to defray the out-of-pocket expenses incurred by the Board in consequence of such use, and on July 18th, 1895, a scale of charges to cover these expenses was adopted.

During the year, 1903, the sum of £311 1s. was received on account of occasional lettings, of which £215 1s. 9d. was for rent, the remainder being paid over to the schoolkeepers for cleaning and moving chairs. In all there were 266 lettings under the "public meetings" regulations, 211 teachers' and schoolkeepers' meetings, and 137 occasional committee and other meetings.

It should be added that under Article 38 of the School Management Code, the Divisional Member in charge of a school is authorised to grant the use of rooms for purposes in connection with the work of the school, such as prize distributions, school entertainments, &c.

### XIV.—PROVISION OF TEMPORARY ACCOMMODATION.

There are at the present time 99 iron buildings which are used for various purposes chiefly for providing temporary day school accommodation and temporary centres of various kinds.

When permanent provision is made in the various districts, and these iron buildings are released, they are transferred to other districts where similar provision is required.

As the cost of erecting these iron buildings is considerable, the Board have lately arranged, in several cases, to provide brick buildings which are suitable for temporary day school accommodation in the first instance, and can ultimately be utilised as permanent centres in connection with the day school when completed.

## XV.—RE-HOUSING.

In the Act of 1899 confirming the Provisional Order (London) Bill for that year, a clause was inserted making the Board responsible for re-housing in the case of any parish in the metropolis where 20 or more houses occupied by persons of the labouring classes had been, or were about to be, scheduled or acquired in that and the preceding four sessions. Under this Act the Board ultimately had to provide accommodation for 1,030 persons, and an arrangement was made with the London County Council by which that body took over the liabilities of the School Board on the payment of a sum of £10,359. Since that date the Board did not, under the terms of the Provisional Order Confirmation Acts become liable for any further re-housing until the session 1902-3, and they are still in communication with the Home Office in reference to the number of persons for whom accommodation will have to be provided in connection with the properties which were scheduled during that session, and it is intended to acquire.

## XVI.—ACCOMMODATION OF SCHOOLS.

For the first few years of the Board's existence the accommodation of the Boys' and Girls' departments of schools erected by the Board, was calculated on the 9 square feet basis, and the accommodation of the Infants' departments on the 8 square feet basis.

In 1877 an arrangement was made with the Education Department by which the accommodation of new schools, the plans of which were subsequently submitted to them, should be calculated in the Boys' and Girls' departments on the number of seats which the rooms were planned to hold—approximately 10 square feet per child. The accommodation of the Infants' departments was still calculated on the 8 square feet basis.

In 1895 the Board determined to reckon the accommodation of all new Infants departments on the seat basis, but this resolution was subsequently rescinded.

In 1898 a memorial was presented to the Education Department, which contained the following paragraph:—

"The Board would willingly reckon all new Infants' departments at 10 square feet per child if the Education Department would recognise the increased cost of building involved by this proposal, as the same space would be reckoned for fewer children."

On January 16th, 1899, the Education Department wrote as follows:—

"My Lords will, in future, reckon the accommodation of Infants' schools to be erected by your Board at 9 square feet per child, and will make this the basis on which loans will be sanctioned. But they will raise no objection to the Board limiting in particular schools the number of children in average

E 2

attendance to those who can be accommodated at 10 square feet, reserving to themselves the right of reckoning, if they deem it necessary or desirable, the accommodation at 9 square feet in the event of a deficiency of accommodation existing in the neighbourhood of the school."

Since that date the Board have calculated the accommodation of Infants' departments on the seat basis (as in the upper floors for boys and girls), but have been allowed to calculate the amount of the loan to be granted on the number of children which the Department would hold if reckoned on the 9 feet basis.

In more recent schools, however, which have, as a general rule, been built on the one storey principle, or with two storeys for boys and girls and a separate Infants' department, the accommodation of the latter department, which is not in this case governed by the size of the Senior departments, has been calculated once more on the 9 square feet basis.

## XVII.—SELECTION OF CONTRACTORS.

In the earlier years of the Board, tenders for building were invited from a list of contractors selected by the Architect. In 1886, the Board decided to invite tenders by advertisement. This plan was adopted until 1889, when the Board decided that tenders for all works, the value of which exceeds £100, should be invited only from a limited and selected list of builders. A list of firms was accordingly prepared for each class of work, and every contractor desirous of being placed on this list, who can show that he is in a position to carry out these works satisfactorily, is added to the list, with a view to increasing the number of firms willing to compete. The Board have, from time to time, by advertisement, invited applications from additional firms, so that the range of selection might be as wide as possible. From the lists so compiled the Works Committee select the particular firms to tender for each contract, or for the supply of furniture. In the case of repairs done on the Board's printed schedule of prices, all the contractors on the list are invited to tender for the groups of schools most convenient to them, and when the schools are to be painted, the contractors are invited to specify the particular schools for the painting of which they desire to tender, marking the schools in the order of preference.

The list of the tenders received in each competition is published in *The Builder*, *The Building News*, *The Architect and Contract Reporter*, *The Contract Journal*, and *The British Architect*, so that each contractor may have the opportunity of seeing his place in the competition.

## XVIII.—RATES OF WAGES.

The Board, as a large employer of labour, both directly and through their contractors, have considered the question of the proper rates of wages to be enforced, and the following is a statement of the action taken by them since 1889, when the matter was first discussed.

On February 7th, 1889, the Board decided that a declaration should be inserted in the form of tender to be signed by the contractor, stating that he would pay to the workmen employed by him not less than the minimum standard rate of wages in each branch of the trade. On June 9th, 1890, it was agreed that the following explanatory footnote should be attached to the declaration :—

The minimum standard rate of wages is to be understood as follows :—Bricklayer, 9½. per hour ; carpenter, 9d. per hour ; mason, 9d. per hour ; painter, 8d. per hour ; plasterer, 8d. per hour ; plumber, 10d. per hour.

On July 9th, 1891, the Board decided that, in lieu of requiring each contractor to sign a declaration in the form of tender, the following clause, with the footnote as above, should be inserted in each contract in future :—

Where the London scale of wages shall apply, the contractor shall pay to the workmen employed by him not less than the minimum standard rate of wages in each branch of the trade. In all other districts where the London scale of wages shall not apply, the contractor shall pay the workmen and all other persons employed by him in connection with his contract, not less than the minimum standard rate of wages which may for the time being be usual and generally paid where such workmen are employed.

This arrangement was in operation until September 29th, 1892, when the Committee reported to the Board that the Central Association of Master Builders had agreed to a general advance in workmen's wages ; and the Board then decided, upon the recommendation of the Committee, that, as other alterations in these rates might be made from time to time, the explanatory footnote, containing the rate of wages, should be omitted.

On April 12th and May 10th, 1894, the Board also passed the following resolution :—

That in all future building contracts there be inserted a clause binding the contractors to pay the rates of wages mutually agreed upon by the Central Association of Master Builders of London and the London Building Trades Federation.

On May 9th, 1895, the Board resolved to insert in each building contract a schedule of wages and hours, particulars of which were then reported to the Board.

On October 1st, 1896, the Board agreed to amend the clause inserted in all building contracts so that it shall read as follows, the words printed in italics being those which were added on this date :—

Where the London scale of wages shall apply, the contractor shall pay to the workmen employed by him *not less than* the rates of wages *from time to time* mutually agreed upon by the Central Association of Master Builders of London and the representatives of the Unions of the various branches of the building trade, the agreed rates of wages *at present recognised being* set out in the schedule hereto. In all other districts where the London scale of wages shall not apply, the contractor shall pay the workmen, and all other persons employed by him in connection with his contract, not less than the minimum standard rate of wages which may for the time being be usual and generally paid where such workmen are employed.

For all and every breach by the contractor of this condition, and notwithstanding the condonation of any prior or other breach, the contractor shall on demand pay to the Board as liquidated damages, and not as a penalty, the sum of £5.

On November 17th, 1898, the Board agreed to amend the schedule of wages now attached to all building contracts by the addition of the trade of ironfounders, with the wage of £2 per week of 54 hours. On December 15th, 1898, the Board agreed to further amend the wages clause in building contracts so that it should, in future, read as follows :—

Where the London scale of wages shall apply, the contractor shall pay to the workmen employed by him not less than the rates of wages from time to time mutually agreed upon by the Central Association of Master Builders of London and the representatives of the Unions of the various branches of the building trade, the agreed rates of wages at present recognised being set out in the schedule hereto ; or in the case of any other trade, not less than such rates of wages as may be recognised by the Board and specified in the schedule. In all other districts where the London Scale of Wages shall not apply, the contractor shall pay the workmen, and all other persons employed by him in connection with his contract, not less than the minimum standard rate of wages accepted between employers and employed. In any case in which there is no recognised standard rate of wages, the contractor shall deposit with his tender the rate which he proposes to pay for the work to be carried out under the contract.

For all and every breach by the contractor of this condition, and notwithstanding the condonation of any prior or other breach, the contractor shall, on demand, pay to the Board as liquidated damages, and not as a penalty, the sum of £5.

In order to give effect to the above resolution, contractors are requested, in the case of tenders for all building work, to furnish particulars with reference to the wages which they intend to pay to any workman or workmen who may be employed for any trade in which there is no recognised standard rate of wages.

The Board, on February 21st, 1901, agreed that the schedule of wages attached to all building contracts shall be inserted also in running contracts for the supply of furniture.

As regulations concerning wages, hours, and overtime for the trade of cabinet-makers had been agreed upon between the Employers' Association and the workmen's Unions, the Board decided on February 21st, 1901, to insert these regulations in the schedule of wages attached to all building contracts.

On May 9th and May 23rd, 1901, the Board agreed that the wages clause, together with the schedule of wages attached to all building contracts, should be inserted also in (i.) Contracts for carrying out repairs to furniture, and (ii.) Contracts for warming apparatus.

On May 23rd, 1901, the Board decided that the agreed rate of wages for smiths and fitters, viz. 9d. to 10d. per hour, should be inserted in the Board's schedule of wages attached to all building contracts.

The Board also, on the same date, resolved to insert in the schedule the increased rates of wages which had then been agreed upon between the masters and men.

The following is the wages clause inserted in all other contracts (not building contracts) :—

*Wages Clause.*—Where the London scale of wages shall apply, the contractor shall pay to the workmen employed by him not less than the minimum standard rate of wages in each branch of the trade. In all other districts where the London scale of wages shall not apply, the contractor shall pay the workmen, and all other persons employed by him in connection with his contract, not less than the minimum standard rate of wages which may for the time being be usual and generally paid where such workmen are employed.

The Board, also on January 20th, 1898, agreed that in future all tar-paving and asphalting contracts should be made subject to the conditions of building contracts, so far as they are applicable.

On November 10th, 1898, the Board, on the recommendation of the Committee, passed the following resolution :—

That where, in any trades, evidence is furnished to the Board of a recognised rate of wages accepted between employers and employed, such rate of wages be filed in the head offices of the Board, and be inserted in the contracts in like manner to the schedule of wages inserted in the building contracts of the Board.

The following are the schedules of wages and hours of employment now attached to each building contract :—

(A) RATES OF WAGES AGREED UPON BY THE CENTRAL ASSOCIATION OF MASTER BUILDERS OF LONDON AND THE REPRESENTATIVES OF THE VARIOUS BRANCHES OF THE BUILDING TRADE.

| Building Trades. | Rate of pay per hour. | Hours of labour per week. | | | Rate of pay for overtime. | | | | |
|---|---|---|---|---|---|---|---|---|---|
| | | Summer. | Winter—13 weeks commencing 2nd Monday in November. | | Week days (except Saturdays). | | | Saturdays. | |
| | | | 3 weeks at beginning and 3 weeks at end. | 6 middle weeks. | Until 8 p.m. | 8 p.m. until 10 p.m. | After 10 p.m. | Until 4 p.m. | After 4 p.m., and Sundays and Christmas Day. |
| | d. | | | | | | | | |
| Carpenters .. .. | 10½ | | | | | | | | |
| Joiners .. .. | 10½ | | | | | | | | |
| Bricklayers .. | 10½ | | | | | | | | |
| Bricklayers (cutting and setting gauged work) | 11 to 11¼ | | | | | | | | |
| Plasterers .. | 11 | | | | | | | | |
| Masons .. .. | 10½ | 50 | 47 | 44 | Time and a quarter. | Time and a half. | Double time. | Time and a half. | Double time. |
| Masons (fixing) .. | 11¼ | | | | | | | | |
| Masons (granite work) | 11½ | | | | | | | | |
| Painters .. .. | 8½ & 9 | | | | | | | | |
| Glaziers .. .. | 8 to 9 | | | | | | | | |
| Smiths & Fitters (including Hot-water Fitters) | 9 to 10 | | | | | | | | |
| Labourers and Navvies | 7 | | | | | 7 p.m. to 10 p.m. time and a half. | Double time. | Time and a half. | Double time. |
| Painters' Labourers .. | 7 | 50 | 47 | 44 | — | | | | |
| Scaffolders .. .. | 7½ | | | | | | | | |
| Plumbers .. .. | 11 | 47 | 44½ | 41½ | — | 8 p.m. to 11 p.m. time and a half. | 11 p.m. to 7 a.m. Double time. | 1 p.m. to 5 p.m. time and a half. | 5 p.m. to 7 a.m. Monday— double time. |
| Plumbers' Mates .. | 7 | | | | | | | | |

(B) OTHER RATES OF WAGES RECOGNISED BY BOARD :—

(I.) *Iron Founders*—£2 per week of 54 hours.

(II.) *Cabinet Makers*—10d. and 10½d. per hour. Working hours—50 hours per week

all the year round. Rules as to overtime and extra payments to be those agreed upon
between the Employers' Association and the Workmen's Unions on August 11th, 1900.

### XIX.—WARMING AND VENTILATION.

The question of the warming and ventilation of the schools by propulsion has given
the Board a considerable amount of trouble. The Board carried out their first experiment in this direction at the Deal-street School, Whitechapel, where what is known as
the "Plenum" system was tried. As might have been expected in the first instance,
the experiment was not a success.

Since the Deal-street school was erected, the Board have employed various
contractors to fit their special systems of warming and ventilation by propulsion at the
following schools, the cost being as stated below:—

| Name of School. | | | | | Accommodation. | Original Actual Cost of Installation. | | |
|---|---|---|---|---|---|---|---|---|
| **HACKNEY.** | | | | | | £ | s. | d. |
| Cassland-road .. | .. | .. | | .. | 816 | 1,565 | 8 | 4 |
| **EAST LAMBETH.** | | | | | | | | |
| "John Ruskin" | .. | .. | . | .. | 1,138 | 1,185 | 0 | 0 |
| Leo-street | .. | .. | .. | .. | 1,138 | 1,185 | 0 | 0 |
| **TOWER HAMLETS.** | | | | | | | | |
| Christian-street | .. | .. | .. | .. | 984 | 926 | 0 | 0 |
| Commercial-street | .. | .. | .. | .. | 912 | 1,300 | 0 | 0 |
| Culloden-street | .. | .. | .. | .. | 1,138 | 1,311 | 2 | 10 |
| Deal-street | .. | .. | .. | .. | 1,200 | 486 | 0 | 8 |
| Old Montague-street | .. | .. | . | .. | 822 | 1,250 | 0 | 0 |
| **WESTMINSTER.** | | | | | | | | |
| St. George's-row | .. | .. | .. | .. | 673 | 622 | 5 | 0 |

In a portion of two other schools—viz., Stanhope-street, Euston-road, and Settles-
street, Commercial-road—similar systems of warming and ventilation have been provided.

The experience of the Board, as represented by the Managers and teachers, has not
been entirely satisfactory. In some cases the system has worked well, and in other cases
it has been a source of constant complaint. Though, as a rule, the scientific observations
show that the air is changed much more frequently than in ordinary schools, and is
purer, it cannot be disputed that the personal testimony of those frequenting the schools
does not agree with the observations recorded by science.

The Board are not at present fitting up any new schools with the propulsion system,
and they feel that this is a question which still needs further attention before a final
solution is arrived at.

## XX.—Lighting.

Until recently all the schools of the Board, with a few exceptions, were lighted by three-light pendants hung in a row over about the centre of the rooms, and fitted with the ordinary flat-flame gas burner. The lighting, however, has not been satisfactory, and it has been found necessary in many cases to increase the number of burners in each room, and to alter the arrangement of the pendants so as to have two rows in each room in order to obtain a better distribution of light. The Board have recently decided to provide incandescent gas lighting in the case of all new schools and enlargements, and also in any rooms in the old portion of a school where for other purposes the lighting has to be altered. Various gas companies have undertaken to provide installations of incandescent gas fittings, as an experiment, and in a few cases their offers have been accepted; the company being given a free hand, with a view to producing the best system of lighting, and due regard being paid to economy in the consumption of gas. In a number of other cases similar installations are being provided by the Board's officers. When these installations shall have been completed, and a sufficient experience of their working gained, a general report should be made as to their comparative value.

In 18 schools, electric lighting has been provided within the last two or three years, but it is clear that this system of lighting is considerably more expensive than that of gas, judging by the experience which has already been acquired.

Drawing classrooms have up to the present been lighted with large Wenham or Siemen lamps, but experiments are now being made with incandescent gas lamps which, if successful, will, it is hoped, prove more economical than the existing arrangements, and quite as efficient.

## XXI.—Opening of Playgrounds.

*Opening of Playgrounds on Saturdays and Sundays.* — There are now 267 schools, the playgrounds of which are opened on Saturdays for the use of children; a sum of 3s. being paid to the schoolkeeper for each Saturday during which these playgrounds are so opened, in order to enable him to provide the necessary supervision.

In accordance with the following resolution passed by the Board on December 8th, 1892, the playgrounds of 45 schools are also opened on Sundays for the use of children, a similar payment being made to the schoolkeeper as in the case of the playgrounds opened on Saturdays :—

That it is desirable to open such playgrounds on Sundays as are needed, owing to the want of open spaces in the neighbourhood, and where the opening will not disturb any Sunday tenancy, provided that means are taken to secure the rest of the schoolkeeper ; and that it be referred to the Divisional Members to recommend suitable cases.

### XXII.—PARTICULARS OF THE COST &c., OF THE SCHOOLS REFERRED TO ON PAGES 43 AND 44.

| Name of School. Division and Sub-Division. | Date on which Tender was accepted by Board. | Amount of Tender. | Recognised Accommodation when Tender was accepted. | Cost per Head. | Remarks. |
|---|---|---|---|---|---|
| 1 " Ben Jonson," (Tower Hamlets N) | 30.10.72 | £11,650 0 0 | 1,500 | £7 15 4 | Designed by outside architect. Central hall on what was then known as the "Prussian" system—a style not at that time adopted by the Board, but tried as an experiment at this school. |
| 2 Northey-street (Tower Hamlets P) | 6.8.73 | 3,210 0 0 | 366 | 8 15 4 | Small central area. |
| 3 Haverstock Hill (Marylebone U) | 12.11.73 | 9,269 0 0 | 1,070 | 8 13 3 | One storey school ; classrooms grouped round central hall ; the first of its type built by the Board. |
| 4 Hawley-cres. (Marylebone L) | 12.11.73 | 7,180 0 0 | 755 | 9 10 2 | — |
| 5 Blackheath-rd.(Greenwich M) | 1.7.74 | 7,283 0 0 | 767 | 9 9 10 | No halls, narrow corridors, but ornate elevation. |
| 6 Hatfield-street (Southwark A) | 2.8.76 | 9,789 0 0 | 1,104 | 8 17 4 | Central area. |
| 7 Barrett-st.(Marylebone E) | 16.5.77 | 8,370 0 0 | 540 | 15 10 0 | — |
| 8 Whitfield-st. (Marylebone D) | 6.3.78 | 7,957 0 0 | 532 | 14 19 1 | — |
| 9 Fleet-rd. (Marylebone AB) | 3.4.78 | 10,114 0 0 | 800 | 12 12 10 | One storey school ; classrooms grouped round central hall. |
| 10 Gillespie-rd. (Finsbury AZ²) | 1.5.78 | 11,257 0 0 | 1,000 | 11 5 1 | No halls, narrow corridors, but rather ornate elevation. |
| 11 Berger-road (Hackney L¹) | 1.5 78 | 12,366 0 0 | 1,200 | 10 6 1 | One hall on ground floor and one on first floor ; corridor on the top. |
| 12 Haggerston-road, (Hackney H) | 15.5.78 | 7,054 0 0 | 800 | 8 16 4 | Hall on ground floor only, lighted from the top. |
| 13 Grafton-rd. (Finsbury BB²) | 26.6.78 | 6,434 0 0 | 802 | 8 0 5 | — |
| 14 Church-st., Kennington (W. Lambeth O) | 23.10.78 | 7,667 11 6 | 800 | 9 11 8 | Central corridor |
| 15 Brackenbury - road, (Chelsea V²) | 23.10.78 | 8,239 0 0 | 800 | 10 6 0 | Hall on ground floor only, lighted from the top. |
| 16 Gifford-st. (Enlargement), (Finsbury T) | 18.12.78 | 10,255 0 0 | 900 | 11 7 10 | — |
| 17 Somerford-street (Hackney T¹) | 16.7.79 | 13,861 0 0 | 1,600 | 8 13 3 | Hall on ground floor only, lighted from the top. |
| 18 Cator-st. (E. Lambeth R) | 4.2.80 | 10,481 0 0 | 1,200 | 9 0 6 | Central corridor. |
| 19 Bath-st. (Finsbury X) | 18.2.80 | 10,347 0 0 | 1,200 | 9 2 5 | Central corridor. |
| 20 Compton-st. (Finsbury S) | 14.7.80 | 12,447 0 0 | 1,400 | 8 7 3 | Central corridor. |
| 21 Sidney-road (Hackney L²) | 4.11.80 | 14,460 0 0 | 1,600 | 9 0 9 | Hall on ground floor only, lighted from the top. |
| 22 Credon-road (East Lambeth N) | 16.12.80 | 14,300 0 0 | 1,600 | 8 18 9 | Do. |

| Name of School. Division and Sub-Division. | Date on which Tender was accepted by Board. | Amount of Tender. | | | Recognised Accommodation when Tender was accepted. | Cost per Head. | | | Remarks. |
|---|---|---|---|---|---|---|---|---|---|
| 23 Crampton-street (East Lambeth D) | 4.8.81 | 12,659 | 0 | 0 | 1,236 | 10 | 4 | 10 | Hall on ground floor only lighted from the top |
| 24 Heber-road (East Lambeth AE) | 10.11.81 | 10,619 | 0 | 0 | 1,000 | 10 | 12 | 4 | Do. |
| 25 Mina-road (East Lambeth K) | 26.5.81 | 13,130 | 0 | 0 | 1,400 | 9 | 7 | 4 | Large halls for two classes of Infants and Boys. Girls on separate floor over hall. |
| 26 Mansford-st. (Hackney S) | 15.12.81 | 13,559 | 0 | 0 | 1,400 | 9 | 13 | 8 | Do. |
| 27 King and Queen-street (East Lambeth B) | 2.2.82 | 12,674 | 0 | 0 | 1,375 | 9 | 4 | 6 | Wide corridors; on top-floor classrooms extending over two staircases forming a large room, 30 ft. wide, divided by a glass partition, available for use as a hall, but calculated in the accommodation. |
| 28 "Latchmere" (West Lambeth BI) | 30.3.82 | 14,270 | 0 | 0 | 1,400 | 10 | 3 | 10 | Hall on the ground floor calculated for 60 Infants, hall on the first floor, and a corridor on the top floor. |
| 29 St. John's-rd. (Hackney Y1) | 11.5.82 | 13,293 | 0 | 0 | 1,170 | 11 | 7 | 3 | Inner hall for Infants, one over for Girls; corridor for Boys round upper part of Girls' hall. |
| 30 Carlton-road (Marylebone U) | 3.8.82 | 19,041 | 0 | 0 | 1,800 | 10 | 11 | 7 | Three storey, with three halls. Each hall originally used for a class. |
| 31 "Lombard Wall" (Greenwich F1) | 12.4.83 | 8,973 | 0 | 0 | 780 | 11 | 10 | 0 | Wide central corridor. |
| 32 "Deptford Park" (Greenwich A1) | 5.7.83 | 8,700 | 0 | 0 | 790 | 11 | 0 | 3 | — |
| 33 Betts-street (Tower Hamlets E) | 10.5.83 | 9,990 | 0 | 0 | 990 | 10 | 1 | 9 | Three storey, with three halls. |
| 34 "Alma" (Southwark V) | 24.1.84 | 10,395 | 0 | 0 | 1,000 | 10 | 7 | 10 | Three storey, with three halls. Each hall originally used for a class. |
| 35 Westville-rd. (Enlargement) (Chelsea AF1) | 23.10.90 | 2,372 | 0 | 0 | 369 | 6 | 8 | 6 | — |
| 36 Trundley's-rd. (Greenwich A3) | 15.10.91 | 15,113 | 0 | 0 | 805 | 18 | 15 | 5 | — |
| 37 Ellerslie-road (Chelsea AE) | 28.7.92 | 15,146 | 0 | 0 | 1,202 | 12 | 12 | 5 | One storey; classrooms grouped round central hall. |
| 38 Enfield-rd. (Hackney G) | 23.3.93 | 15,049 | 0 | 0 | 1,174 | 12 | 15 | 6 | — |
| 39 "Oliver Goldsmith" (East Lambeth Q) | 31.3.98 | 22,957 | 0 | 0 | 756 | 22 | 13 | 3 | Extra expense incurred on architectural features. |
| 40 "Peterborough" (Chelsea Q) | 21 12.99 | 28,954 | 0 | 0 | 1,244 | 23 | 5 | 6 | — |
| 41 Mansfield-rd. (Marylebone AB) | 24.5.00 | 21,654 | 0 | 0 | 772 | 28 | 0 | 11 | — |
| 42 Fulham Palace-road (Chelsea T1) | 26.7.00 | 27,844 | 0 | 0 | 1,080 | 25 | 15 | 7 | — |
| 43 Northwold-road (Hackney B1) | 18.10.00 | 23,948 | 0 | 0 | 918 | 26 | 1 | 8 | — |

Plans of all the above schools as originally designed and erected are given on the following pages (60-70).

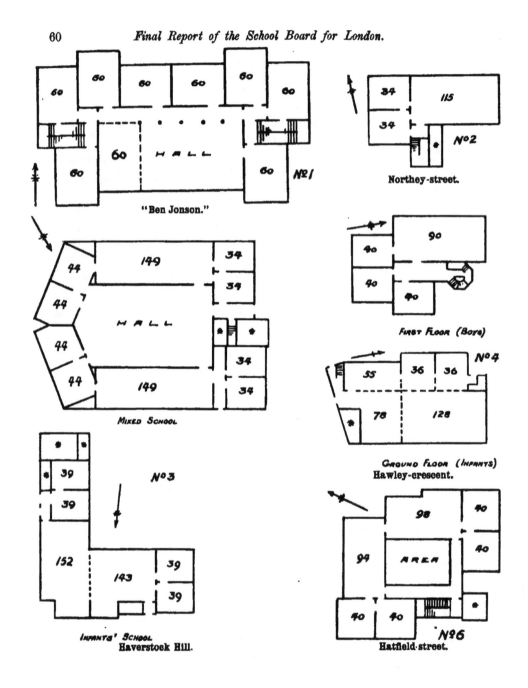

"Ben Jonson."

Nº 1.

Mixed School.

Nº 3

Infants' School
Haverstock Hill.

Nº 2
Northey-street.

First Floor (Boys)

Nº 4
Ground Floor (Infants)
Hawley-crescent.

Nº 6
Hatfield-street.

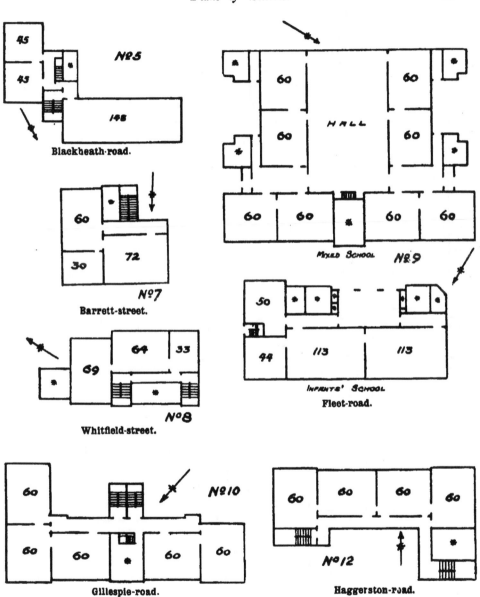

No. 5
45
43
148
Blackheath-road.

No. 7
60
30
72
Barrett-street.

No. 8
64
33
69
Whitfield-street.

No. 9
60 60
HALL
60 60
60 60 60 60
Mixed School

Infants' School
50
44 113 113
Fleet-road.

No. 10
60
60 60 60 60
Gillespie-road.

No. 12
60 60 60 60
Haggerston-road.

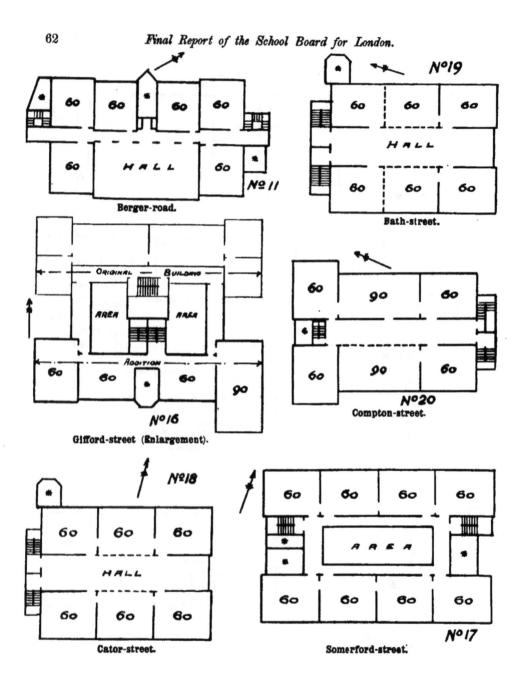

No 11
Berger-road.

No 19
Bath-street.

No 16
Gifford-street (Enlargement).

No 20
Compton-street.

No 18
Cator-street.

No 17
Somerford-street.

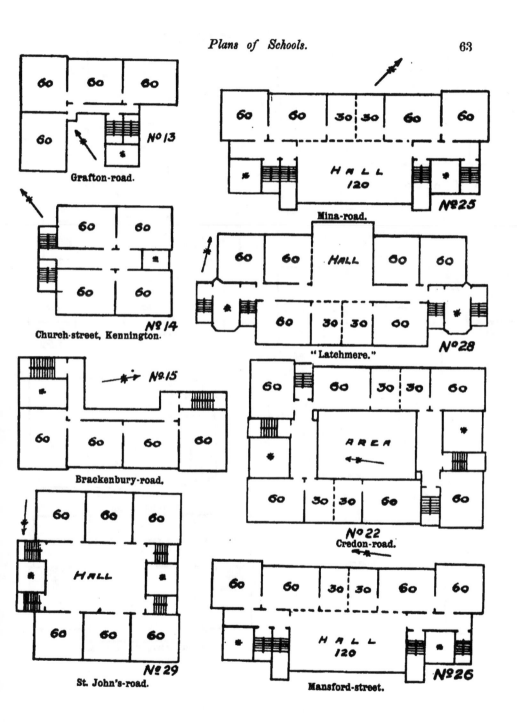

No. 13. Grafton-road.

No. 14. Church-street, Kennington.

No. 15. Brackenbury-road.

No. 29. St. John's-road.

No. 25. Mina-road.

No. 28. "Latchmere."

No. 22. Credon-road.

No. 26. Mansford-street.

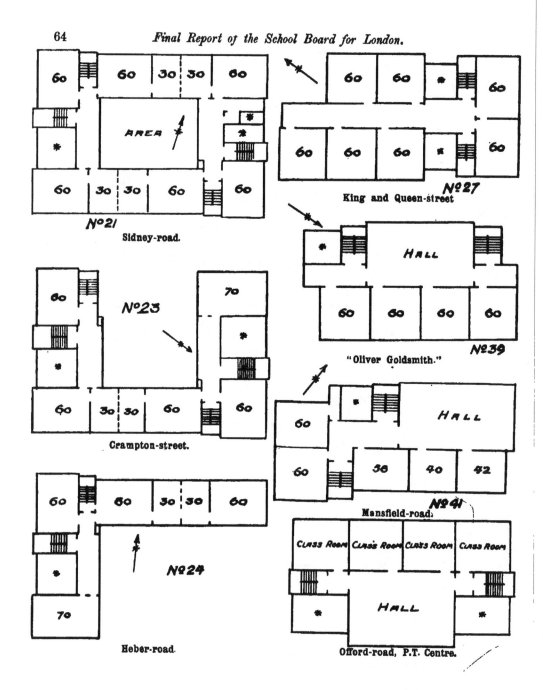

No 21
Sidney-road.

No 27
King and Queen-street.

No 23
Crampton-street.

"Oliver Goldsmith."
No 39

No 24
Heber-road.

No 41
Mansfield-road.

Offord-road, P.T. Centre.

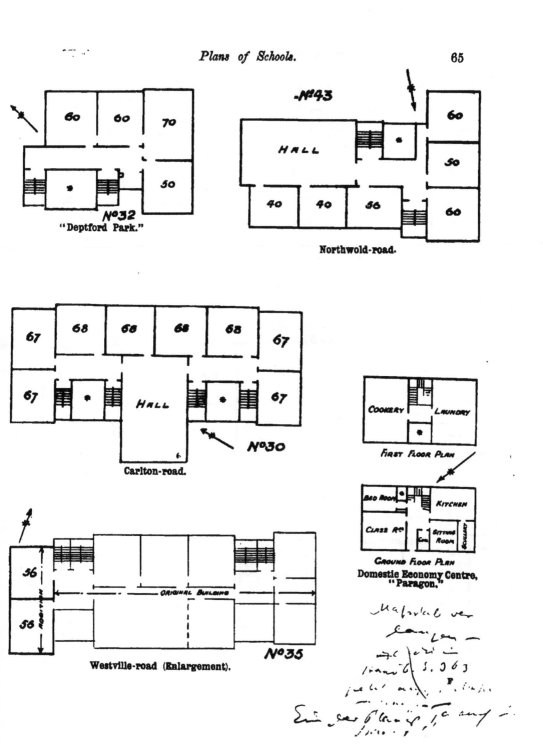

**N⁰32**
"Deptford Park."

-N⁰43

Northwold-road.

Carlton-road.

**N⁰30**

First Floor Plan

Ground Floor Plan
Domestic Economy Centre,
"Paragon."

Westville-road (Enlargement).

**N⁰35**

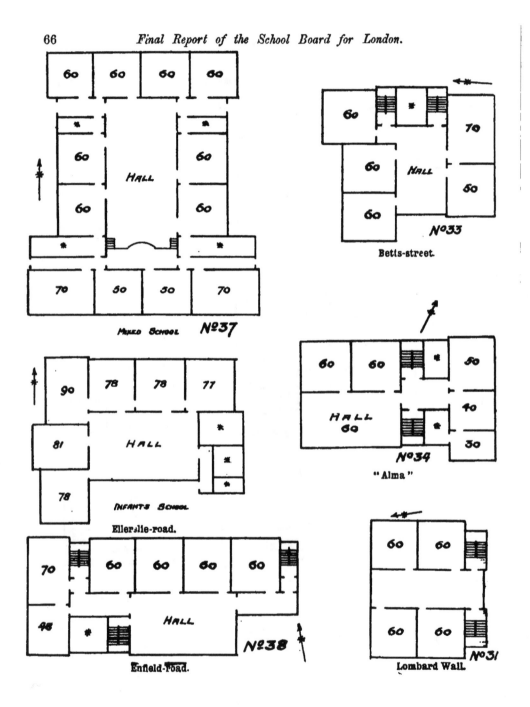

MIXED SCHOOL　Nº37

INFANTS SCHOOL
Ellerslie-road.

Enfield-road.　Nº38

Betts-street.　Nº33

"Alma"　Nº34

Lombard Wall.　Nº31

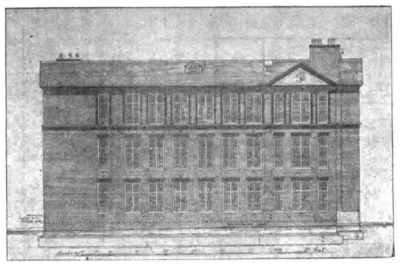

36—Elevation of Trundley's-road School.

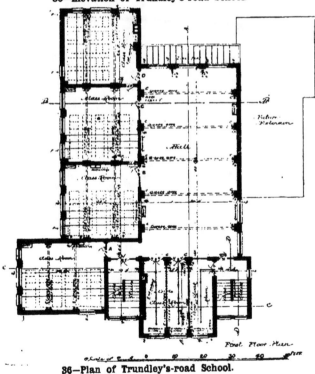

36—Plan of Trundley's-road School.

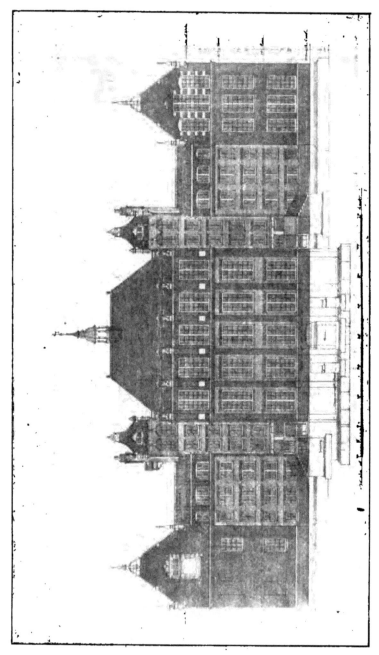

40—Elevation of the "Peterborough" School.

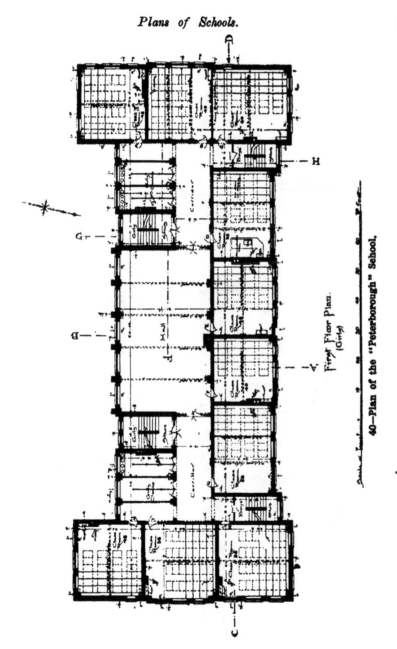

First Floor Plan.
(Girls)

40—Plan of the "Peterborough" School.

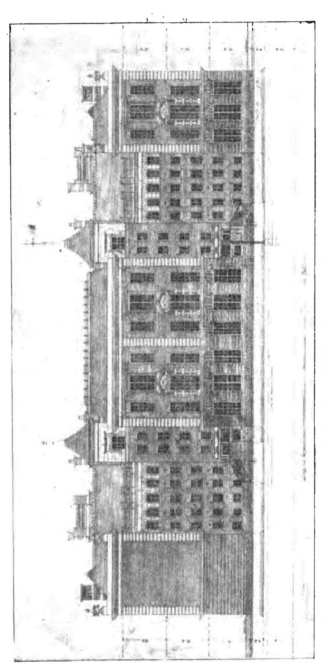

42—Elevation of Fulham Palace-road School.

71

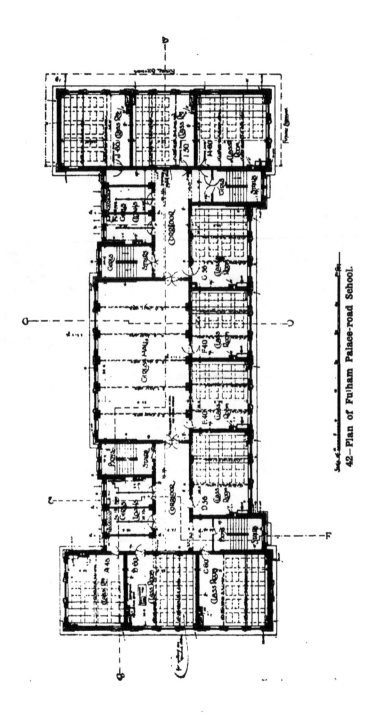

42—Plan of Fulham Palace-road School.

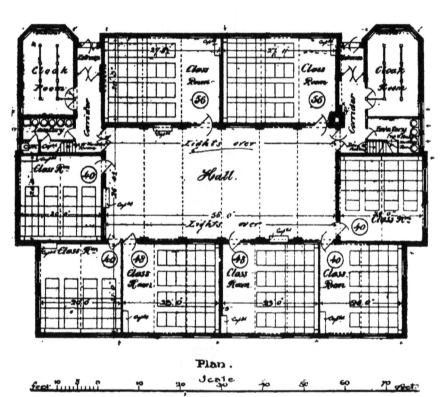

**Plan.**

Typical Plan of Boys' and Girls' School of One Storey.

# ORIGINAL RULES FOR PLANNING AND FITTING UP SCHOOLS.

*As adopted by Board on April 24th, 1872.*

### PRELIMINARY REMARKS.

In planning a schoolroom and the necessary classrooms, the accommodation depends not merely on the superficial area, but on the relations of the classrooms to the general room, their shape, the positions of all the doors, windows, and fireplaces, and the arrangement of the galleries and groups of desks.

As the contemplated use of a building must always govern its plan, the system of teaching contemplated by the *New Code*, 1872, must first be considered.

This [1] divides all schools (above the infant stage) into six grades or "standards," probably commencing at the age of six and a half to seven, and corresponding generally to six successive years.

It contemplates [2] that the number of children to be taught by a certificated teacher, assisted by one pupil teacher, shall be 60. That for every additional 40 children there shall be an additional pupil teacher. And, that for every additional 80 children, the increase of teaching power may be either one assistant certificated teacher, or two pupil teachers.

As experience has shown that the separation or isolation of classes in separate rooms has an important bearing on results, the lessons contemplated under the six standards, should, *as far as practicable*, be taught in separate classrooms. But, as each school is under the general supervision of one master or mistress, this principle must, in some degree, be subordinate to the necessity for such supervision.

In preparing plans it is necessary, always, to consider not only the teaching power required and the most convenient provisions to be founded thereon, but also the *annual working cost* involved throughout, and therefore to provide for the use of such materials and modes of construction as are not liable to involve frequent repair. Under this head, the method to be adopted for warming and ventilating will require special consideration.

For the sake of convenience, in any group of schools, six-fifteenths of the children may be considered as belonging to the Infant department, five-fifteenths to the Junior department (three first standards) and four-fifteenths to the Senior schools together (three highest standards). The calculation assumes that, in London, the Infants will pass to the graded schools soon after the age of six. [3]

The site [4] must contain, according to the Code (unless the price of land is very high) not less than 1,200 square yards, and must be quiet, healthy, and conveniently near the children's homes. In tenure, freehold.

### GENERAL BUILDING RULES.

1. No iron or wooden buildings can be approved.

2. The whole of the external walls of the school and residence, *if of brick*, must be at least one brick and a half in thickness throughout. *If of stone*, at least twenty inches in thickness throughout.

3. The walls of every schoolroom and classroom, *if ceiled at the level of the wall-plate*, to be not less than fourteen feet. If *ceiled to the rafters and collar beam* (as in the case of the top storey)

---

[1] New Code, page 7, par. 28.
[2] *Ib.*, page 7, par. 32 (c).
[3] The Government Statistics of the whole of England show for every thousand children an average of the following numbers, viz.:—
 Between 3 and 4 years of age 111, from 3½ to 4, say 55.
 Between 4 and 5 years of age 110.
 Between 5 and 6 years of age 105.

Between 6 and 7 years of age 103, from 6 to 6½ or 6½ to 7, say 52.
Between 7 and 8 years of age 100.
Between 8 and 9 years of age 98.
Between 9 and 10 years of age 96.
Between 10 and 11 years of age 94.
Between 11 and 12 years of age 93.
Between 12 and 13 years of age 90.
[4] New Code, page 18, par. 29.

they must be at least eleven feet high from the floor to the wallplate, and at least fourteen feet to the ceiling across the collar beam.

4. The window sills should be placed at a height of at least four feet from the floor. The heads should not be much below the line of ceiling. A large portion of each window should be made to open. The upper portion is best. As a general rule, clear glass is best for schools. All windows facing towards a street or otherwise exposed to stone-throwing should be covered externally with strong wire. The precise amount of window surface and its distribution will be governed in some degree by the aspect.

5. Framed and movable wooden partitions should not be generally used between schoolrooms and classrooms unless made double with a clear space between of six inches to stop noise. They should be *hung from the top* on large wheels. No complicated machinery or gearing likely to get out of order can be allowed.

6. Classrooms should be on the same level as the schoolroom, and should never be passage rooms from one part of the building to another, nor from the schoolrooms to the playground or yard. As a rule, they should be entered from the general schoolroom, and the upper panels of the doors should be of clear glass for purposes of supervision.

7. Water closets, and the approaches thereto from the school, must always be separate for the sexes and for Infants. Their best position is outside the school, and approached (where practicable) by a covered way. The number should never be less than two to every hundred children. They must be sub-divided, having a door and light to each sub-division, and be of the simplest possible construction, with ample provision for flushing. Their arrangement in a straight line is best. The drains therefrom must be carefully trapped. There should be a separate w.c. for the master or mistress.

8. The porch must be external to the schoolroom.

9. The lavatories should not be outside the building. They must be supplied with cold water only, and the basins should be numerous, or much time will be lost after an interval of play. About four to each hundred will generally be found sufficient.

10. The cap and bonnet rooms should be separate for each school, and should have two doors, one for ingress, the other for egress, to avoid confusion.

11. A Managers' room should be provided for each group of schools.

12. There should be three playgrounds wherever the size of the site will permit. But in the case of sites of limited sizes the infants' and girls' playgrounds may be in one. Occasionally the Infants' playground may be formed under some part of the main building, but always on a level with the ground. Playgrounds should be properly levelled, drained, enclosed by walls, and laid with tar pavement, asphalte, or other material, to ensure dryness.

13. The principal entrances should be kept as far apart as possible, and, where the site has more than one frontage, the boys' entrance should be from a different street. Each entrance should be marked by name, as boys', girls', or infants'.

14. Staircases should always be of stone or other fireproof material, and should be separate for each school. But for purposes of management, there should either be facility of passing from one school to the staircase of another, or where this is impracticable, an entirely separate staircase for Managers only.

15. The buildings should be designed with regard to the Metropolitan Buildings Act, 18th and 19th Vict. cap. 122, and to the requirements of the Metropolis Local Management Act and Amended Acts as to lines of frontage, etc.

16. In height, they should not, as a rule, be less than two storeys, and should exceed three storeys only in extreme cases.

17. It will generally be found necessary to provide a caretaker's residence of not less than two rooms, applicable to the whole group.

18. It is not desirable that, in new schools, any of the boundary walls should be party walls.

19. The words "*School Board for London. Public Elementary School.* [*Name.*]" should be placed in a permanent and legible manner on the face of each schoolhouse.

## INFANT SCHOOLS.

1. An Infant school should always be on the ground floor, in the case of a single school. Where a second Infant school is intended, it may sometimes be necessary to place it above the other, approached by an easy staircase.

2. It should never be without a playground of ample size, of which a portion must be covered.

3. It is not desirable, that, in London, any Infant school should be organised for less than 120. The maximum number may be taken as 240. And, where the number rises considerably above this, there should be more than one Infant school.

4. In every case there should be two classrooms, one for babies, and another for the most advanced infants. Up to 120, these should be arranged for about 30 each. In the case of a school of maximum size, there should be a third classroom of larger size, and the two smaller classrooms should then be capable of being thrown into one. In consideration of the noise caused by infant teaching, there should be no sliding or wooden partitions in Infant schools other than those necessary for throwing these two smaller classrooms into one.

5. The widths hereinafter laid down as the best for graded schools do not apply to Infant schools.

6. The fittings should always comprise two galleries of unequal size. No gallery in a class-room for infants should hold more than 80 to 90. The large gallery in the schoolroom should be capable of accommodating two-thirds of the infants at one time, for collective teaching. The advanced infant class will require a small group of benches and desks, also a cupboard for books, etc., about 6ft. high.

7. The area of the schoolroom and classrooms together shall be in all cases not less than nine superficial feet for each infant.

## GRADED SCHOOLS.

1. In arranging a school for children of seven years and upwards, the Junior Mixed school should embrace standards one to three and the Senior schools the three higher standards. In point of number, any multiple of thirty, thirty-five, or forty will be found most convenient. Forty, as a unit, is preferred in the classrooms of the first four standards but a smaller number may be adopted for the fifth and sixth.

2. Each school (whether Junior or Senior Boys or Girls) should have a general schoolroom for the assemblage of the whole at one time, calculated at four feet superficial per child, or more, according to circumstances.

3. A school of the largest size should have two double classrooms, calculated at eight to nine feet superficial per child, arranged with sliding partitions, so as to be sub-divisible into four.

Where fewer classrooms are provided, the total area of schoolroom and classrooms together must not be less than ten feet superficial per child. And the schoolroom should then be provided with a sliding partition for sub-division.

4. Where practicable, there should be an additional classroom of large size available for use sometimes for boys and sometimes for girls, and provided with a top light or highly-placed windows so as to be suitable for a Drawing class. It should have provision for placing casts, sculpture, etc.

5. The best width for the general schoolroom is from 18 to 22ft. (This allows for three or four rows deep of benches and desks ranged along one wall). The lighting should be from the back. In all cases there should be "through" ventilation.

...Five rows of benches and desks are allowable in a classroom. The lighting should, if possible, be chiefly from the side.

6. Generally an allowance of 20 inches on each desk and bench will be necessary, otherwise the children will be cramped in writing. The length will, therefore, be as follows, viz. :—

| | Feet. | Inches. |
|---|---|---|
| For 4 children, a length of | 6 | 8 |
| ,, 5 ,, ,, | 8 | 4 |
| ,, 6 ,, ,, | 10 | 0 |
| ,, 7 ,, ,, | 11 | 8 |
| ,, 8 ,, ,, | 13 | 4 |

For Senior classes the provision should be 22in.

Junior Schools should have at one end of the general room a gallery for collective teaching, capable of accommodating about one-half of the school at a time. Also provision in benches and desks for a double class of sixty to eighty. But the room should be so planned that the removal of the gallery and the substitution of benches and desks can easily be effected hereafter if desired.

Senior schools as a general rule do not require the gallery.

Benches and desks are required for all the children (except for one class occupying the gallery), and they should be of various heights according to the varying ages. The desks should be *very slightly* inclined, and the seats should have backs. It is not necessary to fasten the fittings to the floor. They should be either placed on slightly-raised platforms, or (if made to move on castors) should themselves be graduated. Each of the six classes (or standards) should have a cupboard for books, etc., about 6ft. 6in. high.

### ALTERNATIVE SYSTEM FOR GRADED SCHOOLS.

1. Each of the Graded Schools (whether Junior or Senior Boys or Girls) should consist of three or more double classrooms, according to the size of the department.

2. Each double classroom should be capable of accommodating respectively 50, 60, 70, or 80 children, according to the size of the department.

3. As the number of children in Standards V. and VI. will usually be one-fourth and one-third smaller than any of the lower standards, the smaller classrooms should be devoted to these two standards. Thus in the Senior schools, although the space per child will be greater than in the Junior schools, one double classroom may be smaller, and the whole area the same.

4. The entrance should be by a porch to the largest and most central room.

5. Two of the larger rooms should be separated by a movable partition, so as to be thrown together for singing, collective lessons, an address, or any occasion requiring accommodation for the whole (or a large proportion) of the department. As children are placed during collective lessons much closer together than usual, movable partitions are not necessary between all the classrooms, but only between so many as will admit all the children of one department to be closely seated at one time.

6 The entire area should not exceed ten superficial feet per child.

7. Classrooms may be planned with only three or four rows of desks and benches ranged along one wall.

### SCHOOL RESIDENCES.

In cases where the erection of a residence for the master or mistress has been determined on, it should contain a parlour, a kitchen, a scullery, and three bedrooms, of *not less* than the following dimensions, viz. :—

| | | | | | |
|---|---|---|---|---|---|
| (a) For the parlour | ... | ... | ... | ... | 14 ft. by 12 ft. |
| (b) For the kitchen | ... | ... | ... | ... | 14 ft. by 10 ft. |
| (c) For one of the bedrooms | ... | ... | ... | 14 ft. by 10 ft. |
| (d) For two other bedrooms | ... | ... | ... | 10 ft. 6 in. by 8 ft. |

} of superficial area.

(e) The height to be in no case less than 9 ft. to wallplate, if ceiled at the wallplate ; or 7 ft. 6in. to wallplate, and 9 ft. 6 in. to ceiling, if ceiled at the collar.

The residence must be planned so that the staircase should be immediately accessible from an entrance lobby, and from the parlour, kitchen, and each bedroom, without making a passage of any room.

Each bedroom must be on the upper storey, and must have either a fire-place, or proper provision for ingress and egress of air.

The parlour must not open directly into the kitchen or scullery.

There must be no internal communication between the residence and the school.

There must be a yard, with offices separate from the school premises.

### PLANS REQUIRED.

The following plans are required in each case, together with one copy of each, on tracing calico, to remain at the office of the Board. The dimensions of the several parts must be figured, and the respective scales strictly adhered to in the drawings:—

1. *A Block Plan* of the site, drawn to the scale of 20ft. to an inch. This plan should show—
    (a) The position of the school buildings.
    (b) The outbuildings.
    (c) The playgrounds.
    (d) The teachers' residences, if any.
    (e) The drains (collateral and main), with their fall and depth below ground.
    (f) The provision for removal of surface water.
    (g) The entrances.
    (h) The boundary walls, their nature, and the kind of property adjoining.
    (i) The streets or roads.

2. *Ground Plans* drawn to the scale of eight feet to one inch, showing each floor of the school-rooms and teachers' residences (if any). The internal fittings of the schoolrooms (fireplaces, groups of desks and benches, cupboards, etc.) must be accurately shown.

3. *Elevations* of each front and at least two sections. The ceiling, and the mode of warming and ventilation must be clearly shown.

4. *A Specification* of the work detailed for the several trades.

5. *A General Estimate* of cost.

## SCHOOL MANAGEMENT.

IN the history of the Board several experiments have been made in adjusting the relation of the School Management Committee to the whole Board. It has been considered necessary for the purpose of intelligent co-ordination that the educational work—at any rate, in the Day schools—of the Board should be under one general direction, and that the various sections of it should be dealt with by sub-committees of the School Management Committee, rather than by independent committees. The effect, however, of such an arrangement was found to be that a member of the Board who did not belong to the School Management Committee had little opportunity of taking part in educational work in which he might be strongly interested.

For a few months, in 1871-1872, the School Management Committee was a committee of the whole Board. This experiment was again tried in 1894, but it worked thoroughly badly. Although a considerable number of the members who were not specially interested in school management work attended very seldom, the general attendance at the committee meetings was about 40, a number obviously unsuitable for the committee discussion of a long and detailed agenda. In consequence, the work of the Committee fell seriously into arrears, there being—*e.g.* in March, April and May, 1895, an average of 47 pages of "blocked" business per meeting. In 1896 it was decided, upon the recommendation of a special committee appointed by the Board "to consider the expediency of reducing the size and altering the numbers of the committees and sub-committees," that the School Management Committee should consist of its original number of 21, and that members of the Board not belonging to the main committee should be allowed to join the sub-committees up to a number not exceeding one-quarter of the number of the full committee (the sub-committees generally consisting of ten members of the full committee plus five co-opted members). By this arrangement the School Management Committee continued to exercise its powers of general supervision, while at the same time almost all members of the Board had opportunities of taking part in the work of school management. The numbers have been slightly varied in some sub-committees by leave of the Board, and the experiment may be said to have worked, on the whole, very well.

The work of the School Management Committee was further lightened from 1884 to 1891, and from 1899 to the present time, by the appointment of a separate Standing Committee for the Evening Continuation schools, which had been controlled by a sub-committee.

The work of the Evening schools represented a distinct problem and employed, to a certain extent, a separate staff. It was believed that in this case the advantages derived from independent initiative outbalanced the disadvantages involved in the loss of co-ordination. At the same time it was determined that in all cases of misconduct by teachers in the employment of both committees, information should be exchanged.

In 1876 there were four sub-committees of the School Management Committee: three on Cookery, Needlework and Books respectively, and a rota sub-committee, which met weekly to discuss matters of detail and to recommend decisions to the full committee. This last sub-committee was discontinued in 1891, and the work has since been performed by the Chairman of the Committee. The Sub-Committees now number eight, dealing respectively with Teaching Staff, Pupil Teachers, Special Subjects, Domestic Subjects, Special Schools, Requisitions and Stock-taking, Books and Apparatus, and Scripture.

---

## MANAGERS.

### I.—THE STATUS OF MANAGERS.

Before the Act of 1870 became law, the Managers of Elementary Voluntary Schools had sole control over those schools, subject to the regulations of the Code, and to the demands made by the Education Department through, or upon the advice of, its Inspectors. Each school was an independent organism, and its Managers were its official governors. They were personally responsible for the maintenance of the school; upon them rested the duty of raising funds to meet current expenses; they were the recipients of the Government Grant and of the children's fees. They appointed and paid the teachers; they selected the books and apparatus; they controlled the curriculum, and they regulated the general conduct of the school.

Under the provisions of the Act of 1870, School Boards, wherever they were formed (and in London the formation of a School Board was compulsory), were invested with all the powers and duties of Managers in respect to the schools which came under their control. Section 14 of that Act declared that "every school provided by a School Board shall be conducted under the control and management of such Board," in accordance with certain regulations therein laid down. Section 18 provided that "the School Board shall maintain and keep efficient every school provided by such Board." And Section 19 imposed upon the School Board the duty of supplying 'school apparatus and everything necessary for the efficiency of the schools provided by them."

But it was evident that, although the duties of Managers must of necessity be imposed, in the first instance, upon the School Boards, and that those Boards, in the last resort, must be held responsible for the performance of them, they could not effectively render all those smaller and detailed services upon which the efficient conduct of an Elementary school so greatly depends. The members of the larger School Boards could not hope to be able to give that individual attention to minor questions of routine, conduct, and discipline, which was reasonably demanded from the Managers of a Voluntary school. The Act of 1870, therefore, conferred upon School Boards very large powers of delegation to persons who were to be called "Managers."

Section 15 of the Act provided that—

The School Board may, if they think fit, from time to time delegate any of their powers under this Act, except the power of raising money; and, in particular, may delegate the control and management of any school provided by them, with or without any conditions or restrictions, to a body of Managers appointed by them, consisting of not less than three persons.

The School Board may from time to time remove all or any such Managers, and, within the limits allowed by this section, and to or diminish the number of, or otherwise alter the constitution or powers of, any body of Managers formed by it under this section. . . ."

It is to be noted, first, that the power thus conferred was optional; and, second, that it was of very wide scope. There was, as a matter of interpretation, no power except that of raising money that the School Board was not able to delegate to Managers. But it must be noted, also, that the act of delegation did not divest the Board of its duties under the Act, nor release it from the penalties imposed by law for the non-performance of those duties.

## II.—THE EARLIER POLICY OF THE BOARD.

Not long after the formation of the School Board for London, the question of appointment of Managers and of the powers which were to be conferred upon them came under the consideration of the Works and General Purposes Committee; and on May 10th, the following report was presented to and adopted by the Board.

The Board will probably find it expedient to appoint Managers over all schools provided by it, or transferred to it, under such restrictions as it may from time to time see fit to adopt. The 15th Section of the Act gives the Board the power of appointing and removing such Managers, and rules for the "Proceedings of Managers appointed by a School Board" are succinctly prescribed in the third Schedule Upon the judicious selection of Managers much will depend, and in most instances the Board would do well to appoint a certain proportion of the existing Managers. The persons selected should, if possible, be more or less closely identified with the interests of the locality where the school is situated, and should be prepared to undertake personal responsibility for any amounts expended beyond the sanction of the Board.

The duties of Managers appointed by the Board would be similar to those discharged by existing school Managers, with this difference, that the former would be responsible to the Board, not to voluntary subscribers, and would be liable to be removed at its pleasure, if they should neglect or transgress any of its rules. They would probably elect one of their number to act as Secretary, another as Treasurer, and in this way the Board might secure the assistance of volunteers all over the Metropolis without cost to the ratepayers.

It would be the duties of the Managers of a school provided by the Board to visit it periodically, and to see that it was duly provided with suitable desks, maps, books and apparatus; to obtain the sanction of the Board for the purchase of such articles as might be necessary, to receive and examine all tradesmen's bills, to forward them to the Board for payment, to receive from the Teachers the fees paid by the scholars, and to transmit them to the Accountant of the Board; to recommend the appointment and dismissal of Teachers, to consider applications for reduction or remission of Fees, to suggest to the Board what special subjects of instruction would be suited to the neighbourhood, to make periodical reports to the Board upon the general efficiency of the schools, and in short to act as the representatives of the Board in all respects within limits to be hereafter prescribed.

When this Report was adopted, the Board had not a single school under its control. They declined even to entertain proposals for transfers before June 1st, 1871,[1] and the first school erected by them was not opened until July 7th, 1873. The Board had no guidance in preparing their scheme, save the analogy of Voluntary School Managers. They knew that, in the near future, a considerable number of Voluntary Schools would be transferred to them, and that it was expedient to make the way easy for the managers of those schools to adapt themselves to the new order of things. The Board evidently conceived that it would be possible to conduct the schools which they provided under regulations similar to those which had hitherto prevailed in respect to

---

[1] As to the constitution of the body of Managers of a transferred school, see *post*, p. 83.

Voluntary schools. It even appears that members thought it possible to establish a system under which the Managers of Board schools would be primarily liable for expenditure, and that the Board's responsibility would be limited to a fixed grant. Such a plan would not have been practicable, and the whole scheme, when any large number of schools came under the control of the Board, would have led to unnecessary extravagance. Purchases of school furniture, books, and apparatus would have been made locally and at retail prices. Each school would have had its own scale of salaries for teachers. No systematic method of repairs could have been adopted.

Although the Board never in fact entrusted to its Local Managers such vast powers as are disclosed in the Report quoted above, the policy of that Report was never abandoned by any formal act of rescission.[1] Indeed, when nearly a year had elapsed after the adoption of that Report, the Board declined to limit the powers which it had conferred on Managers in one important matter. On April 10th, 1872, a motion was made to deprive Local Managers of the power to furnish and fit up school buildings, and to place the work under the control of the Works and General Purposes Committee. It must be remembered that even at this date the Board were dealing only with transferred schools and the Managers of those schools; and it may have been deemed politic to refrain from limiting too stringently the powers which such Managers had exercised in the days of their independence. The mover stated, very truly, that few Managers knew anything about the purchase of furniture, or how to obtain it in the cheapest market. He wished that "some plan should be adopted by which some one should be made responsible to the Board for the proper performance of this work," and that Managers should "confine their attention to education arrangements." In the course of the debate, one member said that "he believed" the mover of the resolution "was right in saying that a miscellaneous body of men going about in search of school furniture would make worse bargains than a central body like the Board, and although he was not prepared to deprive the existing Managers of any of their powers, he supported the question as a matter of economy."[2] Nevertheless both the speaker and the seconder of the resolution voted against the motion, and the mover remained its only supporter against 27 opponents.[3]

### III.—THE CAUSES OF RESTRICTION OF POWERS.

In practice, the whole course of development of the Board's administrative system has had the incidental effect of diminishing the powers originally conferred upon the Managers. Sometimes this has been the result of steps intended to secure economy

---

[1] In October, 1871, the School Management Committee (then a committee of the whole Board) resumed the power of appointing teachers and fixing their salaries. The policy of the Board, in respect to the powers of Managers, was discussed by three Committees of Inquiry in 1882, 1887, and 1892.

[2] "*School Board Chronicle,*" April 13th, 1872, p. 252.

[3] Board Minutes, Vol. II., p. 246. Within a year of the rejection of the motion quoted above the Board practically adopted it by entering into contracts for the supply of a uniform style of desk [Board Minutes, Vol. III. p. 207], and also for the supply of books, maps, apparatus, &c. [Board Minutes, Vol. II., p. 564.]

and uniformity in the provision of apparatus, &c.; sometimes of the appointment of expert officials, whose advice on technical questions was likely to be taken by the Committees, even if it conflicted with the opinions of the Managers.

A change, possibly more important in its bearing on the influence of the Managers, has also taken place in the position of the head teachers, whose pedagogic responsibility has been increased and defined by the policy both of the School Board and of the Board of Education.   It is, for instance, the head teachers and not the Managers who, subject to the regulations of the Board and of the Code, choose books and settle the curriculum of a school.   The liberty of the individual school, which has always been encouraged in England as a safeguard against official rigidity, has tended insensibly in London to become liberty for the head teachers rather than liberty for the Local Managers of the school.   In educational matters, all Managers are expected to see that no neglect of duty takes place, and they may exercise a valuable stimulating influence ; but the power to give definite orders on questions of curriculum has lapsed.

At the same time, the growth since 1870 of the functions of an Elementary school in the life of a great city has created many new duties and opportunities, a large share of which has fallen to the Managers.   The Managers, in many groups of schools, take a leading part in the organisation of School Clubs, Sports, Excursions, Savings Banks, Children's Country Holiday Funds, &c., and in the relief of distress by meals for underfed children and the supply of clothing.

At first, the Managers used to recommend the appointment of teachers and their salaries.   From the beginning, the Board referred back, from time to time, nominations of teachers, on the ground of youth, or want of qualifications, and refused proposals for apparently excessive salaries.   Ultimately, in 1872, the Board adopted a uniform scale of salaries.   The fixing of uniform school hours and holidays, in 1872, also had the effect of diminishing the powers originally given to the Managers.

The first Board also appointed two Inspectors to examine and report upon the discipline and general efficiency of their schools, and this action naturally involved supervision by the Board over the Managers' work.   This decision brought up again the question of the general position of the Managers.   A motion was moved :—

" That in future no Managers be appointed for new schools established by this Board, but that the schools be managed by Inspectors, who shall visit each school in each fortnight." [1]

The motion was not intended to affect transferred schools, but only the new schools which the Board proposed to establish.   The reasons urged in its favour were : (1) The difficulty of obtaining a sufficient supply of competent Managers ; (2) the greater uniformity and efficiency that would be obtained under an inspectorate ; (3) the more direct control over education that the Board would be enabled to exercise.   The opponents of the proposal objected that it would tend to produce over-centralisation, a too rigid uniformity of method, and to stifle local interest in the schools.   They asserted that, though " instruction " might benefit, " education " would suffer. [2]

[1] May 1st, 1872.   Board Minutes, Vol. II., p. 309.          [2] *School Board Chronicle*, Vol. 5, pp. 362-3.

It was ultimately resolved to refer the question to the School Management Committee for consideration, and on May 29th, 1872, the Board adopted the recommendation of the Committee that management by inspectors was undesirable, but that with a view to widening the experience of Managers, "it was desirable, when practicable, to have several schools under the same Managers, especially when grouped so as to comprise various kinds of schools." [1]

The earliest schools of the Board were transferred Voluntary schools, which, at the time of transfer, had existing bodies of Managers. As soon as the transfer of a school to the Board had been arranged, four persons were nominated for appointment by the Board by the existing Managers of the school and four by the School Management Committee on the recommendation of the Divisional Members.[2] This arrangement lasted until 1874, after which transferred schools were placed under some existing body of Managers, or under a new committee of eight Managers appointed entirely by the Board. These eight persons acted as a committee of Managers for the transferred school, and to them were delegated "the control and management of the school, subject to such conditions and restrictions as the Board might from time to time impose." [3] In the case of new schools provided by the Board, the Divisional Members nominated eight persons for appointment by the Board as Managers.[4] Both as regards new schools and transferred schools, it was a rule that one of the persons nominated by the Divisional Members should be a Member of the Board. [5]

From the first, Divisional Members were instructed to revise the lists from time to time, with a view to filling vacancies, and also with a view to the addition of new Managers where desirable. Managers who had attended less than one-fourth of the total number of their Committee-meetings were considered to have vacated their seats, but were eligible for re-appointment. In 1879, it was decided that this revision should be made annually, and should be subject to the approval of the Board.

In 1876 the Board summarised and codified the different resolutions and directions that it had, during the first six years of its life, issued to the Managers. According to the School Management Code for that year, the duties required from Managers were:—"To nominate head, assistant, and pupil teachers, and schoolkeepers to the Board for appointment; to visit schools whenever convenient; to see that the instruction was given in accordance with the regulations; to examine periodically teachers' returns; to recommend the school fees to be charged; and to exercise a general supervision over the property of the Board." It will at once be noticed how striking was the difference between this modest list of functions, and the ambitious programme of 1871; and how complete had been the change of policy of the School Board. These words, with the exception of the clause on school fees, may still be used to define the position of the Board's Local Managers.

---

[1] Board Minutes, Vol. II , p. 372.
[2] *Ib.*, Vol. I., p. 355. *Ib.*, Vol. II., p. 37.
[3] *Ib.*, Vol. I., p. 342.

[4] Board Minutes, Vol. II., p. 37.
[5] *Ib.*, Vol. II., p. 170.

### IV.—COMMITTEES OF INQUIRY.

Since 1876 three special Committees of Inquiry upon the powers and duties of Managers have been held—in 1882, 1887, and 1893. It may be said that the result of these inquiries, and of the subsequent legislation by the Board, was, first, to narrow and limit, by successive steps, the interpretation placed upon the foregoing clause of the Code; and, secondly, to revise and perfect the machinery by which the Committee of Managers were appointed and renewed.

The first of these Committees was held in the year 1882, and dealt chiefly with questions of the constitution of the Managers' Committees. It was decided that not more than twelve Managers should be appointed for any one school, and not more than twenty for any group of schools. Up to that time eight persons had been nominated as Managers to each school. In cases of a vacancy in their number, the remaining Managers were allowed to nominate candidates to be considered by the Divisional Members. This rule has since been frequently discussed, but is still in force. The existing practice of giving Managers notice of important structural alterations, was also instituted on the recommendation of this committee. Between 1882 and 1887 the Board made a few trifling changes in its rules with regard to Managers. One of these was necessitated by the Government Code of 1884. That Code placed upon the School Board the duty of determining what children, either from mental or physical defect, or bad health, were to be excused from the Government examination. The Board accordingly directed the Local Managers to form small health sub-committees, consisting of at least three persons, one of whom should, if possible, be a doctor, and one a woman.

The Board also, in 1886, resolved :—

"That the Divisional Member in Charge of the School, or the Local Managers with the consent of the Divisional Member in Charge of the school, be empowered to order urgent and slight repairs in schools up to a total amount not exceeding £4 per department in any one year. . . ."

The Works Committee having decided that intermittent applications for repairs to school buildings should be discouraged, and that yearly applications should be sent in by the Managers, it was found necessary to make some provision for cases where slight repairs were urgently needed.

This permission was revoked in July, 1889, when the whole of these arrangements were placed in the hands of local clerks of works.

In 1883, the Local Managers instituted a Central Committee for the discussion of questions affecting the work of their schools. This Committee was known as the "Committee of Representative Managers." It included a representative from nearly every body of Managers, and it met, once a month, at the School Board Offices. It was valuable as a means of conference between the Managers themselves, and as a channel by which their views might be made known to the Board.

The Committee of Inquiry in 1887 chiefly dealt with the important question of the appointment of teachers. It also made recommendations on some minor matters, chiefly questions of the machinery of choosing and organising the different boards of Managers;

and these were, for the most part, finally revised on the recommendations of the third and last committee of inquiry in 1892. In 1887 the maximum number of schools in each group was fixed at three, and in 1888 the minimum at two. In the same year, it was arranged that no person should serve as Manager on more than two groups of schools. It had already been decided, in the previous year, that no person might be chairman of more than two groups of schools. This rule was finally amended in 1893, when the Board resolved that no Manager might be chairman of more than one group of schools.

Both the Special Committees of 1887 and 1892 reported that they found that some persons who had ceased to take any interest in their duties, were still retained on the Committees. The Board consequently resolved, in 1888, that Managers who had attended less than one-third of the meetings, or who had failed to make three visits to their schools in each year, should be struck off the list; and on the receipt of the similar report of 1892, resolved that the maximum number of Managers should be reduced to eight for a single school, twelve for two schools, and fifteen for a group of three schools, the minimum numbers being fixed at five, eight, and twelve respectively. The divisional members were, in 1887, directed to secure that, if possible, two women should be appointed on each Committee of Managers, and in 1893 that one-third of each Committee should be women. Finally, in order to conclude the question of the constitution of Boards of Managers, the Special Committee of 1892 considered how far it was possible to appoint working men as Managers, and made the following report:—

> The question of "securing the services of a fair proportion of working people in the capacity of Managers" was specially mentioned in the reference of the Board indicating the lines of the Committee's inquiry. They think, however, that it is the fitness of the person to serve in that capacity rather than his occupation or social position which should be chiefly considered.
>
> In the Committee's opinion the present Rules and Regulations leave it open to the Divisional Members to nominate desirable persons of the working class.

The rule referred to, was the following resolution passed by the Board in 1889:—

> That it be a recommendation to the Divisional Members that as far as possible, in every group of Managers, where it is not the case already, there be nominated two persons at least, who are, or have been parents of children attending Public Elementary schools.

The practice of appointing working men as Managers has not, however, been adopted generally. It is necessary that the Managers should visit the schools when the children are present, and also, in many cases, attend Committee Meetings in the day time. These duties can only be performed by persons with a certain amount of leisure.

No further change has been made in the constitution of the Committees of Local Managers, except that, on November 25th, 1898, after a discussion upon the large number of clergymen acting as Managers, the School Management Committee decided: "That it be an instruction to Divisional Members in making nominations of Local Managers of schools to have in their minds the avoidance of the preponderance of any one class on the management."

## V.—Appointment of Teachers.

The main question discussed by the Special Committee of 1887 was the appointment of the head teacher. The Committee were convinced, by the evidence submitted to them, that some scheme of systematic promotion had become necessary. It was impossible that Managers, with their purely local experience, should be able to compare the claims of persons from remote districts. The School Management Committee, at that time, kept what was known as a "promotion list." The Committee of Inquiry recommended that teachers possessing the necessary qualifications should be invited to enter their names, and that the Managers should be requested to make their selection from this list.

This vague and permissive resolution having produced no effect, the Board, in 1889, decided to deprive the Managers altogether of the power of appointment. Strong and repeated protests were received both from individual groups of Managers, and from the Committee of Representative Managers, and in 1890 the Board adopted a modification of the scheme. Vacancies were advertised, the names received were considered by a committee of the Board, with the assistance of two Managers. These selected three names, which were submitted to the School Management Committee for final appointment.

This scheme was, however, amended in 1892, when it was decided that a committee of the Board—the Teaching Staff Sub-Committee—should, with the assistance of two Managers, select three names. These were sent to the Local Managers, who chose from them one candidate for nomination. In 1898, the number of Managers at the original selection was reduced to one. In 1899, the arrangements at present in force were introduced. According to this scheme, when a head teacher was to be appointed, every member of the Board, the Board Inspectors, and the Chairman or Vice-Chairman of the local managements were invited to submit a nomination. The list was then considered by the Teaching Staff Sub-Committee, who selected, and saw, seven candidates. From these three were chosen and sent to the Local Managers, who, from among them, made a final selection for approval by the Board. By an amendment of 1900, one Manager was allowed to be present and vote when the matter was under discussion by the Teaching Staff Sub-Committee. To these elaborate arrangements there are, however, several exceptions. In the case of new schools, the Managers are not consulted ; and the choice of teachers in Higher Grade and Higher Elementary schools, is made by a Committee of the Board. A representative of the Managers, however, is allowed to be present and to vote.

The Board have never, expressly, interfered with the Managers' power of nominating assistant teachers. This power has, however, since 1899, been incidentally, but seriously, diminished. In that year, the Board Inspectors were directed to visit the different training colleges, and to obtain the names of suitable women students who were willing to enter the service of the Board. The names of these students were placed upon a list, known as the "College List," and, until all these students had been permanently appointed, the Managers were limited in their choice to teachers·

whose names were on this list. Such students as were not at once permanently engaged were placed on "supply" and paid permanent scale salary until appointments were found for them. By this means the Board were able to secure in advance the services of teachers who might otherwise have applied for other appointments. It was further decided, in 1900, that students who had been seen at the Colleges by the Board Inspectors should not be summoned to attend before the Managers. These decisions caused great dissatisfaction amongst the Local Managers, and many protests were received from various bodies. It would appear, from a letter that the Board received from the Committee of Representative Managers, that the chief grounds of objection were—(i.) the fear that in the course of time the selection of assistant teachers would fall entirely into the hands of the Board Inspectors, and (ii.) the dislike entertained to appointing teachers solely on paper qualifications, without first securing a personal interview. In reply to these protests, the School Management Committee issued an explanatory circular to Managers, calling their attention to the serious interference in the important work of College Students during their last term caused by repeated summonses to attend before Managers, and pointing out that most of the students on the "College List" had been pupil teachers under the Board, and were quite satisfactory as to conduct and intellectual attainments.

In February, 1901, the whole question was raised as to whether the existing practice should be maintained. After very careful consideration by the Board Inspectors, the Teaching Staff Sub-Committee, and finally by the School Management Committee, it was decided that the visits of the Board Inspectors to the colleges should be continued, and that, as before, the Managers' selection of teachers should be restricted to the "College List." The rule as to students not being summoned from college was, however, relaxed, Managers being allowed to require their attendance after the certificate examination. During 1902 about 600 women teachers entered the service of the Board through the agency of the "College List." In 1902 a "College List" was also established for men teachers.

The above brief history of the policy of the Board, with regard to their Local Managers, necessarily leaves untouched all that is voluntarily undertaken by the Managers. As has been said before, in many schools, the Managers take a leading part in social work connected with their schools. They are directed to report annually to the Board upon such subjects as the following :—Excessive illness among teachers or scholars, or any special difficulties of the school; special subjects studied ; condition of the school libraries and the use made of them ; the use made of the halls ; clubs for swimming, games, or natural history ; arrangements for country holidays for children, or provident funds ; any special measures adopted to meet cases of sickness or poverty among the children, or special plans for interesting the parents in the work of the school.

In the words of the School Management Code (adopted from the Government Code) : " the duty of Managers is to foster the schools under their care by every means in their power, to see that the rules laid down for the guidance of teachers are adhered to, to smooth down the difficulties of teachers by constant encouragement and sympathy, to have at heart the mental, moral, and physical welfare of the scholars, and to see that they are brought up in habits of punctuality, of good manners and language, of cleanliness and neatness, and also that the teachers impress upon the children the importance of cheerful obedience to duty, of consideration and respect for others, and of honour and truthfulness in word and act." [1]

### THE BOARD INSPECTORATE.

The question whether the Board should rely in the main for information as to the condition of their schools on officials of its own or on the Inspectors of the Board of Education has been debated from time to time ever since the Board came into existence.

On October 11th, 1871, Professor Huxley, Chairman of the Scheme of Education Committee, moved :—" That Inspectors be appointed by the Board to examine its schools and pupil teachers in all the subjects taught in each school, and to report to the Board from time to time upon the discipline and general efficiency of the schools provided by the Board." He argued that " If there was one thing more important than another for the School Boards, it was that the inspection should be given up by the Government and left to the energy of the School Boards."

An amendment was moved :—" That officers be appointed by the Board to visit its schools, and to report to the Board, from time to time, upon the discipline and general efficiency of the schools provided by the Board."

The seconder of the amendment, said :—" He believed that the feeling was very general that the duty of the Board was to bring schools into existence, and that it was for the Government to see that they were really efficient." [2]

The amendment was supported by the Rev. J. Rodgers (afterwards the well-known Chairman of the School Management Committee) who said :—" When they had the work efficiently done by H.M. Inspectors he did not see that they wanted it done again."

A third alternative was that the Board should obtain certain kinds of information and help from its own inspectors, and rely for other kinds upon H.M. Inspectors. This alternative seems to have been implicitly adopted, and when, in 1872, the Board decided to appoint an inspector of their own, his first duty was stated to be " to assist in organising schools provided by the Board," [3] and the Rev. J. Rodgers stated that he " hoped the Board would not appoint any inspector except such as was contemplated in the report, because, with regard to the intellectual inspection of the schools, the work would be done thoroughly by the Government inspectors." [4]

From the beginning, however, the Board Inspectors assessed and reported on schools much in the same way as H.M. Inspectors, in addition to the administrative work required of them by the School Management Committee, although neither then nor since has any official relation existed between the two bodies of Inspectors.

By the spring of 1885 the Board had seven Inspectors for an average attendance of 285,807. They not only assisted in administration, but held regular individual examinations of scholars on the same lines as the annual examinations of H.M. Inspectors.

[1] Board Minutes, Vol. XXIII., p. 87.   [3] Board Minutes, Vol. II., p. 74.
[2] *School Board Chronicle*, October 14th, 1871.   [4] *School Board Chronicle*, January 27th, 1872.

Early in 1885 the Board, however, decided, in the case of their own Inspectors, to substitute inspection for examination, and, in defining the duties of the Board Inspectors, laid it down " that their annual report on each school should set forth their judgment as gathered from their observations made during visits throughout the school year."

In that summer (1885) two vacancies existed among the Board Inspectorate, and the filling up of these vacancies was postponed. The new Board, which was elected in November, 1885, referred to the School Management Committee a motion, "That in the opinion of this Board the present dual system of inspection is unnecessary . . . " A Special Sub-Committee of the School Management Committee then inquired into the work of the Inspectors, took evidence on the question of inspection and examination, and recommended "that for the next year the existing number (5) of the Board Inspectors be not increased, and that the work be arranged in the direction of inspection rather than examination, so that they may be able to compass that work."

This was adopted by the Board, and the Board further directed that the Board Inspectors should " thoroughly examine and report upon such schools as the Committee shall from time to time suggest." [1]

Soon afterwards a change began in the methods of H.M. inspectors. From 1862 to 1890 each child had been examined in each of the "Three R's." By the Code of 1890 the head teacher was required to divide each standard into three sections, and the Inspector then examined one section in Reading, another in Writing, and the third in Arithmetic.

In 1894 inspection was substituted for examination throughout the Infant schools, and in 1895 the Inspectors were authorised to give notice that the examination due in the following year (1896) would be omitted in any school which had reached a good educational standard. They were instructed to pay at least two visits of inspection without notice during the year to any school excused examination. Notice was so given practically to all the schools of the London Board.

In 1901 the annual examination was definitely abolished, and in the " Instructions " for that year it is laid down: " In future the Inspectors will not follow the practice of past years, and will no longer (except as provided for in the case of an appeal under Article 86 of the Code) hold any examinations of individual scholars except those who require labour certificates."

The Instructions to H.M. inspectors of 1899 and 1900 said:—

Your annual report should not enter into details as to particular portions of the school work, except where some special excellence or defect has to be noted, and you should avoid including in it any personal reflections on the teachers. The annual report should consist of a short description of the general character of the school as regards instruction, organisation, discipline, premises, and apparatus.

Meanwhile the policy of the Government was to increase and make effective the responsibility of the head teacher of each school for the state of his school. The

[1] Board Minutes, April 8th, 1886.

following paragraph (applying then only to schools excused examination) appeared in the " Instructions " for " 1895 " :—

> It will materially assist you in your visits to such schools if the Managers will request the teachers to provide at the beginning of each year a syllabus of instruction for each class, notebooks for containing brief summaries of the chief oral lessons, and a record book in which the head teacher may make brief entries showing the quality of work done throughout the school, as tested by periodical examinations, and progress or mark books as to the individual conduct, application, and advance of the scholars. It would also be advisable that you should be supplied at the beginning of the year with a copy of the time-table for the ensuing year.

The paragraph was afterwards strengthened and generalised, and appeared in the ' Instructions " of 1901 as follows :—

> At the beginning of each year there must be provided a plan of the work to be done in that year, which should set out in outline schemes of work in the different subjects. But if it is necessary in the interests of the scholars, the teacher is at liberty to deviate from any scheme either in the way of omission or enlargement or curtailment of its various parts. There should also be provided notebooks for containing brief summaries of the chief oral lessons, a record book in which the head teacher may make brief entries showing the quality of work done throughout the school as tested by periodical examinations, and progress or mark books as to the individual conduct, application, and advance of the scholars. All these documents are the property of the Managers, and in case of a change of teacher should be left at the school. It may be useful that some short record of the conduct of each scholar should be sent to the parents annually. But such records should not hamper a teacher in varying the work of the school, nor be so detailed as to demand an undue amount of clerical work.

The Board Inspectors in a succession of annual reports from 1896 to 1901 first welcomed the change, then (in 1898) stated that the improvement due to the change "was not equally distributed throughout the schools," and in 1900 and (in stronger language in 1901) warned the Board as to the educational condition of some of the schools.

On receiving the report for 1901, the Board adopted the following resolution :—

> That in view of the very serious statements contained in the report of the Board Inspectors, the School Management Committee be directed to inquire into the causes and extent of the alleged defects, both in teaching and discipline in the schools of the Board, and to report thereon.

The Board received the report of the School Management Committee on 23rd October, 1902, and after considerable debate, passed a series of resolutions. Some of these resolutions aimed at securing to the Board Inspectors the power and the time "to ascertain more fully the condition of departments or classes either chosen by themselves or indicated by the School Management Committee." Other resolutions aimed at making more systematic and effective the system of examinations and records by head teachers.

These objects were further aimed at by resolutions (in 1903) appointing eight sub-inspectors to assist the Board Inspectors and adopting a uniform "Record and Progress Book" for use in the schools.

# CURRICULUM.

## I.—INTRODUCTION.

The Board have never had a free hand in fixing the curriculum of their schools. They are only legally empowered to spend public money in carrying on " Public Elementary schools," and a Public Elementary school must be carried on in accordance with the Government Code of the time being.[1]

The Code contains a list of compulsory subjects, which has varied considerably during the existence of the Board, and of optional subjects, many of which were, until the introduction of the " block " grant, encouraged by " special " grants, and some of which (Manual Training, Domestic Economy, etc ) are still so encouraged.  The list ot optional subjects has had a negative as well as a positive effect on the curriculum, since it has been held by the Local Government Board (*e.g.* in the case of Manual Training, 1886) that the Board are not entitled to spend public money on the teaching of any subject which does not appear either among the compulsory or among the optional subjects in the Code.[2]

But the Board have throughout their history been unwilling to make full use even of the power of regulating the time-tables of their schools which the Government Code has allowed them.  The Board have always believed that a certain freedom should be left to each school in the development of its curriculum, so that experiment may be encouraged and allowance may be made for the special knowledge of the various teachers and the special requirements of various districts.  The Board have from time to time issued directions requiring certain subjects to be taken or dropped, or regulating the time to be given to a particular subject, but apart from these directions and the requirements of the Government Code, large liberty and responsibility in drawing up the time-tables have been left to the head teacher of each school department.  The Board, indeed, have often been content rather to watch and record than to control the growth or decline of subjects of instruction in their schools.

It will be convenient, therefore, to begin this chapter with a short sketch of the variations in the Government Codes since 1871 as far as they affect curriculum.  This will be followed by a general account of the policy of the Board, and by a more detailed account in which the history of the various subjects will be given from the time of their introduction.  The end of the chapter will consist of statistical tables showing the growth and decline of separate subjects of instruction. An account of the curriculum of the Higher Grade and Special Schools is reserved for later chapters.

## II.—OUTLINE OF THE REGULATIONS OF THE GOVERNMENT CODES SINCE 1871 AS AFFECTING CURRICULUM.

The Code of 1871 required as compulsory subjects: (*a*) for children between 4 and 7 instruction suitable to their ages [3] ;  (*b*) for children above 7 :—Reading, Writing and

---

[1] Elementary Education Act, 1870, s. 97.  [3] Article 17 (g).
[2] *Cf*. Regina *v*. Cockerton, L.R., 1 Q.B. 1901, p. 322.

Arithmetic, in which each scholar was required to be presented for examination, and "Plain Needlework and Cutting Out" for the girls.

The optional subjects for which a "special" grant was given for individual scholars in Standards IV.-VI. passing a satisfactory examination were:—Geography, History, Grammar, Algebra, Geometry, Natural Philosophy, Physical Geography, the Natural Sciences, Political Economy, Languages, or "any definite subject of instruction, extending over the classes to be examined in Standards IV., V., VI., and taught according to a graduated scheme, of which the Inspector can report that it is well adapted to the capacity of the children, and is sufficiently distinct from the ordinary reading book lessons to justify its description as a "Specific Subject of Instruction." [1]  No scholar could be presented in more than two of these subjects.

In 1875 the optional subjects were divided into "class" subjects and "specific" subjects.  The "class" subjects were: Grammar, History, Geography, and Needlework, and a grant was given if the classes above Standard I. passed a creditable examination in any two (or in 1878 any one) of them.  This grant was reduced by one-half if 20 per cent.[2] of the children examined in the Elementary subjects were not in or above Standard IV.  The "specific" subjects recognised were: Mathematics, Mechanics, Latin, Animal Physiology, French, Physical Geography, German, Botany, Domestic Economy (for girls); English Literature being added in the following year.  The "specific" grant was given for individual scholars in Standards IV.-VI. who passed an examination by H.M. Inspector.

Under Art. 24 of the Code the attendance of girls at lessons in Practical Cookery for not more than two hours a week was allowed to count as school attendance.[3]

The Code of 1882 was a revolution against the mechanical methods of the earlier codes.  In addition to a fixed grant it offered a "merit" grant, dependent in amount upon the assessment of the school by H.M. Inspector as "fair," "good," or "excellent."  In assessing the merit grant for Infants' departments, regard was to be had to the provision made for  . . .  "simple lessons on objects and on the phenomena of nature and of common life," and "appropriate and varied occupations."  In the upper departments, the assessment of the merit grant depended upon "organisation and discipline, the intelligence employed in instruction, and the general quality of the work, especially in the Elementary subjects."  It also recognised as a "class" subject, Elementary Science, which was defined as "a progressive course of simple lessons  . . .  adapted to cultivate habits of exact observation, statement, and reasoning.  English first appeared in the list of "class" subjects in this Code, and was compulsory if "class" subjects were taken.  English Literature and Physical Geography were also taken out of the list of

---

[1] Schedule IV.
[2] Reduced to 10 per cent. in 1876, raised to 15 per cent. in 1879, and to 20 per cent. in 1880.
[3] A special grant was given by the Government for the teaching of this subject in 1882.  In 1890 a special grant was offered for Laundrywork, and in 1894 "Domestic Economy" was recognised as a "class" subject. From 1877 to 1881 the Government Code made Domestic Economy for girls compulsory in schools where specific subjects were taken.

"specific" subjects, and Chemistry, Physics, the Principles of Agriculture, and any other subject sanctioned by the Education Department were added.

In 1885 Drawing was added to the "class" subjects, and the maximum number of "class" subjects that could be taken was raised from two to three. If two "class" subjects were taken, English, as before, was to be one of them, and if three were taken, Drawing was to be the second. In 1887 Drawing was omitted from the "class" subjects, and the number allowed to be taken reduced to two again.[1]

In 1890 Manual Training was allowed to be included in the time-table and a grant from the Science and Art Department was given for it, and important changes were made in the system of grants for Senior schools. The grant for the compulsory subjects upon the results of individual examination was abolished and a fixed grant was allowed according to the recommendation of the Inspector on the accuracy of knowledge and general intelligence of scholars in those subjects. The head teacher was required to divide each standard into three sections, and the Inspector then examined one section in Reading, another in Writing, and the third in Arithmetic. A grant was also given for organisation and discipline, and subsequently in 1895 this grant was made conditional upon instruction in Drill or Physical Exercises. Drawing was made compulsory for boys, and the requirement that English should be taken as a "class" subject, if any "class" subject were taken was dropped. Shorthand and Bookkeeping were allowed as "specific" subjects.

In 1892 the Code made one "class" subject compulsory, and the grant for "specific" subjects was awarded upon the number of scholars presented for examination in each subject, instead of upon the number of passes.

In 1894 inspection was substituted for examination throughout the Infants' schools, and in 1895 H.M. Inspectors were authorised to give notice that the examination due for Senior departments in the following year (1896) would be omitted in any school which had reached a good educational standard. Notice was so given practically to all the schools of the Board. In the same year "Object Lessons" and "Suitable Occupations" in Standards I. to III were made compulsory, and were also recognised as "class" subjects. In 1896, "Suitable Occupations" ceased to be compulsory, but continued to be a "class" subject.

In 1898 "Object Lessons" was omitted from the list of "class" subjects, but it was required that the first "class" subject in Standards I. to III. should be "taught by means of object lessons." In this year also the system of paying grant for "specific" subjects was modified, grant on examination being superseded by grant on hours of instruction given. This Code also gave grants for Manual Training and Drawing to compensate for the South Kensington grants which were then withdrawn.

In 1900 the "block" grant system was introduced. In Senior schools one "principal" grant took the place of the old principal, discipline and organisation grants; and of

---

[1] Until 1885 Drawing was examined under the regulations of the Science and Art Department (see *post,* p. 108).

the grants for Needlework, Singing, Drawing, "class" subjects and "specific" subjects. The distinction between "obligatory" and "class" subjects disappeared, and a course of instruction including English, Arithmetic, Drawing (for boys), Needlework (for girls), lessons in Geography and History and Common Things, Singing and Physical Exercises was made generally compulsory. One or more of these subjects might be omitted, and one or more of the subjects hitherto known as "specific" might be added, if H.M. Inspector consented. The old grants for Cookery, Laundrywork, and Manual Training were continued, and a new grant for Household Management was offered.

In Infants' schools one fixed grant took the place of the old principal, variable, Needlework and Singing grants, and the compulsory course of instruction included "simple instruction in the Elementary Subjects, Simple Lessons on Common Things, Appropriate and Varied Occupations, Needlework (or Drawing for boys) Singing and Physical Exercises."

Since 1900 there has been no important change in the Code.

### III.—GENERAL SKETCH OF THE POLICY OF THE BOARD WITH REGARD TO CURRICULUM.

An account of the policy of the Board with regard to curriculum may be conveniently divided into three sections dealing with the years (a) 1870-1885, (b) 1885-1896, (c) 1896-1903.

The first period began with the Report of Professor Huxley's Committee on Curriculum.[1] This Report was, as finally adopted, in the following form :—

" In Infants' schools instruction shall be given in the following subjects :—

(a) The Bible and the Principles of Religion and Morality in accordance with the terms of the resolution of the Board passed March 8th, 1871.

(b) Reading, Writing, and Arithmetic.

(c) Object lessons of a simple character, with some such exercise of the hands and eyes, as is given in the Kindergarten system.

(d) Music and Drill.

" In Junior and Senior schools certain kinds of instruction shall form the essential part of the teaching of every school; but others may, or may not, be added to them at the discretion of the Managers of individual schools, or by the special direction of the Board. The instruction in the discretionary subjects shall not interfere with the efficiency of the teaching of the essential subjects.

The following subjects shall be essential :—

(a) The Bible and the principles of religion and morality in accordance with the terms of the resolution of the Board passed March 8th, 1871.

(b) Reading, Writing, and Arithmetic ; English, Grammar and Composition and the principles of Bookkeeping in the Senior schools ; with Mensuration in Senior Boys' schools.

(c) Systematised Object Lessons, embracing in the six school years a course of elementary instruction in Physical Science and serving as an introduction to the science examinations which are conducted by the Science and Art Department.

(d) The History of England.

(e) Elementary Geography.

---

[1] June 14th, 1871, Board Minutes, Vol. I., pp. 155-159.

(*f*) Elementary Social Economy.[1]

(*g*) Elementary Drawing.

(*h*) Music and Drill.

(*i*) (In Girls' school•). Plain Needlework and Cutting Out.

The following subjects shall be discretionary :—

(*a*) Domestic Economy.

(*b*) Algebra.

(*c*) Geometry.

Subject to the approbation of the Board, any extra subjects recognised by the new Code, 1871, shall be considered to be discretionary subjects."

The Report had an important traditional influence on the policy of the Board, but could necessarily have little immediate effect in schools containing a very large proportion of children brought in for the first time from the streets.

In the Report upon the work of the first Board, submitted to the Board by the Clerk on October 29th, 1873, it was stated that effect had been given to the scheme "as far as practicable with the very raw material to be found for the most part in Board schools. It could not, of course, be regarded otherwise than as an ideal ; to which, however, the Board hope that their schools will approximate more and more with each succeeding year."

There is no definite information as to the extent to which instruction was given in the various subjects at the end of 1873, but it would appear that the only subjects taught in the schools of the Board, with very few exceptions, were the three obligatory subjects of the Government Code, with Singing, Drawing, Needlework, and Physical Education. The Government Reports received during the year ended December, 1873, show that only a very small number of children earned grant in the "specific" subjects of the Code. the figures being: Geography, 150 ; Grammar, 70 ; History, 42 ; Algebra, 6 ; Animal Physiology, 2. The statistics given on pages 128-9 show the gradual increase in succeeding years of subjects other than the three R's.

The general policy of the Board from 1871 to 1885 may, perhaps, be described as an effort to put the ordinary subjects on a sound footing with a view to carrying out as far as possible the Huxley Report.

The second period, 1885-1896, was marked by a certain change of aim. The majority who had held power at the Board since 1870, were defeated at the election of

---

[1] In 1883 this subject was transferred from the list of essential subjects to the list of discretionary subjects and the following provisional syllabus of a three years' course was placed in the S.M. Code, and remained there until 1902.

*Stage I.—Production of Wealth.*—The functions of labour and of capital in producing wealth ; the ineffectiveness of each without the other. Contract between employer and employed. Thrift, temperance, and economy ; their bearing not only on individual comfort, but general wages. Honesty, trustworthiness, forethought, &c., in their influence on the wealth of the community, and on individual well-being, and the prevention of destitution.

*Stage II.—Distribution of Wealth.*—Wages, profits,

rent: whence obtained and how regulated. Interest. Credit : its proper and improper employment. Impossibility of increasing wages by law. The qualities of character from which increase in wealth may be expected by the community.

*Stage III.—Exchange of Wealth.*—Division of labour and its advantages ; exchange thus necessitated. The use of credit in promoting interchange dependent upon honesty in business life. Machinery of business ; bills of exchange, &c. Savings banks, building societies, and other ways of making small savings productive. Money. Taxation. The duties of citizens.

[2] Board Minutes, Vol. III., p. 1075.

1885.  The severe depression of trade which commenced in 1879, the sudden development of German competition and the consequent inquiries and legislation of the Government on Technical Education (1883-4), and the agitation against "over-pressure" (1883-4), all united to produce a demand for a less ambitious and less literary education than that indicated by the Huxley Report.  Manual Training, "Hand and Eye," Training, Drawing, Elementary Science and Domestic Economy were all rapidly developed.  Homework for the scholars was practically abolished.

The policy of the Board during this period was largely influenced by the Report of a Special Committee appointed by the Board on March 31st, 1887, "to consider the present subjects and modes of instruction in the Board's schools and to report whether such changes can be made as shall secure that children leaving school shall be more fitted than they now are to perform the duties and work of life before them."

The Committee made recommendations which were adopted by the Board in 1888 in the following form :—

1. That the methods of Kindergarten teaching in Infants' schools be developed for senior scholars throughout the Standards in schools, so as to supply a graduated course of Manual Training in connection with Science teaching and Object Lessons.

2. That the teaching of all subjects be accompanied, where possible, by experiments and ocular demonstration, and that the necessary apparatus be supplied to the schools.

3. That the Board encourage Modelling in Clay in all departments of Schools, both in connection with Drawing as a training of the artistic faculties, and for the illustration of the teaching of Geography and other subjects.

4. That all manual instruction should be given in connection with the scientific principles underlying the work, and with suitable Drawing and Geometry.

5. That, as soon as the Board are permitted by law to give special instruction in manual work, such instruction shall be given to boys in and above the Fourth Standard in schools approved by the School Management Committee, in accordance with Resolution 4.

6. That classes for instruction in Slöjd be established in three selected schools approved by the School Management Committee.

7. That the instruction in the classes for manual work and Slöjd be only given by such teachers as have qualified for that purpose.

8. That, as opportunity offers, accommodation shall be provided in connection with each Boys', Girls', and Senior Mixed Department in which instruction in manual and other practical work shall be given.

9. That the experiments referred to in the Resolution[1] of the Board of May 5th, 1887, be tested in schools in selected districts.

10. That greater attention be paid to the teaching of Mechanics as a "specific" subject, and that models for illustrating the instruction be placed on the Requisition List.

11. That instruction in Practical Geometry be included in the teaching of Drawing, and that Mechanical Drawing to scale with actual measurements be encouraged in all Boys' departments.

12. That instruction in Drawing be given in all Girls' departments, though it be not taken as a subject of examination.

[1] *The Resolution referred to reads as follows:—* "That, subject to the sanction of the Education Department being given to the general principle, the instruction to children in the Fifth, Sixth, and Seventh Standards may, with the consent of the School Management Committee, be given in one School only in each Group of Schools." [*The Education Department, in assenting to the general principle of the proposal, asked that the arrangements proposed in each particular case should be submitted for the approval of the Department.*]

13. That instruction in Cookery be given only to Girls over 11 years of age without regard to Standard, and that the necessary additional Cookery Centres be provided.

14. That the time now given for Dictation be reduced in all Standards, and that in substitution for the part omitted in the lower Standards the reproduction by children in their own words of passages read out to them, and in Standard IV. and upwards original composition be taken.

15. That the teaching of Reading should be specially directed to give children an interest in books, and to encourage them to read for their own pleasure, and that Reading books should be for imparting a knowledge of Geography, History, Social Economy, and facts of common life to all children who may not be able to take such subjects for examination.

16. That, in order to allow time for experimental teaching and manual work, the time now given to Spelling, Parsing, and Grammar generally, be reduced.

17. That the Board authorise the appointment of an Organiser of Teaching, whose duties shall be to assist and advise teachers in the instruction of manual work, and in an improved method of instruction by the development of Kindergarten training.

18. That the Board authorise the appointment of an Officer, whose duties shall be to give instruction in, and to organise, the methods of teaching Mechanical and Geometrical Drawing.

19. That the Board authorise the appointment of four additional Instructors, who shall give instruction on the peripatetic plan in the Science subjects authorised by the New Code.

20. That head teachers of all departments be required to forward before the commencement of each school year, for the approval of the School Management Committee, (a) a scheme of Object Lessons ; (b) a copy of the time-table before being submitted to Her Majesty's Inspector.

21. That teachers be informed that the Board do not pay so much attention to the percentage of passes obtained at the Government Inspection as to the general tone and character of the school work, as set out in the remarks of Her Majesty's Inspector.

22. That the number of Mixed Schools be increased in suitable districts, and that the staff of such Mixed schools, be arranged so that the number of women teachers shall not be less in proportion to the male teachers, than the girls to the boys.

23 That in each Mixed department under a master an appointment be made of a head assistant mistress, who shall be responsible for the teaching of Needlework to girls.

24. That Advanced Evening Classes be established at the various Pupil Teachers' Schools, for instruction in Science and Drawing, Commercial Subjects, and Modern Languages.

25. That the playgrounds attached to schools be used for the formation of clubs for hardy sports, gymnastic exercises and drill, and that the school organisations be used for the establishment of field clubs and swimming classes.

26. That the Chairman of the Board be asked to convene a meeting of local Managers and others to consider the question of organised Physical Education out of school hours, and to request personal help in the work.

27. That, with a view to secure the improvement of Kindergarten in the schools of the Board, the Education Department be requested to grant certificates to teachers after examination, showing that they have been trained in the principles and sound practice of Kindergarten.

28. That application be made to the Education Department that the new Code be revised as follows :

(a) By postponing the individual examination in Spelling till the Third Standard. (*Schedule I.*)

(b) By applying to senior departments the regulation made with regard to infants' departments in Article 106 (b) of the New Code, viz. : that the award of a "merit" grant should have "regard to the provision made for . . . simple lessons on objects, and on the phenomena of nature and of common life."

(c) By providing that more freedom of choice may be given to managers and teachers in the selection of class subjects, in order that the first class subject need not necessarily be English.

(d) By providing that Shorthand shall be recognised as a "specific" subject under Article 15 of the New Code.

H

*e*) By providing for the payment of a grant of 4s. a head in the case of all girls of 11 years of age below Standard IV., who have received efficient instruction in Cookery.

(*f*) By rendering it obligatory upon pupil teachers to exhibit a knowledge of elementary science in some form at their annual examinations. (*Schedule V.*)

(*g*) By providing that in evening classes additional subjects may be taken by scholars who have passed the standard of exemption from Elementary Schools, or exceed the age of 14, without requiring such scholars to pass an individual examination in the elementary subjects.

29. That application be made to the Science and Art Department that their syllabus be remodelled, so as to supply a greater stimulus to Drawing being taken in combination with Geometry and Measurements, and in preparation for manual work.

Throughout this period the initiative of the London Board had an important influence upon the policy of the Department. In 1885, for instance, the Board started a class for boys in Manual Training, and in 1890 the Government Code recognised the subject. In 1889 the Board started Laundrywork, which was also recognised by the Code of 1890. "Hand and Eye" Training was commenced in the schools in 1890, and was introduced into the Government Code in 1895.

During the third period (1896-1903) the curriculum of the London Board Schools was largely affected by those changes introduced into the Government Code which culminated in the "block" grant of 1900. Both the Government and the Board seem to have felt during this period that what was wanted, in the interests both of general and technical education, was not the introduction or encouragement of further separate "subjects," but due co-ordination of the whole time-table in each school. In this period the various "Hand and Eye" subjects were merged in a general scheme of Drawing and Modelling. Cookery, Laundrywork, and Housewifery were united in a general scheme of Domestic Economy.

Object Lessons were largely co-ordinated with, or superseded by, Elementary Science; a general Science Course was in many schools substituted for the teaching of specialised sciences, and special attention was paid to the teaching of Geography and History. Annual educational conferences between the head teachers of the different departments were introduced (1898).

In this period also the Board urged upon its teachers on several occasions the danger of a too exclusive reliance upon oral teaching, and home work was partially re-introduced.[1]

It must be remembered, in considering all three periods, that changes in the policy of the Board with regard to curriculum, especially when they involve the scheduling of land for the erection of "centres" of instruction, require many years for their full development. The decision, for instance, to provide Manual Training for the elder boys was taken in 1890, but more than half the existing Manual Training accommodation has been erected since 1895. The decision that all girls in Standard V. and upwards should learn Cookery was taken in 1882, but it was not till 1891 that half the girls over Standard V. were receiving such instruction. It is very largely true

---

[1] In 1903 the Board decided that in cases where, in the judgment of the head teacher, home work was desirable, school books might be lent to the scholars for use at home.

that each Board has formed plans for its successors and carried out the plans of its predecessors.

## IV.—INDIVIDUAL SUBJECTS.

### 1. *Scripture.*

The resolution referred to in the Huxley Report quoted above was moved by Mr. W. H. Smith, and adopted by the Board by 38 votes to 3, on March 8th, 1871. It ran as follows :—

In the schools provided by the Board the Bible shall be read, and there shall be given such explanations and such instruction therefrom in the principles of Morality and Religion as are suited to the capacities of children, provided always—

(i.) That in such explanations and instruction the provisions of the Elementary Education Act, 1870, in Sections VII. and XIV., be strictly observed both in letter and spirit, and that no attempt be made in any such schools to attach children to any particular denomination.

(ii.) That, in regard to any particular school, the Board shall consider and determine upon any application by managers, parents, or ratepayers of the district who may show special cause for exception of the school from the operation of this resolution, in whole or in part.

On January 25th, 1894, the words " the Christian Religion and of Morality " were substituted by the Board for the words " Morality and Religion." On March 15th, 1894, the Board decided to send a circular to the teachers on religious teaching. This circular was not adopted as part of the School Management Code, and on July 3rd, 1903, the School Management Committee informed a correspondent that the only regulations of the Board at present in force which concern religious teaching in schools of the Board were those contained in Article 200 of the Board's Code.

In June, 1875, the late Mr. Francis Peek, then a member of the Board, informed the Board that he had provided, by an agreement with the Religious Tract Society, a permanent fund to supply yearly prizes to those scholars who might show excellence in Biblical knowledge at a voluntary examination.

For these prizes there has been, since 1876, an annual examination in two parts. The first, or preliminary part, has been conducted by the head teachers of the schools. A percentage of the children in Standards V., VI., VII., and ex-VII., and of the pupil teachers and probationers, has then been selected to compete in a further examination.

The majority of the scholars have annually presented themselves at the preliminary examination. The following table gives the number of children in Standard I. and above, who were present at the examination in 1876 (the first examination held under the scheme) and in 1902 :—

|  | Number in Average Attendance. | Number present at Examination. | |
|---|---|---|---|
|  |  | Preliminary. | Final. |
| 1876 | 67,653 | 43,238 | 2,430 |
| 1902 | 378,953 | 312,977 | 6,957 |

H 2

## 2. *The Obligatory Subjects.*

*Reading.*—In 1877 the School Management Committee were directed by the Board "to inquire into the best method of teaching Reading according to the present or any other system of Spelling, and to bring up a scheme for the purpose of putting the method or methods recommended to the test." The Committee appointed a Sub-Committee, and evidence was taken from teachers who had distinguished themselves by their success in teaching Reading, as to the methods they adopted and the difficulties they experienced. Evidence was also taken from outside experts on the subject. It was decided to try, as an experiment, the following four different methods of teaching Reading at selected schools :—"Sonnenschein's Method," "Pitman's Phonetic Method," "Leigh's Method," and "Robinson's Phonic Method." In a report on the working of this experiment, attention was drawn to difficulties experienced owing to the limited recognition which the Education Department afforded to such schemes. As a result of this report, the Department were petitioned to give greater facilities for the trial of different methods in teaching to read; but, as the reply was unfavourable, the matter was allowed to drop.[1]

During the last two years an attempt has been made to introduce a new method of teaching Reading. The School Management Committee have allowed the author, Miss Nellie Dale, to give lectures in schools where the head teachers have made application, and the system has now been adopted, wholly or partially, in about 100 departments. The system is built up on the phonic powers of the letters, and abstains from teaching the letter-names.

To encourage an interest in reading among the children, the Board in 1877 established lending libraries in connection with every school. There was at first an interchange of books between school and school every six months. Subsequently the libraries were made fixed instead of circulating, and an annual allowance of not exceeding twelve shillings for each department is now made for new books. In 1898 the condition of the scholars' lending libraries engaged the attention of the School Management Committee, and during the next three years the libraries were in rotation overhauled and replenished. The Local Managers were requested to depute one of their number to interest himself in the libraries, and to include in their annual report a short statement on the condition of the library and the use made of it by the scholars.

In 1901 the Board decided to grant facilities for the establishment of Home Reading Union Classes in the schools, and agreed under conditions to pay membership subscription fees and to supply copies of not more than two books on the Union's lists, which books might be taken home by the scholars, but were to remain the property of the Board.

*Writing.*—The Board have never imposed any uniform system of Writing upon their schools. It has, however, been found that inconvenience results from a variation in

---

[1] On November 22nd, 1876, the Board adopted the following resolution :—

"That this Board is of opinion that a great difficulty is placed in the way of education by our present method of Spelling, and that it is highly desirable that the Government should be moved to issue a Royal Commission for considering the best manner of reforming and simplifying it."—Board Minutes, Vol VI., p. 1731.

system among the different departments of any school, and consequently the Board require that this subject shall be considered by the head teachers of the departments of each school when they hold their annual conference.

In July, 1900, it was decided, for hygienic reasons, to stop supplying slates to schools.

The method of teaching Writing in the Infants' schools has been largely influenced of late years by the rapid growth of Blackboard Drawing and "Free Arm" Drawing for Infants.

*Arithmetic.*—From 1871 to 1893 the subject of Arithmetic was examined by H. M. Inspector on the basis of a single graduated scheme, set out in the Government Code In the existing Code that scheme is now called "Scheme A." During that period the syllabus varied very slightly, the only material alteration being the addition of a Seventh Standard in 1882

The Government Code of 1893 allowed an alternative scheme (B) to be taken. The two schemes are substantially the same in the higher Standards. They differ in the lower Standards, partly in the order in which the different rules are taken, and partly in the age at which the children are introduced to the use of large numbers.

In their Annual Report for 1898 the Board Inspectors stated that there was a tendency to substitute Scheme (B) for Scheme (A), and that generally they found more mental activity in the children, but there was a falling off in the accuracy that once obtained with the Arithmetical results.

The following table shows the percentage of passes on the number presented to H.M. Inspector for examination in the three obligatory subjects, triennially, from 1873 to 1891, when individual examination in these subjects was abolished :—

|  | | | 1873. | 1876. | 1879. | 1882. | 1885. | 1888. | 1891. |
|---|---|---|---|---|---|---|---|---|---|
| Reading | ... | ... | 87·9 | 87·1 | 88·2 | 92·1 | 95·1 | 96·0 | 97·4 |
| Writing | ... | ... | 83·3 | 83·7 | 84·7 | 90·0 | 89·2 | 91·1 | 93·3 |
| Arithmetic | ... | ... | 76·8 | 77·9 | 80·0 | 85·0 | 87·4 | 89·0 | 91·1 |

### 3 *English.*

English is, perhaps, the least satisfactory section of the history of the London Board school curriculum. Neither in the time allocated to the subject nor in the character of the scheme of studies has there ever been anything to correspond to the carefully-balanced literary and structural study of language under the names of *la langue Française* and *die Mutter-Sprache* in French and German curricula.

The Government Code, up to 1875, did not contemplate any class study of Language or Literature beyond Reading and Writing, though individual scholars were allowed to earn grant for the undefined subject of Grammar from 1870 to 1875. In 1873 the number of the Board's scholars who earned grant in this subject was 70, and even by 1875 the number was only 465.

In 1875 Grammar became a "class subject," with an almost incredibly meagre schedule, which it is perhaps worth while to give in full.

| STANDARD II. | STANDARD III. | STANDARD IV. | STANDARD V. | STANDARD VI. |
|---|---|---|---|---|
| To point out the nouns in the passage read. | To point out the nouns, verbs and adjectives. | Parsing of a "simple" sentence. | Parsing with analysis of a "simple" sentence. | Parsing and analysis of a short "complex" sentence. |

In 1876 "English Literature," with an almost equally scanty syllabus,[1] became a specific subject.

In 1882 Grammar and English Literature were combined, with no substantial addition to the syllabus, to form the class subject "English." This was made compulsory in every school which took class subjects: that is to say, in almost every London Board school. The effect of this change was, of course, to increase enormously the number of children taking the subject. But the examination standard of H.M. Inspectors, the previous history of the subject, and the want of a full and suggestive syllabus prevented any real development. English as a class subject was meagre, mechanical and unpopular. As a consequence of this it was made optional in 1890, and dropped steadily, being taken by 47·7 per cent. of the children on the roll in 1890, and by 18·6 per cent. in 1900.

The Block Grant Code (1900) included " English, by which is to be understood Reading, Recitation, Writing, Composition and Grammar, in so far as it bears upon the correct use of Language " as one of the compulsory subjects.

The position, therefore, of the subject has returned to that of 1882-1890, when it was practically compulsory, and under the present system of local freedom it may be hoped that, even without help from the Government, an adequate scheme of Language Study may be evolved in London.

### 4. *Object Lessons and Science.*

During the first twelve years of the Board's existence the Whitehall Code made no provision for Science, even in the form of Object Lessons, as part of the ordinary curriculum of an Elementary school. Individual scholars in the upper standards were, it is true, allowed by the Code of 1871 to offer various scientific subjects for examination, but this permission was apparently intended to apply to exceptional cases of talented children working individually. Even when the " class " subjects were introduced, to be taken by the scholars above Standard I., the list did not include either object lessons or any form of Elementary Science. It was not till 1882 that "simple lessons on objects and on the phenomena of nature and of common life, and appropriate and varied occupations " were encouraged in Infants' schools,[2] and " Elementary Science " was made a " class " subject in senior schools.

---

[1] The syllabus was as follows :—

1st Year.—One hundred lines of poetry, got by heart, with knowledge of meaning and allusions. Writing a letter on a simple subject.

2nd Year.—Two hundred lines of poetry, not before brought up, repeated, with knowledge of meaning and allusions. Writing a paraphrase of a passage of easy prose.

3rd Year.—Three hundred lines of poetry, not before brought up, repeated, with knowledge of meaning and allusions. Writing a letter or statement, the heads of the topics to be given by the Inspector.

N.B.—The passages need not be continuous ; and no passages may be brought up which have been learnt for the standard examination.

[2] Government Code, Article 106 (b).

Meanwhile the Board, under the guidance first of Professor Huxley, and afterwards of Dr. Gladstone, was attempting to introduce Elementary Science into the curriculum. Professor Huxley was, during his period of service on the Board, closely connected by his official position with the Science and Art Department, and his policy was to use the examinations and grants of that Department to make up for lack of encouragement in the Whitehall Code. The Huxley Committee (1871) recommended as one of the essential elementary subjects, "systematised Object Lessons embracing in the six school years a course of elementary instruction in Physical Science, and serving as an introduction to the examinations of the Science and Art Department." The circumstances of the early schools of the Board prevented the general carrying out of the Huxley Scheme, but Object Lessons, more or less systematised, were taken in some of the schools by enthusiastic teachers during the first seven years of the Board.

In 1878, when the upper standards were beginning to fill, the Board, on the initiative of Dr. Gladstone, issued a detailed syllabus of science teaching, dealing with Object Lessons in the lower standards, Elementary Science in c nnection with the "specific" subjects of the Whitehall Code in the upper standards, and the more specialised science subjects of the South Kensington Directory for individual children at the top of the school.

It is noteworthy that Animal Physiology, taught entirely by lecturing with the use of a few diagrams, was practically the only science "specific" subject taken. In 1881, for instance, 6,901 children took this subject, as compared with 411 who took Botany, and 51 who took Mechanics, the only other science "specific" subjects offered, unless Physical Geography, taken by 3,342 children, is counted as a science.

In that year (1881) the Board forwarded to the Education Department a memorial, praying "that in the contemplated modifications of the New Code, Object Lessons should be fully recognised, that they should be considered an essential part of the instruction of Infants' schools, and that their introduction into the upper schools should be facilitated," and the changes in the Code of 1882 referred to above were the direct result of that petition. The "class" subject, "Elementary Science," which was then introduced into the Code, was at first hardly ever taken in the schools. Only two "class" subjects could be then taken, of which English was obligatory, and the other was almost invariably either Geography, History, or Needlework. The Board (1882) issued a revised syllabus of Object Lessons in Elementary Science, but the subject in the few schools which took it was left without the stimulus of the "class" subject examination and grant.

By this time the movement for the introduction of a more technical type of instruction was fully begun. In 1883 a Royal Commission on Technical Instruction was appointed, and in the same year the Board appointed a Special Committee "to consider how far the Board might facilitate technical education," of which Dr. Gladstone was chairman. Dr. Gladstone also introduced into the schools an inexpensive box of simple science apparatus for illustrating experimentally the elementary principles of Chemistry and Physics. In order that the teachers might see the best methods of giving lessons illustrated by experiments, the Board in 1885 appointed a peripatetic demonstrator. He took his apparatus from school to school and gave short courses, including both elementary chemical experiments and the beginning of a preparation for the "specific" subject, Mechanics. In 1887 three additional demonstrators were appointed. In consequence of this, the number of children taking Mechanics as a "specific" subject rose rapidly from 174 in 1885 to 3,610 in 1890, those taking Animal Physiology dropping from 8,096 in 1882 to 4,021 in 1890. No other "specific" science was taken by any considerable number of children. As the knowledge of the teachers increased, the demonstrators ceased to demonstrate and became organisers, regulating schemes of instruction, requisitions for apparatus, etc.

The simple lessons on objects, for which, according to the Code of 1882, provision might be made in the middle standards, were still in most schools casual and desultory, and the Board attempted to "encourage this intuitive[1] instruction by providing rarer objects, and by offering a museum cabinet to any school in which a good commencement of a collection has been made."[2]

In 1890 English, as a "class" subject, ceased to be compulsory, and Elementary Science began to be generally taken as a "class" subject. A schedule of graduated alternative courses, including Mechanics, Physiology, Botany, Agriculture, Chemistry, Sound, Light and Heat, and Magnetism and Electricity, under the name of the "class" subject "Elementary Science," was inserted in the Code. A consequence of this change was that the number of children taking Elementary Science as a "class" subject rose from 2,293 in 1891 to 52,982 in 1895, as compared with 168,733 taking English, 168,289 taking Geography, and 20,366 taking History in that year.

In 1895 the Whitehall Code made Object Lessons compulsory[3] in all schools in Standards I., II., and III. The effect of this regulation (which lasted till 1898) was to produce a very rapid fall in the number of children taking English as a "class" subject from 169,046 in 1896 to 100,425 in 1900, and a corresponding increase in Elementary Science from 62,494 in 1896 to 173,462 in 1900.

During this period also the number of children taking Mechanics as a "specific" subject rapidly increased, rising from 3,610 in 1890 to 12,652 in 1898; while Animal Physiology increased very slowly from 4,021 in 1890 to 5,650 in 1898, Chemistry rose from 343 to 1,482 and Magnetism and Electricity from 340 to 1,246.

As the science teaching in the Standards improved pupils in some schools who had passed out of the Standards began to be presented for examination in science subjects under the Directory of the Science and Art Department. The number of passes in 1893 was 520, which by 1896 had increased to 1,955. There were four schools of the Board

---

[1] Apparently a translation of *Anschauungs Unterricht.*

[2] Board's Annual Report, 1887.

[3] The same Code (1895) allowed visits of scholars during school hours to such places as Kew Gardens, the Natural History Museum at South Kensington, and the Zoological Gardens, to count as school attendances. These visits were encouraged by the Board. The Board in 1899 purchased a large collection of 10,000 Natural History specimens from the Shoreditch Museum, and arrangements were made by which the specimens should be sent from school to school, on application being made.

pre-eminent in the number of their available candidates for these examinations and under a clause of the Science and Art Directory these schools received high grants from the Science and Art Department as "Organised Science Schools."[1]

Meanwhile the Board had encouraged their teachers to prepare themselves by taking the advanced Science and Art certificates of South Kensington. At first the teachers attended classes at the City of London College, the Birkbeck, and other Institutes, and afterwards at some of the Board's Evening Schools.

In 1891 it was decided to give special attention to teachers' qualifications for practical science teaching, and the four Science Demonstrators opened classes for teachers in different parts of London. Later these classes were supplemented by others conducted by specially appointed lecturers, and subsequently (1899) pedagogical classes dealing with the methods of science instruction were established under the direction of the School Management Committee.

The eight years since 1895 have been a period of rapid change, and of great, though somewhat confused, development in science teaching. Object Lessons of the old type still survive in the lower standards of many schools, but the growth of kindred work in the Infants' schools may in time allow them to be replaced by more systematic teaching. The course of instruction in the upper standards has been influenced by the "Elementary Science" required for competition for the County Council Scholarships since 1894; by Dr. Kimmins' Report of 1900; by the "block" grant system (1900); by the appointment of a new organiser of the Science teaching in 1902; and by the complete separation of the South Kensington Branch of the Board of Education from all elementary schools which are not "Higher Elementary."

The educational aims both of the Board and of the Board of Education have, during the same period, been largely influenced by the "heuristic" educational principles associated with the name of Professor Armstrong, and by a desire among many who did not adopt Professor Armstrong's principles for an increase in the amount of practical work to be done by individual scholars.

The statistics of scholars taking "optional" subjects in 1903, given on page 128-9, shows that a large number of children, of whom the great majority were boys, were taking a group of vaguely distinguished Physical Sciences: 11,352 taking "Elementary Physics and Chemistry," 11,953 "Elementary Science," 4,105 "Experimental and Practical Science," 17,370 "Mechanics," and 7,498 "Physics."[2] These subjects are generally taken in a classroom provided with a demonstration table for the teacher, less often in one of the 23 fully equipped physical laboratories, or in one of the simply furnished "science rooms," 20 of which have lately been introduced by the Board, and whose number, if the present policy of the Board is continued, is likely to increase. Besides these, 7,510 children, almost all boys, took Chemistry either in one of the 39 chemical laboratories or in one of the "science rooms."

---

[1] The four Organised Science Schools were Medburn-street, St. Pancras (1892), Bloomfield-road, Plumstead (1893), Blackheath-road (1898), and Burghley-road, Highgate-road, N. (1898).

[2] These figures exclude the Higher Elementary, but include the Higher Grade schools.

Amidst this apparent confusion there is therefore a tendency discoverable in the Boys' schools towards the general adoption of courses of generalised Elementary Physics, Chemistry and Mechanics, accompanied invariably by experiments carried out by the teacher, and in a small but increasing percentage of cases by experiments on the part of the scholars. Such a course naturally allies itself with the quantitative work and mechanical drawing in the Manual Training shop.

In Girls' schools it is possible, by ignoring the confusion of names and classification, to detect a corresponding tendency towards the general teaching of Elementary Science on a biological instead of a physical basis. A few girls from the beginning learnt Botany as a "specific" subject, and more took Animal Physiology. Still more took "Domestic Economy," which was taught under the extremely unsatisfactory conditions of the ordinary class-room to 8,906 girls as a "specific" subject in 1882. The "specific" subject "Domestic Economy" fell from this total to 2,909 in 1885, and rose again, till in 1900 32,348 units of twenty-four hours' instruction were given under class-room conditions.

Meanwhile practically the same subject was being taught under better conditions in the Cookery and Laundry "centres," which by 1900 were attended by practically all girls over Standard V.,[1] and, as a result of Lord Reay's committee " on the relation of domestic subjects to other subjects in the curricula," in 1899-1900 the Board decided that Domestic Economy should cease to be taught in the classrooms. In 1898 the Board adopted a syllabus of Domestic Economy teaching for the centres, which contained some elementary Physiology and Biology. In the classrooms and laboratories in 1903, 9,532 girls took Botany, 3,174 Hygiene, 3,064 the awkwardly-named course of "Domestic Science," and about 7,140 "Elementary Science."

The general problem of the relation of the science teaching in girls' schools to that given in the Domestic Economy centres is still under consideration.[2]

### 5. *History and Geography.*

Until the introduction of the "block" grant in 1900, when lessons in History and Geography were made compulsory, History appeared as a separate subject on the time-tables of very few of the Board's schools, although the use of "Historical Readers" was general. Geography was a usual "class" subject. In 1901 the Board decided to issue special suggestions to teachers on the teaching of History under the new conditions, and Professor H. L. Withers prepared, at the request of the Board, a memorandum on the teaching of History in its relation to the other subjects of the curriculum. Copies of this memorandum were forwarded by the Board to the head teachers of all Senior departments.

In 1901 the Board also adopted a scheme for the delivery of lectures on the history of the various London boroughs with lantern slide illustrations. With the permission of the Borough Councils the lectures were given to the Higher Standard children in the Town-halls of the various boroughs, and were repeated in the halls of schools. In

---

[1] See pages 122-126.     [2] See p. 122.

the same year the Board accepted an offer, made by the Rev. A. W. Jephson, of ten prizes, five for boys and five for girls, to be competed for by the children of London in order to encourage a knowledge of London and its history. The Board also encouraged the formation of History and Geography "circles" by which groups of schools were formed for the use of lantern slides, reference libraries, etc., consultative committees being appointed for each group. Three such circles have been formed in the Hackney Division. They further made arrangements for the production of a new shilling atlas specially suitable for use in London Elementary schools. The atlas was published and supplied on requisition, and was also placed on sale for scholars and students.

To encourage the teaching of Geography and History, the Board, on May 7th, 1896, agreed that prizes for the best essays on geographical and historical subjects, should be given to a boy and girl in each Senior department in which there was systematic instruction given in these subjects ; and, further, that superior prizes should be given for the best essays on such subjects, to be competed for by the successful competitors in the individual schools. An excellent method of encouraging an interest in these subjects has been adopted by the teachers of one of the Board's Higher Grade Schools (Bellenden-road, Peckham), who, for eight successive years, have organised "school journeys" to the West of England. In January, 1904, the School Management Committee agreed to arrange a conference on this subject.

### 6. *Drawing, Modelling, &c.*

The Huxley Report (1871) made " Elementary Drawing " one of the " essential " subjects in all senior schools. The first specific regulations as to this instruction were approved by the Board in 1874, when it was decided that Freehand, Model, Geometry, Perspective and Memory Drawing should be taught in Boys' and Girls' schools. The time to be devoted to Drawing was fixed at two hours a week for boys, and one and a-half hours for girls, and the subject was to be taken in all Standards from the first. Drawing was at that time examined and aided, not by the Education Department at Whitehall, but by the Science and Art Department at South Kensington, and the Board passed in 1874 the counsel of perfection:—" That every school submit its pupils to the examination by the Science and Art Examiners in March, and that the results of the examination be laid before the School Management Committee."[1]

The earliest information obtainable as to the extent of the instruction given in the different branches of Drawing is to be found in a table of the results of the South Kensington examination in 1876.

The number of passes in Freehand in that year was 4,028 ; in Geometry, 282 ; and in Model, 264. The number "giving satisfactory evidence of having been taught Drawing" was 37·3 per cent of the total number of scholars in Senior departments, whilst the percentage of passes was only 6 9. In the following year (1877) the results showed a great improvement, the percentage of the number in average attendance taught satisfactorily was 41·6, and the percentage of passes was 12·5.

---

[1] **Board Minutes,** Vol. IV., p. 1190.

Prior to 1882, the Board Inspectors had supervised the instruction in Drawing. It was decided in that year to appoint a Drawing Instructor for one year. The appointment was twice extended, and was finally made permanent. The Drawing Instructor resigned his appointment at the end of 1887, and the office was not filled until 1889. In the same year it was decided to appoint a second Instructor.

At first few teachers possessed the necessary qualifications to teach Drawing, and in January, 1879, it was decided to inform teachers, at the time of their appointment, that if they had not obtained the full Drawing Certificate (D) they were to take steps to obtain that qualification with as little delay as possible. This qualification was from 1874 to 1883 rewarded by an addition of £5 and £2 10s. to the salaries of men and women teachers respectively.

In September, 1883, the Drawing Instructor reported that the Drawing of the children would not greatly improve until the skill of the teachers was considerably increased. A central class was established for the instruction of teachers, and in 1884 a class was formed with a view to enabling teachers to obtain the Art Class Teacher's Certificate. The hall of Saffron Hill school was fitted up as an Art "centre," the instruction being given by the Drawing Instructor.

The policy of the Board and of the head teachers with regard to the teaching of Drawing has throughout been greatly influenced by changes in the relations between the Science and Art Department at South Kensington and the Education Department at Whitehall.

From the first Drawing could be taken, and was taken, by children who were not entered for the South Kensington examination. The Government Code for 1885 provided for these children by allowing Drawing to be taken either for South Kensington or as a "class" subject under Whitehall. In 1887 this policy was reversed, and all grants and examinations for Drawing were confined to South Kensington. Individual examination was confined to the higher work, and grants for "fair," "good" or "excellent" results were given to schools which offered themselves for examination. In 1898 the whole administration of the Drawing grants was transferred to Whitehall, and in 1900 the special grants for Drawing were abolished and the subject became compulsory in Boys' schools and optional in Girls' schools.

Up to 1885 the scope of the instruction required to earn South Kensington grants was indicated only by general instructions in the Directory. On the recognition of Drawing as a "class" subject under Whitehall, a syllabus, graduated for the standards throughout the school, was inserted in the Whitehall Codes for 1885 and 1886. From 1887 till 1897 the syllabus was retained in the South Kensington Directory.

This syllabus for Standards I. and II. consisted of figures made up of straight lines. In Standard III. curved figures were introduced. In Standard IV. Scale Drawing began. In Standards V., VI., and VII. one-third of the time allotted to Drawing was supposed to be devoted to Model Drawing, but on account of the excessive amount of finish required only a few models were practised. Plane Geometry formed part of the curriculum in Standard V. In Boys' departments Solid Geometry was taken in

Standards VI. and VII., and in Standard VII. shading from casts or models was occasionally taken.

It is generally admitted that the syllabus was too rigid, and that the course, especially in the lower standards, was both uninteresting and unintelligent; and as Drawing progressed in the schools of the Board the defect became more serious. In some Infant schools a thoroughly stimulating course of Drawing was being developed out of the Kindergarten occupations, and it was a distinct set-back to children who had gone through such a course to be compelled to spend several years on the South Kensington syllabus from Standards I. to III.

As a rule the syllabus was taken in Boys' schools, and the instruction, narrow though it was, steadily increased in thoroughness. The percentage of departments assessed as "excellent" improved, for instance, from 21 per cent. in 1890 to 62 per cent., in 1898. The Girls' schools, as a rule, did not take the South Kensington syllabus, and the standard reached in the subject was generally unsatisfactory.

In 1883, during the discussion on "Overpressure," a motion was referred to the School Management Committee that Drawing in Girls' schools, which had been nominally compulsory, should be abolished. This motion was rejected, and the policy of the Board on the question varied several times during the next few years. In 1885 Drawing in Girls' schools was made optional; in 1888 it was made compulsory, though the examination was optional. In 1889 it was decided that one and a half hours a week should be given to Drawing in all Girls' schools, but later in the same year the time to be given to the subject was again left optional.

It has already been said that the syllabus issued in 1885 was narrow and uninteresting. The fact that the instruction was confined to the use of the lead pencil prevented any instruction in colour, in the use of chalk and the brush, or in plastic work with clay or cardboard. Any experiment which the Board or their teachers might desire to try, involved the loss of the South Kensington grants. When this was done, freedom was secured, but the stimulus of examination was lost, and drawing necessarily suffered in competition with those sections of the time-table which were the subject of Government reports and on which the reputation of the school depended.

The difficulty of this position is illustrated by the experience of the Board in introducing "Hand and Eye" work, in accordance with the recommendation of Mr. Bousfield's committee (1888).[1] This subject was intended to be connected with the Kindergarten "occupations" in Infant schools and with the Woodwork which was being commenced under the Joint Committee on Manual Training.[2] It consisted of various exercises of drawing and colouring; folding, cutting, and designing in coloured paper or cardboard; modelling in clay and in cardboard; drawing plans and elevations showing forms constructed of Kindergarten material. With the object of enabling teachers to become fully acquainted with the scheme, courses of lectures were given in various districts

---

[1] See *ante*, p. 96.        [2] See *post*, p. 327-8.

of London. This work steadily increased, until in 1897 there were 600 departments taking one or more branches of "Hand and Eye" Training.

All this work was obviously related to Drawing, but it was outside the cognisance of the South Kensington Inspectors, just as the Drawing was outside the cognisance of the Whitehall Inspectors. The confusion was made worse when in 1895—largely as a result of the London experiment—"suitable occupations" were suddenly made a compulsory subject in the Whitehall Code for Standards I. to III., and when next year they ceased to be compulsory and were made a "class" subject for these Standards. An alternative syllabus, including the new subject of "Brushwork," was issued in the Directory for 1895. It was attempted in only one school in London—the Alma.

In 1898 the whole position was changed by the transfer of Drawing to Whitehall. The old South Kensington syllabus remained and was still used in most of the Boys' schools, but by the recognition by the Department of other approved syllabuses, all the best of the hand and eye work could be included in a Drawing course. Moreover, at the same time, the annual examination was abolished and inspection substituted, and this had the effect of encouraging teachers to leave the old lines. In the same year the Board made a step towards correlation by turning the Organiser of "Hand and Eye" Work into an Assistant-Superintendent of Drawing.

Meanwhile the Drawing and Artistic Work in the schools had been greatly influenced by the development of special "art" work in "centres" earning the higher South Kensington grants. When, in 1884, the Board fitted up the Saffron Hill centre as a "School of Art" for the instruction of teachers desirous of taking the Art Master's certificate, it was decided that the centre should also be used for the instruction of boys drawn from schools in the neighbourhood. The boys selected were to be not less than twelve years of age, and to have passed at least two subjects in First Grade Drawing. The instruction was given by a special teacher in the afternoons. At first, drawing from objects and casts, memory drawing, drawing plans and elevations from measurements, designing, and modelling in clay, were taught at these classes. Subsequently the classes were conducted simply as Drawing and Modelling classes, and similar classes were also held for girls. Drawing and Modelling classes were opened at another school in 1885, and in 1889 at a third school. Difficulties arose as to the legality of the registration of attendances of scholars at these classes, and it was not until 1890 that the Education Department agreed to regard an attendance at an Art class or centre as equivalent to an attendance at an Ordinary school.

In 1891 this system of giving central instruction to scholars of exceptional ability was extended. Other centres were opened, additional art teachers appointed, and a direction was inserted in the School Management Code that teachers desiring any of their scholars to attend these centres should make application to the Drawing Instructor for the district. In 1893 a "School of Art" was opened at Medburn-street School.

The Annual Exhibitions of Drawing and other forms of handwork, which were held by the School Board from 1877 onwards, did much to spread the influence of the freer and more advanced work of the Art centres among the schools. Still more in this direction was done in 1898 by the establishment of a new class of Art teacher. In schools where the teaching of Drawing was sufficiently advanced, a visiting Art teacher was allowed for one or more sessions a week to give instruction to the higher standards.

Since 1898 the higher work has rapidly increased, and at the present time there are 278 departments receiving special instruction from eighty-nine visiting teachers of Drawing. The greater freedom of curriculum combined with the special encouragement given by the Board and the influence of the general artistic movement in England has brought about a very marked improvement in the Drawing, Modelling, Design, &c., among the schools of the Board.

The Drawing, Modelling, &c., in Infants' schools have rapidly developed. Clay Modelling has been encouraged in the Senior departments by an annual examination held by the Board, at which, in 1903, 853 obtained certificates. Nature Drawing has been encouraged by the provision of plants, &c., supplied under the Board's Gardener's scheme[1] and the standard reached both in class-work and in the work of individual students has advanced every year.

The present system is, however, avowedly experimental and transitory. The Board, for instance in 1898 and 1899, approved two syllabuses prepared by the Drawing Instructors for their respective districts, the North and the South of the Thames. These, on the request of the Board, have been recognised by the Board of Education, special grants of material, &c., are made, and lectures to teachers are organised by the Instructors on these syllabuses. But they are permissive, and have only been adopted by 327 out of 982 Senior departments. The remaining (322 Boys, 274 Girls, 59 Mixed), take the "South Kensington" syllabus which was originally prepared in 1885, and which remains practically unchanged.

### 7. *Vocal Music.*

On March 22nd, 1871, the Board resolved "that the art and practice of Singing be taught, so far as may be possible in the Board schools, as a branch of elementary education." In the year 1872 it was decided that Singing should be taught by note, and a Singing Instructor was appointed to direct and superintend the teaching of Music. In the early years classes were held for teachers, under the superintendence of the Instructor.

The Board have always left the choice between teaching Singing by the staff or tonic sol-fa notation to the discretion of head teachers. A return obtained by the Board at the beginning of 1898 showed that there were then only 90 departments taking the staff notation.

By the Government Code of 1872, the average attendance grant was reduced if Singing did not form a part of the ordinary instruction. A separate grant for Singing was allowed in 1874 for every child in average attendance, and in 1882 this grant was reduced if Singing was taught by ear, but remained the same if it was taught by note. These conditions remained in force until the adoption of the "block grant" in 1900.

---

[1] See page 121.

The instruction has been given in accordance with a graduated syllabus first adopted in 1876, and which has been revised from time to time, but has remained practically unchanged since 1887.

In 1876 the first performance of music by the Board's scholars and teachers took place at the Crystal Palace on the occasion of the presentation of the Scripture prizes. These Crystal Palace concerts have been continued, at first annually, and afterwards triennially, until the present time.

From 1889 to 1898 concerts held at the Queen's Hall were made the occasion of a competition between schools .Since 1898 displays, but no competitions, have taken place.

In 1898 the School Management Committee reported that they " while conscious of the fact that the sight singing of children in the Board's schools is probably unequalled elsewhere, are yet of opinion that the tone of the children's voices might be considerably softened and improved, and the risk of the adult voice avoided if more attention were paid to the proper voice production." The Committee also called attention to the fact that of the teachers absent from duty, a large number suffered from laryngitis, and to the advantages which would accrue if some steps were taken to instruct teachers on the subject of voice production in speaking.

The Board accordingly arranged courses of lectures to teachers on voice production in the teaching of singing to children and on " voice production with particular reference to the teaching voice and to the cause of teachers' laryngitis."[1]

### 8. *Manual Training in Woodwork.*

It has been very largely due to the action of the School Board for London that Manual Training is now recognised as a Code subject in Elementary schools. Upon the recommendation of the Special Committee appointed in 1883 " to consider how far the Board might facilitate technical education, or co-operate with those bodies which were carrying it on," to which reference has been already made, the Board, on December 18th, 1884, decided :—

> That, as an experiment, arrangements be made for the establishment of a class for the elementary instruction of boys in the use of tools as applied to working in wood, the attendance being voluntary, and out of school hours.

In accordance with this decision a class was commenced in September, 1885, at the Beethoven Street School, Queen's Park Estate. The schoolkeeper of that school, having been a carpenter, gave the practical instruction, under the superintendence of the head master. The boys were selected from the Seventh and ex-Seventh Standards, and the instruction was given on two afternoons a week in a shed which had been erected for the purpose in a corner of the playground.

At that time the Government Code contained no provision for Manual Instruction, and the auditor of the Local Government Board surcharged the payments in connection with this experiment. An unsuccessful appeal was made to the Local Government Board, and the class was discontinued. The School Board therefore appealed, on April 30th,

---

[1] The courses of lectures were attended by over 8,000 teachers.

1886, to the City Guilds for voluntary contributions that would enable them to carry out the work in their own classrooms and buildings, and made application to the Education Department that Manual Training should be regarded as a "Specific" subject, but a reply was received that their Lordships must reserve their decision until the question of Technical Education should have been fully considered by Parliament. In 1887 a Joint Committee was formed of the City Guilds and the Board, who received an annual sum of about £1,250, and had by 1890 six Manual Training centres in Board and Voluntary schools under their control.

Meanwhile the Technical Instruction Act of 1889, which represented the Parliamentary consideration of Technical Instruction referred to by the Education Department in 1886, was passed, and contained a clause forbidding any contribution on behalf of scholars in attendance at Public Elementary schools.

In that year, the Liverpool School Board received an opinion from Sir Horace Davey Q.C., that a School Board might legally give Manual Instruction and defray the costs out of the school fund. The Board, relying upon this opinion, authorised instruction in Manual Training in the Boys' department of Waterloo-road school, such instruction being given by the teachers and entered on the time-table, and informed the auditor of the action taken. Next year, Manual Training was recognised by the Education Department,[1] and the following year a grant was allowed from the Science and Art Department.

Immediately upon the recognition of Manual Training by the Government, the Board took measures for the organisation of this work on a large scale. Suitable rooms were selected where Manual Training in Woodwork could be commenced, and classes for teachers were established. In September, 1891, the Board appointed as permanent organiser and instructor in Manual Training in Woodwork, the organiser under the Joint Committee. In the first instance the instruction was given by one of the ordinary teachers of the school who had specially qualified himself for the purpose. Each class met once a week from 3.30 to 5.30 p.m. and consisted of 20 scholars in Standard V. and upwards, and instruction was given on as many afternoons a week as were necessary to include all scholars in these standards up to 100 in number. By Lady Day, 1892, such classes were being held in 17 schools.

On June 23rd, 1892, the Board decided that the instruction, instead of being given by an ordinary teacher of the school, should be given by special and separate teachers on the "centre" system. The rooms hitherto used for the instruction were utilised as centres, and attended by scholars from neighbouring schools. Two lessons a day were given, lasting the whole of the morning and afternoon sessions respectively. In order that the 20 hours' secular instruction might be shown in the time-table, the Board decided that, in schools from which boys attended a centre for woodwork, the registers should be closed at 9.45 instead of at 9.55 a.m. This system is at present in force. The centres now in use accommodate either 20 or 40. An instructor is appointed to each centre, and an assistant is allowed in the larger centres. There are at present 188 centres under the Board, providing accommodation for 59,880. The staff engaged in teaching

---

[1] *Code of* 1890.

Woodwork consists of 188 instructors and 114 assistant instructors, and the organisation of the work is carried on by the organiser with three assistants.

The following Table shows the number of boys who received instruction in Manual Training in Woodwork in each year from 1893 to 1903 :—

| Year. | No. of Boys who received Instruction. | Year. | No. of Boys who received Instruction. |
|---|---|---|---|
| 1893 | 4,340 | 1899 | 41,940 |
| 1894 | 13,600 | 1900 | 45,136 |
| 1895 | 20 315 | 1901 | 49,880 |
| 1896 | 30,508 | 1902 | 53.664 |
| 1897 | 33,688 | 1903 | 55,107 |
| 1898 | 41,828 | | |

These figures up to and including 1900 include a certain number of scholars who were receiving Manual Instruction in the centres of the Joint Committee.

In 1887, a controversy in connection with Manual Training, not unlike that between the English and Swedish systems of Physical Exercises, seemed likely to arise. The Board's system involved the use of the ordinary English tools, and the production, from working drawings of models in regular forms and capable of exact measurement. Side by side with this in 1887 was established a class in Slöjd, involving the large use of the knife, and the production of moulded forms. The class met with the same fate as the rest when surcharged by the Local Government Board in that year, and though two or three other attempts to carry on Slöjd under the Manual Training section of the Government Code have been made, only one class, that at Brackenbury-road, is now in existence.

### 9. Drill and Physical Exercises.

The systematic physical instruction given in the schools of the Board consists of (a) the free standing exercises ranging from marching to a developed system of " Swedish " gymnastics ; (b) exercises with apparatus, ranging from the use of simple wands to training under superintendents in equipped gymnasia ; (c) swimming instruction given in school hours at the expense of the Board in the large baths provided by the London boroughs, and in a few cases in baths provided by the Board ; (d) the more or less organised games of the playground in and out of school hours and the voluntary clubs for cricket and football.

On the 1st February, 1871, the Board resolved :—

" That it is highly desirable that means shall be provided for Physica Training, Exercise and Drill in Public Elementary schools established under the authority of this Board."

" Drill " was proposed as an " essential " subject in the Huxley curriculum, and in 1871 an instructor was appointed. The instructor held classes for male teachers, and at the end of each course conducted an examination. In 1874 the instructor reported that most of the teachers in Boys' departments were qualified to teach drill.

In February, 1876, the Board inserted the following article in their Code :—

Instruction of girls in Physical Exercises in the schoolroom, and by, or under the eye of, th principal School Mistress, may be provided for in the two hours' secular instruction required by the New Code.

On the 2nd August, 1876, this instruction in Girls' departments was made compulsory by the Board. Classes for female teachers were commenced in November, 1876.

As soon as the subject began to develop, a controversy arose between the supporters of Ling's Swedish system of free standing exercises and those of the so-called English system, founded upon a development of military drill. At first the Swedish system showed itself the stronger.

In 1879 the Board engaged a Swedish teacher to train its mistresses and to superintend the introduction of Swedish exercises into Girls' and Infants' schools. In 1884 the Board decided to introduce Swedish exercises with apparatus, and by means of a gift from Lord Brabazon a Swedish gymnasium was opened at Crampton-street school, and an officer of the Swedish army was appointed to give instruction to teachers.

In 1889, however, the Board decided to recognise the Swedish system and what is known as the English combined system of drill and physical exercises as alternatives in Boys' schools. Instructors of both systems were appointed, the Board's teachers being allowed to choose which system they would learn. In 1892 a second instructor, who had been trained under the combined system, was appointed in place of the instructor of the Swedish system; and in the following year all boys' teachers were required to get the Board's Physical Education certificate in the combined system. The Swedish system continued in Girls' and Infants' schools, and is now taught by four instructresses.

In 1897 the allocation of a definite time in the time-table was made compulsory, and in 1900 the regulation was altered so that the instruction should be given in definite lessons of 20 minutes three times a week in the case of Boys' and Girls', and 15 minutes five times a week in the case of Infants' departments.

Another controversy arose on the question whether dumb-bells, Indian clubs and skipping-ropes should be used. In 1897 it was decided that dumb-bells, &c., should be granted to schools who were certified by one of the Drill Instructors to have obtained proficiency in the free standing exercises. In 1898 it was decided that fixed gymnastic apparatus should not, as a rule, be used in Girls' departments, but that when a Higher Grade school was erected, a gymnasium available for boys and girls should be part of the equipment. Three such gymnasia have been equipped. The School Board encourage their teachers, as far as possible, to make arrangements for organised games out of school hours.[1]

A very important part in the development of Physical Exercises has been played by the organisation of periodical displays. In 1873 the first such display was held in Regent's Park, and from 1876 a banner given by the Society of Arts for Drill was annually competed for, other banners being given in 1887 and 1890. The competition for these banners became very keen, and in 1896 it was decided that the competitive element should be excluded from the displays. Since 1898 these

---

[1] See *ante*, p. 97, resolutions 25 and 26.

displays have been held in alternate years instead of annually, and have taken place in the Albert Hall.

The last ten years have shown an extraordinary development in the teaching of Swimming in connection with the schools of the Board. As early as 1872 the Board had passed a resolution urging managers to give " all reasonable encouragement to those children who desire to bathe and to learn how to swim," and had sent a letter to the Education Department asking that in the amending Act to be promoted in Parliament in 1873, the Department would introduce a clause giving power to School Boards to expend money in providing Swimming Baths and in making payment for instruction of children in swimming.

It was not, however, till 1890 that the Department consented to recognise attendance at lessons in Swimming as school attendances. A few months later they agreed (March, 1891) that the Board might defray the cost of admission and instruction of the children at public baths out of the school funds. Accordingly it was decided by the Board that a fee not exceeding 1d. a child a lesson should be paid to bath proprietors.

In 1892 the Education Department agreed to the proposal of the Board that instruction in swimming should, if so desired, be given out of school hours.

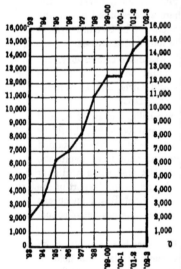

Owing to the inadequate bath accommodation in London, the Board applied to the Education Department for permission to provide four central Swimming Baths of their own (a decision which raised protests from many of the London Vestries.) The Education Department, in March, 1891, replied that they would be prepared to sanction loans for this purpose, and the Board resolved that steps should at once be taken to provide one of these baths. This resolution was rescinded in the following year.

The approval of the Board of Education has since been obtained for the provision of three baths, viz. :—

Marlborough-street, New Cut, opened in 1900.
Lyham-road, Brixton, opened in 1901.
Albion Bath, Dalston, opened in 1901.

But most of the instruction is given in the public baths provided by the Borough Councils, the number of which has been largely increased.

Special Instructors of Swimming have been appointed in cases where there are not sufficient teachers on the school staff capable of giving instruction in Swimming.

The London Schools Swimming Association, founded in 1891 with the object of encouraging swimming among the scholars of Elementary schools within the metropolis, has done admirable work for the teaching of Swimming in the Board's schools by organising competitions and giving certificates and trophies.

The following table shows the number of departments taking Swimming, the number of children instructed, and the number of children taught to swim in each year since 1893:—

| Year. | No. of Departments taking Swimming. | No. of Scholars Instructed. | No. of Scholars taught to Swim. |
|---|---|---|---|
| 1893 | 79 | 5,894 | 2,174 |
| 1894 | 146 | 10,416 | 3,345 |
| 1895 | 237 | 19,322 | 6,296 |
| 1896* | 279 | 23,209 | 7,007 |
| 1897 | 319 | 26,959 | 8,227 |
| 1898 | 391 | 33,380 | 11,039 |
| 1899-00 | 421 | 38,176 | 12,502 |
| 1900-01 | 445 | 39,475 | 12,548 |
| 1901-02 | 496 | 44,354 | 14,330 |
| 1902-03 | 530 | 48,535 | 15,287 |

* The School Management Committee, on April 24th, 1896, agreed that the swimming season, hitherto reckoned from March 25th to September 29th each year, could be extended during the winter months.

## 10. *Needlework.*

Needlework has always been taught in the Girls' schools of the Board. The Government Code of 1871 laid down, as one of the conditions to be fulfilled for the payment of grant, that the girls in the schools should be taught Plain Needlework and Cutting Out as part of the ordinary instruction. In 1876 the Code included darning, mending, marking, and knitting in the term "Needlework," and in 1877 a detailed syllabus was inserted.

The instruction given by the Board closely followed this syllabus, until in 1895 a clause in the Code allowed head teachers to frame their own syllabuses to be approved by H.M.I. The scope of the work has since then much widened, and now includes practical mending, smocking, frock-making, and, when permitted by H.M.I., dress-cutting and dressmaking aided by the sewing machine. Millinery has also been occasionally taken with special permission.

The time given to the subject has varied greatly in different districts, according to the views held by the Government Inspectors for the districts; but the maximum time now allowed by the School Management Committee is three hours weekly.

Needlework was first accorded a separate grant in 1875, and Standards II. to VI. were included in the schemes of instruction. In 1879 Standard I. was also included, and in the same year part of the "average attendance" grant for Infants was made conditional upon their passing a satisfactory examination in Needlework. The Needlework schedule was thus made compulsory throughout all Primary schools, but a choice was allowed to be made between taking Needlework for the "class" subject grant, or for a lower grant on more elementary instruction. In 1900 the Government Code abolished the Needlework grant, and incorporated it with the "block" grant earned by the schools.

The boys in the Infants' schools were at one time taught Needlework with the girls; but this was altered in 1890, the boys now generally taking Drawing, while the girls take Needlework.

No special qualifications have been required for Needlework from the teachers in the ordinary Day schools. Some few, however, work of their own accord for a separate diploma of Needlework, and many sit for examination in Dressmaking under various examining bodies.

At the first, the Board Inspectors were held responsible for the inspection of Needlework, being empowered to ask for assistance of ladies on the Board of Managers of the various schools, and where this was impracticable or inexpedient, to call in other efficient assistance. This arrangement did not continue long, as in 1873 the Board appointed an Examiner of Needlework. An assistant was appointed in 1875. Since 1890 three Examiners have generally been at work.

The materials, which are chosen by the Needlework Examiners, are issued to the schools at cost price, and, after being made into garments, are sold, also at cost price, to the children and their parents at the end of the year's work, after having been seen by the Government Inspectors. No profit is allowed to be made on any of the articles.

### 11. *Method in Infants' Schools.*

The Huxley Report proposed that there should be given in Infants' schools "Object Lessons of a simple character, with some such exercise of the hands and eyes as is given in the Kindergarten system."

In 1873 an Instructor in Kindergarten was appointed, who in the following year began a system of classes for teachers. On December 8th, 1875, she was "authorised to issue a certificate to each teacher whose personal application of her Kindergarten knowledge reaches the standard required by the Instructor."

In their earlier annual reports the Board Inspectors complained that the education given in the Infants' schools of the Board suffered in consequence of insufficient knowledge among the teachers of the principles of Kindergarten, and in 1878 the Kindergarten Instructor reported that she had experienced difficulty in endeavouring "to secure that the principles of the Kindergarten system should be infused as far as possible into the general instruction in Infants' schools," and that the teachers too frequently looked upon Kindergarten "as a subject of instruction like Reading, Writing, &c., rather than as a principle to be applied where possible in every lesson." The Board in 1878 abolished the title of "Instructor in Kindergarten Exercises" and substituted for it the title "Superintendent of Method in Infants' Schools." The Board also defined the duties of the Superintendent, in addition to that of visiting the schools, as follow:—

"To secure, wherever practicable, the application of Kindergarten principles to the teaching of ordinary subjects.

" To give occasional model lessons to the children illustrative of the mode in which the above object might be secured.

" To report once a quarter, or oftener if necessary, the progress made in the extension of Kindergarten methods."

Although the title of the Instructress had been altered, the word " Kindergarten " was still used in the documents of the Board to describe her work. In 1888 the Board asked the Froebel Society to suggest an Examiner who should examine the students in the Board's training classes.

The Education Department, on February 6th, 1893, issued a circular to its Inspectors, saying that " the Department are desirous of giving further encouragement to the employment of Kindergarten methods," and referring to " two leading principles,' namely, " the recognition of the child's spontaneous activity," and " the harmonious and complete development of the whole of a child's faculties," as " a sound basis for the education of early childhood."

In 1895 the Board's Superintendent of Method in Infants' schools resigned, and on the 2nd August of that year the School Management Committee carried the previous question on a proposal of the Special Subjects Sub-Committee to issue an advertisement for a successor.

In 1896 it was found from a return of the Special Subjects Sub-Committee that a large number of teachers in Infants' schools under the Board were without Kindergarten certificates. It was decided by the Board on February 27th, 1896, that teachers entering the service of the Board without a Kindergarten certificate recognised by the Board should be required to attend classes with the view to obtaining such a certificate and on March 4th, 1897, a resolution was passed that assistant teachers in Infants' schools should obtain a recognised Kindergarten certificate before they become eligible for increase of salary under the scale. In the same year the School Management Committee appointed a Special Sub-Committee to advise on the best mode of improving the method and curriculum in the Infants' schools.

The Sub-Committee reported in 1897 that " the witnesses who have given evidence before us are unanimous in declaring that the methods and results of Infant school work have greatly improved during the last twenty years, and that that improvement is due to the influence of ' Kindergarten.' It is clear from the Circular of the Education Department of February 6th, 1893, that the Department is of the same opinion." The Sub-Committee recommended :—

" That a list be prepared of Training Colleges whose certificates will be recognised by the Board . . .

" That the Elementary and the Advanced Certificates issued by the National Froebel Union be recognised by the Board.

" That arrangements be made for the delivery in each year of lectures on Method in Infants' schools ; and for the holding of theoretical and practical Kindergarten examinations based on these lectures . .

"That the Board, on the result of the examinations provided for in the foregoing resolution, issue their own certificate.

"That a Superintendent of Method in Infants' schools be appointed."

These recommendations were adopted.

### 12. *Temperance.*

On April 18th, 1877, the Board resolved :—

That in view of the prevalent evil of intemperance and its serious consequences to the community, advantage be taken as opportunity offers to impart special instruction to the children in Board schools of the dangers arising therefrom.

The School Management Committee accordingly issued a circular to all schools. This circular, in the form finally adopted in 1892, was as follows :—

(i.) Whenever the opening lesson of the day—from the Holy Scripture—supplies a suitable opportunity for the occasional instruction of children, by examples, warnings, cautions, and admonitions, in the principles of the virtue of temperance, the teachers should avail themselves of it.

(ii.) The reading books and copy books for use in schools might be rendered largely helpful in this direction. Such reading books are on the requisition list, and may behad on application. Copy books should be applied for when required.

(iii.) Picture cards, diagrams, and wall-papers illustrative of the subjects of industry, sobriety, and thrift, may be beneficially exhibited as part of the wall furniture of schools.

(iv.) Songs and hymns at the selection of the teacher, on the subject of temperance, should be incorporated with the musical exercises of the school.

(v.) The Board will be recommended to grant, free of charge, the use of their schools both during and after the usual school hours, for illustrated lectures, by well-qualified lecturers, to children attending the schools, but the attendance at such lectures is to be purely voluntary on the part of both teachers and scholars ; the lecturers and their subjects and the syllabus of such lectures, and any books or diagrams used, in each case to be submitted to, and to receive the approval of, the School Management Committee, such approval to be notified beforehand to the school where it is proposed to give such teaching before the lecturer is admitted. For the purpose of this section, "schools" must be taken to include Pupil Teachers' schools.

In 1883 this circular was re-issued, and in 1886 the regulations were embodied in the School Management Code.

In 1892 the subject was again raised upon a notice of motion by the Rev. B. Meredyth Kidson, "that the Education Department be memorialised to make the subject of Temperance a Code subject," and during that year the School Management Committee and the Board gave the whole question prolonged attention, and received deputations from representative temperance bodies. As a result, the facilities for lectures on temperance were granted during the ordinary school hours ; but at the same time the Board decided that the syllabus of the lectures, and any diagrams or books to be used in them, should be approved by the School Management Committee.[1]

The School Management Committee have approved five lecturers provided by the Band of Hope Union, and one lecturer provided by the Guild of St. Matthew. The Band of Hope Union lecturers have given an annual average of 543 lectures in the

---

[1] Board Minutes, Vol. LVI., pp. 988-9.

schools since 1889, and have received an annual average of 38,943 essays written for prizes offered by the Union. The Guild of St. Matthew's lecturer delivered twenty or thirty lectures.

### 13. *Modern Languages.*

On December 16th, 1880, the Board decided to allow the services of a peripatetic French teacher in schools where French was taken as one of the "specific" subjects in accordance with the Code, and where, in the opinion of the School Management Committee the teaching was sufficiently advanced; the instruction, however, was not to be beyond the stages of the Code. During the following year (1881) four schools were allowed the services of a French teacher for two hours a week.

In 1898 the Board granted similar facilities for the teaching of German. Very few schools take this subject, and at the present time a teacher of German is employed in only one school.

In 1899 the School Management Committee decided that where a modern language was taught, a teacher of the country should be allowed earlier in the course, and as low down as Standard V. Instruction, however, has been given lower down than Standard V. in a few schools, and in January, 1904, the Special Subjects Sub-Committee were considering the cases of these schools. It was also decided in 1899 that the School Management Committee should nominate the teachers for appointment instead of the Managers as hitherto.

The number of departments in which French teachers have been engaged has increased from 64 in 1900 to 114 in 1903. The number of children receiving instruction in French had in 1903 reached the large total of 47,808.

### 14. *The Use of Flowers, &c., in Instruction.*

The Board in 1898 having "noted with satisfaction that in several Infants' schools an attempt had been made to interest the children in the phenomena of plant life by growing plants and flowers in the windows of the Infants' schools and in rough boxes placed in the playground," decided to allow an amount not exceeding ten shillings per annum to head teachers of Infants' schools for the purchase of seeds, small flower pots, hyacinth glasses, &c., and of £1 for the purchase of boxes for the playground. This authority was subsequently extended to Girls' departments and Mixed departments under a mistress and to the "special" schools of the Board. In May, 1898, the Board had their attention called to the manner in which flowers gathered in the town gardens in Berlin were placed in the Municipal schools for the purpose of furthering the study of Botany. They made inquiries, and with the considerate co-operation of H.M. Office of Works, were enabled to forward to a number of departments a fortnightly supply of flowers, leaves, cuttings, &c., from the Royal parks, for use in the teaching of Drawing and Botany, and for Object Lessons. A gardener was appointed to carry on this work, and in the following year the operation of the scheme was largely increased, 220 departments being supplied. The scheme has been found especially useful in schools for the physically and mentally defective children and in those for deaf children. In addition to the valuable resources of the Royal parks, the Board were enabled, through the kindness of the various authorities, to place boxes in Kew Gardens, Chelsea Botanic Gardens, and Royal Horticultural Gardens, Chiswick, into which specimens, cuttings, etc., available for the use of the Board were put, the boxes being periodically cleared.

### V. Domestic Subjects (Cookery, Laundrywork and Housewifery).

Practically all girls attending the schools of the Board now receive instruction in Domestic Subjects at specially-equipped centres. This instruction follows, as far as circumstances allow, the three-years' course adopted by the Board in 1902, and modified in detail in 1903  Each girl, during the three years, is expected to attend for one morning or afternoon every week. The course, when fully carried out, provides for two sessions of six months each in a Laundry centre, two sessions in a Cookery centre, and two sessions in a Housewifery centre.[1] There are in all 183 centres, or sections of combined centres, specially equipped for teaching Cooking; 142 centres, or sections of centres, equipped for Laundrywork; and 31 centres for Housewifery. This inequality in the provision of the various kinds of centres prevents the syllabus in most cases from being carried out in its complete form, and Housewifery, in particular, is generally taught under a scheme modified by the fact that the teaching takes place in a Cookery or Laundry centre.[2] The instruction is given by a staff of 358 teachers, giving their full time to the work and possessing special qualifications. No Domestic Economy is taught except in the centres, and an attempt is being made to secure that the Science teaching in the schools shall be carefully differentiated from, and co-ordinated with, the teaching of elementary scientific facts which forms part of the "theoretical" instruction in the centres.

The present system of the teaching of Domestic Subjects has been reached by a series of steps beginning in 1874. These steps may be summed up as consisting of (a) an early experimental stage (1875 to 1877), when instruction was given in a few special centres apart from the school premises; (b) a second stage (1877 to 1882), during which the Government Code developed a system of "Domestic Economy" teaching in the ordinary classrooms, while the Board was erecting special centres for practical work; and (c) a third period (1882 to 1903), during which the Board's policy has been (i.) to remove the teaching of Domestic Subjects from the classrooms to the centres; (ii.) to co-ordinate the separate domestic subjects of Cookery, Laundry, and Housewifery into a connected Household Management course; and (iii.) to correlate the Household Management teaching with the Object Lessons and other forms of Elementary Science in Girls' and Mixed schools.

---

[1] The Housewifery centres are usually small, working-class houses which have been left standing when a site for a school has been cleared. There are, however, seventeen fully-equipped Domestic Economy centres where the Housewifery centre is adjacent to the Cookery and Laundry centres.

[2] This fact has created difficulties, which are not yet settled, between the School Board and the Board of Education as to the payment of the full Household Management grant under Art. 101 (m) of the Government Code.

## 1. *First Period* (1875-1877).

On June 3rd, 1874, the Board, on the motion of Mr. John MacGregor, resolved " that it is desirable to promote a knowledge of Plain Cookery and the household operations connected therewith as part of the elementary education of girls." In the following year the Education Department made it possible for the Board to give such instruction during school hours, since the Code for 1875 made Domestic Economy a specific subject for girls, and laid down that " Attendance of . . . girls at lessons in Practical Cookery, approved by the inspector, for not more than two hours a week, and forty hours in the year, may, in a Day school, be counted as a school attendance."

In the same year the Board opened two Cookery centres in Greenwich and Marylebone, and in 1876 two more in Lambeth and Tower Hamlets. The teachers were selected by the National Training School for Cookery; attendance consisted of two hours once a fortnight, and the right to attend was given to the elder girls and pupil teacher candidates as a reward for regular attendance. In 1876 this teaching was connected with the Domestic Economy of the Government Code by an instruction from the School Management Committee that all girls who had attended at the Cookery centres should be presented for examination in Domestic Economy at the annual inspection of their schools.

## 2. *Second Period* (1877-1882).

On October 20th, 1876, the Board resolved :—

That it is desirable to introduce this instruction (Practical Cookery) into, at any rate, the larger Girls' schools of the Board.

That for this purpose teachers and pupil teachers should be instructed in Cookery, so as to be able to give lessons in their respective schools, and that the simple apparatus required might be supplied at a small expense.

For this purpose it was decided to use the existing centres for the purpose of teaching pupil teachers and other teachers in the service of the Board during the evening, and on January 24th, 1877, the Board resolved that all head and assistant mistresses of Girls' schools who are not already competent to teach Cookery, be strongly urged to attend a course of lessons in that subject, and at the following meeting it was decided to insert the following instruction in the Board's Code:—" One or more mistresses of every Girls' school must be competent to teach Cookery."

The Government Code for 1877 laid down the rule that every girl presented for examination in specific subjects must take Domestic Economy as a subject for examination. This made the subject practically compulsory for the elder girls in all the better schools.[1]

About 600 teachers attended the evening classes for teachers in the four centres, and received certificates.

---

[1] The Syllabus inserted in the Code (Schedule IV., col. 10) was as follows :—

*First Stage.*—Food and its preparation. Clothing and materials.

*Second Stage.*—The dwelling ; warming, cleaning and ventilation. Washing materials and their use.

*Third Stage.*—Rules for health ; the management of a sick room. Cottage income, expenditure and savings.

Meanwhile the policy of the Board was to give the practical lessons in Cookery rather in special centres than in the classrooms, as apparently contemplated by the Government Code. In 1876, for instance, the Works Committee reported that it would be inconvenient and expensive to provide suitable rooms in each new school in which Cookery could be taught practically; and that they were of the opinion that it would be preferable to give theoretical lessons only in the schools themselves, leaving the practical lessons to be taught in special centres, and in 1877 the Board decided to erect Cookery centres in the Finsbury, Southwark, and Tower Hamlets divisions.

On May 29th, 1878, the Board adopted a general scheme for practical lessons at twenty-one centres, such lessons to be given in three-monthly courses of a half-day in each week. For other schools it was decided :—

"That the school in outlying districts, which cannot be included in this system, owing to distance or other causes, be supplied with a simple cooking apparatus, in order that the girls may receive their instruction in Cookery at their respective schools."

### 3. *Third Period* (1882-1904).

In response to two memorials forwarded by the Board to the Education Department the new Code for 1882 abolished the compulsory obligation to take Domestic Economy as a first specific subject in Girls' schools, and also instituted the payment of a special grant for instruction in Cookery. In consideration of the terms of this Code, the rules of the Board were revised. The rule that "one or more mistresses in every Girls' school must be competent to teach Cookery" was deleted on the ground that it had become obsolete. All girls in Standards V. and VI., and all girls over 12 years of age, were required to attend a course of 20 lessons, in two sections, at one of the centres if the schools were sufficiently near, unless satisfactory reasons for their non-attendance was furnished by the managers. Two courses instead of three were to be given in each year, viz., *First Course*, January to June; *Second Course*, July to December.

Several superintendents were appointed as the work grew, and various changes were made by the Board and the Board of Education as to the ages and standards of girls who should be entitled or required to attend at the centres. In 1889 the Board made an arrangement with the Drapers' Company that Laundrywork should be experimentally taught, at the expense of the Company, at several centres, under the same Joint Committee which was superintending instruction in Woodwork.[1]

On February 13th, 1890, it was agreed to ask the Education Department to recognise practical teaching in Laundrywork in the same way as the practical teaching in Cookery.

The New Code for 1890 gave a grant for Laundrywork, and on April 24th of that year the Board resolved themselves to organise instruction in the subject.

In 1891 the Joint Committee began an experimental scheme of Housewifery at William-street School on Saturday mornings, and in 1893 the Government Code recognised Housewifery as a subject which might be taught during school hours.

The existence of the three subjects, Cookery, Laundry, and Housewifery, side by

---

[1] See *post*, pp. 327 *et seq.*

side with the ordinary school subject of Domestic Economy, made some scheme of co-ordination desirable. On March 9th, 1894, the Domestic Subjects Sub-Committee, which had been formed two years before, adopted an experimental scheme of instruction in Domestic Economy and Housewifery, and on May 9th, 1895, the Board adopted the following resolution :—

" That the Board authorise the immediate organisation and instruction in Housewifery in connection with certain selected schools of the Board, and that the School Management Committee be directed to consider and report whether it is not desirable, both educationally and economically, to combine the instruction in the Code specific subject, Domestic Economy, and the special subjects, Cookery, Laundrywork and Housewifery, in one building at each centre, to be called a School of Domestic Economy."

On January 23rd, 1896, the Board granted indemnity to the School Management Committee for having forwarded a letter to the Education Department calling attention to the overlapping existing between the subjects of Cookery, Domestic Economy, Housewifery and Laundrywork in the new Code, and asking for the provision of a combined syllabus with a view to the better organisation of the work proposed in these subjects.

The new Code for 1896 included Domestic Economy as a class subject which might be taught at centres, and on May 8th the School Management Committee appointed a special Sub-Committee to consider the question of teaching Domestic Economy on the centre system. The report of this Sub-Committee was submitted to the Board on October 15th, 1896, was of an exhaustive character, and included reports by the Board's inspectors and the senior superintendents. It was resolved to forward copies of these reports to the Education Department, and ask permission for the experiment of combining instruction, both theoretical and practical, in Domestic Economy, Cookery, Housewifery and Laundrywork to girls mainly in and above Standard IV. in three special centres. It was further agreed to ask that, for the purpose of carrying out this experiment the special grants for Cookery, Laundrywork and Domestic Economy might be commuted in favour of an inclusive annual grant upon the lines laid down for Manual Training in Woodwork for boys.

On July 28th, 1898, a syllabus of instruction in Domestic Economy for a complete three years' course was approved, and the Education Department were asked to allow an inclusive grant of not less than 9s. per head for this combined subject when taught in centres, in lieu of the separate grants for Cookery, Laundrywork, and Domestic Economy ; and in 1899 the Board pointed out to the Education Department that such combined grant under the name of Household Economy was paid under the Scotch Education Code.

In the winter of 1899-1900 a Special Sub-Committee, of which Lord Reay was Chairman, considered the difficult question of the relation of the Domestic Subjects to other parts of the school curriculum. It was decided to discontinue Domestic Economy as a " class " or " specific " subject in the schools, and to reduce the maximum time to be given to Needlework to three hours. It was further decided that girls below 12 years of age, who were also below the Fifth Standard, should not attend the centres. The time given to kindred subjects in the classrooms being thus reduced, and the younger children being withdrawn from the centre instruction, the Committee decided that the time given by the elder girls in the centres should be so far extended

"That in all schools, girls in Standards V., VI., and VII., make one attendance a week at one or other of these centres throughout the year, except that the head teachers in Higher Grade schools be allowed to exercise their discretion as to sending girls in Standards VII. and ex-VII.

It was decided to further develop the work of co-ordination by appointing an Organising Superintendent of Household Management.

Since February, 1901, special half-time courses of instruction in Domestic Economy (lasting for 6 or 12 months) have been held at five centres for girls who would leave school before being able to complete the ordinary course of instruction in Domestic Subjects. The girls attending these classes must be over 13 years of age, and must attend the classes five half-days a week and the ordinary day school the remaining five half-days. It is a further condition that their parents shall give an assurance that the girls shall remain at school until the completion of the course.

Domestic Economy teaching has also been found particularly suitable for the instruction of Blind, Deaf, and Mentally Defective children.[1]

It will be observed that throughout the whole history of these subjects the Board, acting from 1889 to 1900 in conjunction with the Joint Committee, have generally anticipated, rather than followed, the Government. An instance of this may be found in the desire of the Board to teach Cooking to some of the small boys on the Isle of Dogs who were likely to go to sea. In 1898 and in 1900 the Education Department refused to allow such instruction to be given during school hours; and in 1898 it was decided by the Board to take the risk of giving such instruction during the ordinary school hours, but without registration for grant. In 1901 the Code at last legalised such action. It may, perhaps, be hoped that the Board's successors will be equally successful in obtaining recognition and grant for the organised course of Household Management under which all the centres are now working.

NUMBER OF CHILDREN UNDER INSTRUCTION IN COOKERY, LAUNDRY, AND HOUSEWIFERY CENTRES.

| Year. | No. of Cntrs. | COOKERY. | | | | | | No. of Cntrs. | LAUNDRYWORK. | | | | | |
|---|---|---|---|---|---|---|---|---|---|---|---|---|---|---|
| | | No. of Children under Instruction. | | | | | | | No. of Children under Instruction. | | | | | |
| | | Ordinary. | Special. | Blind | Deaf. | Volun-tary. | Total. | | Ordinary. | Special. | Bliud. | Deaf. | Volun-tary. | Total. |
| 1892 | 97 | 31,020 | ... | ... | ... | 174 | 31,194 | 10 | 999 | ... | ... | ... | ... | 999 |
| 1893 | 109 | 31,199 | ... | ... | ... | 267 | 31,466 | 23 | 4,082 | ... | ... | ... | ... | 4,082 |
| 1894 | 122 | 34,867 | ... | ... | ... | 271 | 35,138 | 42 | 7,667 | ... | ... | ... | 28 | 7,695 |
| 1895 | 142 | 40,053 | ... | ... | ... | 333 | 40,386 | 62 | 10,951 | ... | ... | ... | 60 | 11,011 |
| 1896 | 151 | 42,923 | ... | ... | ... | 688 | 43,611 | 83 | 14,678 | ... | ... | ... | 130 | 14,808 |
| 1897 | 160 | 42,826 | 45 | ... | 113 | 1,252 | 44,236 | 95 | 17,869 | 71 | ... | 95 | 224 | 18,259 |
| 1898 | 167 | 43,523 | 125 | ... | 97 | 1,385 | 45,130 | 108 | 18,913 | 156 | ... | 114 | 359 | 19,542 |
| 1899 | 172 | 39,460 | 140 | 8 | 99 | 1,329 | 41,036 | 117 | 17,498 | 267 | ... | 93 | 426 | 18,284 |
| 1900 | 181 | 38,503 | 347 | 8 | 136 | 1,318 | 40,312 | 122 | 19,674 | 291 | ... | 52 | 327 | 20,344 |
| 1901 | 185 | 44,544 | 552 | 24 | 81 | 1,322 | 46,523 | 127 | 19,921 | 319 | 14 | 28 | 172 | 20,454 |
| 1902 | 186 | 45,902 | 1,085 | 75 | 100 | 932 | 48,094 | 132 | 27,568 | 816 | 16 | 85 | 208 | 28,693 |
| 1903 | 181 | 48,857 | 1,457 | 56 | 167 | 462 | 50,999 | 139 | 28,931 | 1,182 | 13 | 71 | 92 | 30,289 |

[1] See *post*, p. 190.

| Year. | HOUSEWIFERY. | | | | | TOTAL FOR THE THREE SUBJECTS. | | | | | | |
| | No. of Centres. | No. of Children under Instruction. | | | | No. of Cntrs. | No. of Children under Instruction. | | | | | |
| | | Ordinary. | Special. | Deaf. | Total. | | Ordinary. | Special. | Blind. | Deaf. | Voluntary. | Total. |
|---|---|---|---|---|---|---|---|---|---|---|---|---|
| 1892 | ... | ... | ... | ... | ... | 107 | 32,019 | ... | ... | ... | 174 | 32,193 |
| 1893 | ... | ... | ... | ... | ... | 132 | 35,281 | ... | ... | ... | 267 | 35,548 |
| 1894 | ... | ... | ... | ... | ... | 164 | 42,534 | ... | ... | ... | 299 | 42,833 |
| 1895 | ... | ... | ... | ... | ... | 204 | 51,004 | ... | ... | ... | 393 | 51,397 |
| 1896 | ... | ... | ... | ... | ... | 234 | 57,601 | ... | ... | ... | 818 | 58,419 |
| 1897 | ... | ... | ... | ... | ... | 255 | 60,695 | 116 | ... | 208 | 1,476 | 62,495 |
| 1898 | 5 | 684 | ... | ... | 684 | 280 | 63,120 | 281 | ... | 211 | 1,744 | 65,356 |
| 1899 | 6 | 1.244 | ... | ... | 1,244 | 295 | 58,202 | 407 | 8 | 192 | 1,755 | 60,564 |
| 1900 | 10 | 2,471 | 15 | ... | 2,486 | 313 | 60,648 | 653 | 8 | 188 | 1 645 | 63,142 |
| 1901 | 20 | 4,416 | 48 | ... | 4,464 | 332 | 68,881 | 919 | 38 | 109 | 1,494 | 71,441 |
| 1902 | 22 | 5 567 | 29 | 10 | 5,606 | 340 | 79,037 | 1,930 | 91 | 195 | 1,140 | 82,393 |
| 1903 | 27 | 5,953 | 17 | ... | 5,970 | 347 | 83,741 | 2,656 | 69 | 238 | 554 | 87,258 |

## VI.—CLASS AND SPECIFIC SUBJECTS.

Average attendance on which Grants for the various Class Subjects were paid for twelve years (1890-1901):—

| Year ended Lady-day. | English. | Geography. | Elementary Science. | History. | Needlework. | Object Lessons. | Total of Units of Payment for Class Subjects. |
|---|---|---|---|---|---|---|---|
| 1890 | 219,749 | 124 492 | 2 224 | 2,468 | 90,504 | ... | 439,437 |
| 1891 | 215,523 | 123,522 | 2,293 | 3,322 | 87,676 | ... | 432,336 |
| 1892 | 193,477 | 136,007 | 26,674 | 9,846 | 90,160 | ... | 456,164 |
| 1893 | 172,824 | 145,139 | 40,208 | 12,716 | 86,124 | ... | 457,011 |
| 1894 | 164 259 | 149,853 | 49,367 | 16,732 | 90,032 | ... | 470 243 |
| 1895 | 168,733 | 168,289 | 52,982 | 20,366 | 94,014 | ... | 504 384 |
| 1896 | 169,046 | 179,984 | 62,494 | 22 553 | 97,790 | ... | 531,867 |
| 1897 | 153,094 | 184,974 | 86,638 | 24,283 | 100,161 | ... | 549,150 |
| 1898 | 127,663 | 182,352 | 70 626 | 26,761 | 98,581 | 75,993 | 581,976 |
| 1899 | 82,245 | 160,945 | 56,183 | 20,765 | 85,355 | 117,187 | 522,680° |
| 1900 | 100,425 | 184,279 | 173,462 | 24,412 | 85,748 | † | 568.326 |
| 1901 | 107,569 | 199,110 | 163,434 | 26,904 | 80,981 | ... | 577,998 |

* The decrease in 1899 is accounted for by there being a less number of schools for which reports were received for that period.

† Object lessons are now shown under the name of the class subjects that have been actually taught.

*Passes or Presentations in " Specific " Subjects on which Grant was received (1876 to Subjects (1899 to 1901), and the Number of Scholars*

| Year ended | Animal Physiology | Botany | Domestic Economy | English Literature | French | Latin | Mechanics | Physical Geography | Mathematics | German | Chemistry | Physics. Sound, Light, and Heat | Physics. Magnetism and Electricity | Principles of Agriculture |
|---|---|---|---|---|---|---|---|---|---|---|---|---|---|---|
| Dec., 1876 | 1,015 | 35 | 372 | 1,109 | 185 | 4 | 36 | 625 | ... | ... | ... | ... | ... | ... *1* |
| ,, 1877 | 1,696 | 125 | 1,161 | 3 137 | 212 | 3 | 10 | 981 | 143 | ... | ... | ... | ... | ... *2* |
| ,, 1878 | 2,754 | 113 | 2,354 | 5,238 | 296 | ... | 5 | 1 536 | 204 | 13 | ... | ... | ... | ... *3* |
| ,, 1879 | 4,115 | 75 | 3.558 | 8,041 | 30⅃ | 1 | 11 | 2,442 | 109 | ... | ... | ... | ... | ... *4* |
| ,, 1880 | 5,417 | 382 | 5.002 | 12,496 | 362 | ... | 23 | 3,005 | 191 | ... | ... | ... | ... | .. *5* |
| ,, 1881 | 6,901 | 411 | 7 026 | 16,336 | 413 | 4 | 51 | 3 342 | 179 | ... | ... | ... | ... | ... *6* |
| ,, 1882 | 8,096 | 571 | 8.906 | 21.307 | 447 | 2 | 33 | 4 327 | 161 | ... | ... | ... | ... | ... *7* |
| Sept., 1883 | 7,922 | 715 | 7 722 | 15,339 | 451 | ... | 30 | 2 921 | 1,235 | ... | 116 | 28 | 429 | 65 *8* |
| ,, 1884 | 6,252 | 690 | 3,8⅃7 | 13 | 742 | ... | 173 | ... | ... | ... | 255 | 207 | 847 | 484 *9* |
| ,, 1885 | 5,000 | 440 | 2,909 | ... | 423 | ... | 174 | ... | ... | .. | 113 | 132 | 478 | 477 *10* |
| Mar., 1887 | 5,209 | 618 | 4.453 | ... | 679 | .. | 844 | ... | ... | ... | 33⅃ | 268 | 711 | 315 *11* |
| ,, 1888 | 5.454 | 468 | 4 597 | ... | 782 | ... | 768 | ... | ... | ... | 341 | 199 | 686 | 265 *12* |
| ,, 1889 | 4,407 | 477 | 4,730 | ... | 927 | ... | 2.407 | ... | ... | ... | 308 | 262 | 670 | 236 *13* |
| ,, 1890 | 4,021 | 492 | 4.750 | ... | 1 067 | ... | 3,610 | ... | ... | ... | 34⅃ | 29 | 340 | 190 *14* |
| ,, 1891 | 3,530 | 500 | 4,868 | ... | 1 007 | ... | 4.806 | ... | ... | ... | 365 | 157 | 384 | 156 *15* |
| ,, 1892 | 3 312 | 562 | 5,025 | ... | 1.413 | ... | 5.931 | ... | ... | ... | 400 | 127 | 405 | 105 *16* |
| ,, 1893 | 3,637 | 668 | 5 903 | ... | 2 139 | ... | 7,748 | ... | ... | ... | 682 | 88 | 468 | 7 *17* |
| ,, 1894 | 3,789 | 790 | 7.590 | ... | 2 675 | ... | 9,584 | ... | ... | 3 | 809 | ... | 758 | ... *18* |
| ,, 1895 | 4,622 | 994 | 8.688 | ... | 2,953 | ... | 10,324 | ... | ... | 13 | 1,087 | 101 | 1,039 | ... *19* |
| ,, 1896 | 4,552 | 1,148 | 9.125 | ... | 3,246 | ... | 11.550 | ... | ... | 17 | 1,091 | 108 | 1,215 | ... *20* |
| ,, 1897 | 5.233 | 1,334 | 10 863 | ... | 3,867 | ... | 11,902 | ... | ... | ... | 1,147 | 34 | 1 098 | ... *21* |
| ,, 1898 | 5 650 | 1,422 | 12,030 | ... | 4,888 | ... | 12,652 | ... | ... | 27 | 1,482 | 152 | 1.246 | ... *22* |
| ,, 1899* | 2,961 | 1,120 | 7,443 | ... | 3,372 | ... | 6,988 | ... | ... | 30 | 1 525 | 94 | 810 | ... *23* |
| ,, 1899† | 3,756 | 1,316 | 10.923 | ... | 5.785 | ... | 12,120 | ... | ... | ... | 685 | 265 | 1,430 | ... *24* |
| ,, 1900 | 11,354 | 4,918 | 32,348 | ... | 18 553 | ... | 31,440 | ... | ... | 178 | 4,767 | 891 | 3,055 | ... *25* |
| ,, 1901 | 14,480 | 6,096 | 26,706 | ... | 28,010 | 162 | 32,595 | ... | ... | 140 | 5,215 | 728 | 3,816 | ... *26* |
| ,, 1902 | 12,253 | 8,710 | 790 | ... | 42,529 | 223 | 16,694 | ... | 175 | 448 | 6,833 | ... | 1,852 | ... *27* |
| ,, 1903 | 11,599 | 9,532 | 896 | ... | 47,868 | 313 | 17,370 | ... | 27 | 863 | 7,510 | 117 | 1,960 | ... *28* |

\* These figures relate only to reports on schools whose school years ended on or before 31st July, 1898.

† These figures are for schools whose school years ended on or after 31st August, 1898.

‡ From 1885 to 1896 there were also a few presentations in Social Economy, the highest number being 48 in 1890.

§ Ambulance work, First Aid, and Home Nursing was taken by 87 children in 1902 and 200 in 1903.

1899), *together with the number of units of twenty-four hours' Instruction given in "Specific"* *receiving Instruction in Optional Subjects* (1902 and 1903).

| | Algebra. | Euclid and Mensuration. | Hygiene. | Shorthand. | Book-keeping. | Natural Philosophy. | Elementary Science. | Experimental and Practical Science. | Domestic Science. | Mensuration. | Elementary Physics and Chemistry. | Euclid. | Physics. | Physiography. | TOTAL. |
|---|---|---|---|---|---|---|---|---|---|---|---|---|---|---|---|
| 1 | ... | ... | ... | ... | ... | ... | ... | ... | ... | ... | ... | ... | ... | ... | 3,381 |
| 2 | ... | ... | ... | ... | ... | ... | ... | ... | ... | ... | ... | ... | ... | ... | 7,481 |
| 3 | ... | ... | ... | ... | ... | ... | ... | ... | ... | ... | ... | ... | ... | ... | 12,500 |
| 4 | ... | ... | ... | ... | ... | ... | ... | ... | ... | ... | ... | ... | ... | ... | 18,654 |
| 5 | ... | ... | ... | ... | ... | ... | ... | ... | ... | ... | ... | ... | ... | ... | 26,878 |
| 6 | ... | ... | ... | ... | ... | ... | ... | ... | ... | ... | ... | ... | ... | ... | 34,663 |
| 7 | ... | ... | ... | ... | ... | ... | ... | ... | ... | ... | ... | ... | ... | ... | 43,850 |
| 8 | ... | ... | ... | ... | ... | ... | ... | ... | ... | ... | ... | ... | ... | ... | 36,873 |
| 9 | 3,470 | 59 | ... | ... | ... | ... | ... | ... | ... | ... | ... | ... | ... | ... | 16,999 ‖ |
| 10 | 2,897 | 102 | ... | ... | ... | ... | ... | ... | ... | ... | ... | ... | ... | ... | 13,145 |
| 11 | 3,546 | ... | 55 | ... | ... | ... | ... | ... | ... | ... | ... | ... | ... | ... | 17,058 |
| 12 | 3,905 | ... | 39 | ... | ... | ... | ... | ... | ... | ... | ... | ... | ... | ... | 17,504 |
| 13 | 3,570 | 8 | 28 | ... | ... | ... | ... | ... | ... | ... | ... | ... | ... | ... | 17,730 |
| 14 | 3,334 | ... | 14 | ... | ... | ... | ... | ... | ... | ... | ... | ... | ... | ... | 18,390 |
| 15 | 3,414 | ... | 9 | 7 | ... | ... | ... | ... | ... | ... | ... | ... | ... | ... | 19,202 |
| 16 | 3,839 | 87 | ... | 156 | 40 | ... | ... | ... | ... | ... | ... | ... | ... | ... | 21,404 |
| 17 | 4,393 | 187 | 11 | 547 | 217 | 66 | ... | ... | ... | ... | ... | ... | ... | ... | 26,761 |
| 18 | 5,169 | 89 | 20 | 1,543 | 370 | 32 | 61 | 45 | ... | ... | ... | ... | ... | ... | 33,327 |
| 19 | 5,124 | 179 | 21 | 2,075 | 441 | 21 | ... | 51 | ... | ... | ... | ... | ... | ... | 37,733 |
| 20 | 6,620 | 296 | 45 | 1,903 | 500 | ... | ... | 129 | ... | ... | ... | ... | ... | ... | 41,585‡ |
| 21 | 7,277 | 321 | 208 | 2,081 | 671 | 165 | 140 | 446 | ... | ... | ... | ... | ... | ... | 46,789 |
| 22 | 9,963 | 202 | 126 | 1,916 | 647 | ... | 389 | 702 | 107 | ... | ... | ... | ... | ... | 53,701 |
| 23 | 6,933 | 57 | 177 | 1,111 | 445 | ... | 428 | 346 | 139 | ... | ... | ... | ... | ... | 33,979 |
| 24 | 10,247 | ... | 102 | 2,397 | 664 | ... | 484 | 1,039 | 278 | 129 | ... | ... | ... | ... | 51,620 |
| 25 | 36,435 | ... | 680 | 6,485 | 2,000 | ... | 623 | 3,187 | 967 | 1,048 | 2,194 | 37 | ... | ... | 161,790 |
| 26 | 43,263 | ... | 1,168 | 5,889 | 2,631 | ... | 223 | 2,965 | 2,018 | 841 | 7,088 | 51 | ... | ... | 184,085 |
| 27 | 29,438 | ... | 3,096 | 5,811 | 2,633 | ... | 5,325 | 1,869 | 2,594 | 2,507 | 7,755 | 3,134 | 5,556 | 70 | 160,382 |
| 28 | 30,382 | ... | 3,174 | 5,483 | 2,451 | ... | 11,953 | 4,105 | 3,064 | 3,807 | 11,352 | 3,997 | 7,498 | 290 | 185,611 § |

‖ The drop in the total for 1883 was due to the changes in the Government Code, by which Literature and Physical Geography were omitted from the list of "specific" subjects. The introduction of a grant for Cookery also had the effect of diminishing the number of passes in Domestic Economy. These changes were also responsible to a much greater extent for the fall in the total for 1884. In 1885 the full force of the changes was felt. It should also be mentioned that in 1885 the number of schools upon which Government reports were received was 170, as compared with 203 in the previous year.

*Diagrams, founded upon the Table given on page 127, showing the number of children in average attendance on which grant for certain class subjects was paid during the years 1890-1901 :—*

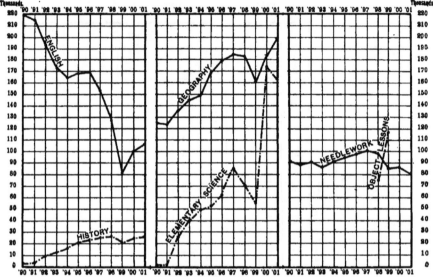

*Diagrams, founded upon the Table given on pages 128 and 129, showing the number of passes per 1,000 children on the Roll in the most popular specific subjects from 1876 to 1882 :—*

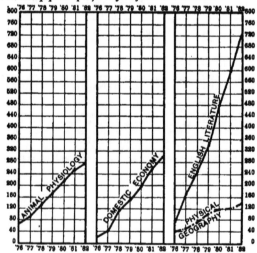

*Diagrams, founded upon the Table given on pages 128 and 129, showing the percentage of passes of children on the Roll in certain specific subjects from 1884 to 1898 :—*

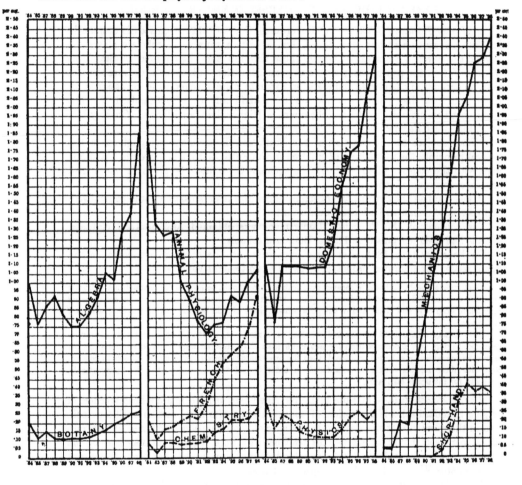

## HIGHER GRADE AND HIGHER ELEMENTARY SCHOOLS.

1. *Higher Standard Schools.*—The Government Code of 1871 recognised Six Standards. In 1882 a Seventh Standard was added, but a certain number of scholars stayed on beyond the Seventh Standard, and both these children and the children in Standards VI. and VII. in the poorer schools were at great educational disadvantages from the fact that, on account of their small numbers, no separate class teacher could be assigned for them, and that they generally either worked individually or with Standard V. The Board met this difficulty by the establishment of Higher Standard schools. On May 5th 1887, the Board decided :—

" That, subject to the sanction of the Education Department being given to the general principle, the instruction of children in the Fifth, Sixth, and Seventh Standards may, with the consent of the School Management Committee, be given in one school only in each group of schools."

It was claimed that by this arrangement difficulties in organisation would be removed, and economy in staff and salaries would result.

The consent of the Education Department was obtained, and by 1889 eighteen schools had been recognised as Higher Standard schools.

On February 19th, 1891, after some opposition on the score of extravagance, the Board passed the following proposals by twenty-two to eight votes :—

That, in the selected schools, wherever practicable, there should be a room for manual instruction, a room for science, and a room for drawing (three rooms in all, the science and drawing rooms being common to both boys and girls), and in the girls' schools there should be facilities for teaching advanced cutting-out.

That in any enlargement of selected schools, or alterations, at least two class rooms should be provided, having seat accommodation for not more than fifty children each ; that where these schools cannot be conveniently enlarged or altered, then the question of erecting junior mixed schools in connection with these schools should be considered, in order to set free accommodation in these schools, specially for the upper standards.

2. *Five o'clock Rule.*—On June 11th, 1891, the Board decided to allow head teachers of Higher Standard schools the option of continuing the afternoon session until 5 o'clock, and in the same year it was decided that a special remuneration calculated at the rate of 5s. per week should be allowed to teachers who were required to stay late by the head teacher.[1]   Since April, 1902, the extended afternoon session has been compulsory for Standards VII. and Ex.-VII. in Higher Grade schools.

Meanwhile " Higher Grade " schools, supported in the main by the large grants of the Science and Art Department, had been established by many School Boards, especially in the North of England.   Such schools, till the Cockerton judgment in 1900, were recognised by the Science and Art Department as " organised Science schools," or (later) schools of Science.

---

[1] Since the adoption of a special scale of salaries for Higher Grade teachers in 1899, this allowance has not been made, except in the case of teachers working in Higher Grade schools, but not receiving salary under the Higher Grade scale.

3. *Higher Grade Schools*—By the year 1898 most Senior departments of Board schools possessed higher standards, and in that year the Board decided to call the Higher Standard schools "Higher Grade" schools. Since that date the Board have given special attention to the staff of Higher Grade schools. Early in 1899 it was decided that the selection of teachers for these schools should rest with the School Management Committee, on the recommendation of the Special Subjects Sub-Committee, and not with the local managers, and in the same year a special scale of salaries was adopted for teachers in Higher Grade schools.

4. *Curricula of Higher Grade Schools.*—The curricula of these schools are drawn up by the head teachers, but the Board have since 1900 prescribed a minimum time for the various subjects. The outline time-table adopted by the Board is as follows:—

### OUTLINE TIME-TABLE.

| HIGHER GRADE BOYS' SCHOOLS. | HIGHER GRADE GIRLS' SCHOOLS. |
|---|---|
| *Time available, 9 to 12 and 2 to 5—30 hours a week.* | *Time available, 9 to 12 and 2 to 5—30 hours a week.* |
| Registration, 10 to 15 mins. daily  1 hr. 15 mins. a week. | Registration, 10 to 15 mins. daily  1 hr. 15 mins. a week. |
| Religious Exercises and Scripture, 30 mins daily ... ... 2 hrs. 30 mins. a week. | Religious Exercises and Scripture, 30 mins. daily ... ... 2 hrs. 30 mins. a week. |
| Recreation ... ... ... 1 hr. 40 mins. a week. | Recreation ... ... ... 1 hr. 40 mins. a week. |
| 5 hrs. 25 mins. a week. | 5 hrs. 25 mins. a week. |
| *Time remaining for Secular Instruction—24 hours 35 minutes a week.* | *Time remaining for Secular Instruction—24 hours 35 minutes a week.* |
| Minimum time for compulsory subjects:— | Minimum time for compulsory subjects— |
| 1. Arithmetic and Mathematics ... 3½ hours a week. | 1. Arithmetic and Mathematics ... 3 hours a week. |
| 2. Experimental Science ... 2  „ | 2. Experimental Science ... ... 2  „ |
| 3. English Subjects (including Composition) ... ... ... 3½  „ | 3. English Subjects (including Composition) ... ... ... 4½  „ |
| 4. History and Geography ... ... 2  „ | 4. History and Geography ... ... 2  „ |
| 5. One Foreign Language ... ... 2  „ | 5. One Foreign Language ... ... 2  „ |
| 6. Drawing ... ... ... ... 2  „ | 6. Drawing ... ... ... 2  „ |
| 7. Systematic Physical Exercises ... 1  „ | 7. Systematic Physical Exercises ... 1  „ |
|  | 8. Needlework for Standard VII. ... 2  „ |
|  | 9. Singing ... ... ... ... ½  „ |
| Total ... ... 16  „ | Total ... ... 19  „ |
| This leaves about 8 hours 35 minutes to be allotted at the discretion of the head teacher. | This leaves about 5 hours 35 minutes to be alloted at the discretion of the head teacher. |

The minimum times apply as a rule to Standards VII. and upwards, but head teachers are required so to arrange the instruction in the lower standards as to lead up to the work covered in the upper standards. The School Board also issued instructions that methods of instruction should be chosen by which the scholars should be forced to develop their powers of self-reliance by individual effort, and that too exclusive reliance should not be placed upon oral instruction.

In most of these schools the instruction is adapted so as to form a suitable preparation for the L.C.C. scholarship and the Oxford and Cambridge local examinations.

The number of Higher Grade schools under the Board increased, until in 1900 there were 79 Higher Grade departments, including four which had been recognised as Science schools under the directory of the Science and Art Department.

5. *Higher Elementary Schools.*—In 1900, after Mr. Cockerton's surcharge, but before

the judgment, the Board of Education issued a minute constituting Higher Elementary schools. The chief conditions for the recognition of a school as a Higher Elementary school were :—

1. The school must be organised to give a complete four years' course of instruction approved by the Board.

2. No child shall be admitted into a Higher Elementary school unless he—

(i.) Has been under instruction at a Public Elementary school, other than a Higher Elementary school, for at least two years; and

(ii.) Has been certified by an inspector of the Board to be qualified to profit by the instruction offered in the Higher Elementary school.

3. The fitness of any child to continue, or be promoted from one year's course to another, in a Higher Elementary school shall be certified by an inspector of the Board.

4. (i.) Attendances may not be recognised in a Higher Elementary school for any scholar who is upwards of 15 years of age; and

(ii.) No scholar may remain in a Higher Elementary school beyond the close of the school year in which he or she is 15 years old.

o    o    o    o    o

7. (a) The school must be shown, to the satisfaction of the Board, to be necessary in the locality; and

(b) The premises must be recognised by the Board as suitable for the purposes of a Higher Elementary school.

The Minute also allowed considerably higher grants for these schools.

The School Board made application for the recognition of the existing seventy-nine Higher Grade departments as Higher Elementary schools. The Board of Education objected to the establishment of so large a number, and stated in effect that the intention of the Minute was that the Higher Elementary schools should conform to a curriculum based on that of the "School of Science." In the course of a long correspondence the Board emphasised their view that in London Higher Elementary schools should be of a less definitely scientific type, but were unable to obtain the concurrence of the Board of Education in this opinion. The Board therefore decided to withdraw their application for the whole of their seventy-nine Higher Grade departments, and to substitute an application for the recognition of fifteen departments, four of which were schools of Science, and in the rest of which the curriculum had been preponderatingly scientific.

Of the fifteen departments for which recognition was sought, the Board of Education and the School Board were ultimately only able to agree to seven.

In these schools the same conditions as to selection of teachers, school hours, &c., apply as in the case of Higher Grade schools; but the curriculum is practically fixed by the Board of Education.

6. *Entrance Examination.*—The new policy of the Board with regard to Higher Grade schools, which accompanied the change of name from "Higher Standard Schools," was extended in 1901, when the Board adopted a competitive scheme of Entrance Examination to Higher Grade and Higher Elementary schools. The intention of the scheme is to secure for the Higher Grade and Higher Elementary schools the most promising scholars from the neighbouring ordinary Board schools. To be eligible for

examination the children must be under twelve or thirteen years of age, and must be fitted for examination in the work of a standard not below IV. On the requirements of the Entrance Examination being satisfied the parents of the successful scholars are asked whether, in the event of their children being admitted, they would be willing to retain them at school up to the completion of the course of instruction of the school.

There has always been a difficulty in the Higher Grade and Higher Elementary schools owing to the fact that they have been grafted on existing fully organised schools and the relation of the Infants' departments and lower standards of these schools to their upper standards has added to the difficulty of drawing from contributory schools. An attempt has been made to get over this difficulty by organising many of the Higher Grade schools with Senior Mixed, Junior Mixed, and Infants' departments. In 1898 the Board made application to the Education Department for permission to build in certain selected districts schools to contain no children below Standard V. Two such schools have been erected, and two others are in course of erection.

## MERIT AND HONOUR CERTIFICATES.

1. *Merit Certificate.*—Until February, 1900, a boy or girl who had passed Standard VII. and had been at least a year in a school, was awarded an Honour Certificate on leaving. On that date the practice was abandoned and an annual Merit Certificate examination was instituted. The examination, which extends over two days, is both written and oral, is open to all scholars who have worked, since the beginning of the current educational school year, in a class not lower than Standard VII., and who are, as a rule, 13 years of age or upwards. A Merit Certificate is awarded to each scholar who obtains half the maximum number of marks. The first Merit Certificate examination was held on June 13th and 14th, 1900. Since that year the examinations have been held in the month of July. Papers were set in all the " class " subjects, and in most of the " specific " subjects in the Code, and in most of the papers candidates were allowed to select eight questions out of ten given. A candidate who fails to obtain 25 per cent. of the maximum marks in any one subject is not allowed to be credited with any marks at all in that subject.

The following table shows the results of the Merit Certificate examinations for the years 1900, 1901, 1902 and 1903 :—

|  |  |  |  |  | Number Presented for Examination. | | Number Awarded Merit Certificates. | |
|---|---|---|---|---|---|---|---|---|
|  |  |  |  |  | Boys. | Girls. | Boys. | Girls. |
| 1900 | ... | ... | ... | ... | 718 | 881 | 280 | 386 |
| 1901 | ... | ... | ... | ... | 1,110 | 1,082 | 338 | 383 |
| 1902 | ... | ... | ... | ... | 1,262 | 1,344 | 703 | 804 |
| 1904 | ... | ... | ... | ... | 3,488 | 3,299 | 1,624 | 1,621 |

In comparing the figures for 1902 with those for previous years, it should be borne in mind that, in consequence of a conference between the examiner and the Board inspectors, the papers were modified in several respects, and a larger selection of questions allowed. Further, the minimum in each subject below which marks were not counted was reduced that year from 33 per cent. to 25 per cent.

In 1902 the Board, having regard to the abolition of the Government examinations in the schools, came to the conclusion that more use should be made of the Merit Certificate examination. They accordingly decided to require all schools to present a very considerable proportion of children who are eligible for the Merit Certificate examination, and to require in every case at least 25 per cent. to be presented. The increased number of candidates in 1903 was due to this fact. At the examination in July, 1904, not less than 33 per cent. of the eligible children are required to be presented.

2. *Honour Certificate.*—When the examination for the Merit Certificate was instituted it was considered desirable that head teachers should be encouraged to enter scholars for the Oxford and Cambridge Local Examinations, and such other examinations as might from time to time be approved by the Board. On the recommendation of the School Management Committee the Board decided to grant Honour Certificates to scholars who passed satisfactorily any of these examinations, provided that such scholars had either obtained the Merit Certificate at least a year before, or had completed a course beyond Standard VII.

The following figures show the number of Honour Certificates awarded each year :—

|  | | | | | 1900. | 1901. | 1902. | 1903. |
|---|---|---|---|---|---|---|---|---|
| Boys | ... | ... | ... | ... | 21 | 25 | 52 | 200 |
| Girls | ... | ... | ... | ... | 117 | 98 | 163 | 318 |

## THE TRAINING OF PUPIL TEACHERS.

### I.—THE PERIOD OF INDIVIDUAL INSTRUCTION BY HEAD TEACHERS.

In 1870 the pupil teacher system had been in existence for twenty-four years. It had been established in 1846 to supersede the discredited monitorial system (under which the elder children taught the younger) and to provide an annual supply of young teachers ready for training. The system was based upon the methods of apprenticeship prevailing in the skilled manual trades. The pupil teacher was "apprenticed" to the head teacher, assisted him in his work, received instruction, and was paid a small but gradually increasing salary. If, after the expiration of his indentures, he was able to pass the Queen's Scholarship Examination, he might apply for admission to a Training College, where his expenses were aided by a "Queen's Scholarship."

In the early days of the Board, London pupil teachers were worse prepared for their future work than those in the country. The apprenticeship system proved to be, under London conditions, as unsuitable a preparation for the teaching profession as it has since then proved to be for the skilled trades. A carpenter's apprentice in the country usually lives as well as works with his master, and is trained in the varied activities of a small workshop. In consequence he finds himself better trained than the London apprentice, who lives far from the shop, and works under a foreman, who never sees him except during working hours. \Similarly the country pupil teacher, living in the teacher's house, with the chief manager's house close by, and carrying on all sorts of responsible occupations in a small school, was at first very much better off than the Board pupil teacher, who worked in a big school, with no master's house near.

It is now easy to see that the solution of both problems was the same—the substitution of carefully organised technical education for the casual and incidental mixture of instruction and imitation which formed the basis of the apprenticeship system. But the whole education system of London is enormously indebted to the Rev. John Rodgers, who recognised this fact thirty years ago, and proposed, in complete outline, the scheme which has since been developed.

In the early years of the Board there were in the London Board schools about two pupil teachers and candidates to one adult teacher.[1] The general condition of their education was well described by Mr. Alderson, H.M. Inspector, in his general report for 1869 on the Eastern and Metropolitan Counties [2]:—

As a body, he said, the "pupil teachers" are useful and well-behaved, and failure to pass their annual examination is rare. But on the other hand, the promise of future professional excellence among them is rare also. Taking the fifth year examination as the highest outcome of their training, I am struck by the crudity and want of thoroughness which it commonly exhibits. It shows a respectable mass of information, but very little mastery of any one branch ; a mechanical familiarity with the various subjects, but no power of handling any of them intelligently. I notice this particularly in reference to the "original composition" which the fifth year pupil teacher has to write. The language is usually grammatical, and the meaning is tolerably well expressed; but the poverty of ideas which the exercise discloses is remarkable. In most cases it may fairly be characterised as an "original composition" wholly destitute of a spark of originality.

A description which dealt with London only would probably have been somewhat darker.

The age of the pupil teachers under the then current Code was not less than 13 at the beginning of their engagement, and the candidates were in some cases still younger. The Code required them to work a daily average of five hours in keeping and teaching the school, and an hour in receiving instruction, in addition to the work of private study. The instruction could only be given by the head teacher [3] who under the then London conditions had enough teaching and organising work to occupy the whole of his time. The instruction, in fact, was almost entirely given in the morning from 7 to 8 o'clock, the pupil teacher and the head teacher taking their breakfast on the premises. Such an arrangement brought a strong temptation to neglect the work to bear upon head teacher and pupil teacher alike.

The defects of such a system were obvious, and Mr. Rodgers desired to remove them by securing (a) that the pupil teachership, with its full day's work in teaching, should begin at an age sufficiently late to secure that the pupil teacher should have received at least the elements of general education ; (b) that instruction should be given by assistant teachers if fully qualified, instead of head teachers only ; (c) that the pupil teachers should

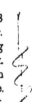

---

[1] In 1903 there were four adult teachers to one pupil teacher.

[2] Education Department Report 1869-70, p. 286.

[3] Art. 70 (c) of the Government Code laid down that the pupil teacher should serve under "the certificated teacher" of the school.

be collected in sufficient numbers to secure tolerable classification and organised instruction; and (*d*) that they should be released from some part of the full day's work in school.

In 1874 Mr. Rodgers, as Chairman of the School Management Committee, brought up a scheme, the essential proposals of which were that no pupil teacher should be engaged under the age of 15; that headmasters should be relieved of the duty of instructing them, and that centres should be established, where a specially-appointed staff should give to the pupil teachers a suitable education.[1]  The first amendment proposed was to alter the age from 15 to 14; this was carried, and then the whole question was referred back to the School Management Committee for consideration and report.[2]

In February, 1875, a revised scheme was submitted by the School Management Committee to the Board, which was eventually adopted, with amendments, in the following June.[3]  It was intended to apply to male pupil teachers only.  The following clauses exhibit the main features of the proposed change:—

(ii.) That no person be engaged as a candidate under 14 years of age.

(iii.) That no pupil teacher be engaged by the Board unless he has served a previous period of probation for six months as a candidate pupil teacher.

(ix.) That the pupil teacher be strictly prohibited from evening school work.

(x.) That no pupil teacher shall be placed in charge of a class as its responsible teacher until he shall have entered upon the last three years of his apprenticeship; but that up to that time he shall assist one of the responsible teachers.

(xiii.) That in each division, wherever possible, one or more groups of schools be formed for the instruction of pupil teachers and candidates, such group or groups to consist of schools within reasonable distance of each other.

(xiv.) That for each of these groups one school be selected as a centre at which pupil teachers and candidates may attend for instruction in given subjects, and that the classes be taught by the head teachers of Board schools.

(xv.) That the payment for instruction be, in the aggregate, the same as at present—viz., a sum equal to £5 for each pupil teacher or candidate who succeeds in passing the Government examination.

Soon after the scheme had been adopted the Board separated for the summer recess. Before the adjournment the School Management Committee made arrangements that the scheme should be put into partial operation when the schools re-opened after the summer holidays.  It was found that, in order to carry out the centre scheme in its entirety it would be necessary to modify the Memorandum of Agreement, and the Board wrote to the Education Department asking that this might be done.  The Education Department replied by a letter, dated the 12th August, 1875, in which they declined to consent to the proposed modification, or to facilitate in any way the adoption of the new scheme.  "My Lords" even went so far as to say that "they saw no reason why the existing system should not continue to produce, though perhaps in larger numbers than at present, a body of thoroughly efficient teachers."[4]

This letter was received during the Board's vacation, and the schools re-opened

[1] Board Minutes, Vol. IV., p. 551.
[2] *Ib.*, pp. 1249, 1250.
[3] *Ib.*, Vol. V. pp. 239, 851.
[4] The whole correspondence will be found in Board Minutes, Vol. V., pp. 1328, *et seq.*

before that vacation had ended. On the 19th October a further communication was received from the Department stating that one of their Inspectors had reported that the scheme was in operation. They reminded the School Board that they had declined to sanction the scheme, and they pointed out that if the private lessons given under it had been substituted for those prescribed by the Memorandum of Agreement, the services of the pupil teachers in the schools no longer fulfilled the requirements of the Code. They added that a reduction from the next grant would consequently have to be made. Upon the receipt of this letter the Board requested the Education Department to receive a deputation on the subject. The Department replied that no deputation could be received until an assurance was given by the School Board that the infringement of the Code had been corrected.[1]

The Board had now no option but to acquiesce. In December, 1875, they decided to cancel the clauses of the scheme which infringed the provisions of the Code. This was, in effect, a cancellation of the scheme itself.[2] A memorial to the Department was approved, after a prolonged debate, which was an apology for the Board's breach of the Code and a defence of the scheme which they had proposed to adopt. The memorial concluded with an appeal to the Department to make such modifications in the Code as would legalise the scheme.[3] In this memorial the School Management Committee stated that their "own experience proved that the pupil teachers, as a rule, entered upon their apprenticeship at too early an age; that for some time after their appointment they had neither the requisite authority nor knowledge to take charge of children, and that to the end of their apprenticeship their instruction by the head teachers under the prevailing system was inadequate and unsatisfactory. With reference to the mode in which instruction was given under the present system, it would seem sufficient to state the case in order to show its defects. A single certificated teacher in a large school may have charge of five or six pupil teachers, in five different years of apprenticeship, independently of candidates. The pupil teachers and the candidates, in strict accordance with the Code, may have to study seven or eight different subjects, independently of the 'additional subjects' for which marks are given at the scholarship examination; and these subjects are graduated according to the years of apprenticeship. It thus becomes apparent that a single teacher in the course of five hours per week may have to deal with pupil teachers under many different conditions. To instruct the pupil teachers properly under such circumstances was simply impossible. The Board accordingly availing themselves of the increased supply of schools, and of the fact that they are themselves the Managers of a large number of schools, resolved (subject to the concurrence of the Department) to combine their schools together, in certain cases, so that the pupil teachers might be classified according to years of apprenticeship and attainments. The teacher who hitherto had been compelled to turn in a few minutes from one pupil teacher working sums in practice to another pupil teacher solving quadratic equations, or from one studying the geography of the British Isles to another studying the

---

[1] Board Minutes, Vol. V., p. 1360.
[2] *Ib.*, Vol. VI., p. 24. The articles cancelled were vi. to viii. and xiv. to xvii.
[3] Board Minutes, Vol. VI., p. 73

geography of America and the Oceans, would now take a class of eight or ten pupil teachers in the same subject—the scholars having consequently the undivided attention of their instructor for half-an-hour or an hour at a time, and having, in addition, the stimulus afforded by common study.  It is obvious, moreover, that, inasmuch as teachers have not all the same taste nor the same capacities, and that one, for example, may prefer languages and another mathematics, the plan adopted by the Board was calculated to enable the teacher to take up that subject with which he was more especially conversant, and, as an inevitable result, to secure that the teaching, instead of being dry and lifeless, should become earnest and animated."  The Department replied somewhat curtly, declining to take any responsibility for the failure of the scheme, and adding that "My Lords will carefully consider the proposals now submitted to them in the memorial before the Code for 1876 is issued ; but, in agreeing to do so, they must not be supposed to give any assent to that proposal." [1]

At a meeting of the Board on October 4th, 1876, it was reported that the Education Department had agreed to alter the Memorandum of Agreement, so that the certificated assistant teachers of the school might legally give instruction to pupil teachers.[2] This small concession did not greatly assist the scheme which the Board had advocated ; but it was evidence that the Department was in a more yielding mood, and, in consequence the Board resolved once more to ask the Department to receive a deputation with reference to the instruction of pupil teachers at centres.[3]

The deputation was received by the Department on March 7th, 1877, and on July 11th, the School Management Committee reported to the Board that the Department had stated that they could not permit the five hours' instruction in secular subjects required to be given to the pupil teachers weekly by a certificated master of the school to be interfered with in any way, but that " (i.) it is not necessary that pupil teachers employ the whole of their time during school hours in ' keeping and teaching ' the school, but that a portion of the school hours may be devoted to their own studies, (ii.) that the pupil teachers may during the portion of the school hours devoted to their own studies, be absent from school for the purpose of receiving instruction from teachers other than the certificated teacher of the school, it being, of course understood that the special instruction during five hours whilst the school is not being held shall be given in accordance with Article 4 of the pupil teachers' Memorandum of Agreement."[4]

These concessions seemed to open the door to a scheme of central teaching, and a proposal for this purpose was brought up to the Board.  It was referred back to the School Management Committee in order that the cost might be reduced, and, in consequence, an amended scheme was brought up on December 12th, 1877.  One clause of this scheme provided for the establishment of central classes at which pupil teachers in the third, fourth, and fifth year should be instructed.[5]  It was proposed that sixteen centres should be established, and that the Board should pay the travelling expenses of

[1] Board Minutes, Vol. VI., p. 190.          [4] Board Minutes, Vol. VII., p. 872.
[2] *School Board Chronicle*, Vol. XVI., p. 332.        [5] *Ib*, Vol. VIII., p. 55.
[3] Board Minutes, Vol. VI., p. 1307.

pupil teachers whose schools were removed from the centres. The Board, on March 13th, 1878, approved the scheme, but instructed the School Management Committee to take counsel's opinion whether the expenses involved could legally be incurred.[1]

The opinion of Mr. John Westlake, Q.C., was first taken, and subsequently that of the then Attorney-General, Sir John Holker. These opinions were entirely adverse to the right of the Board to expend money upon the training of pupil teachers in any manner, or in any subject of instruction which was not recognised by the Code in force for the time being. It is not unimportant to notice, having regard to recent judicial decisions, that the test of legality set up by these eminent legal authorities was the provisions of the Code. It never occurred to them to advise the Board that the establishment of pupil teachers' centres would be illegal even if such centres were recognised by the Code.

In consequence of these adverse opinions the Board sent another deputation to the Education Department. The deputation was favourably received, and it was intimated that changes would be made in the next Code that would enable the Board to establish a system of training pupil teachers at centres.[2] The Code for 1879, however, contained no such provisions.

## II.—The Period of Collective Instruction in Evening Schools.

The efforts of the Board were at last rewarded. The Code for 1880 was altered so as to allow the instruction of pupil teachers to be given by any certificated teacher, instead of, as hitherto, a certificated teacher of the school in which the pupil teacher served.

The Board, therefore, in 1881, adopted a new scheme for the instruction of pupil teachers at central classes. The scheme was brought up by the School Management Committee on October 27th, and on November 3rd it was passed by the Board almost without amendment.[3] Central classes were to be established for the collective instruction of pupil teachers in such schools as should be selected by the School Management Committee. The classes were to be held on Monday and Wednesday evenings from 6 to 8 o'clock, and on Saturday mornings from 9 to 12.30. The subjects of instruction were to be limited to those recognised by the Code, and the classes were to be taught by selected certificated teachers, and by special teachers engaged to teach such subjects, as Languages and Science. Scripture instruction was to continue to be given by the head teachers of the schools in which the pupil teachers served. Travelling expenses were allowed to students who resided more than a mile from their appointed centres. Head teachers were instructed to arrange the school work so as to permit the pupil teachers to leave school early on Mondays and Wednesdays for the purpose of study. The committee also proposed that pupil teachers from Voluntary schools should be permitted to attend the centres on payment of a small fee. This motion was postponed in order that the opinion of the solicitor might be obtained as to whether it was legal. The solicitor reported that the motion was *ultra vires*, and it was therefore dropped. Since 1883, however, the Board have allowed pupil teachers from

---

[1] Board Minutes Vol. VIII., p. 500.  [3] Board Minutes, Vol. XV., pp. 648-699.
[2] *Ib.*, Vol. IX., p. 309.

non-Board schools to attend the central classes for instruction. At first a charge was made equal to their share in the whole cost of the instruction. From 1895 until now the instruction has been given free of charge, but the grants earned by the pupil teachers are retained by the Board. From 1900 to the present time the Board have charged a small fee for probationers from non-Board schools attending the centres. This action was undoubtedly illegal, but was apparently acquiesced in by the Education Department.

This scheme had one great advantage over the system it displaced in that it permitted the classification of pupil teachers for purposes of instruction, so that each subject of the curriculum could be taught by specially qualified teachers; but it increased rather than diminished the strain upon the pupil. It was soon found that the demand that the pupil teachers should work in the day school, attend central classes, and prepare lessons at such times as might be available for the purpose, was too heavy. H M. Inspectors reported unfavourably upon the results. In the general report on the Metropolitan Division for 1885 the following quotations are given from the reports of assistant inspectors :—

> The centre system of instruction of pupil teachers does not appear to secure the objects which its promoters had in view, nor to become more popular either with the masters or mistresses of schools, or with their pupil teachers. Of the evils attending it I spoke in my general report two years ago. Of its success in providing the pupil teachers with the instruction they require, it is sufficient to say that not 20 per cent. of them in this district pass their examination so well as to obtain the higher or 60s. grant.
>
> It may benefit the more intelligent and advanced pupils, but it does not meet the wants of those of average or inferior ability, nor give them the individual attention which they need to make proper progress. Moreover, it withdraws them too much from their school duties, leads them to consider learning more important than teaching, weakens their interest in their class, interrupts the school routine, and sacrifices the valuable influence of the head teacher for the sake of securing, in a limited number of instances only, more efficient instruction than the teachers are supposed to be able to provide.
>
> The diminution in the number of pupil teachers in this district is remarkable. My half-yearly examinations are but little larger than some of the monthly examinations nine years ago ; and the quality does not make up for quantity.[1]

### III.—The Period of Collective Day Instruction at Pupil Teachers' Centres.

Meanwhile the Board had already taken steps to remedy as far as the law then allowed the evils complained of. On April 24th, 1884, a scheme was adopted by which the candidates and the first and second year pupil teachers, called henceforth junior pupil teachers, should attend the school in which they were apprenticed for the "necessary"[2] part of each day and the central classes the other part of the day. Two months later, on July 24th, 1884, a change was made in the same direction in the case of the seniors—third and fourth year pupil teachers. It was further agreed that all pupil teachers should be relieved of the necessity of attending evening classes, and should be required to attend the central classes for instruction on two half-days a week and on

---

[1] Education Department Report 1885-6, p. 307.
[2] The Government Code laid down that the pupil teacher should serve in the school not less than three or more than six hours upon any one day, nor more than 25 hours in any one week.

Saturday mornings. The school teaching in their absence was provided for by a scheme under which the juniors took classes in the absence of the seniors.

There was not sufficient accommodation in the day schools for the instruction of all the pupil teachers, and the consent of the Education Department was obtained to the erection of special classrooms at certain schools. Pending the erection of these classrooms temporary premises were hired. The first permanent centre (Stepney) was opened in August, 1885, and from time to time others were opened, until in 1895 there were twelve centres.

The cost of the working of the new scheme was found to be much in excess of the estimate given when the scheme was first before the Board, and on July 2nd, 1885, Mr. H. Gover moved that the resolution of the Board establishing the new scheme be rescinded. In support of his motion, Mr. Gover, after condemning the scheme on account of its costliness, stated that he believed " the effect of the scheme would be to centre the interest of the young teachers far too much upon their instruction, to the detriment of their work and training as teachers," and pointed out the leakages into other professions from the service of the Board which, in his opinion, would occur at different stages in the course of training and at its close. He did not think that the Board were justified in undertaking the training of teachers at the expense of the ratepayers.

The chief arguments upon the other side were the necessity for making provision for the future supply of teachers, and the need for removing the overpressure which existed under the old scheme.[1] After a long discussion the " Previous Question " was carried by 19 votes against 15.

Mr. Gover made another attempt to rescind the scheme in January, 1886, a new Board having come into office in the previous November. After a long discussion, the Board decided "that the School Management Committee be instructed to present a report at an early date as to the efficiency, cost, and possible amendment of the scheme for the instruction of pupil teachers with any recommendations thereupon, but with the understanding that no system will be satisfactory to the Board which does not provide against the possibility of using the pupil teachers' centre training as a substitute for the training in college."

On the 17th June, 1886, the committee submitted an exhaustive report. They pointed out that there were four courses open for the Board to adopt, viz.: (i.) to abolish pupil teachers, and staff the schools wholly with assistants; (ii.) to revert to the original system of entrusting the education of the pupil teachers to the head teachers of the schools in which they were engaged; (iii.) of re-establishing the evening classes, when the pupil teachers would be engaged in their schools during the whole of the day-time, and receive their instruction on certain evenings, and on Saturdays; and (iv.) of continuing the existing system, by which the pupil teachers devoted part of their time to the schools in which they were engaged, and part to attendance at the pupil teachers' schools.

---

[1] *School Board Chronicle*, July 4th, 1885, p. 5.

Whilst conceding that the plan of staffing schools wholly with assistants was decidedly the best from an educational point of view, the Committee did not recommend its adoption, for the following reasons :—

(a) The increased cost of substituting assistants for pupil teachers ;

(b) the questionable policy of depending entirely upon the provinces for the supply of teachers ;

(c) the extreme improbability that sufficient teachers could be obtained from the outside to supply (i.) what might be called waste, amounting to over three hundred assistants per annum, caused through teachers leaving the service of the Board ; (ii.) the increase from time to time of accommodation in the schools of the Board ; and (iii.) the deficiency of teachers that would be caused in the schools of the Board through the abolition of pupil teachers.

Nor did the Committee recommend the Board to revert to the original scheme whereby the pupil teachers would be engaged in teaching for probably twenty-five hours in each week, and receive their instruction from the head teacher of the school. The instruction of pupil teachers at evening classes was also condemned. If that course were adopted the young pupil teachers (who might be spoken of as children) would, as under the original scheme, be engaged all day long in teaching children Although better results were obtained at the evening classes during the years 1882-4 than had been obtained under the original system, the Committee were of opinion that it was too much to expect that young persons, especially girls, of the ages of 15, 16, or 17 should be required to teach all day in their schools, and then devote their evenings to attendance at the pupil teachers' centres, and to private study. The Committee therefore recommended the continuance of the present scheme, making such modifications in it from time to time as may be desirable. They also reported that they were of opinion that the pupil teachers received more efficient instruction under the new system than under either of the former systems.

With regard to the cost of the maintenance of the pupil teachers' schools, the Committee reported that they hoped it would be reduced by the pupil teachers earning increased grants under the new system from the Science and Art Department and the Education Department ; also that another saving would be effected by the retention of pupil teachers for one year after they had completed their apprenticeship at the salary of ex-pupil teachers, and so take the place of trained assistants.

After an amendment to refer the report back to the School Management Committee for further consideration had been lost by 17 against 16, the Committee's recommendation was passed by 16 to 15.[1]

The Committee also submitted many modifications in the new scheme which were adopted by the Board on July 8th, 1886.[1]

The legality of expenditure by the Board for the maintenance of pupil teachers' centres was questioned in 1886, when the Local Government Board's Auditor disallowed a

[1] For full details of the scheme as finally fixed on July 8th, 1886, see Board Minutes, Vol. XXV., pp. 309,310.

sum of £38 11s. 6d., expenditure incurred for rent, cleaning, gas and fuel in connection with the Lycett Memorial Pupil Teachers' School. The School Board made an appeal to the Local Government Board against this disallowance, and in March, 1887, a letter was received from the Local Government Board stating that the disallowance was made (*a*) because the school was not a Public Elementary school within the meaning of the Education Acts; (*b*) because School Boards were not entitled to maintain schools for the sole instruction of pupil teachers; and (*c*) because they could only incur expenditure for such instruction at a Public Elementary school, and not at any building used exclusively for the instruction of pupil teachers. The Local Government Board, however, stated that they had ascertained that the Education Department were of opinion that the expenditure might be regarded as having been incurred by the School Board for the purpose of fulfilling their obligations under the Memorandum of Agreement with the pupil teachers, and as part of the expenditure which they were entitled to incur in maintaining each of the several schools to which the pupil teachers belonged; and upon this view the Local Government Board reversed the decision of the Auditor.

Since 1886 the Board's system of training pupil teachers has remained in essentials the same, though important changes in details have taken place. These changes have tended on the one hand to decrease both the time given by the pupil teachers to teaching work in school and their responsibility for the conduct of a class, and, on the ther hand, have followed the general educational improvement in the country by taking elder students for a shorter period of apprenticeship, and preparing them for a somewhat wider educational course. On the first point the development was shortly as follows :—

The scheme of 1886 provided that seniors should attend the central classes on two half-days, and on Saturday mornings, in each week, the remainder of their time being spent in school. The juniors were required to spend five half-days a week at classes and five at school; in 1887, they were also required to attend classes on Saturday morning. The time spent by seniors in teaching at the school was shortened in 1891 by one half-day in each fortnight, and when, in 1895, all pupil teachers were allowed a free half-day a week to relieve overpressure, in the case of seniors, it was taken from the school time. After considering the recommendations of the Departmental Committee of 1897-8, it was decided that seniors should attend during the same time as juniors, viz., five half-days a week (including Saturday morning) at centre, and five half-days at school. In February, 1898, with a view to testing their aptitude for teaching, it was decided that candidates should, in the first instance, be required to attend full time at the day school for three months. In the following June, however, this resolution was rescinded, and, since then, the first two or three months' attendance has been half-time at school, and half at centre. Meanwhile, the responsibility which the Board have attached to senior pupil teachers in the schools has also been reduced. Until 1890 they were reckoned for forty children; from 1890 till 1898, for thirty; and since 1898 for twenty. Junior pupil teachers have not been counted for staffing purposes since 1884.

On the second point, with a view to obtaining pupil teachers of higher educational ability, the Board have recognised certain examinations as entitling boys and girls to

L

admission as pupil teachers, viz., the Junior Oxford or Cambridge Local examination, since 1886, and the College of Preceptors' examination since 1897. They have also, since 1893, accepted for shortened periods of apprenticeship candidates who have passed the Senior Oxford or Cambridge Local examination or, since 1896, the London Matriculation examination, and since 1900 candidates possessing the "School of Science" certificate issued by the Board of Education.

But meanwhile, owing to the want of training college accommodation, and the pass examination for the Queen's Scholarship becoming a very severe competitive examination, young teachers tended to stay later at school, in order that, by going in later for the Queen's Scholarship examination, they would get a better place. The Board, therefore, in November, 1901, decided that it was desirable that pupil teachers should sit for the scholarship examination before they were twenty years of age, and, with that view, reduced the full course of training from about 5½ years to about 4½ years.

The danger which was constantly referred to in the debates of the Board (though there does not seem even to have been evidence of its real existence) that pupil teachers would use the course in order to get a general education without becoming professional teachers was met by a pledge that they would go to college, by the "college allowance" as a form of postponed pay, and further, since 1899, by deferring payment of a certain portion of their salary until they entered college. Another danger, viz., that pupil teachers after passing the scholarship examination would take no steps to go to college and would prefer to earn a salary directly as ex-pupil teachers, was provided against, with partial success, by a policy of offering very low salaries under such conditions.

The fact that the scheme of 1884 was severely criticised at the Board on financial grounds, and was ultimately only carried by one vote, made it necessary for the School Management Committee to use every possible means to diminish the expenses of the centres. Such means were provided in the large grants given by the Science and Art Department, and the pupil teachers' course is said to have been at one time largely dominated by the necessity of earning as many grants for as many "sciences" as possible. From at least 1894 to 1904 this consideration seems to have had little weight, and a rather considerable portion of the students now prepare for the London Matriculation examination. This has been facilitated by the fact that the Board of Education has, since 1899, allowed the pupil teachers' centres larger liberty in curriculum, by recognising the certificates of certain examinations to count as qualifications for admission to training colleges; in 1901, by excusing the Board's pupil teachers sitting at the annual Government examination; and in 1904, by accepting the Board's examination for all purposes.

The success of the pupil teachers in the scholarship examination was at first phenomenal. The gradual introduction of the centre system into other towns lessened after a time the disparity between London and the rest of the country. At present the Board's pupil teachers gain about twice as many successes, in proportion, as compared with the rest of the country.

Meanwhile, the supply of pupil teachers is steadily falling off in proportion to the needs of London.

During the last few years, the Board has required about 1,000 new teachers each year, whereas about 550 Board pupil teachers, on an average, have passed the King's Scholarship examination, of whom 80 per cent. at the most become certificated teachers. Not only has the general supply of pupil teachers in proportion to the number of children in the schools diminished, but the proportion of boy pupil teachers to girl pupil teachers has steadily diminished from the beginning (see diagram p. 148), in spite of considerable increases in the salaries of boys,[1] and the increase in the average salary paid to men assistants from £115 6s. 5d. in 1888 to £140 1s. 1d. in 1903.

This tendency is not peculiar to England, and is less marked than in the United States, but it constitutes a very serious subject for consideration by any educational body.

One reason for the difficulty in obtaining pupil teachers, has always been the want of such a supply of training colleges as should ensure that every pupil teacher passing well in the King's Scholarship examination would be able to obtain suitable training college accommodation. The Board, again and again, approached the Education Department on this point,[2] and in 1898 attempted to meet the difficulty in some part by engaging women assistant teachers, who should give half their time to an extended course of preparation for the Certificate examination, and should then be recognised by the Board as trained teachers. These Board's Certificate classes were first opened in 1898, and in 1904 contained 83 students. They were always perhaps of doubtful legality, but the Cockerton Act of 1900 enabled the Board, by a declaration of their illegality, to secure their recognition by the County Council.

---

## BOOKS AND APPARATUS.

The system followed by the School Board with regard to school books and furniture was, like many other important matters of policy, determined during the first four years of the Board's existence, and has not since then suffered any material change. The three main questions of who was to choose the school books and apparatus, how they were to be distributed, and on what terms they should be supplied to the parents, were then settled, and settled upon lines which have not been changed. Apparently, the original intention of the Board was to leave these questions to be settled by the Local Managers. The first Board, in the extensive scheme of delegation, which has before been described, decided that the Managers should see that the school was duly provided with suitable desks, maps, books, and apparatus. The Managers also decided upon what terms the books should be supplied to the parents. This scheme was adopted in 1871; twelve months had not passed before the Board began to take again into its own hands, the powers of which it had intended to deprive itself.

---

[1] See *post*, pp 196-7.
[2] Board Minutes, Vol. XXXVI., pp. 1069, 1096;    Vol. XXXVII., p. 154; Vol. XLIX., pp. 485-6, and 670.

Diagram showing the percentage of boy and girl Pupil Teachers to the total number of
Pupil Teachers from 1873 to 1903.

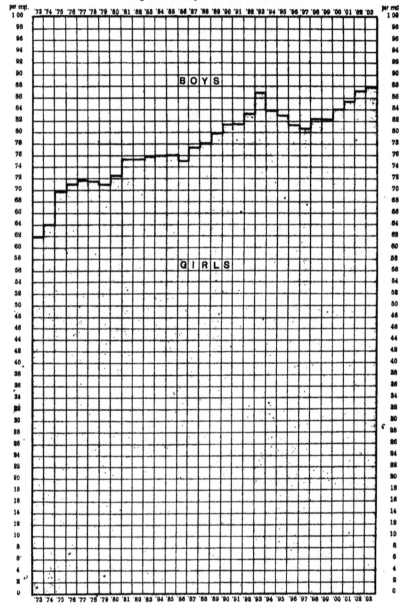

In 1872 the Sub-Committee, appointed to give instruction to Managers, considered the question of school books suitable for adoption by the Board. So seriously dissatisfied were the members of the Board with the existing school books, that it was debated whether the Board should not, itself, prepare and issue its own text-books. The Committee, however, recommended that the decision of this question should be postponed,[1] and the Board should confine itself to exercising supervision over reading books used in the schools. It was accordingly resolved that the Board should draw up a list of suitable reading-books, and that the Managers should be instructed to make their choice from this list. The selection of copybooks, and of the toys and books needed in the Infant school were left to the Managers; and so was that of the books on Grammar, Geography, and Arithmetic. No textbooks were at first supplied in any other subjects.[2] The Board reserved to itself a veto on all books.[3] This partial and incomplete arrangement lasted until 1874, when the rules with regard to reading-books were applied to all other books and school apparatus. The powers of selection are now exercised by a special Sub-Committee of the School Management Committee—the "Books and Apparatus Sub Committee." The school material approved by this Committee are entered on a list, known as the "Requisition List." From this list the head teachers select, subject to certain limits of expenditure, the books and stationery they may require.

The machinery of distribution was the next branch of this question discussed by the first Board. A Special Sub-Committee, that on "Requisitions," was formed to consider the demand received from the different schools for books and apparatus. At first, an agent was appointed to supply the articles requisitioned at a fixed percentage, and to deliver them to the schools. In 1874, however, it was resolved that the Board should establish a central store of their own, on the grounds that economy would be effected by dealing direct with manufacturers and publishers, and that the goods could be delivered to the schools with greater expedition. This store was held, at different times, in temporary buildings, and at the head office of the Board. The present warehouse at Clerkenwell, was completed and occupied in 1896.[4]

The first Board also settled the important question of principle, whether the books and apparatus should be supplied free of charge or not. It appears probable that, originally, the opinion of the first Board was that it was a good and wholesome thing that those who could afford it should pay for the books supplied. The School Management Committee brought up a report, to the effect that children attending a school, where a fee of more than threepence a week was charged, should pay for all that was supplied to them with the exception of reading-books. After some discussion, an amendment was moved in favour of making the fee include a reasonable charge for books and apparatus; and, finally, both the amendment and the original motion were withdrawn, in order that the question might be reconsidered. The debate had brought into prominence the great difficulties which the Board would have to encounter in making a charge for books. It was even doubtful whether such a charge would be legal. The Board, therefore, when

[1] Board Minutes, Vol. II. p. 140.    [3] Board Minutes, Vol. II. p. 184.
[2] *Ib.*, Vol. II. pp. 228-410.    [4] See *post*, p. 357.

it reconsidered the question, resolved "that the use of all books, stationery, and apparatus be allowed in Board schools without any additional charge." It can hardly be doubted that this resolution tended to make the working of the Education Act more easy in London, while it undoubtedly greatly simplified the administrative task of the Board.

Since 1874, as has been said, the work of the Board in connection with school material has proceeded on the lines then laid down. The enlargement of the Board's curriculum, the increase of the teaching of Science, the development of the Kindergarten system, the increased attention given to Modern Languages, the requirements of scholars preparing for County Council and other examinations, have all contributed to swell the Board's requisition list beyond the original modest catalogue of text-books in reading; but the change has been one merely of development and addition.

Since 1886 the Board has arranged that all the books and apparatus on its list should be displayed in a room at headquarters, and has recently (1903) resolved that all head teachers must visit this educational museum before drawing up their annual requisitions.

## REWARD CARDS, PRIZES AND MEDALS.

As early as December, 1874, the Board decided that scholars should receive rewards for regular and punctual attendance, and shortly after that date a scheme was adopted by which " reward cards " were given to scholars, who, during a quarter of a year, had attended punctually 95 per cent. of the school sessions. A scholar who had received two reward cards, received a book prize.

This scheme was abolished in 1886, when the Board adopted a system of reward cards for good attendance during a quarter, prizes for good attendance during a year, and medals for perfect attendance during a year.

In 1901 the Board decided that prizes should not be allowed for attendance only, but that conduct and industry also should be taken into account. An amount based on the average attendance is allowed to each school, and it is left to the head teacher to distribute this amount in accordance with a scheme drawn up by himself and approved by the Local Managers. This system enables teachers to give consideration to the varying circumstances of their schools in drawing up their schemes and ensures every school receiving a certain amount to expend in prizes.

In 1902 the Board decided that reward cards also might be awarded for conduct and industry. Medals are now the only rewards which are given exclusively for regular and punctual attendance.

The following table shows the number of prizes and medals awarded during each year from 1888 to 1903:—

| Year ended March 25th, | Prizes. | | Medals. | |
|---|---|---|---|---|
| | Number awarded. | Percentage on average attendance. | Number awarded. | Percentage on average attendance. |
| 1 | 2 | 3 | 4 | 5 |
| 1888 | 28,034 | 8·7 | 4,442 | 1·4 |
| 1889 | 32,889 | 9·8 | 7,125 | 2·1 |
| 1890 | 35,201 | 10·3 | 9,359 | 2·7 |
| 1891 | 31,653 | 9·2 | 8,702 | 2·49 |
| 1892 | 30,632 | 8·7 | 8,990 | 2·6 |
| 1893 | 32,965 | 8·9 | 9,948 | 2·7 |
| 1894 | 37,282 | 9·8 | 11,667 | 3·05 |
| 1895 | 45,860 | 11·7 | 15,294 | 3·88 |
| 1896 | 52,934 | 13·1 | 19,589 | 4·9 |
| 1897 | 61,211 | 14·8 | 24,291 | 5·9 |
| (a) 1898 | 37,180 | 15·2 | 15,567 | 6·4 |
| 1899 | 70,038 | 16·4 | 33,959 | 7·96 |
| 1900 | (b) 64,775 | (c) 14·9 | 30,010 | (d) 9·8 |
| 1901 | 64,488 | 14·7 | 30,612 | 9·8 |
| 1902 | 70,848 | 15·9 | 33,309 | 10·4 |
| 1903 | (e) | ... | 33,565 | 10·0 |

(a) The low numbers for 1898 are accounted for by the fact that returns were not received from all the schools in consequence of the adoption of a uniform educational year.

(b) The Board in 1899 decided to allow half-yearly prizes to infants below Standard I. Two of these half-yearly prizes have been counted as equivalent to one yearly prize in this table.

(c) The maximum number of absences allowed was reduced from 15 to 12 in 1899, and further reduced to 10 in 1900.

(d) The Board in January, 1898, decided that absences on not more than four sessions should not debar a child from receiving a medal, if notice of the absences had been given; and in December, 1898, that medals should not be given to children below Standard I. in the Infants' Departments. The large increase in 1900 in the percentage is the result of these decisions.

(e) No record is kept of the number of prizes awarded under the new scheme.

## "ORGANISATION."

Two of the regulations of the first School Management Code (1871) were that Infants' schools should be "Mixed," and that Senior schools should be "Separate." There has, however, always been a small number of schools in which the elder boys and girls have been taught together. Since 1888 there has been a growing tendency on the part of the Board in favour of mixed Upper departments, and specific resolutions were adopted in 1888[1] and 1892 with a view to increasing the number of such schools in suitable districts. During the last few years the policy of the Board has been to organise many new schools with Junior Mixed and Senior Mixed departments, and the increase in the number of Mixed departments has been very marked.

The Diagram on the following page shows how the percentage of Mixed departments (including Junior Mixed) upon the total number of Senior departments has varied during the last thirty years. It should be borne in mind that in the early years the schools of the Board were mostly small transferred Voluntary schools, many of which, rather for convenience than on educational grounds, were organised with Mixed departments.

[1] See *ante*, p. 97 : Resolutions, 22 and 23.

*Diagram showing the percentage of Mixed departments (including Junior Mixed) upon the number of Senior departments.*

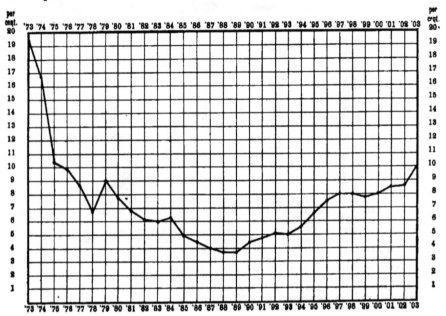

## CLASSIFICATION.

The old system of "payment by results," based on an annual examination of all children, made it possible for the Government to formulate a strict rule of classification by age.

This rule was meant to be enforced in two ways—(*a*) by the requirement that all children over seven years of age should be examined in Standard I., and (*b*) that, as a rule, all children should be advanced a standard a year.[1]

The Government Code relaxed these requirements in 1890 and 1896, and abolished them in 1900 and 1901.

---

[1] *E.g.*, the Government Code of 1882 laid it down that "scholars over 7 years old must, as a rule, be examined in the first standard (Article 107 [c])," and that "every scholar should be presented in a standard higher than the highest in which he has before been presented, whether in his present or in any former school" (Art. 109 [e] V.); in 1884 the qualification, "unless there is a reasonable excuse for treating him exceptionally," being added.  In 1884 Art. (e) also stated that ". . . scholars presented a second time in the same standard without reasonable excuse *will* be considered to have failed in the three (elementary) subjects"; but in 1885 "may" was substituted for "will."

In 1890 the rule that scholars should be presentèd for examination in a higher standard each year was superseded by the following:—" In ordinary circumstances a scholar should be advanced not less than one standard a year."

In 1894 inspection was substituted for examination in infants' schools, and in 1896 in Senior schools; a change which had the indirect effect of giving greater freedom of classification to head teachers.

In 1900 the rule that in ordinary circumstances scholars should be advanced not less than one standard a year was omitted.

In 1901 the requirement that scholars over 7 years of age must, as a rule, be examined in Standard I. was omitted, and all reference to the standards, except for labour certificate examinations, was abolished.

For a long time the regulations of the Board in respect to classification of age were less strict than those of the Government.

It was soon found that the exigencies of accommodation prevented the full carrying out of the Government rule requiring that all children over 7 years of age shall be instructed in the upper departments, and in 1877 the Board decided that, in cases where there was no room in the upper departments for children who would be 7 years of age at the end of the school year, those children should remain in the Infants' department and be presented in Standard I. in that department at the Government examination.

In 1885, upon the recommendation of the Special Committee on Overpressure, it was decided that a review of the children who had been instructed in the First Standard in the Infants' school should be made after the school examination, with a view to keeping in the First Standard in the upper schools those children who were unable to do the work of the Second Standard without overpressure.[1]

But since 1900 the rules on classification in the Board's Code, which were originally a copy or modification of those in the Government Code, have represented the only definite regulations which are binding on head teachers in this respect. The Government Code makes no mention of standards, and simply says that the report of the Inspector as to the "discipline and organisation" of each school shall be considered by the Board of Education when allotting grants.

The Board has retained the reference to the standards, and the rule that a child should commence the work of Standard I. at 6. By a succession of changes between 1900 and 1903 the classification rules in the Board's Code, whilst unchanged in principle, have been made more precise.

At present the essential paragraph of those rules (Art. 142 note) stands as follows:—

Teachers should bear in mind that, as a rule, children who have turned 6 and 7 years of age should be able to commence the work of Standards I. and II. respectively at the beginning of the educational year. The Board Inspectors have instructions to report to the School Management Committee any cases in which, in their opinion, an undue number of scholars who have turned 6 and 7 are not able to commence the work of Standards I. and II. respectively at the beginning of the educational year.

---

[1] Board Minutes, Vol. XXIII., pp. 552-3.

Article 140 of the Board's Code still implies that the old regulation requiring that children must, as a rule, be advanced a "standard" a year is in force.[1]

It is clear from the statistics of the Board that the actual classification of the schools has never coincided with the Government or, later, the Board's regulations. Either those regulations have aimed too high for the average child under the existing conditions, or the classification has been defective.

The bulk of the children have not done the amount of work in the "Standard" subjects represented by "Standard I." by 7 years of age, nor have they proceeded thenceforward at the rate of a standard a year.

The statistics show that in the early years of the Board, in spite of the rigidity of the Government rule, and of the fact that the pay of the teachers depended very largely on "results," the ideal represented by the Government rule was not even approached.

The earliest information as to the proportion of children in the different standards in the Senior departments is given in the Annual Statement of the Chairman of the Board for 1877, where the following table relating to one of the two Board Inspectors' districts is set out:—

| YEAR. | Percentage in each Standard. | | | |
|---|---|---|---|---|
| | I. | II. | III. | IV. and above. |
| 1873 | 79·0 | 13 0 | 5·8 | 2·2 |
| 1875 | 62·5 | 20·0 | 10·0 | 7·5 |
| 1876 | 41·6 | 25·0 | 18·0 | 15·4 |

By 1880 a great improvement had taken place, and of the children in the Senior departments 24·1 per cent. were in Standard I., 26·5 in Standard II., 22·4 in Standard III., and 27·0 in Standard IV. and above.

But if, in 1880, the facts had corresponded to the Government ideal, and if the average child had passed Standard I. at 7, and gone up a standard a year till it left at 13 (if the number kept back annually had been equal to the number advanced more than a standard annually), the result would have been, roughly, that about 17 per cent. of the children of the Senior departments would have been found in each standard from I. to VI. (then the highest standard).

Since then the conditions of the problem have very greatly changed. For instance, since 1886 the school life of the children has increased from an average of 8½ to almost 10 years, and the average attendance from 78·9 to 86·4 per cent. The result is that on an average the children now attend nearly 3,700 school sessions in the course of their school life, as compared with about 2,900 in 1886.

At the same time, the average size of classes has steadily diminished, and the mentally defective children have been removed from the ordinary schools.

[1] Article 140 is as follows :—"In cases where children are advanced more than one standard, or put down into lower standards, or kept in the same standard another year, a report of each case should be entered in the log book, and the reasons for the course adopted should be given. Special attention is to be called to the case of any child to whom promotion has been refused in the previous year."

The returns and diagram on pages 157-9 show that, allowing for the fact that few children now leave before 14, any approximation of the facts to the " ideal" standardisation has been almost imperceptible.

Since 1901 the actual average age of the children in each standard has been obtained, and the figures for 1903 may be considered in detail.

Article 142 of the School Management Code, quoted above, sets out that as a rule children who have turned 6 years of age at the beginning of the educational year should be placed in Standard I. Such promoted children would be at an average age of 6½ years on August 1st (the commencement of the educational year), and at an average age of 7 years 2 months on March 25th following. There would further be, if this rule were carried out exactly, neither more nor less than a year's batch of children (about 58,000) in Standard I., most of whom would be in Infants' schools. If at the end of a year these children passed into Standard II., there would be about the same number in Standard II. of an average age of 8·2. The returns show that, taking Infants' and Senior departments together, there were on March 25th, 1903, 85,268 (instead of £8,000) children in Standard I. of an average age of 7·9 (instead of 7·2), and 70,502 (instead of 58,000) in Standard II. of an average age of 9·3 (instead of 8·2), or an average retardation of more than a year, due partly to the fact that the average child entered Standard I. later than the age laid down in the Board's Code, and partly to the fact that he stayed in Standard I. more than a year.

The statistics are still more significant when one examines separately the figures for the Infants' and the Upper departments. In the Infants' departments there were 39,242 children in Standard I. averaging 7·3 years of age, but on the other hand (on the assumption that the ages of individual children were equally spread through the months of the year) there were 24,436 children who ought by age to have been in Standard I., but were not. In the Senior departments there were 46,026 children in Standard I., aged 8·5 (as compared with an average of 7·3 in the Infants), of whom only 5,114, or 1 in 9, were (on the assumption made above) of the age indicated by the School Management Code. In the same year, for Standard II. in the Infants' departments, the average age was 8·5 years, and of Standard II. children upstairs the average age was 9·3 years.[1]

The further average ages in the higher standards would have been as follows if the children had been all promoted to Standard I. in accordance with Article 142, and afterwards promoted on the average a standard a year : –

Standard III. 9·2      IV., 10·2      V., 11·2      VI., 12·2      VII., 13·2

The actual average age of the Standards as compared with this ideal is as follows:—

|  | Std. III. | IV. | V. | VI. | VII. |
|---|---|---|---|---|---|
| Actual age   ...   ...   ... | 10·4 | 11·4 | 12·2 | 12·8 | 13·3 |
| Ideal age as above   ...   ... | 9·2 | 10·2 | 11·2 | 12·2 | 13·2 |

[1] See School Management Committee's Report for 1903, p. 397.

The apparent recovery in Standards VI. and VII. is due to the fact that comparatively few children reach those standards. Comparing ages with standards, we find in our schools (1903):—

| Ages | ... | ... | 9-10 | 10-11 | 11-12 | 12-13 | 13-14 |
|---|---|---|---|---|---|---|---|
| | | | 55,903 | 56,104 | 54,364 | 52,492 | 48,267 |
| Standard... | | ... | III. | IV. | V. | VL. | VII. |
| | | | 65,059 | 58,560 | 48,215 | 33,076 | 18,432 |

The figures for 1903 show that the number of children of the "ideal" age for Standard I., but below that standard, had in that year somewhat markedly declined. Some allowance must be made for the fact that the result of this will be to make a temporary increase in the numbers in Standard I., which will not be due to an excess of time spent by the children in that standard.

Diagram A opposite shows by the red lines the percentage of the number of children below Standards I., II., III., IV., and V., and by the black lines the approximate percentage of the number of children who should be below those standards according to age; allowance being made for the changes in the date of the educational year.[1] If the Board's ideal were realised the red and black lines should coincide, and the space between the lines shows the extent to which the ideal has failed. It is most noticeable that the red curve II. nearly coincides with the black curve III., showing very clearly that the children have always been on an average about a year older than the ideal age before they entered Standard II. The sudden rise in all the curves in 1898 is due to the introduction of the uniform educational year, and should not be taken into account.

The whole problem suggested by these figures is an extremely difficult one, and has engaged much of the attention of the School Management Committee since 1901.[2] The question of "freedom of classification," the relation between the Senior and Infants departments, and that between the "standard" subjects and other subjects on the curriculum, as well as the question whether the ideal aimed at by the Board's regulations is too high, are all involved.

---

[1] From 1886 to 1897 the school year ended at different times of the year. In 1898 a uniform educational year was fixed, which ended on June 30th until 1901, and on July 31st since 1901. It has been assumed that from 1886 to 1897 one-half of the children between six and seven years of age, at Lady-day, would be under six at the beginning of the school year, and that from 1898 to 1900, three-quarters, or, since 1901, two-thirds, of such children would be below six at the beginning of the educational year. A similar assumption has been made in the case of the older children.

[2] See e.g., the Annual Report of the Board Inspectors for 1901; Lord Stanley's Memorandum on "Backward Children in Infant Schools," June 21st, 1901, with the Board Inspector's report on it; the Board Inspectors' General Report for 1901; the Report of the Special Committee of Enquiry on that Report, submitted to the Board on 23rd October, 1902; the revised Memorandum by the Chairman of the School Management Committee on the "Standard and Ages" Returns for 1901, 1902, and 1903; and other memoranda submitted to a conference of Members, Board Inspectors, and Teachers, held on January 14th, 1904.

# A
## STANDARDS AND AGES.

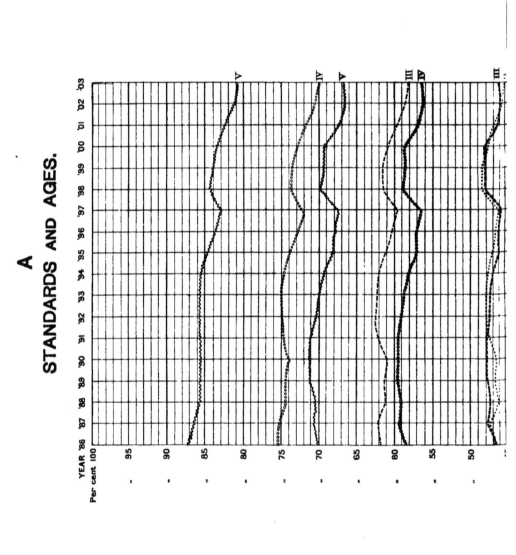

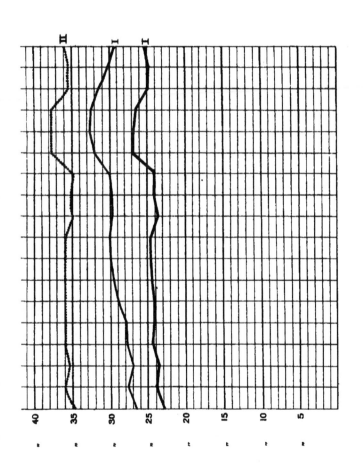

I shows percentage of children below 8td.    I
II    „    „    „    „    „    II
III    „    „    „    „    „    III
IV    „    „    „    „    „    IV
V    „    „    „    „    „    V

shows percentage of children at the
I    beginning of the educational year below    6
II    „    „    „    „    „    7
III    „    „    „    „    „    8
IV    „    „    „    „    „    9
V    „    „    „    „    „    10

To face page 156

## AGES AND STANDARDS OF CHILDREN.

### A.—AGES TABLE.

Number and percentage of children of the various ages on the Roll for 18 years.

| At Lady Day. | Under 3 years. | 3 and under 4 years. | 4 and under 5 years. | 5 and under 6 years. | 6 and under 7 years. | 7 and under 8 years. | 8 and under 9 years. | 9 and under 10 years. | 10 and under 11 years. | 11 and under 12 years. | 12 and under 13 years. | 13 and under 14 years. | 14½ ears and over. | 15 yrs and over. | Totals. |
|---|---|---|---|---|---|---|---|---|---|---|---|---|---|---|---|
| 1886 | 380 | 8661 | 21073 | 34563 | 42756 | 45241 | 44033 | 45165 | 43642 | 40322 | 32387 | 14223 | 3141 | ... | 375587 |
| | ·1 | 2·3 | 5·6 | 9·2 | 11·4 | 12·1 | 11·7 | 12·0 | 11·6 | 10·8 | 8·6 | 3·8 | ·8 | | |
| 1887 | 436 | 10934 | 24922 | 38873 | 45687 | 49653 | 46940 | 46364 | 46241 | 42643 | 35074 | 14825 | 3380 | ... | 405972 |
| | ·1 | 2·7 | 6·1 | 9·6 | 11·3 | 12·2 | 11·6 | 11·4 | 11·4 | 10·5 | 8·6 | 3·7 | ·8 | | |
| 1888 | 360 | 10763 | 24416 | 39846 | 46280 | 50838 | 48709 | 48066 | 46879 | 44431 | 36413 | 15117 | 3492 | ... | 415610 |
| | ·1 | 2·6 | 5·9 | 9·6 | 11·1 | 12·2 | 11·7 | 11·6 | 11·3 | 10·7 | 8·8 | 3·6 | ·8 | | |
| 1889 | 438 | 11622 | 26949 | 41908 | 48542 | 52098 | 50222 | 50713 | 48581 | 44432 | 37264 | 15114 | 3425 | ... | 431308 |
| | ·1 | 2·7 | 6·2 | 9·7 | 11·3 | 12·1 | 11·6 | 11·8 | 11·3 | 10·3 | 8·6 | 3·5 | ·8 | | |
| 1890 | 407 | 11737 | 27142 | 42590 | 48777 | 54019 | 50650 | 51726 | 50326 | 45794 | 36881 | 14734 | 3273 | ... | 438056 |
| | ·1 | 2·7 | 6·2 | 9·7 | 11·1 | 12·3 | 11·6 | 11·8 | 11·5 | 10·5 | 8·4 | 3·4 | ·7 | | |
| 1891 | 458 | 12019 | 27600 | 43242 | 50482 | 54409 | 52956 | 51969 | 51130 | 47885 | 38155 | 14570 | 3232 | ... | 448107 |
| | ·1 | 2·7 | 6·2 | 9·6 | 11·3 | 12·1 | 11·8 | 11·6 | 11·4 | 10·7 | 8·5 | 3·3 | ·7 | | |
| 1892 | 407 | 13198 | 29572 | 44982 | 51895 | 55658 | 52626 | 53931 | 52036 | 48725 | 42207 | 16150 | 3755 | ... | 465142 |
| | ·1 | 2·8 | 6·3 | 9·7 | 11·1 | 12·0 | 11·3 | 11·6 | 11·2 | 10·5 | 9·1 | 3·5 | ·8 | | |
| 1893 | 423 | 13491 | 30407 | 46819 | 52727 | 55518 | 53465 | 53736 | 53743 | 49821 | 43145 | 18218 | 4310 | ... | 475823 |
| | ·1 | 2·8 | 6·4 | 9·8 | 11·1 | 11·7 | 11·2 | 11·3 | 11·3 | 10·5 | 9·1 | 3·8 | ·9 | | |
| 1894 | 454 | 12812 | 30478 | 47544 | 54640 | 55479 | 54080 | 54598 | 53235 | 51826 | 45088 | 19858 | 4968 | ... | 485060 |
| | ·1 | 2·6 | 6·3 | 9·8 | 11·3 | 11·4 | 11·1 | 11·3 | 11·0 | 10·7 | 9·3 | 4·1 | 1·0 | | |
| 1895 | 329 | 12785 | 29818 | 47151 | 54577 | 56639 | 53878 | 55287 | 55242 | 52280 | 48358 | 23000 | 5776 | ... | 495120 |
| | ·1 | 2·6 | 6·0 | 9·5 | 110 | 11·4 | 10·9 | 11·2 | 11·1 | 10·6 | 9·8 | 4·6 | 1·2 | | |
| 1896 | 400 | 14457 | 32419 | 48596 | 53718 | 56963 | 55346 | 55851 | 55392 | 54182 | 49337 | 25182 | 6246 | | 508089 |
| | ·1 | 2·8 | 6·4 | 9·6 | 10·6 | 11·2 | 10·9 | 11·0 | 10·9 | 10·7 | 9·7 | 4·9 | 1·2 | | |
| 1897 | 348 | 14215 | 32341 | 50091 | 54341 | 56964 | 55762 | 56687 | 55797 | 54261 | 51065 | 28625 | 6602 | ... | 517099 |
| | ·1 | 2·7 | 6·3 | 9·7 | 10·5 | 11·0 | 10·8 | 10·9 | 10·8 | 10·5 | 9·9 | 5·5 | 1·3 | | |
| 1898 | 295 | 13742 | 32274 | 51282 | 55689 | 55711 | 54798 | 56385 | 56646 | 54557 | 51307 | 29806 | 6519 | ... | 519011 |
| | ·1 | 2·6 | 6·2 | 9·9 | 10·7 | 10·7 | 10·6 | 10·9 | 10·9 | 105 | 9·9 | 5·7 | 1·3 | | |
| 1899 | 214 | 14411 | 32435 | 51808 | 56559 | 57577 | 54377 | 56079 | 56474 | 55535 | 52598 | 32688 | 7074 | ... | 527829 |
| | ·1 | 2·7 | 6·2 | 9·8 | 107 | 10·9 | 10·3 | 10·6 | 10·7 | 10·5 | 10·0 | 6·2 | 1·3 | | |

| At Lady Day. | Under 3 years. | 3 and under 4 years. | 4 and under 5 years. | 5 and under 6 years. | 6 and under 7 years. | 7 and under 8 years. | 8 and under 9 years. | 9 and under 10 years. | 10 and under 11 years. | 11 and under 12 years. | 12 and under 13 years. | 13 and under 14 years. | 14 and under 15 years. | 15 years and over. | Totals. |
|---|---|---|---|---|---|---|---|---|---|---|---|---|---|---|---|
| 1900 | 255 | 13269 | 32488 | 51427 | 56566 | 57941 | 55631 | 55302 | 55908 | 54962 | 53191 | 33276 | 5888 | 1075 | 527179 |
| | ·1 | 2·5 | 6·2 | 9·8 | 10·7 | 11·0 | 10·5 | 10·5 | 10·6 | 10·4 | 10·1 | 6·3 | 1·1 | ·2 | |
| 1901 | 174 | 12589 | 31770 | 52021 | 55109 | 58460° | 55956 | 56572 | 55031† | 53879 | 53180 | 40675 | 6015 | 1171 | 532602 |
| | ·1 | 2·3 | 5·9 | 9·7 | 10·3 | 11·0 | 10·5 | 10·6 | 10·5 | 10·1 | 10·0 | 7·6 | 1·2 | ·2 | |
| 1902 | 191 | 12686 | 31738 | 52515 | 55589 | 58277° | 55799 | 56942 | 55760† | 53662 | 52935 | 48762 | 6192 | 966 | 542014 |
| | ·1 | 2·3 | 5·8 | 9·7 | 10·3 | 10·7 | 10·3 | 10·5 | 10·3 | 9·9 | 9·8 | 9·0 | 1·1 | ·2 | |
| 1903 | 181 | 13936 | 32927 | 53488 | 55446 | 59311° | 54909 | 55903 | 56104† | 54364 | 52492 | 48267 | 6105 | 1042 | 544475 |
| | ·1 | 2·5 | 6·0 | 9·8 | 10·2 | 10·9 | 10·1 | 10·3 | 10·3 | 10·0 | 9·6 | 8·9 | 1·1 | ·2 | |

° This number includes all children in Boys', Girls', and Mixed departments who were of any age under 8 years.
† This number includes all children in Infants' departments over 10 years of age.

B.—STANDARDS TABLE.

Number and percentage of children below Standard I. and in each Standard on the Roll for 18 years.

| At Lady-Day. | Below I. | I. | II. | III. | IV. | V. | VI. | VII. | Ex.-VII. | Total. |
|---|---|---|---|---|---|---|---|---|---|---|
| 1886 | 99757 | 75287 | 56633 | 51267 | 44038 | 29201 | 14805 | *4599 | ... | 375587 |
|  | *26·6* | *20·0* | *15·1* | *13·7* | *11·7* | *7·8* | *3·9* | *1·2* | ... |  |
| 1887 | 111599 | 80716 | 59819 | 53028 | 45695 | 32453 | 17154 | °5508 | ... | 405972 |
|  | *27·5* | *19·9* | *14·7* | *13·1* | *11·2* | *8·0* | *4·2* | *1·4* | ... |  |
| 1888 | 111911 | 80369 | 62319 | 54541 | 46778 | 33777 | 19276 | 5953 | 686 | 415610 |
|  | *26·9* | *19·3* | *15·0* | *13·1* | *11·3* | *8·1* | *4·7* | *1·4* | *·2* |  |
| 1889 | 119813 | 81293 | 62715 | 56545 | 48725 | 34501 | 20368 | 6583 | 765 | 431308 |
|  | *27·8* | *18·9* | *14·5* | *13·1* | *11·3* | *8·0* | *4·7* | *1·5* | *·2* |  |
| 1890 | 121968 | 81364 | 62878 | 57179 | 50222 | 36134 | 20494 | 6791 | 1026 | 438056 |
|  | *27·8* | *18·6* | *14·4* | *13·1* | *11·5* | *8·3* | *4·6* | *1·5* | *·2* |  |
| 1891 | 129241 | 83161 | 64203 | 57115 | 49410 | 36365 | 20784 | 6748 | 1080 | 448107 |
|  | *28·9* | *18·6* | *14·3* | *12·8* | *11·0* | *8·1* | *4·6* | *1·5* | *·2* |  |
| 1892 | 137492 | 85710 | 66474 | 58471 | 50126 | 36376 | 21309 | 7552 | 1632 | 465142 |
|  | *29·6* | *18·4* | *14·3* | *12·6* | *10·8* | *7·8* | *4·6* | *1·6* | *·3* |  |
| 1893 | 142612 | 85542 | 67626 | 60919 | 50631 | 36632 | 21676 | 8026 | 2159 | 475823 |
|  | *30·0* | *18·0* | *14·2* | *12·8* | *10·6* | *7·7* | *4·6* | *1·7* | *·4* |  |
| 1894 | 145477 | 87020 | 68794 | 61154 | 52160 | 37263 | 22363 | 8285 | 2544 | 485060 |
|  | *30·0* | *17·9* | *14·2* | *12·6* | *10·8* | *7·7* | *4·6* | *1·7* | *·5* |  |
| 1895 | 147028 | 85672 | 70403 | 62835 | 53445 | 39226 | 23673 | 10060 | 2778 | 495120 |
|  | *29·7* | *17·3* | *14·2* | *12·7* | *10·8* | *7·9* | *4·8* | *2·0* | *·6* |  |
| 1896 | 151344 | 84188 | 70830 | 64057 | 55056 | 41470 | 25899 | 11521 | 3724 | 508089 |
|  | *29·8* | *16·6* | *13·9* | *12·6* | *10·8* | *8·2* | *5·1* | *2·3* | *·7* |  |
| 1897 | 155270 | 83170 | 69140 | 64555 | 56494 | 43569 | 27591 | 13017 | 4293 | 517099 |
|  | *30·0* | *16·1* | *13·4* | *12·5* | *10·9* | *8·4* | *5·4* | *2·5* | *·8* |  |
| 1898 | 167296 | 83520 | 67963 | 63160 | 54790 | 41563 | 25517 | 11529 | 3673 | 519011 |
|  | *32·2* | *16·1* | *13·1* | *12·2* | *10·6* | *8·0* | *4·9* | *2·2* | *·7* |  |
| 1899 | 171205 | 83463 | 69812 | 63348 | 54736 | 42706 | 26142 | 12552 | 3865 | 527829 |
|  | *32·5* | *15·8* | *13·2* | *12·0* | *10·4* | *8·1* | *4·9* | *2·4* | *·7* |  |
| 1900 | 170433 | 81945 | 68286 | 62990 | 55857 | 42616 | 27498 | 13336 | 4218 | 527179 |
|  | *32·3* | *15·5* | *13·0* | *12·0* | *10·6* | *8·1* | *5·2* | *2·5* | *·8* |  |
| 1901 | 167120 | 82928 | 68130 | 64002 | 56159 | 45262 | 29220 | 15382 | 4399 | 532602 |
|  | *31·4* | *15·6* | *12·8* | *12·0* | *10·5* | *8·5* | *5·5* | *2·9* | *·8* |  |
| 1902 | 163061 | 83817 | 69000 | 65343 | 57562 | 47679 | 32736 | 18103 | 4713 | 542014 |
|  | *30·1* | *15·5* | *12·8* | *12·1* | *10·6* | *8·8* | *6·0* | *3·3* | *·8* |  |
| 1903 | 160064 | 85268 | 70502 | 65059 | 58560 | 48215 | 33076 | 18432 | 5299 | 544475 |
|  | *29·4* | *15·7* | *12·9* | *11·9* | *10·8* | *8·9* | *6·1* | *3·4* | *·9* |  |

* Number of children in Standards VII. and Ex-VII.

## AVERAGE NUMBER OF CHILDREN IN ATTENDANCE PER TEACHER.

The average number of children per adult teacher—illustrated by the Diagram on the opposite page—has been calculated by dividing the number of children in average attendance by the number of adult teachers, including Head teachers, and excluding Pupil Teachers and Instructors in Manual Training, Domestic Subjects, &c.[1]

[1] See Table on page 160.

Diagram showing the number of children in attendance per adult Teacher—1874-1906.

It will be seen that the number of children per adult teacher has decreased from 80·5 in 1873 to 41·9 in 1903—*i.e.* the proportion of adult teachers to scholars has almost doubled. The improvement is still greater if the number of special teachers be taken into account. If all the teachers of Domestic Subjects and Manual Training, and half the number of peripatetic teachers of Drawing and Modern Languages, were added to the total number of adult teachers, the number of children per adult teacher would be 80·5 in 1873, 58·9 in 1883, 48·2 in 1893, and 39·4 in 1903.

## GENERAL STATISTICS.

### CALCULATED TO LADY-DAY EACH YEAR.

| Year. | No. of Schools. | No. of Departments. | | | | | *Average Number in Attendance. | No. of Adult Teachers (including Head, Asst. and Supply, and Ex-P.Ts.). | | | No. of Children in Average Attendance per Adult Teacher. | No. of P.Ts., Candidates, and Probationers. | | |
|---|---|---|---|---|---|---|---|---|---|---|---|---|---|---|
| | | Boys. | Girls. | Mxd. | Infnts. | Total. | | Men. | Women. | Total. | | Boys. | Girls. | Total. |
| 1873 | 138 | 71 | 50 | 29 | 57 | 207 | 22145 | 109 | 166 | 275 | 80·5 | 247 | 401 | 648 |
| 1874 | 169 | 100 | 81 | 37 | 83 | 301 | 47346 | 212 | 343 | 555 | 85·3 | 421 | 748 | 1169 |
| 1875 | 195 | 137 | 121 | 30 | 130 | 418 | 76941 | 393 | 655 | 1048 | 73·4 | 511 | 1181 | 1692 |
| 1876 | 216 | 164 | 146 | 34 | 142 | 486 | 98146 | 523 | 838 | 1361 | 72·1 | 509 | 1250 | 1759 |
| 1877 | 238 | 188 | 168 | 34 | 177 | 567 | 119729 | 647 | 1038 | 1685 | 71·1 | 516 | 1312 | 1828 |
| 1878 | 272 | 228 | 207 | 31 | 214 | 680 | 152668 | 885 | 1493 | 2378 | 64·2 | 499 | 1252 | 1751 |
| 1879 | 299 | 248 | 218 | 46 | 226 | 738 | 168167 | 1074 | 1790 | 2864 | 58·7 | 455 | 1121 | 1576 |
| 1880 | 305 | 257 | 234 | 41 | 240 | 772 | 186813 | 1177 | 1989 | 3166 | 59·0 | 393 | 1036 | 1429 |
| 1881 | 301 | 262 | 242 | 37 | 252 | 793 | 197718 | 1241 | 2115 | 3356 | 58·9 | 361 | 1110 | 1471 |
| 1882 | 310 | 279 | 257 | 35 | 270 | 841 | 225654 | 1352 | 2333 | 3685 | 61·2 | 379 | 1167 | 1546 |
| 1883 | 324 | 289 | 271 | 36 | 280 | 876 | 242394 | 1497 | 2590 | 4087 | 59·3 | 360 | 1136 | 1496 |
| 1884 | 357 | 318 | 296 | 41 | 304 | 959 | 275330 | 1692 | 3069 | 4761 | 57·8 | 342 | 1081 | 1423 |
| 1885 | 371 | 337 | 316 | 34 | 325 | 1012 | 285807 | 1916 | 3595 | 5511 | 52·1† | 399 | 1269 | 1668 |
| 1886 | 384 | 354 | 338 | 33 | 344 | 1069 | 295753 | 2076 | 4065 | 6141 | 48·3 | 407 | 1236 | 1643 |
| 1887 | 397 | 365 | 353 | 30 | 360 | 1108 | 319848 | 2185 | 4288 | 6473 | 49·8 | 407 | 1407 | 1814 |
| 1888 | 393 | 368 | 361 | 28 | 369 | 1126 | 328405 | 2207 | 4359 | 6566 | 50·4 | 430 | 1530 | 1960 |
| 1889 | 396 | 370 | 365 | 28 | 374 | 1137 | 342321 | 2319 | 4579 | 6898 | 50·1 | 396 | 1560 | 1956 |
| 1890 | 404 | 373 | 367 | 34 | 376 | 1150 | 345746 | 2396 | 4770 | 7166 | 48·8 | 344 | 1527 | 1871 |
| 1891 | 410 | 381 | 371 | 37 | 382 | 1171 | 347857 | 2476 | 4974 | 7450 | 47·4 | 324 | 1450 | 1774 |
| 1892 | 413 | 382 | 372 | 41 | 388 | 1183 | 362585 | 2574 | 5166 | 7740 | 47·5 | 308 | 1552 | 1860 |
| 1893 | 419 | 385 | 379 | 40 | 398 | 1202 | 379445 | 2606 | 5188 | 7794 | 49·2 | 277 | 1819 | 2096 |
| 1894 | 426 | 392 | 384 | 46 | 405 | 1227 | 390812 | 2724 | 5470 | 8194 | 48·5 | 328 | 1705 | 2033 |
| 1895 | 433 | 393 | 387 | 55 | 414 | 1249 | 400912 | 2883 | 5796 | 8679 | 46·7 | 385 | 1868 | 2253 |
| 1896 | 448 | 404 | 396 | 65 | 427 | 1292 | 415771 | 3014 | 6079 | 9093 | 46·3 | 427 | 1862 | 2289 |
| 1897 | 457 | 409 | 404 | 73 | 437 | 1323 | 4219 0 | 3103 | 6367 | 9470 | 45·3 | 435 | 1818 | 2253 |
| 1898 | 464 | 417 | 412 | 72 | 445 | 1346 | 429853 | 3197 | 6545 | 9742 | 44·7 | 416 | 1947 | 2363 |
| 1899 | 472 | 425 | 422 | 72 | 455 | 1374 | 438434 | 3276 | 6614 | 9890 | 45·3‡ | 506 | 2345 | 2851 |
| 1900 | 481 | 430 | 427 | 75 | 463 | 1395 | 439744 | 3458 | 7080 | 10538 | 42·6 | 459 | 2435 | 2894 |
| 1901 | 487 | 431 | 430 | 79 | 468 | 1408 | 446866 | 3532 | 7291 | 10823 | 42·0 | 405 | 2414 | 2819 |
| 1902 | 501 | 444 | 440 | 83 | 483 | 1450 | 462840 | 3668 | 7567 | 11235 | 42·2 | 363 | 2477 | 2840 |
| 1903 | 509 | 441 | 438 | 97 | 490 | 1466 | 475150 | 3769 | 7832 | 11601 | 41·9 | 339 | 2465 | 2804 |

* From 1873 to 1878 the figures relate to the quarter ended Lady-day ; from 1879 to 1886, to the half-year ended Lady-day ; and from 1887 to 1903, to the year ended Lady-day.

† After 1884 one-half of the number of supply teachers has been deducted in calculating the average size of classes. Previously the number of supply teachers could not be ascertained with reliability.

‡ The apparent increase in the average size of classes in this year is due to the fact that in consequence of a change in the date of the Scholarship examination in 1894, and in the apprenticeship of pupil teachers, only a small number of pupil teachers became ex-pupil teachers in the early part of 1899.

## TEACHERS' SALARIES.

### I.—Temporary Arrangements—1870-1872.

The first schools with which the Board had to deal were transferred Voluntary schools. It has been pointed out elsewhere that the policy of the Board was to make as little alteration as possible in the management of these schools, in order to avoid friction during a period of transition. In pursuance of this policy the Board decided to leave to the Managers the power to fix the salaries of teachers.[1]

The method of payment adopted in nearly all Voluntary schools prior to 1870, was dictated by necessity rather than by convenience. The funds of the Voluntary Managers consisted in School Fees, Subscriptions, and Government Grant. The amount of the latter, which generally formed the larger part of the income of the school, was liable to fluctuate with the results of examination. It would have been difficult in such circumstances for the Managers to pay their teachers an adequate fixed salary. The plan usually adopted was to pay a small fixed salary periodically and to give the teachers a share of the grant.

This system was financially advantageous to the Managers, because it interested the teachers in the amount of grant earned; but it intensified the evils inherent in "payment by results." It was inevitable that a teacher, with the best intentions, should be driven to look upon the pupil as a grant-earner. From the teacher's point of view the system was no less unsatisfactory. His fixed income was but a pittance; his comfort was dependent upon chances over which he had but imperfect control.

### II.—The First Scale of the Board—1872-1883.

It soon became evident that the Board could not permanently permit the amount of teachers' salaries to be fixed by the Managers of the individual schools. Under such a method there could be no fair adjustment of remuneration to services throughout the schools as a whole, and this caused inequalities which were certain to give rise to discontent. In October, 1871, the School Management Committee decided that they would fix the salaries of teachers; and early in 1872 the Committee recommended the establishment of a scale of salaries for all the teachers in their service.

The scale was based upon the method of payment adopted in Voluntary Schools. It provided for a fixed salary, paid monthly, and in the case of teachers, in Boys' and Girls' departments, a share of the Government grant, paid annually. The teachers in Infant schools were to receive, instead of a share of the Government grant, a payment of 5s. for each child who was passed into a Junior school on the report of a School Board Inspector, and was qualified in point of age to be presented in the First Standard at the first examination held after he had entered the Junior school.[2]

One-half of the Government grant, in schools other than Infant schools, was paid to the head teacher, and the other half was divided among the assistant teachers,

---

[1] See *ante*, p. 82.　　　　[2] Board Minutes, Vol. II., pp. 104, 115, 207.

**M**

according to the discretion of the Managers, after consultation with the head teacher; but only one-fourth was to be given in schools where only one assistant teacher was employed. In addition a teacher might receive £5 a year for the instruction of each male pupil teacher, and £4 for the instruction of each female pupil teacher; but, as a rule, no teacher was to instruct more than six pupil teachers. A further sum of £20, together with half the Government grant, was to be allowed for holding an Evening school. But as the first attempt of the Board to establish Evening schools was a failure, and was abandoned in 1875, this last allowance did not prove a very fruitful source of income.

The scale of salaries was based upon the assumption that the Board would not provide residences for the teachers, and this has never been done in the schools built by the Board. The scale was as follows:—

| | Fixed Annual Salary. | |
| --- | --- | --- |
| | Males.<br>Maximum. | Females.<br>Maximum. |
| | £ | £ |
| HEAD TEACHERS :— | | |
| Being Certificated (Art. 53) :— | | |
| First Class (Art. 54 & 63) ... ... ... ... ... ... | 200 | 110 |
| Second Class :— | | |
| (a) Stamped Certificate (Art. 104) ... ... ... ... | 120 | 70 |
| (b) Unstamped Certificate (Art. 46) ... ... ... ... | 110 | 65 |
| Third Class (Art. 57) ... ... ... ... ... ... | 100 | 60 |
| ASSISTANT TEACHERS :— | | |
| Being Certificated Teachers ... ... ... ... ... ... | 100 | 60 |
| Being Probationers (Art. 51) :— | | |
| First Division ... ... ... ... ... ... ... | 80 | 50 |
| Second Division ... ... ... ... ... ... ... | 75 | 45 |
| Third Division ... ... ... ... ... ... ... | 70 | 42 |
| Fourth Division (Art. 49) ... ... ... ... ... ... | 65 | 40 |
| Being Ex-Pupil Teachers (Art. 79 and 80) | | |
| Second and subsequent years ... ... ... ... ... | 55 | 35 |
| First year ... ... ... ... ... ... ... | 45 | 30 |
| | Weekly Salary. | |
| | Males. | Females. |
| PUPIL TEACHERS :— | | |
| First year of Apprenticeship ... ... ... ... ... | 6s. | 4s. |
| Second ,, ,, ... ... ... ... ... ... | 7s. | 5s. |
| Third ,, ,, ... ... ... ... ... ... | 8s. | 6s. |
| Fourth ,, ,, ... ... ... ... ... ... | 10s. | 8s. |
| Fifth ,, ,, ... ... ... ... ... ... | 12s. | 10s. |

The scale did not provide either a graduation of salary for head teachers according to the amount of accommodation, or for fixed increases of salary from a minimum to a maximum. But some informal graduation according to the qualifications of teachers was evidently intended beyond that indicated in the scale. The School Management Committee, in their covering report, stated:—

That it is not intended that the maximum of the fixed annual stipend should be given to any except teachers of experience and tried ability. Beyond the distinctions pointed out by the possession of certificates of different classes. there will be found amongst teachers a very wide diversity of qualifications. Some can teach Music, Drawing and Drill ; some can teach one, or the other, or none of these subjects. The Board must evidently reserve a margin for the use of discretionary power to meet such a variety of cases, which really can be met only as they arise.

This, however, formed no part of the scheme as adopted by the Board. It appears that the fixed scale was treated practically as a maximum scale, and that salaries were awarded within the maxima, after consideration of the individual qualifications of the candidate for appointment.

The most noticeable feature of the scale is the disparity between the salaries of male and female teachers. Before the year was out this disparity was remedied by a revision of the scale, which considerably raised the salaries of all female teachers except head teachers of the first class. The salaries of male ex-pupil teachers were also raised and a more elaborate classification of head teachers was adopted.

The allowance in lieu of grant to the head teacher of the Infant school was changed, payment being made under the following resolution:—"Five shillings for each child who has attended school not less than 80 times and who is reported by the School Board Inspector to be fit to pass into a Junior school in respect of the three subjects of Reading, Writing and Arithmetic. If, however, a child fails to pass in more than two subjects, the head teacher is to receive a fee of only 3s. in respect of such child, and if the child fails to pass in more than one subject, a fee of only 1s."

On July 29th, 1874, owing to the difficulty experienced in securing assistant mistresses, the fixed salary of female assistant teachers with certificates of the 1st or 2nd class, and of those on probation for a 2nd class certificate was further increased, and in the following November an addition was made to the salaries of certain female assistants, and to the salaries of male assistant teachers who held additional Drawing and Science qualifications ; distinction was also made, for the first time, in the amount of salary paid to trained and untrained teachers. The report of the School Management Committee of this date recommending the appointment of teachers, contained a provision that in the case of students at college the salary under the scale should be diminished by £5 in cases of students who failed to obtain the full Drawing certificate, and by £5 or £2 10s. in the case of male and female assistants respectively who failed to pass in the first division of the Certificate Examination.[1]

This policy of allowing increased salary to teachers who possessed additional qualifications was further developed on the 9th December, 1874. Male teachers received an increase of £10 per annum, and female teachers an increase of £5 per annum, who held the following addditional qualifications :—

    (i.) The full Drawing certificate.

    (ii.) (In the case of males) three Advanced Science certificates.
            (In the case of females) one Advanced Science certificate.

---

[1] Board Minutes, Vol. IV., p. 1241.

When only one additional qualification was held, male teachers were granted an increase of £5, and female teachers an increase of £2 10s. The scale was also amplified by further distinction being made in point of fixed salary between teachers trained for two years, trained for one year, or untrained.

Another important change was effected in July, 1875. For the fixed annual salary paid to assistant teachers a slightly rising scale was substituted, increases of £5 men and £3 women being allowed on the receipt of parchment certificate, and for each subsequent good report, to the maximum of £110 men and £90 women. In the case of head teachers the minimum commencing salaries were fixed at £110 for men and £90 for women, together with an allowance for parchment certificate and for each good report of £10 for men and £6 for women, and increases were granted of £10 and £6 respectively, to the maximum of £210 for men and £150 for women.

The annual salary in the case of both head and assistant teachers was also increased for the possession of Drawing and Science certificates, and an additional amount of £10 was allowed for the possession of the B.A. degree in the case of men, or in the case of women of five special certificates of Higher Proficiency granted by the London University.

These changes represent the final development of the first scale of the Board, which was based upon a fixed payment, augmented by a share of the Government grant. The following table shows the result of them:—

SALARIES FOR HEAD TEACHERS.

| | Male. | Female. |
|---|---|---|
| | £ | £ |
| Subject to the rule that the commencing salary of a head teacher shall in no case be less than ... ... ... ... ... ... ... ... ... | 110 | 90 |
| The amount of salary on appointment will be based upon the result of the Certificate Examination as set out in Table I., together with an increase for receipt of parchment of ... ... ... ... ... ... | 10 | 6 |
| And such further increase, in consideration of valuable experience and proved superior ability, as may seem proper to the School Management Committee, in each case, considered on its merits; such addition, however, not to exceed in any case ... ... ... ... ... ... ... | 60 | 40 |
| After appointment the increase will be for each "Good Report"... ... ... | 10 | 6 |
| So as to rise to a maximum of ... ... ... ... ... ... ... ... | 210 | 150 |

SALARIES FOR ASSISTANT TEACHERS.

| | Fixed Annual Salary. | |
|---|---|---|
| | Male. | Female. |
| A.—Ex-Pupil Teachers:— | £ | £ |
| In 1st year ... ... ... ... ... ... ... ... ... | 55 | 50 |
| In 2nd, or higher year ... ... ... ... ... ... ... | 60 | 55 |
| (Subject to same Rules as at present) | | |

| | Fixed Annual Salary. | |
|---|---|---|
| | **Male.** | **Female.** |

| | Male £ | Female £ |
|---|---|---|
| B.—Teachers under Probation :— | | |
| (a) Teachers who have passed the Certificate Examination, but who have not been Pupil Teachers nor trained :— | | |
| 3rd Division ... ... ... ... ... ... ... ... | 60 | 55 |
| 2nd ,, ... ... ... ... ... ... ... ... | 65 | 60 |
| 1st ,, ... ... ... ... ... ... ... ... | 70 | 65 |
| (b) Teachers who have been Pupil Teachers, and who have passed the Certificate Examination, but who have not been trained, or— | | |
| (c) Teachers who have been trained for one year, or— | | |
| (d) Teachers who have been trained for two years, but have taken the first year's papers :— | | |
| 3rd Division ... ... ... ... ... ... ... ... | 65 | 60 |
| 2nd ,, ... ... ... ... ... ... ... ... | 70 | 65 |
| 1st ,, ... ... ... ... ... ... ... ... | 75 | 70 |
| (e) Teachers who have been trained for two years, and have taken the second year's papers :— | | |
| 3rd Division ... ... ... ... ... ... ... ... | 70 | 65 |
| 2nd ,, ... ... ... ... ... ... ... ... | 75 | 70 |
| 1st ,, ... ... ... ... ... ... ... ... | 80 | 75 |
| C.—Teachers with Parchments :— | | |
| The above Salaries will be increased on the receipt of parchment, and on every subsequent "Good Report," by ... ... ... ... | 5 | 3 |
| So as to rise to a maximum of ... ... ... ... ... | 110 | 90 |

The annual salary in the case of both assistant and head teachers, as determined above, will be further increased for the following qualifications :—

| | Male. £ | Female. £ |
|---|---|---|
| Full D ... ... ... ... ... ... ... ... ... ... ... | 5 | 5 |
| Three or more advanced Science Certificates... ... ... ... ... ... | 5 | 5 |
| One advanced Science Certificate ... ... ... ... ... ... | ... | 2 10 |
| A Bachelor's Degree in Arts in any University of Great Britain or Ireland, or, in the case of women, five Special Certificates of higher proficiency (of which not more than two shall be for languages) granted by the London University ... ... ... ... ... ... ... ... | 10 | 10 |

### PAYMENT FOR INSTRUCTION IN DRAWING.

The whole of the Drawing grant, with the exception of £1 granted by the Science and Art Department for expenses incurred in conducting the examination, will be divided amongst the actual teachers of Drawing, other than pupil teachers, in proportion to the amounts earned by their pupils respectively, provided always that the teachers are qualified by the Science and Art Department to teach in respect of the branch or branches of Drawing which they have actually taught.

Under this scale the qualifications for Headships were further defined. As a rule only candidates who had been trained for two years, and had passed in the first or second division on second year's papers, and had received the parchment certificate, were eligible.

This somewhat complex scheme was evolved out of the simple scale of 1872 in less than four years, but the only salient changes were the approximation of the salaries of women towards those of men, and the introduction of a scale of increases of salary.

### III.—The Second Scale of the Board, 1883-1899.

The scale of salaries thus laboriously evolved remained unaltered, in any material respect, for eight years. During that period changes took place which tended to make the scheme unsatisfactory. In 1875 the Board had erected 93 schools. In 1883 the number had increased to 260. These schools varied greatly in accommodation ; most of them were much larger than the transferred schools controlled by the Board when the first scheme of salaries was formulated. A scale for head teachers, therefore, which paid no regard to the size of the school had become an anomaly. In 1872, when it was decided to base the scheme of salaries upon a fixed salary, augmented by a share of the Government grant, the Board calculated that the grant would average between six and nine shillings per child. In 1874 the actual average grant per scholar was 5s. 4d. In 1883 it had risen to 15s. 8d. The teachers' shares, and more especially the head teachers' shares of this grant had increased very rapidly ; and in some of the larger schools the head teachers were receiving incomes far larger than had been contemplated when the scheme was adopted. A further defect was to be found in the fact that the better class of school, which was easier and more attractive to work in, earned a higher grant than the poorer school, situated in a dismal locality, and attended by waifs and strays.

Some of these considerations had evidently pressed themselves upon the Board so early as 1878, for in February of that year the Board passed the following resolution :— " That the School Management Committee be requested to consider and lay before the Board some plan by which its teachers may be paid more generally and to a larger degree by fixed salaries, and also to suggest some means by which those teachers who distinguish themselves in small schools, or schools of peculiar difficulty, may, in time, be promoted to more desirable positions.[1]

One of the main obstacles to the adoption of any such revision of the scale was the fact that the teacher, on appointment, acquired a vested interest in a share of the Government grant. In order to meet this difficulty the Board, in the following November, resolved :— " That the School Management Committee do notify to the teachers to be now or hereafter appointed that the Board, having under consideration the present scale of salaries of teachers, their appointments will be subject to such alteration of that scale as may be hereinafter determined upon by the Board."[2]

The School Management Committee considered the subject for more than five years, and during that period they presented two schemes to the Board which were rejected. The difficulties which the Committee had to encounter related chiefly to the

---

[1] Board Minutes, Vol. VIII., p. 317.        [2] Board Minutes, Vol. IX., p. 677.

scale of salaries for head teachers; and it was upon the proposals for the salaries of head teachers that both schemes were eventually wrecked.

The first scheme was brought forward in March, 1879.[1]  With infinite pains the Committee had fixed a maximum and minimum salary for the head teacher of each department of every school under the control of the Board, based upon the accommodation of that department.  Annual increases were to be given at the rate of £10 for men, and £6 for women, upon a "good" report; and of £5 for men, and £3 for women, upon a "moderately good" report.  But if the Education Department made deductions from the grant on account of faults of instruction, discipline, or for other specified reasons, the head of the department so fined was to make good such deductions out of salary to the extent of £20.  A fixed and graduated scale of salaries, with annual increases, was proposed for assistant teachers.  After some discussion the scheme was referred back to the School Management Committee for further consideration, with instructions to bring up a "more detailed report as to the financial effects of the scale."[2]

The reference back proved the death-blow of the proposed scale.  No further suggestion was made by the School Management Committee for more than a year.  In June, 1880, a new scheme was propounded, based upon somewhat different principles.  Instead of attempting to fix a salary for each head teacher it provided a graduated scale in the following form :—

1. Head masters of departments with accommodation :—
      Under 200, £1 per school place.
      201 to 400, £200 and 10s. for each school place beyond 200.
      401 to 800, £300 and 5s. for each school place beyond 400.
      801 and over, £400 and 2s. 6d. for each school place beyond 800.

2. Head mistresses (Girls).—Three-fourths of the salary of a head master of a department with the same accommodation.

3. Head mistresses (Infants).—Three-fourths of the salary of a head master of a department which provided three-fourths the accommodation of the Infants' department.

It was further provided that no head master should receive a less salary than £150, and no head mistress a less salary than three-fourths of £150.  The Board was to be empowered to give annual bonuses, upon good reports, of £20 to a head master and £15 to a headmistress.

For assistant teachers a graduated scale was provided, with power to grant an annual bonus, upon good reports, of £10 to a male and £8 to a female teacher.[3]

The scale was to apply to all teachers appointed since November 20th, 1878.[4]

A prolonged debate took place upon these proposals, which lasted until November 11th, when the whole scheme was referred back to the School Management Committee for further consideration.

This second failure to produce an acceptable scheme seems to have caused a distaste

---

[1] Board Minutes, Vol. X., p. 652.  For the scheme, see pp. 847 *et seq.*
[2] May 14th, 1879, Board Minutes, Vol. X., p. 1001.
[3] Board Minutes, Vol. XIII., pp. 114, 127.
[4] See *ante*, p. 166.

for the question. It still remained under the consideration of the School Management Committee, but the Board left it severely alone for two years. Then, in May, 1882, the Committee, mindful of past difficulties, invited the Board to lay down certain definite principles upon which a scheme might be based, and they recommended :—

1. That, as a rule, the salaries of the head teachers shall vary with the accommodation of the school.

2. That a special addition be made to the salaries of teachers in schools of special difficulty." [1]

To the first of these proposals an amendment was carried substituting the words " average attendance " for " accommodation," and in this altered form the recommendations were approved. [2]

This resolution did not stand long unaltered. In the following July a proposal was made to rescind it, and eventually the following resolution was adopted :—

" That the School Management Committee be instructed, in the proposed new scheme of teachers' salaries, to propose, for each department, a commencing salary for the head teacher, regard being had, in fixing such salary, to accommodation, to average attendance as compared with accommodation, to locality, and to surrounding circumstances. [3]

Shortly before this resolution was adopted the School Management Committee had brought up a report dealing solely with the question of the commutation of the salaries of teachers who had received a share of the Government grant under the scheme which it was proposed to repeal. It will be remembered that these teachers fell into two classes : first, those who were appointed prior to the resolution of the Board of November, 1879 ; and, second, those who were appointed after that date, with notice that their salaries were subject to any alteration that the Board might make in the scale. [4] When that resolution was passed it was assumed that a new scale would be adopted in a very short time ; but five years had elapsed and no change had been effected. It seemed therefore unreasonable that these teachers should suffer any diminution of a stipend so long enjoyed, and the Committee therefore proposed that all teachers permanently engaged at the time when the new scale should be adopted should receive their old fixed salaries and in addition a commuted payment in lieu of Government grant. The commutation was to be based upon the average of the Government grant for the previous three years. [5]

The Board discussed this proposal until October, 1882, when the inevitable amendment to refer the question back to the Committee was moved: " with instructions to bring up a complete and amended scale of salaries." [6] Before the Board could adequately discuss this proposal, the Committee produced their completed scheme. [7]

The new scale was adopted on December 20th, 1883, and was made to apply to all teachers who were appointed to commence work on or after the preceding October 1st.

It provided that certificated assistant teachers should receive commencing salaries

[1] Board Minutes, Vol. XVI., p. 845.
[2] *Ib.*, p. 918.
[3] *Ib.*, Vol., XIX., p. 422.
[4] See *ante*, p. 166.
[5] Board Minutes, Vol. XIX , p. 245.

[6] Board Minutes, p. 655.
[7] Dec. 6th, 1883. The amendment to refer back was thereupon withdrawn. Board Minutes, Vol. XX., pp. 30, 44.

varying from amounts of £60 to £115 for men and £50 to £100 for women, according to training and certificate qualifications and teaching experience, and that these salaries should rise by increase of £5 for men and £3 for women, for each report after the receipt of the parchment certificate which, in the opinion of the School Management Committee, was a good report, to the maximum of £155 and £125 respectively.

Head Teachers received salaries on the basis of the accommodation of the department, the grades being:—

| I. | Accommodation | 180 or under. |
|---|---|---|
| II. | „ | 181 to 280 inclusive. |
| III. | „ | 281 to 380 inclusive. |
| IV. | „ | 381 to 500 inclusive. |
| V. | „ | over 500 |

The commencing salaries of head teachers of Grade I. schools were: masters £150, mistresses (Girls', Mixed, or Infants') £120, and the maxima of the various grades were reached by increases of £5 for men and £4 for women.

The maxima of Grade V. head teachers were, for masters of Boys' or Mixed departments £400, mistresses of Girls' departments or Mixed £300, mistresses of Infants' departments £240.

With regard to the teachers in the Board's service prior to October 1st, 1883, the following resolution was adopted:—

" That, in the case of all certificated assistant teachers and head teachers permanently appointed to commence work before October 1st, 1883, if the average salary received by them is more than the amount due under the new scheme, they be paid that average salary until the salary under the new scheme amounts to that sum; but that any teacher now in the service of the Board may elect to come under the new scheme if he wishes. A head teacher in the service of the Board previous to October, 1883, whose average salary falls between the minimum and maximum of the scale of his school under the new scheme, shall come immediately under the new scheme, and shall proceed by the usual annual rises to the maximum salary of his class."

The scale provided for the recognition of certain schools as of special difficulty, the head teachers of which were to receive £20 and assistant teachers £10 in addition to the ordinary scale salary.

From this date the standard of certificate and other qualifications was gradually raised. On November 14th, 1889, the Board decided " that untrained teachers who have been placed in the third division on the first year's papers will not be appointed by the Board in future. The provisions of this rule do not apply to ex-pupil teachers now in the service of the Board under conditions to the Board rules."

Following on the regulation in the Education Department's Code of 1890 that after January 1st, 1891, only those teachers who had passed the Certificate Examination in the second year's papers would be recognised as certificated, and only those teachers who had passed in the first or second division on the second year's papers would be entitled to superintend pupil teachers, the Board agreed that teachers who at the 1891 or any subsequent Certificate Examination should be placed in the third division on the second year's papers should be appointed only under the condition of sitting again at the Certificate Examination to raise their status and be paid the salary of "Supply" teachers until they had raised their status and were qualified by examination to superintend pupil teachers. This later regulation was on the division of the Certificate Examination into parts in 1897 amended by requiring that for permanent appointment a teacher must have passed in the two parts not lower than equal to the second division —i.e. must be qualified to superintend pupil teachers.

Until 1897 increases of salary were not dependent upon the acquisition of additional qualifications. On March 4th in that year the School Management Committee reported to the Board that they had been considering "the question of requiring teachers entering the service of the Board with low qualifications to take steps to improve their status. They consider it important that, in certain cases of future appointments, teachers should be under the obligation to add to their qualifications, and are of opinion that this end would be obtained by making increases of salary depend upon the teachers increasing their educational attainments up to a certain level."[1] They therefore proposed, and the Board adopted, the following resolution :—

"Assistant teachers appointed to the permanent service of the Board after March 4th, 1897, will not be entitled to any increase of salary prescribed by the scale of the Board (except that for receipt of parchment certificate) unless or until they shall have obtained five points of additional qualifications, as follows[2] :—

Three of these five points were obligatory. All were required to possess or obtain a Drawing subject and the Board's Physical Education certificate. The third obligatory point in the case of teachers in the Senior departments was an Advanced Science certificate, and in the case of teachers in the Infants' departments a recognised Kindergarten certificate. The remaining two points were left to the option of the teacher out of a long list of possible qualifications.

On Lady Day, 1903, there were still 74 head and 5 assistant teachers under the old commuted scale of 1883. The highest salary ever paid under this scale was £460.

## IV.—THE THIRD SCALE OF THE BOARD, 1899.

Except for the small changes which have been enumerated, no attempt was made for nine years to alter fundamentally the scale adopted in 1883. In 1892 the question was resuscitated. On October 6th a motion was made to increase the maximum salary of all male assistants from £155 to £175 by annual increments of £5 for each year of satisfactory service.[3] The "Previous Question" was moved and lost[4] ; and then a second amendment, to refer the question to a Special Committee for consideration and report, was carried. Immediately afterwards another motion was moved and carried, "That it be an instruction to the Special Committee, agreed to be appointed,

---

[1] Board Minutes, Vol. XLVI., p. 892.          [3] Board Minutes, Vol. XXXVII., p. 709.
[2] *Ib.*, 933.          [4] *Ib.*, p. 796.

to further consider and report whether any, and if so, what, alterations should be made in the existing scale of salaries for teachers."

This Special Committee reported to the Board on June 15th, 1893 They dealt with the question of head teachers' salaries. They tested the opinion of the Board on two main propositions. First, that average attendance be the basis of calculation of the salaries to be paid to head teachers. Second, that the maximum salary of a head master shall in no case exceed £350.[1]

The first resolution was defeated by an amendment to refer it back to the Special Committee for consideration and report, " with instructions that the Board are not prepared to deal with a partial scheme for varying the scale of salaries."[2] This amendment, on becoming the main question, was negatived, and thus the proposal to base the salaries of head teachers upon average attendance disappeared. The second proposal of the Special Committee was adopted by the Board, with an addition to the effect that it was only to apply to future appointments.[3]

On November 8th, 1894, the Special Committee complied with the request of the Board for a complete scheme of salaries for men teachers. The scale for head masters was based upon school accommodation.[4]

Head assistant masters were to receive a special salary of £10, in addition to the scale amount, and the maximum of the higher qualified assistant was to be raised to £175. After a considerable amount of debate the whole of the motions arising out of the report, together with all the proposed amendments, were referred to the School Management Committee as an open question, for consideration and report.[5]

The School Management Committee then took up the task, and on October 31st, 1895, they presented a report which dealt only with the salaries of assistant masters. The policy of the proposed scheme was to reduce the minimum salary by £5 and to increase the maximum to £175. Accompanying the report was a detailed statement of the financial effect of the scale.[6] This statement showed that although a slight economy would be effected at first, the scale would eventually prove more costly than that which was then in force. To the first of the twenty motions in which the scheme was propounded an amendment was moved to refer the whole proposal back to the Committee, with an instruction " to refrain from bringing before the Board any proposals for altering the scale of salaries, the effect of which is to increase the aggregate cost payable by the rate-payers."[7] This amendment was lost ; but an amendment quite as fatal to immediate progress was carried, referring the whole of the resolutions back to the Committee, "in order that they may reconsider the financial effect of the proposals and report again to the Board."[8]

A year afterwards the School Management Committee came back to the Board with

[1] Board Minutes, Vol. XXXIX., p. 36.
[2] Ib. p. 1387.
[3] Ib. p. 1389.
[4] Ib. Vol. XLI. p. 1448.
[5] December 13th, 1894, Board Minutes, Vol. XLII., p 99. A motion to increase the maximum salary of male assistants to £175 was also referred to the School Management Committee on January 24·b, 1895. Ib. p. 235.
[6] Board Minutes, Vol. XLIII., pp. 1063, 1082.
[7] Ib., p 1484.
[8] Ib., Vol. XLIV., p. 146.

a proposal that this reference back should be discharged, but even this motion was referred back to them for reconsideration.[1] It was evidently impossible for the members of the Committee to come to any agreement upon the subject. In February, 1897, the Committee once more asked the Board to discharge the reference.[2] But the Board was inexorable. An amendment was carried referring the proposed resolution to a special committee of five.[3]

In January, 1898, the question of a scale for male assistants was again referred to the School Management Committee for consideration and report.[4] It was in reply to this reference that a report was brought up, on May 19th, 1898, which was the basis of the scale adopted in the following year.

Under this scale, which was passed by the Board on March 9th, 1899, the maximum of trained and certificated assistant teachers was raised from £155 to £175 in the case of men, and in that of assistant mistresses from £125 to £140, the commencing salaries, however, in each case, being £5 per annum lower than those under the previous scale.

A distinction was made between the ultimate salaries of teachers trained, and those untrained or trained for one year only; male assistants not fully trained rising to a maximum of £160 and female assistants to a maximum of £130.

The standard of qualification was raised, no certificated teacher who had passed on the second year's papers lower than the equivalent of the second division being eligible for permanent appointment. On the other hand, graduates of a university who had qualified for recognition as certificated teachers were given a place in the scale, and a special salary was provided for graduates who might enter the Board's service with the intention of qualifying for recognition as certificated teachers. An additional commencing salary of £5 was given to teachers who had undergone three years' training or who held a B.A. degree.

The system of grades for assistant teachers was discontinued, and increase of salary was to be granted on the completion of school years of satisfactory service only. The raising of the maximum for assistant teachers necessitated an alteration in the minima and maxima in some of the lower grades of head teacherships. The minima of Grade I. head masters and mistresses were accordingly raised to £175 and £140 respectively, and the restriction to £350 maximum of head masters in the highest grade was removed.

The basis of grading founded on accommodation was varied, and the new grading was fixed as follows:—

|  |  |  |  |  |  |
|---|---|---|---|---|---|
| Grade I. | Accommodation | 200 or under | (former | limit | 180) |
| „ II. | „ | 201 to 300 | ( „ | „ | 181 to 280) |
| „ III. | „ | 301 to 400 | ( „ | „ | 281 to 380) |
| „ IV. | „ | 401 to 600 | ( „ | „ | 381 to 500) |
| „ V. | „ | over 600 | ( „ | „ | over 500) |

A scale was also fixed for teachers in the Higher Grade schools. Teachers appointed under the Higher Grade scale from the ordinary schools were allowed—men £20, and

---

[1] November 19th, 1896. Board Minutes. Vol. XLV., p. 1457.
[2] *Ib.*, Vol. XLVI., p. 814
[3] Board Minutes, Vol. XLVII., p. 157.
[4] *Ib.*, Vol. XLVIII. p. 398.

women £15, in addition to the salaries they were then receiving. The commencing salaries of teachers appointed from outside the Board's service under the Higher Grade scale were fixed at £115 men, and £100 women, and the maximum of all assistants under the Higher Grade scale at £10 higher than that of an assistant teacher in an ordinary school of the Board. The salaries of head teachers of Higher Grade schools were also increased on the same scale, with the proviso that the maxima of Grade V. should not exceed £400 head masters, and £300 head mistresses.

All certificated assistant teachers were allowed to apply to be placed on the new scale, and such of them as were favourably reported on by the Board Inspector were transferred thereto, an arrest of increase amounting to £5 being made so as to bring their salaries into line with the scale, starting from a lower minimum.

The procedure was varied, however, in the case of the teachers in the Board's service who had become certificated after passing the Certificate Examination only on the first year's papers, or in the third division on the second year's papers prior to 1891, and also of those who prior to 1891 had passed the Certificate Examination satisfactorily, but had not been trained. The teachers in this class, in addition to the favourable report on their capabilities from the Board Inspector, were also required to have improved their qualifications to the satisfaction of the School Management Committee.

The Board, in May, 1901, further considered the case of the teachers in this category who, on account of the non-possession of the approved special qualifications had not been transferred to the new scale, and decided that those among them who were reported on as exceptionally good teachers should be allowed to rise to the higher maximum under the new scale.[1]

The salaries of assistant teachers in the Board's Pupil Teachers' schools were also increased in March, 1899, the men assistants rising from £150 to £200 in place of from £148 to £175, and the women assistants rising from £130 to £165 in place of from £125 to £150.[2]

In March, 1902, in consequence of the increasing difficulty which was experienced in obtaining assistant teachers, the Board reconsidered the amounts of commencing salaries fixed for trained teachers entering their service after a period of service elsewhere, and also for untrained teachers.

The commencing amounts of such teachers with varying lengths of experience were raised in nearly every case, and whereas no higher commencing salary had been allowed for more than six years of satisfactory service, the scale now allowed of a proportionately higher salary for eight or ten such years of service. Also the regulation under which the first increase of salary had hitherto been given only on the completion of a school year of service was altered to allow of teachers receiving increase at the end of twelve months' service. The benefit of these adjustments as granted to those teachers who had entered the Board's service after the passing of the scale of 1899. As a consequence of the change in the scale for teachers in the Board's ordinary schools, the Higher Grade scale was varied in October, 1902, the salary of new entrants to the Board's service being

---

[1] Board Minutes, Vol. LIV., p. 1525.  [2] Board Minutes, Vol L., pp. 1248, 1252.

no longer a fixed amount without regard to experience, but an amount £20 for men, and £15 for women in excess of the commencing salary under the ordinary scale paid to teachers with similar training and certificate qualifications and experience.[1]

Two months later[2] a rising scale for "Unattached" teachers was agreed to. These teachers had hitherto been paid the yearly salaries of "Supply" teachers under the scale in force prior to March 9th, 1899, and were also allowed a sum for travelling expenses while at work at the rate of £2 per month. The fixed salaries could not, however, exceed the amounts of £95 men, and £85 women. An amount of £5 per annum for possible travelling expenses is allowed under the new "Unattached" scale, and for each year of satisfactory service increase of salary is granted and teachers rise to the maximum of the ordinary scale if possessing full training and certificate qualifications, otherwise—for teachers ineligible for permanent appointment are accepted for the ' Unattached " list—the maxima are £135 and £112 respectively.

The following is the existing scale of salaries for head and assistant teachers in Ordinary schools.

### A.—HEAD TEACHERS.

| Accommodation. | | | | | Head Masters of Boys' or Mixed Schools. | Head Mistresses of Girls' or Mixed Schools. | Head Mistresses of Infants' Schools. |
|---|---|---|---|---|---|---|---|
| | | | | | £ | £ | £ |
| Grade 1—200 or under | ... | ... | ... | ... | 175—200 | 140—150 | 140—150 |
| " 2 200 to 300 | ... | ... | ... | ... | 200—250 | 150—185 | 150—160 |
| " 3 301 to 400 | ... | ... | ... | ... | 250—300 | 185—225 | 160—180 |
| " 4 401 to 600 | ... | ... | ... | ... | 300—350 | 225—260 | 180—210 |
| " 5 over 600 | ... | ... | ... | ... | 350—400 | 260—300 | 210—240 |

### B.—ASSISTANT TEACHERS.

1.—ASSISTANT TEACHERS APPOINTED WHEN ON PROBATION FOR THE PARCHMENT CERTIFICATE.

*Annual commencing Salary.*

| | Men. | Wom. | |
|---|---|---|---|
| (a) Probationers who have been trained for two years, and have passed the Certificate Examination on the second year's papers in the 1st or 2nd Division. (b) Probationers (other than class (d)) being persons who are recognised as certificated teachers under Article 60 (b) of the Board of Education's Day School Code. (c) Probationers (other than class (d) ) being graduates, or persons being qualified by examination to become graduates in Arts or Science of any university in the British Empire recognised by the Board of Education under Article 60 (b) of the B.E. Code, who have passed the Certificate Examination on the second year's papers in the 1st or 2nd Division. | £90 | £80 | An increase of £5 (men), and £4 for the 1st year, 2nd year and 3rd year, and thereafter £3 (women) will be allowed for each year of satisfactory service under the Board up to a maximum of £175 (men) and £140 (women), but the increase after the third year of service shall depend upon the teacher gaining qualifications according to the regulations set out in Section (12) of Article 101 of the Board's Code. |
| (d) Probationers who have been trained for three years, or who have taken a university degree or who have taken a university degree or other equivalent Higher Educational Certificates, approved by the Board, requiring not less than three years' study. | 95 | 85 | |

[1] Board Minutes, Vol. LVI , pp. 983, 1017. [2] May 15th, 1902. Board Minutes, Vol. LVI., p. 1471.

2.—ASSISTANT TEACHERS APPOINTED AFTER OBTAINING THE PARCHMENT CERTIFICATE.

(*a*) If trained two years and having passed on the second year's papers in the 1st or 2nd Division.

(*b*) Persons (other than class (*d*)) who are recognised as certificated teachers under Article 60 (*b*) of the Board of Education's Day School Code.

(*c*) Persons (other than class (*a*), being graduates, or persons being qualified by examination to become graduates, in Arts or Science of any University in the British Empire recognised by the Board of Education under Article 60 (*b*) of the B.E. Code. who have passed the certificate examination on the second year's papers in the 1st or 2nd Division.

*Annual Commencing Salary* (*a*), (*b*), (*c*) :—

|  | Men. | Women. |
|---|---|---|
| If with parchment alone ... ... ... | £95 | £85 |
| If with parchment and two years of subsequent satisfactory service... ... | 100 | 90 |
| If with parchment and four years of subsequent satisfactory service... ... | 105 | 94 |
| If with parchment and six or more years of subsequent satisfactory service ... | 110 | 98 (6 yrs.) |
|  | 115 (8 yrs.) | 102 (8 yrs.) |
|  | 120 (10 yrs. or more) | 106 (10 yrs. or more) |

An increase of £5 (men) and £3 (women) will be allowed for each year of satisfactory service under the Board up to a maximum of £175 (men) and £140 (women), (see Section (40) of this article), but the increase after the third year of service shall depend upon the teacher gaining qualifications according to the regulations set out in Section (12).

(*d*) Persons who have been trained for three years, or who have taken a University degree or other equivalent higher educational certificates, approved by the Board, requiring not less than three years' study.

*Annual Commencing Salary* (*d*) :—

A commencing salary £5 (men and women alike) higher than the amounts set out above.

(*e*) If trained one year, or untrained (not possessing qualifications set out in (*b*), (*c*) or (*d*) ), and having passed the second year's papers in the 1st or 2nd Division.

*Annual Commencing Salary* (*e*) :—

|  | Men. | Women. |
|---|---|---|
| If probationers ... ... ... ... | £80 | £75 |
| If with parchment alone ... ... ... | 85 | 80 |
| If with parchment and two years of subsequent satisfactory service... ... | 90 | 85 |
| If with parchment and four years of subsequent satisfactory service ... ... | 95 | 89 |
| If with parchment and six or more years of subsequent satisfactory service ... | 100 | 93 (6 yrs.) |
|  | 105 (8 yrs.) | 97 (8 yrs.) |
|  | 110 (10 yrs. or more) | 101 (10 yrs. or more) |

The same increase and conditions as above for teachers with parchment but the maximum of these classes is £160 (men) and £130 (women).

In October, 1903, the Board resolved that the following resolution be referred to the School Management Committee for consideration and report : "That the School Management Committee be instructed to take immediate steps to find teachers for the rapidly increasing vacancies; and that, if necessary, the Committee be empowered to bring up recommendations varying the conditions of service and scales of salary, in order to attract additional teaching staff." This Instruction was referred to a Special Sub-Committee of the School Management Committee. This sub-committee prepared certain statistical tables, showing the general condition of the Board's service, and the

done by the Board for the various classes of the "unfit" may be chronologically grouped in three periods :—

### 1. *First Period : Before delegation to a Sub-Committee.*

This initial stage of the instruction of the blind and deaf covers the period from February, 1872, to June, 1877. On the earlier date the Board passed their first resolution respecting blind and deaf children, instructing the Statistical Committee to ascertain what provision existed for the education of such children.[1] That resolution was, in due course, followed by the adoption of schemes to provide instruction for both blind and deaf, which were carried out under the immediate direction of the School Management Committee.

### 2. *Second Period : Sub-Committee on Blind and Deaf.*

In 1877 it was decided to delegate the superintendence of the teaching of the blind and the deaf to a Sub-Committee, the first meeting of which took place on June 13th, 1877, when Sir Charles Reed (then Chairman of the Board), who had from the first taken great interest in the work, was elected Chairman of the Sub-Committee. This second period, which lasted till 1891, differed but little from that which preceded it. No legislative changes were effected, but the work was carried on with the formal sanction of the Education Department. No grant was received for the scholars taught, and, even if expenditure on classes not receiving grant were legal, there were other items of expenditure, such as guides and travelling, which were probably liable to surcharge. The most important event of this period was the appointment of the Royal Commission on the Blind, the Deaf and Dumb, &c., in July, 1885, the Report of which was issued in 1889. That Report recommended legislation, the need for which had already been pointed out to the Education Department by the London School Board.

### 3. *Third period : Work of Sub-Committee extended to other Defectives.*

In July, 1891, the School Management Committee decided that the Sub-Committee on the Blind and Deaf should also undertake the provision of special instruction for mentally and physically defective children, and the name of the sub-committee was altered to the "Special Schools Sub-Committee." This period—July, 1891, to the present time—includes the most important part of the work done, because three Acts of Parliament dealing with defective children—the Elementary Education (Blind and Deaf Children) Act, 1893 ; the Elementary Education (Defective and Epileptic Children) Act, 1899 ; and the Elementary Education (Defective and Epileptic Children) Amendment Act, 1903—gave powers for dealing with these classes of children.

The importance of the Special Schools cannot be gauged by the number of cases dealt with, or by the cost at which the work is carried on. Happily the "unfit" are few compared with normal children ; the blind and deaf together number about one in a thousand. the physically and mentally defective one in a hundred, and epileptics one

---

[1] Board Minutes, Vol. II., pp. 83, 103.

in two thousand, making a total of children capable of receiving education, but below the normal standard, of over eleven in the thousand. These, through the varying degrees of their infirmities, require almost individual treatment. Cases occur which, by reason of their combination of defects, are difficult, even impossible, to classify. The care of these defective children often involves questions of a peculiarly technical character, as the number and variety of matters on which the Sub-Committee have had to consult the Board's Solicitor and Medical Officer testify.

The schools for the Blind and the Deaf were under separate superintendents until the end of 1900, when one superintendent of both classes of schools was appointed, with an assistant superintendent for the Blind schools. The schools for Physically and Mentally Defective children are under a superintendent, who has two assistants, one of whom was specially appointed for the Physically Defective schools.

There is considerable difference of opinion as to the relative values of Day schools and Residential institutions for the Blind and the Deaf. The Act of 1893 gave the school authority power to adopt either system. The Board of Education sanctioned a system of boarding blind and deaf children with foster-parents, in order that they might attend at certified Day schools, and the School Board adopted this system in 1895 for some cases and sent others to voluntary institutions at which accommodation was available. It was soon found, however, that this method would not meet the needs of all cases. There was not always the amount or the kind of voluntary accommodation available which the Board required; while the boarding-out system often proved uncertain and unsuitable. The School Board was from the first in favour of children attending Day schools where home circumstances made it possible; but it soon became evident that proper classification, and therefore, satisfactory results, could only be obtained in many cases by means of boarding-schools. The only chance of success in teaching the blind and deaf is to ensure healthy conditions of living and regular attendance at school. This consideration, together with the distance some of the children lived from the Day schools, induced the Board to provide Residential schools for the elder blind and deaf children, and also for those blind and deaf who suffer from combined defects. The use of voluntary institutions and boarding-out was continued, to a limited extent, and the Day schools were retained. It was intended to extend the residential system so as to include certain mentally defective cases.

## II.—The Blind.

The expression "blind" means too blind to be able to read the ordinary school books used by children.[1]

The teaching of the blind has been surrounded with considerable difficulties, and has been carried on with varying success. The blind have in some instances proved themselves capable of attaining high places in the ranks of scholarship, but the teaching of the blind in the Board's Special schools has made slow progress. This is accounted for by the exceptional difficulties which have been encountered.

---

[1] 56 and 57 Vict., c. 42, s. 15 (1).

The blind, as a class, had been educationally neglected. The provision which had been made for them was by way of charity only, and was more in the nature of care than instruction, as the names of the oldest schools—" asylums "—indicate. Therefore, when the Board, in February, 1872, decided to provide teaching for the blind, they had little in the way of experience to guide them, and they embarked on a work of which the experimental stage lasted nearly twenty years. The first great difficulty was that of types. The earliest plan was the appointment of a peripatetic teacher to visit the various schools once or twice a week to give a lesson to blind children by aid of the Moon type, and this teaching was supplemented by an occasional lesson at home from the agent of a voluntary society, In 1876 it was found that the Moon type was unsuitable for teaching the young blind, so after trying Roman type, the Board decided to adopt the Braille type for reading and writing. The next seventeen years showed a slow but sure improvement in results. In 1890 the School Board brought under the notice of the Education Department the unsatisfactory state of things that existed with regard to the day classes for the blind and deaf, and obtained as a concession the recognition of these classes for purposes of grant; but no improvement was possible until the Act of 1893 was passed, giving wider powers to the School Authority. Prior to this Act, the Poor Law Guardians possessed permissive powers to teach and maintain blind and deaf children.[1] The Act of 1893 cancelled those powers,[2] laid the obligation on the School Authority without allowing an option, and made the attendance of blind children at school compulsory between the ages of 5 and 16. It also enabled the School Board to place blind children in Residential schools, and until the Board could provide such schools, they utilised places in voluntary institutions. By this means and by boarding out other cases with foster-parents, the schools for the Blind have been reduced from 26 in 1893 to 10 in 1903. This reduction has facilitated the better classification of the pupils.

The School Board in 1897 acquired the Royal Normal College for the Blind at Norwood as a Residential school; but owing to many difficulties in working a school the main object of which was to teach adults, the Board in 1899 re-transferred that institution to the Voluntary Committee from which they had taken it over. In 1900, they decided to acquire two Residential schools for the elder blind children between the ages of 12 and 16, one for girls and one for boys. The girls' school at West Norwood, and the boys' at Wandsworth Common were both opened in 1902.

Special attention is paid in these schools to Industrial and Manual Work, in order to teach the children, during their final years of school life, some occupation by which they may become to some extent self-supporting. In 1901 the Board decided to appoint a sighted teacher in each school for the Blind, and agreed that the younger children, instead of spending half time in the ordinary schools, as hitherto, should be taught entirely in the schools for the Blind, those in Standard IV. and upwards still continuing to attend at the ordinary schools three half days a week. To complete the

[1] 4 & 5 Will. IV. c. 76, s. 56.        [2] Except pauper children.

accommodation required for the blind, the Board have recently acquired premises at Hackney Downs for a Residential school for those Blind who are also Deaf, or who are too defective to be taught in the ordinary blind schools.

Many of the blind who have been instructed in the Board's classes have afterwards obtained scholarships which have enabled them to continue their studies, and amongst these are some who have become teachers of the Blind. There are numerous instances of good results obtained, notwithstanding the difficulties under which this work has been carried on. It may, therefore, be hoped that with the greater advantages now available far better results will yet be shown.

### III.—THE DEAF.

The expression " deaf" means too deaf to be taught in a class of hearing children in an Elementary school.[1]

The education of the deaf was commenced before that of the blind, and has perhaps attracted more attention, firstly because the deaf are more numerous, and secondly because, having at one time been classed with idiots, the discovery that they could be taught excited interest in their behalf. The French system, known as the " sign," or " manual," system and the German, or " oral," system, promulgated respectively by the Abbé de l'Epée and by Heinicke, became generally known by the middle of the 18th Century, although as late as 1871 the oral system was but little used in England. Both systems have their advantages and their limitations, but it is generally conceded that if the ideal of the oral system can be realised the weight of evidence is in its favour. This is shown by the following excerpts from Board of Education reports :—

There are, generally speaking, two distinct methods of teaching the deaf—the pure oral and the manual. Combined systems are merely modifications of these, and vary considerably in detail. The oral method aims at teaching the deaf to speak intelligibly and to follow and understand the speech of others by watching the motions of the mouth and the expression of the features, by " lip-reading," as it is inadequately termed in this country. If the deaf can acquire these arts, they are no longer secluded from general society, but can mix freely with their fellow creatures. By the manual method, language is taught in signs only (writing, which is practised in both kinds of schools, is a sign), thus the deaf taught by this kind of method express themselves in signs and understand signs only ; they are, therefore, able to converse with the very small number of persons who are acquainted with the language of signs, for a conversation conducted in writing is hardly conceivable.[2]

There is no doubt that the deaf child who has received sufficient command of spoken language at school to enable it to make further progress by its own effort is certain of a brighter and fuller life than one who, with the same linguistic attainments, can only communicate by gesture or by writing.

At the same time we must not delude ourselves as to the possibilities of the oral method. We shall never make the deaf speak with the facility, the breadth of idiom, and with the voice and intonation of the hearing. But we can do much in the direction of such an ideal, and thereby enrich and enlighten lives which would otherwise languish dull and inert. There will always remain a proportion of deaf not amenable to oral teaching.[3]

In 1872 the London School Board first considered the question of instructing the

[1] 56 & 57 Vict., c. 42, s. 15 (1).       [3] Board of Education Report, 1900-1, p. 161.
[2] Education Department Report, 1898-9, p. 305.

deaf and dumb, and in 1874 they established their first class, on the "sign" or manual system   In 1877, it was decided that two classes should be commenced on the "oral" system, and this gradually spread to other schools.  Although from July, 1877, the "combined system" began to give place to the "oral" system, it is only in quite recent years that the latter has had a fair trial, and it is doubtful even yet whether its possibilities have been attained.  The disadvantages under which the "oral" system has suffered may briefly be summarised as: (1) The adverse influence of children being lodged in "homes" where communication was by means of signs; (2) The advanced age of pupils when they first came under instruction; (3) The presence in the oral classes of children of defective intellect.

With regard to the first disadvantage, the closing of the Stainer homes in London has, to some extent, prevented the orally taught children from communicating entirely by signs out of school.  The second disadvantage has been obviated by compulsory attendance at school required by the Elementary Education (Blind and Deaf Children) Act, 1893, which has ensured that the children commence instruction at an earlier age. Unfortunately however, the minimum age fixed by the Act is 7, and the importance to the deaf child, who is to be taught on the oral system, of the four or five years' teaching before the age of 7 is very great.  The Board have admitted children to schools for the deaf at 3 years of age with good results, and we shall probably find that the system now being tried in Philadelphia, of teaching the deaf child speech at the same age as the hearing child is the only fair condition under which the oral system may be judged.  The third disadvantage has been dealt with by providing separate accommodation for the defectives, resulting in the segregation of about 10 per cent. of the deaf children whose instruction is carried on by means of writing, finger-spelling, and speech, not less to their own benefit than to the benefit of those from whom they have been separated.

On January 1st, 1894, it became legal for School Authorities to provide and maintain Residential as well as Day schools for the Blind and Deaf, and to pay for guides and travelling.  Rules were issued by the Education Department under the Act to allow the boarding of blind and deaf children near certified Day schools under Boarding-out Committees.  The only difference between the blind and deaf made in the Act is the regulation referred to above by which the deaf child cannot be compelled to attend school till the age of 7.  Soon after the Act came into operation, the Board decided it was desirable that a Residential school should be provided, and they submitted plans to the Education Department for the provision of such a school at Anerley; but in consequence of conditions required by the Department the proposal was, for the time, dropped.  In March, 1898, it was decided to adapt premises at Homerton for a Residential Deaf school, and in December, 1899, the Board submitted fresh plans for a Residential school at Anerley, which were accepted by the Education Department.  In August, 1900, the Board's first Residential school for the Deaf was opened at Homerton to receive cases which, for various reasons, were unfit to be boarded-out.

In 1898 the Board, for the first time, made a definite attempt to introduce Drawing into the schools for the Deaf, and not only afforded facilities for the teachers to qualify in this subject, but also caused a special Drawing scheme to be prepared for the schools for the Deaf. In furtherance of the same policy the Board in 1903 appointed a teacher of Drawing to visit all the schools periodically.

In 1902 the Board considered a scheme for training the elder deaf children, and they decided that two schools should be provided, one for elder boys and the other for elder girls, to give definite technical training. It was agreed that the cottage homes and school, then being built at Anerley, should be used for the Technical Training school for boys, to accommodate 60 residential and 30 day scholars, and that the Residential and Day school for training the elder deaf girls should be provided at Wandsworth Common. The defective deaf were to be accommodated at the Homerton school, where, by an extension of the buildings, 40 residential and 30 day scholars have now been provided for. It now only remains to open the Training school at Wandsworth Common for elder girls, so that it may reasonably be hoped that this entire scheme will be working satisfactorily in the course of the present year.

## IV.—THE MENTALLY DEFECTIVE.

These are defined as children who, not being imbecile and not merely dull or backward, are by reason of mental defect incapable of receiving proper benefit from the instruction in the ordinary Public Elementary schools, but not incapable of receiving benefit from instruction in special classes or schools.[1]

In January, 1888, the reference to the Royal Commission on the Blind was enlarged so as to include "the deaf and dumb. as well as such other cases as from special circumstances would seem to require exceptional methods of education." In the Report of the Commission it is stated that the Royal Commission on the Elementary Education Acts suggested that the feeble-minded would come within the terms of the reference. Evidence was therefore taken, and recommendations were submitted, respecting that class of children. One of the recommendations was that feeble-minded children should be separated from ordinary scholars in Public Elementary schools in order that they might receive special instruction. In 1890 the School Management Committee had before them a report on the "separate school" established in Elberfeld-Barmen, and the Board, in November, 1890, instructed the School Management Committee to prepare a scheme for the establishment of special classes for mentally and physically defective children. In March, 1891, the Board resolved that special schools should be established for those children who, by reason of physical and mental defect, could not be taught "in the ordinary standards or by ordinary methods."[2] The first two schools for such children were opened in July, 1892. The Education Department sanctioned the schools, allowing them to rank for the purposes of grant as ordinary Infant schools, and the general report of the Senior Chief Inspector for 1895 contains the following reference to the scheme :—

The classes for the special instruction of mentally defective children are among the

---

[1] 62 & 63 Vic., c. 32, s. 1 (1) (a).       [2] Board Minutes, Vol. XXXIV., p. 254.

most interesting classes under the Board, and the example is being followed in other large centres of population. These children vary very greatly in such mental power as they possess ; some can be so far developed that they can hold their own fairly when transferred to an ordinary school, though with scholars generally younger than themselves ; others can be so far assisted that they can, with some little supervision, take care of themselves ; but there still remains a considerable residuum who are only fit for the asylums for idiot children.[1]

A Departmental Committee on Poor Law schools reported in 1896 respecting separate schools for defectives as follows :—

As the result of our enquiries on this branch of the subject we consider that, in fairness to the normal children, as well as for the benefit of the feeble-minded, separate provision should be made for their education, with a view to the development of the backward brain and the awakening of the dormant moral sense.

In 1894, and again in 1896, the School Board called the attention of the Education Department to the desirability of legislating for defective and epileptic children, and in consequence a Departmental Committee was appointed to consider the matter. In 1898 this Committee submitted their Report, which contained very valuable information respecting defectives, and recommended legislation mainly on the lines of the Blind and Deaf Act of 1893. The recommendations were, to a large extent, adopted in the Elementary Education (Defective and Epileptic Children) Act, 1899, and the Minute of the Education Department of February 2nd, 1900. The Act differs chiefly from the Blind and Deaf Act by being permissive with regard to its obligations on the School Authority. The School Board decided to put the Act into operation in London as far as it applied to defective children, and they have now for four years been providing special schools where they were needed, and bringing existing schools into conformity with the regulations of the Act.

The curriculum of the Special school differs mainly from that of the ordinary Elementary school in the greater elasticity of the time-table, shorter lessons, and the larger amount of manual occupations, the afternoon session being principally devoted to handwork. The Government reports show that good and steady work has been done, and the fact that during the past two years 184 and 258 children respectively have been promoted from the special to the ordinary schools, shows that the special schools have served a useful purpose.

Two important developments of this work have been decided on : Firstly, to provide residential accommodation for two kinds of defectives : (1) Homes for those who, while needing for various reasons, to be removed from their parents, are not cases of such gravity as to preclude their attendance at a certified Day Special School. (2) Custodial institutions for those whose bad habits and want of moral sense make it desirable to separate them from other children. A home for boys and one for girls of the first kind is now being provided, and a site is being sought outside the London district for the erection of the custodial institutions. The second development is the opening of " training" schools for elder mentally

---

[1] Education Department Report, 1895-6, p. 13.

defective boys, where manual instruction of a more specialised character is to be provided during their last three or four years of school life. Three such schools have been opened, and another is about to be opened.

## V.—PHYSICALLY DEFECTIVE.

These are defined as children who, not being imbecile and not merely dull or backward, are by reason of physical defect, incapable of receiving proper benefit from the instruction in the ordinary public Elementary school, but not incapable of receiving benefit from instruction in special classes or schools.[1]

The Royal Commission on the Blind did not consider the question of the physically defective, and although physical as well as mental defect is mentioned in the scheme approved by the Board in 1891 for the establishment of Special schools, children suffering only from physical defect were not then looked upon as a separate class, but they were from that time onward frequently admitted to the Special schools with the mentally defectives. Physical defect is not mentioned in the reference to the Departmental Committee on Defective and Epileptic Children, appointed in 1896; but the report of that Committee, issued in 1898, includes a section on physically defective children in which they say :—

" We recommend that physically defective children shall be admitted to special classes if, owing to chronic ill-health they are not capable of receiving proper benefit from instruction in the ordinary school while capable of benefiting from instruction in the special classes." [2]

Later in the same report the class for physically defectives then being carried on in Southwark is referred to as " a fair field for voluntary effort," but for which the recognition of the Department is not recommended. In 1898 a committee connected with the Passmore Edwards Settlement in Tavistock Place made an application to the Special Schools Sub-Committee for the establishment of an Invalid Children's school in rooms belonging to the Settlement. They pointed out that some invalid children's classes already existed in London, carried on by voluntary workers. The committee submitted a schedule of 25 children—9 of whom were exempt from school attendance, and the remainder attending irregularly—who could be admitted if the school were established. The Board agreed to the proposal, which involved purely educational expenses only, the Settlement Committee providing the ambulance and nurse. The sanction of the Education Department was given on January 26th, 1899, and the school was opened on February 28th, 1899. On November 10th, 1899, the School Management Committee adopted a resolution requiring lists of all cripples of school age not attending school to be furnished to the Special Schools Sub-Committee. On February 26th, 1900, a return of 620 such children was considered, and referred for medical report. On July 2nd, 1900, the Medical Officer's report on 606 cases was submitted, and referred for consideration to a Committee of members of the Board and specialists. This Committee reported on October 26th, 1900, in favour of the establishment of separate schools for

---

[1] 62 & 63 Vict., c. 32, s. 1 (1) (a).  [2] Page 29, s. 76, last paragraph.

the physically defective of normal intelligence. This recommendation was accepted by the Board ; the Board of Education approved the proposal, and consented to the provision of schools for physically defectives in districts where the accommodation was required. Cripple or invalid children who are also mentally defective are not admitted to these schools, but it has been decided, where possible, that children suffering from the double affliction shall be taught at the schools for the Mentally Defective, whither they are to be taken by ambulance. Each Cripple school is managed by a local committee, has a trained nurse and helper, and one or two ambulances, according to the number of children to be collected.

Drawing is being made a feature in the instruction of these children, and an Art teacher attends at each school to give the more advanced teaching. The work of the Cripple schools is supplemented by a voluntary society, called the " Cripple Children's After-Training and Dinner Society," which, in addition to arranging for a midday meal at each school, endeavours to provide special training for cripples on reaching 16, or to apprentice them to suitable trades. A school for children under treatment at the Orthopædic Hospital has been organised on the same system as that carried on in connection with the convalescent home at West Kirby. The Board of Education have sanctioned this school as an experiment, on the condition that it is not certified as a Special school under the Act of 1899, but is considered a part of the nearest ordinary Board school.

### VI.—Defective Children for whom no Instruction has been provided.

1. *Epileptics*—Children, not being idiots or imbeciles, who are unfit by reason of severe epilepsy to attend the ordinary public Elementary schools,[1] either on account of serious danger to themselves, to other children, or disturbance to the school work caused by such attendance.

The representation respecting defectives made by the School Board to the Education Department in 1896, drew particular attention to children capable of receiving education who, by reason of severe epilepsy were excluded from ordinary and special schools, and the Departmental Committee on Defective Children recommended that special provision should be made for such children by means of Residential schools. The Elementary Education (Defective and Epileptic Children) Act, 1899, and the Minute of the Board of Education of February 19th, 1900, empowered school authorities to make such provision.

This Act is permissive so far as the School Authority is concerned, and the Board decided not to avail themselves of its provisions with regard to epileptics, because the limitation it contained as to the size of homes was unsatisfactory. No establishment could consist of more than four homes for fifteen children each. A Special Sub-Committee was appointed by the Board to consider the matter, and the Board's Medical Officer was requested to examine all the children throughout London who were reported as epileptic, in order that trustworthy information might be available both as to the number

---

[1] 62 & 63 Vict., c. 32, s. 1 (1) [*b*].

and the severity of the cases. The Medical Officer's report, showing 114 cases fit for a Residential school, was forwarded to the Board of Education, together with a memorial from the School Board objecting to Section 2, Sub-section 6 of the Act, on the ground that it would ultimately require five establishments to deal with the epileptic children in London. The Act has remained a dead letter so far as epileptic children are concerned.

In 1903 an amending Act was passed[1] giving the Board of Education power to submit rules to Parliament under which schools might be certified without regard to the limit in size imposed by the Act of 1899. After this amendment the Board decided to make provision for epileptics, and they asked the Board of Education for their sanction to provide the accommodation needed. The National Society for the Employment of Epileptics was also communicated with as to the possibility of the provision required being made at their colony at Chalfont St. Peter.

The Board of Education (August 24th, 1903) replied stating that they regarded the general scheme of the Board with favour ; but they suggested, in view of the approaching transfer of the powers of the School Board to the County Council, that the Council should be consulted as to the details of the scheme, and as to the best place for the proposed homes. The Board accordingly referred the matter to the County Council.

2. *Imbeciles*—Children not capable of receiving proper benefit from instruction either in Ordinary schools or in Special schools.

The Royal Commission on the Blind reported that they considered that power should be given to the County or Town Councils, jointly or severally, to provide institutions for imbeciles out of the funds at their disposal wherever there is either insufficient or no accommodation.

The Departmental Committee on Defective and Epileptic Children suggested in 1898 that the medical examination held by the School Authority should be utilised as a mode of admission for imbecile children to suitable institutions.

The School Board have considered the need for special action with regard to imbecile children, and in December, 1899, they sent a deputation to the Home Office on the subject. In February, 1902, the County Council, the Metropolitan Asylums Board, and the School Board held a conference, at which the following resolutions were passed, and were afterwards confirmed by each of the three authorities :—

" (1 That it is desirable that public provision be made for all imbecile children (i.e. children under 16 not capable of receiving proper benefit from instruction in an ordinary school or in special classes conducted under the provisions of the Elementary Education (Defective and Epileptic Children) Act, 1899, for whose care efficient and suitable provision is not otherwise made.

" (2) That a parent or guardian who voluntarily sends or is called upon to part with the custody of an imbecile child, should be required to contribute a reasonable amount towards maintenance, but should not, by reason of so parting with a child, be considered to be in receipt of Poor Law relief.

---

[1] 3 Edw. 7, c. 13.

" (3) That the county or county borough should be suggested as the area for this purpose."

It was agreed to ask the President of the Board of Education, the Home Secretary, and the President of the Local Government Board to receive a joint deputation on the matter, and a memorial was forwarded showing the desirability of making provision for imbecile children, and giving particulars of many typical cases which had come under the notice of the Board.

## VII.—STATISTICS.

The following Statistics for the year ended March 20th, 1903, show the work carried on under the Special Schools Sub-Committee :—

| | Schools Existing. | | | Schools Projected. | | No. of children scheduled. | Roll. | Av. Attendance. | Percentage of Av. Attendance on Roll. | Staff. | | Sent to Outside Schools as Day Scholars |
|---|---|---|---|---|---|---|---|---|---|---|---|---|
| | Residential. | Day. | Total Accom. | Residential | Day. | | | | | Teachers. | *Other Officers. | |
| Blind ... ... | 2 | 8 | 271 | 1 | 4 | 307 | 233 | 205 | 88·0 | 23 | 15 | ... |
| Deaf ... ... | 2 | 15 | 804 | 1 | 3 | 618 | 569 | 516 | 90·7 | 68 | 25 | 38 |
| Mentally Defective | ... | 60 | 3,219 | 4 | 15 | 2,942 | 3,063 | 2,480 | 81·0 | 159 | 25 | ... |
| Physically Defective | ... | 8 | 360 | ... | 19 | 1,733 | 321 | 244 | 76·0 | 18 | 23 | ... |
| Total ... ... | 4 | 91 | 4,654 | 6 | 41 | 5,900 | 4,413 | 3,445 | ... | 268 | 88 | 38 |
| | | | | | | | | | | 356 | | |

| | ** Maintained. | | | | Grant. | | Cost. | |
|---|---|---|---|---|---|---|---|---|
| | Residential Schools. | | Boarded with Foster Parents to attend Day Schools. | | | | | |
| | Board's Residential Schools. | Sent to Outside Residential Schools. | Board's cases. | Other cases. | Total. | Average per Head. | Total. | †Net per Head. |
| | | | | | £ | £ s. d. | £ | £ s. d. |
| Blind ... ... | 47 | 13 | 17 | 5 | 984 | 4 16 0 | 6,200 | 25 8 10½ |
| Deaf ... ... | 79 | 11 | 43 | 13 | 1,811 | 3 10 2¼ | 13,068 | 21 16 3¾ |
| Mentally Defective | ... | ... | ... | ... | } 9,717 | 3 11 4 | 28,985 | 7 1 5⅛ |
| Physically Defective | ... | ... | ... | ... | | | | |
| Total ... ... | 126 | 24 | 60 | 18 | £12,512 | ... | £48,253 | ... |
| | 150 | | 78 | | | | | |
| | | 228 | | | | | | |

\* Including Domestic Staff, Bathing-women, Helpers, Caretakers, &c.

\*\* The numbers shewn under this heading are included in the Roll, Average, &c.

† The amounts contributed by parents towards maintenance have not been deducted from the net cost per head.

### VIII.—THE SPECIAL SCHOOL.

1. *The Children.*—The children are brought to the notice of the Sub-Committee mainly by the head teachers of ordinary Elementary schools; but sometimes by the Divisional Superintendents or by parents or friends. Medical examination is not required under the Blind and Deaf Act, but if there is a doubt in any case as to the child being sufficiently blind or deaf for the Special school, the Board of Education make a medical certificate a condition of retention. A certificate by an approved practitioner is required for the admission of the physically or mentally defective. In the schools for "Defectives" admissions are made by the Board's Medical Officers twice a year, and they visit the Schools for the Blind and Deaf at least once a year. The children admitted to the Special schools vary considerably in degree of defect, some being only just below the standard suitable for instruction in ordinary Elementary schools, while some belong to the lowest grade of children who are capable of receiving education.

2. *The Teachers.*—The teachers are, as a rule, trained and certified Elementary school teachers, Kindergarten and drawing qualifications being generally required. A few teachers who do not hold the Government certificate are engaged, such as "Higher Froebel" certificate teachers, and those holding the certificate of Teacher of the Deaf, which is not a Government certificate. These latter have mostly the certificate of the Ealing or Fitzroy Square Training Colleges, or of the Examining College of Teachers of the Deaf. Some of the blind teachers also have not the Government certificate. Only adult teachers are engaged, and, as a rule, they are not engaged on first leaving college, but are required to have had first some experience of ordinary school work. All the teachers in the schools for Defectives are women, except in the three schools for elder boys. In the Special schools the responsible teacher is called "teacher in charge."

3. *The Records.*—The Board of Education have prescribed a form for keeping the medical records in the Schools for the Defectives. These records are entered in a book known as the "Family History and Progress Book," which is considered confidential and is kept under lock and key. The Board's Medical Officer twice a year makes an entry on each child in these books. Keeping uniform records in the schools for the Blind and Deaf has recently been commenced, but these are educational rather than medical.

4. *The Managers.*—Two Local Managers are appointed for each Special school, and the schools are grouped into districts—three or four schools comprising each group. The Managers hold quarterly meetings and make their recommendations to the Special Schools Sub-Committee. The Residential schools and the schools for Physically Defectives are not grouped with the other Special schools, but generally one local committee manages two schools and meets fortnightly, monthly or bi-monthly. Where blind or deaf children are boarded with foster-parents the Local Managers act as a boarding-out committee.

5. *The Curriculum.*—The subjects of instruction vary considerably in the different Special schools. Reading, Writing, and Arithmetic are common to all, and the subjects in the schools for the Blind and the Physically Defective are those taken in the ordinary

Elementary schools.   Leaving methods of instruction out of the question, the main difference between the Special schools and the Ordinary schools is the much larger amount of attention given to the individual pupil and the training in handwork.   The Government regulations require that a minimum of six hours a week in the schools for Defectives and four in the schools for the Blind and the Deaf shall be given to manual or industrial work.   In some of the Special schools this amount of time is considerably increased ,and in the case of the elder scholars at the Blind and Deaf schools, nearly half the time is devoted to the manual side of the school work.   The handwork at the various schools includes Drawing and Brushwork, Clay-modelling, Macramé-work, and Chair-caning ; while for boys Woodwork, Shoemaking, Basket-making, Tailoring and Saddlery are taken ; and for girls Cookery, Laundrywork, plain and fancy Needlework and Millinery.   The Art side of the work is being developed in the Physically Defective schools, and much care is now bestowed upon the Physical Exercises at all the schools. In the Residential schools the gymnasia are being used with good results.

6. *Aims and Results.* —While forming the mind and training the touch are aimed at, the teacher of the sub-normal child cannot hope, as a rule, to see great success according to the ordinary standard.   The exceptions are too rare to be counted upon.   From the outset it is as well to accept the fact that four senses are not equal to five, and that the very best that can be done for the afflicted child will generally leave it in a worse position from a worker's point of view than the normal child.   But if brilliant results are not to be expected from the Special schools work, it is still true that a limit is placed upon total failure, and that many from these schools do become capable workers.   The recent extension of the manual work by providing specialised training for the elder children, and the attempt at "after care" by means of voluntary committees, will increase the chances of the success of the Special schools.

### IX.—CONCLUSION.

Much has been done for the various classes of defective children ; but much remains to be done.   Legislation is required to meet the needs of the certifiable imbeciles, and for the extended, and in some cases permanent, care of the class immediately above imbecile.   Accommodation under the existing law is required for epileptics, and perhaps an extension of legal powers to deal with some cases after 16.   The homes which the School Board have decided to provide for the mentally defective of the low grade type are badly needed, and there should be power to retain some of these cases beyond 16. The accommodation now provided and projected will fairly meet the needs of Blind, Deaf and Physically Defectives, except that London will no doubt see the need to secure a seaside school for convalescent cripples as Birmingham is about to do.   The Mentally Defectives are not yet fully provided for by the existing and projected accommodation, and it is probable that the future extensions in the accommodation for this branch should be in the nature of training schools for the elder scholars. Border-line cases in each section have caused, and will continue to cause, difficulty.

# CENTRES. SHEET I.

**Chelsea.**
1. Ashburnham, C. M.T.
2. Marlborough Road, C. L. M.T.
3. Park Walk, C. M.D. L. M.T.
4. Walton Street, M.D.

**Fulham.**
5. Ackmar Road, C. D. M.D.
6. Fulham Palace Road, H. M.T.
7. Hilford Road, C. M.T.
8. Hugon Road, M.T.
9. Kingswood Road, C. M.D.
10. Langford Road, C. M.D.
11. Lillie Road, C. L.
12. Munster Road, G.
13. North End Road, C.
14. Sherbrooke Road, M.D. M.T.
15. St. Dunstan's Road, H. M.T.
16. William Street, C. P. L. M.T.

**Hammersmith.**
17. Brackenbury Road, C.
18. Brook Green, P. M.D. M.T.
19. Eyot ... A. C.
20. Kenmont Gardens, C. L.
21. Latimer Road, C.
22. Westgrove Road, L. M.T.

**Kensington.**
23. Broomsleigh Street, C. L.
24. Fleet Road, C. M.T.
25. Holmslaw Road, M.D.
26. Pangbourne Street, C.
27. ... Terrace, L.
28. ... Road, C. M.D.
29. For... C. M.T.
30. Oxford ... M.T.
31. Portland ... C. H.
32. Nelle ... L.
33. ... Road, C. M.D.
34. Wornington Road, L. M.T.

**Paddington.**
35. Amberley Road, M.T.
36. Beethoven Street, C. M.T.
37. Essendine Road, C. P.D.
38. Kilburn Lane, C. L. M.T.
39. Moberly, C. M.D. L.

**Marylebone.**
40. Capland Street, C. D. M.T.
41. Marylebone Central, M.D. M.T.
42. Shroton Street, C. L.
43. Stephen Street, M.I.
44. Barnsbury Road, C. P.T.

**St. Pancras.**
45. Camden Hall, M.D.
46. Camden Street, L. H.
47. Carlton Road, C. M.T.
48. Great College Street, C.
49. Haverstock Hill, M.D. M.I.
50. Holmes Road, L.
51. Mansfield Road, C. M.T.
52. Medburn Street, C. M.T.
53. Prince... Row, L.
55. Stanhope Street, B. L. M.I.

**Westminster.**
57. Buckingham Gate, C. M.T.
58. Christ Cross Road, C. M.T.
59. Mitcham ... M.D. M.I.
62. National Training Sch.

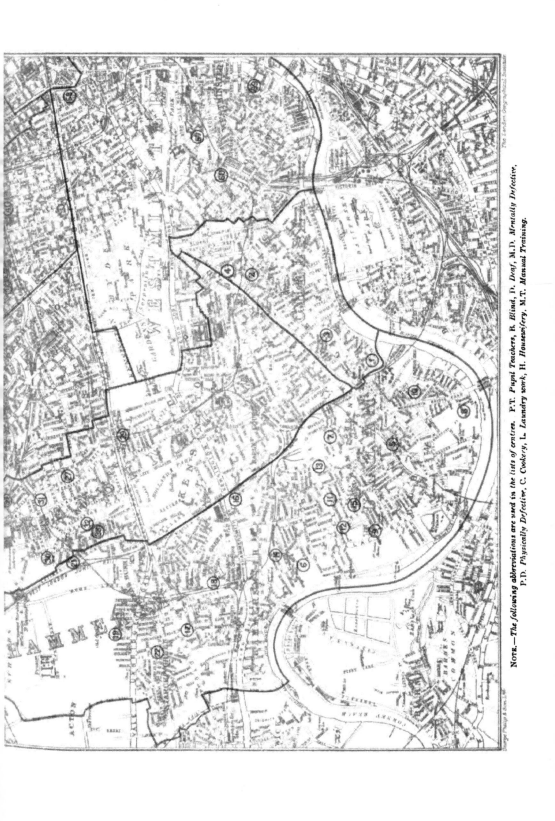

NOTE.—*The following abbreviations are used in the lists of centres.  P.T. Pupil Teachers, B. Blind, D. Deaf, M.D. Mentally Defective, P.D. Physically Defective, C. Cookery, L. Laundry work, H. Housewifery, M.T. Manual Training.*

**City of London.**
1. Gravel Lane, L., H.
**Bermondsey.**
2. Albion Street, C., L.
3. East Lane, C., L., M.T.
4. Fair Street, C.
5. Keeton's Road, C., M.T.
6. Laxon Street, C., L.
7. Riley Street, M.D.
**Bethnal Green.**
8. Abbey Street, C., M.D., L., H., M.T.
9. Bonner Street, L.
10. Cliosenhale Road, L.
11. Columbia Road, C.
12. Cranbrook Road, M.D.
13. Daniel Street, C., M.D., L., M.T.
14. Mansford Street, C., P.D., L., M.T.
15. Mowlem Street, C., M.T.
16. Olga Street, C.
17. Portman Place, C., M.D.
18. Summerford Street, D.
19. Wilmot Street, C.
**Finsbury.**
20. Baltic Street, C., M.T.
21. Bath Street, C., M.D.
22. Chequer Street, L.
23. Hugh Myddelton C., D., M.D., L., M.T.
24. Risinghill Street, M.T.
**Hackney.**
25. Baileys Lane, C., L., M.T.
26. Benthall Road, C., M.T.
27. Berger Road, M.D., M.T.
28. Casslaud Road, M.T.
29. College Lane, P.D.
30. Eleanor Road, M.T.
31. Enfield Road, M.D., M.T.
32. Gainsborough Road, M.T.
33. Gayhurst Road, L.
34. Glyn Road, C., L., M.T.
35. Homerton, D.
36. Homerton Row, C.
37. Lamb Lane, M.D.
38. Lauriston Road, C., L.
39. Millfields Road, C., L., M.T.
40. Morning Lane, B.
41. Northwold Road, M.D.
42. Queen's Road, C., L., M.T.
43. Sigdon Road, C., L., M.T.
44. Sydney Road, L.
45. Tottenham Road, C., P.T., L., H., M.T.
46. Wilton Road, C.
47. Windsor Road, C., M.D., L.
**Holborn.**
48. Drury Lane, M.T.
49. Great Wild Street, C., M.T.
50. Princeton Street, C., L.
51. Tower Street, M.T.

**Islington.**
52. Ambler Road, M.D., L.
53. Blackstock Road, C., M.T.
54. Buckingham Street, C., L.
55. Canonbury Road, C.
56. Duncombe Road, L., M.T.
57. Ecclesbourne Road, M.D., L., M.T.
58. Gifford Street, C., M.T.
59. Grafton Road, C.
60. Hargrave Park, C.
61. Hungerford Road, L., M.T.
62. Montem Street, C., L., M.T.
63. Newington Green, C., L., M.T.
64. Offord Road, P.T.
65. Queen's Head Street, C.
66. Richard Street, C., L.
67. Rotherfield Street, C.
68. Station Road, L.
69. Thornhill Road, C., M.T.
70. Upper Hornsey Road, M.D., L., M.T.
71. Vittoria Place, C., M.T.
72. Warbourne Road, C., M.T.
73. Yerbury Road, L, M.T.
**Lambeth**
74. Waterloo Road, L.
**Poplar.**
75. Atley Road, M.T.
76. Bow Creek, C., L.
77. Bromley Hall Road, C.
78. Culloden Street, C., M.D., L., H., M.T.
79. Fairfield Road, C., L., M.T.
80. Knapp Road, M.T.
81. Malmesbury Road, M.T.
82. Millwall, M.T.
83. Montcith Road, C., L.
84. Old Ford Road, M.D.
85. Old Palace, C., L., M.T.
86. Ricardo Street, C., L.
87. Roman Road, M.T.
**St. Pancras.**
88. Prospect Terrace, C., M.T.
**Shoreditch.**
89. Canal Road, C.
90. Catherine Street, L., M.T.
91. Gopsall Street, C., L., H., M.T.
92. Maidstone Street, C., M.D.
93. Napier Street, L., M.T.
94. St. John's Road, C., M.D., M.T.
95. Scawfell Street, C., M.T.
**Southwark.**
96. Chaucer, M.D., M.T.
97. Hatfield Street, M.T.
98. Orange Street, C., L., M.T.
99. Pocock Street, C., M.D.
100. Westminster Bridge Road, C., M.T.
**Stepney.**
101. Baker Street, C., L., M.T.
102. Bedford Street, M.T.
103. Ben Jonson, C., L.
104. Berner Street, C., L., M.T.
105. Broad Street, M.T.
106. Buxton Street, M.T.
107. Cable Street, C., M.D., L., M.T.
108. Chicksand Street, C.
109. Collingwood Street, C.
110. Commercial Street, P.D.
111. Deal Street, M.D.
112. Dempsey Street, M.T.
113. Essex Street, P.T.
114. Farrance Street, D., L.
115. Highway, B.
116. Lower Chapman Street, H.
117. Northey Street, M.D., M.T.
118. Old Castle Street, M.T.
119. St. James', M.D.
120. St. Paul's Road, L.
121. Sidney Square, H.
122. Smith Street, C., M.D., M.T.
123. South Grove, C.
124. Thomas Street, C., H., M.T.
125. Trafalgar Square, C., P.T., M.D., L.
**Stoke Newington.**
126. Church Street, L.
127. Oldfield Road, L., M.T.
128. Princess May Road, M.D.
129. Wordsworth Road, C., M.T.
**Westminster.**
130. Crown Court, M.D.

**Battersea.**
1. Basnett Road, C., M.T.
2. Battersea Park Road, L., M.T.
3. Ethelburga Street, C., L.
4. Gideon Road, M.T.
5. Honeywell Road, C., L., M.T.
6. Latchmere, C.
7. Lavender Hill, P.T., L., M.T.
8. Linden Lodge, B.
9. Mantua Street, C.
10. Plough Road, C.
11. Raymond Road, C.
12. Shillington Street, C., B., M.D., L., M.T.
13. Sleaford Street, L.
14. Surrey Lane, D., H., M.T.
15. Tennyson Street, C., J.H.

**Bermondsey.**
16. Alma, P.T., H., M.T.
17. Galleywall Road, C., M.D.
18. Monnow Road, C., L., M.T.
19. Pages Walk, L., M.T.

**Camberwell.**
20. Arthur Street, C., M.T.
21. Boundary Lane, B.
22. Choumert Road, C., M.D., L., M.T.
23. Cobourg Road, C., M.T.
24. Colls Road, C., M.T.
25. Crawford Street, C., M.T.
26. Croxton Road, L.
27. Daley Street, P.D.
28. Dulwich Hamlet, C., L., M.T.
29. Friern, L., H.
30. George Street, C.
31. Gloucester Road, M.D., M.T.
32. Goodrich Road, C., M.D., M.T.
33. Grove Vale, M.T.
34. Heber Road, M.T.
35. Ilderton Road, C., M.T.
36. Leo Street, C., M.D., L., H.
37. Mawbey Road, M.T.
38. Nunhead Passage, C., L., M.T.
39. Oliver Goldsmith, M.T.
40. Peckham Park, L., M.T.
41. Rolls Road, L.
42. Southampton Street, L.
43. Sumner Road, C., P.T., L., M.T.

**Lambeth.**
44. Cormont Road, M.D.
45. Elm Court, B.
46. Hackford Road, C., P.T., L., M.T.
47. Kennington Road, C.
48. Lollard Road, M.T.
49. Priory Grove, C., M.D.
50. Surrey Hill, C., L., M.T.
51. Stockwell Street, M.D., M.T.
52. South Lambeth Road, M.T.
53. Sunlight, L., M.T.
54. Stockwell Road, C., L.
55. Sussex Road, C., L., M.T.
56. Upper Kennington Lane, C., L., M.T.

**Lewisham.**
57. Sydenham Hill, C.

**Southwark.**
58. Blackfriars Street, H., M.T.
59. Cranmer Street, L., M.T.
60. Lion Street, L.
61. Mint Buildings, M.T.
62. Old Kent Road, D., P.D.
63. Paragon, C., L., H., M.T.
64. Penrose Street, C., M.T.
65. Sandford Row, L., M.T.
66. Sawyer Street, C., M.D., L.
67. Surrey Square, C.
68. Victory Place, C.
69. Westmorland Road, C., M.T.
70. West Square, C., L., M.T.

**Wandsworth.**
71. Brandlehow Road, C., L., M.T.
72. Cavendish Road, C., D., L., M.T.
73. Eardley Road, C., L.
74. Ellingham Street, L., M.T.
75. Freecroft Road, C., L., M.T.
76. Garratt Lane, M.D.
77. Haselrigge Road, C., L., M.T.
78. Merton Road, G., L.
79. New Park Road, C., L., H.
80. Oldridge Road, M.D.
81. St. Andrew's Street, L., M.T.
82. Smallwood Road, C., L., H.
83. Sunnyhill Road, C., L.
84. Swaffield Road, C., L., H.
85. Wald on Road, M.T.
86. Wandle Way, C., M.T.
87. West Hill, M.D., M.T.

George Philip & Son, Ltd.

NOTE.—*The following abbreviations are used in the lists of centres.* P.T. *Pupil Teachers*, B. *Blind*, D. *Deaf*, M.D. *Mentally D*

The London Geographical Institute

P.D. *Physically Defective*, C. *Cookery*, L. *Laundry work*, H. *Housewifery*, M.T. *Manual Training*.

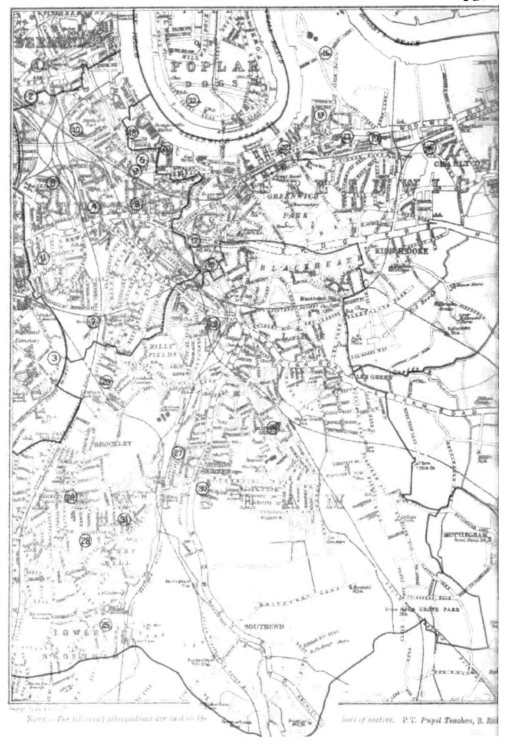

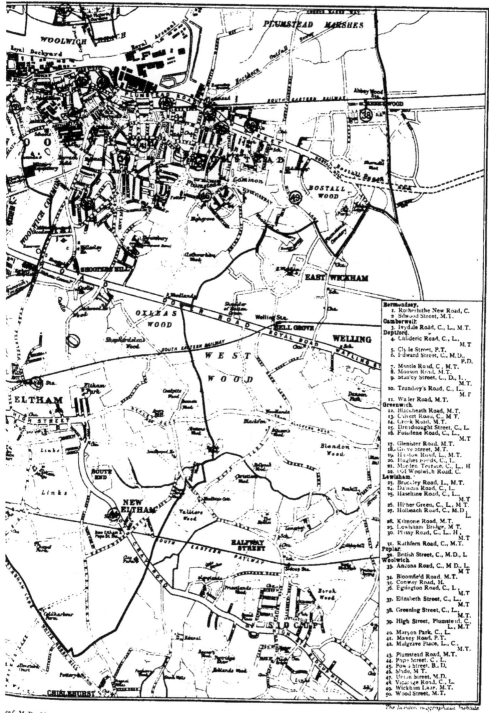

The London Topographical Institute

The time may come when the School Authority will think fit to act upon a suggestion which years ago was considered by the Special Schools Sub-Committee—viz. of dealing with the "intermediate" cases, which, while below normal are not serious enough to admit to Special schools. For example, by the introduction of this system an "aural" class and a "seeing" class could be formed for scholars, who while not properly suited to ordinary schools, are not deaf or blind enough for the Special schools. Separate classes might also be an advantage for children who although mentally feeble are of too high a grade to place with the ordinary mentally defectives. The "After Care" Voluntary Committees which have been started for the Physically Defective, the Blind and the Deaf, should be encouraged to continue their work, and if possible to extend it to other defectives. The extension of the work of the Voluntary Committee which arranges the mid day meal at Physically Defective schools to all other Special schools —perhaps through the help of the Local Managers—would be most useful.

Technical Training schools for the Blind and Deaf over 16 are required, and the provision of municipal workshop accommodation for the Blind, with perhaps a modification of the "Saxon system," so far as it is applicable in London, would probably enable that class to become largely self-supporting.

# SCHOOL ATTENDANCE.

## I.—THE INTRODUCTION OF COMPULSORY EDUCATION.

SOME of the most important provisions of the Elementary Education Act of 1870 were those contained in Section 74, which gave powers to School Boards to frame Bye-laws for the purpose of enforcing the attendance of children at school. The debates in Parliament clearly show that the Government of the day had come to the conclusion that the time had not arrived when it would be expedient to adopt a system of universal compulsion. It was, therefore, left to the discretion of the Boards elected under the Act to decide whether or not they would take advantage of the powers conferred upon them by Section 74 to frame Bye-laws for the purpose of enforcing attendance at school. Moreover, even if a School Board decided to enforce attendance, they were given a very wide latitude as to the limits of age within which compulsion should be operative, the only provision being that no child could be compelled to attend school under the age of five or over the age of thirteen.

Section 74 of the Elementary Education Act of 1870 is as follows :—

*Attendance at School.*

Every School Board may from time to time, with the approval of the Education Department, make Bye-laws for all or any of the following purposes :—

(1) Requiring the parents of children of such age, not less than five years nor more than thirteen years, as may be fixed by the Bye-laws, to cause such children (unless there is some reasonable excuse) to attend school:

(2) Determining the time during which children are so to attend school; provided that no such Bye-laws shall prevent the withdrawal of any child from any religious observance or instruction in religious subjects, or shall require any child to attend school on any day exclusively set apart for religious observance by the religious body to which his parent belongs, or shall be contrary to anything contained in any Act for regulating the education of children employed in labour:

(3) Providing for the remission or payment of the whole or any part of the fees of any child where the parent satisfies the School Board that he is unable from poverty to pay the same:

(4) Imposing penalties for the breach of any Bye-laws:

(5) Revoking or altering any Bye-law previously made;

Provided that any Bye-law under this section requiring a child between ten and thirteen years of age to attend school shall provide for the total or partial exemption of such child from the obligation to attend school if one of Her Majesty's Inspectors certifies that such child has reached a standard of education specified in such Bye-law. Any of the following reasons shall be a reasonable excuse; namely,

(1) That the child is under efficient instruction in some other manner;

(2) That the child has been prevented from attending school by sickness or any unavoidable cause;

(3) That there is no Public Elementary school open which the child can attend within such distance, not exceeding three miles, measured according to the nearest road, from the residence of such child, as the Bye-laws may prescribe.

The School Board, not less than one month before submitting any Bye-law under this section for the approval of the Education Department, shall deposit a printed copy of the proposed Bye-laws at their office for inspection by any ratepayer, and supply a printed copy thereof gratis to any ratepayer, and shall publish a notice of such deposit.

The Education Department before approving of any Bye-laws shall be satisfied that such deposit has been made and notice published, and shall cause such inquiry to be made in the school district as they think requisite.

Any proceeding to enforce any Bye law may be taken, and any penalty for the breach of any Bye-law may be recovered, in a summary manner; but no penalty imposed for the breach of any Bye-law shall exceed such amount as with the costs will amount to five shillings for each offence, and such Bye-laws shall not come into operation until they have been sanctioned by Her Majesty in Council.

It shall be lawful for Her Majesty, by Order in Council, to sanction the said Bye-laws, and thereupon the same shall have effect as if they were enacted in this Act.

All Bye-laws sanctioned by Her Majesty in Council under this section shall be set out in an appendix to the annual report of the Education Department.

Within a few weeks of the election of the School Board for London, the Board passed a resolution confirming the necessity of enforcing attendance at school; and, on February 15th, 1871, a Special Committee was appointed to draft Bye-laws under Section 74 of the Act. That this Committee went into the matter with extreme care is shown by the following report, which they submitted to the Board on June 28th, 1871:—

Your Committee entered upon their duties under a strong sense of the responsibility devolved upon them by the Board, and with a conviction that the compulsory clauses of the Act form one of its most important features, as marking a new epoch in the history of national education in England, and as affording the only means of making that education universal.

Your Committee deemed it advisable to ascertain how the principle of compulsion operated in countries where it had been tried, and its probable operation in this Metropolis. For this purpose they invited several gentlemen to give evidence before them, to whom they are indebted for very valuable information. Four sittings were occupied in taking this evidence. In addition to this several members of your Committee acquainted themselves with the reports of Mr. Matthew Arnold and Rev. Mark Pattison on education, with special reference to its compulsory aspect on the Continent, and also with the report of Bishop Fraser on the same subject with reference to America.

The conviction of the Committee that, although the compulsory clauses are the true expression of a decided public opinion, this opinion has been gradually formed, and, pronounced with some hesitation, has influenced the Committee in arriving at the practical conclusions which are embodied in the Bye-laws and regulations submitted with this Report.

Compulsion, although adopted in the Factory Act and other more recent legislation, is, in its direct application, new in England, and should, therefore, be carried out, especially at first, with as much gentleness and consideration for the circumstances and feelings of parents as is consistent with its effective operation.

Your Committee have thought it advisable to make a distinction between the Bye-laws which have a permanent character and cannot be changed without the sanction of the Queen in Council, and the machinery for carrying them into effect, which may be modified by the Board from time to time, according to local circumstances and experience. They have, therefore, with the aid of the Solicitors of the Board, framed a code of Bye-laws, in accordance with the instructions contained in the Act, and have prepared a scheme for their enforcement.

Your Committee have endeavoured to provide against the evil, widely felt, of habitual irregularity, as well as of total non-attendance, while at the same time admitting the total or partial exemption of children who have attained a fair amount of education, or who are necessarily at work during part of the day.

Your Committee, by a small majority, have decided that, in order to carry out Section 74, some provision must be made for the payment and remission of fees. But they are unanimously of opinion that the power given by Bye-law viii. should be most cautiously and sparingly used, and that the utmost care should be taken to avoid conveying to the poor the impression that they are to be relieved from the obligation of paying their children's schooling. Your Committee submit that the encouragement of anything like a general expectation on the part of the parents that, as a matter of course, and on the untested allegation of inability to pay the fees, they will be relieved, at the cost of the ratepayers, from their duty to their children, would be a great evil, as tending to pauperise a class of the population who should rather be stimulated to a sense of their duty, and to a manly spirit of independence. It is but justice to express the conviction that a large proportion of the wage-earning classes concur in these views.

Your Committee have had considerable discussion as to the meaning to be attached to the word "School." Eventually, your Committee resolved that the following definition should be inserted in the Interpretation Clause: The term "School" means either a Public Elementary school, or any other school at which efficient Elementary instruction is given.

Your Committee are convinced that the successful working of any code of Bye-laws must depend mainly on the means adopted for carrying it out. They have accordingly aimed at devising a machinery which shall take cognisance of all the children to be dealt with, and which shall only reach the last resort of legal proceedings in extreme cases of parental neglect, after passing on gradually through the stages of inquiry, remonstrance, and formal notice of the consequences of such neglect, if persevered in.

In pursuance of this view, they have recommended the appointment of Visitors to assigned districts, with defined duties. They suggest that, as a general rule, but not exclusively, these agents be women who have had experience in similar work, as District Visitors, etc. There is reason to believe that there are ladies who would gladly give their time to this work at a comparatively small cost, and the Committee are of opinion that by employing women it would be possible to secure the services of persons of a higher class than could otherwise be obtained, while the advantage would be gained of making a distinction between this class of officers and those employed in looking after the street children under the Industrial Schools Act. It is also recommended on the grounds (1) that the chief part of the work will consist in visiting the mothers of truant children, and in considering such excuses for non-attendance as want of clothes and other domestic difficulties, which can be most fitly dealt with by women; and (2) that the visits of a class of persons with whom the poor are already familiar, will be the least likely to excite resistance.

Your Committee have further recommended, for the purposes of supervision and of dealing with cases requiring to be brought under the action of the Law, that Divisional Committees be appointed, to be sub-divided into Local Committees, and that with a view to obtaining the advantage of local knowledge and support, persons resident in the division and interested in education, be invited to serve, with the Members for the Division, on these Committees. In order to secure coherence and stability, it is proposed that each Divisional Committee should appoint either one of their own number or a paid officer, to be responsible for arranging meetings of the Local Committees at convenient times and places, and to superintend the visitors.

Your Committee now beg leave to submit a code of Bye-laws in pursuance of the reference to them, and a system of administration which they believe will secure their effective operation.

### II.—THE FIRST BYE-LAWS.

The Committee then submitted nine Bye-laws.

In the first, the term "School" was defined as "a Public Elementary school or any other school at which efficient elementary education is given." A number of the Members of the Committee dissented from this definition, and expressed the opinion that the compulsory regular attendance of all children at school was more likely to be introduced with the willing acquiescence of the parents if complete freedom of choice were left to them as to the schools to which they might send their children. Upon this proposal there was considerable difference of opinion amongst the Members of the Board, but the Committee's definition was ultimately approved by the Board.

The second Bye-law dealt with the period of compulsion. The Act permitted this period to extend from five to thirteen years of age; and the Committee recommended that the Bye-laws should cover the whole period sanctioned by the Act. After amendments, moved with a view to curtailing the period of compulsion, had been lost at the Board, an amendment was moved which would have had the effect of postponing the operation of this Bye-law until the Education Department had certified that suitable efficient accommodation had been provided in the Metropolis. In consequence of the great deficiency of accommodation in London, it is evident that, had this amendment been adopted by the Board, compulsion would have been inoperative for some years. After an interesting discussion, this amendment was, however, withdrawn, and the Bye-law was approved.

The third Bye-law suggested by the Committee provided that the school to which a child might be sent could be selected by the parent. This provision was found to be unnecessary, and it was consequently withdrawn.

The next Bye-law suggested by the Committee laid down that a child should be required to attend school during the whole of the time that the school was open for instruction, with a clause making provision for withdrawals from religious instruction. This Bye-law is numbered 3 in the set finally approved.

A Bye-law dealing with the remission of fees was the subject of prolonged debate, it being discussed at no less than six different meetings of the Board. The greatest opposition was to a proposal that fees should be paid in denominational schools. Many amendments were proposed, and finally the whole Bye-law was withdrawn. By means, however, of a resolution of the Board, provision was made that for twelve months fees should be remitted, or paid, in Public Elementary schools "exceptionally on proof of urgent temporary need, each case being dealt with on its own merits, without prejudice to the principles involved on either side, it being understood that such remission or payment of fees is not to be considered as made in respect of any instruction in religious subjects."

After discussion, ranging over many meetings of the Board, the Bye-laws were finally adopted in the following form, and they were approved in an Order in Council dated December 21st, 1871 :—

o 2

*Bye-Laws of the School Board for London.*

I.—In these Bye-laws: Terms importing males include females.

The term "School" means either a Public Elementary school or any other school at which efficient elementary instruction is given.

The term Public Elementary school means a school or department of a school at which elementary education is the principal part of the education given, and at which the ordinary payments in respect of instruction do not exceed ninepence a week, and which is conducted in accordance with the regulations contained in the 7th Section of the Elementary Education Act.

The term Board or School Board means the School Board for London.

II.—The parent of every child of not less than five years, nor more than thirteen years of age, is required to cause such child to attend school, unless there be some reasonable excuse for non-attendance.

III.—Except as hereinafter provided, the time during which every such child is required to attend school, is the whole time for which the school selected shall be open for the instruction of children, not being less than twenty-five hours a week, except on Sundays, and except also that nothing herein contained shall prevent the withdrawal of any child from any religious observance or instruction in religious subjects, or shall require any child to attend school on any day exclusively set apart for religious observance by the religious body to which his parent belongs.

IV.—(1) A child of not less than ten years of age, who has obtained from one of Her Majesty's Inspectors a certificate that he has reached a standard equivalent to the Fifth Standard of the Government New Code of 1871, shall be altogether exempt from the obligation to attend school, and

(2) A child of not less than ten years of age who shows, to the satisfaction of the Board, that he is beneficially and necessarily at work, shall be exempt from the obligation to attend school during the whole time for which the school shall be opened as aforesaid, but every such child is required to attend school for at least ten hours in every week in which the school is opened as aforesaid, and in computing for the purpose of this section the time during which a child has attended any school there shall not be included any time during which such child has attended either,

(a) In excess of three hours at any one time, or in excess of five hours on any one day, or

(b) On Sundays.

V.—Provided always, that if and whenever Bye-laws III. and IV., or either of them, shall be contrary to, or inconsistent with the regulations affecting any child subject thereto contained in any Act for regulating the education of children employed in labour, the said regulations shall prevail, and the said Bye-law shall affect such child only to such extent as they are consistent with the said regulations.

VI.—In addition to the reasonable excuses for the non-attendance of a child at school mentioned in the Act, viz.:

(1) That the child is under efficient instruction in some other manner.

(2) That the child has been prevented from attending school by sickness or any unavoidable cause,

It shall be—

(3) A reasonable excuse for his non-attendance that there is no Public Elementary school open which such child can attend within one mile, measured according to the nearest road from the residence of such child.

VII.—Every parent who shall not observe, or shall neglect, or violate these Bye-laws, or any of them, shall upon conviction be liable to a penalty not exceeding 5s., including costs, for each offence.

## 1. *First Arrangements for Enforcing the Bye-Laws.*

Immediately after deciding upon their Bye-laws, the Board proceeded to consider the arrangements which were suggested by the Special Committee for giving effect to them. Under the Act of 1870, London was divided into ten divisions. In each division the Board agreed to form a Committee consisting of the Members for the division and of such other persons, " being inhabitants or ratepayers of that division, as the Board shall from time to time appoint." Every Divisional Committee was given power to nominate directly to the Board a duly qualified person to act as Clerk to the Committee and as Superintendent of the Visitors within the division. The Divisional Committees were also given the power to sub-divide their divisions and to form Sub-Committees, provided that full particulars were submitted to the Board for confirmation. The Sub-Committees were at first given powers similar to those of the Divisional Committees for specified areas. Every Sub-Committee had power to enforce the Bye-laws ; to divide its sub-division into districts, so that each district might be of such size and population as to be manageable by one Visitor ; to nominate for appointment by the Board as many Visitors as were deemed to be necessary ; to direct and control the Visitors ; and to fix its own quorum. After a very short time it was found that the plan of delegating to these Sub-Committees such full powers did not work satisfactorily ; and on July 3rd, 1872, the Board considered a motion to dissolve forthwith the whole of these Sub-Committees. After some discussion, it was, however, agreed to allow the Sub-Committees to continue, but to restrict their duties to dealing with absenteeism in its early stages. They were required to report to the Divisional Committees the results of their action, and their power to report directly to the Board, and to act independently of the Divisional Committees, was cancelled. Thenceforth the Divisional Committees had the general direction of the detailed work of the divisions, subject to the authority of the Central Committee at the Head Office.

The arrangements also defined the duties of a Visitor, and it is extremely interesting to note that, even at this early period, the Board realised the importance of the Visitors being called upon to keep a Schedule of the names and addresses of the whole of the children who should be required to attend school. It was decided that the Schedule should show the names of the children who were expected to attend school ; the school which each child should attend ; the names of the children said to be receiving efficient instruction in some other manner, particulars to be given of this instruction so that the Committee might be able to judge of its efficiency ; the names of the children not attending school, and the reasons given for their non-attendance. The Visitors were also required to investigate and report upon all applications from parents for the remission of school fees ; to report all cases of infringement of the Bye-laws within their district to the Committee for the division ; to report to the proper Authority any infringement of the Workshops' Act which might come under their notice ; and to call the attention of the Superintendents to all cases of children coming under their notice liable under the Industrial Schools Act to be sent to a certified Industrial school. The Board decided that it should be considered a breach of the Bye-laws if a child of less than 10 years of age were absent from school for more than one whole day or two half days in one week, or where there was frequent irregularity in the attendance of a child at school, unless sickness or some other reasonable cause could be shown for the non-attendance.

It should be here stated that two notices were drafted and approved by the Board, designated Notices A and B respectively. Up to 1874 both these notices invited the parents to attend before a Committee to explain the cause of the absence of the child. But after 1874 only the " B," or second notice, gave the parents the opportunity of appearing before a Committee.

When an infringement of the Bye-laws had been reported by the Visitor, he could be authorised by the Committee or the Divisional Superintendent to serve one of these notices, and it is worthy of remark that, at this period, he was given special instructions to read over and explain such notices to the parents, and to impress upon them the consequence of neglecting to comply with the warning. Other general arrangements were made for dealing with details of the Visitors' work.

In those early days there can be little doubt that the Board were convinced that to ensure the successful working of the compulsory clauses of the Act it was necessary to deal with cases of neglect with the greatest leniency. Indeed, the Special Committee made a point of reporting that they had aimed at devising machinery which should take cognisance of all children dealt with, but which should only reach the last resort of legal proceedings in extreme cases of parental neglect, after passing on gradually through the stages of inquiry, remonstrance, and formal notice of the consequence of such neglect if persisted in by the parents.

### 2. *The Early Machinery for Enforcing the Bye-Laws.*

By May, 1872, the Board had appointed a Superintendent to each of the ten divisions. At this period 47 Visitors had been appointed; and even at the end of 1872 there were only 92 Visitors at work, of whom 25 were women. The number of children in charge of a Visitor at this time varied from 2,500 to 18,100. One of the causes of this great disparity in the numbers was probably due to the fact that it had been left to the various Sub-committees within the divisions to recommend such officers as they deemed necessary; but the records of the Board show that even the Members of the Board did not at first realise the magnitude of the work and the fact that so large a number of Visitors as was subsequently found to be necessary would be required to perform the duties efficiently. In November, 1872, after further experience, the Board came to the conclusion that the staff of Visitors would have to be very greatly augmented, and they decided that additional Visitors should be appointed. The practical effect of their decision was to prevent an officer having more than 5,000 children under his charge. In consequence of this resolution, the number of Visitors employed at the end of 1873 had increased to 130. At this period the attendance could only be enforced in comparatively few districts, and the work of the staff was greatly restricted by the want of school places. Despite this fact, however, considerable efforts had been made to improve attendance wherever schools existed; and, during the year 1872, in addition to the service of a large number of cautionary notices, 478 summonses were issued, most of which were conducted by the Board's Solicitor. But the fact that in less than one-half of these cases convictions were obtained, clearly indicates the attitude of the Magistrates to School Board cases in these early days. In the following year (1873) there was some improvement, for out of 4,559 prosecutions, 3,155 fines were inflicted. Still, many Magistrates were unwilling to convict in School Board cases, as is shown by a report of a Divisional Superintendent, received in November, 1873, wherein he stated that out of 83 cases taken in three months he had only obtained one conviction, although some of the parents had been previously summoned two or three times.

In March, 1873, the Board constituted a Standing Committee, known as the Bye-Laws Committee, to deal with the enforcement of the attendance of children at school. This Committee continued to perform these duties until November, 1891, when the work of that Committee was transferred to the School Accommodation and Attendance Committee, which has ever since directed the work. Upon the recommendation of the Bye-Laws Committee, the Board, in July, 1874, further reduced the number of children to be allotted to each Visitor from 5,000 to 3,000. In view of the fact that in many parts of London there was still a great deficiency of accommodation, it was understood that this arrangement should apply only to the districts where there was suitable accommodation for the children.

As additional school accommodation was provided, the staff was able gradually to deal with an increased number of cases. Still for many years the Board was considerably hampered by the lack of sufficient Police Court facilities.

### III.—SCHEDULING.

It has already been stated that the Board from the first made it a condition that the Visitors should keep Schedules of the children requiring elementary instruction in their districts; but in many cases the Visitors were in charge of such huge districts—sometimes containing as many as 18,000 children—that it must have been impossible for them to have kept anything resembling a complete record. The first real attempts to secure in the Visitors' Schedules anything like a correct statement of the children requiring elementary education must have been made subsequently to July, 1874; for it was in this year that the Board decided to make the Visitors' districts a reasonable size by reducing the number of children allocated to each Visitor from 5,000 to 3,000. It was, moreover, in this year that the first general rule was issued to the Visitors as to the class of property which should be scheduled, the Committee deciding that the Schedules should include " all houses rated at £25 or less; all houses rated at a higher rating than £25, for which the landlord is rated; all houses which are let in lodgings to weekly or monthly tenants; all servants' dwellings, such as gardeners' cottages, stables with living rooms, &c.; all houses containing a child on the roll of a Public Elementary school, as well as any others ascertained to contain or likely to contain children of a similar class, or any children of a higher class whose education, it is supposed, has been neglected."

In consequence of the number of children returned by the Visitors being greatly under the number which required elementary instruction, according to an estimate based on the Registrar-General's returns, the Bye-Laws Committee, in 1878, went very exhaustively into the matter, and they called upon each Divisional Superintendent to report fully upon the figures furnished for his division. It is clear, from these reports, that an adequate number of Visitors had not been appointed to deal with both visitation and scheduling. In these reports appears for the first time a suggestion that, in addition to the Visitor for the district, there should be Special Visitors appointed for dealing with street cases. The Divisional Superintendents reported that very great difficulty was experienced in tracing the poorest families; that frequently the parents did their very best to evade the officers; and that, upon removing from one district to another, it was no infrequent occurrence to find that the parents withheld the names of their eldest children, so that, if possible, these children might be sent to work. Moreover, it was pointed out that the Visitors had not scheduled the whole of their districts simultaneously, and many of the Superintendents were of opinion that this was the chief cause of the discrepancy. The time of the Visitors would seem to have been almost entirely taken up in visiting absentees, and up to this time the scheduling had been looked upon as a secondary matter. In consequence, no doubt, of the inquiry which had been instituted by the Bye-Laws Committee, it was resolved that there should be each year a simultaneous scheduling of the whole of London.

Up to 1877, the figures supplied by the Visitors had not been considered sufficiently reliable to be quoted in the Board's returns, but the result of the first simultaneous scheduling of 1878 was given in the Board's official returns. From this time forward great attention was paid to the scheduling. Increased efforts were made to trace families from place to place, and Visitors were required to obtain the particulars of each family from the officer in whose district the family last resided, and thus ensure that the whole of the children of school age were placed in the Schedule; and, at a later date, Special Visitors were appointed to pick up children in the streets and to trace families.

It must be borne in mind, however, that the work was still hampered by lack of school accommodation. As, however, more school places were provided, and the Visitors became more accustomed to the work, the results improved; until, in 1892, the number of children returned by the Visitors exceeded the estimate based upon the Census by nearly 11,000; and ever since that date the returns of the visitors have shown a greater number of children requiring elementary education than the estimate based upon the Registrar-General's figures.

The diagram on the opposite page shows a comparison of the estimated number of school places required (1) on the basis of calculation that one-sixth of the population require elementary school places, and (2) on the Board's method of calculation approved by the Board of Education from time to time, based on the figures obtained from the Visitors' schedules.

*Diagram showing, from 1871 to 1903, the estimated number of school places required upon the basis of (1) the assumption that one-sixth of the population require elementary school places, and (2) the methods adopted by the Board.*

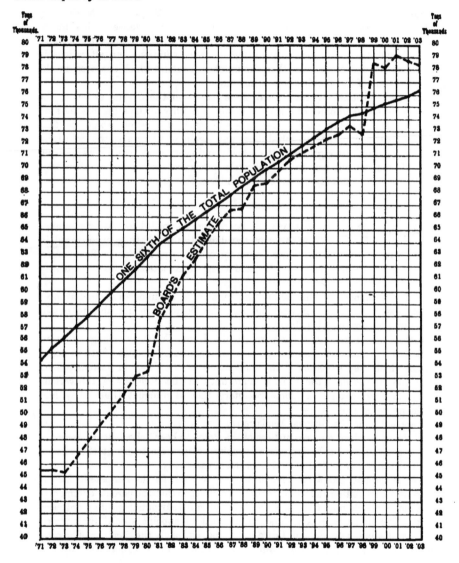

The Board have for a long period considered a correct Schedule to be the very basis of the Visitor's work, and they have attached very great importance to this branch of the work. Each Visitor is required to make corrections, where necessary, day by day, and, in migratory districts, there are frequently many more additions and alterations in the Schedule at the end of the year than the number of entries which appeared in the Schedule at the time of the simultaneous scheduling.

Now that the Visitors' figures exceed those based on the Census estimate, the question might be asked whether or not there is any possibility of the schedules showing more children than actually exist. The answer to such a question would be that immediately after the simultaneous scheduling, and again at Christmas, the Schedules are verified by the duplicate registers of the schools, and every child's name not appearing on the roll of the schools has to be definitely accounted for in some other way. Consequently the Schedules cannot show more children than actually exist.

### IV.—POLICE COURT DIFFICULTIES.

At a very early stage of their existence the Board were compelled to make representations to the Home Office in consequence of the difficulties which they experienced in obtaining adequate facilities at the Police Courts for the hearing of School Board cases. The first representations were made in 1873, and these representations were frequently repeated.

Probably in consequence of this action the number of summonses allowed at most Police Courts was somewhat increased, but still the Board were not able to obtain adequate facilities for dealing with their cases.

In 1889, the Board presented a Memorial to the Home Secretary calling attention " to the evils and dangers attending the present arrangements "; setting forth in detail the difficulties which they experienced in consequence of the delay in bringing their cases before the Magistrates; the want of uniformity in the decisions of the various Magistrates ; and reminding the Home Secretary that at different times they had suggested the following remedies:—

(1) The appointment of additional Magistrates;

(2) Facilities to be given for two Justices of the Peace to hear School Board cases ;

(3) The appointment of a Peripatetic Stipendiary Magistrate to sit at the various Courts in rotation in order to deal with School Board cases only.

The Board suggested that arrangements should be made for the Peripatetic Magistrate to hold his Courts either in the Vestry or Town Halls, so that the parents summoned under the Education Acts might be spared from the criminal surroundings of an ordinary Police Court. The Home Secretary, however, declined to appoint special Stipendiary Magistrates for dealing with School Board cases, and, although the facilities offered to the Board were slightly improved, great difficulty continued to be experienced by the Board.

In 1891 the Board availed themselves of an offer which was made by the Justices of the Tower Division to deal, as an experiment, with summonses issued under the

Education Acts; but, in July of the same year, the Justices suspended the hearing of these cases, in consequence of a communication which they had received from the Home Secretary. In 1894 the Justices arranged to resume their Petty Sessions at the Town Hall, Hackney, for hearing School Board cases, and they have continued to deal with the Board cases from the Tower Hamlets Division, and from the greater portion of the Hackney Division, down to the present time with excellent results to school attendance.

Moreover, in 1896, arrangements were also made with the Justices of the Kensington Petty Sessions to deal with cases under the Education Acts. Since that date practically the whole of the School Board cases for the Chelsea Division have been heard by these Justices, and the results have been entirely satisfactory.

By these arrangements the Divisions of Chelsea, Hackney, and Tower Hamlets were supplied with ample facilities for the hearing of their cases; and the wish of the Board that the parents summoned should not have criminal surroundings when appearing before the Magistrates has thus far been fulfilled. Still, within recent years, the Board have been compelled to call the Home Secretary's attention to their difficulty in securing a sufficient number of cases in some parts of London. The last representation which the Board made to the Home Secretary with regard to the lack of Police Court facilities was in 1898, when a deputation from the Board was received by the Home Secretary, and, at his request, a summary of the procedure which was adopted in absentee cases was forwarded to the Home Office.

A Committee was soon afterwards appointed by the Home Office to consider the whole question of the jurisdiction of the Metropolitan Police Magistrates and County Justices respectively, and certain Members of the Board gave evidence on behalf of the Board. As a result of the deliberations of the Committee a Bill was introduced into Parliament, which, if passed, would have provided greater facilities for the hearing of School Board cases. Unfortunately, through pressure of business, the Bill was dropped by the Government, and it has not since been introduced.

Nevertheless, during the last few years the Board have been able to obtain a greater number of summonses. This probably has been due more to the great change in the attitude of the London Magistrates towards School Board cases than to any other cause, most of the Magistrates now being anxious that the Board shall experience no difficulty in securing an adequate number of summonses.

With regard to the number of cases dealt with, it is well worth recording that, now that the Board have the opportunity of dealing with the cases immediately they consider it necessary to take legal proceedings, it has been found that the number of cases needing prosecution is greatly decreasing. In 1900, the Board issued 28,836 summonses, and obtained no less than 26,119 convictions. But since this period the number of summonses has decreased year by year, until in the year 1903 the number was reduced to 20,584.

It is not claimed that this reduction in the number of summonses is wholly due to the fact that the Board have now facilities for dealing with their cases as they arise; for it is no doubt partially attributable to the fact that the Act of 1900 enables Magistrates to inflict a fine up to 20s., whereas, prior to that date, they were limited to a maximum penalty of 5s. for non-attendance. Probably even a more potent reason for the reduction in the number of summonses would be found in the increase of the Visitorial staff, and the instructions which they have received to deal with absenteeism in *its earliest stages.*

## V.—EMPLOYMENT OF CHILDREN OF SCHOOL AGE.

One of the great obstacles to regular attendance at school has been the employment of children of school age out of school hours. Although the Act of 1876 provides that such employment shall not interfere with the efficient elementary instruction of a child, yet it has, nevertheless, been found extremely difficult to deal with even the most excessive cases of child labour, where a child has attended with fair regularity at school. From a return which was obtained by the Board in 1899 from 112 schools, the following results were obtained :—

1,143 children worked from 19 to 29 hours per week,
729 children worked from 30 to 39 hours per week, and
285 children worked 40 hours and above per week.
Of these 309 children were employed at house-work and domestic work for 8,309 hours per week, and received a total sum of £21 9s. 3½d., which is an average of 27 hours each child at ½d. per hour;
719 children were employed at newspaper and milk delivery for 21,662 hours per week, and and received a total sum of £94 1s. 10d., which is an average of 30 hours each child at 1d. an hour;
1,056 children were employed at shop and factory work and errands for 31,923 hours per week, and received a total sum of £121 4s. 11d., which is an average of 30 hours each child at 1d. per hour; and
69 children were employed at various other employments for 2,001 hours per week, and received a total sum of £9 12s. 6d., which is an average of 29 hours each child at 1¼d. per hour.

The reports of the head teachers, which accompanied the returns from the schools, in many cases showed that the children who were subjected to so many hours of labour were quite unfit to receive instruction. Indeed, one head master stated that some of the lads were "so tired when they came to school in the morning that the teacher has enough to do to keep them awake."

In view of the state of affairs disclosed by this return, the Board decided that it was desirable to limit the out of school employment of school children, and a representation was made to the London County Council with the view of determining what should be the limitations to such employment, and also whether the powers of the Council would enable them to put such limitations into operation, or whether it would be necessary for them to apply for further Parliamentary powers. This question received very careful consideration from the London County Council, and they made a special report containing a number of suggestions for dealing with the question.

In the year 1900, when the Elementary Education Bill of that year was before Parliament, an amendment was on the Paper which provided that no person should take into his employment any child between the ages of 5 and 14, unless such child had previously obtained a licence to labour or trade. The amendment also outlined a method by which the licences could be obtained; and there was a provision that no licence for street trading should be given to any child under the age of 14.

The Board petitioned Parliament in favour of this amendment, but the Government refused to accept the proposals contained therein. They, however, appointed an Inter-Departmental Committee of the Home Office, the Board of Education, and the Board of Trade to consider the whole question of the employment of school children. Before this Committee two Members, and many of the Officers of the Board gave evidence.

The Report of the Inter-Departmental Committee was issued in November, 1901, and in March, 1902, the Board addressed a letter to the First Lord of the Treasury, urging that facilities should be given for legislation dealing with the limitation and regulation of the employment of children.

Subsequently a Bill dealing with this subject was introduced into the House of Commons, but on the 16th October, 1902, in consequence of pressure of business, this Bill was withdrawn.

Early in 1903, the Board had before them suggestions which had been submitted to the Home Secretary with regard to the matter by a deputation which had waited upon him urging the re-introduction of a Bill dealing with this subject. The Board, after approving these resolutions, forwarded a copy of them to each of the London Members of Parliament. A Bill dealing with the subject was introduced by the Home Secretary, and it occupied a considerable amount of time in Parliament during the year 1903. During its various stages the Bill was considerably modified. As finally passed, it gave to Local Authorities power to make Bye-laws prescribing for all children, or for boys and girls separately, the age below which employment is illegal; the hours between which employment is illegal; and the number of daily and weekly hours beyond which employment is illegal. It also permitted Local Authorities to make Bye-laws prohibiting absolutely, or permitting subject to conditions, the employment of children in any specified occupation. It further gave Local Authorities the power to frame Bye-laws with respect to Street Trading by persons under the age of sixteen, and permitted the Local Authorities to grant licences and to generally regulate Street Trading One particular provision contained in this part of the Act was that Local Authorites in making Bye-laws should have special regard to the desirability of preventing the employment of girls under the age of 16 in streets or public places. The Act also provided that no child under the age of 11 years should be employed in Street Trading. Moreover, it enacted that no child employed half-time under the Factory and Workshop Act should be employed in any other occupation. The Act also contains a general restriction that a child shall not be employed between the hours of nine in the evening and six in the morning unless special provision is made for any specified occupation. It further enacted that a child should not be employed in any occupation likely to be injurious to life, limb, health, or education.

Under this Act the authority for the City of London will be the City Corporation, and for the rest of the Metropolis the London County Council. It is understood that the City Corporation have framed Bye-laws, and that the County Council have the question before them, and at an early date they will no doubt submit Bye-laws to the Home Office.

*Principal Alterations since* 1870 *in the Law Relating to School Attendance.*

The first Act amending the Act of 1870 was that passed in 1873. The only section in this Act which affected school attendance was a provision that, where out-relief was given by Guardians to any parent of a child between 5 and 13 years of age, it should be a condition that such child, unless exempt from school attendance, should attend school, and that such further relief as might be necessary should be given to enable the child to attend school.

The next Education Act was passed in 1876. Clause 4 of this Act provides that it shall be the duty of the parent of every child to cause such child to receive efficient elementary instruction in Reading, Writing, and Arithmetic. Section 5 enacts that no person shall take into his employment a child under the age of 10 years, or any child above that age who has not obtained a certificate exempting him from school attendance. The maximum penalty for the illegal employment of a child was fixed at 40s. This Act also introduced the principle of what is generally known as the "Dunce's Certificate" of exemption, such exemption being allowed in virtue of a given number of attendances made by a child for a certain number of years. The number of attendances fixed by this Act was 250 for each year.

In order that a child might claim exemption under this Act it was necessary in the years 1877 and 1878 that it should have passed the Second Standard, or should have made 250 attendances in not more than two schools during any two years after reaching the age of 5. In the year 1879 the Standard was raised to the Third, and the number of years for attendances to three. In the following year the Standard remained the same, but the 250 attendances must have been made for each of four years. From that year onwards, until the passing of the Act of 1900, a child could be exempted from school attendance by having made 250 attendances (in not more than two schools in each year) for five years after having reached the age of 5, or by having passed the Fourth Standard, provided that the child was not amenable to the Bye-laws in force for the time being. The practical effect was that in London from 1881 the "Dunce's Certificate" could not be claimed unless a child had reached the age of 13.

It is worthy of notice that the Bye-laws of the School Board for London in force in 1877 did not permit of the exemption of a child under the age of 13, unless, being over 10 years of age, it had passed the Fifth Standard, although exemption could then be claimed under the Act of 1876 for a child who was 10 years of age if it had made 250 attendances for two years.

Sections 11 and 12 of the Act of 1876 gave power to School Boards to deal with cases of children habitually neglected by parents, or found wandering and consorting with criminals or disorderly persons, and it is under these Sections that the cases of habitual truancy are dealt with.

It will be remembered that the Act of 1870 left it to the discretion of School Authorities to frame Bye-laws. In 1880, however, an Act was passed which made it compulsory for the Local Authority for education to frame Bye-laws for their district.

After the passing of the Act of 1876 the Board experienced great difficulty with some of the Magistrates in London, who held that, where a parent pleaded that a child was beyond control, a prosecution could not be instituted under the Bye-laws, but must, of necessity, be taken under the Act of 1876. Section 4 of the Act of 1880 definitely enacted that proceedings might be taken by the Local Authority for punishing a contravention of a Bye-law, notwithstanding that the act, or neglect, or default, alleged as such contravention, constituted habitual neglect to provide efficient elementary education within the meaning of Section 11 of the Act of 1876.

In 1891 an Act was passed which enabled education to be made free.

The Board, even before the Bill had been passed, decided that, should Parliament give them the power, they would abolish the fees in the whole of their schools, and make education entirely free so far as their schools were concerned.

Until the year 1893 the education of the Blind and the Deaf was not made obligatory; but in that year an Act was passed which made it compulsory for a Blind child between the ages of 5 and 16, and of a Deaf child between the ages of 7 and 16, to receive education; and the attendance of these children at school could be enforced as if it were required by the Bye-laws made under the Acts of 1870-1891.

In the year 1893 a short Act of Parliament was passed prohibiting the exemption from school attendance of any child under the age of 11.

During 1899 the Defective and Epileptic Children Act became law. This Act gave School Authorities powers to enforce the education of a Defective or Epileptic child between the ages of 7 and 16 wherever suitable provision had been made for the instruction of such children.

It was also in the year 1899 that Parliament enacted that the minimum age for exemption from school attendance should be 12.

In this Act a provision was made that, if a Local Authority fixed 13 as the minimum age for exemption for children to be employed in agriculture, in such district children over 11 and under 13 who had passed the standard fixed for partial exemption should not be required to attend school more than 250 times in any year. It also provided that a child should be entitled to obtain partial exemption from school attendance on attaining the age of 12, if such child had made 300 attendances in not more than two schools during each year for five preceding years, whether consecutive or not.

In 1900 an Act was passed which allowed Bye-laws to cover all children up to the age of 14; increased the number of attendances required in each year under the Act of 1876 from 250 to 350, and also increased the maximum penalty for non-attendance at school from 5s. to 20s.

The only other Act which affects school attendance is the Employment of Children Act, which has already been dealt with.

The following table will show the qualifications necessary for total or partial exemption at different periods since the establishment of the School Board (a) according to the requirements of the Bye-laws of the School Board for London, and (b) according to the Elementary Education Acts:—

REQUIREMENTS FOR PARTIAL AND TOTAL EXEMPTION.

| | ACCORDING TO THE BYE-LAWS. | | | | ACCORDING TO THE ELEMENTARY EDUCATION ACTS. | | |
|---|---|---|---|---|---|---|---|
| Periods. | Conditions for Partial Exemption. | | Conditions for Total Exemption. | | Act. | Partial. | Total. |
| | Age. | Qualification. | Age. | Qualification. | | | |
| From Nov., 1871 to Nov., 1873 | Not less than 10 years | Beneficially and necessarily at work* | Not less than 10 years | Having reached St. V. | 1870 | ... | Bye-laws to provide for partial or total exemption of a child between 10 and 13 years if child has reached standard of education specified in Bye-laws. |
| From Nov., 1873 to May, 1879 | Do. | Do.† | Do. | Do. | 1876 | ... ... | A child could be employed in 1877 if over 9 years, and subsequent years if over 10 years, under following conditions:—<br>In year　Passed<br>1877　St. II.　Or made 250 attendance in not more than two schools for two years.<br>1878　St. II.　Do.<br>1879　St. III.　Do. for three years.<br>1880　St. III.　Do. for four years.<br>1881　St. IV.　Do. for five years.<br>and onwards. |
| From May, 1879 to July, 1891 | Between 10 and 13 years | Having reached Stan. III., and beneficially and necessarily at work‡ | Between 10 and 13 years | Having reached St. VI. | | | |
| From July, 1891 to Feb., 1894 | Do. | Having reached Stan. IV., and beneficially and necessarily at work | Do. | Do. | | | |
| From Feb., 1894 to July, 1898 | Between 11 and 13 years | Do. | Between 11 and 13 years | Do. | 1893 | Minimum age raised to 11 years | Minimum age raised to 11 years. |
| From July, 1898 to Feb., 1900 | Do. | Having reached Stan. V., and beneficially and necessarily at work | Do. | Having reached St. VII. | 1899 | Between 12 and 13 if reached Stan. V. or made 300 attendances in not more than two schools for five years | Minimum age raised to 12 years. |
| From Feb., 1900 to Dec., 1900 | Between 12 and 13 years | Do., Or having made 300 attendances in not more than two schools during each year for five preceding years after 5 years of age whether consecutive or not | Between 12 and 13 years | Do. | 1900 | Maximum age raised to 14 years | Maximum age raised to 14 years, and 350 attendances substituted for 250 attendances mentioned in Act of 1876. |
| From Dec., 1900 to present time | Nil | Nil | Between 12 and 14 years | Do. | | | |

* Not required to attend more than ten hours a week; attendance however could not be counted for more than three hours a session, or more than five hours a day, or for Sunday. † Attendance on Saturday added to the time for which attendance could not be counted. ‡ Child to make five attendances a week.

## VI.—THE STAFF AND ITS DUTIES.

From 1874 until 1901 the rule that a Visitor should have charge of about 3,000 children of the Elementary school class was in force. In July, 1901, the School Accommodation and Attendance Committee were urged by the Members for certain divisions to recommend the appointment of a number of Visitors beyond that which could be allowed under the existing rule. During this year the Committee were also informed by their Principal Clerk, in his yearly report upon Divisional Office Administration that the visitation of children making only eight attendances a week varied very considerably in the different divisions, and even in different districts of the same division. He reported that, wherever there had been a systematic visitation of children losing two attendances a week, the results were most satisfactory. He, however, informed the Committee that comparatively few of the Visitors could spare the time to visit such cases, and that in some of the most difficult districts the Visitors were hardly able to cope with the cases losing three attendances and more a week. The Committee were impressed with the importance of securing the systematic visitation of the parents of children who lost two half-days in the week; and, after very carefully considering the question, the Committee at first recommended that the number of children to be allotted to a Visitor should be reduced to 2,700. This proposal, however, was taken back from the Board, and after further consideration the Committee modified their proposal, and recommended that, in future, the average number of children requiring elementary education to be allotted to each Visitor should be 2,800. This recommendation met with the approval of the Board. At the same time, the Board adopted a recommendation of the School Accommodation and Attendance Committee that an additional Visitor for special purposes should be allowed for each division. It was understood that the services of this officer should be utilised in districts of a specially difficult character, or where the percentage of attendance was below 80. It was, however, left to the discretion of the Divisional Committees to use the services of these Visitors wherever they were of opinion that the work of additionally experienced officers would be beneficial and desirable.

In increasing the staff it was understood that the Visitors would in future visit the parents of children who lost two attendances a week. In their last Report, the School Accommodation and Attendance Committee stated that they had received with great satisfaction a report from their Principal Clerk " that in many divisions not only are cases making 80 per cent. of attendances visited, but that a considerable number of cases of 80 to 90 per cent. of attendances is also dealt with by the Visitors." The Committee further reported that they were of opinion that " this class of visitation prevents many cases becoming chronic absentees, and they believe that, by this means, the number of prosecutions will be still further decreased."

There is a consensus of opinion amongst the Divisional Superintendents that the work of the Special Visitors has been a great success.

Prior to January, 1899, there were attached to the Industrial Schools Department

P

at the Head Office a number of officers who dealt with the cases reported by the Visitors and Divisional Superintendents to the Industrial Schools Committee as suitable cases for Truant and Industrial schools.   These officers were empowered to charge any cases which they met with in the streets coming under the provisions of the Industrial Schools Act of 1866.   They also made full inquiries into all the cases of children of school age who were charged by the Police, and submitted the results of these inquiries to the Industrial Schools Committee.

In December, 1898, the School Accommodation and Attendance Committee acquiesced in a recommendation of a Special Sub-committee which had been appointed by the Industrial Schools Committee that these officers should be placed under the supervision of the Divisional Superintendents, and ever since this date they have formed part of the School Attendance staff.

In May, 1901, the attention of the School Accommodation and Attendance Committee was called to the desirability of the systematic patrol of the streets in certain parts of London during the evening and night by some of the most experienced of the School Board's Visitors.   From information which was supplied to the Committee, they came to the conclusion that if this work were performed many facts could be obtained which could not be discovered by their officers during the daytime, and that in all probability the special information obtained during the night would be the means of rescuing many children from evil and criminal surroundings.   They then requested their Chairman to confer with the Chairman of the Industrial Schools Committee.

As a result of this conference, a scheme was approved by the School Accommodation and Attendance Committee for the work to be conducted as an experiment for six months.   Each Divisional Superintendent was authorised to select from his staff four officers, it being understood that the work should be performed in each division at least three evenings in a week, and that, as a general rule, the officers should not be engaged for more than one evening in each week.

At the end of six months the Committee received reports from all the Divisional Superintendents.   From these reports it was ascertained that during the first six months of the experiment 196 children had been charged by the officers engaged upon the night work ; that of this number no fewer than 93 had been sent to Industrial schools, and that the remaining 103 children had been discharged by the Magistrates.   The results thus obtained were so extremely satisfactory that the work has been continued up to the present time.

During the last year 827 children were charged by the officers, and of these 126 were sent to Industrial schools ; 199 were discharged, two cases being on remand when the return was submitted.   It should be pointed out that, even when a case is discharged by the Magistrate, it is kept under the closest possible observation ; and that the Divisional Superintendents require from the Visitors special reports from time to time upon all these cases.   Consequently many of these children are dealt with under the Education Acts.

In the last Report of the School Accommodation and Attendance Committee it is stated that the Divisional Superintendents are unanimously of opinion that the work has had a most beneficial effect, and that a number of Superintendents draw special attention to the fact that the Police and other Public Officials have stated that the number of children found in the streets during the night begging or selling articles has very greatly decreased since the Board's Officers have been doing the night work.

In addition to the duties which have been previously outlined, the collection of all contributions from Parents and Guardians towards the maintenance of Blind and Deaf children, and also the collection of the contributions for children in Day Industrial Schools, is now performed by the Visitors; and it is satisfactory to be able to state that, since this work has been in the hands of the Attendance Staff, a far greater proportion of the amounts due has been collected than heretofore.

Up to the year 1901 the system adopted throughout London for dealing with absentee and irregular cases was to obtain from all Board schools, and, wherever possible, from Voluntary schools, duplicate registers showing the names, addresses, and particulars of each child's attendance. From this duplicate was abstracted and entered in a book the particulars of each absentee case. The Visitor concerned then placed in his book, at the house, the reasons for absence, and, later in the week, entered these reasons on the duplicate register. It will be readily understood that this system involved a very considerable amount of clerical work.

For some two and a-half years the Board have, however, been testing, in certain divisions of London, the plan of having the duplicate register in the form of a slip for each child.

Under this system the head teachers enter on a separate slip for each child the same particulars as are given on the duplicate register. The slips are sent to the Visitor in the order of the children on the register, and are numbered consecutively. When the Visitor receives the slips from the schools he places a distinctive mark on the last slip in each class, and at once sorts the slips of absentees from those of children who have been regular in their attendance. He retains the slips for the children residing in his own district, and hands to the Visitors in whose districts the other children reside the slips for the remaining absentee cases. When the Visitor has received the whole of the slips for his irregular cases, he at once proceeds to arrange them into the order in which he desires to use them in his visitation. He places on the slip, when making his visit, the alleged reasons for the absence of the child. When he has completed his visitation, the Visitor in charge of the school is responsible for seeing that all slips are placed in proper order, and that no slips are missing. They are then returned to the school. Provision has been made on the slip, as on the duplicate register, for the block and page in the Visitor's schedule to be shown. In short, the "Slip" system is in effect the "Duplicate Register" system, only in slip form. By this method the copying out of the absentee cases in a book is entirely dispensed with, the result being that the clerical work is considerably less than under the "Duplicate Register" system.

The Board, after carefully considering the results of the experiment which they had caused to be made, decided that the "Slip" system should be adopted throughout London.

The present staff of each of the several divisions is as follows:—

City and Westminster—1 Divisional Superintendent, 1 Assistant Superintendent, 1 Clerk, and 15 Visitors.

Chelsea—1 Divisional Superintendent, 1 Assistant Superintendent, 5 Clerks, 1 Office Youth, and 37 Visitors.

Finsbury—1 Divisional Superintendent, 1 Assistant Superintendent, 5 Clerks, and 42 Visitors. (An Italian Visitor is also employed 3 days a week.)

Greenwich—1 Divisional Superintendent, 1 Assistant Superintendent, 4 Clerks, 2 Office Youths, and 38 Visitors.

Hackney—1 Divisional Superintendent, 1 Assistant Superintendent, 4 Clerks, 1 Junior Clerk, and 40 Visitors.

East Lambeth—1 Divisional Superintendent, 1 Assistant Superintendent, 4 Clerks, 2 Office Youths, and 33 Visitors.

West Lambeth—1 Divisional Superintendent, 2 Assistant Superintendents, 4 Clerks, 2 Office Youths, and 53 Visitors.

Marylebone—1 Divisional Superintendent, 1 Assistant Superintendent, 4 Clerks, 2 Office Youths, and 36 Visitors.

Southwark—1 Divisional Superintendent, 1 Assistant Superintendent, 2 Clerks, 2 Office Youths, and 25 Visitors.

Tower Hamlets—1 Divisional Superintendent, 1 Assistant Superintendent, 5 Clerks, 2 Office Youths, and 45 Visitors.

Total—10 Divisional Superintendents, 11 Assistant Superintendents, 38 Clerks, 1 Junior Clerk, 13 Office Youths, and 364 Visitors. An Italian Visitor is employed 3 days a week.

Each Divisional Superintendent is responsible for the efficient administration within his division of the Bye-laws and Acts of Parliament relating to school attendance, and also for the supervision of the Visitors and the Clerical Staff. It is his duty periodically to examine the work of the Visitors, to see that all their books and records are properly kept, and to pay visits without notice from time to time to them upon their districts He is also required to report at once to the Divisional Committee any serious breach of discipline or good conduct on the part of any member of his staff, and to report directly. to the School Accommodation and Attendance Committee any second offence.

The Principal Clerk of the School Accommodation and Attendance Committee, or his Head Assistant, has for some years been required to visit each of the divisional offices at least once a year; to see the Clerical Staff and Visitors at work; to confer with the Divisional Superintendent; and to report his impressions and suggestions to the School Accommodation and Attendance Committee.

## VII.—Some Results of School Attendance Work.

From a return submitted to Parliament in 1876 it has been ascertained that in the year 1871 there was accommodation in the efficient Elementary schools in London for 262,259 children; that at the same period the average number on the rolls of these schools was 222,518, and that the average attendance was 174,301. It was estimated that there were at this period 574,693 children of the Elementary school class.

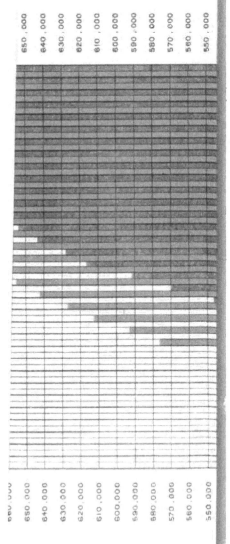

650,000
640,000
630,000
620,000
610,000
600,000
590,000
580,000
570,000
560,000
550,000

**NOTE.** The estimated number of school places required was based upon the Registrar General's figures down to the year 1878. From that year the figures have been based upon the returns obtained from the visitors' schedules.

To face page 243

From these figures it will be seen that only 38·7 per cent. of the children were on the rolls of efficient schools, and that, although it is reasonable to assume that the children actually in attendance at these schools came from parents who valued education, and who would, therefore, take pains that their children should attend as regularly as possible, yet the percentage of average attendance at this period was only 78·3.

The Diagram on page 214 shows how, year by year, the numbers have grown, until in 1903, the number of children of the Elementary school class was 884,003, the total existing accommodation in all permanent and temporary efficient schools was 789,737, the average number on the roll at the same period was 762,974, and the average attendance 653,124. The percentage of the number of the children on the roll compared with the number scheduled in 1903 was 86·3, as against 38·7 in 1871; and, although in 1903 practically every child of compulsory age requiring elementary education had been enrolled, the percentage of average attendance had reached 85·6, as compared with 78·3 in 1871.

In 1871 the accommodation in Voluntary schools was 261,158, the number on the roll was 221,401, and the average attendance 173,406. According to the method of calculation adopted by the School Board for London in 1903, the Voluntary schools in London provided accommodation for 217,088; the number on the roll was 213,297; and the average attendance 177,974. From this it will be seen that, whereas the accommodation, and the number on the roll had decreased, the average attendance had increased no less than 4,568 in Voluntary schools.

In the year 1871 the Board had provided no permanent accommodation, but they had in Transferred schools accommodation for 1,101 children. In the year 1903 they had accommodation in temporary and permanent buildings for 572,649 children. The total number on the rolls of these schools was 549,677, and the average attendance 475,150. These facts, together with the progress made year by year during the existence of the Board, are illustrated by the Diagram on page 215.

The estimated number of school places required in London in the year 1871 was 454,783, and the total number on the rolls of Elementary schools was 222,518, or a percentage of 48·9. In the year 1903 the number of school places required was estimated at 784,355, and the number on the rolls of all schools, including schools for the blind, deaf and special instruction, was 767,160, or a percentage of 97·8. In valuing this percentage it must be borne in mind that the estimated number of school places required includes children 3 to 5 years of age, over whom the Board have no compulsory powers, and a very great proportion of whom are not enrolled. It is true that the Board make a deduction of 12½ per cent. for all causes of absence from the total number of children scheduled 3 to 13, but it is found that the number of children not enrolled between the ages of 3 and 5 amounts to nearly 12½ per cent. of the whole of the number of the children scheduled. The progress year by year from 1871 to 1903 is shown on the Diagram marked B, the estimated number of school places required being shown by red columns, and the number of children on the rolls of Elementary schools being shown by grey columns.

*Diagram showing the number of children of the Elementary school class, and the accommodation, roll and average attendance at all efficient schools :—*

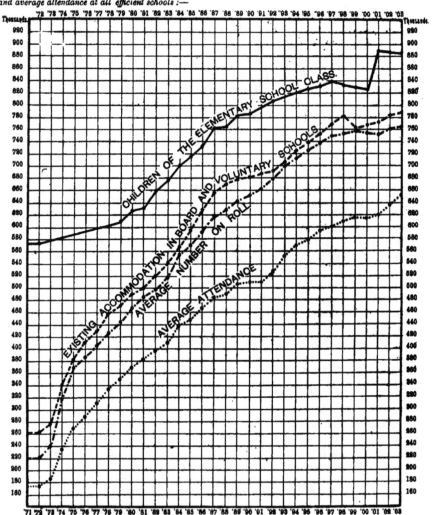

1. There was no return of the children of the Elementary school class in the years 1872 to 1877 inclusive, an no simultaneous scheduling by the Visitors in the years 1891, 1893, and 1894.

2. From 1871 to 1885 the returns of accommodation, &c., were made up each year to December, and from 1887 to 1903 to March. For the purpose of comparison the December returns have been treated as though they were made up to March of the following year.

3. In the year 1899 the apparent reduction of accommodation is mainly due to the fact that the accommodation of the Senior departments of Voluntary schools, which had previously been reckoned generally at 8 sq. ft. per child, was then, for the first time, reckoned at 10 sq. ft. per child.

*Diagram showing the accommodation, roll, and average attendance at Board and Voluntary schools from 1871 to 1903 :—*

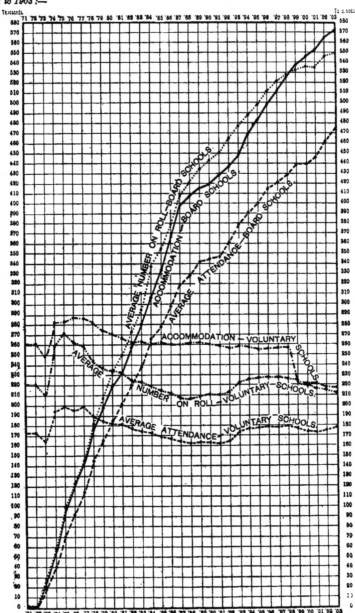

The total number of children scheduled by the Visitors year by year, from 1871 to 1903, with the total number of children on the rolls according to the scheduling returns, is illustrated in the Diagram on page 217. Perhaps it is well to point out that the number of children on the rolls of the schools as returned by the Visitors from their schedule books differs in some slight degree from the number on the rolls according to the returns from the schools, and that this difference is attributable to the fact that the school returns since 1887 have been made up to Lady Day, whilst the scheduling figures are supplied after the verification of the schedules, at a period varying from six to eight weeks after the receipt of the school returns. It is at this period that large numbers of young children are, for the first time, sent to school.

It is hardly necessary to point out that there will always be a large number of children who, for various causes, cannot be compelled to attend school. In the Annual Report for the year 1903 it was found that in the Metropolis there were 122,159 children between the ages of 3 and 14, and 100 defective children from 14 to 16 years of age, who were not on the rolls of any schools. These children were accounted for in the following manner:—

| | |
|---|---:|
| Receiving efficient instruction at home ... ... ... ... ... ... | 859 |
| Attending schools not recognised as efficient ... ... ... ... ... ... | 601 |
| Under 5 years of age, and cannot, therefore, be compelled to attend school ... | 100,817 |
| | 102,277 |
| Wholly exempt ... ... ... ... ... ... ... ... ... ... | 765 |
| Blind, Deaf, Defective, Epileptic, and other special cases temporarily absent from school ... ... ... ... ... ... ... ... ... ... | 1,121 |
| Permanently disabled ... ... ... ... ... ... ... ... ... | 738 |
| In the country ... ... ... ... ... ... ... ... ... ... | 2,390 |
| Ill, or delicate, or residing in houses where there is infectious illness ... ... | 4,368 |
| Out of school for want of accommodation, or unsuitable accommodation ... | 3,708 |
| Under surveillance of the respective Divisional Committees ... ... ... | 6,678 |
| Unclassified ... ... ... ... ... ... ... ... ... ... | 214 |
| | 19,982 |
| Total ... ... ... ... ... | 122,259 |

In the Diagram on pages 218 and 219 the particulars of the children scheduled and the children on the rolls of schools according to the schedules are shown separately for the children 3 to 5 and 5 and upwards.

The Diagram marked C illustrates the facts shown in the preceding diagram by percentages. The percentage of the children 3 to 5 is shown in light red, the percentage of the children 5 and upwards in dark red, and the percentage of the two is shown in grey.

The Board have ascertained that the proportion of the total child population of the Metropolis attending Elementary schools has greatly increased since the establishment of the School Board. In the year 1871 the total child population of the Metropolis between the ages of 3 and 14 was estimated to be 740,952, whilst at this period there were on the rolls of efficient Elementary schools only 222,518, or a percentage of 30·0. In the year 1903, whilst the total child population between these ages was estimated at 968,007, the number of children on the rolls of efficient Elementary schools had risen

RDS 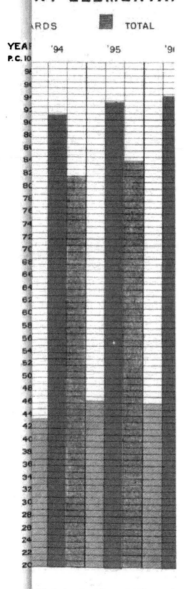 TOTAL

YEAI    '94         '95         '9
P.C. 10

been repeated in 1891, and

*Diagram showing the total number of children scheduled by the Visitors, and the total number of children on the rolls of Elementary schools from 1872 to 1903 :—*

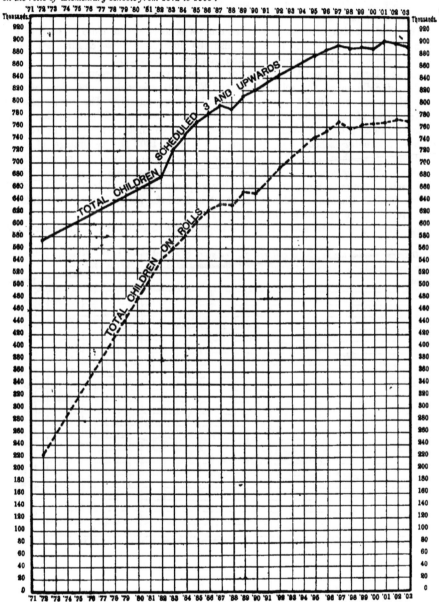

to 767,160, or 79·2 per cent. The increase in the proportion of children attending Elementary schools in London for each year from 1871 to 1903 is illustrated by the Diagram on page 220.

The total number of children on the rolls of schools at the close of each of the years ended Lady Day 1886 to 1903, and also the number of these children who were over the age o f 10 years, are shown in the Diagram on page 221.

In the Diagram marked D is shown for the same years the percentage of the total number of children on the rolls of efficient Elementary schools at the close of each year, who were over 10, 12, and 13 years of age respectively. The percentages of children over 10 are shown by dark red columns; those over 12 by light blue; and those over 13 by grey. In 1886 the percentage of the children over 10 on the rolls of efficient Elementary schools was 35·6, but in the year 1903 the percentage of these children had reached 40·3. The percentage of the children over 12 on the rolls of efficient Elementary schools in 1886 was 13·2, and in the year 1903 it had reached 19·9. The greatest difference, however, is shown in the percentage of children over 13 on the rolls of efficient Elementary schools, for whilst in 1886 the percentage of such children was only 4·6, in the year 1903 it had reached 10·3.

It should, however, be stated that these figures are based upon returns according to

*Diagram showing the number of children of 3 to 5 years of age scheduled by the Visitors, together with the number of such children on the rolls of efficient Elementary schools from 1871 to 1903 :—*

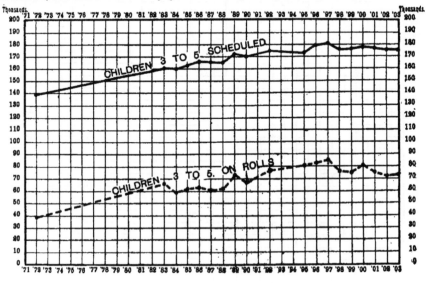

# D

Diagram showing at Lady-Day of each year, from 1886 to 1903, the percentage of children on the rolls of efficient elementary schools, who were over 10, 12 and 13 years of age respectively.

■ over 10          ▧ over 12          ■ over 13

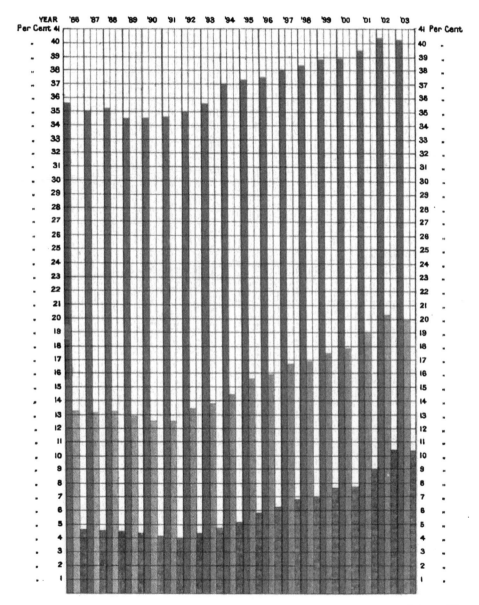

*Diagram showing the number of children of 5 years of age and upwards, scheduled by the Visitors together with the number of such children upon the rolls of efficient Elementary schools :—*

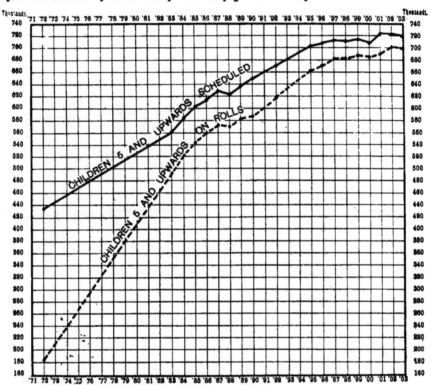

1  In regard to the Diagram on page 218 opposite, it must be observed that children between the ages of 3 and 5 cannot be compelled to attend school.

2  There were no complete returns for the years 1873 to 1882 inclusive ; and no simultaneous scheduling by the visitors in the years 1891, 1893, and 1894.

Diagram showing the entire child population aged 3 to 14 (higher line), and the number on the rolls of efficient Public Elementary schools (lower line) from 1870 to 1903.

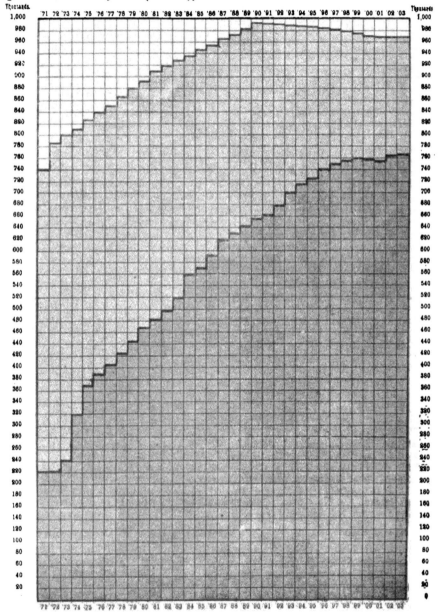

| ember, 1892. | December, 1883. | December, 1884. |
|---|---|---|
| 78475 (1882) | 700894 (1883) | 716532 (1884) |
| 593666 ct. '82) [Ages, on st Jan., 1883] | 613282 (Nov. '83) [Ages, on 1st Jan., 1883] | 627235 (1884) [Ages on 1st July, 1884. |
| 280275 263617 | 307330 260906 | 33430 26207 |
| 543892 | 568236 | 596384 |
| 295833 223297 | 337855 219707 | 35598 21506 |
| 519130 | 557562 | 57028 |
| 238205 174723 | 266013 173845 | 278924 169011 |
| 412928 | 439858 | 447235 |
| 80·5 78·2 | 78·7 79·1 | 784 785 |
| 79·5 | 78·8 oo | 784 |
| ... ... | 41·1 88·0 | 364 882 |
| 79·6 | 77·5 | 774 |

of the Education Department
except in case of death), unless
the child had left the school

th, 1891, the Board resolved th
the year 1892, and thenceforws
an annual simultaneous sched
regulation of the Education De
uous absence of four weeks,
ained, came into force in July.

lation required ;

| December, 1885. | June, 1886. | |
|---|---|---|
| 734700 (1885) | 749686 (1886) | 7 ( |
| 642862 [July '85] [Ages, on 1st July, 1885] | 655976 (Dec. '86) [Ages, on 1st July, 1886] | 6 (O [A 1 |
| 367639 | 378464 | 3 |
| 260597 | 260158 | 2 |
| 628236 | 638622 | 6 |
| 379931 | 384346 | 4 |
| 212490 | 207219 | 2 |
| 592421 | 591565 | 6 |
| 298317 | 303715 | 3 |
| 167242 | 163477 | 1 |
| 465559 | 467192 | 4 |
| 78·7 | 79·0 | |
| 78·5 | 78·8 | |
| 78·5 °°° | 78·9 | |
| 37·9 | 38·1 | |
| 89·9 | 91·1 | |
| 78·8 | 79·8 | |

t no child's name should
e Managers had ascerta
neighbourhood, came

he next simultaneous s
riennially. On Februar
l.
tment that children's n
fter due inquiry, the Vi
l. (Board Minutes, July

ages supplied from the Board's schools, and as no such returns have ever been received from the Voluntary schools, it has been assumed for the figures set out in Diagrams 8 and 9 that the proportion of children of those ages is the same in the Board and Voluntary schools.

The accompanying Table shows in detail for each year from 1871 to 1903 (except when those figures could not be obtained) the number of children scheduled by the Visitors; the accommodation required according to the Board's estimate; the accommodation provided in Board and Voluntary schools respectively; with the average number on the roll, the average attendance and percentage of average attendance on the average number on the roll, for Board and non-Board Schools separately; and the percentage of the number of children scheduled by the Visitors who were on the rolls of efficient Elementary schools, as taken from the schedules. From this Table it will be seen that since the establishment of the School Board for London the Elementary school population has increased by 55·7 per cent.; but that, during this period, the accommodation in efficient Elementary schools has increased by no less than 201·1 per cent., the average number on the roll by 242·8 per cent., and the average attendance by 274·7 per cent.

The Table also discloses the fact that the percentage of average attendance for the last three years has risen year by year, although that reached in 1901 was higher than that ever before recorded, the figures for the three years being 82·5, 83·7, and 85·6 for the years 1901, 1902, and 1903 respectively.

It is satisfactory to note that, whilst these results have been obtained, the

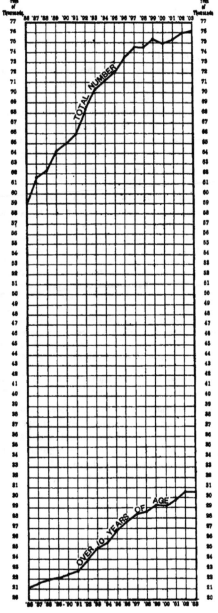

percentage of children on the rolls of schools as compared with the number of childre[n]
scheduled has, during the past two years been considerably higher than at any othe[r]
period in the history of the Board, the percentage for the children of compulsory ag[e]
now standing at 97·1.

When due weight is given to the fact of the enormous difficulties which have to b[e]
encountered in London in consequence of the migratory habits of a great number of th[e]
people living in the poorest districts, who often have special reasons for endeavourin[g]
to prevent all possible means of their whereabouts being known, it is considered a[n]
excellent result that so large a number of children should have been enrolled.

The School Accommodation and Attendance Committee in their last Annual Repor[t]
stated that they had the greatest satisfaction in submitting to the Board the result[s]
which have been herein summarised, and they called special attention to the followin[g]
observations of the late H.M. Senior Chief Inspector of Schools in his last General Repor[t]
which is the latest report dealing with London :—

On the whole, it appears that the task of bringing all the children of London to school has bee[n]
accomplished as rapidly and completely as possible.

The next point to consider is the regularity of the attendance at school.    The Board expre[ss]
moderate satisfaction that the " percentage of attendance "—*i.e.* the percentage of children enroll[ed]
that attends daily—has increased from 81.2 in 1900 to 82.5 in 1901.   (The percentage for Board schoo[l]
is 83.4, and for non-Board schools 80.2.)   An examination of the figures on which this calculation[ is]
based shows that the actual attendance of children above the age of infancy is much more regular th[an]
these results indicate.    The table which refers to Board schools only (the Board schoo[ls]
educate five-sevenths of the children of London; the precise number of scholars enrolled on Mar[ch]
31st, 1901, was : Board schools, 532,602 ; non-Board schools, 217,098) shows that the attendance [of]
boys is very good, that girls, who are necessarily required at home more than boys, attend well ; b[ut]
that the infants, of whom many cannot be compelled to attend at all, and who are more exposed [to]
sickness and other causes of occasional absence, attend less frequently, and thus bring down t[he]
summary percentage.

It seems therefore that the Board hardly takes credit to itself for the admirable work that h[as]
been done.   Impartial observers will say, " Go on and prosper."

It is with deep satisfaction that the Board are able to record that, so far as they ha[ve]
been permitted, they have gone on and prospered in their efforts to improve sch[ool]
attendance ; for, since the above report was issued, the percentage of the number [of]
children on the rolls of schools, as compared with the number scheduled, and t [he]
percentage of average attendance, have both materially increased.

# INDUSTRIAL SCHOOLS.

## I.—INTRODUCTION.

THE establishment of the Industrial school system in England originated between 1835 and 1855, in a movement in favour of remedial measures for the prevention of juvenile crime. In a lecture entitled "Encouragements and Experiences of Fifty Years' Work," Mr. Henry Rogers, who was for many years H.M. Assistant Inspector of Reformatory and Industrial schools, states that it was painful to contemplate the statistics of juvenile crime about the year 1851, and that the number of juveniles of the very neglected and degraded class, in London alone, amounted to 30,000. He adds that "thoughtful and right-minded men and women of that age were deeply shocked at the revelations made from time to time of what was really going on under the surface." One of the results of this alarm was that some of the philanthropic leaders of the time resolved to take steps to remedy this terrible state of things.

The movement in England had been anticipated in Scotland by the establishment, in Aberdeen, of a Boys' Industrial Feeding School, which was opened on October 1st, 1841. A similar school for girls was opened in the same place on January 5th, 1843. In England the Manchester Industrial School was established in 1845-6; in Birmingham an Industrial school was opened in 1846; on August 1st, 1846, Miss Mary Carpenter opened her ragged school in Bristol, and schools were opened in succeeding years in Liverpool, York, Newcastle, and other places.

During this time no Industrial school had been established for the reception of London children, but the ragged school system had been founded by Lord Shaftesbury, James Smithies, and others, and did good work in the darkest and most neglected parts of London.

In 1852, upon the report of a Committee of Inquiry appointed by the Government, legislation was promised. For the next few years action was chiefly directed to the Reformatory movement as distinct from the Industrial schools movement, but the latter followed as a natural consequence.

Conferences were held in Birmingham in 1851 and 1852 which resulted in the passing in 1854 of the first Reformatory Act and of the first Industrial Schools Act, the latter applying to Scotland only. This was followed by the Industrial Schools Act of 1857, which applied to England. Children under this Act were to be between the ages of 7 and 14 on admission, and were not to be detained beyond the age of 15 years. It was discovered, however, that if anything effectual was to be accomplished, a new Act was needed; and it was not until the year 1861 that the Industrial school system was really brought into operation in England, when an Act was passed repealing the Act of 1857 by a consolidating Act, which soon began to exert a beneficial influence. This Act provided for giving board, lodging, and clothing, as well as education, to the neglected and vagrant children who were to be found in large masses of population, and a distinction was drawn between Reformatory and Industrial schools by the provision that no child should be sent to an Industrial school if previously convicted of felony. The inferior limitation of age (7) was removed by this Act.

In 1866 the Scotch and English Acts were consolidated by the Act which is now in force[1] By this Act the Industrial schools of England and Scotland were placed on the same footing, and for England the Local Authority was declared to be the Prison Authority. Children were allowed by this Act to be detained up to the age of 16 years.

The principal sections of this Act are the following, which relate to the classes of children who may be sent to Industrial schools :—

*Section* 14.—Any person may bring before two justices or a magistrate any child apparently under the age of fourteen years that comes within any of the following descriptions, namely—That is found begging or receiving alms (whether actually or under the pretext of selling or offering for sale anything), or being in any street or public place for the purpose of so begging or receiving alms: That is found wandering and not having any home or settled place of abode, or proper guardianship, or visible means of subsistence: That is found destitute, either being an orphan, or having a surviving parent who is undergoing penal servitude, or imprisonment: That frequents the company of reputed thieves.

The justices or magistrate before whom a child is brought as coming within one of those descriptions, if satisfied on inquiry of that fact, and that it is expedient to deal with him under this Act, may order him to be sent to a certified Industrial school.

*Section* 15.—Where a child, apparently under the age of twelve years, is charged before two justices or a magistrate with an offence punishable by imprisonment or a less punishment, but has not been in England convicted of felony, or in Scotland of theft, and the child ought, in the opinion of the justices or magistrate (regard being had to his age, and to the circumstances of the case), to be dealt with under this Act, the justices or magistrate may order him to be sent to a certified Industrial school.

*Section* 16.—Where the parent or step-parent or guardian of a child, apparently under the age of fourteen years, represents to two justices or a magistrate that he is unable to control the child, and that he desires that the child be sent to an Industrial school under this Act, the justices or magistrate, if satisfied on inquiry that it is expedient to deal with the child under this Act, may order him to be sent to a certified Industrial school.

Additional provisions have been made by later enactments as follow :—

Prevention of Crimes Act, 1871,[2] *Section* 14.—Where any woman is convicted of a crime, and a previous conviction of crime is proved against her, any children of such woman, under the age of fourteen years, who may be under her care and control at the time of her conviction for the last of such crimes, and who have no visible means of subsistence, or are without proper guardianship, shall be deemed to be children to whom in Great Britain the provisions of the Industrial Schools Act, 1866, and in Ireland the provisions of the Industrial Schools (Ireland) Act, 1868, apply, and the Court, by whom such woman is convicted, or two justices or a magistrate, shall have the same power of ordering such children to be sent to a certified Industrial school, as is vested in two justices or a magistrate by the fourteenth Section of the Industrial Schools Act, 1866, and by the eleventh Section of the Industrial Schools (Ireland) Act, 1868, in respect of the children in the said Sections described.

Elementary Education Act, 1876, *Section* 11.—If either (1) The parent of any child above the age of five years, who is under this Act prohibited from being taken into full time employment, habitually

---

[1] 29 & 30 Vict., c. 118.     [2] 34 & 35 Vict., c. 112.

and without reasonable excuse neglects to provide efficient elementary instruction for his child; or (2) Any child is found habitually wandering or not under proper control, or in the company of rogues, vagabonds, disorderly persons, or reputed criminals, it shall be the duty of the local authority, after due warning to the parent of such child, to complain to a Court of Summary Jurisdiction, and such Court may, if satisfied of the truth of such complaint, order that the child do attend some certified efficient school willing to receive him, and named in the order, being either such as the parent may select, or if he do not select any, then such public Elementary school as the Court think expedient, and the child shall attend that school every time that the school is open, or in such other regular manner as is specified in the order. An order under this section is in this Act referred to as an attendance order. Any of the following reasons shall be a reasonable excuse: (1) That there is not within two miles, measured according to the nearest road, from the residence of such child, any public Elementary school open which the child can attend; or (2) that the absence of the child from school has been caused by sickness or any unavoidable cause.

*Section* 12.--Where an attendance order is not complied with, without any reasonable excuse within the meaning of this Act, a Court of Summary Jurisdiction, on complaint made by the local authority, may, if it think fit, order as follows:

(1) In the first case of non-compliance, if the parent of the child does not appear, or appears and fails to satisfy the Court that he has used all reasonable efforts to enforce compliance with the order, the Court may impose a penalty not exceeding, with the costs, five shillings; but if the parent satisfies the Court that he has used all reasonable efforts as aforesaid, the Court may, without inflicting a penalty, order the child to be sent to a certified Day Industrial school, or if it appears to the Court that there is no such school suitable for the child, then to a certified Industrial school; and (2) In the second or any subsequent case of non-compliance with the order, the Court may order the child to be sent to a certified Day Industrial school, or, if it appears to the Court that there is no such school suitable for the child, then to a certified Industrial school, and may further in its discretion inflict any such penalty as aforesaid, or it may for each such non-compliance inflict any such penalty as aforesaid without ordering the child to be sent to an Industrial school; provided that a complaint under this section, with respect to a continuing non-compliance with any attendance order shall not be repeated by the local authority at any less interval than two weeks.

A child shall be sent to a certified Industrial school, or certified Day Industrial school, in pursuance of this section, in like manner as if sent in pursuance of the Industrial Schools Act, 1866, and when so sent, shall be deemed to have been sent in pursuance of that Act, and the Acts amending the same; and the parent, if liable under the said Acts, to contribute to the maintenance and training of his child when sent to an Industrial school, shall be liable so to contribute when his child is sent in pursuance of this section.

Industrial Schools Acts Amendment Act, 1880.--1. Section 14 of the Industrial Schools Act, 1866, and Section 11 of the Industrial Schools Act (Ireland), 1868, shall be respectively read and construed as if, after the four several descriptions therein respectively contained, there were added the following descriptions—namely, That is lodging, living, or residing with common or reputed prostitutes, or in a house resided in or frequented by prostitutes for the purpose of prostitution: That frequents the company of prostitutes.

A serious defect in the Act of 1866 is the omission of effective machinery for putting it in force. Section 14 says that "any person" *may* bring cases before a magistrate; but a duty left to "any person" to perform generally results in its neglect; and this proved to be the case. The principal cause of inaction was that before a child could be sent away, a school had to be found which was willing to receive it. Inasmuch as the Treasury contribution towards the maintenance of a child only covered a portion of the cost, the Managers of a School were unable to accept a child unless the balance was supplied from some other source.

The Industrial Schools Act up to the year 1870 was, therefore, practically inoperative, at any rate, so far as London was concerned. One or two societies for the reclamation of children now and then took action in isolated cases, and a few private individuals occasionally tried to bring cases before the Courts, but with very little success.

## II.—The Commencement of the Board's Industrial Schools Work.

The Elementary Education Act, 1870, conferred on School Boards the powers which prison authorities already possessed, of contributing to the establishment and maintenance of Industrial schools, and also powers which the prison authorities did not then possess, of themselves establishing Industrial schools. The duty of taking action was imposed upon them by the following section of the Elementary Education Act, 1876:—

*Section 13.*—Where the local authority are informed by any person of any child in their jurisdiction who is stated by that person to be liable to be ordered by a Court under this Act to attend school, or to be sent under this Act, or the Industrial Schools Act, 1866, to an Industrial school, it shall be the duty of the local authority to take proceedings under this Act or the Industrial Schools Act, 1866, accordingly, unless the local authority think that it is inexpedient to take such proceedings.

Provided that nothing in this section shall relieve the local authority from the responsibility of performing their duty under the other provisions of this Act.

The Board were also empowered to appoint officers to enforce the Industrial Schools Act in their districts. The machinery which was lacking in the Act of 1866 was thus provided.

The Board, soon after 1870, began to exercise the powers thus conferred upon them. The work was first undertaken by a Sub-Committee of the School Management Committee; but in the year 1873 a standing committee was appointed for the purpose, and since that date the work has been continuously carried on by the Industrial Schools Committee.

In June, 1871, two Industrial Schools officers commenced work, one on the north side of the Thames and one on the south side. The duties of these officers were to bring before magistrates cases suitable for Industrial schools; to make inquiries into cases reported by the police; to attend the meetings of the Committee for the purpose of giving information as to the cases submitted; and to furnish the magistrates at the police courts with particulars as to the children coming before them, and the suggestions of the Committee as to their disposal.

## III.—Conditions Prevailing in 1870.

The children who were brought before the Industrial Schools Committee were of the very lowest type. The streets swarmed with waifs and strays who had never attended school, a large number of whom habitually frequented the riverside, the London railway termini, the purlieus of Drury-lane and Seven Dials, streets and courts off Holborn and the Strand, and the neighbourhood of the Borough, Whitechapel, and many similar parts of the Metropolis. These children slept together in gangs in such places as the Adelphi arches, on barges, on the steps of London Bridge, in empty boxes and boilers at

Bankside, in empty packing-cases, down the "Shades"; covered over with tarpaulins and old sacks. A very favourite haunt of street-arabs was George's Coffee House. *alias* the "House of Lords," in Upper Thames-street, where a room was specially set apart for their accommodation.

The following account of the social condition of the Boundary-street area by the School Board visitor for the district illustrates the social condition of an East end district in 1870:—

In the district comprising the Boundary Street area, Bethnal Green, there were twenty-three public-houses and beershops. Two general shops where spirits could be obtained at any time by those in the secret. Many of the public-houses had a way right through, so that persons could escape at the back, and be easily lost in the streets behind. Examples of these were the "Old Fountain, in High Street, Shoreditch; the "Five Ink-h rns," New Nicol Street; and the "Admiral Vernon," in Old and New Nicol Streets. The "Five Ink-hor s" was kept for several years by James Napper, the pugilist, and his children attended Nicol Street Board School.

A number of the streets had many private houses through which persons could pass with little difficulty into other streets. The occupation of the women was chiefly matchbox making, and the manufacture of small articles for selling in the streets, and in these occupations the children had to bear a constant part.

The whole moral tone was inconceivably low. The people's lives consisted of constant deception and concealment. There was scarcely a family but appeared to have some reason for fearing the police, and a large proportion of the men were on "ticket of leave." The entire population entertained an absolute dread of fresh air and cleanliness. Except upon the occurrence of a funeral (for these people paid more respect to the dead than to the living), rooms and passages were reeking in filth for months, and even years. . . . .

Pickpockets, burglars, dog-stealers, and pugilists here abounded. They might frequently be observed examining their tools on the window sills, and practising robbery from upper windows. Jim Smith, the pugilist, lived in Old Nicol Street, and attended Nicol Street Board School. Bill Goode, also—whose father was, perhaps, the most famous dog-stealer of his time—lived in New Turnville Street; Burdett, of Boundary Street, had "done time" for horse stealing: his wife's father was concerned, with two others, in a burglary at Muswell Hill, when a young man was murdered, and they were arrested in the "Barley Mow," in Boundary Street; James Baker, hanged for shooting a police inspector, after burglary, lived in the district. A murder was committed at 4, Old Nicol Street.

The children's lives were a constant round of sunless drudgery—they never played as children play, they never seemed even to think; they were prematurely old, and the victims of an awful cruelty. They worked at matchbox making many hours, and at other times assisted their parents in disposing of their wares in the streets. The mortality among the young children was appalling.

## IV.—CONSIDERATION OF CASES OF CHILDREN.

It soon became apparent that the three officers appointed for the purpose of bringing cases before the Committee were unable to cope with the work. Additional officers were accordingly appointed, two in 1873, one in 1875, one in 1892, and one in 1895, making eight in all. They were attached to the Industrial Schools Department, and were under the direct control of the Industrial Schools Committee. In January, 1899, the Board decided that in lieu of the plan of employing a separate staff of officers, the inquiries into and the conduct of cases at the various police-courts should be carried on under the direction of the respective Divisional Superintendents. The Industrial schools officers were accordingly transferred to the various Divisions.

These officers attended the meetings of the Committee, reported the cases which had come before them, and took the instructions of the Committee as to their disposal. In January, 1877, however, it was decided that the officers' cases should in future be heard weekly by three members of the Committee, who were summoned in rotation, and this method has been continued up to the present time. As children are constantly being charged at the police-courts, it is necessary that cases should be dealt with every week throughout the year; and in order to cause as little inconvenience as possible to members during the recesses, cases are at these times considered by two members of the Committee.

The cases which come before the Rota Sub-Committee are received from various sources. Some are charged by the Industrial school visitors, or by the ordinary visitors, who have instructions to give into custody any suitable cases with which they become acquainted while performing their regular duties. Some are charged by the police and are referred by the Magistrates to the Board's Officers for inquiry and, ir necessary, for a school to be found for them. From whatever source they are received, each case is carefully considered by the Rota Sub-Committee, who strive to elicit all the facts which bear upon the case; and, whilst they act primarily for the child's welfare, they endeavour to ensure that the provisions of the Act are not abused by unscrupulous persons for the purpose of ridding themselves of their children.

Out of a total number of 64,000 cases which have been considered by the Committee since the Board was established, about one half have been sent to schools.

It frequently happens that cases which are brought before the Rota Sub-Committee charged under one of the clauses of Section 14 of the Act of 1866 are upon the border-line between Industrial schools cases and cases which should be dealt with by the Guardians. For instance—

    (a) A child charged with wandering, etc., father or mother dead, surviving parent in prison.

    (b) A child charged with begging, etc., parents living, but without any home.

It is often objected that such children should not be sent to an Industrial school, but should be dealt with by the Guardians. If, however, the case is left to be dealt with by the Guardians, and the child is sent to the workhouse, it can at any time be withdrawn therefrom on the demand of the parent. It thereupon returns to its former bad surroundings and it probably gets charged with theft, or with some other offence punishable by imprisonment. The only way therefore to save such a child is to deal with it in the first instance by sending it to an Industrial school.

It is true that under Section 1 of the Poor Law Act of 1899, Guardians of the Poor may, in certain specified cases, adopt children until they reach the age ot eighteen years, but this power is very rarely exercised.

Section 39 of the Act of 1866, provides that the parent, step-parent, or other person for the time being liable to maintain a child detained in a certified Industrial school shall, if of sufficient ability, contribute to its maintenance and training therein a sum not exceeding five shillings per week. This power is rigidly enforced by the Government, who, for the year 1901, under magistrates' orders, collected the sum of £20,000.

## V.—AGREEMENTS WITH VOLUNTARY INDUSTRIAL SCHOOLS.

As the Board did not at first possess any Industrial schools of their own, and also, probably, because they thought that it would be more advantageous to London children to be sent to voluntary institutions in the country, they entered into agreements with the Managers of many of the Industrial schools then existing in London and the country for the reception of London cases. The agreements with the majority of these schools are still in force.

Subsequently the Board decided to establish a few schools under their own control; but as time went on, and they gained experience, they became convinced of the wisdom of the policy of distributing the children as widely as possible. This policy has sometimes been questioned; but, owing to the bad character of the surroundings and of the parents of the majority of the children, it is usually desirable that such children should be removed to a distance. It is also a decided advantage for London children to be transferred to the healthier environment afforded by the Institutions in the country; and, in addition, a larger number of people become interested in their welfare, and better means of disposal are secured. Upon this point Mr. Legge says, in his Report for the year 1900:—

Lastly, we come to the most common method of classification, and one by no means to be commended, viz., classification by locality. Last year attention was called to the dangers and difficulties involved in bringing together, in the same schools, children from the same locality. Hope of reform largely depends on the influences of new associations. Obviously these influences must be weaker when a child, on being removed from the court or alley in which he has hitherto spent his existence, finds himself in company with others who left the same court or alley, or neighbouring ones, a year or two before. The effect is as bad on the old hand as on the newcomer. Difficult, indeed, as it is to prevent a child on leaving school from reverting to the slum from which it came, the difficulty can only be aggravated when there is so much in the school to keep alive the memory and associations of the past. It is not surprising that one should find the proportion of re-convictions in connection with such schools above the normal. During the past five years this consideration has been a frequent topic of conversation between H.M. Inspector and the superintendents of schools, and only a single one has been found to favour the sending of boys to a reformatory near their homes. The argument he used was simply this: in his opinion the boys settled down with more tranquillity, were easier to manage, and less inclined to abscond, when they knew their own home was but a mile or two off. With this exception, all the practical men and women whose opinions have been taken, have been in favour of receiving only a proportion of local cases to be mixed up with children brought from a distance. The fact is—to use a homely simile, so apt as to be irresistible—a good school is like a good salad, and should be compounded of the most varied ingredients.

It is a matter for congratulation that of the immense number of Industrial school children for whom the London School Board is responsible, at least three-fourths are dealt with, not in London tself, but in different localities on the outskirts, and as far away as Lancashire, Norfolk, and Cornwall. The gain is reciprocal, both to the London child and the school to which he is sent, for of all the constituents of a good school, there is none more pungent than the London boy; he seems to quicken and to flavour every school he enters. It will be a hard task to break down this classification by locality; the origin of the schools has to be remembered. In the case of Voluntary schools, people, aroused by the contemplation of juvenile delinquency in their own districts, have collected subscriptions and donations to found an Industrial school to cope with the needs of their own district. They naturally find a difficulty in inducing subscribers to continue their subscriptions in favour of strange children from a distance. Similarly where County Councils and School Boards have founded schools, they are, as a rule, most anxious to keep in them the children for whom they are responsible. But there is reason to believe that, as the conditions of the problem are better understood, the authorities in the various localities, whether voluntary managers or ratable authorities, will see no hardship in a reasonable arrangement by which, adequate provision having been made for the needs of a particular district, some of that is devoted to children from other districts for whom room is made by transferring to those other districts local children in whose case it is eminently desirable that a final severance from the past should be effected.

The Board have now agreements with 64 schools: 38 for Boys and 26 for girls The following list gives the names and localities of these schools, together with the total accommodation and the number of Board children in the School on the 31st December, 1903 :—

| Name of School, &c. | Address. | Total Accommodation of School. | No. of Board Childr'n in Schools on Dec. 31st, 1903 | Remarks. |
|---|---|---|---|---|
| *Schools for Boys other than Roman Catholic.* | | | | |
| Albert ... ... ... ... | Corporation-road, Birkenhead | 120 | 16 | |
| Ardwick Green... ... ... | Ardwick Green, near Manchester | 200 | 108 | Sixty places secured for 15 years from 1902. |
| Barnes Home ... ... ... | Heaton Mersey, near Manchester | 275 | 99 | Sixty places secured for 15 years from 1900. |
| Bath ... ... ... ... | Twerton, Bath ... ... | 180 | 58 | |
| Blandford [Dorset County Council] | Milborne St. Andrew's, near Blandford | 60 | 32 | |
| Boys' Home ... ... ... | Regent's Park-road, N.W.... | 120 | 112 | |
| Buxton ... ... | Buxton Lamas, nr. Norwich | 90 | 30 | |
| Church Farm Boys' Home ... | East Barnet | 65 | 38 | |
| Clifton ... ... ... ... | Hotwells-rd., Clifton Wood, Bristol | 200 | 90 | |
| Desford [Leicester School Board] | Desford, near Leicester ... | 200 | 57 | |
| East London ... ... ... | Brookbank-road, Lewisham, S.E. | 150 | 151 | This School was formerly located in Whitechapel. |
| Essex ... ... ... ... | Primrose Hill, Chelmsford | 150 | 1 | Boys over 7 and under 10 only received in sound physical and mental health. |
| Field-lane ... ... ... | Hillfield-road, West Hampstead, N.W. | 140 | 128 | |
| "Formidable" ... ... ... | Off Portishead, near Bristol | 350 | ... | |
| "Havannah" .. ... ... | Grange-road, Cardiff ... | 100 | 19 | |
| Hayes ... ... ... ... | Hayes, Middlesex ... ... | 60 | 47 | For Jewish cases only |
| Hereford ... ... ... | Bath-street, Hereford ... | 115 | 79 | |

| Name of School, &c. | Address | Total Accommodation of School. | No. of Board Childr'n in Schools on De-. 31st, 1903 | Remarks. |
|---|---|---|---|---|
| Leeds (Shadwell) [Leeds School Board] | Moortown, Leeds ... ... | 180 | 16 | |
| Macclesfield ... ... ... | Brook-street, Macclesfield | 150 | 71 | |
| Mayford [London County Council] | Near Woking, Surrey ... | 180 | ... | |
| Middlesbrough [Middlesbrough School Board] | Linthorpe, Middlesbrough | 60 | 11 | |
| Milton Children's Home ... | Farnborough, Hants ... | 100 | 28 | This School is now restricted to children described as Protestant Nonconformist. |
| "Mount Edgcumbe" Industrial School Ship | Saltash, Cornwall ... ... | 250 | 92 | |
| Purbrook, Boys' Farm Home... | Purbrook, Cosham, Hants... | 95 | 26 | |
| Shustoke [Birmingham City Council] | Coleshill, near Birmingham | 160 | 43 | |
| Standon Bridge Boys' Farm Home | Standon Bridge, near Eccleshall, Stafford | 90 | 9 | |
| Stockport ... ... ... | Offerton, Stockport ... | 150 | 19 | This School is now, by direction of the Home Office, restricted to cases of Protestant Nonconformist boys. |
| Toxteth Park ... ... ... | 77, Grafton-street, Toxteth Park, Liverpool | 200 | 43 | |
| Walsham-le-Willows ... ... | Near Bury St. Edmunds, Suffolk | 40 | 26 | |
| Werrington [Staffordshire County Council] | Werrington, near Stoke ... | 160 | 10 | |
| York ... ... ... | Marygate, Bootham, York | 120 | 40 | |
| *Roman Catholic Boys.* | | | | |
| Bishop Brown Memorial ... | Stockport ... ... ... | 80 | 19 | |
| Cannington ... ... ... | Cannington, nr. Bridgwater | 100 | 51 | |
| St. John's ... ... ... | Walthamstow, Essex ... | 150 | 114 | |
| St. Nicholas ... ... ... | Manor House, Little Ilford, Essex | 250 | 124 | |
| St. Vincent's ... ... ... | Dartford, Kent ... ... | 200 | 175 | |
| Do., Branch School for Little Boys | Whitstable ... ... | 30 | 45 | |
| *Truant School for Boys.* | | | | |
| Lichfield... ... ... ... | Beacon-street, Lichfield ... | 100 | 3 | Under the management of the Burton-on-Trent, Walsall, and West Bromwich School Boards. |
| *Schools for Girls other than Roman Catholic.* | Total (Boys) ... | 5420 | 2030 | |
| Bath ... ... ... ... | 17, Walcot-parade, Bath ... | 80 | 29 | |
| Cold Ash ... ... ... | Hill House, Cold Ash, near Newbury | 30 | 12 | For cases under Amendment Act of 1880. |
| Elm House (late School of Discipline) | Parson's Green, Fulham, S.W. | 40 | 24 | |
| Fakenham, Norfolk County I.S. and Orphanage [Now closed] | Fakenham, Norfolk ... | 50 | ... | Girls under 12 only admitted. |
| Greenwood ... ... ... | Halstead, Essex ... ... | 70 | 42 | Girls under 12 only received, and under 10 in Amendment Act cases. |

| Name of School, &c. | Address. | Total Accommodation of School. | No. of Board Childr'n in Schools on Dec. 31st,1903 | Remarks. |
|---|---|---|---|---|
| King Edward's ... ... ... | Andrews-road, Cambridge Heath, N.E. | 120 | 89 | |
| Leeds, Beckett Home ... ... | Meanwood, Leeds ... ... | 30 | 17 | |
| Lichfield [Staffordshire County Council] | Lichfield ... ... ... | 55 | 16 | |
| Liverpool ... ... ... | 27, Northumberland-terrace, Liverpool | 100 | 12 | Under 10 if sent under Sec xvi. |
| Maurice Girls' Home ... ... | 22, Charlotte-st., Portland-place, W. | 12 | 10 | |
| Newton Stewart ... ... | Newton Stewart, N.B. ... | 50 | 3 | |
| Plymouth ... ... ... | 13 and 14, Portland-villas, Plymouth | 55 | 37 | |
| Poole ... ... ... ... | West-street, Poole, Dorset | 100 | 28 | |
| Portsmouth and South Hants | Waterlooville, Cosham, Hants | 36 | 22 | For cases under Amendment Act, 1880, between the ages of 6 and 9. |
| Princess Mary's Village Homes | Addlestone, nr. Weybridge | 140 | 35 | |
| Sale ... ... ... ... | Sale, near Manchester ... | 100 | 27 | |
| Shipton-under-Wychwood (previously at Hemel Hempstead) | Oxfordshire... ... ... | 30 | 18 | For cases under Amendment Act of 1880. |
| Stanhope House ... ... | 14, Somerset-street, Kingsdown, Bristol | 60 | 37 | |
| Stockport ... ... ... | Dialstone-lane, Stockport... | 60 | 5 | This School is now by direction of the Home Office, restricted to Protestant Nonconformist girls. |
| Thorparch [Leeds School Board] | Thorparch, near Leeds ... | 100 | 18 | |
| York ... ... ... ... | Lowther-street, York ... | 50 | 27 | Girls over 10 preferred. |
| *Roman Catholic Girls.* | | | | |
| Nazareth House ... ... | Isleworth, Middlesex ... | 120 | 40 | |
| St. Elizabeth's ... ... | Salisbury ... ... ... | 65 | 8 | |
| St. Joseph's ... ... | Howard, Hill, Sheffield ... | 120 | 12 | |
| St. Margaret's ... ... | Mill Hill, Hendon ... ... | 100 | 46 | |
| St. Mary's ... ... | Wellesley-road, West Croydon | 150 | 75 | Special accommodation for little girls. |
| | Total (Girls) ... | 1923 | 689 | |
| | Total (Boys and Girls) | 7343 | 2719 | |

## VI.—GRANTS AND CONTRIBUTIONS BY BOARD TO INDUSTRIAL SCHOOLS.

Section 27 of the Elementary Education Act of 1870 gives power to a School Board to contribute such sums of money, on such conditions as they think fit, towards the establishment, building, alteration, enlargement, or re-building of an Industrial School, or towards the support of the inmates or the management of such a school.

1. *Maintenance Contributions.*—The agreements generally entered into with the managers of Industrial Schools on account of maintenance between 1871 and 1902, provide for the payment by the Board, in the case of each child sent at their

instance, of such a sum per week as will, with the Treasury contribution, make up a total sum of seven shillings per week. In the latter year the Board decided, having regard to the greatly increased cost of maintenance, to increase their grant so as to make a total of eight shillings per child per week, subject to the compliance by the Managers with certain conditions, including the appointment of a representative of the Board on the Committee of Management, the maintenance of the school in every department in such a state of efficiency as shall satisfy the Industrial Schools Committee, and the inspection of the school at any time by a a member or officer of the Board. This increased maintenance grant has been accepted by the Managers of thirty schools, and the opportunity was taken of bringing these Schools under a new agreement which embodied the foregoing conditions.

2. *Maintenance Grants for Young Children.* — Where special and separate provision is made for the reception of very young children, the Board, in order to meet the extra expense incurred in such cases, contribute a weekly sum sufficient to make up a total of 10s. per week in the case of each child under 10 years of age, and of 9s. per week in the case of each child over that age, until it is removed to a Senior school.

The following Table shows the amounts contributed by the Board and the Treasury respectively in each case :—

| | BOARD'S CONTRIBUTIONS. | | | | | TREASURY CONTRIBUTIONS. | | | | |
|---|---|---|---|---|---|---|---|---|---|---|
| | Industrial Schools Act, 1866. | | | Elementary Education Act, 1876. | | Industrial Schools Act, 1866. | | | Elementary Education Act, 1876. | |
| | Sec. 14 | Sec. 15 | Sec. 16 | Sec. 11 (1) | Sec. 11 (2) | Sec. 14 | Sec. 15 | Sec. 16 | Sec. 11 (1) | Sec. 11 (2) |
| | s. d. | s. d. | s. d. | s. d. | s. d. | s. d. | s. d. | s. d. | s. d. | s. d. |
| *Ages 6 to 10§—* | | | | | | | | | | |
| New Agreements ... ... | 5 0 | 5 0 | 6 0 | 6 0 | 5 0⎫ | 3 0 | 3 0 | 2 0 | 2 0 | 3 0 |
| Old Agreements ... ... | 4 0 | 4 0 | 5 0 | 5 0 | 4 0⎬ | | | | | |
| *Ages 10 to 15—* | | | | | | | | | | |
| New Agreements ... ... | *4 6 | *4 6 | 6 0 | 6 0 | 4 6⎫ | ‡3 6 | ‡3 6 | 2 0 | 2 0 | 3 6 |
| Old Agreements ... ... | †3 6 | †3 6 | 5 0 | 5 0 | 3 6⎬ | | | | | |
| *Over 15 if* **LESS** *than 4 years under detention—* | | | | | | | | | | |
| New Agreements ... ... | *4 6 | *4 6 | 6 0 | 6 0 | 4 6⎫ | ‡3 6 | ‡3 6 | 2 0 | 2 0 | 3 6 |
| Old Agreements ... ... | †3 6 | †3 6 | 5 0 | 5 0 | 3 6⎬ | | | | | |
| *Over 15 if* **MORE** *than 4 years under detention—* | | | | | | | | | | |
| New Agreements ... ... | 3 0 | 3 0 | 6 0 | 6 0 | 3 0⎫ | 3 0 | 3 0 | 2 0 | 2 0 | 3 0 |
| Old Agreements ... ... | 4 0 | 4 0 | 5 0 | 5 0 | 4 0⎬ | | | | | |
| Special Schools for reception of children under 9 years of age. | | | | | | | | | | |
| Ages 6 to 10§ ... ... | 7 0 | 7 0 | 8 0 | 8 0 | 7 0 | 3 0 | 3 0 | 2 0 | 2 0 | 3 0 |
| Over 10** ... ... | ¶5 6 | ¶5 6 | 7 0 | 7 0 | 5 6⎬ | ‡3 6 | ‡3 6 | 2 0 | 2 0 | 3 6 |

* In cases of Schools certified before 1872, this amount is 3s.
+ In cases of Schools certified before 1872, this amount is 2s.
‡ In cases of Schools certified before 1872, this amount is 5s.
¶ In cases of Schools certified before 1872, this amount is 4s.

§ If children are committed *under* the age of 6 years no Treasury contribution is paid until they attain that age and the full contribution of 7s., 8s., or 10s. per week, as the case may be, is therefore paid by the School Board.
** These children are transferred to a Senior school as soon after reaching 10 years of age as may be desirable.

3. *Education Grants.*—In May, 1899, the Board decided, with a view to enabling the Managers of schools to improve the education, and to increase the efficiency of the teaching staff, to make a grant not exceeding 1s. per child per week for the appointment of duly qualified teachers, or the appointment of additional teachers, or for increasing the remuneration of existing teachers. The payment of this grant was, however, subject to the acceptance by the Managers of conditions similar to those mentioned in connection with the increased maintenance grant. Grants of this character were made to 20 schools, but at a later date they were in 15 cases discontinued in favour of the increased maintenance grants, with the result that education grants are now being paid to the Managers of five schools only.

4. *Licensing Allowance.*—An allowance is made by the Board to assist Managers in the supervision of children on licence at the rate of 2s. per week for a maximum period of 13 weeks, and 1s. per week for a maximum period of 26 weeks; but these payments cease in all cases when a child attains the age of 16 years.

5. *Disposal Grants.*—A contribution of £3 towards the provision of a suitable and sufficient outfit is made to the Managers in the case of each child placed in some situation or otherwise disposed of to the satisfaction of the Board.

6. *Contribution towards Emigration Expenses.*—In cases approved by the Industrial Schools Committee a sum of £9, in addition to the £3 mentioned above is paid to the Managers in the case of each child emigrated to one of the British Colonies.

7. *Special Grants.*—Applications are from time to time received from Managers for assistance to enable them to meet exceptional expenditure, either in regard to the apprenticeship of a child, the purchase of special surgical appliances, expenses connected with particular cases of sickness, the cost of hospital treatment, temporary residence in a convalescent home, or funeral expenses.

8. *Building Grants.*—In order to secure places permanently for the use of the Board in Industrial schools and to enable Managers to improve their buildings, grants have from time to time been made at the rate of £10 for each bed. The main conditions governing these grants have been as follow:—

The places are to be reserved for Board cases so long as the school shall exist.

In the event of the school being discontinued within a period of 10 years after the payment of the grant, repayment is to be made to the Board according to the following scale: within 3 years, 75 per cent.; within 7 years, 50 per cent.; within 10 years, 25 per cent. The Managers are to give security for carrying out their agreement as to repayment.

In the year, 1899, the Board decided that in special circumstances grants might be made at a higher rate than £10 per bed; but in these cases the term during which Managers are liable on the closing of the school to repay to the Board a proportion of the grant is increased from 10 to 20 years, viz.: within 7 years, 75 per cent.; within 12 years, 50 per cent. and within 20 years, 25 per cent. The regulations with regard to building grants were at the same time amended by the addition of conditions identical with those mentioned under the heading of "Maintenance Contributions."

The following table gives particulars of the building grants made to schools (£25,217 10s.), and of the number of vacancies secured (1,930), &c. It will be noticed, however, that some of the schools have now been closed, and the number of places available is therefore now only 1,550 :—

| School. | Year. | Amount. | | No. of Beds secured. | Date of termination of liability for re-payment. | Object of Grant. | Remarks. |
|---|---|---|---|---|---|---|---|
| | | £ | s. | | | | |
| East London ... | 1872 | 700 | 0 | 70 | 1883 | Alteration of premises at Whitechapel. | |
| ,, ... | 1884 | 500 | 0 | 50 | 1895 | Premises at Lewisham | |
| ,, ... | 1895 | 100 | 0 | 10 | 1906 | Alteration and enlgt. | |
| ,, ... | 1900 | 520 | 0 | — | 1921 | ,, ,, imprvmt. | |
| St. Paul's ... | 1872 | 1,000 | 0 | 100 | 1883 | Alteration and enlgt. | £250 repaid on closing of School in 1881. |
| King Edward ... | 1872 | 600 | 0 | 80 | 1883 | ,, ,, | This branch of School closed in 1888. |
| ,, ... | 1875 | 500 | 0 | 60 | 1886 | ,, ,, | |
| ,, ... | 1879 | 500 | 0 | 20 | 1890 | ,, ,, | 30 beds had previously been secured without payment. |
| ,, ... | 1893 | 300 | 0 | — | — | New drains, &c. ... | |
| St. Stephen's ... | 1872 | 700 | 0 | 80 | 1883 | Alteration and enlgt. | School closed in 1887. |
| St. Vincent's ... | 1872 | 300 | 0 | 30 | 1883 | ,, ,, | |
| ,, ... | 1873 | 400 | 0 | 40 | 1884 | ,, ,, | |
| ,, ... | 1876 | 800 | 0 | 80 | 1887 | New premises ... | |
| ,, ... | 1898 | 300 | 0 | 30 | 1909 | Swimming bath ... | |
| ,, ... | 1900 | see remarks | | — | — | To pay interest and reduce debt | £1 per head per year for 6 years |
| Milton ... ... | 1874 | 1,000 | 0 | 100 | 1885 | Establishmt of School | } Total accom. of School |
| ,, ... | 1879 | 200 | 0 | 20 | 1890 | Alteration and enlgt. | } now reduced to 100. |
| Church Farm ... | 1874 | 100 | 0 | 10 | 1885 | ,, ,, | |
| ,, ... | 1878 | 50 | 0 | 5 | 1889 | ,, ,, | |
| Surrey ... ... | 1874 | 500 | 0 | 50 | 1885 | ,, ,, | School transferred to Mayford. |
| Essex ... ... | 1875 | 50 | 0 | 5 | 1876 | ,, ,, | |
| "Formidable" ... | 1875 | 100 | 0 | 20 | 1880 | Purchase of a Tender | Beds secured for 5 years only. |
| Field Lane (Boys) ... | 1875 | 500 | 0 | 50 | 1886 | New premises ... | |
| ,, ... | 1891 | 800 | 0 | 80 | 1902 | Alteration and enlgt. | |
| St. Francis, Shefford | 1875 | 200 | 0 | 20 | 1886 | Enlargement ... | School now closed. |
| St. Swithun's ... | 1892 | 172 | 10 | 80 | 1903 | ,, ... | School closed in 1899, repayment clause waived. |
| Clifton ... ... | 1893 | 250 | 0 | 25 | 1904 | Purchase of School buildings | |
| ,, ... ... | 1894 | 250 | 0 | 25 | 1905 | Alteration and enlgt. | |
| ,, ... ... | 1899 | 1,900 | 0 | 50 | 1920 | ,, ,, | |
| ,, | 1900 | 500 | 0 | — | 1921 | ,, ,, | |
| Boys' Home ... | 1893 | 300 | 0 | 80 | 1904 | Alteration & imprvmt. | |
| ,, ... | 1898 | 400 | 0 | 40 | 1909 | New Band Room. | |
| ,, ... | 1899 | 100 | 0 | — | 1920 | New Band Room, &c. | |
| Hereford ... ... | 1894 | 600 | 0 | 60 | 1905 | Alteration and enlgt. | |
| ,, ... | 1902 | 2,500 | 0 | 20 | 1923 | ,, ,, | |
| York (Boys') ... | 1894 | 300 | 0 | 30 | 1905 | ,, ,, | |
| Stanhope House ... | 1895 | 250 | 0 | 25 | 1906 | ,, ,, | |
| ,, ... | 1900 | 200 | 0 | 10 | 1921 | ,, imprvmt. | |

| School. | Year. | Amount. | No. of Beds secured. | Date of termination of liability for repayment. | Object of Grant. | Remarks. |
|---|---|---|---|---|---|---|
| | | £ s. | | | | |
| Plymouth ... ... | 1896 | 100 0 | 10 | 1907 | Purchase of new premises. | |
| ,, ... ... | 1899 | 300 0 | 10 | 1920 | ,, ,, | |
| St. Joseph's ... | 1896 | 200 0 | 30 | 1907 | Alteration & imprvmt. | |
| Stockport (Boys') ... | 1897 | 400 0 | 40 | 1908 | Site & new buildings | 30 beds secured in Boys' School and 10 in Girls' School. |
| Fakenham ... ... | 1899 | 200 0 | 30 | 1910 | New Schoolroom ... | School closed in 1903. £100 repaid. |
| Barnes Home ... | 1899 | 600 0 | 60 | 1910 | Alteration & imprvmt. | Beds secured for 15 years only. |
| "Mount Edgcumbe" | 1899 | 1,000 0 | 100 | 1910 | Purchase of a Tender | |
| Macclesfield... ... | 1900 | 2,000 0 | 60 | 1921 | Alteration & imprvmt. | Board also have right to claim 40 additional beds when there are vacancies Last instalment of £500 not yet paid. |
| St. John's ... ... | 1901 | 1,875 0 | 75 | 1922 | ,, ,, | |
| Ardwick Green ... | 1902 | 600 0 | 60 | 1923 | ,, ,, | Beds secured for 15 years only. |

## VII.—REQUIREMENTS OF THE HOME OFFICE.

When it is proposed to establish an Industrial school, the approval of the Home Secretary must be obtained in writing. To secure this approval it is necessary to satisfy him that the site and position of the school will be such as to allow of a sufficient amount of ground being attached to it for the exercise and recreation of the inmates, and to insure free ventilation and good drainage in the internal space. Plans of the proposed school must be approved by him, showing the area, height and connection of the rooms, and details of the drainage, ventilation and the arrangement of the offices. The regulations further provide that in the dormitories the allowance for each inmate shall be not less than 36 square and 360 cubic feet of space; and in the school and day rooms, not less than 10 square and 100 cubic feet; that boys and girls shall not be boarded together in the same institution; and that, unless the special sanction of the Secretary of State is obtained, the number of inmates shall not exceed 150. When the school is completed a notification of the fact must be sent by the managers to the Secretary of State, who then directs the Inspector of Industrial schools to examine into the condition of the school. If the report of the Inspector be satisfactory, the Home Secretary issues a certificate under his hand, and the school thereupon becomes a certified Industrial school.

Every school must be inspected at least once a year by one of His Majesty's Inspectors of Industrial schools; but, in addition to this annual visit, of which notice is given, the schools are usually visited without notice once or oftener in a year.

Schools are conducted in accordance with rules and regulations which must be approved in writing by the Secretary of State.

## VIII.—EDUCATION AND INDUSTRIAL TRAINING.

### 1. *Education.*

In the early days the Industrial schools were looked upon as semi-penal institutions, and the inmates were treated more like prisoners than school-children. Corporal punishments were severe, and solitary confinement was not uncommon.[1] Education in the school-room was of a low type, and industrial training was considered the more important part of the work.

The unsatisfactory nature of the school-work was the outcome of circumstances over which the Managers had no control. It may have been partly due to the low standard then adopted by the Home Office. The following is an extract from a Home Office Report written in 1881 :—

> I would strongly advise that a limit be set at the Fifth Standard. This is about as much as we can attain to in schools of this character, and with the limited time allotted to school education. To attempt to go beyond this generally results in failure, and has a damaging influence in exactness and accuracy throughout the school.

As a witness before the Royal Commission on Industrial schools one of the Home Office Inspectors, speaking of the teachers in Industrial schools, said "The majority of the men are not certificated, they have not had proper training; but they are fit to teach so far as we want them to go." Another said of the education in these schools: "I do not think there is any necessity whatever for improving it." The Royal Commission answered this by reporting :—

> If they (*i.e.*, the Industrial school children) are not to be under heavy disadvantages as compared with their competitors in after life, they should receive an elementary education similar, and as far as circumstances admit, not inferior to that which the law obliges other children to receive at the Public Elementary schools.

In the year 1880 the Board's Inspectors were instructed to visit the Industrial schools with which the Board had agreements, as well as the schools under the direct control of the Board, and to report not only on the educational and industrial training, but also on the staff, the condition of the buildings, the sanitary and domestic arrangements, food and clothing, health, conduct, punishments, how the children were placed out, and their subsequent history. For about six years the duty was divided, but, at the end of the year 1886, it was devolved upon one Inspector, who since that time has yearly inspected the schools, and has examined the children sent to them at the instance of the Board.

During the fifteen years following 1880 there does not appear to have been much

---

[1] "I strongly recommend the establishment of two rooms for occasional separate confinement not to exceed three days in any case."—*Government Inspector's Report*, 1880.

improvement in the Industrial schools so far as school-work was concerned. The Board Inspector reported in January, 1893 :—

Though some schools have improved considerably of late, in the majority there is little or no attempt to awaken and develop intelligence. Reading is not taught with a view to inspire love for reading, neither for the interest it awakens, nor the delight it affords. Composition, even of the simplest kind, is practically unknown. Arithmetic is a matter of rule rather than a process of reasoning, and mechanical accuracy the all important goal. We usually, not always, miss Recitation, Drawing, Object Lessons, Singing by Note, English, Geography, History ; and, in fact, most of those things which tend to make a school efficient, and withal pleasing and attractive.

And again he writes in May, 1894 :—

Are the scholars in the Industrial schools receiving an education similar, and as far as circumstances admit, not inferior to that given in the Public Elementary schools? Are the intellectual faculties being trained and the latent tastes and powers developed by a suitable course of elementary teaching?

His answer was :—

Admitting exceptions—a few of them notable exceptions—decidedly not. The education is distinctly inferior. There is but a very scant training of the intellectual faculties, and latent tastes and powers are very little developed. The work is good of its kind, and rubbed in, in many cases, with a persistence and a perseverance worthy of a better cause. It is the quality, not so much the quantity, which is at fault. To the uninitiated it is the education in the standards as prescribed by the Day School Code; to the initiated it is the dry bones of the Standard work.

An analysis of the Home Office Blue Book, 1893, shows that out of a total of 109 schools in England and Wales, 16 schools taught a little Geography, 10 took Drawing, 3 a little English, and 7 Recitation.

Even at this period it was considered unnecessary to attempt to carry children beyond the Fifth Standard, no matter to what extent they were gifted with ability and natural capacity.

In consequence of the persistent pressure of the Board, and of the direct pecuniary assistance given by it in the form of an Education Grant, and also, of the more liberal policy which has been adopted by the Home Office, the educational progress in these schools during the past decade has been very marked, and at the present moment the work in an Industrial school is probably as good as in the average Board School.

An analysis of the Blue Book for the year 1903 shows that 116 Industrial schools were carried on in England and Wales, and that 87 of these schools have a Standard VI. with nearly 1,200 scholars, and 28 have a Standard VII. with over 200 scholars. In addition to Reading, Writing, Spelling and Arithmetic, all the schools took Mental Arithmetic, Geography and Singing ; 110 took Recitations, 101 Composition, 96 Object Lessons, 65 Drawing, and 9 English Grammar ; while 52 schools use History reading books, 12 Domestic Economy reading books, and 9 Elementary Science reading books with a view to giving the children some elementary notions in these subjects. Shorthand, Typewriting and Bookkeeping are also taught in one or two of the girls' schools.

## 2.—*Industrial Training.*

The character of the industries taught is determined in a great measure by the situation of the school—whether it is a town or a country school. In both cases, however, three main industries are generally adopted in boys' schools, viz., Tailoring, Shoemaking, and Bread-making. The reason for the choice of these industries is that each, besides being useful to the children, is of pecuniary advantage to the schools, because the labour is utilised in clothing and feeding the inmates. Another consideration in the case of both classes of schools is the possibility of disposing of the results of the labour profitably. In town schools such industries as the following are also adopted: Basket-making, Wood turning, Brush-making, Printing, Paper Bag-making. Wood-chopping was at one time extensively carried on, as it was a very remunerative occupation, but as the boys engaged in this work were not benefited thereby, it has been discouraged both by the School Board and by the Government, and has, except in a few cases, been discontinued. In country schools other occupations are possible, the chief of which are Farming and Market Gardening. In many schools, both in town and country, Carpenters' Shops are established, in which manual instruction is given; and other shops in which instruction, practical and technical, is given in Metalwork, Blacksmith's Work, Plumbing, House Decoration and Designing. In the girls' schools the chief industries are Laundrywork, Dressmaking, Cooking, and General Housework.

In order to give the various kinds of industrial training in the most efficient and thorough manner, the several disciplinary officers of the schools are carefully selected with regard to their proficiency in the trades followed, and to their capacity to impart such knowledge to the children. They are all practical men, masters of their respective trades, and, in many instances, possess certificates from technical schools certifying to their knowledge of and capacity for imparting technical instruction. It is one of the conditions for the recognition of an Industrial school that all the shops shall be suitable for their purpose with respect to space, light, and air, and that they shall be adequately equipped with the necessary tools and materials. Great care is exercised by the Governors of the various institutions in deciding upon the particular trade or industry which shall be taught to the children. Consideration is given, so far as circumstances permit, to the bent or wish of the children themselves, and to their apparent capacity for or adaptability to any particular occupation.

The following is a quotation from the Government Report of 1901 :—

Industrial training continues to improve. Year by year more schools come into line, and now in a large proportion of them children will be found who have more than a merely empirical knowledge of the handicraft in which they are engaged. These young carpenters, saddlers, shoemakers, tailors, and others, can not only cut, chip, saw, hammer, press, or stitch, they can also draft out their work on paper, wood, cloth, or leather; tell a visitor the nature, uses, and quality of the tool or material they are handling, and will display an interest and pride in their work which indicate influences at work far more effective for the formation of character than volumes of sermons or years of dangling on a nurse's knee. What these schools are succeeding in doing is to apply to all the trades they engage in the principles on which are based the courses of Manual Instruction in

Woodwork in many Elementary schools, and in Metalwork in a few.  But they do not forget that after all it is practice which makes perfect, and they have no fastidious contempt for the humbler occupations in which many an honest livelihood is gained.  In an age of conflicting authorities and ideas, they may well hold fast to Goethe's maxim: "In all things to serve from the lowest station upwards is necessary.  To restrict yourself to a trade is best.  For the narrow mind, whatever he attempts is still a trade; for the higher an art; and the highest in doing one thing, does all; or, to speak less paradoxically, in the one thing which he does rightly, he sees the likeness of all that is done rightly."

### IX.—Physical Training and Recreation.

The inmates of Industrial schools have in many cases been the victims of underfeeding and neglect from their infancy.  A large proportion of them, therefore, require in the first instance specially nourishing food, until they have been brought into a healthy condition.  When the child's health has been fairly established, it is maintained and developed by suitable exercise and recreation, conducted, as far as possible, in the open air.  Constant occupation is essential to the discipline of an Industrial school, therefore the children must always, when not at meals or in bed, be engaged either in school, at work, or at drill, physical exercises, organised games, or play.  The children are kept doing something as much as possible during their waking hours.  In all schools a certain amount of drill and physical exercise forms an important part of the school curriculum.  This is the case to a greater extent in town schools, where industrial occupations are mostly of an indoor character, than in country schools where a large proportion of the boys are engaged in outdoor pursuits.  Physical training by organised exercises has everywhere assumed greater importance of late years than was formerly the case.  Apart from the development of public opinion in the matter, the result is due, in a great measure, to the support of H.M. Inspector and the Home Office.  In a large proportion of the boys' schools and in some of the girls' schools, an excellent display of gymnastics can be given, which would include practically the whole of the children and not a few specially selected squads.  The result is the improved physique of the children.  The system of instruction followed in the case of boys is usually that adopted for the Day Schools of the Board.  A large number of boys' schools possess a swimming bath and a gymnasium, and a qualified gymnastic instructor is now, as a rule, a member of the school staff.

Mr. Legge says, in his report for 1897 :—

Experience, particularly in this class of school, goes to show that in order to keep a boys' school sweet and clean there is absolutely nothing so efficacious as a gymnasium in proper use.

In some of the schools advantage is taken of proximity to an Army Depôt for the engagement two or three times weekly of an Army staff instructor, with results which must be seen to be adequately realised.

With a view to stimulating the Managers of Industrial schools to take a greater interest in physical training, and to improve the methods employed at their own institutions, the Board in the autumn of last year, held a public display of Drill and Gymnastics.  The whole of the boys' schools within a reasonable distance of London sixteen in number, were invited to take part in the display, and fourteen (including the Board's own schools) accepted the invitation.

### 1. *Organised Games.*

Of equal importance in the physical training of the children are what may be collectively termed "Organised Games" and athletics, such as cricket, football, swimming, running, jumping, and boxing, The fostering of cricket and football has been greatly promoted of late years by the warm encouragement of H.M. Inspector, and by the formation of leagues among the Home Office schools, divided into North and South of England. The matches between the various schools in the Leagues are contested with the greatest keenness, and are marked by sportsmanlike behaviour, good temper, and unselfishness on the part of the players. This is one of the best features of the contests. Not only are the teams interested in the matches, but this interest is shared by the rank and file of the schools, and it causes among the youngsters an amount of emulation to qualify for selection which has a most beneficial effect upon them, and constitutes one of the best aids to discipline. It possesses many other advantages, such as mixing with boys of other schools; giving them self-confidence, and increasing their self-respect. Mr. Legge has observed that "an incidental advantage of this spirit in our schools is the attraction it offers for masters in sympathy with boy-nature, who thoroughly understand and enjoy a game themselves, and take a pride in working up to efficiency the material they have in hand. Many a good fellow finds himself heartened for his work in the schoolroom by the consciousness that by directing and joining in the boys' sports he has won their confidence and affection as he could have done in no other way."

Physical training is not such a prominent feature in girls' schools, but it is making good progress. In the Government Report for 1898, Mr. Legge writes :—

"Nor have girls been neglected. Quite as striking as anything seen at boys' schools has been the improvement in the gait and deportment of the girls in many schoo's, owing to the more sustained practice of well-designed extension and marching exercises. A glimpse at the raw material in any schools will show how important and how difficult the work must be. Among Industrial schools it is fair to mention two which have especially distinguished themselves by the excellence of the training given in them: they are St. Margaret's, Mill Hill, and Gordon House, Isleworth. The Leeds School Board's school at Thorparch is the only one at which systematic gymnastic instruction is being given to girls, and the results there will be watched with much interest. At several schools regular instruction in swimming is being given."

### 2. *Summer Camps.*

Another feature of Industrial school life is the annual summer holiday at the seaside, or in camp in the country. This change is particularly beneficial to children in town schools; and it has its advantages even for children in country schools : for it provides them with a change of scene and air. It permits the school buildings, to be cleansed. It also brightens the children's lives, enlarges their experience, and gives them something to look back upon, and something to anticipate. Many of the schools have permanent

R

auxiliary homes at the seaside, to which batches of children can be sent, in rotation, all the year round.

## X.—Control of Children who have Left School.

### 1. *Disposals or Placing Out.*

The training of a child in the school during the term of its detention is directed to fitting it to support itself at the end of it. This is the most critical stage in the child's career. In order to bridge over the earlier portion of this period by keeping in comparatively close touch with the children, the Industrial Schools Act, 1866, authorises a system of licensing them "to live with any trustworthy and respectable person named in the licence, and willing to receive and take charge of them." In practice, this means to an employer, or to some person who is willing to provide a home for the child whilst engaged in suitable employment. The licence can only be in force for three months, but it may be renewed for further periods of three months, until the period of the child's detention has expired—*i.e.* at the age of 16. In the case of unsatisfactory conduct the licence may be revoked. In 1894, Parliament, with the view of further protecting children after the term of their detention had expired, extended the provisions with regard to licensing, by certain sections in the "Industrial Schools Acts Amendment Act,"[1] which gives Managers of Industrial schools supervision of the children until they have reached the age of 18, and also gives them power, where necessary, to revoke the licence of such children, and to recall them to the school for a period not exceeding three months at any one time.

As a rule, it is disadvantageous to the child to remain in the school to the limit of its term of detention. In the case of boys it has been found better to release them on licence at about 15 years of age, or even still earlier. Boys of the labouring class begin to work at 14 or sooner; and, as such boys are paid about an equal rate of wages at the beginning, regardless of age, it is unfair and discouraging to the elder children. It is found that a lad takes to outside work more kindly, and is more amenable to control at 15 than at 16. Moreover, at the latter age he is too old for apprenticeship; and he is, generally, not sufficiently competent to go as an "improver" and earn his living at the trade which he has been learning in the school. It is now, therefore, the general practice to license boys out at about 15 years of age. In former years it was deemed to be of advantage to girls to remain in school until 16, so that they could be better trained for domestic service; but now, even in their cases, it is usually found to be desirable that they should be licensed at 15 or 15½.

### 2. *Kinds of Disposal.*

The employments into which children are placed upon leaving school vary considerably, according to the children's tastes and capacities, and to the locality of the school and the opportunities of the superintendents and managers.

Girls usually enter domestic service, and this kind of disposal is generally considered

[1] 57 and 58 Vict., c. 33.

to be the best for the majority of girls. Some, however, have successfully entered higher employments as Teachers, Milliners, Shop Assistants, Art Students, Art Needle-workers.

The range of occupations is much larger for boys, and the choice more varied. Among the most popular are the following:—Army, Farm-service, Emigration, Domestic Service, Mercantile Marine, and trades of various kinds. A larger number enter the Army than any other employment. They go as Band boys, for which they have been prepared by the school Bands. Nearly every boys' school has its Band, and in many this is one of the most important "Industries." The band-masters of regiments are glad to get such recruits, in consequence of their knowledge of music, and because they have been accustomed to discipline. A number enter the Royal Navy, but the facilities for their joining this branch of the Service are not equal to those of the Army.

Both employments are considered to be exceedingly good for Industrial School boys, as they are given opportunities of advancement, and are removed from the many pitfalls which beset boys in civil employment.

Mr. Legge, in the Government Report for 1899, says:—

> There is not the slightest doubt that enlistment in the Army and Navy is to be commended as a means of disposal for the boys in Home Office schools. These boys are the stuff out of which good sailors and soldiers are made; they are quick-witted, full of courage, reckless even to a fault, and the open-air life and steady discipline are just what suits them. On enlistment they are saved from returning to the surroundings which proved their bane in childhood. Finally, there is a fitness in boys who owe much of their education to the State repaying their debt in service to the State.

A large number, mostly from training ships, enter the Mercantile Marine; and many boys take employment upon farms, where they live with the farmer as a member of the family. Mr. Legge, in the Report for 1901, points out:—

> As Industrial training improves, the number of those engaged in skilled employment must increase. The most arduous, and not the least important, of a superintendent's duties is the placing out of boys. But hard work reaps its reward, and once a good connection is established with three or four large employers of labour, the task is easier. Instead of having to find employers for boys, boys have to be found for employers. The secret of success in several cases has been a study of the kind of boys wanted here or there, and of the precise training likely to be useful, followed by a resolute effort to give boys that precise training. Finally comes the struggle to keep hold of lads, who are qualified for skilled employment, and prevent them from drifting back into the vicious circle from which they originally came. It cannot be too often repeated that the Working Boys' Home is the most valuable auxiliary a school can have; and the growth of these homes in connection with schools is one of the most hopeful signs for the future.

Very great care is taken by the managers and superintendents of schools in placing children in suitable employment. In the cases of London boys sent from schools in the country to employment in London, an officer of the Board visits the proposed employer, and must report favourably, both with regard to him and to the respectability of the proposed residence and surroundings of the child before the Board will consent to the disposal.

R 2

In a few cases the children are allowed to return to their friends; but this is only permitted if the parents and home surroundings are satisfactory and some suitable employment is found for them.

In many cases no communication whatever passes between the child and its parents during the whole of its term of detention until just before its close. Then the parental anxiety to be united to his child is quite remarkable. The child is anxious to respond to the new-found love of its formerly indifferent or cruel parents, and expresses a desire to return home, refusing to be disposed of in any other manner. If the desire be granted, disillusionment, as a rule, speedily follows. Many superintendents, therefore, before licensing out a child, in the event of its desire to return home, give it a fortnight's holiday, so that it may obtain a clearer appreciation of the meaning of " home " in its case. The effect of such a visit is generally to remove the illusion, and to secure the ready sanction of the child to its disposal by the Managers in some more suitable manner.

It is most important that children should be placed in situations which afford prospects of future advancement and an ultimate means of livelihood, even at comparatively low commencing wages, rather than that they should be placed in unskilled employment in which the immediate remuneration is comparatively high. These latter posts are easy to obtain; they rarely lead to permanent employment; the lad in a few years has to make way for younger boys at lower wages, and he probably drifts into merely casual labour, and may even degenerate into the ranks of the so-called " Hooligans." For this reason the Committee have discouraged, as much as possible, the practice of licensing boys to the latter class of situations; and the Managers are now resorting to them only as a last resource for those boys who are very dull, or who have some slight physical defect which unfits them for better positions.

### 3. *Emigration.*

For many Industrial school children emigration forms the most effective of all disposals. The children suitable for emigration are those of worthless parents, or who have no parents, and consequently no homes. They must be physically strong, and must not have retained any criminal tendencies. The Colonies refuse to be the dumping ground for physical or moral refuse. This means of disposal has been freely adopted by many Industrial schools, and the results have been so good that the number of children sent to employment in the Colonies increases yearly.

At present Canada is the only Colony which is effectually open for the emigration of Industrial school children. The Legislatures of Ontario, Manitoba, and Quebec have passed Acts regulating the emigration of children from England; but the Quebec Act is practically inoperative.

Mr. Legge, in his report for 1898, makes the following observations upon this subject :—

Emigrants for the period 1896-7 numbered 102, as against 34 for the period 1894-6. This is a decided improvement. Emigration under proper safeguards—and the Colonial authorities have wisely done their best to secure these—is one of the best means of disposing of such girls as these. The advantage of emigration to the girls is obvious; they may be rescued from evil influences at home, and get a fresh start and a fair one abroad. Nor is the advantage to the Colonies of getting a steady supply of well-selected, carefully-trained girls from the mother country less obvious. In 1898 the Glasgow Juvenile Delinquency Board sent over to Canada a lady to visit girls who have been emigrated from Maryhill to that Colony. Her report was thoroughly satisfactory; the girls were doing well, and were appreciated.

### 4. *Certified Working-Boys' Homes.*

A valuable aid in cases of disposal is found in working homes for boys or girls. These homes are not required in the case of those children who are placed in the country, as they usually reside with their employer, or the employer provides a home for the child. In the case of boys placed in employment in London, the existence of a home is invaluable. In most town employments it is impossible for the *employé* to sleep where he works. Therefore, unless he has respectable parents residing in the town, lodgings must be found for him. The greatest difficulty is that at the outset the boy's earnings are insufficient to support him What he needs, therefore, is a home in which he can live until he can support himself. This need is supplied by the various homes for working boys which have been established, some in connection with a particular school, and others by independent bodies.

The boys can be kept in communities of fifteen or twenty much cheaper than they can keep themselves individually. For every boy licensed to a certified home before the expiration of his term of detention, the Home Office make a payment of 2s. 6d. per week, and the School Board also contribute 2s. 6d. per week for every boy so sent by them. Whilst resident in the home the lad is subject to certain necessary rules as to conduct, and he has to contribute a proportion of his wages each week towards the expenses of his maintenance.

### 5. *Keeping in Touch.*

One of the most important duties of Managers of Industrial schools is to keep in touch with the children after they have left the school. Nothing contributes more effectually to their successful establishment in life. Various means are adopted by Managers and superintendents for keeping in touch with their children.

The first, easiest and, in cases of those at a distance, the only means, is by correspondence. This, however, although of great value, is insufficient. Accordingly, most bodies of Managers arrange that, at least once a year, the superintendent or some member of the Committee shall personally visit the children to see how they are getting on, to give advice or assistance, and to show sympathy. These visits are highly appreciated both by the children and by the employers.

When children are sent a long distance from the school it is customary to enlist the interest of some lady or gentleman in the district, who looks after the children, and reports from time to time to the school how they are progressing. Another valuable means of keeping in touch is the annual reunion of old boys or girls. These meetings are very popular, and are attended frequently for many years by former inmates of a school, even after they have been married and have become parents of families.

The Board employs a visiting officer for the "Shaftesbury" Training Ship, whose whole time is occupied in the visitation of old boys, and in reporting upon their work and condition. The captain-superintendent of the ship keeps up a correspondence with these boys, and the letters received from them are periodically forwarded to the Head Office of the Board. In the case of Gordon House the superintendent keeps in touch with the girls by correspondence and by visits.

Girls licensed or discharged to domestic service in London, either from Gordon House, or from the other girls' Industrial schools in the neighbourhood of London, receive great assistance from the Metropolitan Association for Befriending Young Servants. For the payment of a small fee this association undertakes the work of supervision, and reports annually upon the girls. The Association also admits any girls into their lodging-homes who may be out of a place, or during illness or holidays. It is expected that the girls in service should pay part of their cost when staying at these homes, but in cases of sickness they are admitted free. The homes are certified by the Home Office, and if the licence of a girl is revoked she may be legally recalled to the home.

### XI.—Improved Condition of the Schools.

It is admitted that during the last quarter of a century a great improvement has been effected in the condition of Industrial schools. It has already been pointed out that greater importance is attached to education. In addition, the health, comfort, and industrial training of the children have received more consideration; a higher standard has been required in respect of the structural suitability and sanitary condition of the buildings; the dietary and clothing have been improved. Greater variety has been imparted to the life of the children. Endeavours have been made to develop and strengthen character by training them to be self-reliant and trustworthy, and to approximate the conditions of their lives more nearly to those of ordinary children. A great improvement has been effected by attention to the recreation and occupations of the children when not engaged either in school or at work. More personal liberty is accorded to the children within the homes. The result has been to raise the tone of the Industrial schools, and to improve the physical, mental and moral development of the children. Such improvement has only been possible at a considerably increased cost of maintenance, and in this respect indispensable assistance has been given by the various Local Authorities, who have contributed an increased maintenance allowance.

Evidence in proof of the above facts is afforded by the following extracts from letters which have been received from some of the schools with which the Board have agreements :—

*Essex Boys' Industrial School.*

About 20 influential ladies and gentlemen from the town come up to this school regularly every Sunday evening to take classes, and during the week to help with the Band of Hope, Boys' Library, Band of Mercy, and in other ways. The teachers have special classes, so that they become acquainted with, and take special interest in, one particular lot of boys, and in connection with this the lads are invited out to tea, etc., by the teachers. They thus come in frequent contact with persons in good positions. We find this has a valuable effect in elevating the moral tone and general behaviour of the lads in the school.

### York Boys' Industrial School.

The School Board for London have exhibited an interest in their children beyond any other authority, and this interest has been shown in such a manner that the school Managers and superintendents with whom they have agreements, have found it a pleasure to comply with their suggestions for the mental and physical improvement of the children under their care while in the institutions; and for the care and oversight of them subsequently.

For my part, I feel deeply grateful for the help and consideration shown by the Board; and but for that help and consideration, I am convinced that the York school would be vastly below its present standard of attainments.

### St. Vincent's R.C. (Boys), Dartford.

Comparing the present time with twenty years ago, the Industrial schools show an immense advance. The inmates are not now the rough, uncouth, and very often vicious, material one had then to deal with. The School Board officer has evidently been abroad, and he hasn't been idle. The increased generosity of the contributing authorities has enabled Managers to better equip the various departments of their institutions, also to command the influence of a more intelligent class of instructors, and so to bring the education—technical and literary, as well as the physical and moral culture—of the youngsters up to the high standard aimed at by the inspectors and other officials. The responsible bodies, one is pleased to see, have come to recognise more fully the very important place the Industrial schools of the country should hold in their administration, and certainly the metropolis has, as is only fitting, shown the lead in this matter.

### St. Nicholas R.C. (Boys), Manor Park, Ilford.

The intercourse between the different schools brought about by the South of England Home Office Schools Athletic Association; the visits necessitated by out and home cricket and football matches between the various schools, by inter-school athletic sports, etc.; the consequent meetings of the different superintendents to arrange the same, and the interchange of visits and views; also the very great interest aroused by these games and sports are amongst the most important of all the beneficial influences alluded to.

It is, in my opinion, difficult to overrate the good done by these cricket and football matches and sports, etc., and such meetings as the recent gymnastic display in Holborn Town Hall.

Not only do they engender feelings of healthy emulation, and, consequently, self-respect in the boys themselves, but the ideas and views of officers and superintendents are enlarged and stimulated; the use and benefit of physical training becomes understood alike by boys and masters, and drill, gymnastics, and games have ceased to be merely mechanical, and are inspired by a life, spirit, and energy which has made this school, at any rate, a different place from what it was.

### Portsmouth and South Hants Industrial School.

The liberal additional payment of the London School Board, by enabling the schools to obtain a higher class of women as teachers and matrons, and to provide better clothing, food, and appliances, and so raising the standard of industrial training and mental and physical development of the children as well as their comfort in every way, has, I consider, been one of the main causes. I think the Industrial schools owe much to the London School Board, and will be sorry when their liberal and just reign is over.

*King Edward School.*

As the claims in the general cause of humanity have advanced, and the study of "child life" has engaged the attention of those interested in the work of education, the elimination of the retributive or punitive element from our particular branch is a powerful influence in alleviating the necessarily restricted life in an Industrial school. To make the children happy and useful is the intention of every effort, and any measures that tend to remove the stigma incurred by detention in such a school should be encouraged.

## XII.—Provision of Special Accommodation for Young Children.

This question was brought under the consideration of the Industrial Schools Committee in December, 1901, by a letter from the Managers of the St. Vincent's Junior Industrial School at Whitstable. In this letter the Managers called attention to the fact that, in consequence of the number of young and delicate children sent to St. Vincent's, Dartford, in 1898 and 1899, who required special treatment and female supervision, which could not be provided at Dartford, this Junior school was opened as an experiment in 1899. It was pointed out that the agreement for renting the house would shortly terminate, that the buildings at Whitstable, although fairly comfortable for the children, were inadequate for the accommodation of the staff, and that the Managers had to decide whether or not they could build a permanent school.

It was added that the Home Office would not allow more than fifty children in a Junior school, and as the expense of such a small institution for this particular class of child works out at a greater cost per head than that of older children, the Managers would not feel justified in building a permanent school, unless an amount of at least 10s. per week per child could be assured.

The Managers explained that they had been able to carry on this school with 7s. per head for the time, because the Sisters were willing to try the experiment of the Junior establishment without receiving any remuneration; but that if the Institution is to be permanent it would be necessary to pay them. The Managers therefore asked the Board to give these matters their early consideration.

In order to have the question fully laid before them, the committee placed the matter n the hands of their Chairman, who submitted the following Memorandum :—

I have for a considerable time been impressed with the undesirableness of sending very young children who have been committed for no fault of their own, and whose moral character is not bad, to mix with older children, committed for their own misdemeanours. In dealing with such young children it has been the practice of the Rota Sub-Committee, as far as possible, to send them to selected schools where they would receive treatment suitable to their tender age. Cases of children who are not Roman Catholics have up to the present been dealt with as follows:

Boys have been, as far as possible, sent to the Davenport Hill Boys' Home, but for some time past, owing to the accommodation at Margate being limited, the number of cases which could be received at this school has been reduced from 100 to less than 80.

Girls are, as far as possible, sent to Gordon House.

Special provision for Roman Catholic boys has, as an experiment, been made at the Junior school at Whitstable, which is connected with the St. Vincent's School, Dartford, but no special provision has yet been made for girls.

When the places in the schools mentioned above have all been filled, it has not been possible to do much in the direction of providing specially for young children, inasmuch as the selection of the committee is limited to the particular schools which may have vacant places at the time.

I am strongly of opinion that the time has arrived for the Board to consider the question of making proper provision for these young children.

Two alternative methods present themselves for dealing with this problem. One is the establishment of a limited number of schools to which only children under eight years of age should be sent, such children to remain in the same school during the whole period of their detention ; and Board, however, to reserve to themselves the right, in exceptional cases, to transfer children to other schools for the purpose of learning a trade or for any other reason; and the other is the establishment of a smaller number of such schools to which the children should be sent, but from which they should be transferred on attaining the age of, say, ten years, to other special schools reserved for the reception of such children. After careful consideration, I am of opinion that the first-named is the more desirable.

In both cases it would be essential that special arrangements should be made for the treatment of these young children in respect of the general equipment of the school, the character of the staff (which should largely consist of women), the organisation for purposes of recreation, the dietary, clothing, etc.

In view of the fact that none of the children would, on committal, be morally bad, the association of the young children afterwards admitted with those who had grown up in the school would not be open to the objection which at present exists to the association of young children with the ordinary senior inmates of Industrial schools. Moreover, I consider that it would be an advantage for such children to remain under the care of the persons who had charge of them in their infancy; who had laid the foundations of their moral character; and whom the children would have become accustomed to regard in the light of parents. In the latter alternative, viz., the transfer of children when they arrived at the age of ten to another school, although they would still be kept from the association with children of previous bad character, the good influence which had grown up in the schools to which they had first been sent would be interrupted or broken; the new methods and influences would probably be of a somewhat different character, and, in the end, not really so beneficial for the development of the child. In support of this view, I would quote the following extract from the last report of H.M. Inspector, Mr. Legge : —

'Objections may be raised to entirely separate Junior schools. It cannot be good for a child first of all to wrench it from however an unsavoury bed in the slums and plant it in a Junior school, and then later on, at eleven or twelve, to pluck it up by the roots again and transplant it into a Senior school. The hold that a school will get of a child is very much greater than is sometimes supposed; school ties may, and do, become like family ties, and it is desirable to interfere as little as possible with their natural growth. The passage from a Junior to a Senior department in the same school is an easy one, and there can be no objection to Junior departments. They are to be encouraged.'

I am convinced that in order to make this scheme work with the greatest possible degree of success, it is necessary that these Special schools should belong to the Board, and be under their own direct management. It is, therefore, greatly to be regretted that the Home Secretary withheld his sanction to the provision of a new school to replace the Davenport Hill Boys' Home at Brent-wood, which might have been devoted entirely to the reception of young children. In the event, however, of the transference to the Board of the London County Council Industrial schools, it might be practicable to carry out the scheme, either by removing the whole of the present inmates of the Mayford School to Feltham, and reserving the former school entirely for the reception of young children, or by setting apart a portion of the premises at Feltham for the purpose. I should strongly favour the former plan.

It may be, however, that neither plan will prove feasible, and I would, therefore, propose, as a further alternative, that arrangements should be made, if possible, with two schools with which the Board have agreements—one for girls and one for boys—for the transference of the whole of their present children to other schools, and for these two schools to be specially reserved for the reception of very young children, under conditions to be laid down by the Board.

I am of opinion that it is undesirable and unnecessary to retain the boys, who have been committed when very young, after they reach fourteen years of age, and I would, therefore, recommend that as a general rule boys committed to these schools be licensed out as soon as possible after reaching the age of fourteen. The Committee will remember that this principle was adopted some years ago in the case of the Davenport Hill Boys' Home, and that the present regulations respecting the matter provide that in the cases of boys who have been under detention for more than six years, who have passed Standard VI., and who are not suffering from any physical disability, the age for licensing shall, as a general rule, be fourteen and a half years.

I do not feel able to make the same recommendation in the case of girls, as they would not, at the age of fourteen, be old enough for domestic service. If, however, after inquiry, it was found that the homes had improved and that the parents were fit to receive the girls, it might be considered whether or not they should then be licensed to them, control being retained over them until they reached the age of eighteen.

It must be borne in mind that the expense of the maintenance of schools entirely for the reception of young children will be proportionately greater than that of an ordinary school. For instance, a more numerous as well as a specially selected staff will be required, firstly to minister to the special requirements of such young children, and, secondly, because the school will be deprived in a great measure of the assistance which in ordinary schools is rendered by the children in the usual domestic work of the institution, as they would both enter and leave at an early age. Clothing also will be more costly, inasmuch as the whole of the garments will have to be purchased outside the institution instead of being made by the children. The dietary will be a special one, but need not, I think, cost more than usual.

For the reasons given above, it will be absolutely necessary, in the event of the proposal being carried out in this way, that the contribution of the Board shall be fixed at a rate considerably higher than that for ordinary schools, and I do not think that anything less than a total weekly payment of 10s. from both sources will be sufficient.

In the case of the Roman Catholic boys, I think that the arrangement now in force in connection with the St. Vincent's school, by which special provision is made for young children at Whitstable, is the best which can be devised, and that it should be continued, but that the Board should undertake to raise the contribution to 10s., in order that the Managers might be justified in taking the steps which they propose to enlarge the present buildings or to provide new buildings for the accommodation of a total number of fifty young children.

Similar arrangements should be made for providing accommodation for the younger Roman Catholic girls, and I suggest that I may be authorised to communicate with the Roman Catholic authorities, with the view of ascertaining the steps which they will be prepared to take in the matter.

Although not coming strictly within the scope of the present memorandum, it may not be out of place to call attention to the fact that Mr. Legge, in his last report, mentioned the question of also providing special accommodation for boys who are over twelve years of age when committed, and expressed the opinion that it is a question whether the difficulty of dealing with these cases, though not so clearly recognised, is not the more serious difficulty of the two. He added: "Very few boys of twelve and a half and thirteen, committed to an Industrial school, are sent until they are more or less hardened offenders. In the school they at once take their place amongst the oldest and biggest. Instead of being led by others who have come under the influence of wholesome discipline, they are in danger of leading others, and leading them astray."

The Committee, after giving the foregoing memorandum very full and careful consideration, forwarded to the Board recommendations which were formally adopted on February 20th. 1902, in the following resolutions:—

(1) That a letter be addressed to the Home Secretary, asking whether he would be prepared to sanction the provision by the Board of a school, or schools, specially for the reception of children under nine years of age, either (in the event of the London County Council schools being transferred to the Board) (a) by the utilisation of the buildings at Mayford, or the provision of special accommodation at the Feltham Industrial School; or (in the event of the London County Council schools not being transferred to the Board) (b) by the provision by the Board of two new schools, one for boys and one for girls; and by a special arrangement with the Managers of two or more existing schools with which the Board have agreements.

(2) That (in the event of the sanction of the Home Office being obtained to the latter part of the alternative proposal (b)) the Board authorise the committee, if necessary, to make arrangements with the Managers of certain existing schools with which the Board have agreements, for the reception only of children under nine years of age, and that in such cases the Board agree to make to the Managers, in respect of each child sent by the Board, a contribution at the following rates:—

(a) Whilst the child is under the age of ten years such an amount as will, with the Treasury grant, make up a total sum of 10s. per week.

(b) When the child attains the age of ten years, such an amount as will, with the Treasury grant, make up a total sum of 9s. per week.

The Home Secretary approved of the scheme in principle.

Arrangements were made in existing schools for the reception of young Roman Catholic children, boys being provided for at Whitstable, in the Junior section of the St. Vincent's Industrial School, Dartford, and special accommodation being provided for girls in the St. Mary's Industrial School, Croydon. Efforts were made to find Protestant schools the Managers of which were able to fulfil the requirements of the Board, but they were unsuccessful. A communication was therefore forwarded to the Home Secretary, asking him to authorise the Board, as an experiment, to secure two large houses in the neighbourhood of London which would accommodate from twenty to thirty little boys and girls respectively, these houses to be placed under Matrons and female officers, and the children to be sent to public Elementary day schools in the neighbourhood. The Home Secretary required some information in detail, and in January, 1903, a reply was received stating that, if suitable buildings were provided for the purpose, the Home Secretary would be prepared to grant temporary certificates for the homes. Immediate steps were taken to secure such buildings, but great difficulties were encountered. None could be hired, and it became necessary to obtain the approval of the Board to the purchase of buildings; but it was not until the end of June that the Committee were successful in acquiring a suitable house in Clapham Park.

The certificate of the Secretary of State was received on November 21st, 1903, and was granted for a period of two years for the reception of 30 little boys. The Home was opened on December 29th, when a number of little boys, who had been temporarily accommodated in schools with which the Board have agreements, were sent into residence.

The provision of a similar school for little girls remains in abeyance for a time, as it is found that there is sufficient accommodation in existing schools to provide for present needs.

### XIII.—TRUANT SCHOOLS.

In the year 1876 the Board decided that it was desirable to ascertain whether the difficulties occasioned by incorrigible truants and children otherwise uncontrollable by their parents could be advantageously met by the establishment of special schools where such children, with the consent of their parents, except under very special circumstances, and by order of some competent authority, might be detained for short periods under suitable discipline; or whether any other suggestion could be made for the attainment of the same ends. They also appointed a special committee to consider and report whether it appeared desirable that any representation should be made by the Board on the subject to the Education Department or the Home Office. The Special Committee reported to the Board that they considered it proved

that there is a class of boys numerous enough to demand serious attention which are not satisfactorily met either by the Bye-laws or by the ordinary application of the Industrial Schools Act. These are the cases of parents who sincerely desire to obey the law, but who, through feeble health, widowhood, or absence at work, cannot prevent the wilful and perverse truancy of their children. In such cases the Bye-laws are sometimes felt to operate with harshness, if not injustice; while a long detention of the children in an Industrial school seems disproportionate to the circumstances, disturbs family life to an unnecessary extent, and involves an excessive expense to the public.

The Board thereupon asked the Home Secretary and the Education Department for authority to make provision for not more than fifty boys, as an experiment, under the Industrial Schools Acts, either in a school already existing, or in a school to be provided by the Board. They further decided that no boy should be sent to the school, except by express desire of his parents, and on the joint application of such parents and the Board.

The Home Secretary approved of the proposed Truant school on the understanding that children should be sent thither for short periods ranging from one week to a month.

Inquiries were thereupon made with the view of finding suitable buildings in which the proposed school could be established, with the result that Upton House, Urswick road, Homerton, capable of accommodating sixty boys, was purchased and furnished, and the necessary staff was appointed.

The intention was that all cases should be sent to the school under Section 16 of the Industrial Schools Act, which provides that a child may be sent to an Industrial school by a magistrate, on the representation of a parent or guardian that he is unable to control him. It was further proposed that the period of detention should be from one week to a month; that there should be an absolute prohibition of conversation among the boys, and that no play should be allowed, but that the necessary exercise should be derived from the drill.

In February, 1878, a letter was received from the Home Secretary stating that a point of law had unexpectedly been raised in connection with the control and detention of children in the proposed school, upon which he had felt bound to consult the law officers of the Crown, and forwarding a letter from Sir James Ingham, the chief magistrate, stating that the majority of the magistrates were of opinion that a school established in conformity with the proposed rules could not be deemed to be an Industrial school, and that an order could not be made under Section 16 of the Industrial Schools Act for the detention of a child therein.

The Board forwarded to the Home Secretary an appeal against the statement that the school could not be legally established. Pending the decision of the Home Secretary, they gave notice to the officers already appointed for the termination of their engagements.

A reply from the Home Office was received at the end of March, stating that the law officers of the Crown were of opinion that an order for the detention of a child for so short a period as a month or six weeks was at variance with the spirit, though not with the letter of the Industrial Schools Act. The Board thereupon withdrew their application for a certificate for a Truant school; but they asked that, as the building had been purchased and the officers appointed in reliance on the preliminary sanction granted by the Home Secretary, the school might be certified as an ordinary Industrial school.

The Board further resolved that the Upton House School should be reserved for cases sent under Section 12 of the Elementary Education Act of 1876, and the Home Secretary was so informed. The result of this decision was that the school would be an ordinary Industrial school; but that only truant boys would be admitted, the section referred to giving power to a court to send children to an Industrial school for the breach of an order to attend an ordinary Elementary school.

In October, 1878, the Secretary of State issued a Certificate for the school for sixty boys under the Industrial Schools Act, the school to be used for the reception of cases sent to it under Section 12 of the Elementary Education Act of 1876, so that the school became in effect what it had been in name—an Industrial school reserved for the reception of truant boys—or in other words a Truant school.

The school was soon filled, and in February, 1880, a report was laid before the Committee calling attention to the fact that a large number of cases were waiting for admission, but that there were no vacancies. No action was then taken; but in the following May the question of the necessity for additional accommodation was again under consideration and an application was made to the Managers of all schools within the district of the metropolis with which the Board had agreements, asking whether they were willing to provide accommodation for truant cases on the usual terms of payment. The answers being in the negative, it was decided to recommend the Board to provide additional accommodation for truant cases.

Some idea of the results achieved in the reclamation of truant boys during the short time which had elapsed since the opening of Upton House may be gathered from the following report from the superintendent of the East Lambeth division, which was made in the early part of 1880 :—

I had a social meeting with the Visitors last week to discuss various points of their work, and, *inter alia,* the results manifested in the conduct of those boys who had been sent to, and remitted from, Upton House. I was surprised by the strength and unanimity of testimony to the beneficial effect on these lads (and, indirectly through them, upon other boys inclined to be irregular) from their temporary detention at this school. Twelve boys in all have passed to the home from this division, and been discharged on licence (this is now more). In only one case has there been a failure on a first release. In all other instances the effect of detention has been most beneficial. The boys licensed out are amongst the most sprightly, well-conducted, and punctual of scholars, and some instances were signalised where the change in appearance and conduct was spoken of as "surprising," "most gratifying." As visitor after visitor spoke of the good result upon his own cases, I could not but feel convinced, even if not fully so before, that the Board have a highly remedial institution in Upton House for the evil it is designed to meet, and it will be a matter of great interest to me to see other incorrigible youngsters removed there, and to watch the results also in their cases.

Subsequent observation and experience have strengthened my conviction of the value of such an institution. I have spoken to some of the boys who have been consigned to this home and subsequently released, and to their parents and teachers. The universal testimony has been as to the radical improvement effected in the conduct of these boys. One mother was especially fervent in her thanks to the Board for the great good done to her wilful boy by some weeks' residence at the institution, and the magistrates view with favour the disciplinary character of such a home in the numerous cases brought before them where parents plead that the irregularity is entirely the fault of the children, and not their own. I look forward with expectancy to the early establishment of a similiar Truant school for the large metropolitan area south of the Thames.

Upton House proved to be inadequate for the accommodation of sixty boys, and also unsuitable for permanent use as a Truant school. At the beginning of 1883, therefore, it was decided at once to reduce the number of inmates from sixty to forty-six. The necessary additional land having been acquired, it was further decided to pull down the old buildings and to erect on the site a new school to accommodate 100 boys. The new buildings were completed, and the Home Secretary's certificate was received in February, 1885. Accommodation for forty more boys was provided in 1887 by utilising as dormitories rooms in the main building which had been occupied as an infirmary, and by erecting a new infirmary in the playground.

Up to this time no accommodation had been available for truant Roman Catholics, and the only way in which the worst of such cases could be dealt with was by sending them to ordinary Roman Catholic Industrial schools. A portion of the additional accommodation was therefore devoted to Roman Catholic boys. At a later date some additional property was purchased adjoining the school in order to improve the accommodation and to provide a gymnasium and a swimming bath. On the completion of this work in May, 1901, the certificate was extended so as to allow of the accommodation of 150 boys.

Section 16 of the Industrial Schools Act, under which boys are sent to Truant schools, provides that :—

The order shall specify the time for which the child is to be detained in the school, being such time as to the justices or magistrate seems proper for the teaching and training of the child, but not in any case extending beyond the time when the child will attain the age of 16 years.

Provision is made by which a child may be licensed out at any time after the expiration of one month's detention, on condition that he attends an ordinary Day school. In the event of a breach of this condition, the licence may be revoked, and the child may be re-admitted to the Truant school.

Up to the end of the year 1892 there was no uniformity of practice at the various Metropolitan Police Courts as to the period during which orders for the detention of children in Truant schools should have effect. The practice at most of them was to order a child to be detained until he reached the age of 14 (the maximum age at which he would in ordinary circumstances be liable to the provisions of the Education Acts), but in some it was 16. At a few of the courts, however, the magistrates made their orders of detention for varying short periods of about three months, and in some cases for so short a period as six weeks. The fact of a boy knowing that he could only be detained for a short time was found to be prejudicial to the discipline of the Truant school. Moreover in such cases the Managers had no opportunity of releasing boys on licence under penalty that, if they failed to attend a Day school. the licence would be revoked, and they would be taken back to the Truant school for a further period of detention. The necessity of a uniform practice was therefore apparent. The Board accordingly asked the Home Secretary to make provision by legislation for this course to be adopted, and that in the meantime he would make a representation to the magistrates at the courts in question as to the desirableness of meeting the views of the Board.

In March, 1893, a reply was received from the Home Secretary, stating that at a fully-attended meeting of magistrates it had been decided that children should be formally committed to Truant schools until they attained the age of fourteen, subject to their being allowed out on licence at any time before reaching that age.

Before this time the need of still further accommodation for truant boys had become very pressing. Many new cases could not be dealt with, and cases in which it was necessary to revoke the licences of boys for non-attendance at a Day school could only be dealt with after very great delay.

In 1884 the Board entered into an agreement for the reception of cases with the Managers of the North London Truant School at Walthamstow, and in 1887 with the Managers of the West Ham Truant School at Fyfield. In July, 1887, the Committee reported to the Board that these schools were all full, and that there were over 100 cases waiting for admission or re-admission. The Home Secretary thereupon sanctioned the establishment by the Board of a second Truant school to accommodate from 120 to 150 boys. A site was purchased at Anerley ; but as the new school could not be completed for at least two years, and the need for additional accommodation was very great, steps were taken to provide temporary accommodation. The Board had purchased the old House of Detention at Clerkenwell for the site of a new Board school, and an application was made to the Home Secretary for permission to use temporarily a wing of the building for a Truant school. A reply was received in August, 1888, stating that the Secretary of State was unable to sanction the proposal.

In March, 1890, the Board made an application to the Home Office for authority to make temporary arrangements for truant cases pending the building of the new Truant school. The Home Secretary approved of the proposal, and steps were taken to secure a suitable building. The attention of the committee was called to a building at Highbury, which had been used as a "Church Missionary Children's Home." This building, proved to be so suitable for the purpose that the Board decided to purchase it, and to apply to the Home Secretary for permission to use it for a permanent Truant school in lieu of the school formerly authorised at Anerley.[1] In March, 1891, the certificate of the Home Secretary was received, authorising the reception of 150 boys, with a margin up to 160. In October, 1892, the certificate was amended so as to authorise the admission of 175 boys; and, in August, 1893, the certificate was again amended so as to enable the school to receive its full complement of 200 boys as from January 1st, 1894.

The school is provided with an excellent bakery, and with shops for the teaching of Shoemaking, Tailoring and Matmaking, all of which have been specially erected for the purpose. The provision of a swimming bath and an enlarged gymnasium has been sanctioned. There is also a detached infirmary for the accommodation of children suffering from minor ailments. Any infectious cases would be at once removed to a hospital.

Further provision for truant boys had, during this time, been made by entering into agreements with the Managers of the Holme Court Truant School, Isleworth; and, in February, 1895, an agreement was entered into with the Managers of a new Truant school at Lichfield.

In January, 1895, the attention of the Committee was called to the fact that the available accommodation was still insufficient, and to the necessity for a third Truant school which should be situated in South London. They obtained the approval of the Board, and of the Home Office, to this proposal. A house at Barnes, known as St. Ann's was, with the approval of the Secretary of State, purchased for the purpose. In December, 1898, however, the Board decided that this house was not suitable, and, with the approval of the Home Office, they instructed the Works Committee to dispose of it. Before this date, however, the difficulty of dealing with the cases of boys who were re-admitted to a Truant school for the fourth, fifth, or sixth time, was brought under the notice of the Committee. Experience having shown that in these cases it was useless to continue licensing the boys out, it was proposed that they should remain under detention until they reached the age of 14, not in an ordinary Truant school, but in a separate school, which would be conducted as an ordinary Industrial school. An alternative suggestion as to dealing with such cases was that they should, on re-admission to the Truant school, receive full-time school instruction. The Board decided to forward these alternative proposals to the Home Secretary, and to inform him that, in the event of his approving of the first suggestion, the Board proposed, so soon as a suitable building had been secured for a third Truant school, to ask his consent to one of the Board's Truant schools being specially set apart for the purpose.

---

[1] The Anerley site was subsequently utilised for the erection of a school for the Blind.

A reply was subsequently received from the Home Office stating that the proposals had been referred to a Committee which was then inquring into the working of the Reformatory and Industrial school system.

The matter was again brought before the Board in May, 1898, when the Board passed the following resolutions :—

That where boys have been admitted to a Truant school three times, and all efforts have failed to secure their attendance at a day school, and it is necessary to revoke the licence and admit the boy for the fourth time, it is desirable that the boys should then be transferred to a separate school until the expiration of the period of detention, such school to be conducted on the lines of an ordinary Industrial school.

That a building (St. Ann's, Barnes) having now been acquired for the purpose of a third Truant school, the Home Secretary be asked to approve the school, when ready, being set apart for the above purpose, on the understanding that he will be willing to sanction a set of rules specially applicable to the proposed school which will authorise the detention of the boys until they reach the age mentioned in the Order of Detention without further licences.

In April, 1899, the Home Secretary stated that he was prepared to approve of the proposal on condition that the school was conducted as an ordinary Industrial school. In the meantime, however, the proposal to occupy St. Ann's, Barnes, as a Truant school had been abandoned.

A further proposal to use the buildings belonging to the Board at Brentwood was also abandoned; and in March, 1899, the Board asked the Home Secretary to approve of the purchase of a site at Hither Green, upon which the proposed school for incorrigible truants might be erected in conjunction with an ordinary Industrial school to replace the Brentwood school. Plans and an estimate of the cost of the proposed schools were submitted to the Home Secretary; but, owing to the large amount of the expenditure involved, he did not see his way to agree to the proposal. Ultimately, on February 28th, 1901, the Board, decided that no further steps should be taken for the erection of a school for incorrigible truants until the result of the two Day Industrial schools which the Board had previously decided to establish at Brunswick-road and Ponton-road should have been seen. The various means adopted for dealing with truancy, however, have been so successful that the provision of further accommodation is now unnecessary.

It will be remembered that early in 1896 the Board adopted an alternative proposal for dealing with incorrigible truants—viz. that they should receive full-time school instruction; but that beyond forwarding the resolution to the Home Office, no action had been taken upon it. In March, 1897, the Board applied to the Home Office for permission to amend the time-table of Upton House as an experiment for one year, so as to admit of boys who returned to the school for a fourth, fifth or sixth time receiving, as a rule, full-time instruction, together with such industrial training as might be thought desirable. This proposal was agreed to by the Home Secretary, and was put in force. At the conclusion of the experiment the Committee came to the decision that the system was good, and at their request, the Home Secretary sanctioned it permanently. The proposal to establish a school specially for incorrigible truants having been

s

abandoned, it became necessary to take other steps for dealing with such cases A report was accordingly presented to the Board, in which it was pointed out that boys who were committed to the Board's Truant schools were usually detained in the first instance for a period of about twelve weeks, and were then licensed out to attend ordinary elementary schools. If it were necessary, in consequence of continued non-attendance, to re-admit them, the term of detention was increased, and they were kept for periods varying from sixteen weeks to twenty-six weeks, according to the number of times each boy had been re-admitted, and having regard to the other circumstances connected with the case. A small number of boys who had succeeded in evading the Board's officers, were not committed to the Truant school until they reached the age of thirteen years. It was generally found in these cases that the boys were very backward in their education. This was also true of boys who, although committed at an earlier age, would not attend school when placed out on licence, and had to be re-admitted to the Truant school. It was desirable in such cases that the boys should receive as much instruction as possible before becoming exempt, and that any boy who on admission or re-admission was over thirteen years of age should be retained until he became exempt. In consequence of the pressure on the accommodation it had not previously been possible to carry such a proposal into effect; but the number of truants had, for some time past, been steadily diminishing, so that it was possible to retain these older children in the schools for a longer period without prejudice to new cases for admission. The Home Secretary was therefore asked that truants who are admitted or re-admitted in their fourteenth year might be retained, so far as the accommodation permitted, until they attained fourteen. The Home Secretary consented to the proposal as an experiment for two years.

In the earlier years the discipline adopted in the Truant schools was of a punitive and corrective character, but experience proved that this was undesirable, and the severity of the discipline has, been gradually relaxed, with good results. That this change of system receives the hearty approval of H.M. Inspector is shown by the following extract from his Report for the year 1899 :—

I am convinced that the dread of making the Truant school too agreeable a place rests on no solid foundation. The idea of making life in a Truant school so horrible that the terrors of recall to it will keep a boy regular in attendance at any Day school, however unattractive or unsuited to him, is not one that can commend itself to the pedagogic authorities of to-day. The imagination shrinks from contemplating the sort of man such a regimen would be likely to produce—an anarchist, not a citizen. For the genuine truant, the discipline of such a school as Highbury is quite severe enough. The absolute insistence there on hard work in the schoolroom, in the shops, or at exercise, on punctuality, cleanliness, and obedience, the fact that almost every moment of the day is mapped out for you, that you have continually to be stifling your own inclination—all this is not punishment, but the most excellent of medicines. The self-willed little boy and the easy-going individual from a slovenly home do not like it, but it is good for them, just what they want in fact. If a very few doses of the medicine do not suit the boy, then the probability is that his complaint has not been properly diagnosed. The disease may be a worse one than truancy; on the other hand, there may be no disease at all in the boy himself, the seat of it may be in his home, or in the school which he refused to attend. In either event the Truant school is not the proper place for him, and a heavy responsibility lies on the Managers of such a school to secure a fair trial for every boy brought before them. If it were possible for boys to form a union, the National Union of Scholars might employ a legal gentleman to properly represent before a magistrate the boys' side of a case; we should then be much better informed than we are at present of the conditions of life at home, in the Day school, or in the streets favouring truancy.

Up to the year 1895, the practice of the Committee was to apply to the Home Secretary for the formal discharge from the Truant school of any boy who, after being licensed out, attended regularly at a day school for a period of nine months. In that year, however, they came to the conclusion that it was undesirable to forfeit the power over a boy which was secured by the warrant of commitment; and they decided that, if a boy made satisfactory attendances for a year, the weekly card by which his attendances are reported to the office should be discontinued, but that his name should be retained on the books of the Truant school, so that, if he relapsed into truancy, he might be re-admitted without further legal proceedings.

The Industrial Training in the Truant Schools comprises Tailoring, Shoemaking, Gardening, Laundrywork, and a class of smaller boys is employed in Darning. The clothing, boots, and slippers are made and repaired at the schools. The boys at Highbury are taught, in addition, Mat-making, and receive Manual Training in Wood. Drawing as applied to industrial training is taken at both schools with much success. The Physical Training of the children comprises Military Drill, Physical Exercises, Gymnastics, and Swimming.

Of the 11,000 boys committed to the Board's Truant schools since their establishment, about one-half have been permanently cured by a first detention, and of the remainder about one-half have been cured by a second detention. The average percentage of attendance of boys on licence during the whole period has been about 86 per cent., and at the present time it is over 90 per cent.

The decrease in the number of admissions steadily continues. This is attributable to the following causes :—

(1) The raising of the maximum fine for non-attendance from 5s. to £1 by the Education Act, 1900. This has caused parents to exercise greater control over children with truanting tendencies. Consequently, the number of summonses necessary to be issued has decreased, and this, together with the decision of the Board to reduce the number of children for whom each visitor was responsible, has enabled the visitors to take immediate action for the visitation of parents whose children make only eight attendances per week.

(2) The appointment of a visitor in each division, to be employed in districts of a specially difficult character, or where the percentage of average attendance falls below 80, or in any district where the Divisional Committee are of opinion that the services of an additional officer with great experience would be beneficial.

(3) The deterrent effect of the Truant schools themselves, not only upon children who have been inmates of those schools, but also upon other children who would have become truants but for the fear of being committed to them.

(4) In the earlier days of the Board many of the parents of the children who

s 2

were liable to attend school cared little as to whether their children attended or were absent. Many of the scholars of those days are the parents of the children now attending school, and the majority of them are anxious for the education of their children.

No Truant school accommodation has been provided for girls. The Committee in 1894, considered the question why so small a number of girls came under the provisions of Sections 11 and 12 of the Elementary Education Act of 1876. It was decided to ascertain from the Divisional Superintendents whether this was because there was no accommodation for girls of the Truant school class. The replies received were unanimous in stating that the number of girl truants was so small that no special provision of the kind was needed. Some few cases of girl truants do, from time to time occur. The Magistrate usually commits them to an ordinary Industrial school.

### XIV.—DAY INDUSTRIAL SCHOOLS.

The origin of the present system of Day Industrial schools was the old Ragged Day Feeding schools. These schools were the result of the voluntary efforts of philanthropists, and were mainly supported by them, although in some instances the Committee of Council on Education contributed grants in aid. The attendance was voluntary, but the inducements of food and warmth, and sometimes of clothing, were sufficiently strong to attract a large number of poor and neglected children.

The subject of Day Industrial schools has been before the Board on several occasions. As early as 1872 the Board instructed the Industrial Schools Committee to report on the subject. The Committee in their report stated that:

However useful such schools might be made when properly conducted by private management with an unfettered power of selection of cases and application of funds voluntarily subscribed, it appears clear to the Committee that if these schools were to be managed by the Board, and paid for by the rates, the effect would be to cast upon the school rate a burden which ought to be borne by the poor rate, and to pauperise or demoralise many persons who could not readily be excluded from availing themselves of public funds. Moreover, any action in this direction by the Board would require previous legislation.[1]

In 1873, the Board referred to the Industrial Schools Committee a proposed memorial to the Education Department which had been forwarded by the Bristol School Board, asking that powers might be given to School Boards to establish Day Industrial Schools. The Committee reported:

That while the difficulties mentioned therein are acknowledged to exist to some degree, the committee do not consider the remedy proposed would be adequate or satisfactory.[2]

Again, in 1875, the Committee reported to the Board on the subject, and their report concludes with a statement that:

Because the Day Industrial Feeding school is unsuitable for most of the children who are difficult to deal with, and to send children to it would entail a serious additional cost to the Board for the others (unless a Treasury grant were to be part of the scheme), the Committee are unable to recommend even a trial of the proposal in London.

---

[1] Board Minutes, Vol. II., p. 351.     [2] Board Minutes, Vol. III., p. 566.

The establishment of Day Industrial schools was authorised by the Elementary Education Act of 1876, Section 16 of which provides that:

If a Secretary of State is satisfied that, owing to the circumstances of any class of population in any school district, a school in which industrial training, elementary education, and one or more meals a day, but not lodging, are provided for the children, is necessary or expedient for the proper training and control of the children of such class, he may, in like manner, as under the Industrial Schools Act, 1866, certify any such school (in this Act referred to as a day Industrial school) in the neighbourhood of the said population to be a certified day Industrial school.

In February, 1878, and again in 1885, the Industrial Schools Committee recommended the establishment of Day Industrial schools, but their proposals were rejected by the Board.

In March, 1890, the Committee reported to the Board that, in their opinion, the time had arrived to carry out the provisions of the Act of 1876 respecting Day Industrial schools, and they recommended the establishment of two such schools with accommodation not exceeding 100 children each, one on the south, and one on the north side of the river. The question was referred back to the Committee for further information. This was supplied, and the recommendation of the Committee was adopted with the omission of the words limiting the accommodation in each case to 100. Legislation on the subject was expected at this time, and action was therefore delayed to see whether the resolution of the Board would thereby be affected.

In February, 1892, a motion was moved at the Board with a view of immediate steps being taken to establish the two schools; but the matter was referred to the Committee to reconsider the whole question, and to advise the Board whether the original proposal should be carried out. The Committee then recommended the establishment of one Day Industrial school only: such school, if practicable, to be opened in some suitable building which was already under the control of the Board, and this recommendation was adopted by the Board. No such building was, however, then available. In 1894 the Board closed the Drury-lane school as a Public Elementary school, and, in the following year, they opened it as a Day Industrial school for 200 children, with the consent of the Education Department and of the Home Office.

In May, 1898, the Board sanctioned the establishment of a second Day Industrial school. The necessary consents were obtained to the adaptation of buildings in Brunswick Road, Poplar, which had previously been used as a Public Elementary school On September 12th, 1901, the Secretary of State issued his certificate authorising the school as a Day Industrial school for 150 inmates.

In June, 1900, the Boys' and Girls' departments of the Ponton Road School, Nine Elms, were discontinued as Day schools, and were opened, in April, 1902, as a Day Industrial school, the Secretary of State having certified them for 150 children.

In October, 1898, the School Accommodation and Attendance Committee forwarded to the Industrial Schools Committee a report from the Tower Hamlets Divisional Committee, calling attention to the number of homeless children in that division, and recommending that a Day Industrial school should be opened in Whitechapel for such children.  In May, 1899, the Board, agreed to this proposal, provided a suitable building could be obtained at a reasonable cost, and the consent of the Home Secretary was obtained.  In May, 1900, the Committee reported that they had been unable to secure a building within the district.  The Board thereupon instructed the Works Committee to furnish an estimate of the cost of acquiring a site and erecting a suitable building to accommodate 200 children.  This cost proved to be too heavy, and the Board did not proceed further in the matter.

### 1. *Parental Contributions.*

Parental contributions are regulated by Section 16, sub-section 6, of the Elementary Education Act of 1876, and an Order made thereunder, which provide that where a child is sent to a Day Industrial school under an order of detention, the parent or guardian shall contribute towards his maintenance a sum of not exceeding two shillings per week.  Where a child is sent under an attendance order, or without an order of Court, the parental contribution must be a sum of not less than one shilling, nor more than two shillings, per week.  The number of cases of the latter description is very small.  In the cases of children attending under an order of detention the majority of the parents pay their contributions with regularity.  When difficulty is experienced in obtaining the amount, on account of the poverty of the parents, leniency is shown and time is given in which to pay off the arrears.  In cases where it seems hopeless to obtain payment arrears are remitted.

The Treasury contribution for attendance is paid quarterly, and for proficiency, discipline, and organisation annually.  It may amount in all to a sum of 52s. a year, or one shilling a week per child in cases under order of detention, and to half these sums in attendance order or voluntary cases, according to the following table :—

|  | For children sent under order of detention. | For children attending otherwise. |
|---|---|---|
| *Quarterly* for average number in attendance  ...  ...  ...  ... | 10s. | 5s. |
| *Annually*— |  |  |
| For *proficiency* in Reading, Writing, and Arithmetic  ...  ... | 6s. | 3s. |
| Do.  in Special subjects, viz.: Recitation and Elementary Geography or Grammar  ...  ...  ...  ...  ... | 2s. | 1s. |
| For *Discipline and Organisation,* on a satisfactory report from Inspector  ...  ...  ...  ...  ...  ...  ...  ... | 4s. | 2s. |
|  | 52s. a year. | 26s. a year. |

Year by year it has become more and more apparent that the Day Industrial schools supply a need which is not met either by the residential Industrial school or by the Truant school.  Mr. Henry Rogers, late Assistant Inspector of Industrial schools, wrote of them in 1897 as follows :—

I can testify, however, that the Day Industrial schools now at work have been so organised, so managed, and controlled, and the children's necessities so thoroughly felt and understood, that it has been nothing else than a keen sense of satisfaction to enter their doors, and gaze on the spectacle presented.  No matter what the outward condition or aspect of the poor children or the sufferings and privations to which they had been or are exposed, within the walls of this refuge there may be found harmony, rest, and peace.  In no class of schools I have ever entered have I witnessed more encouraging scenes of good order, discipline, and quiet control. Time after time, year after year, in all these schools, the triumph of good feeling, quiet persuasion, kindly Christian influence, and patient forbearance has been exceedingly made manifest, and has surprised me in a high degree.

And Mr. Legge, in the Government Report of 1900, says:—

As suggested last year, it is eminently desirable that these schools should increase in number. They afford a welcome relief from the conventional type of day school, and are eminently suited for an ever-growing class of children whose poverty leads to truancy, and thence by too easy a transition to juvenile delinquency.

Day Industrial schools are not intended for the homeless, destitute child, nor for the child with an immoral or criminal home, nor for mere truants; but for a class between the Truant school class and the Industrial school class. The children must have a fairly decent and respectable home, however poor. They have frequently only one parent, who perhaps is absent all day at work, or they may have father and mother both out at work all day. Such children often find their home, even until late at night, in the streets. The result is almost inevitable. The child gets out of hand, becomes a truant, and is sometimes upon the verge of being a criminal. These children are often intelligent and self-reliant. After admission to the school they develop into diligent, obedient, and even affectionate, children, and are, perhaps, the most interesting of the three classes of Industrial school children.

### 2. *The School Work.*

The "half-time" system of school work is adopted in the Day Industrial School, the other portion of the day being devoted to Industrial Training. Experience has proved that in this kind of school the literary part of the education does not suffer from its combination with industrial work. In certain cases children make greater progress with the industrial instruction than with the school work. Some of them have a positive distaste for the latter, whilst at manual work, they are interested and capable.

Notwithstanding the fact that many of these children compare favourably in intellect with the average London child, the majority of them on admission to the school are very backward. It is found necessary to place nearly 50 per cent. either in the First Standard, or in the preparatory class. As the result, however, of perfectly regular attendance, of a state of physical comfort, and of a carefully-prepared curriculum of short and attractive lessons, the interest of the children is engaged and maintained, habits of attention and concentration are developed, and the scholars make rapid, and in some instances, remarkable progress.

### 3. *Industrial Training.*

The Industrial occupations at these schools are necessarily limited in number. Those for boys comprise Carpentry, Shoemaking and Printing. The girls, who form only a small proportion of the whole, receive instruction in Cookery and Laundry-work, and are taught the various details of household work, such as cleaning, waiting at table, knitting and darning, and the making, mending and altering of garments. All these occupations have a beneficial effect upon the children. Besides making them proficient in the particular branch of labour, they inculcate habits of industry and precision which, apart from their value in the formation of character, are frequently of practical use in securing situations for them after leaving the schools. Some of the boys become competent to make a pair of boots or shoes throughout, and possess a technical and theoretical knowledge of the processes of the manufacture of leather, of the art of cutting out, and of the several kinds of leather employed in different sorts of work. In order to give variety of experience, a small number of private orders are executed in addition to the boots and shoes made and repaired for the inmates of some of the Board's Residential Schools.

The Printing Department at Drury Lane has turned out boys who are able to set up plain work and printed forms. Some of the official forms used in the Industrial Schools Department of the Head Office are printed by them. Moreover, the Governor, by this means, finds a ready opening for boys on leaving school, employers in the neighbourhood being glad to secure their services.

The most recently established industry is the band. Of its results it is too early yet to speak; but it is expected that, in addition to other advantages, it will be exceedingly valuable as a means of disposing of boys by securing their admission to Army bands directly upon leaving school.

Of these schools, Mr. Legge writes in the Government Report for 1901 :—

As regards industrial training and its corollary—viz. effective disposal, Drury Lane school in London is still pre-eminent, though it will soon be run hard by its younger brother, the new school at Brunswick Road, Poplar. These London schools deserve study by all interested in social questions. A casual visit to them is not enough; they will repay the most careful investigation.

### 4. *Period of Detention.*

Every child sent to a Day Industrial school is committed for a period of three years or, if over the age of 11, until such time as it shall reach the age of 14. Permission however, is given to license a child, after having been detained for one month, upon the condition of regular attendance at an ordinary Public Elementary school; but, in practice, a much longer period is necessary before a child is licensed out. A considerable class of children cannot well be let out on licence at all, such as children of widows or of widowers who do work which takes them from home; children of negligent parents, in whose case the greatest efforts are made to enforce the payments of the contributions. Other children are retained because it is proved that they would still be truants if licensed to an Ordinary school. On the other hand, the experience of the London Day Industrial schools has been that the children released upon licence make almost perfect attendances.

The legal duties of the Managers of a Day Industrial school cease when the child reaches the age of 14; but anxiety for the interests of the children, and the desire to prevent the care which has been bestowed upon them from being lost, cause the superintendents not only to interest themselves in procuring situations for ex-scholars, but also to visit and supervise them, and report upon their subsequent career.

### XV.—BOARD'S INDUSTRIAL SCHOOLS.

In the case of each Industrial school established by the Board, the Industrial

Schools Committee have been appointed as a body of Managers for the school. The meetings of the Managers are held at the Board Offices fortnightly as part of the proceedings of the Industrial Schools Committee.

In addition a Sub-Committee has been appointed to supervise each school. These Sub-Committees meet monthly (as a general rule at the respective institutions) for the purposes of inspecting the school and its inmates, and of transacting business relating thereto. They then report to the full Committee and submit such recommendations as may be necessary in cases where expenditure is involved.

The Board have established 9 Industrial schools, the following being the names of the schools and the dates of their establishment :—

1. Brentwood Industrial School, Essex, 1874.
2. "Shaftesbury," Industrial Training Ship, off Grays, Essex, 1878.
3. Upton House Truant School, Homerton, 1878.
4. Highbury Truant School, Highbury Grove, 1891.
5. Day Industrial School, Goldsmith Street, Drury Lane, 1895.
6. Gordon House Girls' Home, Isleworth, 1897.
7. Day Industrial School, Brunswick Road, Poplar, 1901.
8. Day Industrial School, Ponton Road, Nine Elms, 1902.
9. Home for Little Boys, King's Road, Clapham Park, 1903.

The following schools of the Board have not been described in the foregoing pages :—

### 1. *Brentwood Industrial School.*

In the year 1873 the Board came to the conclusion that, in addition to sending boys to schools with which they had agreements, it was desirable that they should themselves establish Industrial schools. A building at Brentwood, Essex, was purchased, and was opened in 1874, accommodation being provided for 100 inmates.

The late Miss Davenport-Hill, who was for a long time a member of the Board, took a very great interest in the school, and was Chairman of the Sub-Committee for a period of twelve years. When, in 1897, she ceased to be a member of the Board, it was decided, in order to commemorate her connection with the school, that it should in future be known as the "Davenport-Hill Boys' Home."

For many years the children received at the school were those who would not be received at other schools, either on account of their extreme youth, or of some physical or mental defect. On admission they were frequently sickly and feeble, and required great care and attention. During their residence they usually improved steadily, with the result that, when the time came to leave the school, on attaining the age of 14 or soon after, they were, with few exceptions, well-grown and healthy, and capable of earning their own living.

In 1892 the Board Inspector reported :—

There is one feature in this school which deserves special mention, viz., the large number of children in the Upper Standards. Standards IV., V., and VI. include more than half of the boys, and the number in Standard VI. is pretty nearly one-quarter of the whole school. I know of no other institution of this kind which can show the same proportionate number in the higher standards.

The occupations carried on were Tailoring, Shoemaking, Breadmaking, Gardening and Woodwork. There was also an excellent Brass Band.

About 50 per cent. of the boys, on leaving the school, were placed in Army Bands, and have done exceedingly well. One boy, who left in 1883, is now Bandmaster of the regiment in which he was placed, and others have also attained that rank. One old boy, who joined the 20th Hussars, writing from the Punjab, states that he has been six years in India, and during that time has been a Bandmaster and a Schoolmaster ; that he is now a Clerk in the Army Headquarters of the India Adjutant-General's Department, with the rank of Sergeant, and has good prospects of obtaining a commission.

Reports received respecting boys who joined the Army at a later date are equally satisfactory, and all the boys who joined the Army bands during the years 1883 to 1898 are doing well.

For a period of over 20 years the inmates enjoyed almost uninterrupted immunity from sickness of an epidemic nature. At the end of that time, however, several outbreaks of illness occurred, and consequently the boys were removed to temporary premises at Margate in October, 1898. Whilst there the majority of them were taught to swim, and received instruction in life-saving methods.

The value of this instruction was demonstrated in August, 1899, when a boy named Henry Pentlow, 10½ years of age, saved a school-fellow and the Labourmaster of the school from drowning. For this action he was awarded the certificate of the Royal Humane Society.

Steps were taken to replace the school at Brentwood by the erection of a new permanent building upon a site at Hither Green, but in consequence of the high cost the proposal was abandoned. In the year 1902 the Home Secretary decided that he could no longer sanction the use of the temporary premises at Margate. The older children were therefore placed out in life, and the remainder were transferred to other Industrial schools.

### 2. *Training-Ship "Shaftesbury."*

The Board, finding that a considerable proportion of the boys sent to Industrial schools were suitable for a seafaring life, in the first instance entered into agreements with existing training ships for the reception of boys ; but in the year 1877 they decided to establish an Industrial school training-ship of their own. After an unsuccessful application to the Admiralty for the loan of a ship, an iron vessel called the *Nubia* was purchased from the Peninsular and Oriental Steam Navigation Company, and was adapted for the purpose of an Industrial school training-ship. In commemoration of the great services rendered by the late Lord Shaftesbury to destitute and poor lads in London, the ship was re-named the *Shaftesbury*. She was certified for 500 boys, but this number was subsequently reduced to 400, of whom 100 may be Roman Catholics.

The vessel was moored off Grays, Essex, in a position which had been dredged for her by the Thames Conservancy, and she remained there until January, 1881. On the 18th of that month, during the great blizzard, the ship parted her bow moorings, and tugs had to be hired to stand by her to ensure the safety of the vessel and crew. Notwithstanding this precaution the *Shaftesbury* drifted on shore, and heeled over on her beam ends. So dangerous was her position, that it was necessary to clear the ship of officers and boys. The order was therefore given to "leave the ship." This, in the circumstances, was a dangerous operation, but perfect discipline was maintained, and, within about twenty minutes from the time the order was given, the whole of the ship's company were safely transferred to the tugs in attendance. As the tide rose the *Shaftesbury* righted herself, and the crew were re-transferred to her. She was then removed for a time to temporary moorings, and was subsequently re-moored, with additional anchors and cables, at a short distance from her former position. Here she remained until the summer of 1901, when, as she had been continuously in the water for twenty-three years, it was considered necessary that she should be placed in dry dock for general overhaul outside and inside. The necessary painting and repairs having been carried out, the vessel returned to her moorings, and the officers and boys, who had during this time been in camp in the play-field on shore, returned on board.

Attached to the *Shaftesbury* is the Tender *Themis*, a top-sail schooner of 145 tons. During the summer months the *Themis*, with three officers and thirty boys, cruises about the River Thames, and a voyage is generally made down the English Channel, touching at the various ports as far as Plymouth.

The principal industrial occupation is seamanship. Boys on entry are placed in the lowest class and are examined quarterly with a view of advancement to the higher classes. The syllabus is as follows:—

| 4th Class. First Instruction. | 3rd Class. Second Instruction. | 2nd Class. Third Instruction. | 1st Class. Fourth Instruction. |
|---|---|---|---|
| Slight knowledge of names of spars, rigging, and parts of sails. Boat duty. Making clothes stops. Compass. Lead and line. Hammock drill. Coiling ropes. Bends and hitches. | A good knowledge of First Instruction. Bends and hitches. Models and sail drill. Names of International Code. Signal Flags. Reeving running rigging. | A good knowledge of First and Second Instruction. Knots and splices. Anchor and cask. Grummets and cringles. Pointing and whipping ropes. Loosing and furling sails. Sending top - gallant masts and yards up and down. Reefing topsails. Reeving running rigging. Signalling by flags and semaphore. | A good knowledge of previous Instructions. Fitting rigging, setting up the same. Use of palm and needle. Sail-making. Making mats. Rule of the Road at sea. Use of log-line. Heaving the Lead. Steering by compass and sails. Sailing a boat and the Tender. Bending and unbending sails. Figures to denote the force of the wind. Letters to denote the state of the weather. |

The school-work is conducted on the half-time system, according to the Government Code for public Elementary schools, and includes Writing, Spelling, Arithmetic, English

History, Geography, Vocal Music, Drawing, Object Lessons in Elementary Science, and a special course of practical navigation.

Of 160 boys who left the ship for employment during the year ended in July, 1903, 6 were in Standard ex-VII. ; 13 in Standard VII., 41 in Standard VI., 52 in Standard V., 40 in Standard IV., 13 in Standard III. and 1 in Standard II.

There is a full military band numbering 45 performers. In addition, all the boys are taught singing on the Tonic Sol-fa system. The boys are also instructed or engaged in the following trades :—Shoemaking, Tailoring, Sailmaking, and Cooking. The senior boys assist the ship's carpenter in carrying out the painting and small repairs of the ship, the tender, and the boats, and also in building new boats. There is a special class for Manual Training in Wood, the practical part being taught by the ship's carpenter and the theoretical part by one of the schoolmasters. A few of the boys are also engaged as captain's steerage boys, and others assist the ship's engineers by acting as stokers.

The boys are trained in Gymnastics by an officer holding a first-class Aldershot certificate. He also teaches Swimming, the instruction being given during the summer months in a large covered bath 100 ft. by 50 ft., in the playfield. A Swimming and Diving Competition is held annually, the funds for purchasing prizes being obtained from the interest on a legacy which was left to the ship many years ago. Dumb Bell and Indian Club exercises are also taught by the Chief Officer. The whole of this work is periodically supervised by the Board's Organiser of Physical Education for boys. All boys intended for Sea Service are instructed in Gun, Rifle, and Cutlass drill, a special officer, who was previously a Chief Petty Officer and Instructor in the Royal Navy, being attached to the ship by the Admiralty for the purpose.

Football and Cricket are played in their seasons, and the boys take part in the League competitions connected with Industrial schools. The Ship's Infirmary and Isolation Ward are under the care of a Matron, who is a trained nurse. The majority of the boys admitted are sent on account of minor ailments, or for slight surgical matters. Infectious or contagious cases are removed to one of the hospitals of the Metropolitan Asylums Board.

The field has also been used on two occasions for the purposes of a camping ground whilst the ship was under repair, when the whole ship's company lived under canvas for a period of six or eight weeks. The camps were organised on military lines, a guard being mounted night and day. This change from the ordinary routine of ship life has been found to be very beneficial, not only by improving the health of the boys, but by enabling the vessel to be disinfected, aired and ventilated in a much more thorough manner than is possible in ordinary circumstances.

In February, 1895, the River Thames was frozen over, and for a time the ship was ice-bound. Much discomfort and inconvenience were experienced ; the fresh water supply ran short, and a tug had to be hired to keep up communication with the outside world. Messages for the shore had to be telephoned from the ship to the Head Office, and re-telephoned to Grays.

In June, 1900, a boy accidentally fell overboard. Mr. King, Master-at-Arms, attempted to save him; but the boy clung to him, and both were drowned. Mr. King had served on the ship for 22 years, and was previously in the Navy for a similar period. To perpetuate the memory of his heroism the Board affixed a brass tablet on the ship.

As soon as a boy reaches the age of 15, the question of his suitable disposal is considered by the Committee, who have before them the boy's wishes and general fitness, the suggestion of the captain-superintendent, and also a report by the visiting officer of the ship with reference to the character and surroundings of the parents. All these matters having been considered, a decision is arrived at, and in due course the boy leaves the ship on licence. Up to the present over 3,300 boys have left the ship. Of these, over 50 per cent. have gone to sea in the Royal Navy or the Mercantile Marine; 25 per cent. have gone into the Army; and the remaining 25 per cent. have either been placed in employment on shore, returned to their friends, or have emigrated. Of the boys discharged, over 80 per cent. are doing well in after life. Some have reached positions of trust and responsibility. One is a bandmaster in a distinguished regiment. Two have received their certificates of competency for Mates in the Mercantile Marine. One is in charge of the telegraph station in Georgetown, Tasmania. Many are to be found amongst the petty officers of the Royal Navy, or the non-commissioned officers of the Army. Now and again old boys visit the ship wearing two, and sometimes three, medals for active service in the Army or Navy.

### 3. *Gordon House Girls' Home.*

Owing to the difficulty of finding sufficient suitable accommodation for girls, the Board, in the year 1897, decided to establish a girls' school of their own. A building was secured at Isleworth, and the necessary alterations having been completed, it was opened in December, 1897, for fifty girls. A cottage home in the grounds was subsequently erected for twenty children, and the school now provides accommodation for seventy. The school is devoted chiefly to the reception of very young children whom it is necessary to remove from the custody of parents of bad character, or from immoral homes.

The training given to the girls is practical and thorough, and on leaving, no difficulty is found in placing them in good situations; in fact, the demand for the girls is greater than the supply.

Up to the present thirty girls have left the Home, and have gone to situations; all of them are doing well. As an incentive to girls to remain in their situations the Board give prizes to those girls under 18 years of age who remain in satisfactory employment, not necessarily in one situation, to the value of 5s. for the first year, 7s. 6d. for the second year, and 10s. for the third year.

### 4. *School at Portslade.*

In addition to the schools mentioned above, the Board, in conjunction with the Brighton Education authority, have established a joint Industrial school at Portslade, near Brighton, for 120 boys. The school was opened in 1902, and was at once filled by the transfer of the Brighton boys, who had previously been accommodated in old and unsuitable buildings at Chailey, and by the admission of London boys who had been inmates of the Davenport Hill Boys' Home.

## XVI.—RETURN OF CHILDREN SENT TO SCHOOLS.

The following return shows the number of children sent by the Board to Industrial schools, Truant schools and Day Industrial schools respectively, year by year.

| | ORDINARY INDUSTRIAL SCHOOLS. | | | | | | |
|---|---|---|---|---|---|---|---|
| YEAR. | Industrial Schools Act, 1866. | | Industrial Schools Acts Amendment Act, 1880 | Elementary Education Act, 1876 | TRUANT SCHOOLS | DAY INDUSTRIAL SCHOOLS. | GRAND TOTAL. |
| | XIV.—XV. | XVI. | | | | | |
| Year ended 25th December, 1871 ... | 176 | 4 | ... | ... | ... | ... | 180 |
| ,,        ,,        1872 ... | 287 | 22 | ... | ... | ... | ... | 309 |
| ,,        ,,        1873 ... | 527 | 138 | ... | ... | ... | ... | 665 |
| ,,        ,,        1874 ... | 442 | 154 | ... | ... | ... | ... | 596 |
| ,,        ,,        1875 ... | 422 | 286 | ... | ... | ... | ... | 708 |
| ,,        ,,        1876 ... | 510 | 288 | ... | ... | ... | ... | 798 |
| ,,        ,,        1877 ... | 573 | 199 | ... | 8 | ... | ... | 780 |
| ,,        ,,        1878 ... | 519 | 170 | ... | 21 | 35 | ... | 745 |
| ,,        ,,        1879 ... | 491 | 129 | ... | 112 | 133 | ... | 865 |
| ,,        ,,        1880 ... | 386 | 68 | ... | 138 | 96 | ... | 688 |
| ,,        ,,        1881 ... | 417 | 59 | 7 | 152 | 169 | ... | 804 |
| ,,        ,,        1882 ... | 341 | 75 | 7 | 84 | 166 | ... | 673 |
| ,,        ,,        1883 ... | 447 | 97 | 50 | 177 | 116 | ... | 887 |
| ,,        ,,        1884 ... | 397 | 74 | 47 | 118 | 122 | ... | 758 |
| ,,        ,,        1885 ... | 369 | 50 | 28 | 99 | 409 | ... | 955 |
| ,,        ,,        1886 ... | 388 | 52 | 7 | 67 | 459 | ... | 973 |
| Fifteen months ended 25th Mar., 1888 | 520 | 68 | 16 | 86 | 466 | ... | 1156 |
| Year ended 25th March, 1889 ... | 527 | 71 | 11 | 32 | 418 | ... | 1059 |
| ,,        ,,        1890 ... | 529 | 59 | 18 | 11 | 325 | ... | 942 |
| ,,        ,,        1891 ... | 490 | 81 | 22 | 19 | 311 | ... | 923 |
| ,,        ,,        1892 ... | 483 | 101 | 34 | 24 | 928 | ... | 1570 |
| ,,        ,,        1893 ... | 337 | 73 | 40 | 16 | 678 | ... | 1144 |
| ,,        ,,        1894 ... | 461 | 90 | 56 | 13 | 688 | ... | 1308 |
| ,,        ,,        1895 ... | 514 | 87 | 69 | 20 | 632 | ... | 1322 |
| ,,        ,,        1896 ... | 602 | 177 | 72 | 35 | 557 | 64 | 1507 |
| ,,        ,,        1897 ... | 548 | 134 | 61 | 34 | 633 | 120 | 1530 |
| ,,        ,,        1898 ... | 696 | 146 | 17 | 50 | 626 | 87 | 1622 |
| ,,        ,,        1899 ... | 601 | 114 | 30 | 50 | 688 | 116 | 1599 |
| ,,        ,,        1900 ... | 513 | 82 | 30 | 65 | 645 | 155 | 1490 |
| ,,        ,,        1901 ... | 530 | 146 | 31 | 75 | 601 | 145 | 1528 |
| ,,        ,,        1902 ... | 574 | 133 | 26 | 100 | 580 | 164 | 1577 |
| ,,        ,,        1903 ... | 434 | 79 | 36 | 104 | 424 | 268 | 1345 |
| ,,        ,,        1904 ... | 385 | 69 | 33 | 106 | 376 | 135 | 1104 |
| | 15,436 | 3,575 | 748 | 1,816 | 11,281 | 1,254 | 34,110 |

Of these children 30,378 have been discharged, and at Lady Day, 1904, 3,732 remained under detention. The latter are distributed thus :—

Board's Industrial schools ... ... ... ... ... 412

„ Truant „ ... ... ... ... ... 322

„ Day Industrial schools ... ... ... ... 277

Total ... ... 1,011

Schools with which the Board have agreements ... ... 2,721

Grand total ... ... 3,732

In addition to the 34,110 cases which have been sent to Industrial schools at the instance of the Board, the Committee have inquired into 29,868 further cases, which have been mainly disposed of as follows:—Some were sent to Industrial schools, irrespective of the Board; some were referred to parish authorities; and some were referred to the Divisional Committees of the Board for action under the Bye-laws or the Education Act of 1876.

## EVENING CONTINUATION SCHOOLS.

### I.—Introduction.

THE history of this branch of the Board's work falls into two periods—namely, from 1870 to 1882, and from 1882 to 1904.

### 1. *First Period*: 1870 to 1882.

The following extract from the "Work of the London School Board," issued in 1900 describes fully what was attempted by the Board in the first period:—

It was the intention of the Board to establish evening schools concurrently with day schools. The evening school which had existed previously to 1870 was a school in which young persons who had passed school age, and were earning their living during the daytime, might obtain those rudiments of education during the evening which they had failed to acquire in their childhood. The instruction given was usually of the most elementary character, and the idea of the evening school as an institution in which well-instructed youth could continue and expand the education of their school days was not even conceived. The uneducated were too many and the half-educated too few for such a plan to be practicable. It could only be dreamt of as a future possibility when the day schools had raised a more educated generation.

The Education Department recognised evening schools, and assisted them with a grant, but the only grant-earning subjects were reading, writing, and arithmetic. The Elementary Education Act of 1870 did not specifically empower School Boards to conduct evening schools; but it did not define the hours during which schools were to be open, and there was, therefore, nothing in the Act to prevent the establishment of evening classes. But a difficulty arose in regard to the question whether there was any limit of age beyond which it was illegal for the Board to provide a young person with educational facilities. The Act fixed no maximum age to limit the legality of the Board's expenditure upon a child's education; it merely fixed an age beyond which it was illegal to compel the child's attendance at school. The Education Department paid no grant for a child who had passed the highest standard of the Code for the time being in force, but there was no legal obligation upon the Board to refuse education to a child who had ceased to be a grant-earning pupil. Thus neither age nor attainments fixed a limit which, when reached, excluded the child from voluntary attendance at school. These questions so perplexed the first Board that it referred them to its solicitor for advice. He arrived, with great hesitation, at the conclusion that if there was any such limit, it was at the age of sixteen. When evening schools were being started, the question of age limitation again arose. The solicitor was once more consulted. This was in 1872, and the Code of that year defined the maximum age of scholars both in day and evening schools as eighteen. It still remained doubtful whether the new regulation was merely a bar to the earning of the grant, or a more general prohibition of expenditure upon the education of adults who were over the specified age. The solicitor, therefore, advised the Board that if it educated persons above the age of eighteen, without charging a fee which covered the whole cost of their education, it was liable to have the cost disallowed by the Local Government Board. Acting upon this advice, the Board resolved that, without incurring any expense in the matter, it would grant the use of its schoolrooms to properly constituted committees for the purpose of carrying on evening schools for persons over eighteen years of age.

The Committee on the Scheme of Education was not less sanguine in its hope of introducing a liberal curriculum into evening schools than it had been in regard to the day schools; but in the case of the former a more complete disappointment was in store for them. "Evening Schools," said the Committee, "are of great importance, partly as a means for providing elementary education for those who, for various reasons, fail to obtain sufficient instruction in Elementary day schools, and partly because it is easy to connect with such schools special classes in which a higher kind of instruction than that contemplated by Standard VI. can be given to the more intelligent and elder scholars. In this manner the advantages of further instruction may be secured by those scholars who are unable or unwilling to go into Secondary schools, but who are both able and willing to pay for instruction of a more advanced kind than that given in primary schools."

The Committee, therefore, advised, and the Board resolved, that the curriculum for evening schools for young persons under the age of eighteen should be of the same character as that which had been adopted for the day schools, and the Managers of evening schools were advised to adapt the instruction given to the requirements of the localities in which the schools were situated. It was further resolved that science and art classes should be established, if possible, in connection with the Science and Art Department.

The early relations between the School Board and the Science and Art Department are interesting in view of the hostile attitude which that Department has recently assumed in relation to the Board's work. In November, 1871, the Department asked the School Board to co-operate with it in organising the conduct of its examinations and in appointing local secretaries for the several school divisions of London. Such a request would not have been made unless the Science and Art Department were willing, if not eager, to establish a connection between itself and the schools under the Board. To this the Board replied that its hands were so full of its own special work that it was unable to accept the Department's invitation, but that if it were renewed next year the Board would be ready to consider the invitation afresh. In September, 1873, the Board resolved that permanent schools might be used for Science and Art Evening Classes, provided that all expenses were met without any demand upon the funds of the Board, and that they did not interfere with any ordinary evening classes which it might be considered desirable to establish.

This resolution was passed under the influence of the enforced prudence which immediately precedes a triennial election. It seems evident from the report of the Committee on the Scheme of Education that so restricted a co-operation with the Science and Art Department was not originally contemplated. It is not a little curious that in 1872-3 the Department should have wooed the Board in vain, and that of late years, when the Board made the advances, the Department should have proved so coy.

In the first enthusiasm of the moment the Board instructed the School Management Committee to consider and report upon the desirability of opening evening schools during the winter of 1871-2. The result was that the Committee, in December, 1871, directed the Sub-Committee for the Instruction of Managers to urge Managers to establish evening schools wherever practicable, at as early a date as possible. The notice was a short one, and Managers were fully employed in the re-organisation of the day schools. Very few evening schools were opened during that winter. In December, 1872, a return of the number of evening schools already opened was laid before the Board. That return cannot now be found, but it evidently showed that very little had been done to establish evening schools, for in January, 1873, the Board requested the School Management Committee to consider and report whether more evening schools could not with advantage be opened. The Committee replied with a somewhat ambiguous declaration that they would be prepared to consider any application for the establishment of such schools which was properly recommended by a duly constituted body of Managers. In the pressure of other work, evening schools were evidently being crushed out of consideration.

In September, 1873, the Board furnished a scheme for the conduct of evening schools. The only important portion of it was the declaration that no evening school should be opened unless at least forty names were entered on the register, or continued if the average attendance of the previous month fell below twenty. This resolution gave the final blow to the first attempt to

T

establish evening schools under the School Board for London, and to the liberal curriculum which had been formulated for them by the Scheme of Education Committee. The plan which had originally been proposed was somewhat. ahead of the requirements of the time. To bring it to fruition, and to attract pupils to the schools, a long period of nursing was essential. The evening schools required to be forced into popularity. To refuse to establish such a school because forty scholars could not be at once enrolled, and to insist upon closing such a school because the average attendance fell in any one month below twenty was to deny the scheme a chance of success. The attendance at an evening school must of necessity be irregular. The scholars attend it after a long day's labour, and many of them, under pressure, are compelled to work overtime at their callings. It is no evidence of waning interest in their evening studies if they sometimes, or even frequently, fail to attend at the evening class.

Under such uncongenial influences evening schools had no chance of springing into healthy existence. Their end came in a somewhat unexpected manner. In January, 1875, the Board directed the School Management Committee to reconsider the method of remunerating the teachers in evening schools. The Committee did not report until the end of June. They then declared that the Board desired that children subject to the Bye-laws should make their attendances at day schools, and that evening schools should not be specially created to meet the case of half-timers. They, therefore, recommended that the resolutions of the Board for establishing evening schools should be rescinded; that no such schools should be carried on directly by the Board; but that the use of the Board's schools should be granted for evening classes to voluntary agencies at a small charge for rent. These recommendations were adopted by the Board, apparently without challenge or debate.

The reason for the Board's action is difficult to explain. The recommendation to discontinue evening classes was outside the limits of the reference which the Board had sent down to the School Management Committee. The alleged reason can hardly be taken as explaining the real motive; for the existing Bye-laws of the Board precluded a half-timer from making his necessary attendances after six o'clock in the afternoon. The Press appears to have taken no notice of a resolution which, although it passed through the Board without discussion, was one of considerable educational importance. The only probable explanation of the Board's action is that the evening classes had not proved successful; that the Board was, at the time, incurring very severe criticism on account of its alleged lavish expenditure, and that, therefore, it was resolved to destroy, with as little publicity as possible, a branch of the work which was costly without being popular. The work of the Board in connection with evening schools was not revived until 1882.

## 2. *Second Period*: 1882 *to* 1904.

This period witnessed the successful establishment of the schools. The first steps towards their opening were taken in 1879, when the Board, on the 5th November, instructed the School Management Committee to report upon the general question of grading elementary education and of providing higher elementary education, including the provision of night schools and night classes in connection with the City Guilds and other voluntary agencies; such classes to lead up to the proposed Technical Schools and Colleges. The arguments brought forward in the discussion of this subject were that there was need for such instruction to enable scholars to fit themselves for receiving instruction in the proposed Technical Schools and Colleges; that it was necessary to provide means by which scholars who had left the day school could recover the knowledge that had been forgotten through neglect to continue their education; that the Board had spent vast sums of money upon elementary education but the effect upon the life of the scholars was to a great extent lost owing to the lack of means to continue it; that the period immediately after leaving the day school was one of the most dangerous periods in a child's life; and that the schools would be well-nigh self-supporting. The School Management Committee did not—apparently from pressure of work in connection with the day schools—present a report to the Board. On July 23rd, 1881, the attention of the Board was drawn to this inaction of the School Management Committee, and it was moved:—

That a Special Committee be appointed to consider and report upon the best means of organising evening classes for ordinary and science subjects in the schools of the Board.

This motion was adopted, but again there was a long delay before any further action was taken. At last on July 20th, 1882, the Special Committee made a report to the Board, in which they asked for powers to establish classes in

(a) Elementary instruction under the conditions of the new Code (Elementary Classes), and

(b) Instruction in subjects recognised by the Science and Art Department and by the City and Guilds of London Institute, and in such other special subjects as the Board may from time to time approve (Advanced Classes).

These latter classes, the Committee explained, had been carried on, to some extent, in the schools of the Board by persons who rented rooms for that purpose.

The following paragraph in the Committee's report indicates the principle upon which the Board proposed to conduct their evening schools in the earlier years of the movement:—

Your Committee think that the cost of establishing and maintaining these classes other than that arising from the use of the rooms, cleaning, fuel, gas, and educational appliances, should be met by the fees of the scholars, the Government Grant, and such other assistance as may be supplied from voluntary sources. It is further necessary to state that in the working of classes not recognised in the Code no charge whatever can be made on the school fund.

On this basis the evening schools were begun in 1882 and have made progress in nearly every session, as the table on page 277 shows.

But the crisis through which the evening schools passed in consequence of what is known as the "Cockerton judgment" (1901) demands special notice. The details concerning this legal decision are given elsewhere [1]; it is only therefore necessary to allude briefly to the result of the judgment in its relation to evening schools. In effect, the decision was that the Board could not charge upon the rates the cost of (i.) Science and Art classes conducted under the directory of the Science and Art Department, South Kensington, and (ii.) or of instructing persons who were not "children" within the meaning of the Education Acts. Consequently the Board could not, without new legislation, effectually carry on the evening schools. In the Parliamentary Session of 1901 the Government introduced a Bill which contained provisions in relation to these schools.

On the second reading of this Bill, the Vice-President of the Committee of Council

---

[1] See *post*, p. 321.

on Education made a speech which, in the opinion of the Board, contained inaccuracies concerning the evening schools. The Board replied to his comments in the form of a memorandum which was sent to the Board of Education and Members of Parliament. The Vice-President complained of undue competition with Polytechnics and Schools of Art—the Board pointed to the growth of evening classes in Polytechnics and Schools of Art, as shown in a report of the Technical Education Board of the London County Council : he spoke of the education given in the Board's evening schools as being " cheap and shoddy "—the Board quoted the favourable reports of H.M. Inspectors on individual schools, drew attention to the high rate of grants received by the schools, and pointed to the percentage of passes in Science and Art as a proof that the work in the schools was efficient. He stated that, with some exceptions, most of the schools were purely recreative—the Board remarked that the bulk of the work done in the evening continuation schools consisted of instruction in subjects recognised and paid for under the Code, but, conformably with Clause V. of the Explanatory Memorandum of the Evening Continuation School Code, experiments had been tried in order to render the schools " more attractive," but in not more than 20 schools out of about 395 was Dancing taught, and in these instances it had been approved by H.M. Inspectors.

The Bill brought forward by the Government was dropped, but a short Act was passed, enabling County Councils to authorise School Boards to continue schools, including evening schools, which had been held to be illegal,[1] for a period of one year. At the same time a Minute was issued by the Board of Education setting forth the conditions under which grants would be paid to schools carried on by School Boards for persons under 15 years of age, and also the regulations under which grants would be paid to schools conducted under the above Act. The Board considered that it would be futile to open schools merely for persons under 15 years of age, and decided to apply to the London County Council for authority to continue the schools without any distinction as to the ages of the students. The Council acceded to this application, and the Board were thus enabled to carry on the work for another year. One important point remains to be added to this brief record of some of the effects of the judgment— namely, evening schools were no longer subject to the Elementary Education Acts, and hence the work of administration was transferred from the Board of Education (Whitehall) to the Board of Education (South Kensington), and the regulations for the schools were issued by the latter. The operation of the Enabling Act was extended to July 31st, 1903, by a Renewal Act passed in the Session of 1902,[2] and it has been further extended by the Education Act, 1902, and the Education (London) Act, 1903, until the appointed day. Acting under the powers thus conferred upon them, the London County Council have authorised the continuance of the schools until the 30th April, 1904.

---

[1] 1 Edw. 7, c. 11 (see *post*, p. 320).          [2] 2 Edw. 7, c. 19.

TABLE SHOWING THE ATTENDANCE, &c., AT THE SCHOOLS.

| Session. | No. of Schools. | No of Pupils admitted. | Average No. the Rolls. (Winter Terms). | *Average No. Present at all (Winter Terms). | Percentage of Average No. present at all on the Average No. on the Rolls. |
|---|---|---|---|---|---|
| 1882—1883 | 83 | 9,064 | 2,692 | | ... |
| 1883—1884 | 74 | 5,563 | 2,394 | | ... |
| 1884—1885 | 84 | 9 346 | 4,642 | | ... |
| 1885—1886 | 114 | 13,968 | 7,292 | | ... |
| 1886—1887 | 128 | 16,050 | 8,695 | | ... |
| 1887—1888 | 128 | 16,320 | 9,077 | These figures were not prepared in these years. | ... |
| 1888—1889 | 135 | 15,732 | 8,645 | | ... |
| 1889—1890 | 159 | 18,268 | 10,454 | | ... |
| 1890—1891 | 232 | 31,015 | 17,037 | | ... |
| 1891—1892 | 239 | 34,562 | 18,180 | | ... |
| 1892—1893 | 242 | 34,797 | 18,334 | | ... |
| 1893—1894 | 265 | 40,858 | 20,125 | 14,613 | 72·6 |
| 1894—1895 | 271 | 48,512 | 23,920 | 17,444 | 72·9 |
| 1895—1896 | 271 | 50,218 | 25,693 | 19,633 | 76·4 |
| 1896—1897 | 276 | 52,804 | 27,832 | 21,326 | 76·6 |
| 1897—1898 | 280 | 57,586 | 30,730 | 24,350 | 79·2 |
| 1898—1899 | 321 | 109,121 | 56,412 | 42 109 | 74·6 |
| 1899—1900 | 368 | 125,640 | 65.060 | 47,965 | 73·7 |
| 1900—1901 | 395 | 146,971 | 78.658 | 58,682 | 74·6 |
| 1901—1902 | 398 | 133,191 | 73,796 | 55,238 | 74·9 |
| 1902—1903 | 376 | 126,753 | 76,182 | 57,800 | 75·9 |

* This figure represents the average number of individual pupils who attended the schools in each week.

The progress made in the attendance of students may be seen from the diagram on the following page.

In considering the attendance at evening schools, it must always be remembered that long, and often exhausting, hours of labour prevent the students from attending the schools regularly, and prevent many from joining at all. It was calculated in the Session 1901-2 that of the population of London between 14 and 21, only 15 per cent had enrolled themselves in the Board's evening schools. In order to minimise one of the chief hindrances to a better attendance, the Board have on two or three occasions taken action on the question of long hours of labour. In 1892 the Royal Commission on Labour was asked to receive written statements showing that young people were prevented, by their long hours of labour, from joining evening schools. Two years later the Board petitioned Parliament in favour of a bill limiting the working hours of young people under 16 years of age to eight hours a day. In 1900, when the Factories and Workshops Bill was before Parliament, a petition was presented to the House of Commons asking for the amendment of the Bill in certain particulars, so that young people might be better able to attend evening schools; and in the same year the Board forwarded a petition to Parliament, asking that seven o'clock might be fixed as the latest hour to which young people should be permitted to be retained in employment, unless in special circumstances the Home Secretary saw fit to make an exception.

Diagram showing the number of students admitted to Evening schools from 1882-83 to 1902-03 :—

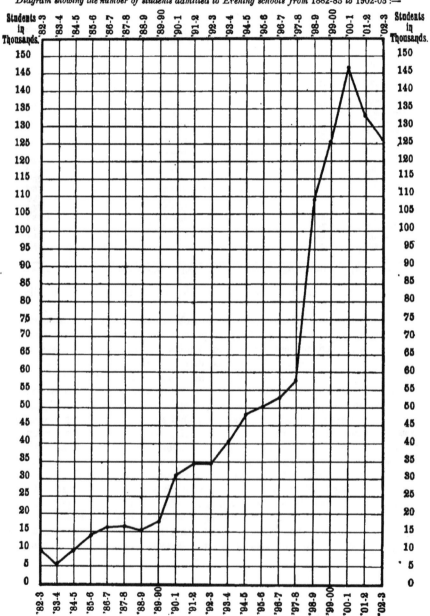

It will be observed that, except in four sessions, there has been an uninterrupted increase in the number of pupils admitted to the schools, and that there were two sessions in which the increase was abnormal—viz. in the Session 1890-91, when the numbers admitted increased by 69·8 per cent., and in the Session 1898-99, when they rose by 89·5 per cent. The improvement in the first case was due to changes in the Government Code,[1] and in the second case chiefly to the abolition of the fees.[2] The increase in two other sessions must also be noted—viz. : Sessions 1893-94 and 1894-95. These followed the introduction of the separate Code for evening continuation schools.[3] On the other hand, there were four sessions in which the numbers fell off. In the second session, 1883-84, the number of pupils admitted decreased by 38·6 per cent. This was attributed to the insufficient advertising of the schools and to the fact that the novelty which attended their opening for the first time had died away. The falling off in 1888-89 by 3·6 per cent. was wholly due to the charging of a fee of 1s. a week to adults in the first few weeks of the session The next decrease took place in 1901-2, when the number admitted fell by 9 4 per cent. This falling off was attributed to (1) the uncertainty that prevailed as to whether the schools would be continued after the decision in the case of "Rex v. Cockerton"; (2) the disparaging statements—the accuracy of which was disputed by the Board—made in Parliament by the Vice-President of the Committee of Council on Education concerning the work done in the evening schools; and (3) a new regulation of the Board of Education [South Kensington] discontinuing the recognition of the attendance of day school scholars in evening schools. In the fourth instance of a decrease (Session 1902-03) the number admitted fell by 4·8 per cent., but the average number present at all rose by 4·6 per cent. A sessional fee was charged in most schools this session.[4]

In the second column of the Table the number of schools opened each session is given. These numbers do not necessarily represent separate buildings, as in many instances two schools, one for male and one for female students, are held under separate responsible teachers in the same building; but this was not the case in the first years of the work, when each sex met in a separate building. The first step in the direction of mixed schools was taken in 1889 by allowing a school for female pupils to meet in a building where a male school was being held, but in that case the two schools were not allowed to meet on the same floors. In the next year, however, a mixed school was opened : the arrangement worked well, and gradually the number of mixed schools has been increased, until now there are 191 such schools. and even where there are two schools held in one building under separate responsible teachers the male and female students meet together for instruction in some of the subjects.

The Board have not restricted the opening of evening schools to their own buildings. Following the example of the Manchester School Board, schools have been conducted since 1899 in Voluntary school premises with the co-operation of the Managers. One of the members of the day school staff has generally been appointed responsible teacher of

---

[1] See p. 287.    [2] See p. 309.    [3] See p. 288.    [4] See p. 310.

the evening school, and the Board have paid the Managers a sum to cover the cost of fuel, light, &c. The number of these schools in the Session 1902-03 was 20 and the attendance was fairly satisfactory.

The table does not indicate the various types of schools which have been conducted by the Board: indeed, there has not generally been any official distinction made between one school and another; but the various needs of the students have determined the differences in the character of the schools. Whilst this is true of the schools generally, and especially up to the year 1898, there have since been established types of schools which differ from the majority. These are the Commercial and Science and Art schools, schools in poor districts, and schools for the Deaf, which are described under the head of Curriculum.[1]

In most of the schools an attempt has been made to teach adults in rooms separate from the younger students, but no attempt was made until the year 1897 to open separate schools for persons of given ages. One was started in that year and was well attended, the conditions being exceptionally favourable to the experiment. Many schools have been opened since then for juniors or seniors, the dividing line being generally the age of 18. In the Session 1902-03, there were 12 schools for junior students and 19 for seniors; the tendency of late, however, has been in the contrary direction, as several of these schools have during the last two or three years been unsuccessful.

The ages of the students have varied from 12 to 70 or even 80. No one has been refused admission on account of old age, but some restrictions have been made in the contrary direction. The Government regulations have only recognised the attendances of scholars who are exempt from the legal obligation to attend a day school. Most of the scholars are under 21, the age at which they chiefly attend being between 14 and 15, as the following admissions according to ages in the Session 1902-03 show: under 14, 1,721; 14 to 15, 28,964; 15 to 16, 25,356; 16 to 17, 13,225; 17 to 18, 10,244; 18 to 21, 19,274; over 21, 27,969. Total 126,753.

The session of the schools extends from the third week in September until about the end of July in the following year; but the chief work of the session comes to an end at Whitsuntide. The schools which are continued beyond that time usually meet only on one evening a week, and the chief subject of instruction is Swimming and Life-saving. The session has not always lasted so long. After the first session, when the attendance beyond Easter was unsatisfactory, the classes were closed at Easter for several years, that is to say until the Session 1889-90, but from that time until the present, the session has extended from September to July.

The usual number of evenings a week on which the schools have met has been three, but there are at the present time many exceptions, especially in the case of the Commercial and Science and Art schools, which meet on four, and even five, evenings a week. Some classes attached to the schools are taught on what are called "off" evenings, that is to say, evenings on which the whole schools are not meeting: these classes are

---

[1] See pp. 290-2.

for the most part held at centres, such as Cookery, Laundrywork, Manual Training, Gymnastics, &c.

The ordinary hours of meeting are from 7.30 to 9.30, although there are many exceptions, especially in the case of the Commercial and Science and Art schools, whose period of meeting is more than two hours, generally two and a-half hours, from 7 to 9.30.

### 3. *The Committee.*

From 1882, when the evening schools were first opened, until 1884, the administrative part of the work was entrusted to a Special Committee. In the latter year the Special Committee was constituted a Standing Committee of the Board as the "Evening Classes Committee," but in 1891 the work was transferred to the School Management Committee on the adoption of a general scheme for the re-organisation of committees, and it remained under the charge of that Committee until 1899, when the Board decided that there should again be a Standing Committee for evening schools.

### 4. *Advertising the Schools.*

Attendance at evening schools is not compulsory, and it has been necessary to make known the schools to those for whom they have been opened. To this end various means have been employed. In the Session of 1882 posters announcing the opening of the schools were placed on the walls of the school buildings and playgrounds; but this was not again permitted, as the bills were a disfigurement, and boards were provided for them. Posters have been displayed on street hoardings; but this method has been discarded, as it was found to be of little value. In 1893, a directory giving full particulars of the schools was published, but was found to be ineffective as an advertising medium. For three or four sessions a book, entitled "Old Scholars Book," was kept in each senior department of the day schools, and the scholars were asked to enter their names therein when leaving school: the responsible teachers consulted this book, and sent invitations to the ex-scholars to join the evening schools, but the plan was abandoned after a time, as many scholars failed to enter their names and responsible teachers sometimes found difficulty in gaining access to the book.

The present means of making known the schools consist in the printing of a handbill for each school, which is distributed under the direction of the responsible teacher. Leaflets announcing groups of schools are distributed throughout London by boys under the supervision of the visitors; posters are placed on the notice-boards attached to the school buildings, and a specially designed poster is displayed on railway stations; small bills are provided for shop windows and factories, where the responsible teachers are able to secure their display; and a prospectus is also printed and sent to ministers of religion, Sunday-school superintendents, Managers of day and evening schools, and others who are interested in evening school work. At certain times of the year head teachers of day schools are required to send to the Head Office a list of the names and addresses of the scholars who have left the schools. These lists are sent to responsible teachers of evening schools in the neighbourhood, and their duty is to send a circular letter of invitation to the scholars to join the evening schools. Another means of making known the schools exists in public meetings for the distribution of prizes, towards the expenses of which the Board grant the sum of £1 per school.

The cost of advertising has fluctuated. In the first session the only cost appears to have been the printing of the posters placed on the walls of the schools. The amount now voted by the Board for advertising is £3 10s. per school, and in the Session 1902-3 the total sum amounted to £1,330.

## II.—CURRICULUM.

There are three periods into which this subject may be divided—from 1882 to 1889; 1890 to 1897; and 1898 to 1904.

### 1. *First Period*: 1882 *to* 1889.

The original scheme of the Board, adopted in 1882, contemplated the establishment of two kinds of classes, that is to say :—

(*a*) Classes providing elementary instruction under the conditions of the Code of the Education Department;

(*b*) Other classes, termed " Advanced Classes," in subjects recognised by the Science and Art Department and by the City and Guilds of London Institute, and in such other special subjects as the Board might from time to time approve.

These latter classes were opened in 1883; but as the Board could not legally spend money upon this higher work, they merely lent rooms for the meetings of the classes at a nominal charge, to persons who were designated " superintending teachers." These persons were, in some cases, responsible teachers of the " Elementary evening classes"; the others had no connection with the rest of the Board's evening school work. The subjects were chiefly those recognised by the Science and Art Department, and Bookkeeping, Carpentry and Joinery, French, German, Greek, Latin, Mechanical Engineering, Needlework, Plumbing, Shorthand, Singing and the Violin. In return for the nominal charge at which the superintending teachers were allowed to have the use of the rooms, their proposals as to subjects, fees, &c., were submitted to the Evening Schools Committee for approval; but as the Board could give no financial help to the classes, the Committee could not effectively initiate or control the provision of this higher instruction. The classes were practically independent of the Board : the plan was makeshift in character, and when the Code of 1890 enabled the Board to provide higher instruction, this temporary expedient was abandoned.

The Board were able to defray the cost of Elementary evening classes out of the rates; but they were, during the first four or five years, of opinion that those classes should be practically self-supporting. The title, " Elementary evening classes," needs some explanation. They provided elementary instruction under the conditions of the Code of the Education Department. The subjects that were included in the Codes from 1882 to 1889 were the elementary and additional subjects. The elementary subjects were Reading, Writing, and Arithmetic, and the additional subjects were Algebra,

Animal Physiology, Botany, Chemistry, Domestic Economy, Drawing, Elementary Science, Euclid and Mensuration, English, French, Geography, History, Latin, Mechanics, Physics, Principles of Agriculture, and Singing. Such a list of subjects suggests something beyond elementary instruction; but as the Code provided that no scholar could take up additional subjects without being examined in Reading, Writing, and Arithmetic, there was little scope for giving more than Elementary instruction. Some progress was nevertheless made in the character and extent of the curriculum. A comparison of the two sessions beginning and ending this period shows that the schools were developing, although perhaps slowly :—

TABLE SHOWING THE SUBJECTS OF INSTRUCTION AND THE NUMBER OF PASSES IN THE SESSIONS 1882-3 AND 1889-1890.

| Subjects. | Number of Passes. | |
|---|---|---|
| | Session 1882–1883. | Session 1889–1890. |
| **ELEMENTARY.** | | |
| Reading ... ... ... ... ... | 1,114 | 5,175 |
| Writing ... ... .. ... ... | 965 | 4,874 |
| Arithmetic ... .. ... ... ... | 744 | 3,730 |
| °Total ... ... ... ... ... | 2,823 | 13,779 |
| **ADDITIONAL.** | | |
| Algebra... .. ... ... ... | 21 | 150 |
| Animal Physiology ... ... ... ... | 17 | 93 |
| Bookkeeping ... ... ... ... ... | ... | 334 |
| Botany... ... ... ... ... ... | ... | 6 |
| Chemistry ... ... .. ... ... | ... | 15 |
| Cookery ... ... ... ... ... | ... | 25 |
| Domestic Economy ... ... ... ... | 19 | 231 |
| Drawing ... ... ... ... ... | ... | 818 |
| Elementary Science ... ... ... ... | ... | 44 |
| English... ... ... ... ... ... | 189 | 957 |
| French... ... ... ... ... ... | ... | 198 |
| Geography ... ... ... ... ... | 124 | 682 |
| History... ... ... ... ... ... | 17 | 24 |
| Magnetism and Electricity ... ... ... | ... | 40 |
| Mechanics ... ... ... ... .. | 28 | 27 |
| Sound, Light, and Heat ... ... ... | 27 | ... |
| Total ... ... ... ... ... | 442 | 3,644 |
| Grand Total ... ... ... ... | 3,265 | 17,423 |

* In the Session 1883-4 the standard in which most of the students (353) were presented, was the fifth, but in the Session 1889-90, the standard in which the highest number of pupils (2,037) was presented, was the seventh.

A record of this time would not be complete without some reference to the assistance rendered by the Recreative Evening Schools Association. The London Trades Council asked the Board in 1885 that recreative and practical subjects (such as Musical Drill, Singing, Drawing, Modelling, Carving, Cookery, Sewing, &c.), oral teaching, and object lessons illustrated by the lantern might be introduced into the schools. The Board consented to give effect to these suggestions as far as practicable, and to accept voluntary help in the schools. The Recreative Evening Schools Association was formed, and in the Second Term of the Session 1885-6 they began to carry out some of these proposals in a few of the schools. The Association continued to give this assistance in subsequent sessions, and the Evening Schools Committee expressed their appreciation of this help in their annual reports to the Board. The term " Recreative " is perhaps somewhat misleading, for the chief part of the work of the Association was to supply lanterns and slides to be used in connection with the teaching of Geography, and in promoting the teaching of Musical Drill by providing wands, bar-bells, dumb-bells, musical instruments, and, in a few cases, by supplying voluntary teachers. A misconception has existed in reference to this work, the impression being that these classes were conducted apart from the ordinary evening schools. The fact is that the persons taught were pupils of the schools, but doubtless others were drawn into the schools by the efforts of the Association.

Although the Board were able to expand the work to some extent owing, amongst other causes, to slight changes in the Code, they were unable to develop the schools in such a way as to meet the needs of those who wished to continue their education after leaving the day school. The conditions of the Code prevented the Board from accomplishing the chief purpose of an evening school. Consequently they asked the Education Department to alter the Code in such a way as to permit the establishment of a type of evening schools which would be more suited to the needs of pupils who were becoming better educated year by year in the day schools.

In December, 1884, the Board asked that there should be special schedules of subjects, including Drawing and the first grades of some Science subjects; that the ground covered by the students in one year should be reduced, as the requirement of the Department that an evening school scholar should cover as much ground as a day school scholar was unreasonable, because of the comparatively short time which the evening school scholar is able to devote to study; and that the attendances of scholars who had passed through the standards might be recognised without requiring them to submit themselves again to the standard examinations in the elementary subjects. On the other hand, the Board desired that scholars might be presented in a standard as low as Standard II., as it was found that many who attended the evening schools were unable to pass a higher standard.

No changes were made by the Department, except that the subject of Elementary Drawing was added to the Code in 1885, and removed in 1887 to the Directory of the Science and Art Department, under which the Board were able to continue instruction in the subject. Accordingly the Board determined in 1887 to approach the Royal Commission on the working of the Education Acts which was then sitting, and in July they adopted a memorial that embodied the representations which had been made to the Education Department in 1884. The Board's later experience led them also to suggest that scholars above Standard IV., and not merely those above Standard VII., should be allowed to take up additional subjects without being compelled to sit for examination in the elementary subjects. They also suggested that the method of examination adopted for the day schools was not suitable for evening schools.

In February, 1889, the Board expressed their approval of certain representations which were included in a memorial to the Prime Minister and the Lord President of the Council. The parts of the memorial relating to evening schools were as follows :—

Both the reports of the recent Royal Commission on Education have unanimously reported in favour of three important improvements in the system of national education.

\* \* \* \* \*

That continuation schools shall be made an integral part of the elementary system of education, and that these schools shall be adapted to the needs of working boys and girls, so as to attract and interest tired children, and prepare them for actual duties of life.

We beg to submit for the consideration of the Government our reasons for making these proposals and respectfully to urge their great and even paramount importance.

\* \* \* \* \*

At present, working boys and girls are exposed, during the most important period of their life—from 13 to 16—to great dangers, especially during the evening. Continuation schools of the kind recommended by your Commissioners would help to protect them, elevate their tastes, inform their minds, and give useful and practical training.

\* \* \* \* \*

If, because more scholars go to evening continuation schools, there be an increase in the grant to these scholars, it should be readily given, inasmuch as a great waste of public money is prevented, and so many public benefits are attained.

Endeavours were also being made in Parliament at this time to promote a Technical Education Bill, the object of which was to enable School Boards to provide technical education in their schools, either day or evening. Technical Education was defined as follows :—

(i.) Any of the branches of Science and Art with respect to which grants are for the time being made by the Department of Science and Art.

(ii.) The working of wood, clay, metal, or other material for the purpose of art or handicraft.

(iii.) Commercial Arithmetic, Commercial Geography, Modern Languages, Bookkeeping, and Shorthand.

(iv.) Any other subject applicable to the purposes of agriculture, trade or commercial life and practice, which may be sanctioned by a minute of the Department of Science and Art made on the representation of a School Board or Local Authority that such form of instruction is suited to the needs of the district.

The Board expressed their approval of this Bill, and they asked the Education Department to support it. There was, however, no longer any need for this Bill on the passing of the Technical Instruction Act of 1889 and the adoption of the new Code for 1890. Soon after the passing of that Act the Board determined to open a few classes in subjects specified in it. One or more subjects of Science or Art or Manual Training were taught in four schools; but difficulties arose with the Education Department, and consequently the Board gave up the attempt to conduct classes under the Act. The objection of the Education Department was that the classes would not be Elementary schools under the Elementary Education Act of 1870. The Board, in their reply to the Education Department, pointed out that it was not their intention to establish these classes as separate schools, but to give the proposed instruction as a part of the curriculum of the ordinary evening schools, and that they would confine themselves to instruction in the subjects recognised by the Code. An important point arose in the correspondence with the Science and Art Department concerning these classes. The Department were asked whether scholars in evening schools who had passed Standard VII. could earn grants under the Technical Instruction Act. The reply was practically in the affirmative; but it was added that "it must be clearly understood that the Science and Art Department had no authority to construe an Act of Parliament, and that, therefore, any action the School Board may take, must be on their own responsibility."

In February, 1890, the Board made a further attempt to induce the Education Department to modify the Code. The Leeds School Board organised a deputation on the subject, and on their invitation the London Board authorised the Evening Schools Committee to appoint representatives to join the deputation. At the same time the Recreative Evening Schools Association prepared a memorial and asked the Board to adopt it, or a modification of it. A memorial was passed by the Board asking for amendments similar to those which they had previously suggested, and emphasising the need for the proposed changes by the following quotation from the final report of the Royal Commission on the working of the Public Elementary Education Acts :—

That the necessity for having some form of evening school for the purpose of fixing and making permanent the day school instruction is almost self-evident ; and that it would be worth the while of the State to spend more money on such schools.

That the evening school system should be thoroughly revised ; that a special curriculum and special schedules of standards and subjects should be allowed, suitable to the needs of the locality, and the Local Managers should be encouraged to submit such schedules to the Department for approval ; that the provision embodied in the Code requiring all scholars in evening schools to pass in the three elementary subjects as a condition of taking of additional subjects should cease to be enforced ; and that no superior limit of age should be imposed on the scholar.

That the success of evening schools will largely depend upon great freedom being given to their managers and teachers, and the Department should take ample securities for their educational efficiency, and that, if this is done, more money might be given as a fixed grant, and less made to depend on the results of individual examination.

That the evening schools of the future should be regarded and organised chiefly as schools for maintaining and continuing the education already received in the day school, but that, for some years to come, it will be necessary in many places to repeat in the evening schools, in greater or less proportion, the course of instruction previously given in the day school.

## 2. *Second Period:* 1890 *to* 1897.

The persistent representations which had been made from many quarters to the Education Department were at last, to a considerable degree, effectual. Important changes were made in the Code of 1890, which marked a new era in the history of the schools. There was now a possibility of making them serve as centres where those who had left day schools might continue their education, instead of being merely places where the work was mainly confined to a repetition of that of the day school. This change was not brought about so much by the introduction of new subjects as by a new rule which permitted scholars who had passed Standard V. to take up additional subjects without submitting themselves for examination in the three R's. Scholars below Standard V., who were still obliged to be examined in the three elementary subjects, could take up any two other subjects, and students could be presented in one standard for one subject and in another standard for another subject, whereas previously they could not be presented in more than one standard. The list of recognised subjects was also enlarged by the inclusion of Shorthand, German, Needlework, and Laundrywork; and instruction in Science and Art, Manual Training and Physical Exercises was encouraged by the recognition of tuition in these subjects in the minimum time constituting a recognised attendance.

The chief objects contemplated in these changes are explained in the revised instructions to H.M. Inspectors, 1890, in which the Department stated that they were " to provide for the continuation of the teaching given to the scholars who have left the day schools by giving greater variety and attractiveness to the course of instruction in evening schools, and by withdrawing the condition that all evening scholars shall necessarily be examined in the standard subjects." The liberty to present scholars in additional subjects necessitated an amendment of the Education Act of 1870, and consequently a short Act, entitled the Education Code Act, 1890, was passed which provided that elementary education need not form the principal part of the education given in evening schools.

The Board were now able to proceed with the development of the curriculum in the direction which had so long been felt to be necessary. One of their first acts was to discard the advanced classes, which were conducted more or less independently of the Board, and the chief result of this was the teaching of Science and Art subjects under the Directory of the Science and Art Department. This section of the work consisted at first in teaching ten Science subjects and seven Art subjects. The other subjects which were subsequently introduced under the New Code were Shorthand, German, Needlework, and Laundrywork, Manual Training in Wood, Physical Exercises, and Swimming. Of these Shorthand was the most popular, more students taking this subject than any other: only a few selected German. Needlework, as taught in the day schools, attracted a fair number of students, and Manual Training in Wood, which was first taught in the 1892-93 Session, was chosen by many. Little information can be given concerning Physical Exercises, as there are no statistics available except as to Swimming, which was started in a tentative way in the summer of 1891 by the teaching of some 500 scholars, whose admission to the baths was not however, in the first instance, paid by the Board.

Before passing from a review of this time, some allusion may be here made to suggestions received from the National Home Reading Union. A deputation waited on the Board and presented a memorial suggesting various ways in which the work of the Union might be aided by the Board in the day and evening schools. The Board promised to adopt the scheme of the Union as far as practicable, and if a teacher has desired a class to be attached to the Union, they have purchased the books issued by the Union, and have also paid a small affiliation fee; but the plan has not found much favour in the schools.

At Christmas, 1892, the Recreative Evening Schools Association withdrew the help which they had given to the Board for some years past. The Association stated that they felt no longer justified in continuing to throw on a few generous contributors a burden which might now be legally met by an insignificant addition to the rates, and they asked that the Board should purchase their stock. On receiving this intimation the Board resolved :—

That the best thanks of the Board should be accorded the Recreative Evening Schools Association for the valuable assistance which they have rendered to the Board's evening schools during the past seven years.

The Board also decided to purchase the apparatus of the Association for use in the schools.

The next important event was the issue of the separate Code for Evening Schools in 1893. Hitherto the regulations for evening schools had been incorporated with those for day schools. They were now issued in a separate form and the title was changed from "Evening Schools" to "Evening Continuation Schools."

In the words of the memorandum in the Code, the new regulations were

designed generally to meet the requirements of scholars who are no longer subject to the law of compulsory attendance at school, and who desire to prolong their education, either in the ordinary school subjects or in some special subjects in order to fit themselves for some industrial career. Evening continuation schools will have to meet various needs, as, for instance :—

(a) The case of the smaller schools which are intended mainly to supply defects in early elementary instruction, and to continue such instruction with a view to the ordinary pursuits of daily life.

(b) The case of schools, especially in the more populous districts, in which the general education of the scholar is prolonged, and combined with some form of useful and interesting employment.

(c) The case where the principal part of the work will be preparatory to the special studies directed by the Science and Art Department, or to lectures established by the County Councils, University Extension lectures, or other forms of secondary or higher education.

The principal changes made by this Code in the curriculum were that alternative syllabuses of instruction might be submitted; pupils were allowed almost unfettered liberty in the choice of subjects, but were limited to a certain number; and inspection of schools took the place of examination of individual scholars.

Encouraged by these new conditions, the usefulness of the schools was steadily extended during the remainder of this period. New subjects were introduced and the instruction in old subjects was developed.

One of the special features of the Code of 1893 was the introduction of a syllabus on " The Life and Duties of the Citizen." The syllabus is very comprehensive, dealing with Representative Government, Empire, and Industrial and Social Life and Duties. In some preliminary notes to the syllabus it is suggested that:—

The object of the teachers should be to proceed from the known and familiar, such as the police-man, the rate collector, the board of guardians, and the town council, to the history of, and reasons for, our local and national institutions, and our responsibilities in connection with them.

The subject was taught in a few schools by the ordinary staff and the Board thought that special lecturers should also be employed. A somewhat meagre response to the efforts of the Board was made by the scholars themselves. The actual number of students cannot be stated : the nearest approach to statistics is the number of complete twelve hours for which grant was paid—viz. 1,175 in the Session 1893-4, and 454 in the Session 1897-8. Another subject which failed to attract students was History, including Literature. The new Code did not specifically suggest instruction of this kind, but it could be given under the syllabus for History. The subject was taught by special lecturers, but the attendances fell from about 150 in the Session 1894-95 to about 50 in the Session 1897-98. The cause of the failure of these subjects is mainly the desire on the part of the students to receive instruction in subjects which they consider to be of practical utility. As an example of the demand for instruction of this kind Typewriting may be mentioned. In 1894 the Board agreed to hire twenty-four machines ; but the desire on the part of the pupils to be able to typewrite grew year by year, so that in 1897 the number of machines hired by the Board had increased to ninety-six. A subject that appealed to the female students was Dress-cutting and Dress-making. The syllabus for Needlework was altered in the Code of 1893 so as to permit of the teaching of Dress-cutting and Dress-making as part of Needlework, and the Board lost no time in providing instruction in this subject. The aim was not to teach the trade, but to enable scholars to cut out and make their own dresses. Large numbers of students availed themselves of these classes, grant being paid on as many as 6,586 complete twelve hours' instruction in Needlework in 1897. Whilst students were, for the most part, inclined to take up subjects which would assist them in their occupations, a considerable number availed themselves of instruction in subjects of another character. For instance, a substantial number of students took up Vocal Music which, on the passing of the Code of 1893, the Board were able to teach in the schools, and also at centres where it was possible to combine the various voices. Small beginnings were also made in teaching the Violin, Gymnastics, Life-saving and First Aid, but the numbers did not attain any considerable proportions until the period from 1898 onwards. An interesting attempt was made to teach Navigation. The Shipmasters' Society had represented to the

U

Board that shipwrecks and other disasters at sea were frequently traceable to a want of technical knowledge among the officers of the mercantile marine, and had suggested that a class should be opened at one or more schools on each side of the Thames, where the sons of watermen, pilots, masters, mates, marine engineers, and seamen of all grades might have an opportunity of acquiring a theoretical knowledge of Navigation. The Board decided to teach the subject in the Gill-street, Limehouse, day school, and also in two evening schools; but the experiment in the latter schools was not successful, as those who needed the instruction were not long enough on land to be able to attend the classes with profit.

The growth of the curriculum of this period may be gauged from the table on the opposite page.

### 3. *Third period*: 1898 *to* 1904.

Great progress has been made during this period in the development of the curriculum. The energy with which the work has been carried on has been responsible for this advance. The activity has not been, and indeed could not be, devoted so much to the increase in the number of subjects as to the improvement of those which had been attempted in a somewhat hesitating manner in the previous years. Nor have the efforts made to improve the schools been confined to any particular side of the work; the object being to make the schools centres for the mental, physical, and social well-being of the students.

(1) *Commercial and Science and Art Schools.*—One of the first and most important steps taken by the Board in this period was the opening of schools for instruction in Commercial subjects, in Science and Art, and in both. This specialisation was not brought about so much by the opening of new schools as by developing a few of the existing schools. The Commercial side consists chiefly of subjects which those employed in commercial life require to know. The Science and Art subjects are mainly those recognised by the higher regulations (old Directory) of the Board of Education South Kensington; but in both kind of schools other subjects of general benefit to the students are also taken, such as Gymnastics, Swimming and Life-saving, First Aid and Vocal Music. The teachers are specialists in their subjects and are paid higher salaries than the rest. The number of these schools in the Session 1898-1899 was 10 and the number of pupils admitted was 6,588: in the completed Session 1902-1903 there were 25 schools and 17,581 pupils admitted; thus there were increases of 15 schools and 10,993 pupils. There are now (1903-04 Session) 13 Commercial schools, 10 Science and Art and Commercial Schools, and 4 Science and Art Schools.

(2) *Schools in Poor Districts.*—Schools have been opened in poor districts and conducted in such a way as to induce the rougher element of the neighbourhood to attend. No fees have been charged in these schools. Examples of the subjects taught in two of these schools will indicate the character of the curriculum. In one of the schools for male pupils instruction is given in Gymnastics, Swimming, History, Geography, Drawing, First Aid, Metalwork, Elementary Science, and Reading,

TABLE SHOWING THE GROWTH OF THE CURRICULUM FROM 1889 TO 1897.

CURRICULUM.

| Session 1889-90. | Session 1897-98. |
|---|---|
| Algeora | Algebra |
| Arithmetic | Ambulance |
| Book-keeping | Arithmetic |
| Botany | Art |
| Chemistry | Book-keeping |
| Cookery | Botany |
| Domestic Economy | Building Construction |
| D awing | Chemistry |
| Elementary Science | Commercial Correspondence |
| English | Commercial Knowledge |
| French | Composition |
| Geography | Cookery |
| History | Domestic Economy |
| Magnetism and Electricity | Domestic Science |
| Mechanics | English |
| Physiology | French |
| Reading | Geography |
| Writing | Geology |
| | Geometry |
| | German |
| | History |
| | History, including Literature |
| | Hygiene |
| | Laundrywork |
| | Life and Duties of the Citizen |
| | Machine Construction and Drawing |
| | Magnetism and Electricity |
| | Manual Training in Wood |
| | Mathematics |
| | Mechanics |
| | Mensuration |
| | Navigation |
| | Needlework and Cutting-out |
| | Physical Exercises (Life-saving, Swimming, Gymnastics, Drill, etc.) |
| | Physics |
| | Physiography |
| | Physiology |
| | Reading |
| | Recitation |
| | Science of Common Things |
| | Shorthand |
| | Sound, Light, and Heat |
| | Steam |
| | Violin |
| | Vocal Music |
| | Writing |

Writing, and Arithmetic: in a school for female pupils Needlework and Dress-cutting, Gymnastics, Cookery, Laundrywork, Singing, Reading, Home-Nursing, Writing, and Composition are taught. The male pupils are labourers, stablemen, costermongers, bricklayers, watermen, carmen, milk boys, street orderly boys, boys employed in telegraph works, soap works and candle works, boys on barges, and errand boys. The students in the school for female pupils are employed in cap making and packing, card, fancy and tie box making, machining blouses, trousers and buttonholes, envelope folding and stamping, paper bag making, sack making, bookbinding, sewing and folding, cigar making, cigarette packing, show-card making, carpet sewing, toy making, packing perfumery and washing perfumery bottles, sieve making, feather curling, and making umbrellas. One of H.M. Inspectors, in a report upon one of the male schools, stated: "This difficult school continues to be admirably conducted, and a highly beneficial influence is undoubtedly exercised upon those who attend." The following also is the report of one of H.M. Inspectors upon a female school:—"The marked feature in this school is the improvement in the behaviour and appearance of the very rough class of girls that attend it, and reflects great credit on the responsible teacher."

(3) *Schools for the Deaf.*—These schools were transferred from the School Management Committee to the Evening Schools Committee in 1901, as they were deemed to belong more properly to the evening school work. There were nine at that time; there are now (1904) ten, and the number of pupils admitted (433) in the Session 1902-03, shows that they are appreciated by these afflicted students. The scholars may be classified thus:—those under 16 who are still in the day classes, those over 16 who have left the day classes, and those who have become deaf in later years. The classes are held in the same buildings as the day schools for the deaf, and the attendance of a scholar in the evening is recognised as an attendance at a session of the day school. The instruction given in the classes enables the scholars to become more proficient in expressing their thoughts in speech, and in the art of lip-reading, and they receive tuition in certain subjects selected from the following list:—Arithmetic, Cookery, Drawing, English Language, First Aid, Manual Training in Wood, Metalwork, Needle-work, including Dressmaking, Physical Exercises (Swimming and Gymnastics), Reading and Writing.

### 4. Subjects of Instruction.

*Typewriting.*—The increase in the use of typewriters in offices has increased the demand for a knowledge of the machine, consequently it has become necessary to increase the number of machines, and to adopt a scheme providing that as a rule the instruction should be given at centres, and only to those pupils who are able to write shorthand at the rate of forty words a minute, and to transcribe the same correctly. No other students may be taught without the special permission of the Committee.

*Languages.*—The Tables on pages 299 to 301 show that 12,473 pupils have been taught in the language classes during the Session 1902-3. All the languages named in the table except Russian were taught prior to 1898, but not to the same extent. Russian was first of all taught voluntarily in one school, but latterly the Board have defrayed the cost of the two classes which are now in existence. Special efforts have been made to improve the teaching of French. An organising teacher was appointed on October 4th, 1900, to look after these classes. Only those teachers are allowed to teach the subject who have obtained a First-Class Certificate at the Board's French examination which was first held in 1900 This examination is oral as well as written, and much attention is given in the schools to pronunciation. Classes suitable for teachers have been taught on the Gouin system in two or three schools, and a similar number of special classes have been taught on the system of Phonetics. In other schools special courses of lectures, or causeries, have been given by some of the best qualified teachers, the lectures being delivered in French and followed by conversation between the students and the lecturer on the topic of the evening. Some of the results of the instruction iven in the classes may be found in the "Results of Examinations" given on pages 303 to 308.

The Evening Schools Committee recently decided to open a class in Gaelic, but the Board resolved that the class should not meet until they had given their sanction. Soon after this a memorial was received from the Catholic League of South London, asking that Gaelic might be taught, and stating that it was already taken in the evening schools of the Manchester School Board. The Committee then proposed to open a class in the Greenwich Division, but the Board rejected the proposal by 20 votes to 19.

*Science and Art.*—The tables on pages 299 to 301 shows what subjects were taught during the Session 1902-03. The term "Science and Art," as used in this connection applies only to the classes formerly taught under the Directory of the Science and Art Department, South Kensington, and recently under certain divisions of the regulations of the Board of Education, South Kensington. There were other classes in Science and Drawing which were taught for a long time under the Whitehall Code, and recently under the new South Kensington Rules and Regulations. The chief difference between the two kinds of classes is that in the "Science and Art" classes more advanced instruction has been, and is, being given. The development of the Science and Art classes is evidenced by the fact that the number of passes in the advanced stages of the subjects has risen from 360 in the Session 1897-98 to 1,076 in the Session 1902-03. Until the year 1899, Steam, Applied Mechanics, Advanced Building Construction, Advanced Machine Construction and Drawing, and Advanced Magnetism and Electricity were taught, but from that time instruction in these subjects, except in two or three instances, has not been given, in consequence of a resolution at which the Board arrived, as the result of a conference between representatives of the Board and of the Technical Education Board of the London County Council on the question of overlapping in evening classes. The resolution was as follows :—

The School Board will not conduct classes in technological subjects—*e.g.* Steam Engine, Mechanical Engineering, Telegraphy, Telephony, Advance Machine Design (not the drawing of simple pieces of mechanism, etc.), and will not offer instruction specially intended for University degrees.

In the interpretation of this resolution the School Management Committee further decided :—

That the Board make no application to the Science and Art Department for Classes in Advanced Building Construction, Advanced Machine Construction, and Drawing, Advanced Magnetism and Electricity, Applied Mechanics, Steam and Agriculture.

In regard to the other classes in Science and Drawing, not "Science and Art," information as to subjects taught, the number of pupils, etc., in the Session 1902-03, will be found in Table I, pages 299 to 301; but a few particulars concerning Experimental Science, Natural Science, Free-arm Drawing and Preliminary Mechanical Drawing may be given here.

The Experimental Science Classes were opened in 1899, chiefly for teachers employed in the day schools of the Board. The objects of the classes were to provide instruction in the elements of Experimental Science, to familiarise students with the use and con-struction of simple apparatus, and to enable teacher-students to demonstrate scientific facts to their scholars. The course of instruction consisted, in the first instance, of 40 lessons, latterly of 48 lessons, and was intended to be preparatory to a course of pedagogical lectures arranged by the School Management Committee. In the Session 1902-03 courses were delivered in 11 schools. Since that time only one new class has been opened, there being insufficient teachers to form classes in other schools under a new scheme which has recently been adopted by the School Management Committee.

Somewhat similar classes in Natural Science were opened in 1890. The syllabus chiefly consisted of elementary instruction in Geology, Botany, and Zoology, and as much practical work as possible was done in the classes. Classes were held in four schools in the Session 1902-03, when the courses came to an end. No other classes have been opened since the adoption of the new scheme above mentioned.

Nature Study has also been recently introduced into two or three schools. The syllabus of instruction deals with various natural objects and phenomena in their proper season, and the lessons are, as far as possible, illustrated by specimens, the microscope, and lantern.

Free-arm Drawing classes were opened for teachers in order that they might become acquainted with the best methods of teaching Drawing. They were held in 1899 and 1900 and were attended by a considerable number of teachers; but since then they have been provided by the School Management Committee. Special classes in Elementary Mechanical Drawing were opened in 1898: in the Session 1902-03 they were held in 55 schools, and 1,663 pupils joined them.

*Literature.—* In the Session 1898-99 special lecturers were first employed to give oral descriptions of the works of poets, dramatists, and prose writers, with a view to creating and fostering an appreciation of literature. Lectures were delivered in 22 schools to some 2,500 students. In the Session 1902-03 the number of schools had increased to 53, but the attendance had fallen to 1,826. It is needful, however, to remember that the ordinary staff of the schools also taught this subject, although not by quite the same methods.

To encourage the study of Dramatic Literature, the Rev. Stewart D. Headlam, the Chairman of the Evening Continuation Schools Committee, has given a prize for the best class since the Session 1898-99. A competition for the prize has been held annually; scenes from Shakespeare's plays have been rendered, and the class which has been deemed best by the judge has been awarded the prize.

The number of students taking up Literature cannot be stated with exactness, as the attendances in the classes are included under the various heads of Literature, Recitation and Reading.

*History.*—To stimulate interest in History special lecturers have been employed in a few schools, but the plan has not been successful, the number of classes dwindling from 16 in the Session 1900-01 to 6 in the Session 1902-03. The subject has, however, also been taken up by the ordinary staff, and illustrated in most cases by lantern slides. The total number of schools in which History was taught in the session 1902-03 was 66 and the number of students who joined the classes was 3,572.[1] Another attempt to create an interest in recent history, was the appointment, in the Session 1903 04, of a lecturer to give a series of popular lectures on the "Reign of Queen Victoria," illustrated by slides of *Punch* cartoons. The number of schools in which the lectures were given up to Christmas, 1903, was four, and the average attendance was 73.

The above remarks refer to English History in general. Some attempts were also made to interest students in the history of their own city. The Rev. Arthur W. Jephson, offered book prizes for the best papers on "London History," but only twelve students competed; four prizes were awarded, and no further competition has taken place. Coming still nearer to their homes, an attempt has been made to acquaint scholars with the history of their own neighbourhoods. A plan has been adopted similar to that in force in the case of the day school children. Special lecturers have been employed to give lectures on "Local History," illustrated by special slides. These lectures have been given at 20 schools to about 1,500 students in the Session 1902-3, the last completed session under the Board.

*Music.*—Instruction in both Vocal and Instrumental Music has been developed in the past few years. In the Session 1897-98 the schools in which Vocal Music was taught numbered 80; in the Session 1902-03 there were 235. An advance has also been made in the character of the instruction. Choirs have been formed in individual schools and have given proof of their capabilities at local gatherings, exhibitions, &c.; and classes have recently been gathered together at centres for rehearsing standard works (Haydn's "Creation," Spohr's "St. Cecilia's Day," Gaul's "Joan of Arc"), which have been given in public halls and at the Alexandra Palace. Instruction has been given to day school teachers and others to enable them to obtain the School Teachers' Music Certificate. In the Session 1902-03, 133 teachers obtained this certificate, and the knowledge acquired has been of much value in the teaching of the scholars in the day and evening schools. Instrumental Music classes were held in 24 schools in the Session 1902-03 : the instruction

---

[1] See Table on page 300.

has chiefly been devoted to the violin, but a considerable number of orchestral classes are also now in existence.

*Manual Training.* — Woodwork and Wood-carving classes have considerably increased in the last few years, the total number having increased from 203 in 1897-98 to 586 in 1902-03. In the latter session the number was made up of 367 Woodwork and 219 Wood-carving classes. Special classes in Wood-carving have been opened for the instruction of teachers and Manual Training instructors, in order to qualify them to teach the subject in the evening schools. Four of these classes were opened in 1899; nine are now being held and are preparing qualified teachers to carry on the work.

The classes in Metalwork were not started until 1899, although the subject was recognised by the Government Code for many years prior to that date. Under the designation of "Metalwork" three different branches have been taught, namely: (i.) Elementary Metalwork, such as forge-work, chipping, filing and shaping metal, either by hand or in the lathe, or by the use of machine tools; (ii.) Repoussé work or metal embossing and chasing, in which sheet-metal is either driven back from the face, or hammered out from the back into relief and finished on the front surface with fine punches and graving tools; and (iii.) Sheet Metalwork, comprising the lining out, shaping, turning up and soldering sheet-metal into geometrical solids and models, and folded, lapped, and riveted joints. The figures for these classes are given in the Table on page 300.

*Housewifery.* — A beginning has been made in teaching Housewifery in a practical way by opening classes in the Housewifery centres under teachers who are employed in the day classes. In the Session 1902-1903 four classes were held, and although the number of students who were desirous of receiving practical instruction was small, yet there will no doubt be an improved attendance when the character of the instruction becomes better known.

*Millinery.* — Many students have been taught Millinery as a part of the syllabus of Needlework during the last few years. The object of the instruction has not been to train the students to become milliners; but chiefly to enable them to make their own clothes. The exact number of students who have availed themselves of this tuition cannot be stated, as they have been included in the figures for Needlework.

*First Aid and Home-Nursing.* — These subjects were begun in earnest in 1898, when medical practitioners were engaged to deliver courses of lectures, each course consisting of about twelve lectures (six being given by the medical practitioner, and six by a member of the ordinary staff) and at the end of the course the students were examined by the St. John Ambulance Association. This scheme remained in force without change until 1900, when the Board decided to hold an examination of their own; to appoint a medical superintendent to organise and supervise the work and to allow no First Aid class to be taught by anyone who was not a medical practitioner, except that, in the case of Home-Nursing, persons approved by the Committee might teach the subject, as for example, trained nurses. It was also decided, in order to obtain qualified assistants, that classes should be opened for the teachers who were to assist the medical practitioners;

that certificates should be granted to those who had successfully passed the examination at the end of the course; and that, later on, only those teachers who possessed the certificate should be allowed to assist the doctors. The latest available figures for these classes are set out in the Table on page 300. Amongst the number taught are many policemen, whose instruction is being vigorously and systematically proceeded with in conjunction with the authorities at New Scotland Yard, and it was hoped that in time every policeman in London would, as a result of this instruction, be able to render First Aid to those who need immediate help.

*Health.*—Efforts were made between 1899 and 1903 to teach the simple Laws of Health. A few instructors possessing special knowledge and experience were engaged to give the lessons, and the ordinary staff attempted in some classes to inform the minds of the students on this important subject, but only a meagre result followed these efforts. In 1903 the Board decided to employ medical practitioners to lecture in twenty centres according to a syllabus which the medical superintendent had drawn up, which included such subjects as Ventilation, Ill-chosen Food in Childhood, Clothing, Cleanliness, and Removal of Refuse in Health and in Sickness. The instruction has been illustrated by diagrams and accompanied by practical demonstrations. The experiment was so far successful in the earlier part of the Session that the Board decided to increase the number of classes to eighty in the second part.

*Physical Education.*—Much has been done in the direction of Physical Culture, notwithstanding that the Board of Education, South Kensington, did not, when they took over the administration of the evening continuation schools in 1901, follow the practice of the Whitehall Branch of allowing grant for Physical Exercises. The work, however, continued uninterruptedly with the sanction of the London County Council, but unaided by the Government.

*(a) Gymnastics.*—Prior to 1898, Gymnastics was only taught in a few schools, but in that year instruction was given in connection with 135 schools to 13,986 pupils and the numbers have now (1902-03) grown to 276 schools and 20,343 pupils. The classes are held in the halls of the schools. As a rule, a class is equipped with parallel bars, horizontal bar, vaulting-horse, dumb-bells, bar-bells, and Indian clubs. The following extracts from reports of instructors indicate the value of the work that has been done :—

Most of the pupils are at work in factories and workshops in the neighbourhood of the school. More squad drill than gymnastics has been taken, as so many of the girls suffered from anæmia and round shoulders. Last year the class at Carlton Road won a silver challenge cup in a competition, and at a competition for medals this year the work was so good that the judges found it difficult to choose the winners. Girls are sent to the class by doctors, and instances can be given where pupils suffering from anæmia have been cured.

The class at Gopsall Street was composed of boys drawn from the slums of the district. They were at first very much opposed to discipline or anything in the shape of order. It was certainly the most "raw" class that he (the Instructor) had ever seen. In the mass drill, the boys were hardly able to distinguish between left and right, and could not, even with a run, vault over the low horse from the spring board. At the end of the season, the results were very satisfactory. The boys could perform marching evolutions and mass drill with a greater precision and in better style than he (the Instructor) has seen in some gymnasia where the classes have been composed of older pupils, and where they have had two nights a week instruction. The apparatus work improved in a like manner.

Students were carefully examined and measured at the commencement of the session. Some few had to be rejected, and others, with spinal curvature, hollow chest, weak heart and lungs, were given suitable work. The season's work has been very beneficial and, in some cases, quite beyond expectation, having regard to the adverse conditions of work and home surroundings. The greatest increase in chest measurement was 3¾ inches, and in lung measure 57 cubic inches; and there were, in cases, increases of 2¼ and 30 inches respectively. The pupils showed a much better carriage of the body, greater strength with a higher degree of health and quickened growth in all parts; and there was a great improvement in their conduct and moral tone.

In the second part of the Session 1903-04 the work of the classes was tested by a competition. The character of the work done at this competition was of a somewhat unusual kind, the marks being awarded for (1) the rational and beneficial character of the movements ; (2) the graceful and erect carriage of the pupils; and (3) the general form, all-round excellence, and discipline displayed throughout the lesson.

(*b*) *Swimming and Life-Saving.*—Swimming was first taught in 1890 and was supplemented in 1898 by Life-Saving, that is to say, students have been taught the best means of rendering aid to those in danger of drowning and of resuscitating those apparently drowned. Although no Government grant has been paid for Physical Exercises since 1900, the Committee thought that the Board of Education might be willing to aid instruction in Life Saving as part of First Aid, and they asked for official recognition of this work, but the Board of Education declined to sanction any instruction which involved the teaching of Swimming. The School Board, nevertheless, proceeded with the whole of the scheme for Life-Saving, and the number of students who have benefited by these classes has increased from about 3,500 in the Session 1897-98 to 11,961 in the Session 1902-03, an increase which, amongst other causes, was brought about by the payment by the Board of the charge for the admission of the pupils to the baths.

(*c*) *Drill, &c.*—Other exercises have been practised in the form of various kinds of Drill and also, in a few instances, of Dancing. There are, however, no figures available to show the progress that has been made in these forms of Physical Exercises. In the first few years there is no record of anything being done in the matter of the physical education of the students except in the direction of Musical Drill, which was begun by the Recreative Evening Schools Association. Until 1890 the Government recognised Military Drill, but in that year "suitable Physical Exercises" were substituted, and from that time to the present Drill of some kind has been taught in most of the schools. Dancing has also been introduced into some schools in conformity with a suggestion in the Codes, that "My Lords will be interested to learn from the reports of H.M. Inspectors, the results of any successful experiments by which Evening Continuation Schools have been rendered more attractive—e.g. by means of . . . gymnastics, or other employments of a more or less recreative character." Notwithstanding this suggestion, the teaching of this latter exercise was commented upon unfavourably by the Vice-President of the Committee of Council on Education, in a speech made in the House of Commons on May 7th, 1901. At that time Dancing had been approved by Government Inspectors in twenty-four schools, but it was dropped out of the school curriculum in the Session 1901-02.

*Tables of Subjects.*—The following tables show the subjects taught in the Session 1902-03, and the number of scholars who received instruction :—

I.—ALL CLASSES EXCEPT THOSE HELD UNDER DIVISIONS II. AND IV. OF THE REGULATIONS OF THE BOARD OF EDUCATION, SOUTH KENSINGTON.

| SUBJECT. | No. of Schools. | Total No. of Pupils who received instruction during the Session excluding those who attended for one evening only. | Total No. of Pupils who received 14 or more hours' instruction during the Session. [14 is the minimum number for which grant is paid.] |
|---|---|---|---|
| (1) | (2) | (3) | (4) |
| Accountancy and Auditing ... ... ... ... | 1 | 24 | 17 |
| Algebra ... ... ... ... ... ... | 11 | 383 | 159 |
| „ and Arithmetic ... ... ... ... | 2 | 100 | 42 |
| Arithmetic ... ... ... ... ... | 177 | 11,225 | 3,799 |
| „ Commercial ... ... ... ... | 33 | 2,150 | 869 |
| „ and Composition ... ... ... | 1 | 108 | 31 |
| „ and Mensuration ... ... ... | 1 | 50 | 19 |
| „ Reading and Writing ... ... ... | 136 | 10,915 | 4,284 |
| „ Commercial, Reading and Writing... ... | 1 | 52 | 15 |
| „ and Writing ... ... ... ... | 32 | 2,304 | 967 |
| „ Commercial and Writing ... ... | 1 | 90 | 51 |
| „ Writing and Composition ... ... | 2 | 170 | 85 |
| Book-keeping ... ... ... ... ... | 309 | 16,554 | 8,142 |
| Brushwork ... ... ... ... ... | 1 | 45 | 13 |
| Chemistry ... ... ... ... ... | 18 | 911 | 213 |
| „ and Light, Practical ... ... ... | 1 | 49 | 24 |
| „ „ Theoretical ... ... | 1 | 49 | 12 |
| „ as applied to Photography ... ... | 3 | 76 | 34 |
| Cookery ... ... ... ... ... ... | 179 | 5,629 | 2,582 |
| °Correspondence, Commercial, and Office Routine ... | 47 | 2,009 | 764 |
| Domestic Economy ... ... ... ... | 7 | 232 | 69 |
| Drawing (see also Mechanical Drawing) ... ... | 141 | 6,628 | 2,058 |
| English Citizenship ... ... ... ... | 4 | 91 | 21 |
| English Language... ... ... ... ... | 27 | 1,162 | 478 |
| English Literature—(Taught by special lecturers) ... | 53 | 1,826 | 718 |
| „ „ (Taught by ordinary teachers)... | 25 | 993 | 389 |
| Ethics ... ... ... ... ... ... | 1 | 32 | 10 |
| Euclid ... ... ... ... ... ... | 1 | 30 | 17 |
| ‡First Aid—(Taught by medical practitioners and ordinary teachers) ... ... ... ... | 189 | 6,482 | 2,421 |
| ‡First Aid—(Taught by ordinary teachers) ... ... | 6 | 161 | 41 |
| French ... ... ... ... ... ... | 195 | 10,488 | 4,947 |
| Geography ... ... ... ... ... | 132 | 6,761 | 1,733 |
| „ Commercial ... ... ... ... | 27 | 1,298 | 508 |
| „ and History ... ... ... ... | 61 | 4,214 | 1,138 |
| „ „ Commercial ... ... ... | 2 | 115 | 48 |
| Geology ... ... ... ... ... ... | 1 | 32 | 14 |
| German ... ... ... ... ... ... | 36 | 1,387 | 772 |

For Footnotes see p. 301.

| Subject. | No. of Schools. | Total No. of Pupils who received instruction during the Session, excluding those who attended for one evening only. | Total No. of Pupils who received 14 or more hours' instruction during the Session. [14 is the minimum number for which grant is paid.] |
|---|---|---|---|
| (1) | (2) | (3) | (4) |
| Health ... ... ... ... ... ... ... | 2 | 66 | 33 |
| History ... ... ... ... ... ... ... | 66 | 3,572 | 938 |
| „ Commercial ... ... ... ... | 9 | 318 | 120 |
| „ Contemporary ... ... ... ... ... | 7 | 321 | 114 |
| ‡Home Nursing (Taught by medical practitioners and ordinary teachers) ... ... ... ... | 85 | 2,274 | 1,066 |
| ‡Home Nursing (Taught by trained nurses) ... | 57 | 1,597 | 584 |
| ‡Home Nursing (Taught by ordinary teachers) ... | 3 | 36 | 15 |
| Horticulture ... ... ... ... ... | 1 | 54 | 45 |
| Housewifery ... ... ... ... ... | 4 | 42 | 16 |
| Italian ... ... ... ... ... ... | 4 | 104 | 65 |
| Latin ... ... ... ... ... ... | 10 | 173 | 78 |
| Laundrywork ... ... ... ... ... | 66 | 1,304 | 530 |
| Law, Commercial ... ... ... ... ... | 12 | 225 | 127 |
| Machine Construction ... ... ... ... | 3 | 62 | 48 |
| Machinery of Business ... ... ... ... | 3 | 96 | 49 |
| Magnetism and Electricity ... ... ... | 19 | 775 | 240 |
| Manual Training in Metalwork ... ... ... | 30 | 879 | 435 |
| „ „ Wood-carving ... ... ... | 139 | 4,527 | 2,274 |
| „ „ Woodwork ... ... ... | 203 | 11,130 | 4,938 |
| Mathematics ... ... ... ... ... | 12 | 435 | 164 |
| Mechanical Drawing, Preliminary ... ... ... | 55 | 1,663 | 730 |
| Mechanics ... ... ... ... ... ... | 2 | 28 | 11 |
| Mensuration ... ... ... ... ... | 7 | 275 | 104 |
| Metalwork (Elementary Leadwork) ... ... | 4 | 118 | 50 |
| „ (Repoussé) ... ... ... ... | 22 | 652 | 336 |
| †Millinery ... ... ... ... ... ... | 49 | 2,158 | 1,015 |
| Music, Instrumental ... ... ... ... | 24 | 846 | 460 |
| „ Theory of ... ... ... ... ... | 2 | 52 | 27 |
| Nature Study ... ... ... ... ... | 2 | 73 | 3 |
| Needlework ... ... ... ... ... | 1 | 17 | 17 |
| „ (including Dressmaking) (See also Millinery) | 227 | 15,286 | 8,406 |
| „ (including Dressmaking and Millinery) ... | 10 | 952 | 538 |
| Physical Exercises— |  |  |  |
| §Swimming and Life-Saving ... ... ... ... | 291 | 11,961 | 872 |
| Gymnastics ... ... ... ... ... | 276 | 20,343 | 10,207 |
| Drill, &c. ... ... ... ... ... | 90 | 5,948 | 1,925 |
| Physics and Chemistry ... ... ... ... | 6 | 161 | 74 |
| Political Economy ... ... ... ... ... | 5 | 69 | 30 |
| Précis Writing ... ... ... ... ... | 1 | 40 | 15 |
| Portuguese ... ... ... ... ... ... | 1 | 18 | 7 |
| Reading ... ... ... ... ... ... | 29 | 1,173 | 384 |
| „ and Composition ... ... ... | 8 | 642 | 328 |
| „ and Recitation ... ... ... | 10 | 429 | 162 |
| „ and Writing ... ... ... ... | 68 | 5,451 | 1,672 |
| „ Writing, and Composition ... ... | 2 | 112 | 23 |
| Recitation ... ... ... ... ... | 8 | 198 | 89 |
| Russian ... ... ... ... ... ... | 2 | 30 | 14 |
| Science (Elementary) ... ... ... ... | 10 | 431 | 92 |
| „ (Experimental) ... ... ... ... | 15 | 487 | 284 |
| Science (Natural) ... ... ... ... ... | 4 | 44 | 36 |
| Science of Common Things ... ... ... ... | 24 | 1,686 | 364 |

For Footnotes see p. 301.

| SUBJECT (1) | No. of Schools. (2) | Total No. of Pupils who received instruction during the Session, excluding those who attended for one evening only. (3) | Total No. of Pupils who received 14 or more hours' instruction during the Session. [14 is the minimum number for which grant is paid.] (4) |
|---|---|---|---|
| °Shorthand ... ... ... ... ... ... | 315 | 28,729 | 16,082 |
| Spanish ... ... ... ... ... ... | 11 | 273 | 176 |
| Tailoring ... ... ... ... ... ... | 3 | 83 | 49 |
| °Typewriting ... ... ... ... ... ... | 62 | 2,829 | 1,673 |
| Violin ... ... ... ... ... ... | 11 | 314 | 140 |
| Vocal Music ... ... ... ... ... ... | 235 | 14,590 | 6,515 |
| Writing ... ... ... ... ... ... | 1 | 37 | 9 |
| „ and Composition ... ... ... ... | 86 | 6,285 | 2,013 |

\* Typewriting formed generally a part of a course of instruction in Shorthand or Commercial Correspondence.
† Millinery was also taught under the title of Needlework.
‡ The course of instruction covered a period of about three months.
§ Instruction in this subject was given mainly in the summer months, the lessons were necessarily limited in duration to about half an hour, and their total number was, of course, comparatively small.

## II.—CLASSES HELD UNDER DIVISIONS II. AND IV. OF THE REGULATIONS OF THE BOARD OF EDUCATION, SOUTH KENSINGTON.

| SUBJECT. (1) | No. of Schools. (2) | Total No of Pupils who received instruction during the Session, excluding those who attended for one evening only. (3) | Total No. of Pupils who received 14 or more hours' instruction during the Session. [14 is the minimum number for which grant in paid.] (4) |
|---|---|---|---|
| Art ... ... ... ... ... ... ... ... | 54 | 3,079 | 1,996 |
| Biology ... ... ... ... ... ... ... | 2 | 25 | 19 |
| „ Practical ... ... ... ... ... ... | 1 | 51 | 41 |
| Botany ... ... ... ... ... ... ... | 7 | 298 | 188 |
| „ Practical ... ... ... ... ... ... | 2 | 100 | 71 |
| Building Construction ... ... ... ... | 14 | 396 | 246 |
| Chemistry, Inorganic, Practical ... ... ... ... | 27 | 852 | 468 |
| „ „ Theoretical ... ... ... | 25 | 737 | 333 |
| Geology ... ... ... ... ... ... | 1 | 22 | 15 |
| Geometry, Practical, Plane and Solid ... ... ... | 12 | 365 | 191 |
| Heat, Advanced ... ... ... ... ... | 1 | 14 | 6 |
| Hygiene ... ... ... ... ... ... | 10 | 525 | 346 |
| „ Practical ... ... ... ... | 1 | 28 | 22 |
| Machine Construction and Drawing ... ... | 12 | 557 | 376 |
| Magnetism and Electricity ... ... ... ... | 10 | 306 | 138 |
| Mathematics ... ... ... ... ... | 17 | 752 | 427 |
| „ Practical ... ... ... ... | 1 | 8 | 3 |
| Mechanics, Applied ... ... ... ... ... | 1 | 56 | 25 |
| „ Theoretical, Fluids ... ... ... | 1 | 13 | 5 |
| „ „ Solids ... ... ... | 3 | 67 | 34 |
| Physiography ... ... ... ... ... | 10 | 249 | 143 |
| „ Practical ... ... ... ... | 1 | 23 | 15 |
| Physiology, Human ... ... ... ... | 11 | 746 | 491 |
| „ Practical ... ... ... ... | 5 | 145 | 85 |
| Sound, Light, and Heat ... ... ... ... | 3 | 40 | 23 |

NOTE.—In these Tables a student has been counted for as many subjects as he, or she, studied, and may therefore appear more than once. The figures are approximate, as the return from one school has not been received.

### 5. *Social Life in the Schools.*

Although the Board have never been able to spend money to promote the social side of the schools, they have, since 1892, sought to encourage the efforts of the teachers in this direction. In that year the Board decided to allow social gatherings to be held not oftener than once a month on an evening when the school was not meeting, and to grant the free use of the rooms for this purpose. Gatherings have been held occasionally in some schools and regularly in others, and have tended to bring about friendly relations between the teachers and students, and amongst the students themselves. The proceedings at these gatherings have taken the form chiefly of vocal and instrumental music, recitations and readings, dramatic recitals, exhibitions of work, opportunities for conversation, and dancing. The students and the teachers and their friends have been the chief contributors in providing the entertainment. Various clubs have also been formed for cricket, football, tennis, and cycling. Some teachers have accompanied their pupils in country rambles and to places of interest in the City; and circles for the study of French have been recently started. To the teachers generally is due the credit of developing this phase of the evening school movement.

### III.—GOVERNMENT REPORTS AND GRANTS.

The Annual Reports of H.M. Inspectors have, with a few exceptions, testified to the efficiency of the schools, and the grants, which have nearly always been paid at the higher rates, have also shown that the schools have been conducted to the satisfaction of the Board of Education. Apart from these Reports, a Blue Book was issued in July, 1903, by the Board of Education, consisting of general reports of H.M. Inspectors on Higher Education for the year 1902. Two of these Inspectors dealt at some length with the evening schools conducted by the Board, and many of their criticisms were unfavourable. The Board's Inspectors drew up replies, and the Board, on November 19th, 1903, decided to send them to the Board of Education with a covering letter, of which the following is a copy:—

The School Board for London have noted with concern the strictures on the conduct of the evening schools under their charge contained in the Reports on Higher Education, published by the Board of Education.

As, however, the School Board for London have no communication from the Board of Education on the subject of these Reports, which are, moreover, at variance with the Reports received by them for the year 1901-2 on individual schools, they assume that the Reports embody the opinions of the particular inspectors concerned, and not those of the Board of Education.

The School Board for London, however, would wish the Board of Education to be under no misapprehension of the facts of the case; they therefore forward for the information of the Board of Education the Reports of their own Board Inspectors on the matter referred to in the said Reports.

In 1893 a much more liberal scale of grant was allowed to evening schools. Whereas in the previous session, 1892-3, the amount per head was only 11s. 9d., the sum received in the following session, 1893-4, rose to £1 6s. 8¾d. On the other hand, the grants fell somewhat (8d. per head) when the Board of Education, South Kensington, took over the schools from the Whitehall Branch in 1901, as the scale of grants was then reduced, and nothing was paid for Physical Exercises. The basis on which grants were paid in 1893 was aggregate attendances in subjects in place of average attendance and the results of the annual examinations.

### Results of Examinations.

The benefit which the students have derived from the schools cannot be shown by results of examinations alone. Nevertheless, some indication of the work done in the schools may be gathered from the following Tables, which show that the total number of entries in the Session 1902-03 was (excluding the Science and Art, South Kensington, Examinations) 12,867, compared with 290 in the Session 1893-94, the first session in which there is any record of students sitting at examinations of outside bodies. Prior to the Session 1893-94, all the students were examined by the Government Inspectors in the ordinary course of the examination of the schools.

TABLE SHOWING THE RESULTS OF VARIOUS EXAMINATIONS (except those of the Board of Education, South Kensington) at which the students presented themselves voluntarily and in all cases paid the examination fee where the various examining bodies charged fees, Session 1902-03 :—

| Examining Body and Subject. (1) | Number Presented. (2) | Passes. (3) | Examining Body and Subject. (1) | Number Presented. (2) | Passes. (3) |
|---|---|---|---|---|---|
| *Bankers, Institute of—* | | | *Chamber of Commerce—* | | |
| Preliminary ... ... ... | 5 | 4 | Algebra (Juniors) | 10 | 3 |
| Intermediate ... ... ... | 2 | 2 | Arithmetic „ | 26 | °4 |
| Final ... ... ... ... | 2 | 1 | Book-keeping „ | 174 | §50 |
| Economics ... ... ... | 1 | §°1 | Chemistry „ | 9 | ‖7 |
| | | | Drawing „ | 17 | ‖12 |
| | 10 | 8 | English „ | 13 | 8 |
| | | | Euclid „ | 4 | †4 |
| *Banks & Assurance Companies—* | | | French „ | 72 | †‖41 |
| Clerks ... ... ... ... | 3 | 3 | Geography „ | 13 | 9 |
| | | | „ Commercial „ | 5 | 2 |
| *Borough Councils—* | | | „ and History (Com- | | |
| Clerks ... ... ... ... | 4 | 4 | mercial) „ | 4 | 3 |
| | | | German „ | 42 | †°17 |
| *British College of Physical Edu-* | | | Italian „ | 1 | ... |
| *cation—* | | | Latin „ | 6 | °2 |
| Gymnastic Diplomas ... | 3 | ‖†3 | Mathematics „ | 1 | °1 |
| | | | Portuguese „ | 2 | ... |
| | | | Russian „ | 1 | 1 |
| *Browne, Miss Prince—* | | | Science, Elementary „ | 3 | °1 |
| Millinery ... ... ... | 5 | 5 | Shorthand „ | 233 | °†82 |
| | | | Spanish „ | 15 | °◁10 |
| *Cambridge University—* | | | Typewriting „ | 113 | ††58 |
| Higher Local (Arithmetic, French, Drawing) | 1 | 1 | Juniors ... ... | 764 | 315 |

For Footnotes see p. 307.

| Examining Body and Subject. (1) | Number Presented. (2) | Passes. (3) | Examining Body and Subject. (1) | Number Presented. (2) | Passes. (3) |
|---|---|---|---|---|---|
| *Chamber of Commerce*—cont. | | | *Civil Service Commissioners, &c.* —cont. | | |
| Arithmetic ... (Seniors) | 1 | 1 | Second Division Clerk ... | 1 | 1 |
| Banking and Currency ,, | 2 | 1 | Sorters ... ... ... ... | 80 | 62 |
| Book-keeping ... ,, | 281 | §§179 | Sorter Tracer ... ... | 1 | 1 |
| Chemistry ... ... ,, | 7 | §5 | Supplementary Clerks ... | 2 | 1 |
| Drawing ... ... ,, | 6 | δ4 | Telegraph Learners ... | 138 | 104 |
| Economics ... ... ,, | 2 | — | Telephone Clerks ... | 5 | 5 |
| English ... ... ,, | 2 | †2 | Writers in Navy ... | 2 | 2 |
| French ... ... ,, | 65 | †¶41 | | | |
| Geography(Commercial),, | 1 | 1 | | 537 | 431 |
| German ... ... ,, | 18 | †§15 | | | |
| Italian ... ... ... ,, | 3 | δ‖3 | | | |
| Latin ... ... ... ,, | 2 | δ2 | | | |
| Law (Commercial) ... ,, | 33 | ‡16 | *Dock Companies*— | | |
| Machinery of Business ,, | 46 | δδ42 | Assistants (Junior) ... ... | 4 | 4 |
| Mathematics ... ,, | 5 | 3 | Clerks ... ... ... ... | 3 | 3 |
| Political Economy ... ,, | 6 | δ3 | Messengers ... ... ... | 3 | 2 |
| Portuguese ... ... ,, | 1 | — | | | |
| Russian ... ... ,, | 1 | δ§1 | | 10 | 9 |
| Shorthand ... ... ,, | 108 | δ†59 | | | |
| Spanish ... ... ,, | 12 | δ‖10 | *Lambeth, East—Evening Con-* | | |
| Typewriting ... ... ,, | 63 | †32 | *tinuation Schools Swimming* | | |
| | | | *Association*— | | |
| Seniors ... ... | 665 | 420 | Certificates ... ... ... | 17 | ‡§17 |
| | | | | | |
| Total ... ... | 1,429 | 735 | *Law Society (Incorporated)*— | | |
| | | | Preliminary ... ... ... | 2 | 2 |
| *Chartered Accountants, Institute* | | | | | |
| *of*— | | | *Life-Saving Society*— | | |
| Entrance Examination ... | 1 | 1 | Scholars' Certificates ... ... | 61 | 56 |
| | | | Teachers'(Elementary)Certifi- | | |
| *City and Guilds of London In-* | | | cates ... ... ... ... | 13 | 12 |
| *stitute*— | | | Proficiency Certificates ... | 30 | 27 |
| Cabinet-making ... ... | 2 | 2 | Instructor's Certificate ... | 1 | 1 |
| Dressmaking ... ... ... | 55 | 54 | Medallions ... ... ... | 18 | 16 |
| Millinery ... ... ... | 30 | 25 | | | |
| Woodwork ... ... ... | 17 | 17 | | 123 | 112 |
| | | | | | |
| | 104 | 98 | *London County Council*— | | |
| | | | Clerks ... ... ... | 2 | 2 |
| | | | Domestic Economy Scholar- | | |
| *Civil Service Commissioners, &c.*— | | | ships ... ... ... ... | 3 | 3 |
| Assistant Surveyors of Taxes | 2 | 2 | Evening Exhibitions in Art ... | 2 | 1 |
| Boy Copyists ... ... ... | 66 | 50 | Evening Exhibitions in Science | | |
| Customs ... ... ... | 1 | 1 | and Technology ... ... | 47 | 29 |
| Excise ... ... ... | 4 | 1 | | | |
| Naval Ordnance Writers ... | 3 | — | | 54 | 35 |
| Police— | | | | | |
| Inspectors ... ... ... | 39 | 37 | *London School Board*— | | |
| Station Sergeants ... ... | 2 | 2 | Clay Modelling ... ... | 28 | 25 |
| Sergeants ... ... ... | 106 | 101 | First Aid ... ... ... | 1,941 | 1,489 |
| Postmen ... ... ... | 84 | 60 | Home-Nursing ... ... | 1,031 | 824 |
| Prison Clerk (2nd Class) ... | 1 | 1 | | | |

For Footnotes see p. 307.

| Examining Body and Subject. (1) | Number Presented. (2) | Passes. (3) | Examining Body and Subject. (1) | Number Presented. (2) | Passes. (3) |
|---|---|---|---|---|---|
| *London School Board*—cont. | | | *National Union of Teachers* —cont. | | |
| Mechanical Drawing (Pre- | | | German (Intermediate) | 5 | 5 |
| liminary) ... ... ... | 284 | 217 | Shorthand ,, | 164 | ‡¶126 |
| Office Youths ... ... ... | 3 | 3 | Typewriting ,, | 4 | 4 |
| | 3,287 | 2,558 | Intermediate | 345 | 289 |
| *London Schools Swimming Asso-* | | | Arithmetic (Advanced) | 9 | 7 |
| *ciation*— | | | Book-keeping ,, | 66 | 44 |
| Scholars' Certificates... ... | 248 | ‡‖229 | French ... ... ,, | 20 | §‡15 |
| Teachers' Certificates ... | 33 | 28 | German ... ,, | 4 | 4 |
| Medallions ... ... | 1 | 1 | Needlework and | | |
| | | | Cutting-out ,, | 2 | 2 |
| | 282 | 258 | Shorthand ... ,, | 66 | ‡†40 |
| | | | Typewriting ... ,, | 4 | 3 |
| | | | Woodwork ... ,, | 2 | ¶†2 |
| *London University*— | | | Advanced... ... | 173 | 117 |
| Botany... ... ... ... | 1 | ‖†1 | | | |
| Matriculation ... ... ... | 1 | 1 | | | |
| ,, (English and | | | Domestic Economy ... ... | 1 | — |
| French) ... ... ... | 2 | 2 | Dressmaking ... ... ... | 25 | 23 |
| Matriculation (Latin, French, | | | Shorthand (Reporting) ... | 1 | 1 |
| and Mathematics) ... ... | 1 | 1 | | 27 | 24 |
| | 5 | 5 | | | |
| | | | Total ... ... | 1216 | 960 |
| *National Training School of* | | | | | |
| *Cookery*— | | | *National Union of Typists*— | | |
| Domestic Economy Scholar- | | | Typewriting ... ... ... | 3 | 2 |
| ship ... ... ... ... | 1 | 1 | | | |
| *National Union of Teachers*— | | | *Phonographic Society (Incor-* | | |
| Arithmetic (Elementary) | 52 | ‡°36 | *porated)*— | | |
| Book-keeping ,, | 228 | 205 | Shorthand, Elementary ... | 18 | 18 |
| Correspondence | | | ,, Theory ... ... | 42 | 28 |
| (Commercial) ,, | 11 | 6 | ,, Speed ... ... | 106 | ‡‡78 |
| French ,, | 126 | 106 | | 166 | 124 |
| Geography ,, | 22 | 16 | | | |
| German ,, | 19 | 17 | | | |
| Shorthand ,, | 191 | 124 | *Pitman, Sir Isaac, & Sons*— | | |
| Typewriting ,, | 14 | 13 | Shorthand, Elementary ... | 626 | 592 |
| Woodwork ,, | 8 | 7 | ,, Theory ... ... | 224 | 206 |
| Elementary | 671 | 530 | ,, Speed ... ... | 91 | §‡65 |
| | | | Teachers' Registration | | |
| Arithmetic (Intermediate) | 16 | 16 | Certificates ... ... | 2 | 2 |
| Book-keeping ,, | 107 | 93 | | 943 | 865 |
| Correspondence | | | | | |
| (Commercial) ,, | 2 | 2 | | | |
| French ,, | 47 | 43 | | | |

For Footnotes see p. 307.

W

| Examining Body and Subject. (1) | Number Presented. (2) | Passes. (3) | Examining Body and Subject. (1) | Number Presented. (2) | Passes. (3) |
|---|---|---|---|---|---|
| *Preceptors, College of*— Associate (Arithmetic, English and History) ... | 1 | 1 | *Secretaries, Institute of (Incorporated)*— Associate ... ... ... | 1 | 1 |
| Class I. ... ... ... | 1 | 1 | | | |
| „ II. ... ... ... | 5 | 5 | | | |
| | 7 | 7 | *Society of Arts*— Arithmetic Grade I. | 104 | 75 |
| | | | „ (Commercial) „ | 1 | 1 |
| *Railway Companies*— | | | Book-keeping „ | 373 | 193 |
| Boy Clerks ... ... ... | 5 | 5 | French „ | 143 | 81 |
| Junior Clerks ... ... ... | 7 | 7 | Geography and History (Commercial) „ | 3 | 2 |
| Clerks ... ... ... ... | 17 | 17 | German „ | 59 | 35 |
| | 29 | 29 | Handwriting and Correspondence „ | 49 | 23 |
| *Royal Arsenal*— | | | Shorthand „ | 655 | 424 |
| Trades Examinations ... | 30 | 15 | Typewriting „ | 115 | 81 |
| | | | Violin „ | 5 | 4 |
| *Royal Horticultural Society*— Horticulture ... ... ... | 1 | ‖†1 | Grade I. | 1,507 | 919 |
| | | | Arithmetic Grade II. | 24 | 23 |
| *Royal Humane Society*— | | | Book-keeping „ | 1 035 | 862 |
| Certificate ... ... ... | 1 | 1 | Economics „ | 3 | 3 |
| | | | English „ | 19 | 14 |
| | | | French „ | 125 | 105 |
| *Royal Navy*— | | | Geography „ | 10 | 9 |
| Engineer Artificer ... ... | 1 | 1 | German „ | 45 | 37 |
| | | | Italian „ | 1 | §°1 |
| | | | Portuguese „ | 2 | 1 |
| *St. Andrew's University*— | | | Précis Writing „ | 8 | 7 |
| L.L.A. (Commercial Geography and Economics) | 1 | 1 | Russian „ | 2 | §‖1 |
| L.L.A. (French) ... ... | 4 | 4 | Shorthand „ | 1,013 | §†662 |
| | 5 | 5 | Spanish „ | 23 | §¶22 |
| | | | Typewriting „ | 99 | 86 |
| *St. John Ambulance Association*— | | | Violin „ | 2 | °2 |
| Certificates ... ... ... | 47 | 45 | Grade II. | 2,411 | 1,835 |
| Medallions ... ... ... | 3 | 3 | | | |
| | 50 | 48 | French, *vivâ voce* ... ... | 134 | ¶¶109 |
| *Sanitary Institute*— | | | German „ ... ... | 19 | ¶14 |
| Inspectors ... ... ... | 2 | 1 | Harmony ... ... ... | 1 | 1 |
| | | | Music, Higher Rudiments of | 3 | 3 |
| | | | „ Rudiments of, Elementary ... ... ... | 7 | 5 |
| *Script Shorthand Society*— | | | Music, Theory of, Advanced | 7 | 7 |
| Shorthand—Speed ... ... | 28 | ‖§23 | | 171 | 139 |
| | | | Total ... | 4,089 | 2,893 |

For Footnotes see p. 307.

| Examining Body and Subject. (1) | Number Presented. (2) | Passes. (3) | Examining Body and Subject. (1) | Number Presented. (2) | Passes. (3) |
|---|---|---|---|---|---|
| *Society of Musicians (Incorporated)*— Music, Higher Rudiments of | 1 | †*1 | *Tailor's Academy*— Dressmaking ... ... ... | 14 | 12 |
| *Society of Shorthand Teachers (Incorporated)*— | | | *Tonic Sol-fa College*— Elementary ... ... ... | 94 | 93 |
| Elementary ... ... ... | 5 | 2 | Intermediate ... ... ... | 36 | 35 |
| Theory ... ... ... | 9 | 6 | School Teachers' Music ... | 149 | 133 |
| Speed ... ... ... ... | 94 | ‖ 62 | Staff Notation ... ... | 15 | 15 |
| | | | | 294 | 276 |
| | 108 | 70 | Grand Totals ... | 12,867 | 9,621 |

* One with distinction.
† Two with distinction.
‡ Three with distinction.
§ Four with distinction.
‖ Five with distinction.
¶ Six with distinction.
** Ten with distinction.
†† Thirteen with distinction.
‡‡ Fifteen with distinction.
§§ Twenty with distinction.
‖‖ Twenty-one with distinction.
¶¶ Twenty-three with distinction.
*† Thirty-one with distinction.
*‡ Thirty-nine with distinction.

*§ One with double distinction.
*‖ Two with double distinction and one with distinction.
*¶ Two with double distinction and five with distinction.
†* Three with double distinction and six with distinction.
†§ Five with double distinction and eight with distinction.
†‖ Seven with double distinction and three with distinction.
†¶ Sixteen with double distinction and fourteen with distinction.
‡* One with honours

‡† Three with honours.
‡§ Ten with honours.
‡‖ Thirteen with honours.
‡¶ Twenty-seven with honours.
§* Prize of £2.
§† Prize of £3.
§‡ Bronze medal.
§‖ Bronze medal and first prize of £3.
§¶ Bronze medal and third prize of £2.
‖* Silver medal.
‖† Gold medal.
‖§ Gold, silver, and bronze medals.

The following Table shows the results of all examinations held under Divisions II. and IV. of the Regulations of the Board of Education, South Kensington, for the Session 1902-3:—

| SUBJECTS. (1) | Total No. presented for examination. (2) | Elementary Stage (or in case of Mathematics, Stage I.). | | | Advanced Stage (or in case of Mathematics, Stage II., unless otherwise stated). | | | Total. (9) |
|---|---|---|---|---|---|---|---|---|
| | | 1st Class. (3) | 2nd Class. (4) | Fail. (5) | 1st Class. (6) | 2nd Class. (7) | Fail. (8) | |
| *Science*— | | | | | | | | |
| Biology ... ... ... ... | 10 | ... | ... | 1 | 1 | 6 | 2 | 10 |
| Botany ... ... ... ... | 68 | ... | 7 | 6 | 7 | 35 | 13 | 68 |
| Building Construction ... ... | 74 | 26 | 37 | 11 | ... | ... | ... | 74 |
| Chemistry, Inorganic, Practical... | 168 | 18 | 20 | 23 | *10 | 38 | *59 | 168 |
| " " Theoretical ... | 173 | 30 | 33 | 19 | 7 | 54 | †30 | 173 |
| Geology ... ... ... ... | 9 | ... | ... | ... | 6 | 3 | ... | 9 |
| Geometry (Practical, Plane, and Solid) | 80 | 14 | 31 | 25 | 2 | 6 | 2 | 80 |
| Heat ... ... ... ... | 5 | ... | ... | ... | 2 | 3 | ... | 5 |
| Human Physiology ... ... | 288 | 27 | 34 | 9 | ‡36 | 118 | †64 | 288 |
| Hygiene ... ... ... | 247 | 17 | 6 | ... | 28 | 161 | ‡35 | 247 |
| Machine Construction and Drawing ... | 123 | 45 | 35 | 43 | ... | ... | ... | 123 |
| Magnetism and Electricity ... | 39 | 11 | 12 | 16 | ... | ... | ... | 39 |
| Mathematics ... ... ... | 149 | 17 | 21 | 19 | ‡‡9 | ‖50 | §33 | 149 |
| " Practical ... ... | 2 | ... | 2 | ... | ... | ... | ... | 2 |
| Mechanics, Applied ... ... | 2 | ... | ... | 2 | ... | ... | ... | 2 |
| " Theoretical, Solids ... | 24 | 6 | 5 | 2 | 1 | 4 | 6 | 24 |
| " " Fluids... | 6 | 2 | 4 | ... | ... | ... | ... | 6 |
| Physiography ... ... ... | 83 | 11 | 3 | 3 | ‡20 | 37 | 9 | 83 |
| Sound, Light, and Heat ... ... | 10 | 5 | 4 | 1 | ... | ... | ... | 10 |
| Total for Science ... | 1,560 | 229 | 254 | 180 | 129 | 515 | 253 | 1,560 |

* Includes 3 Honours' Stage, Part I.  † Includes 2 Honours' Stage, Part I.  ‡ Includes 1 Honours' Stage, Part I.
‡‡ Includes 1, Stage III.  ‖ Includes 13, Stage III.  § Includes 9, Stage III.

W 2

| SUBJECTS. | Total No. presented for examination. | Elementary Stage (or in case of Mathematics, (Stage I.). | | | Advanced Stage (or in case of Mathematics, Stage II., unless otherwise stated). | | | Total. |
|---|---|---|---|---|---|---|---|---|
| | | 1st Class. | 2nd Class. | Fail. | 1st Class. | 2nd Class. | Fail. | |
| (1) | (2) | (3) | (4) | (5) | (6) | (7) | (8) | (9) |
| *Art—* | | | | | | | | |
| Freehand Drawing ... ... ... | 191 | ... | ... | ... | 40 | 64 | 87 | 191 |
| Model Drawing ... ... ... | 194 | ... | ... | ... | 24 | 81 | 89 | 194 |
| Light and Shade Drawing ... | 355 | ... | ... | ... | 43 | 151 | 161 | 355 |
| Antique, Drawing from ... ... | 4 | ... | ... | ... | ... | 4 | ... | 4 |
| „ Modelling ... ... ... | 5 | ... | ... | ... | ... | ... | 5 | 5 |
| Blackboard, Drawing with Chalk on ... | 200 | 119 | 70 | 11 | ... | ... | ... | 200 |
| Design ... ... ... ... | 35 | 7 | 10 | 3 | ... | 1 | 14 | 35 |
| „ Modelling ... ... | 5 | ... | ... | ... | ... | 2 | 3 | 5 |
| Geometrical Drawing ... ... | 61 | 19 | 24 | 18 | ... | ... | ... | 61 |
| Life, Drawing from ... ... | 2 | ... | ... | ... | ... | ... | 2 | 2 |
| „ Still, Painting from ... | 4 | ... | ... | ... | ... | 1 | 3 | 4 |
| „ Modelling Head from ... ... | 2 | ... | ... | ... | 1 | ... | 1 | 2 |
| Ornament, Painting ... ... | 17 | ... | ... | ... | 1 | 7 | 9 | 17 |
| „ Principles of... ... | 12 | ... | ... | ... | ... | 4 | 8 | 12 |
| Perspective ... ... ... | 117 | 15 | 55 | 47 | ... | ... | ... | 117 |
| Plant Form, Memory Drawing of ... | 23 | ... | ... | ... | ... | 10 | 13 | 23 |
| Total for Art ... ... | 1,227 | 160 | 159 | 79 | 109 | 325 | 395 | 1,227 |
| Total for Science and Art ... | 2,787 | 399 | 413 | 259 | 238 | 840 | 648 | 2,787 |

## IV.—PRIZES AND CERTIFICATES.

The Board have, from the beginning, awarded certificates to the students and since 1884 have also given prizes. The basis on which these have been granted has varied from time to time. On the opening of the schools in 1882 those pupils who passed the Annual Government examinations were granted certificates: in 1884, those who were regular and punctual in attendance, who showed exceptional diligence in their studies and were successful in the Government examinations, were awarded prizes in the form of books, educational instruments, etc., within the sum of £50 for the whole of the schools. It was then thought that by these means, the attendance would be improved and higher results obtained at the Government examinations. The amount of £50 was found to be inadequate, but the Committee did not ask for more money from the Board, as they believed that they could obtain voluntary contributions. However, there appears to have been no money forthcoming from that source, for soon afterwards the Board adopted a scheme without restricting its operation to a defined amount, except that the prizes were to be of a certain value and awarded under specified conditions. This scheme was, subject to some slight modifications, continued until 1893, when it was supplemented by a scheme of prizes, ranging in value from 4s. to 10s., for those who passed the examinations of the Science and Art Department, but in 1899, the teacher-students were debarred from receiving these prizes. In 1894 the certificate had to be changed owing to the alterations in the Government Code. From this date, a certificate was granted to those pupils who had received at least twelve hours' instruction in a subject, and had made diligent progress in it. The principle on which prizes had been awarded up to 1900 was changed in that year, except in the case of scholars under 16 years of age and students of all ages in certain schools in poor districts. In the case of students over 16 (other than teacher-students) prizes were awarded for passing certain examinations of outside bodies, and also those held by the responsible teachers, provided that the students attended the classes for a certain number of times. This scheme is now in operation, and the gross value of the prizes awarded in the Session 1902-3 amounted to £860.

## V.—FEES.

A uniform fee of 3d. per week, or 3s. a quarter, was charged when the schools were first opened in 1882 ; but the Board soon found it necessary to depart from uniformity. From the second session (1883-84) until the abolition of fees in 1898 the number of schools charging 2d. per week in the first few years and 2d. or 1d. per week in the latter years, was increased almost every session; the normal fee was, however, 3d. per week. The term or quarterly fee of 3s. charged in schools with a weekly fee of 3d. was reduced in the second session to 2s., and a corresponding reduction was made in the schools where a lower weekly fee was charged. On the other hand, a higher fee not exceeding 6d. per week was imposed in a few schools ; but, as a rule it did not remain long in force. An extra fee for French was also charged in five sessions, and students of Cookery were also required to pay an extra amount in one or two sessions. For a few weeks of the Session 1888-89 a fee of 1s. a week was charged to adults. The circumstances which led up to this action were that the Auditor and the Local Government Board held that the Board could not legally instruct adults; and the Evening Schools Committee, acting in the recess, and in the spirit of a resolution which the Board had already adopted, agreed to charge a fee of 1s. per week to cover the cost of instructing the students; but the Board decided, when they reassembled after the recess, that the adults should be admitted on the same terms as the juniors. Meanwhile, however, the number of men and women students had fallen off considerably and the loss was not recovered until some two or three years afterwards. The schools were freed in 1898, but before that time attempts had been made in the direction of abolishing the fees. The Board on July 9th, 1891, decided:—

That in the event of the Free Education Bill now before Parliament becoming law in all the schools of the Board in which fees are now charged, all scholars shall be admitted without requiring any fee from and after the day on which the Act shall come into force.

On July 23rd, however, the Board agreed to suspend the operation of this resolution for a period not exceeding six months in the case of the evening schools. Later on, the Committee recommended the Board to rescind the suspensory resolution of July 23rd, but eventually the original resolution that the evening schools should be free was rescinded. In the Session 1893-94, the fees in two schools were abolished, the reason assigned being that the young people of the neighbourhood could not afford to pay fees. At the end of the session a return of attendance was submitted to the Board, which showed that there was an increase in the total number of students, but a falling off in the percentage of attendance. A proposal to augment the number of free schools by opening two in each division was discussed and rejected by the Board. Some suggestions however arose out of this debate. One was that fees should be returned, in the form of deposits in the Post Office Savings Bank, to pupils who made a certain percentage of attendance. The proposal was not carried out, as the Education Department did not approve of it, and the Local Government Board held that the School Board could not legally carry out the projected scheme. The Board thereupon adopted a suggestion made by the Education Department. The Board therefore divided the session into two parts, and decided to charge no fees for the second part to those students who attended a certain number of times in the first part. This plan was in operation for one session only (1897-98), for in the next session (1898-99) the schools were freed. The effect of this change on the number of students is shown in the following Table :—

| Session. | Total No. of pupils admitted during the Session. | Average No. on the Roll during the Winter period of the Session. | Average No. present at all during the Winter period of the Session. | Percentage of av. No. present at all on the average No. on the Rolls. |
|---|---|---|---|---|
| 1897-98 (Fee) ...... ...... | 57,586 | 30,730 | 24,350 | 79·2 |
| 1898-99 (Free) ........... | 109,121 | 56,412 | 42,109 | 74·6 |

Figures for the succeeding sessions in which no fees were charged are given on page 311. They show that, contrary to the experience of the provinces, the attendance rose after the fees were abolished.

The schools remained free until 1902-03. In the preceding session (1901-02) the South Kensington Branch of the Board of Education took over the administration of the evening schools from the Whitehall Branch — a transfer of duties that arose out of the judgment in the case of Rex *v.* Cockerton—and the new authorities intimated, when approving the arrangements for that session, that it was not to be understood that they would in future recognise schools in which no fees were charged; but they would be prepared to consider arrangements providing for the remission of fees in the case of individual scholars. In view of this attitude of the Board of Education it was, of course, necessary to consider what arrangements should be made for the ensuing session. The Evening Schools Committee appointed a sub-committee to receive evidence and to submit recommendations on the whole question of fees. Their report was considered by the Committee and placed before the Board, who came to the conclusion that the present system of free evening schools, which had worked so well, should not be interfered with, but if fees were to be re-imposed—

(i.) No scholars under 18 years of age should be charged a fee.

(ii.) That pupils attending certain schools in poor districts should pay no fees irrespective of age.

(iii.) That in the remaining schools a sessional fee should be charged to persons over 18 years of age as follows:—

    (a) Ordinary schools, 1s.

    (b) Commercial schools, 2s. 6d.

    (c) Science and Art schools, 5s.

The Board of Education demurred to the free education of scholars under 18 years of age, but they eventually sanctioned the scheme, with the substitution of 16 for 18. Two or three modifications have been subsequently approved. Soldiers in uniform are admitted free to all schools: in Commercial and Science and Art schools students pay 5s. a session for Science and Art subjects taught under Divisions II. and IV. of the Regulations of the Board of Education, and 2s. 6d. a session for the other subjects: and the schools for the Deaf are free. The scheme, with these modifications, is in force at the present time: the number of free schools is 76, and fees are charged in 298. The effect of the change is shown in the following table:—

TABLE SHOWING EFFECT PRODUCED BY THE CHARGING FEES.

| Session. | No. of Pupils admitted during the Session. | | | *Average No. on the Rolls. (Winter Terms). | | *Average No. Present at all. (Winter Terms). | | Percentage of Av. No. Present at all on the Av. No. on the Rolls. | |
|---|---|---|---|---|---|---|---|---|---|
| | Under 16 (Free). | Over 16 (Free Schools). | Over 16 (Fee Schools). | Free Schools. | Fee Schools but pupils under 16 free. | Free Schools. | Fee Schools but pupils under 16 free. | Free Schools. | Fee Schools but pupils under 16 free |
| (1) | (2) | (3) | (4) | (5) | (6) | (7) | (8) | (9) | (10) |
| 1902-1903 ... (Fee) | †56,041 | 11,784 | 58,928 | 9,878 | 66,304 | 7,250 | 50,550 | 73·4 | 76·2 |
| 1901-1902 ... (Free) | 41,516 | 11,350 | 80,325 | 9,151 | 64,645 | 6,765 | 48,473 | 73·9 | 75·0 |
| Increase ... | 14,525 | 434 | ... | 727 | 1,659 | 485 | 2,077 | ... | 1·2 |
| Decrease... | ... | ... | 21,397 | ... | ... | ... | ... | ·5 | ... |

* It is not possible to give these figures according to the ages of the Pupils, but the Committee obtained a return from the Schools in the week ended May 9th, 1903, which showed the following result:—

| | Free Pupils. | Paying Pupils |
|---|---|---|
| No. admitted in the period from September 22nd, 1902, to November 22nd, 1902 | 52,044 ... | 46,931 |
| No. present at all in the week ended May 9th, 1903 ... ... ... ... | 21,901 ... | 20,937 |
| Percentage of the No. present at all on the number admitted ... ... ... | 42·1 ... | 4·48 |

† Of this Number 47,170 were admitted to the Fee Schools and 8,871 to the Free Schools.

## VI.—TEACHING STAFF.

The Teachers who are employed in the evening schools are now appointed each session, and have been, for the most part, chosen from the assistant teachers of the day schools; indeed, preference has been given to those who are engaged in the buildings in or near to which the evening school is held; the object being to induce ex-day scholars to return to their teachers. Head teachers of day schools have never been disqualified from service in the evening schools : some have been appointed as responsible teachers, but the number has been diminishing of late years.

The day school staff has supplied most of the teachers ; but others have been engaged to teach such subjects as Shorthand, Bookkeeping, Typewriting, Gymnastics, First Aid, Home-Nursing and Health.

The salaries of the teachers have increased considerably. In 1882, when the schools were first opened, the responsible teachers were paid an inclusive sum of 4s. per evening of two hours : now the salary works out from about 8s. 6d. to 16s. per evening *plus* extra remuneration based on the average attendance. The more highly paid responsible teachers—*i.e.* responsible teachers of the Special schools, work for about three hours per evening. The assistants received 2s. 6d. per evening in 1882 : now the salaries of assistant teachers and instructors vary from 4s.. to 10s. 6d. per evening, and doctors, who have only been employed during the last three or four years, receive £1 1s. for an evening of about two hours. The principle has been to pay teachers a fixed sum, and to add to it an amount depending chiefly upon the attendance in the schools or classes. Instructors, as distinguished from assistants, have been paid a fixed sum, which has been determined mainly by the subject which they teach.

.The amount of staff allowed in a school depends upon its size. A school which reaches an average attendance of 65 is allowed three assistants ; one of 140 has six assistants. This amount of staff works out at the rate of 21·7 students on an average for each assistant teacher in the case of a school of 65, and 23·3 in the case of a school of 140 ; but the responsible teacher does not count on the staff, and teachers of certain subjects—those in which only a comparatively small number of students can be taught at one time—are counted as half teachers.

If the students fell away in their attendance the staff was reduced. Thus a school with three assistants lost an assistant when the numbers fell below 45 for two weeks, and one with six assistants was reduced by one assistant when the numbers fell below 120 ; but reductions were deferred in all cases where the circumstances required it. The teacher whose services could best be spared received notice to leave : for a while the teacher last appointed had to leave, but as this plan sometimes involved the leaving of a teacher who could least be spared, the system which had previously obtained was reverted to.

## VII.—LOCAL MANAGERS.

Some of the duties of the management of the schools have been entrusted to separate bodies of Local Managers. Originally there was only one body of Managers for each division, except in the Greenwich and Tower Hamlets divisions, where the day school Managers also acted for the evening schools.

The divisional system was abandoned in 1885 ; bodies with smaller areas were formed, and steps were taken to secure the services of day school Managers, local employers of labour, and working men and women. The latter, it was believed, would be willing

**Chelsea.**
1. Ashburnham
2. Cook's Ground
3. Marlborough Road
4. Park Walk

**Fulham.**
5. Elberter Road
6. Fulham Palace Road
7. Halford Road
8. Langford Road
9. Lillie Road
10. Munster Road
11. Peterborough Road
12. William Street

**Hammersmith.**
14. Avonmore (Gardens)
15. Brackenbury Road
16. Flora Gardens
17. Kenmont Gardens
18. Lindsey Road
19. Wendell Road

**Hampstead.**
21. Heathbrook Street
22. Netherwood Street

**Kensington.**
23. Bisson Street
24. Fox Road
25. Silver Street

**Paddington.**
28. Amberley Road
29. Gaythorne Road
30. Harrow Road
31. Kilburn Lane

**St. Helens.**
33. Marett Street
34. Barrow Hill Road
35. Chapel Street
36. St. Mary's by Day Square

**St. Pancras.**
37. Stephen Street
38. Stanley Road
39. Camden Street
40. Gordon Road
41. Grove College Street
42. Maresfield Road
43. Medburn Street
44. Kings Street
45. Winchester Street

**Westminster.**
47. Brownlow, Manchester Street
48. Buckingham Gate
49. Charing Cross Road
50. Millbank
51. Palace Street
52. St. Martin's Row.
53. Soho Girls' Club.

George Philip & Son, Ltd.

EVENING CONT

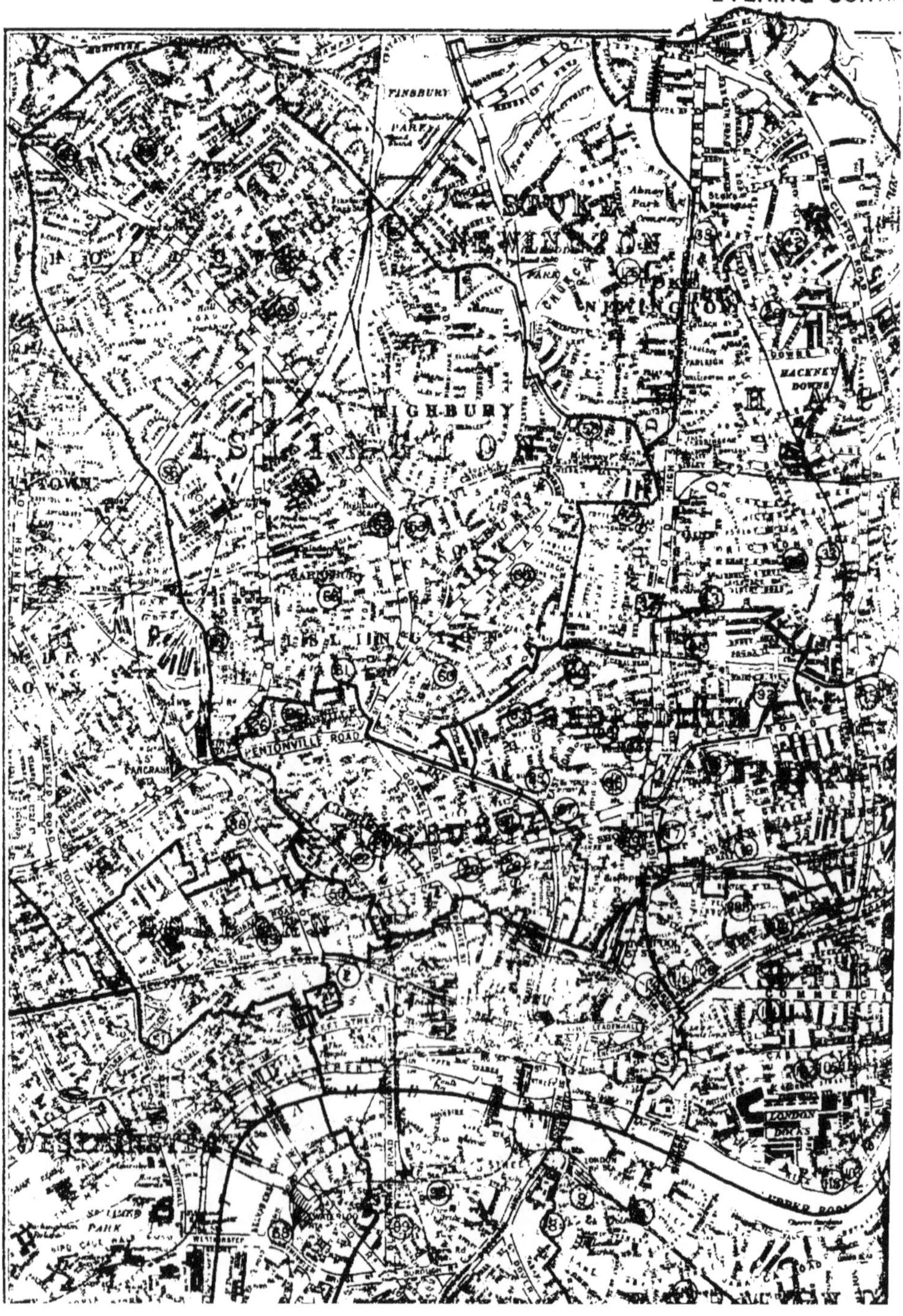

City of London.
1. Gravel Lane.
2. Cripplegate Place.
3. Swan Street.
Bermondsey.
4. Abbots Street.
5. Fair Street.
6. Holy Trinity, Rotherhithe.
7. Keetons Road.
8. Lucey Street.
9. Major Street.
10. Neckinger Road.
Bethnal Green.
11. Chisenhale Road.
12. Columbia Road.
13. Globe Terrace.
14. Mansford Street.
15. Rowden Street.
16. Portman Place.
17. Rochelle Street.
18. Summerford Street.
19. Weal Close.
Finsbury.
20. Baltic Street.
21. Bath Street.
22. Bunhill Green Lane.
23. Chequer Street.
24. Hugh Myddelton.
25. Risinghill Street.
26. Winchester Street.
Hackney.
27. Bailey's Lane.
28. Baxton Road.
29. Benthal Road.
30. Berger Road.
31. Cassland Road.
32. College Lane.
33. Elsmere Road.
34. Enfield Road.
35. Gainsborough Road.
36. Gayhurst Road.
37. Glyn Road.
38. High Street, Stoke Newington.
39. Lauriston Road.
40. Millfields Road.
41. Morning Lane.
42. Northwold Road.
43. Queen's Road.
44. Rushmore Road.
45. Sidney Road.
46. Sigdon Road.
47. Tottenham Road.
48. Windsor Road.
Holborn.
49. Princeton Street.
50. St. Peter's, Lt. Saffron Hill.
51. Tower Street.

Islington.
52. Blackstock Road.
53. Canonbury Road.
54. Dancombe Road.
55. Ecclesbourne Road.
56. Hungerford Road.
57. Monsell Street.
58. Newington Green.
59. Pakeman Street.
60. Queen's Head Street.
61. Richard Street.
62. Station Road.
63. Thornhill Road.
64. Upper Hornsey Road.
65. Westbourne Road.
66. Whittington.
67. York Road.
Lambeth.
68. Addington Street.
Poplar.
69. Bow Creek.
70. Bromley Hall Road.
71. Byron and Bright Streets.
72. Culloden Street.
73. Glengall Road.
74. Knapp Road.
75. Malmesbury Road.
76. Millwall.
77. Monteith Road.
78. Oban Street.
79. Old Palace.
80. Rogan Road.
81. St. Leonard's Road.
82. St. Saviour's, Poplar.
83. Stroud Road.
84. Upper North Street.
85. Woolmore Street.
St. Pancras.
86. Prospect Terrace.
Shoreditch.
87. Calvert Street.
88. Charham Gardens.
89. Curtain Road.
90. Gopsall Street.
91. Haggerston Road.
92. Maidstone Street.
93. Napier Street.
94. Redvers Street.
95. St. John's Road.
96. St. Monica's.
Southwark.
97. Marlborough Street.
98. Orange Street.
99. Pocock Street.
Stepney.
100. Ben Jonson.
101. Berner Street.
102. Betts Street.
103. Brewhouse Lane.
104. Broad Street.
105. Cable Street.
106. Commercial Street.
107. Dalgleish Street.
108. Deal Street.
109. Dempsey Street.
110. Farrance Street.
111. Gill Street.
112. Hamlet of Ratcliff.
113. Highway.
114. Limehouse Roman Catholic.
115. Old Castle Street.
116. Old Montagu Street.
117. Rutland Street.
118. St. Patrick's, Wapping.
119. St. Paul's Road.
120. Settles Street.
121. Single Street.
122. Smith Street.
123. Thomas Street.
124. Trafalgar Square.
Stoke Newington.
125. Oldfield Road.
126. Princess May Road.

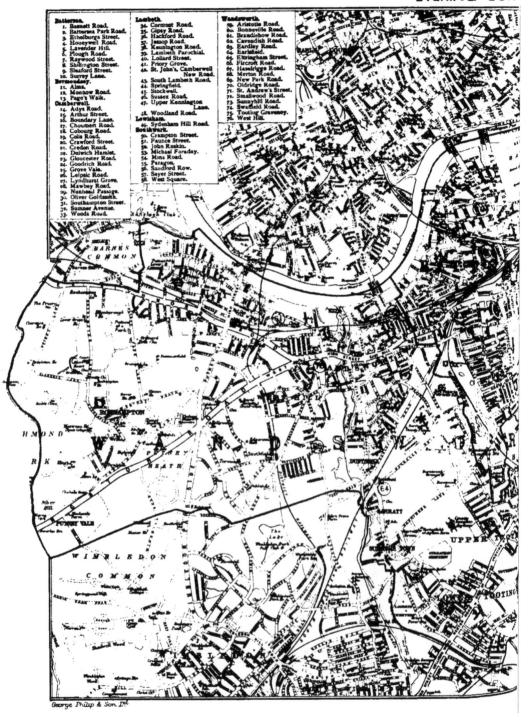

**Battersea.**
1. Basnett Road.
2. Battersea Park Road.
3. Ethelburga Street.
4. Honeywell Road.
5. Lavender Hill.
6. Plough Road.
7. Raywood Street.
8. Shillington Street.
9. Sleaford Street.
10. Surrey Lane.

**Bermondsey.**
11. Alma.
12. Monnow Road.
13. Page's Walk.

**Camberwell.**
14. Adys Road.
15. Arthur Street.
16. Boundary Lane.
17. Choumert Road.
18. Cobourg Road.
19. Colls Road.
20. Crawford Street.
21. Credon Road.
22. Dulwich Hamlet.
23. Gloucester Road.
24. Goodrich Road.
25. Grove Vale.
26. Leipsic Road.
27. Lyndhurst Grove.
28. Mawbey Road.
29. Nunhead Passage.
30. Oliver Goldsmith.
31. Southampton Street.
32. Sumner Avenue.
33. Woods Road.

**Lambeth.**
34. Cormont Road.
35. Gipsy Road.
36. Hackford Road.
37. Jessop Road.
38. Kennington Road.
39. Lambeth Parochial.
40. Lollard Street.
41. Priory Grove.
42. St. John's, Camberwell New Road.
43. South Lambeth Road.
44. Springfield.
45. Stockwell.
46. Sussex Road.
47. Upper Kennington Lane.
48. Woodland Road.

**Lewisham.**
49. Sydenham Hill Road.

**Southwark.**
50. Crampton Street.
51. Faunce Street.
52. John Ruskin.
53. Michael Faraday.
54. Mina Road.
55. Paragon.
56. Sandford Row.
57. Sayer Street.
58. West Square.

**Wandsworth.**
59. Aristotle Road.
60. Bonneville Road.
61. Brandlehow Road.
62. Cavendish Road.
63. Eardley Road.
64. Earlsfield.
65. Eltringham Street.
66. Fircroft Road.
67. Haselrigge Road.
68. Merton Road.
69. New Park Road.
70. Oldridge Road.
71. St. Andrew's Street.
72. Smallwood Road.
73. Sunnyhill Road.
74. Swaffield Road.
75. Tooting Graveney.
76. West Hill.

George Philip & Son Ld.

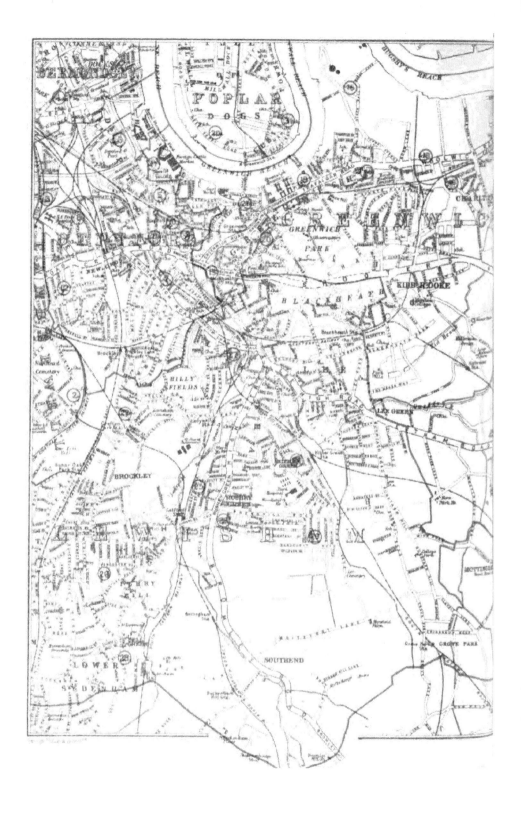

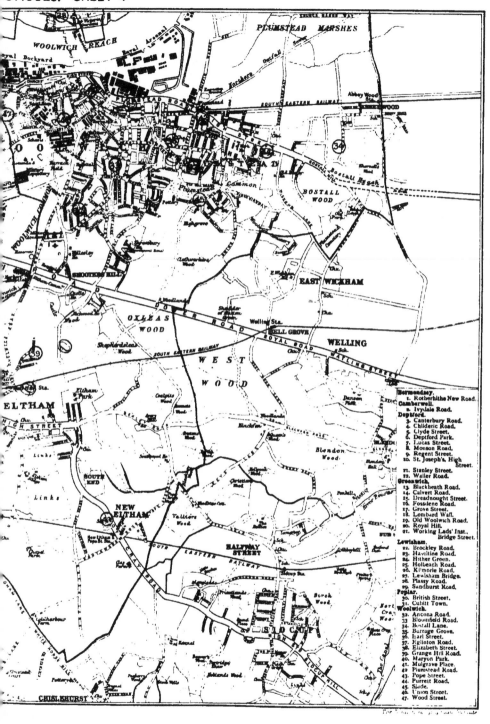

to serve, as the representatives of the trade societies had assured the Board of the interest felt by working men and women in the evening school movement. In the Greenwich Division, but not in the Tower Hamlets, the day school Managers continued to act for the evening schools, and later on similar arrangements were made in the case of schools in other divisions.

The duties of the Managers are, to visit the schools, to see that the regulations of the Board and Government are carried out, to nominate teachers, to test the registers, and, generally, to promote the success of the schools.

At the first, one of the Managers usually acted as Honorary Correspondent; later on these duties were taken over by the Organisers and Correspondents, and finally in 1895, the work was transferred to the Official Correspondents of the day schools.

Whilst the foregoing statement is applicable to most of the schools, deviations from the general rule have been made since the establishment of the Commercial and Science and Art schools in 1898. Some of these schools have no Local Managers, others have Managers who have not the power to nominate teachers, and two or three have visiting Managers only.

The list of Managers is revised annually, and those who have not made a sufficient number of visits to the schools or attendances at the Managers' meetings, are struck off the list, unless the Divisional Members recommend their retention.

## GENERAL PURPOSES.

ON December 4th, 1891, the Board, with a view of condensing its business, redistributed its work so as to compress its scattered branches, and reduced its then eleven Standing Committees to six. Among other decisions, one resolution connected therewith was as follows:—"That there shall be a Standing Committee for general purposes, to be called the General Purposes Committee, to conduct the legal work, the work in connection with Minuting and Educational Endowments, the work of the Salaries Committee, and office control." Prior to the passing of the above resolution, these matters had been controlled by three separate Committees.

On July 21st, the Board added the duty of considering and reporting to the Board upon all proposals for any variation, either in the number or the grade of the Office Staff of any department of the Board, or in the scales of salary.

The new Committee was therefore required to take up the duties enumerated as follows:—

 I. Minuting and Preparation of Business Papers and Minutes of the Board: Index for the latter: Revision of the Standing Orders (Rules and Regulations).

 II. Educational Endowments—Inquiries into Trusts: Analysis of Schemes of the Charity Commissioners, and preparation of histories of the Trusts to which the Schemes refer: suggestions for the variation and appropriation of the funds of such Trusts.

 III. Legal Work—Conduct of litigation: directing the Board's Solicitor: reporting results to the Board.

 IV. Salaries (grading of the staff; and office control).

 V. General matters not connected with the duties specified for any other Standing Committee, which have developed from time to time—such as (a) Underfed Children, (b) Medical department, (c) Licensing matters, voting, &c., (d) Introduction of Manual Training.

### I.—MINUTING.

The Minutes of the Proceedings of the Board form a centre round which all the Standing Committees work. The Standing Committees receive instructions from the Board to consider subjects which relate to the special work with which they are appointed to deal. These Committees in turn furnish the required information on the subjects referred to them, giving the conclusions at which they have arrived and the reasons therefor, and conclude by making such recommendations as they deem fit; the Chairman of the Committee moving at the Board the adoption of such recommendations for acceptance by the Board. These Minutes of Proceedings also record communications from Government and outside bodies and persons, on which the Board deliberate, and in most cases, refer to the various Committees to be discussed and reported upon. They also record the decisions of the Board, and the instructions given,

Thus they form a centre from which instructions radiate to the several Committees, and on which the deliberations of the Committees, with their recommendations, are focussed, and the Board's approval, rejection, or modification of such recommendations. All matters to be considered by the Board are recorded on the Business Papers, being collected from the various Standing Committees, and from outside sources. The Business Papers[1] from the first meeting of the Board, meetings of the Board in Committee, &c., are recorded in 44 volumes. The Minutes of the Proceedings which record all the deliberations of the Board, printed in six annual volumes up to 1878, and in half-yearly volumes subsequently, form 60 foolscap volumes containing 78,578 pages of Minutes, and 13,012 pages of Index; a grand total of 91,590 pages.

1. *Index to Board Minutes.*—An important feature of the Minutes is the index to each half-yearly volume. This index extends on an average to about 150 pages, but its magnitude does not in any way destroy its lucidity. In the case of debates there is not merely given an indication of the subject under discussion, but each phase of the subject, each amendment or modification, and the ultimate result of the proposal, is clearly and concisely shown. This detailing of debates is very useful to those acquainted with the Board's work, and one Chairman of the Board was wont to remark that he could get all the information he required from the index without going through the more lengthy process of reading the actual Minutes. For the convenience of reference certain collective headings are employed, such as " Correspondence," " Motions, Amendments, &c.," " Subjects of Instruction." Every item contained in the Minutes from the appointment of a pupil teacher or a teacher " on Supply " to the most important debate on the religious question or the Education Bill is to be found in the index; yet, owing to the manner in which all these items are condensed, and to the use of distinctive types of print, not a trace of overcrowding or elaboration presents itself, but on the other hand research is greatly facilitated.

The preparation of this index involved a very considerable amount of work; but as each weekly number of the Minutes appeared its contents were dissected by the indexers, and the index, as a whole, made its appearance shortly after the completion of the half-yearly volume of Minutes. As many as 10,000 slips of manuscript were sometimes sent to the printers for the compilation of one volume of index.

---

[1] There were two Business Papers issued in advance of each ordinary meeting—one on the Saturday preceding the meeting of the Board, the other on the Tuesday preceding such meeting (the Board meetings were held on Thursday). The Preliminary Business Paper of the meeting recorded the recommendations of the various Standing Committees respecting the subjects which were to be reported upon, correspondence from all sources—Government and otherwise—and all matters which require four a days' notice, such as matters requiring the consent of the Education Department, and all matters which involved new expense, to comply with the requirements of the Elementary Education Act, 1873, Schedule 3 (G); together with notices of motion received from Members. The detailed Paper issued on the Tuesday preceding the meeting of the Board contained a repetition of the matters appearing on the Preliminary Paper; and gave complete reports of the Special Committees with full information respecting the subjects and the reasons for their findings, and reasons given for making the recommendations which had been set forth in the Preliminary Paper, together with such notices of motion and correspondence as might have been received since the issue of the Preliminary Business Paper.

In addition to the printed index, a manuscript index, in book form, was also prepared, so as to furnish a ready means of reference to Resolutions passed since the issue of the last printed volume, and pending the publication of the one in course of preparation. This index is kept for current use in the Department.

2. *References.*—It was one of the duties of the Minuting section to peruse carefully the Board business paper, and to inform the various Committees concerned of the decisions of the Board. When any modification took place at the Board of any portion of a Committee's report, or an instruction was implied in any independent motion carried by a Member, it again devolved upon the Minuting section to inform the Committee concerned of such modification or instruction.

## II.—EDUCATIONAL ENDOWMENTS.

On May 10th, 1871, the Board resolved that measures should be taken to ascertain whether any, or if so, what, Charitable or other Endowments in the London School district ought to be applied, wholly or in part, to the augmentation of the School Fund. On May 24th of the same year, it was decided to appoint a Committee for ascertaining what was to be known concerning Endowments and Bequests available for Education. Various draft schemes in connection with Endowments were consequently reported upon, and on February 3rd, 1875, the Board resolved to appoint a select Committee. This Committee was constituted on February 10th of that year, and instructed " to consider and report whether, and in what degree, Endowments available for the purposes of education within the area of the jurisdiction of the Board can properly be rendered instrumental in providing for the higher education of scholars in Elementary schools, and especially for the development of technical instruction ; and what measures can be taken by the Board to bring under the consideration of the governing bodies of Endowed Schools and of the Charity Commissioners the claims of the Metropolitan Elementary Schools in this respect." [1] The short title of which Committee was the " Educational Endowments Committee."

Various documents were prepared by this Committee from Parliamentary and other official returns, from incidental information in books, from inquiries from the Charity Commissioners, and from private sources, and these documents were placed in the library of the Board. There was no comprehensive or exhaustive document published from which information could be drawn respecting the conditions of the educational foundations of the Metropolis, and endowed institutions did not manifest any willingness to answer inquiries made by the officer who was appointed to elicit information.

1. *City Parochial Charities.*—The Educational Endowments Committee proceeded to investigate the charities which were under the care of the rectors and vestries of the City parishes. A letter was addressed to the clerks of the 106 City parishes which possessed charities, each letter enclosing schedules containing such accounts of the several charities held by each City parish as were available to the Board. There was no published document containing even a list of the names of the donors,

---

[1] Board Minutes, Vol. V., p. 230.

so that the information contained in the schedules had to be obtained from various private sources and from scattered references in books treating of other subjects. The charities were found to be left for the benefit of particular parishes, and the information was available only to the parish authorities: indeed, it was found that the clerks knew practically nothing of the charity affairs of other parishes than their own. The letters addressed to the Clerks of the various parishes contained courteous requests for further information as to the particular charities, and inquiries as to the willingness of the trustees to make a useful disposition of the same. Of the 106 City parishes to which these letters were sent on behalf of the School Board for London, only 35 replied: 71 City parishes took no notice whatever of them. Of the 35 parishes which acknowledged the receipt of the letter and schedules, no less than 32 declined to comply with the request made. Only three parishes out of the 106 furnished the Committee with any additional information, and in one of these cases the information was only partially complete. The most immediate channels of information being closed to the School Board, the Committee availed themselves of two other sources of information—first, published documents making meagre reference to the endowments; and, secondly, the annual statements of income and expenditure which the trustees are bound by law to furnish to the Charity Commissioners and the Commissioners courteously allowed the Board's officer to investigate. The inquiry lasted through a period of about three years, and resulted in the discovery that the City parishes possessed 1,330 trusts, the total income of which was over £104,000 per annum, and their minimum capital value £2,339,204. Many of these charities had become obsolete: others were appropriated for Church purposes, such as maintenance of churches, payment of church officials, and whatever is considered part of church management, to the amount of £36,000 yearly: for endowments for clergymen and lecturers to deliver special sermons, &c., as memorials on the anniversary of the founder's death; obits; masses for souls; commemoration of the defeat of the Spanish Armada; expression of thankfulness for the failure of the Gunpowder Plot; the reading of prayers, to the amount of over £6,000 per annum: for educational purposes, over £18,000: apprenticeship, over £2,000: in payment towards poor rates, £10,000: for distribution in bread, coals, money, clothing, &c., over £31,000, giving a total of £104,102 a year.

The facts thus elicited were recorded in the newspapers, and steps were then taken to appoint a Royal Commission to conduct a further inquiry, armed with powers of summoning witnesses, and the administration of oaths. The report of the School Board was, however, published prior to that of the Royal Commission, and the findings of the Royal Commission appeared to justify the investigation conducted by the School Board. The outcome of this was the passing of the City Parochial Charities Act, 1883, and the redistribution of the funds arising from the endowments in the manner provided by the Act, for applying "general charity property" (*i.e* all with the exception of ecclesiastical charity property) to (a) the promotion of the education of the poorer inhabitants of the Metropolis by means of exhibitions, technical instruction, secondary education, art education, evening lectures, or otherwise, at the discretion of Commissioners: (*b*) the establishment and maintenance of libraries, museums, art collections, &c., so as to be useful to the poorer inhabitants: (*c*) the preservation of open spaces and recreation grounds or drill grounds: (*d*) the promotion of provident institutions and of institutes for working men and women of the poorer classes: (*e*) the establishment of convalescent hospitals: (*f*) and generally the improvement of the physical, social and moral condition of the poorer inhabitants of the Metropolis.

2. *City Companies' Charities.*—Arising out of the reference of the Board already mentioned, the Committee made a similar investigation into the Trusts placed in the care of the City Companies for administration, but not forming part of the Companies' funds. There have been 109 Companies founded, some of which have decayed, leaving only 89 in existence at the present time. Of this number, 78 are in possession of trusts, the income from which was shown to be about £186,000 per annum. This applies only to charities which have been left to be administered as Trusts by the Companies. The Report of the Committee, together with a concise history of these charities constituting a Volume with Appendices of about 340 pages, was published by the Board in February, 1881. When this Report was nearly completed, in July, 1880, a Royal Commission was appointed to inquire not only into the charities of the City Companies, but also into the affairs of the Companies themselves. That Commission reported in 1884, and, in concluding the summary of the results of their inquiry, they thanked the School Board for their valuable report on the subject of the charities administered by the Companies. They stated that it was exceedingly elaborate, and expressed pleasure in testifying to its excellence and in acknowledging the assistance they had derived from it.

3. *Schedule of Endowed Schools and Educational Endowments.*— In March, 1886, the Board instructed the Educational Endowments Committee to prepare a Return of the number of Elementary school places in the Endowed schools of the Metropolis, together with the fees charged ; also of the Endowed schools in the Metropolis which have ceased to provide elementary education under schemes sanctioned by the Endowed schools and the Charity Commissioners since 1869 ; and of Endowed schools in the Metropolis, in regard to which schemes have been proposed for reducing the number of places for Elementary Education. Great difficulty was experienced in obtaining the required information. The Charity Commissioners were applied to for special information regarding schemes either in operation or likely to be put into operation, but they were unable to offer any assistance, as their office did not afford the materials for supplying with any approach to exactness the information desired with regard to the past reduction of Elementary school places. The result of the investigation showed that a large number of school places existed which were distinctly used for elementary purposes ; but many Endowments, originally intended for the education of the children of the poor, were largely used by others. Finally a Return was published by the Board of 174 trusts, each having an income of over £100 a year.

4. *Educational Charities in the School Board Divisions of Greenwich, East Lambeth, West Lambeth.*—The Educational Endowments Committee having decided that it was desirable to collect and classify information as to the existing funds available for educational purposes within the Metropolitan area, a Return of such funds was prepared so far as regards the School Board Division of Greenwich, and was presented to the Board on May 21st, 1885.

On March 4th, 1886, a Return, relating to the Educational Charities in the East Lambeth Division was presented to the Board.

On February 17th, 1887, a Return, relating to the Educational Charities in the West Lambeth Division was presented to the Board.

A question having arisen as to the legality of expending money in printing the returns referred to, the Committee in these circumstances did not proceed with the records of remaining Divisions.

5. *Schemes Promoted by the Endowed Schools Commissioners and the Charity Commissioners.*—From time to time draft schemes have been forwarded to the Board, at first by the Endowed Schools Commissioners, and afterwards by the Charity Commissioners for the re-organisation of Educational Trusts in the Metropolis, and the Board's criticisms were invited. The Board usually referred these schemes to the Committee for consideration. Such schemes, when published by either the Commissioners or by the Education Department, have been examined from time to time, and the recommendations of the Board in many instances have resulted in securing the extension of the area of competition for Exhibitions and Scholarships to children in Public Elementary schools, and in obtaining other advantages. Several of the larger Educational Trusts have been proved to be very complicated in character, and have called for a great amount of research in respect of their history and financial details. Some very extensive records, with analytical statements, both as to the histories of the trusts and the provisions of the schemes, have been issued from time to time respecting Christ's Hospital, Dulwich College, &c. In addition to the specific trusts already mentioned, the Committee have considered and reported upon 316 schemes relating to 156 trusts.

## III.—LEGAL WORK.

1. *Disputes with Contractors.*—During the early years of the General Purposes Committee's existence, several claims of contractors for repairs executed under a schedule of prices were contested, and the Board were invariably successful in getting such claims reduced. The Committee have also conducted from time to time, with varying success, a considerable number of actions for breach of contract by various contractors.

2. *Prosecutions for Theft and Damage to School Buildings.* — The Committee have continually dealt with cases of theft and wilful damage to school buildings, and in nearly all instances, have been successful in obtaining convictions. The Board considered that it was most important to prosecute the offenders wherever possible, as they were convinced that this action had a deterrent effect on others, especially in rough

neighbourhoods, where the schoolkeeper would otherwise have had great difficulty in preventing these occurrences.

3. *Compensation for Injuries to Children.*—These cases have been very numerous, and have ranged from requests for payment of small amounts to cover doctors' fees to substantial claims for compensation. The Committee adopted a rule which permitted the payment of doctors' fees for the first attendance in simple accident cases, provided the child was taken to the doctor by a teacher. In cases of prolonged attendance by the doctor, or where claims were made for compensation, the Committee, when of opinion that the Board were clearly liable, endeavoured to settle amicably with the claimant by payment of a small sum to cover the doctors' charges or incidental expenses. Claims which the Committee considered were unjust or unreasonable, and could not be sustained in law, were usually contested. In many instances the Board's contentions were upheld by the Courts; but very often, especially when the cases were tried by jury, the tendency has been to sympathise with the children injured and their parents, rather than to consider the case as an abstract point of law. This tendency has probably been accentuated by the fact that the expense would fall on a public body, and not on a private individual.

4. *Assaults on Teachers and other Officers.*—The General Purposes Committee have also investigated cases in which their teachers or other officers had been subjected to assault or abuse from the parents of children; and the practice of the Committee has been either to instruct the Board's solicitor to assist the teacher or officer in a prosecution, or to allow legal expenses up to £3 3s. in the event of a conviction being obtained. These assault cases have not lately been so numerous as formerly, probably owing to the fact that parents are aware that the Board has always endeavoured to protect their *employés* from assaults, and to the fact that the people are more alive to the benefits that the children derive from the schools, and do not encourage the children to magnify the small inconveniences that occur in school life.

5. *Legality of Board's Expenditure on Teaching of Science and Art in Elementary Schools and in connection with the Pupil Teacher Centre System.*—During the last two or three years the Board have been engaged in two actions which call for special mention, and have arisen out of decisions of the Auditor to disallow and surcharge certain items, in one case, in the Board's expenditure in connection with the teaching of Science and Art subjects in Elementary schools.

The Auditor's contention, with reference to the teaching of Science and Art, was that the Elementary Education Acts did not empower School Boards to spend money on these subjects. The Board contended that the Education Department had always encouraged this kind of expenditure, and had, moreover, made provision in their Codes for the teaching of the subjects in question. To ascertain whether the Board's contention was right, a test case was commenced in the Queen's Bench Division of the High Court. The Court upheld the decision of the Auditor. It declared this teaching to be secondary education and outside the scope of the Elementary Education Acts, and gave judgment accordingly.[1] The Board appealed against this decision,

---

[1] Reg. v. Cockerton, L.R. [1901] 1 Q.B., p. 322.

but the Court of Appeal concurred in the judgment of the Court below, and further declared that it was also illegal to conduct Evening Continuation schools for persons who were not children at the expense of the School Fund.[1] Notice of appeal to the House of Lords against that decision has been lodged. The Government recognised the difficult and serious position in which School Boards were placed by these decisions, and a short Act was passed to enable School Boards, with the consent of the Council of the County or Borough, to continue, for a period of one year, to maintain Training Schools and Classes which they had maintained at any time during the twelve months preceding July 31st, 1901, to the maintenance of which the school fund was not lawfully applicable.[2]

The other case referred to arose out of the Auditor's decision, on the representation of certain ratepayers, to disallow and surcharge several items of expenditure in connection with the building of a pupil teachers' centre at Hilldrop-road, Islington. The ratepayers contended that the Board were acting illegally in building and carrying on such centres out of rates raised for Elementary school purposes, on the ground that the Elementary Education Acts only permitted the instruction of pupil teachers at the schools in which they were employed.

As the Board continued the centres, and also proceeded with the erection of the Hilldrop-road centre, these ratepayers brought an action to restrain the Board from continuing the building. This action was decided against the Board, and the judgment declared that it was illegal for the Board to make any more payments in connection with the contract for building the Hilldrop-road centre, or to continue the Pupil Teacher centre system.[3] Under the enabling Act before mentioned it became necessary for the Board to obtain the permission of the London County Council to continue the system in existing schools, and this permission was immediately granted.

This decision of the Court led to very untoward results. The contractor for the erection of the Pupil Teachers' centre at Hilldrop-road, brought an action against the Board for damages for breach of contract; and the freeholder of the site—the Board having acquired only a leasehold interest—sued the Board for recovery of possession of the property, on the ground of the breach by the Board of the covenants of the lease.

The freeholder was successful in his action, but the Board have given notice of appeal against the decision. The action of the contractor has not yet been heard.

### IV.—OFFICE STAFF.

1. *Salaries (Grading of the Staff, &c., and Office Control).*—One branch of the Committee's work consisted in the supervision of the office staff and of office control. Before this work was allotted to the General Purposes Committee it was performed by the Salaries Committee, which consisted of the Chairmen and Vice-Chairmen of

---

[1] Rex. *v.* Cockerton, L.R. [1901], 1 Q.B., p. 726.
[2] 1 Edw. VII., c. 11. For the extensions of the operation of this Act see *ante*, p. 276.
[3] Dyer *v.* the School Board for London, L.R. [1902], 2 Ch., p. 768.

x

the Standing Committees; and, prior to that, the various Committees each considered their own staff and office requirements. The term "office staff" included all officers immediately under the direction of any Committee of the Board.

The plan of referring all staff questions to one Committee worked well, and led to a more impartial and uniform method of treatment than could have resulted from each Committee dealing with its staff separately.

*Scales of Salaries.*—During the Committee's existence the scales of salaries for the clerical staff were twice revised, and are at present as follow:—

|  | Minimum. | Annual Increase. | Maximum. |
|---|---|---|---|
| Third Class Clerks ... | £70 0 0 | £7 10 0 | £140 0 0 |
| Second Class Clerks ... | 140 0 0 | 7 10 0 | 180 0 0 |
| First Class Clerks ... | 180 0 0 | 10 0 0 | 250 0 0 |

with higher posts of Heads of Rooms (£300), Head Assistant Clerks (£350 and £400).

2. *Additions to the Staff.*—Additions were made to the staff by the appointment of Third Class Clerks, and vacancies arising in the higher ranks were filled by competition from the grade below. Prior to the year 1898, Third Class Clerks were selected from applicants in reply to advertisements issued in the newspapers. Since that date candidates for these clerkships have been required to pass a qualifying examination. The examination in two parts, comprised:—OBLIGATORY SUBJECTS—Arithmetic, English Grammar and Composition, English History, Geography, Shorthand, and Orthography. OPTIONAL SUBJECTS—Algebra, Euclid, Chemistry, Physics, Latin, French, German; Geometrical, Perspective, Architectural and Freehand Drawing, Book-keeping, and Typewriting. The age limit for these appointments was 17 to 24 years.

## V.—GENERAL.

1. *Underfed Children Attending School.*—The question of the methods of dealing with the underfed children attending school has engaged the attention of the Board from time to time. In 1889 a Special Sub-Committee was appointed to inquire into the whole question, and to submit a report to the Board. Among other conclusions the Sub-Committee arrived at was one that the Board should encourage the formation of the existing associations into a central organisation with a view to a more economical and efficient system for the provision of cheap or free meals for the poor children attending the Public Elementary schools of London. In accordance with this suggestion, a meeting was convened of the representatives of the various associations, Managers and teachers of schools, and other persons interested in the subject in November, 1889. At this meeting the London Schools Dinner Association was formed. In December, 1894, the Board appointed a Committee to ascertain the number of children attending school who were insufficiently fed, and to report to the Board any further remedies or suggestions which they might deem advisable. The general consensus of opinion was that the Board might materially assist the efforts made by keeping a continuous record of all children receiving meals.

Again, in July, 1898, the Board resolved that inquiry should be made as to the number of children attending Public Elementary schools in London who were underfed, and how far the voluntary provision of school meals was effectual; and a Special Sub-Committee was appointed to investigate and report. A large number of witnesses were examined, and reports as to the various methods of feeding children were obtained from the United States, Belgium, France, Germany, Italy, Norway, Sweden, and Switzerland. In the Report which was submitted to the Board in November, 1899, it was stated that the number of children who, in a severe winter, would probably need relief, was about 55,000 : some 31,000 of these belonging to Board Schools, and the rest to Voluntary schools.

The School Board, in a resolution passed on March 1st, 1900, laid down that Sub-Committees should be appointed by the Local Managers of all schools containing necessitous children for the purpose of (a) drawing up lists of underfed children and verifying the reality of their need; (b) reporting periodically the numbers of children on this list; (c) taking necessary steps to procure funds for their relief by application to Charitable Associations or individuals; and (d) arranging for the distribution of meals to the underfed children. By the same resolution they created a Joint Committee to supervise this organisation. The functions of this Committee were to receive periodical reports of the working of the School Sub-Committees and the numbers of children fed, to draw attention to any apparent defect or excess in the operations of the Sub-Committees, to assist any schools in want of funds by helping them to become connected with one of the Charitable Associations existing for this purpose, and generally to keep the public informed of what was being done to provide relief for underfed children and to stimulate public interest in the work. This Committee was composed as follows :—

Eight members of the School Board, together with representatives of the London Diocesan Board of Education, of the Rochester Diocesan Board of Education, of the Committee of Representative Managers of London Board Schools, of the Board School Children's Free Dinner Fund,[1] of the London Schools Dinner Association, of the Destitute Children's Dinner Society, and of the *Referee* Fund. This Joint Committee held its first meeting on July 16th, 1900.

In June, 1901, the Joint Committee published their first annual report, in which it was shown that the period of feeding extended to, as a maximum, twenty weeks during the winter, while a weekly average of 18,857 children received a daily average of 19,531 meals.

In June, 1902, the Joint Committee issued their second annual report, which showed that a weekly average number of 20,085 children had received a weekly average of 46,619 meals.

In June, 1903, the Joint Committee issued their third annual report, which showed that 22,206 children had received a weekly average of 54,572 meals. This was a slight increase over the return for 1900-1 and 1901-2, but the number of schools reporting was larger.

In the fourth annual report, which is being prepared and will shortly be issued, it is

---

[1] This Fund is now incorporated with the London Schools Dinner Association.

*[handwritten annotations]*

expected that similar figures for children and meals will reach approximately 24,000 children and 59,000 meals.

These figures showed a great reduction on the 55,000 children who were reported in 1899 to be probably in danger of being underfed; but that total included Voluntary schools, whereas the number above quoted came from Board schools only, and the figure of 55,000 was an estimate of what might be needed in a severe winter, whereas the winters of 1900-1 and 1901-2 were mild, and comparatively free from distress. There was also abundance of employment in consequence of the large number of men who had been drafted to the war.

The main principle accepted by the Board in March, 1900, was that private charity, properly organised, is competent to make provision for the wants of the underfed children in the schools, and that it is not necessary to have recourse to the rates for that provision. That principle has been borne out by the events of the three past winters. The first function of the Joint Committee was to be a means of communication between Managers of schools who are in want of funds and the Societies which exist for the purpose of supplying funds. That duty has been effectively performed, and wherever application has been made, the Joint Committee has been able to arrange for affiliating such schools to one or other of the chief Societies, and their wants have been satisfactorily supplied.

The second duty of the Joint Committee was to establish a Sub-Committee for each school or group of schools containing necessitous children. When the School Board resolved that a Sub-Committee should be appointed by the Local Managers in every such school, the possibility of reluctance or refusal to carry out this instruction had been overlooked. It has been necessary in some cases to apply to the School Management Committee to issue definite orders to the Local Managers that a Relief Sub-Committee must be appointed.

In those schools where Sub-Committees have been appointed and have continued to act, with the cordial co-operation of Local Managers, the result encourages the belief that the machinery devised by the Board is capable of successfully performing the work and of eliminating from the list of underfed children those not really in need of food, whilst securing that those in real want should receive meals.

One of the chief difficulties encountered has arisen from the existence of benevolent associations which supply meals and distribute a fixed number of tickets to the schools, thus placing the head teachers in a dilemma between refusing to utilise all of the tickets, or being obliged to give them to children who are not really necessitous. Efforts have been made to induce such Associations to issue tickets only in accordance with an authorised list of necessitous children.

The General Purposes Committee act as the link of communication between the Board and the Joint Committee on Underfed Children.

After three years' experience the Joint Committee reported that where the instructions of the School Board laid down in their Resolutions of March 1st, 1900, had been efficiently carried out with the assistance of the Local Managers, considerable improvement in the administration of charitable relief to school children has followed; but they were of opinion that to ensure the maintenance and increase of this improvement it is essential that the instructions of the Board should be strictly complied with, and that in all cases where relief is given in a Board School, the due appointment of a Sub-Committee as directed by the Regulations should be insisted upon. They also found that the opinion which the Board expressed in 1900, that the relief of underfed children can be effectually dealt with by organising the resources of private charity has been justified by the results of the last three years.

. 2. *Medical Officer's Department.*—In 1890 the Board appointed a medical officer at a salary of £400, rising to £600, per annum. In 1898 two assistant medical officers were appointed provisionally for one year to examine defective children, each to give an equivalent of half-time to the work, at a salary of £250 per annum. One of these was a lady, and it was provided that she should examine all female teachers, officers, and candidates for appointment by the Board. In 1902 the medical officer resigned, and the Board decided to raise the salary of the office to £800, rising by £25 per annum to £1,000, the medical officer to give his whole time to the Board, and not to hold or accept any other office, appointment or engagement. Under these conditions a new medical officer was appointed. The number of assistant medical officers was raised to three: one, a lady, half-time for the examination of female candidates for employment and crippled children, and of defective children in spare time, and two assistants for the examination of defective, blind and deaf children.

*Oculists.*—The Board, in 1901, decided to appoint two oculists for one year for the purpose of testing the eyesight of the children in senior departments of schools of the Board. It was, however, found impossible for two persons to get through the work in the time named, so it was resolved to appoint eight oculists for one year, each to examine a certain number of schools, at a remuneration of 50 guineas each.

On March 12th, 1903, the General Purposes Committee presented to the Board a report of the Medical Officer on the Testing of the Eyesight of School Children. Upon the facts therein set out, the Board, on March 19th, 1903, authorised the appointment of a certain number of oculists for one year, namely, one for half-time at £250, and five others for three half days a week at £125 each, so that twenty sessions a week might be given to the work.

*Ringworm.*—Six nurses were appointed to inspect any children submitted by the head teacher. They also occasionally inspect a whole class individually. They report on special matters when required, and confer with the teachers on general questions of cleanliness; pay visits to the homes of children who are absent or excluded owing to supposed disease or parasitic infection. They take no part in the treatment of cases. In several instances objections have been taken to the action of the nurses in advising teachers to exclude children, more especially in cases of ringworm. The judgment of a nurse who has had long experience in dealing with this disease is sufficient for the protection of the majority of the children and for the promotion of cleanliness. A few suspicious cases which are not ringworm may be excluded; a mistake which is easily remedied by detailed examination. In many cases of ringworm, however, cure is an exceedingly difficult matter, and if the disease is neglected the child may be out of school for many months.

*Diphtheria.*—In January, 1895, the Board requested the medical officer to report generally on the prevalence of diphtheria in London and elsewhere, and its alleged connection with Elementary schools. In April, 1896, the medical officer presented to the Board a report containing certain recommendations. Appended to the report were tables showing the age and sex incidence of diphtheria in every sanitary area in London since 1890; also plates showing the etiology of diphtheria, the geographical distribution of diphtheria mortality from 1861 to 1895 ; and charts showing notifications. In January, 1903, laboratory accommodation was provided for the purposes of bacteriological testing. The questions of infectious disease as affecting attendance, the ventilation of schoolrooms, the testing of eyesight, the presence of ringworm have been considered. In May, 1903, the medical officer of the Board issued his first annual report, in which these and other medical questions were dealt with.

It has always been a question how far the Board are authorised to spend public money on the medical care of children. On the one hand suggestions have been made for the inspection of their teeth, and the treatment of cases of anæmic condition and arrested development. On the other hand, a legal opinion has been expressed that the Board are not entitled to do anything, or to take any measures except such as spring from the fact that the attendance of the children is compulsory. On this account it has been thought right to take action only in those cases in which, on account of contagious disease, it is necessary to exclude children from school.

3. *Intermediate and Secondary Education.*—In 1892 the Board forwarded a petition to the Education Department, praying the Government to appoint a small commission to inquire into the state of intermediate and secondary education in England and Wales. A circular was also forwarded to every School Board representing a population of over 30,000, urging them to present similar petitions. After many delays, the Government appointed a Royal Commission on Secondary Education, consisting of 17 members. The report of the Commission was issued in October, 1895.

4. *Electoral Divisions.*—The Committee have, at various times, devoted a large amount of consideration to this subject. It was felt that the large, unwieldy School Board divisions caused the members of the Board to be largely out of touch with their constituents. Several attempts were made, by the introduction of Bills in Parliament to abolish the old School Board divisions and to substitute the divisions for Parliamentary and County Council purposes, at the same time abolishing the cumulative system of voting.

5. *Sale of Intoxicating Liquors to Children of Elementary School Age.*—The Committee have from time to time had under consideration the question of the hindrance to school work resulting from the sale of intoxicating liquors to children of school age. The Board, on November 12th, 1898, addressed a circular letter to all

the Licensing Justices in London, calling attention to the fact that the work which was being done in the schools, at great cost, to promote the mental and moral training of the children was imperilled to a very great extent by their familiarity with the sights and sounds which are associated with public-houses ; strongly condemning the sale of intoxicating liquors to children of school age; and asking the Justices to take such steps as would prevent such sale. Since this action of the Board, an Act dealing with the matter has been placed on the Statute Book; and it is now illegal to supply young persons under 14 years of age with intoxicants.[1]

6. *Fresh Licences for the Sale of Intoxicating Liquors in Neighbourhood of Board Scho ls.*—The Board, on February 20th, 1902, authorised the General Purposes Committee to communicate with the managers of all Board Schools, asking them to report, after conferring with head teachers, upon any new licences applied for in the immediate neighbourhood of the schools in their charge, with their reasons, if any, for opposing the granting of such licences. These reports were brought before the Committee, who, if they agreed with the representations of the Managers, took immediate steps to oppose the granting of the licences by the magistrates, without involving the Board in any financial liability.

7. *Return of Board Members.*—A return of the number of members who have been appointed on the Board, with an account of their periods of service, and other particulars, was made by this Committee. From the commencement of the School Board for London 326 persons have been Members of the Board. This number includes sixty-eight members appointed to fill casual vacancies, sixty-one vacancies having been filled by co-optation and seven by bye-election, the latter method of election being in force prior to January 1st, 1877.

## VI.—THE JOINT COMMITTEE ON MANUAL TRAINING.

The last fifteen years of the nineteenth century have witnessed a remarkable development in the aims and in the methods of elementary education. From 1885 and onwards the gradual steps of this movement can be distinctly traced. At about that period, in the United States, as in England, a dissatisfaction with the ordinary course of instruction in Public Elementary schools was prevalent. The curriculum had become too literary. It dealt too much with books and too little with things. It gave the scholars a dislike for manual labour. The number of those seeking employment as clerks and shopwomen far exceeded the demand, and neither boys nor girls had the aptitude or the training necessary to enable them to be of use in the more skilled work of artisans.

This general tendency, proceeding from the school, was also met by the results of the decay of the apprenticeship system in the workshop. Whilst that system lasted it counterbalanced and enlarged the training of the school. When it fell into desuetude the lack of balance in school instruction became obvious, and the need for re-adjustment

---

[1] 1 Edw. VII., c. 27.

became imperative.  A Committee of the School Board which was appointed in March 1887, inquired into and made recommendations with reference to the subjects and modes of instruction in Public Elementary schools.[1]   This may be taken as the starting-point of this record.  Amongst other things that Committee reported:—

"That Special Manual instruction should be given under the following principles:

"(1) That manual work be always taken in connection with school teaching of underlying Sciences and of Drawing;

"(2) That no special trade be taught."

An account of the events which led to the constitution of the Joint Committee on Manual Training have been given in an earlier section of this Report.[2]

### 1. *Boys.*

The Joint Committee commenced their work in October, 1887, and from that time until the opening of the first Manual Training class on January 10th, 1888, they were engaged in formulating schemes for the practical introduction of the work into the schools, examining the buildings proposed to be used, and gradually clearing the ground for the actual experiment.  Two instructors, one an artisan and the other a trained schoolmaster, were appointed, it being felt that the practical contrast of these two essentially different individualities would assist in the establishment on a sound basis for the instruction which was to be adopted.  In January, 1888, six classes were opened for giving instruction to boys in Woodwork.  The schools were equally divided on each side of the River Thames, and non-Board as well as Board school children were to be received.  Each class consisted of about twenty boys.  The attendance for each boy was to be for three hours per week, and to continue for the remainder of their school career.  At first the centres were opened in two cases one day a week, and in four cases two days a week.  These sessions were gradually increased until each centre was opened five days a week.  In a little more than two years from the commencement of the experiment (1890), Manual Training in Woodwork was included in the Code of the Education Department.  The educational scheme of instruction in Woodwork increased in favour both with educationists and savants.  In 1892, so great were the strides made that the Joint Committee, mindful of the interests of non-Board schools, rented a classroom at the Central Higher Grade schools, St. Marylebone, and took over the classes which had been established there in Wood and Metalwork.  With a view of extending their usefulness, especially in the direction of Metalwork, they caused an inquiry to be made of various institutions in the British Isles, and also on the Continent; and sent their clerk and organising instructor to the Allen Glen School, Glasgow, and the Central (Higher) Board Schools, Sheffield, for the purposes of personal investigation and report.  The result of that report was that the apparatus and tools at the Central Higher Grade schools were augmented, and an advanced syllabus was formulated.  To facilitate this object a gas engine was provided for working the lathes, &c.

[1] See *ante*, p. 96.        [2] See *ante*, pp. 112, 113.

The Joint Committee then established classes for training teachers in Wood and Metalwork. Many of the teachers trained by the Committee are now instructors in different parts of England, the colonies, and in foreign countries.

### 2. *Girls.*

The subject of handwork in the case of girls presented greater difficulties than in the case of boys, and it seemed as if there were less scope for it. Under the Education Code, School Managers were permitted to teach Cookery and were compelled to teach Needlework; and Needlework absorbed a very considerable portion of a girl's school-time. Yet it was felt that it was desirable to extend a girl's training so as to cover the ordinary duties of home. Four Laundry centres were opened for the instruction of girls, and for classes for the training of teachers. Each class consisted of twelve girls : they received three hours' instruction in each week, and the course of instruction extended to twelve weeks. In the homes of the children the experiment was deservedly popular when its results were seen. That popularity increased the demand for it, and at length it, too, was inserted in the Education Code of 1890 as a subject which might be taught in Elementary schools. The instruction, like that for boys, was wide in its scope, and was left much to the discretion of the Teacher. So soon as the instruction was legalised, the School Board for London and other authorities built Laundry centres as rapidly as they could. Again, there was a need for Teachers; and again the Teachers trained in the Joint Committee classes supplied the need.

The final development of the Committee's work for girls was the establishment of a Housewifery school. In the first instance, three rooms were fitted up exactly as in the home of an artisan, one as a kitchen, one as a sitting-room, and the other as a bedroom. Here a selected number of girls were taught on Saturday mornings to perform the duties of home life. They were taught how to ventilate and to clean a room ; how to polish and arrange its furniture and utensils ; how to arrange and to serve a meal ; how to make a bed and to clean and arrange a bedroom. In all these operations the utmost cleanliness and neatness were insisted upon. The pupils were taught the reason for the manner in which a fire was lighted, why ventilation was needed and how it could be obtained, and generally all the essentials which make up a healthy home. The success of this experiment was attested by the inclusion of the subject in the Education Code of 1893.

The Committee desired to place the range of instruction in Elementary Schools upon a wider basis; to give it a practical tendency ; to use it for building up a habit of daily exactness and thoroughness in handiwork which might re-act upon character; and through it to utilise much unused mental material, as well as to give a more perfect equipment for the duties of daily life. Through the instruction given to the girls there has been generated a desire for cleanly homes, as well as the skill to obtain them, which, if extended as largely as opportunities offer, must minister to the general happiness and comfort of the people.

The expenditure of the Joint Committee from the commencement of their work has been £15,558, and the receipts, independent of grants from the Drapers' Company and the City and Guilds of London Institute, have been respectively £1,698 and £619, the former amount being Government grants and the latter fees, &c. The total income of the Committee was £15,778, and the expenditure being £15,558, there remained a balance in hand of about £200.

The School Board, having been authorised to undertake the work, now conduct it at the expense of the School Fund. The Joint Committee have, therefore, relinquished the pioneer work, and have transferred to the School Board the balance in hand, representing £225 in Consols, the income from which is to be applied in the encouragement of boys and girls in connection with Manual Training.

# FINANCE.

THE finances of the Board were regulated by section 53 (now repealed) of the Elementary Education Act, 1870,[1] which is as follows:—

"The expenses of the School Board under this Act shall be paid out of a fund called the School Fund. There shall be carried to the School Fund all moneys received as fees from scholars, or out of moneys provided by Parliament, or raised by way of loan, or in any manner whatever received by the School Board, and any deficiency shall be raised by the School Board as provided by this Act."

For practical purposes the School Fund is divided into two parts, the "Maintenance Account" and the "Loan Account."

## I.—MAINTENANCE ACCOUNT.

This part comprises the Board's ordinary expenditure and receipts, the expenditure including the repayment of loans and the payment of interest.

### 1. EXPENDITURE.

The Maintenance Account expenditure may be divided into: (1) Maintenance of Day Schools; (2) Maintenance of other Schools, Enforcement of School Attendance, &c.; (3) Repayment of, and Interest on, Loans. The following table shows the expenditure year by year under each division. The Board's financial year ended on March 25th:—

| Year ended March 25th. | Maintenance of Day Schools. | Maintenance of other Schools, Enforcement of School Attendance, &c. | Repayment of, and Interest on, Loans. | Total. |
|---|---|---|---|---|
| 1 | 2 | 3 | 4 | 5 |
| | £ | £ | £ | £ |
| 1871 | — | 428 | — | 428 |
| 1872 | 1,450 | 9,523 | 14 | 10,987 |
| 1873 | 43,187 | 22,167 | 1,002 | 66,356 |
| 1874 | 84,595 | 44,310 | 8,901 | 137,806 |
| 1875 | 163,920 | 81,060 | 39,815 | 284,795 |
| 1876 | 240,504 | 84,697 | 60,250 | 385,451 |
| 1877 | 252,928 | 72,311 | 88,931 | 414,170 |
| 1878 | 391,723 | 77,737 | 110,804 | 580,264 |
| 1879 | 474,650 | 94,682 | 124,571 | 693,903 |
| 1880 | 561,694 | 110,269 | 158,914 | 830,877 |
| 1881 | 571,123 | 98,701 | 171,766 | 841,590 |
| 1882 | 623,978 | 107,999 | 195,141 | 927,118 |
| 1883 | 704,476 | 109,149 | 220,285 | 1,033,910 |
| 1884 | 723,471 | 146,516 | 245,684 | 1,115,671 |
| 1885 | 849,912 | 221,296 | 280,995 | 1,416,681 |
| 1886 | 984,953 | 131,189 | 319,065 | 1,435,207 |
| 1887 | 1,016,525 | 133,315 | 348,657 | 1,498,497 |
| 1888 | 1,060,068 | 122,047 | 361,845 | 1,543,960 |

[1] 33 & 34 Vict., c. 75.

| Year ended March 25th. | Maintenance of Day Schools. | Maintenance of other Schools, Enforcement of School Attendance, &c. | Repayment of, and Interest on, Loans. | Total. |
|---|---|---|---|---|
| 1 | 2 | 3 | 4 | 5 |
| | £ | £ | £ | £ |
| 1889 | 1,090,785 | 113,752 | 374,516 | 1,579,053 |
| 1890 | 1,187,942 | 139 922 | 383,833 | 1,711,697 |
| 1891 | 1,265,454 | 151,721 | 396,804 | 1,813 979 |
| 1892 | 1,288 655 | 188,152 | 405,367 | 1,882,174 |
| 1893 | 1,361.486 | 198,265 | 418,052 | 1,977 803 |
| 1894 | 1,417,056 | 189 373 | 436,673 | 2,043,102 |
| 1895 | 1,501,889 | 202,327 | 467,046 | 2,171,262 |
| 1896 | 1,630,428 | 230.734 | 486,269 | 2,347,431 |
| 1897 | 1.665,189 | 233,421 | 515,553 | 2,414,163 |
| 1898 | 1,733.072 | 243,667 | 532 124 | 2,508,863 |
| 1899 | 1,829.614 | 266,960 | 551,835 | 2,648 409 |
| 1900 | 1,920 531 | 295,091 | 574,871 | 2,790,493 |
| 1901 | 2,010.514 | 346,303 | 597.132 | 2,953,949 |
| 1902 | 2,117 446 | 368,550 | 632,555 | 3.118.551 |
| 1903 | 2,204,437 | 395,706 | 654,737 | 3,254,880 |
| | 33,038,133 | 5,231,340 | 10,164,007 | 48,433,480 |

Note to Column 4.—The amounts in this column include some comparatively small payments for stamp duty and charges in connection with loans, and for interest in connection with the purchase of sites.

### 1. *Maintenance of Day Schools.*

The expenditure for the Maintenance of Day Schools was distributed under various heads, and the following statement shows the average annual cost per child under each head since the year 1889-1890:—

| Year ended Mar. 25th. | Average Attendance. | Salaries of Teachers. | Pupil Teachers' Schools and Training Classes. | Books, Apparatus and Stationery. | Special Subjects of Instruct on, Inspection. &c. | Repairs to Buildings and Furniture. | School-keepers and Cleaning. | Fuel, Light, and Water. | Rates, Rents, &c. | Average Annual Gross cost per Child. | Average Annual Net cost per Child. |
|---|---|---|---|---|---|---|---|---|---|---|---|
| 1 | 2 | 3 | 4 | 5 | 6 | 7 | 8 | 9 | 10 | 11 | 12 |
| | | s. d. | s. d. | s. d. | s. d. | s. d. | s. d. | s. d. | s. d. | £ s. d. | £ s. d. |
| 1890 | 345,746 | 50 6 | 0 9 | 2 11 | 1 10 | 4 4 | 2 8 | 1 6 | 4 2 | 3 8 8 | 2 1 8 |
| 1891 | 347.857 | 52 4 | 0 10 | 3 0 | 2 1 | 5 11 | 2 9 | 1 7 | 4 3 | 3 12 9 | 2 5 11 |
| 1892 | 362,585 | 52 5 | 0 9 | 2 11 | 2 5. | 4 1 | 2 9 | 1 6 | 4 3 | 3 11 1 | 2 4 5 |
| 1893 | 379,445 | 52 7 | 0 9 | 2 10 | 2 5 | 4 7 | 2 8 | 1 10 | 4 1 | 3 11 9 | 2 2 3 |
| 1894 | 390,812 | 52 11 | 0 9 | 3 2 | 2 9 | 4 6 | 2 8 | 1 4 | 4 5 | 3 12 6 | 2 3 1 |
| 1895 | 400,912 | 54 4 | 0 9 | 3 2 | 3 5 | 4 4 | 2 8 | 1 9 | 4 6 | 3 14 11 | 2 4 1 |
| 1896 | 416,367 | 56 4 | 0 9 | 3 5 | 4 2 | 4 5 | 2 9 | 1 10 | 4 8 | 3 18 4 | 2 7 5 |
| 1897 | 422.691 | 57 7 | 0 9 | 3 3 | 4 2 | 3 10 | 2 9 | 1 8 | 4 9 | 3 18 9 | 2 6 9 |
| 1898 | 430,737 | 58 8 | 0 9 | 3 6 | 4 4 | 4 0 | 2 9 | 1 9 | 4 8 | 4 0 5 | 2 8 4 |
| 1899 | 439,684 | 59 8 | 0 10 | 3 11 | 4 10 | 4 7 | 2 10 | 1 9 | 4 10 | 4 3 3 | 2 12 8 |
| 1900 | 441.315 | 62 2 | 1 0 | 3 11 | 5 6 | 4 6 | 2 11 | 1 10 | 5 2 | 4 7 0 | 2 14 10 |
| 1901 | 446,866 | 64 2 | 1 1 | 3 10 | 5 3 | 4 10 | 2 11 | 2 4 | 5 7 | 4 10 0 | 2 18 1 |
| 1902 | 462,840 | 63 11 | 1 1 | 4 1 | 5 6 | 5 3 | 2 11 | 2 6 | 6 3 | 4 11 6 | 2 18 3 |
| 1903 | 475,123 | 64 8 | 1 1 | 4 2 | 5 10 | 5 2 | 2 11 | 2 4 | 6 8 | 4 12 9 | 3 2 0 |

The net cost per child (column 12) equals the gross cost (column 11) after deducting the income per child, which last is shown in column 6 of the table on p. 339.

Certain heads require special notice—namely, Salaries of Teachers, Special Subjects of Instruction, and Rates, Rents, Taxes, and Insurance.

*Salaries of Teachers.*—This was the largest of all the items of the Board's expenditure. In the year 1902-3 it amounted to upwards of £1,500,000, having risen more than £500,000 since 1892-3. This increase was due to two causes—first, the increase in the teaching staff, caused partly by the growth in the number of children in average attendance, which rose by nearly 100,000 during the ten years, and partly by the reduction of the size of the classes, the average number of children under the instruction of each teacher, not including Head Teachers, having decreased from 57 in 1892-93 to 47 in 1902-03; and secondly, the increase in salaries due to the operation of the scale by which they rise by yearly increments, and to alterations in that scale. Up to the year 1883 the teachers received a comparatively small annual salary, with the addition of a share of the Government Grant paid in one amount after the close of the School year. This plan was inconvenient, as they received only a small fixed amount monthly, while at some uncertain date a further sum was received which, in the case of head teachers, often exceeded the fixed annual salary. Furthermore, this variable amount was likely to be materially altered in any year by a change in the Education Code.[1] The Board, therefore, in 1883, resolved that this mode of payment should be altered to a fixed salary of a higher amount, without any share of the Grant; and a scale of salaries was laid down. Changes have been made in the scale from time to time, in each case leading to an increase of expenditure; but the full effect of these revisions will not be felt until normal conditions have been attained: when the staff of teachers has reached its full development and the efflux of teachers retiring at maximum salaries is equalled by the influx of teachers coming in at minimum salaries.

*Special Subjects of Instruction.*—These subjects are, for Girls: Domestic Economy (consisting of Cookery, Laundrywork, and Housewifery); and, for Boys: Manual Training in Woodwork or Metalwork. Particulars with reference to the growth and present condition of the instruction in these subjects will be found in the section on School Management,[2] and it is only necessary here to give some information in regard to the expenditure. The expenditure for Cookery commenced in the year 1874-75, when two small centres for instruction were opened; and in November, 1876, the first Cookery Instructor was appointed. It is impossible to give any trustworthy details of the expenditure before 1894-95, as until then that expenditure was not shown separately, but was included in the ordinary expenditure for the Schools. In that year £17,224 was spent on account of 142 centres. Instruction in Laundrywork was commenced in 1890-01, and in 1894-95 the number of Laundry Centres was 62, and the cost amounted to £4,687. These two subjects were subsequently combined with Housewifery under the title of "Domestic Economy." The expenditure under this head in 1902-03 was £41,383; and there were then 188 Cookery Centres, 139 Laundry Centres, and 27 Housewifery Centres. The expenditure for Manual Training commenced in 1891-92; in 1894-95 it amounted to £13,206, and in 1902-03 it had risen to £42,133, being an increase of £28,927. The Centres increased in number from 72 for

---

[1] See *ante*, pp. 161, *et seq.*    [2] See *ante*, pp. 112, 122-127; and 327-330.

Woodwork, in 1894-95, to 195 in 1902-03, of which 188 were for Woodwork and 7 for Metalwork. In addition to the foregoing expenditure, for some years a small sum has been spent annually in teaching Swimming, and in 1902-03 this amounted to £3,035. Whilst there can be no doubt that the instruction in these subjects is of considerable benefit to the children in after life, it must, nevertheless, be pointed out that the expenditure increased from an amount equal to about a farthing in the £ in 1894-95 to about a halfpenny in the £ in 1902-3. The Grant received from the Board of Education is to some extent a set-off against the expenditure, and the amount of such Grant per child has been increased since 1894-05 by alterations in the Code; but the increase has not been in proportion to the increase of expenditure.

*Rates, Rents, Taxes and Insurance.*—The Rents paid by the Board do not as a rule exceed £2,500 a year, and the schools are practically exempt from Taxes. Amounts are from time to time paid into the Board's Insurance fund, in which most of the schools are insured from fire, particulars of which are given on pages 359, 360. But these three items form a comparatively small proportion of the expenditure under this head, nearly the whole of it being for local rates. During the year 1892-93 the total expenditure was £77,558, or 4s. 1d. per child, whilst in 1902-03 it amounted to £159,232, or 6s. 8d. per child, being an increase of £81,674, or 2s. 7d. per child. This increase was partly due to the number of new schools opened during the ten years, but chiefly to the rates being higher. If the cost per child had remained the same as in 1892-03, the amount for 1902-03 would have been £97,004, an increase of about £20,000 only, so that the remainder of the increase, about £60,000, was almost entirely due to the rise of local rates. This expenditure for rates cannot fairly be considered as forming part of the Board's ordinary expenditure, for it is virtually a return to the rating authorities of a portion of the sums paid by them to the Board in satisfaction of precepts. Since 1897 the voluntary schools have been exempt from rates. On pages 361, 362 information is given as to various steps which have been taken by the Board from time to time with a view to obtain reductions in the assessments of their schools, and so to lessen the expenditure for rates.

### 2. *Maintenance of other Schools, Enforcement of School Attendance, &c.*

This expenditure is distributed under various heads—namely, Special Schools; Evening Continuation Schools; School Buildings, &c., not chargeable to Loan Account; Enforcement of School Attendance; Industrial Schools; Office Expenses; Legal Expenses; and Superannuation. The first, second, and last heads require special notice.

*Special Schools.*—Under this head are included schools for Blind, Deaf, and Mentally and Physically Defective children. Information as to the character of these schools and the instruction given in them will be found in the section relating to School Management.[1] In addition to the ordinary schools for these children there are also Residential schools for some of the blind and deaf, and it has been decided to establish four such schools for some of the defective. Further, in the case of the blind and deaf,

---

[1] See *ante*, pp. 177 to 191.

since November, 1895, children have been boarded out with "foster parents" in order that they may not be at too great a distance from the schools at which they receive instruction. A charge is made on the parents of the children, according to their means, for the children's maintenance, but the receipts from this source are much less than the payments made by the Board to the "foster parents."

Instruction of the blind commenced in 1872, although little was then done in this direction. The first school for the deaf was also opened in 1874, but for a considerable time the accounts were not kept separate, being included in those for the ordinary Day schools. An Act of Parliament of 1893,[1] which came into operation on January 1st, 1894, marked the beginning of official recognition of schools for the blind and deaf: and in 1894-5 the Board commenced an independent record of the finances of these schools.

The number of schools for the blind in 1894-95 was 9, and the amount expended was £1,177; in 1902-03 there were 10 schools, including two Residential schools, Elm Court and Linden Lodge, and the expenditure was £6,200. This amount included £1,732 on account of the two Residential schools, which were opened in that year; but in both cases the expenditure was in excess of the normal cost of maintenance, owing to extra charges connected with the starting of the schools. Elm Court, which was opened on June 2nd, 1902, cost £1,272, and Linden Lodge, opened a few months later, on December 15th, cost £460. In 1894-95 no grant was received except a small amount which cannot now be ascertained, as the attendance on which it was calculated formed part of the average attendance in the Day schools, and the grant was included with the Day school grants. In 1902-03 the amount received was £984.

In 1894-95 the number of schools for the deaf was 17, and the expenditure was £5,197; whilst in 1902-03 there were still 17 schools, two of them being Residential, and the amount expended was £13,068, including £1,249 for the Homerton Residential school and £1,834 for the Anerley Residential school. The latter amount was for a portion of the year only, as the school was not opened until December 1st, 1902, and it was slightly in excess of the normal cost of maintenance owing to extra charges connected with the starting of the school. As regards the grant for 1894-95, the same remark applies as in the case of the Blind. In 1902-03 the grant was £1,811.

In addition to the Government grant, £1,865 was received in 1902-03 from the parents of blind and deaf children placed with "foster-parents" or in institutions, whilst the expenditure for these particular children, which is included with that for the blind and deaf generally, was £3,131.

The first school for mentally and physically defective children was opened in 1892, but it was not until 1899 that the sanction of the legislature[2] was given for the special and separate instruction of such children. In 1902-03 there were 60 schools for the mentally defective and 8 for the physically defective, and the expenditure was £28,985. No separate grant was received until 1900-01, for up to that year it formed part of the

---

[1] 56 & 57 Vict., c. 42.   [2] 62 & 63 Vict., c. 32.

ordinary Day school grants for Infants. In 1902-03 the grant amounted to £9,717. At present there is no Residential school for these children.

The total expenditure for all these children amounted, in 1894-95, to £6,374, and, in 1902-3, to £49,653, from which latter sum, however, must be deducted the receipts, £14,384, leaving a net expenditure chargeable of £35,269. This work has been imposed upon the Board by two Acts of Parliament passed in recent years, and the expenditure connected with it has accordingly been unavoidable.

*Evening Continuation Schools.*—The Board first took in hand the work of providing Evening Continuation Schools in 1882; but for some years the progress made was slow, and by 1889-90 there were not more than 159 schools with 6,779 scholars in average attendance. The following table shows the number of schools and scholars, the expenditure and receipts, and the cost per scholar, in each year since 1889-90:—

| Year ended March 25th. | Number of Schools. | Average Number of scholars "present at all." | Gross Expenditure. | Receipts. | | | Net Expenditure. | Gross cost per scholar. | Receipts per scholar. | Net cost per scholar. |
|---|---|---|---|---|---|---|---|---|---|---|
| | | | | Grants. | School Fees and Sundries. | Total. | | | | |
| 1 | 2 | 3 | 4 | 5 | 6 | 7 | 8 | 9 | 10 | 11 |
| | | | £ | £ | £ | £ | £ | £ s. d. | £ s. d. | £ s. d. |
| 1890 | 159 | 6,779 | 10,640 | 3 088 | 2,134 | 5,222 | 5,418 | 1 11 5 | 0 15 5 | 0 16 0 |
| 1891 | 232 | 10,118 | 20,722 | 3,613 | 3 497 | 7,110 | 13,612 | 2 0 11 | 0 14 0 | 1 6 11 |
| 1892 | 239 | 10,736 | 26,347 | 5,176 | 4 013 | 9,189 | 17.158 | 2 9 1 | 0 17 1 | 1 12 0 |
| 1893 | 242 | 11,532 | 37.862 | 5,618 | 4,131 | 9,749 | 28,113 | 3 5 8 | 0 16 11 | 2 8 9 |
| 1894 | 265 | 14,613 | 32,767 | 5,938 | 4,236 | 10,174 | 22,593 | 2 4 10 | 0 13 11 | 1 10 11 |
| 1895 | 271 | 17,444 | 36 553 | 9,853 | 5,151 | 15,004 | 21,549 | 2 1 11 | 0 17 2 | 1 4 9 |
| 1896 | 271 | 19,633 | 42 719 | 11,440 | 5,454 | 16,894 | 25,825 | 2 3 6 | 0 17 2 | 1 6 4 |
| 1897 | 276 | 21,326 | 42 245 | 13,549 | 5,779 | 19,328 | 22,917 | 1 19 7 | 0 18 1 | 1 1 6 |
| 1898 | 280 | 24,350 | 48 115 | 14,122 | 5,180 | 19,302 | 28.813 | 1 19 6 | 0 15 10 | 1 3 8 |
| 1899 | 321 | 42.109 | 73,339 | 17,191 | 819 | 18.010 | 55,329 | 1 14 10 | 0 8 7 | 1 6 3 |
| 1900 | 368 | 47,965 | 86,202 | 21,812 | 12 | 21,824 | 64,378 | 1 15 11 | 0 9 1 | 1 6 10 |
| 1901 | 395 | 58.682 | 105,614 | 27,108 | 11 | 27.119 | 78,495 | 1 16 0 | 0 9 3 | 1 6 9 |
| 1902 | 398 | 55,238 | 106,558 | 33,692 | 24 | 33,716 | 72,842 | 1 18 7 | 0 12 3 | 1 6 4 |
| 1903 | 376 | 57,800 | 115 467 | 31,705 | 4,184 | 35,889 | 79,578 | 1 19 11 | 0 12 5 | 1 7 6 |

Note to Column 3—prior to 1893-94 the Average Attendance is given, there being no record for these years of the number "present at all."

The above figures do not appear to call for any special remark, as particulars with reference to the Evening Continuation Schools are given in the Section relating to those schools.[1] It will be observed, however, that whereas in 1897-98 the school fees, &c., amounted to £5,180, in the succeeding year they dropped to £819; and in the following three years no fees at all were received, the small amounts shown in those years arising from the sale of Needlework. The cause of this sudden fall in receipts was a decision of the Board of February 17th, 1898, to make all the Evening Continuation Schools free from September, 1898—*i.e.* the beginning of the 1898-99 Session. But in 1902 the Board of Education (South Kensington) required that fees should be charged to pupils over sixteen years of age, except in a certain number of schools, and in that year the receipts from fees amounted to £4,184. In 1898-99 the average number "present at all"

[1] See *ante*, pp. 272, *et seq.*

rose from 24,350 to 42,109, the effect of the abolition of the fees being to immediately improve the attendance; but the re-imposition of fees in 1902 did not have a contrary effect, for the attendance, instead of falling, rose from 55,238 to 57,800.

Under the Education Act, 1902,[1] all Evening Schools are treated as part of the system of education other than Elementary.

*Superannuation.*—Up to March 25th, 1903, the Board's expenditure in connection with their Superannuation Fund, beyond the office expenses involved in the clerical work of the fund, had amounted to less than £250. Particulars of the fund, of the Superannuation Act obtained by the Board in 1902, and of the expenditure since March 25th, 1900, when the fund was divided between officers and teachers, are given on pages 363 to 367.

### 3. *Repayment of, and Interest on, Loans.*

The Maintenance Account is not concerned with the expenditure on land and buildings, this being provided for by loans and forming the Loan account. But the repayment of the loans, and the interest thereon, are a charge on Maintenance Account. The repayments of principal and the payments for interest year by year are shown below.

| Year ended March 25th. 1 | Repayments of Principal. 2 | Interest. 3 | Total. 4 |
|---|---|---|---|
| | £ | £ | £ |
| 1872 | ... | ... | ... |
| 1873 | ... | 265 | 265 |
| 1874 | 1,615 | 5,593 | 7,208 |
| 1875 | 7,868 | 28,884 | 36,752 |
| 1876 | 11,619 | 44,893 | 56,512 |
| 1877 | 17,219 | 67,661 | 84,880 |
| 1878 | 22,371 | 86,270 | 108,641 |
| 1879 | 25,281 | 97,622 | 122,903 |
| 1880 | 32,301 | 121,735 | 154,036 |
| 1881 | 38,877 | 131,065 | 169,942 |
| 1882 | 45,199 | 148,413 | 193,612 |
| 1883 | 56,566 | 161,907 | 218,473 |
| 1884 | 67,778 | 175,363 | 243,141 |
| 1885 | 81,072 | 195,777 | 276,849 |
| 1886 | 95,371 | 220,201 | 315,572 |
| 1887 | 110,716 | 235,837 | 346,553 |
| 1888 | 119,291 | 242,014 | 361,305 |
| 1889 | 124,732 | 247,097 | 371,829 |
| 1890 | 132,676 | 251,155 | 383,831 |
| 1891 | 139,839 | 256,036 | 395,875 |
| 1892 | 147,438 | 256,312 | 403,750 |
| 1893 | 153,091 | 264,079 | 417,170 |
| 1894 | 162,805 | 272,319 | 435,124 |
| 1895 | 179,578 | 285,556 | 465,134 |
| 1896 | 188,413 | 296,046 | 484,459 |
| 1897 | 206,313 | 307,042 | 513,355 |
| 1898 | 217,071 | 312,651 | 529,722 |
| 1899 | 230,157 | 318,165 | 548,322 |
| 1900 | 242,936 | 325,909 | 568,845 |
| 1901 | 259,694 | 335,820 | 595,514 |
| 1902 | 282,405 | 347,959 | 630,364 |
| 1903 | 295,664 | 357,326 | 652,990 |
| | 3,695,956 | 6,396,972 | 10,092,928 |

## 2. RECEIPTS.

The Maintenance Account receipts may be divided into: (1) Government Grants and Miscellaneous Receipts on account of Day Schools; (2) all other Maintenance Account Receipts, except Precepts; (3) Precepts. The following table shows the receipts year by year under each division:—

| Year ended March 25th. | Maintenance of Day Schools. | All other Maintenance Account Receipts, except Precepts. | Precepts. | Total. |
|---|---|---|---|---|
| 1 | 2 | 3 | 4 | 5 |
| | £ | £ | £ | £ |
| 1872 | | 265 | 40,000 | |
| 1873 | | 100 | 75,000 | |
| 1874 | | 1,249 | 62,000 | |
| 1875 | | 106 | 149,808 | |
| 1876 | | 1,943 | 263,713 | |
| 1877 | | 2,168 | 398,867 | |
| 1878 | | 2,339 | 506,353 | |
| 1879 | | 2,710 | 506,306 | |
| 1880 | | 3,913 | 551,247 | |
| 1881 | 4,075,221 | 5,682 | 643,791 | 14,783,515 |
| 1882 | | 9,641 | 676,579 | |
| 1883 | | 12,424 | 679,340 | |
| 1884 | | 12,802 | 801,210 | |
| 1885 | | 12,518 | 950,804 | |
| 1886 | | 12,469 | 1,044,592 | |
| 1887 | | 15,182 | 1,125,034 | |
| 1888 | | 20,254 | 1,070,315 | |
| 1889 | | 18,686 | 1,028,884 | |
| 1890 | 467,539 | 17,890 | 1,158,554 | 1,643,983 |
| 1891 | 467,487 | 24,680 | 1,403,280 | 1,895,447 |
| 1892 | 483,545 | 22,549 | 1,483,174 | 1,989,268 |
| 1893 | 560,010 | 19,124 | 1,444,290 | 2,023,424 |
| 1894 | 575,214 | 18,913 | 1,422,570 | 2,016,697 |
| 1895 | 618,891 | 21,460 | 1,468,510 | 2,108,861 |
| 1896 | 643,985 | 23,238 | 1,631,612 | 2,298,835 |
| 1897 | 677,553 | 30,618 | 1,800,684 | 2,508,855 |
| 1898 | 692,269 | 32,639 | 1,851,703 | 2,576,611 |
| 1899 | 671,985 | 31,896 | 1,873,012 | 2,576,893 |
| 1900 | 709,291 | 35,254 | 2,050,702 | 2,795,247 |
| 1901 | 712,453 | 41,381 | 2,168,613 | 2,922,447 |
| 1902 | 768,835 | 57,180 | 2,339,294 | 3,165,309 |
| 1903 | 729,593 | 61,726 | 2,436,138 | 3,227,457 |
| | 12,853,871 | 572,999 | 35,105,979 | 48,532,849 |

### 1. *Receipts on account of Day Schools.*

The receipts on account of Day schools consist almost entirely of Government grants of various kinds. The following statement shows the average annual income per child under each head of these receipts since the year 1889-90 :—

| Year ended 25th March. 1 | Average Attendance. 2 | Education Grants. 3 | | | School Fees and Fee Grants. 4 | | | Other Receipts. 5 | | | Average Annual Income per Child. 6 | | |
|---|---|---|---|---|---|---|---|---|---|---|---|---|---|
| | | £ | s. | d. | £ | s. | d. | £ | s. | d. | £ | s. | d. |
| 1890 | 345,746 | 0 | 19 | 0 | 0 | 7 | 0 | 0 | 1 | 0 | 1 | 7 | 0 |
| 1891 | 347,857 | 0 | 19 | 1 | 0 | 6 | 9 | 0 | 1 | 0 | 1 | 6 | 10 |
| 1892 | 362,585 | 0 | 18 | 8 | 0 | 6 | 10 | 0 | 1 | 2 | 1 | 6 | 8 |
| 1893 | 379,445 | 0 | 19 | 0 | 0 | 9 | 5 | 0 | 1 | 1 | 1 | 9 | 6 |
| 1894 | 390,812 | 0 | 18 | 3 | 0 | 9 | 10 | 0 | 1 | 4 | 1 | 9 | 5 |
| 1895 | 400,912 | 0 | 19 | 7 | 0 | 9 | 10 | 0 | 1 | 5 | 1 | 10 | 10 |
| 1896 | 416,367 | 0 | 19 | 4 | 0 | 9 | 10 | 0 | 1 | 9 | 1 | 10 | 11 |
| 1897 | 422,691 | 1 | 0 | 2 | 0 | 10 | 0 | 0 | 1 | 10 | 1 | 12 | 0 |
| 1898 | 430,737 | 1 | 0 | 3 | 0 | 9 | 11 | 0 | 1 | 11 | 1 | 12 | 1 |
| 1899 | 439,684 | 1 | 0 | 0 | 0 | 9 | 8 | 0 | 0 | 11 | 1 | 10 | 7 |
| 1900 | 441,315 | 1 | 1 | 5 | 0 | 9 | 11 | 0 | 0 | 10 | 1 | 12 | 2 |
| 1901 | 446,866 | 1 | 1 | 5 | 0 | 9 | 9 | 0 | 0 | 9 | 1 | 11 | 11 |
| 1902 | 462,840 | 1 | 2 | 8 | 0 | 9 | 11 | 0 | 0 | 8 | 1 | 13 | 3 |
| 1903 | 475,123 | 1 | 0 | 5 | 0 | 9 | 10 | 0 | 0 | 6 | 1 | 10 | 9 |

Note to Column 4.—The School Fees ceased, and the Fee Grants commenced, in 1891-2.

All three heads require special notice.

*Education Grants.*—These are the grants awarded in accordance with the Code which is periodically issued by the Board of Education. Many changes have been made by the Government in the manner of awarding these grants. In 1871 there was a fixed grant of 6s. per scholar in average attendance, an Examination grant of 8s. or 10s. for infants and 12s. for older children, and a further 3s. for each scholar passing in certain higher subjects, or, as they were called, "specific" subjects. From that time to 1882 small alterations were made in details, but the principle remained practically the same. In 1882 the whole system was revised. For Infants the fixed grant was increased to 9s. or 7s. and a "merit" grant of 2s., 4s., or 6s., dependent upon H.M. Inspector reporting the school as "fair," "good," or "excellent," was instituted. Needlework and Singing grants, of 1s. each, were also given; thus making a total of 16s. or 17s., which was about the same as before. The system for the older children was somewhat similar, although the amounts differed considerably. There was a fixed grant of 4s. 6d., a "merit" grant of 1s., 2s., or 3s., Needlework and Singing grants of 1s. each, and various other grants for elementary, class, and "specific" subjects, the general effect being that the grants were slightly raised. Small changes were made in 1885 and 1887; principally in connection with Drawing. In 1890 the grants for the older children were again considerably altered in character, a "principal" grant of 12s. 6d. or 14s. per scholar being instituted in place of the fixed and "merit" grants; whilst the other grants for class and "specific" subjects were continued with slight variations. These arrangements, with subsequent small alterations, were in force until 1900, when the whole scheme of grants was altered. The special feature of the new arrangement was the simplification of the existing elaborate system by the substitution of one "principal" grant (higher or lower) for the old "principal" and most of the other grants. Courses of instruction were laid down for Infants and for older children; and provided these were observed, and the character and quality of the instruction, the staff, and the discipline and organisation, were satisfactory, a grant of 17s. or 16s. per scholar was given for Infants, and 22s. or 21s. for older children. Grants were also made of 4s. for each girl for Cookery, and 2s. for Laundrywork, or, as an alternative, 7s. for those two subjects and Practical Housewifery combined under the one head of Household Management; and 6s. or 7s. for Manual Instruction for boys. The effect of these changes was slightly to increase the grants for infants and slightly reduce them for the older children. Some change in the curriculum for the older children was made in the Code of 1901, but in all other respects this simplified scheme was in operation on March 25th, 1903.

With the Education grants were formerly included grants from the Science and Art Department, but these ceased in 1901 owing to a legal decision that the Board had no power to teach the subjects for which they were awarded. Grants are still received in connection with the instruction of Pupil Teachers, but they are comparatively small, and the amount has never exceeded £5,000 in any one year.

The average annual income per child for Education grants, as shown in the table on page 339 is calculated on the amount actually received in each year; but this is not the true amount, or, in other words, the amount falling due within the year. The grants do not come in with uniform regularity, and the amount received in any year invariably includes grants earned during the preceding or succeeding year, or, on the other hand, does not include grants which belong to the year. The following table gives the true income per child for the last five years, calculated on the amount earned (whether actually paid or not), compared with the income calculated on the amount actually paid by the Board of Education, as given in the above statement:—

| Year ended 25th March. | Average annual income per child from Education Grants. | |
| --- | --- | --- |
| | Calculated on amount earned. | Calculated on amount actually received. |
| 1 | 2 | 3 |
| | £  s.  d. | £  s.  d. |
| 1899 | 1  1  0 | 1  0  0 |
| 1900 | 1  1  7 | 1  1  5 |
| 1901 | 1  1  8 | 1  1  5 |
| 1902 | 1  1  4 | 1  2  8 |
| 1903 | 1  1  5 | 1  0  5 |

*Fee Grants.*—From the commencement of the Board until the year 1891-92 fees ranging from 1d. to 9d. per child were charged in all their schools. In 1891, an Act[1] was passed empowering School Boards, if they so desired, to provide free education, and instituting a fee grant to take the place of the school fees; and it came into operation on the 1st September of the same year. The Board at once availed themselves of the Act, and the change was of considerable benefit to their finances. The average annual

---

[1] 54 & 55 Vict., c. 56.

income per child from school fees had been gradually falling; in 1880-81 it stood at 8s. 3d. per child, whereas in 1890-91 it was only 6s. 8d. As the new fee grant was 10s. per child, the immediate gain to the Board exceeded 3s. per child; and in 1902-03 the financial advantage was equal to a rate of a halfpenny in the £. Moreover, there is little doubt that free education has been a great help to the Board in enforcing the attendance of children at school.

*Other Receipts.*—An amount of about £5,000 is realised annually by the sale of Needlework. The material is supplied to the schools from the Board's store, the teachers being held responsible for it; and the garments and other articles made up by the children in the course of their instruction are sold, usually to their parents, at cost price. A receipt of about £2,500 also arises annually from letting schools for Sunday-school purposes, educational classes, elections, and meetings of various kinds. No profit is made, as the amounts charged are calculated merely to reimburse the Board for fuel and light, and wear and tear. Neither of these two receipts has varied to any considerable extent during the last ten years.

### 2. *All other Maintenance Account Receipts, except Precepts.*

These receipts are comparatively small, and never exceed 2 per cent. of the total receipts in connection with Maintenance Account. The Government grants for blind, deaf, and mentally and physically defective children, for Evening Continuation schools, and for Industrial schools, form nine-tenths of these receipts, the remainder being the payments by parents in aid of the education and maintenance of Blind and Deaf children boarded out or in Residential institutions, and of children in Day Industrial schools, and the fees from scholars in Evening Continuation schools.

### 3. *Precepts.*

The expenditure on Maintenance Account, and the receipts, with the exception of precepts, have now been dealt with. The precepts are the demands periodically served by the Board on the Rating Authorities of the Metropolis in pursuance of Section 54 of the Elementary Education Act, 1870, which provides that "any sum required to meet any deficiency in the School Fund, whether for satisfying past or future liabilities, shall be paid by the Rating Authority out of the Local Rate."[1]

Since March 25th, 1872, an Estimate showing the Maintenance Account "deficiency," or, in other words, the amount of the difference between the estimated expenditure and receipts of the financial year, has been drawn up each year and submitted to the Board for approval. The method of preparing these Estimates, and the basis on which they are calculated, have been varied from time to time. In the earlier years of the Board they were prepared by the Finance Committee, and after passing through the other Committees, were forwarded to the Board for approval. Two grounds of objection were taken to this system: one, that the Estimates were prepared under no direct responsibility, and were often inaccurate, the expenditure frequently

---

[1] 33 & 34 Vict., c. 75.

being considerably in excess of the Estimates; and the other, that they were open to the suspicion of being manipulated for party purposes, the Rate being kept low when it seemed desirable to do so, regardless of the fact that the School Board would be involved in a deficit unless there was a corresponding reduction in the expenditure, which never occurred. An important change was accordingly made in May, 1897, and under the new arrangement the Estimates were drawn up by the Accountant of the Board, after consultation with the Principal Clerks of the various departments, the figures being based upon the approximate expenditure and receipts of the preceding financial year, subject to any alterations which appeared to be necessary. The Estimates were then submitted to the Standing Committees concerned in the expenditure, and, after being considered by them, were laid before the Finance Committee, who had power to approve, alter, or revise them, and who finally submitted them to the Board for approval and adoption. In this way all suspicion of manipulation for party purposes was removed and a much greater degree of accuracy in the forecast of both receipts and expenditure was attained. Moreover, the expenditure was divided into eighteen branches, to which the principle of water-tight compartments was applied; a watch was kept on the expenditure of each of these branches, and if there was danger of its exceeding the budget allotment, the Finance Committee was obliged to go to the Board with a Supplementary Estimate to obtain an increased allotment of money, the additional expenditure being met by appropriating for this purpose a portion of the amount set aside for the year as a Working Balance and Contingency Fund. The first Estimate wholly prepared under the new arrangement was that for the year 1898-99, and in the following table are shown, for that year and succeeding years up to 1902-03, the percentages of variation between the estimated and the actual expenditure :—

| Year ended March 25th. | Estimated expenditure. | Actual expenditure. | Expenditure more than Estimate. | Expenditure less than Estimate. | Variation per cent. |
|---|---|---|---|---|---|
| 1 | 2 | 3 | 4 | 5 | 6 |
| | £ | £ | £ | £ | |
| 1899 | 2,680,900 | 2,648,409 | ... | 32,491 | − 1·21 |
| 1900 | 2,795,800 | 2,790,493 | ... | 5,307 | − 0·19 |
| 1901 | 2,938,300 | 2,953,949 | 15,649 | ... | + 0·53 |
| 1902 | 3,092,900 | 3,118,551 | 25,651 | ... | + 0·83 |
| 1903 | 3,250,000 | 3,254,880 | 4,880 | ... | + 0·15 |

In 1874-75, which may be taken as the first normal year in the work of the Board, the precept amount was £149,866, and, as the assessable value was £20,565,446, the rate was therefore 1·75d. in the £. By 1902-03 the precept amount had risen in the proportion of one to sixteen, to £2,437,772, but, the assessable value then being £39,968,714, or nearly double its former amount, the rate in the £ was only 14·66d., or eight times the rate of 1874-75, the doubling of the assessable value enabling the Board to collect sixteen times the amount with a rate only eight times as large. A rate of a penny in the £ produced £85,689 in 1874-75, and £166,536 in 1902-03. In the following table the amount of the precept, of the assessable value, and of the rate in the £, is shown for each year since 1874-75 ; and, further, in order to admit of the progress of the increase in each case being closely followed and compared, the three amounts are expressed as 100 in 1874-75 and proportionately in subsequent years :—

| | | | | Proportionate growth in | | |
|---|---|---|---|---|---|---|
| Year ended March 25th. | Precept amount. | Assessable Value. | Rate in the £. | Precept amount. | Assessable Value. | Rate in the £. |
| 1 | 2 | 3 | 4 | 5 | 6 | 7 |
| | £ | £ | d. | | | |
| 1875 | 149,866 | 20,565,446 | 1·75 | 100 | 100 | 100 |
| 1876 | 263,713 | 20,903,377 | 3·03 | 175 | 102 | 173 |
| 1877 | 398,867 | 21,308,984 | 4·49 | 267 | 104 | 257 |
| 1878 | 506,353 | 23,251,702 | 5·23 | 338 | 113 | 299 |
| 1879 | 506,306 | 23,584,728 | 5·15 | 338 | 115 | 294 |
| 1880 | 551,247 | 24,065,174 | 5·50 | 368 | 117 | 314 |
| 1881 | 643,791 | 24,605,926 | 6·28 | 430 | 120 | 359 |
| 1882 | 676,579 | 26.380,342 | 6·15 | 451 | 128 | 351 |
| 1883 | 679,595 | 27,521,473 | 5·93 | 453 | 134 | 339 |
| 1884 | 801,210 | 28,012,248 | 6·86 | 535 | 136 | 392 |
| 1885 | 950,804 | 28,541,916 | 8·00 | 634 | 139 | 457 |
| 1886 | 1,045,365 | 29,025,534 | 8·64 | 698 | 141 | 494 |
| 1887 | 1,128,046 | 30,621,411 | 8·84 | 753 | 149 | 505 |
| 1888 | 1,070,325 | 30,692,418 | 8·37 | 714 | 149 | 478 |
| 1889 | 1,028,883 | 30,981,825 | 7·97 | 687 | 151 | 455 |
| 1890 | 1,158,554 | 31,251,704 | 8·90 | 774 | 152 | 509 |
| 1891 | 1,403,280 | 31,485,120 | 10·70 | 936 | 153 | 611 |
| 1892 | 1,483,174 | 32,331,555 | 11·01 | 990 | 157 | 629 |
| 1893 | 1,447,413 | 33,227,619 | 10·45 | 966 | 162 | 597 |
| 1894 | 1,424,093 | 33,492,853 | 10·20 | 950 | 163 | 583 |
| 1895 | 1,469,850 | 33,753,569 | 10·45 | 981 | 164 | 597 |
| 1896 | 1,631,663 | 34,064,689 | 11·50 | 1,089 | 166 | 657 |
| 1897 | 1,800,926 | 35,027,648 | 12·34 | 1,202 | 170 | 705 |
| 1898 | 1,852,326 | 35 961,325 | 12·36 | 1,236 | 175 | 706 |
| 1899 | 1,872,729 | 36,332,812 | 12·37 | 1,250 | 177 | 707 |
| 1900 | 2,049,582 | 36,789,317 | 13·37 | 1,368 | 179 | 764 |
| 1901 | 2,172,047 | 37.278.038 | 13·98 | 1,449 | 181 | 799 |
| 1902 | 2,339,540 | 38,642.744 | 14·51 | 1,561 | 188 | 829 |
| 1903 | 2,437,772 | 39,968,714 | 14·66 | 1,627 | 194 | 838 |

It remains to explain how the precepts have been collected from the rating authorities of the Metropolis. In the first place, so soon as the amount of the deficiency had been ascertained it was apportioned amongst the rating authorities according to the assessable values (practically the ratable values in London) of their respective districts, as set out in the Metropolitan Valuation Lists published by the Metropolitan Asylums Board till the year 1888, and since then by the London County Council. In the earlier years of the Board a single demand was made annually on each rating authority for the amount apportioned to it, but the later practice has been to issue two half-yearly precepts, chiefly because the Board were thus able to calculate the second one on the new valuation list which comes into force annually on April 6th and which, ns it always brought an appreciable addition to the assessable value of the Metropolis, lowered thereby to some extent the rate in the £ represented by the Board's requirement for the year. The first precept, for the first half of the financial year, from March 26th to September 29th, was issued in December, three months before the beginning of the year, but it was merely in the nature of a vote on account, the last precept issued (for the second half of the then current financial year) being made to serve as a guide for the amount. When the financial year arrived, and so soon as the accounts of the preceding financial year were made up, an estimate was prepared as described above, and the second precept was then issued, usually in June, for the second half of the year, from September 30th to March 25th. The amount of this precept was the estimated deficiency for the year after deducting the amount already demanded for the first half of the year.

## II.—LOAN ACCOUNT.

This was the second of the two great parts into which the School Fund was divided. It was an account of the expenditure for the purchase of land and the erection of buildings, and of the funds, raised by loans, to meet this expenditure.

The Elementary Education Act, 1870,[1] empowered School Boards to incur expenditure in providing or enlarging schools and to borrow money to meet that expenditure, and, with the consent of the Education Department, to spread the repayment over several years, not exceeding fifty. By section 10 of the Elementary Education Act, 1873,[2] the consent of the Education Department was required before School Boards could exercise their power to borrow money, and such consent was not to be granted unless proof were given, to the satisfaction of the Department, that the additional accommodation which it was proposed to supply was required in order to provide for the educational wants of the district. This section, which has been repealed by the Education Act, 1902,[3] made the Education Department, and not the School Boards, the controlling power in the provision of new accommodation. Before a loan for the erection of a new school was authorised, the consent of the Department had to be obtained, not only to the estimate of the number of children for which the school was to be erected, but also to the plans for the school, which were often subjected to severe examination. The negotiations frequently caused considerable delay in the erection of new schools.[4] By subsequent enactments the powers conferred upon School Boards in regard to providing or enlarging schools were extended to schools transferred to Boards, to Residential schools for deaf, blind, and mentally and physically defective children, to Industrial schools (with the consent of the Home Office, instead of the Education Department) and to offices. The following table shows the amounts which the Board have expended year by year under these powers:—

---

[1] 33 & 34 Vict., c. 75.
[2] 36 & 37 Vict., c. 86.
[3] 2 Edw. 7., c. 42.
[4] See *post*, p. 346.

Table showing the amounts expended out of Loan Account under various heads from 1872 to 1903:—

| Year ended March 26th. | Schools. | Industrial Schools. | Offices (including Stores). | Total. |
|---|---|---|---|---|
| 1 | 2 | 3 | 4 | 5 |
|  | £ | £ | £ | £ |
| 1872 | 11,800 | — | — | 11,800 |
| 1873 | 150,988 | — | 18,348 | 169,336 |
| 1874 | 481,806 | — | 9.037 | 490 843 |
| 1875 | 506,858 | — | 25,790 | 532,648 |
| 1876 | 527,910 | — | 15,777 | 543,687 |
| 1877 | 659,976 | — | 647 | 660 623 |
| 1878 | 424,084 | 15,723 | — | 439,807 |
| 1879 | 371,960 | 34.133 | — | 406,093 |
| 1880 | 433,062 | 1,064 | — | 434,126 |
| 1881 | 395,421 | 1.920 | — | 397,341 |
| 1882 | 454,787 | [890]° | — | 453,897 |
| 1883 | 424,752 | 3.407 | 11,539 | 439,698 |
| 1884 | 559,433 | 5,276 | 3,603 | 568,312 |
| 1885 | 663,995 | 8,736 | 11,585 | 684,316 |
| 1886 | 611,077 | 4,923 | 7,032 | 623,032 |
| 1887 | 458,588 | [2,083]° | 242 | 456,747 |
| 1888 | 234.763 | 1,110 | — | 235,873 |
| 1889 | 196,064 | 1,015 | — | 197,079 |
| 1890 | 173,654 | 184 | 30,781 | 204,619 |
| 1891 | 238,763 | 12,868 | — | 251,631 |
| 1892 | 349,607 | 6,582 | 7,585 | 363,774 |
| 1893 | 432,229 | 1,509 | 17,184 | 450,922 |
| 1894 | 448,316 | 566 | 39,430 | 488,312 |
| 1895 | 491,043 | 626 | 16,857 | 508,526 |
| 1896 | 525,301 | 18,764 | 18,874 | 562,939 |
| 1897 | 535,036 | 2,587 | 16,568 | 554,191 |
| 1898 | 487,203 | 17,773 | 5,045 | 510,021 |
| 1899 | 505,793 | 31,795 | 19,115 | 556,703 |
| 1900 | 580,207 | 17,404 | — | 597,611 |
| 1901 | 552,653 | 3,941 | [504]° | 556,090 |
| 1902 | 602,538 | 20,901 | 183 | 623,622 |
| 1903 | 551,273† | 24,563 | 1 | 575,837 |
|  | 17,200‡ | — | — | 17,200 |
|  | 14,058 | 234,397 | 274,719 | 14,567,256 |

° A credit ; being an amount transferred as a charge on Maintenance Account.

† The actual expenditure for the year was £578,631, but from it has been deducted £27,358 received from the Penge School Board on account of two schools transferred from London to Penge, in consequence of changes of boundary under the London Government Act, 1899.ı

‡ This amount is shown separately because it was not expended by the Board in the usual way, but represents loans taken over from the Hornsey School Board, in the year 1900-1, with a school transferred from Hornsey to London, in consequence of changes of boundary under the London Government Act, 1899,

The following amounts have been borrowed to meet the above expenditure :—

| 1 | Amount borrowed. |
|---|---|
| | £ |
| Schools ... ... ... ..., ... ... ... ... | 14,265,929 |
| Do. ... ... ... ... ... ... ... ... | 17,200° |
| | 14,283,129 |
| Industrial Schools... ... ... ... ... ... ... | 191,024 |
| Offices (including Stores) ... ... ... ... ... | 274,603 |
| Total amount borrowed ... ... ... ... | 14,748,756 |
| Unexpended balance in hand March 25th, 1903 ... | 181,500 |
| | 14,567,256 |

° Loans taken over from the Hornsey School Board.

The money has usually been borrowed in large sums, such as £100,000 or £200,000, made up by aggregating in one amount the various loans required at the time for projected schools, for which consents had been obtained from the Education Department (or the Home Office, if an Industrial school). To procure these consents the plans of the proposed building, together with full particulars of the cost (based on the builder's tender), had to be forwarded to the Government Department, and as a rule the Board were not at liberty to proceed with the work until the plans and the cost had been approved and a loan sanctioned. No limit was imposed in regard to the cost of the land, for that is obviously dependent on the character of the neighbourhood and position of the site; but the cost of the buildings was kept within limits by a system of "allowances." In the first place, the Education Department allowed £10 for each child to be accommodated. It was soon found, however, that although this amount might serve for the country, in London, with heavier charges for labour and materials, and often with peculiar difficulties arising from unsuitable soils and closely hemmed-in sites, it was not sufficient, and various other allowances were added from time to time, until they formed a considerable addition to the £10 per child. Beyond these, however, further special allowances had to be made for certain new classes of expenditure which were obviously outside the £10 limit and the allowances augmenting it. The following is a list of all these allowances :—

### ALLOWANCES FOR ORDINARY SCHOOLS.

(*a*) Principal (original) allowance—£10 per child accommodated.

(*b*) Central halls or hall-corridors—£1 per square foot.

(*c*) Teachers' rooms—15s. per square foot.

(*d*) Glazed bricks for inside walls, up to a certain height—the cost of the same.

(*e*) Mechanical warming and ventilation—the cost of the same.

(*f*) Extra depth of foundations below the usual 4 or 5 feet—the cost of the same.

(*g*) Boundary walls, entrances and gates—the cost of the same.

(*h*) Tar pavement, latrines, playgrounds and drainage—the cost of the same.

(*i*) Forming playground on top of school—the cost of the same. [This is done where the site is limited in area, the extra cost being more than met by the saving in the outlay for land.]

(*j*) Placing buildings on arches so as to form covered playgrounds underneath—the cost of the arches. [The above remark applies in this case also.]

(*k*) Preparing sites for building—the cost of the same.

(*l*) Work to existing buildings—the cost of the same.

(*m*) Sanitary and drainage work to old schools for the purpose of bringing them up to modern requirements—the cost of the same.

### SPECIAL ALLOWANCES FOR OTHER CLASSES OF EXPENDITURE.

(*a*) Manual Instruction room—15s. per square foot.

(*b*) Cookery centre—£500.

(*c*) Laundry centre—£1 per square foot.

(*d*) Science room, laboratory, or drawing-class room—£1 per square foot.

(*e*) Any other Special rooms—£1 per square foot.

(*f*) Schools for blind, deaf, and mentally or physically defective children—£1 per square foot.

(*g*) Schoolkeeper's house—£500.

In addition to the cost of the building work, the allowances were intended to cover also the cost of the furniture and fittings of a permanent character, and the outlay, estimated at 3½ per cent. on the total cost for architect, clerk of works, and general superintendence of the work. The allowances were usually sufficient to cover the cost of the building, when a loan for the full amount was sanctioned. Sometimes, however, it happened that the proposed cost exceeded the allowances, in which case the Department sanctioned a loan only up to the amount of the allowances and ordered that the excess should be paid out of Maintenance Account, although in some cases they have required the plans to be amended with a view to reduce the cost and bring it within the allowances. These excess payments out of Maintenance account are included in the expenditure under the sub-head of that account, entitled " School Buildings, &c., not chargeable to Loan Account."[1] This sub-head is for expenditure which is not defrayed by loans, because the Board of Education does not sanction loans for it, but which is nevertheless for work of such a character that it is not properly chargeable to "Repairs to Buildings."[1]

The loans have been obtained partly from the Public Works Loan Commissioners and the remainder from the Metropolitan Board of Works and their successors, the London County Council. The following table shows the amount borrowed in each case and the amount outstanding at March 25th, 1903:—

| 1 | Amount borrowed. 2 | Amount outstanding. 3 |
|---|---|---|
| | £ | £ |
| Public Works Loan Commissioners ... | 3,693,804 | 2,422,960 |
| Ditto ditto ... | 17,200* | 15,385* |
| | 3,711,004 | 2,438,345 |
| Metropolitan Board of Works ... ... | 4,246,752 | 2,649,255 |
| London County Council ... ... ... | 6,791,000 | 5,965,199 |
| | 14,748,756 | 11,052,799 |

\* Loans taken over from the Hornsey School Board.

[1] See p. 331, under " Maintenance of other Schools, Enforcement of School Attendance, &c."   [2] See p. 332, column 7 of the table under " Maintenance of Day Schools."

The Board are repaying these loans by two methods—the first, on the basis of a fixed equal annual payment for principal and interest in each year of the period for which the money is borrowed; the second, by an equal annual repayment of principal, according to the term for which the money is borrowed, and interest upon the balance outstanding. In the case of the Public Works Loan Commissioners, with the exception of four small loans, the Board have borrowed all the money under the first method, the effect of which is to lighten the repayment of principal in the earlier years of the loan, but to very much increase it in the later years, and in the end to impose a much larger sum for interest. In the year 1891 a calculation was made, from which it appeared that, on the sums then owing to the Public Works Loan Commissioners, the additional interest would in this way amount to no less than £450,000. It will be seen at once that the second method is the sounder financially, and it is that upon which loans have always been obtained from the Metropolitan Board of Works and London County Council.

In the following table the loans from each of the three bodies are grouped according to the years in which they were borrowed, and the rates of interest charged. The average rate of interest has been 3½ per cent. in the case of the Public Works Loan Commissioners and 3¼ per cent. in the case of the Metropolitan Board of Works and London County Council:—

| 1 | Years in which borrowed. 2 | Rates of Interest. 3 | | | Amounts borrowed. 4 | |
|---|---|---|---|---|---|---|
| | | £ | s. | d. | £ | |
| Public Works Loan Commissioners ... | 1872-9 | 3 | 10 | 0 | 3,519,641 | |
| | 1880 | 4 | 0 | 0 | 50,828 | |
| | 1880-2 | 3 | 15 | 0 | 80,940 | |
| | 1899 | 3 | 0 | 0 | 42,395 | |
| | | | | | 3,693,804 | |
| | | | | | 17,200* | |
| | | | | | | 3,711,004 |
| Metropolitan Board of Works ... ... | 1872-3 | 3 | 17 | 6 | 90,000 | |
| | 1880-1 | 3 | 15 | 0 | 700,000 | |
| | 1881-9 | 3 | 10 | 0 | 3,456,752 | |
| | | | | | | 4,246,752 |
| London County Council ... ... | 1889 | 3 | 10 | 0 | 91,000 | |
| | 1889-91 | 3 | 2 | 6 | 550,000 | |
| | 1892-4 | 3 | 5 | 0 | 1,350,000 | |
| | 1894-5 | 3 | 2 | 6 | 350,000 | |
| | 1895 | 3 | 0 | 0 | 200,000 | |
| | 1895-8 | 2 | 13 | 0 | 1,500,000 | |
| | 1898-9 | 2 | 17 | 6 | 650,000 | |
| | 1899 | 3 | 1 | 6 | 200,000 | |
| | 1900-3 | 3 | 7 | 6 | 1,900,000 | |
| | | | | | | 6,791,000 |
| | | | | | | £14,748,756 |

* Loans taken over from the Hornsey School Board.

The periods for which the loans have been borrowed are as follow :—

| Period of loan. | Public Works Loan Commissioners. | Metropolitan Board of Works. | London County Council. | Total. |
|---|---|---|---|---|
| 1 | 2 | 3 | 4 | 5 |
| Years. | £ | £ | £ | £ |
| 50 | 3,364,060 | 3,874,200 | 4,706,783 | 11,945,043 |
| 49 | 55,000 | 350,000 | ... | 405,000 |
| 48 | 9,542 | ... | ... | 9,542 |
| 47 | 15,307 | ... | ... | 15,307 |
| 46 | 11,000 | ... | ... | 11,000 |
| 40 | 50,828 | ... | 1,593,124 | 1,643,952 |
| 30 | 170,827 | 22,552 | 442 380 | 635,759 |
| 20 | 1,450 | ... | 27,242 | 28,692 |
| 10 | 15,790 | ... | 21,471 | 37,261 |
| | 17,200° | ... | ... | 17,200 |
| | 3,711,004 | 4,246,752 | 6,791,000 | 14,748,756 |

° Loans taken over from the Hornsey School Board.

Loans for periods of over 40 years comprise nearly 12½ millions of the total amount borrowed. By Section 10 of the Elementary Education Act, 1873,[1] the Board were empowered, with the consent of the Education Department, to spread the repayment of borrowed money over a period of not exceeding 50 years. Up to 1900 the practice of the Board was to borrow for the maximum period, but in that year they decided to reduce the term for future loans to 40 years, the object being to lessen the expenditure for interest. Money was also borrowed for periods of 49, 48, 47 and 46 years; but these loans were for works connected with, or supplementing, building operations for which 50 years' loans had already been obtained, and the Education Department stipulated in each case that the period of the supplemental loan should be shortened to the necessary extent (varying from one to four years), so that both loans might be finally extinguished on the same date. About two-thirds of the 30 years' loans were for small additions and structural alterations to schools, and drainage, tar pavement, &c., for which the Education Department would not allow a longer period; the remainder were on account of Industrial schools, the rule of the Home Office being to allow only 30 years' loans for these schools. The 20 and 10 years cases were chiefly for inconsiderable improvements or other works of a less permanent character than those already mentioned, and for contributions made by the Board in aid of the repair or improvement of Industrial schools not belonging to them, but to which they send children for whom there is not accommodation in their own Industrial schools.

Apart from a small loan taken over from the Hornsey School Board which was repaid in 1901, the first year in which the repayment of a loan will be completed will be 1907, and this repayment of loans will go on in succeeding years until the year 1949, when all the loans will have been extinguished. The following table shows the years in which

[1] 36 and 37 Vict., c 86.

the final repayments will be made and the amounts of the loans thus completed in each year :—

| Years in which loans will be extinguished. 1 | Public Works Loan Commissioners. 2 | Metropolitan Board of Works. 3 | London County Council. 4 | Total. 5 |
|---|---|---|---|---|
| | £ | £ | £ | £ |
| 1901 | 29° | ... | ... | 29 |
| 1907 | ... | ... | 12,916 | 12,916 |
| 1908 | 30,000 | ... | ... | 30,000 |
| 1909 | 50,522 | ... | ... | 50,522 |
| 1910 | 15,050 | ... | ... | 15,050 |
| 1911 | 40,390 | ... | 8,555 | 48,945 |
| 1912 | 25,500 | ... | ... | 25,500 |
| 1914 | 190° | ... | ... | 190 |
| 1917 | ... | ... | 8,080 | 8,080 |
| 1918 | ... | 22,552 | ... | 22,552 |
| 1919 | { 1,450 3,100° | ... ... | ... | } 4,550 |
| 1920 | { 50,828 2,730° | ... ... | ... | } 53,558 |
| 1921 | ... | ... | 7,144 | 7,144 |
| 1922 | 60,458 | 40,000 | ... | 100,458 |
| 1923 | 605,542 | 50,000 | 12,018 | 667,560 |
| 1924 | 387,700 | ... | ... | 387,700 |
| 1925 | 679,385 | ... | ... | 679,385 |
| 1926 | { 538,702 11,151° | ... ... | ... ... | } 549,853 |
| 1927 | 520,242 | ... | 42,447 | 562,689 |
| 1928 | 433,000 | ... | 50,830 | 483,330 |
| 1929 | 255,035 | 250,000 | 71,761 | 576,796 |
| 1930 | ... | 250,000 | 74,294 | 324,294 |
| 1931 | ... | 400,000 | 100,733 | 500,733 |
| 1932 | ... | 400,000 | 37,755 | 437,755 |
| 1933 | ... | 500,000 | 66,377 | 566,377 |
| 1934 | ... | 850,000 | ... | 850,000 |
| 1935 | ... | 600,000 | ... | 600,000 |
| 1936 | ... | 459,200 | ... | 459,200 |
| 1937 | ... | 200,000 | ... | 200,000 |
| 1938 | ... | 225,000 | ... | 225,000 |
| 1939 | ... | ... | 491,000 | 491,000 |
| 1940 | ... | ... | 675,706 | 675,706 |
| 1941 | ... | ... | 783,568 | 783,568 |
| 1942 | ... | ... | 762,245 | 762,245 |
| 1943 | ... | ... | 621,605 | 621,605 |
| 1944 | ... | ... | 600,000 | 600,000 |
| 1945 | ... | ... | 600,000 | 600,000 |
| 1946 | ... | ... | 450,000 | 450,000 |
| 1947 | ... | ... | 586,557 | 586,557 |
| 1948 | ... | ... | 449,670 | 449,670 |
| 1949 | ... | ... | 278,239 | 278,239 |
| | 3,711,004 | 4,246,752 | 6,791,000 | 14,748,756 |

\* Various loans (£17,200 in all) taken over from the Hornsey School Board.

The question whether it is better to pay for land and buildings at once, or to borrow the money and spread the repayment over a term of years, has been so long settled that it appears useless to re-open it. But it may be interesting to point out that whereas up to March 25th, 1903, the Board had expended £14,567,256 out of Loan Account, out of Maintenance Account they had paid £6,396,972 for interest on loans and repaid principal to the amount of £3,695,956, making a total of £10,092,928. So that, of the total loans of £14,748,756, the amount of £10,871,300 was still owing, although the Board's payments for interest and principal had reached the sum of £10,092,928. If the Board had from the first met their liabilities for land and buildings at once, the effect would have been to increase the School Board rate during the first fifteen years by an average of about threepence in the £, but in course of time the rate would have gradually been reduced, and at the present moment it would have been less than it is by about a halfpenny in the £. In 1902-3 the amount paid for interest and principal was equal to about 4d. in the £, whereas about 3½d. in the £ would have met the expenditure on land and new buildings and alterations in that year. These facts illustrate the financial effect of relying on the power of borrowing, even at low rates of interest.

### III.—THE FINANCES AS A WHOLE.

It may be convenient to give here a brief *résumé* of the principal figures which have been treated above in greater detail.

#### 1. EXPENDITURE.

| | |
|---|---:|
| The expenditure on Maintenance Account, that is on everything except land and buildings, since 1871, has been ... ... .. | £48,433,480 |
| The expenditure on Loan Account, on land and buildings, has been | 14,567,256 |
| Making together a total expenditure of ... ... ... ... | £63,000,736 |
| From this total expenditure, however, must be deducted the amount paid off the loans, as it is included twice therein, once in the Maintenance Account (as repayment of loans) and again in the Loan Account (as expenditure on land and buildings) ... | 3,695,956 |
| Showing that the actual expenditure on both Accounts since 1871, has been ... ... ... ... ... ... ... ... | £59,304,780 |

As regards the Maintenance Account expenditure, the Board have paid their way year by year; that is to say, the expenditure has been met out of money in hand. As to the expenditure on land and buildings, which has been met out of Loans amounting to 14½ millions (of which about 3½ have been paid off), the Board have a valuable asset in the freehold land they have acquired and the schools and offices they have erected, the schools and other buildings numbering in all close upon 500; and, although the buildings will deteriorate in course of time, the land is a permanent asset, the value of which, judging from past experience, may be expected to increase rather than diminish.

## 2. Receipts.

| | |
|---|---|
| The Government grants and other Maintenance Account receipts, except the Precepts, since 1871, have amounted to ... ... | £13,426,870 |
| The Precepts, or money collected from the Rating Authorities to make up the difference between the expenditure and receipts, have amounted to ... ... ... ... ... ... ... | £35,105,979 |
| Making together a total receipt in connection with the Maintenance Account of ... ... ... ... ... ... ... ... | 48,532,849 |
| The amount borrowed for Loan Account purposes since 1871 has been ... ... ... ... ... ... ... ... | 14,748,756 |
| And the total receipt on both Accounts has therefore been ... | £61,590,029 |

If the balance in hand on Maintenance Account at March 25th, 1903, which was £99,369, together with the £181,500 in hand on Loan Account at the same date, be deducted from the total receipt of £63,281,605, the remainder will be £63,000,736, which is shown on page 351 as the total expenditure since 1871.

## 3. The Day School Finances.

The prime duty of the Board, the chief work for which it was brought into existence, was the elementary education of the children in the Day schools, and it has naturally absorbed the greater part, actually about two-thirds, of the expenditure upon Maintenance Account. Commencing in 1874-5, the first normal year in the work of the Board, this greater part—i.e. the expenditure for the maintenance of Day schools, has amounted to £32,955,086, whilst the expenditure on the Maintenance Account as a whole has been £48,217,903. The difference of £15,262,817 has been expended on other objects than the ordinary Day schools—e.g. the repayment of, and interest on, Loans (the largest item), Industrial schools, Evening Continuation schools, &c. It is clear, therefore, that the only Maintenance Account expenditure which has a definite relationship to the average attendance of the children in the Day schools, and can be properly compared with it, is the expenditure for these children, in other words, for the maintenance of the Day schools.

The average attendance in the Day schools has increased year after year, without a single break, during the whole period of the Board's administration, until, in 1902-03, it reached nearly half-a-million; and the expenditure for carrying on the schools (the maintenance of Day schools) has naturally risen also, but its rise has been greater than that of the average attendance, because the expenditure per child has gradually increased. The expenditure from Loan Account for providing the schools has not increased in a similar manner. In 1874-5 the Board commenced building at its maximum strength, and, except for a period of five years in about the middle of its career, it has maintained virtually the same rate of building until 1902-03, with the result that the expenditure has remained at much the same level throughout. It must be pointed out, however, that during the last five years the Loan Account expenditure on Day schools has been swollen to the extent of about £450,000 in all for overhauling the drainage systems of many of the earlier schools and improving their structural arrangements, so as to bring them up to the modern standard of requirement in these respects.

These three matters—the average attendance, the cost of maintaining the Day schools, and the cost of erecting them—have been the largest and most important factors in the Board's finances. In the following table the attendance and the expenditure are shown side by side for each year since 1874-75 (the first normal year), and these statistics are illustrated by a diagram in which they may be compared and followed more readily than by the bare enumeration of the figures.

| Year ended 25th March. | DAY SCHOOLS. | | |
| | No. of Children in average Attendance. | Cost of Maintaining and carrying on the Schools. | Cost of providing the Schools (Land and Buildings). |
| 1 | 2 | 3 | 4 |
| | | £ | £ |
| 1875 | 68,250 | 163,920 | 506,858 |
| 1876 | 92,201 | 240,504 | 527,910 |
| 1877 | 113,642 | 252,928 | 659,976 |
| 1878 | 144,132 | 391,723 | 424,084 |
| 1879 | 163,763 | 474,650 | 371,960 |
| 1880 | 184,745 | 561,694 | 433,062 |
| 1881 | 198,395 | 571,123 | 395,421 |
| 1882 | 219,459 | 623,978 | 454,787 |
| 1883 | 240,008 | 704,476 | 424,752 |
| 1884 | 268,784 | 723,471 | 559,433 |
| 1885 | 279,304 | 914,390 | 663,995 |
| 1886 | 294,764 | 984,953 | 611,077 |
| 1887 | 319,848 | 1,016,525 | 458,588 |
| 1888 | 328,405 | 1,060,068 | 234,763 |
| 1889 | 342,321 | 1,090,785 | 196,064 |
| 1890 | 345,746 | 1,187,942 | 173,654 |
| 1891 | 347,857 | 1,265,454 | 238,763 |
| 1892 | 362,585 | 1,288,655 | 349,607 |
| 1893 | 379,445 | 1,361,486 | 432,229 |
| 1894 | 390,812 | 1,417,056 | 448,316 |
| 1895 | 400,912 | 1,501,889 | 491,043 |
| 1896 | 416,367 | 1,630,428 | 525,301 |
| 1897 | 422,691 | 1,665,189 | 535,036 |
| 1898 | 430,737 | 1,733,072 | 487,203 |
| 1899 | 439,684 | 1,829,614 | 505,793 |
| 1900 | 441,315 | 1,920,531 | 580,207 |
| 1901 | 446,866 | 2,010,514 | 552,653 |
| 1902 | 462,840 | 2,117,446 | 602,538 |
| 1903 | 475,150 | 2,204,437 | 551,273 |

In the following diagram the progress of the attendance and of the two classes of expenditure is exhibited by three lines, and it will be seen that the line of expenditure for maintaining and carrying on the schools rises more rapidly than that of the average

z

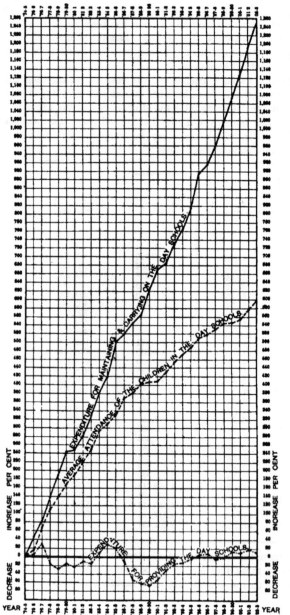

attendance, for the reason that, as already mentioned, the cost per child gradually increased. The divergence between the two lines is the measure of this increase. The line of expenditure for providing the schools, for land and buildings, has, on the other hand, no continuous rise or fall, and this accords with the observations already made in regard to the virtual uniformity of these disbursements throughout the whole period of the Board's existence.

## IV.—MISCELLANEOUS

There are certain other matters, five in number, which remain to be dealt with—namely (i.) Savings Banks in Board Schools; (ii.) the Store for school books, apparatus and stationery; (iii.) the Board's Insurance Fund; (iv.) the Assessment of the schools to local rates; and (v.) Superannuation. The first two matters have not yet been referred to; the last three were mentioned in dealing with the expenditure on Maintenance Account, but as there is much to be said with regard to them beyond what pertains to expenditure, it is desirable to treat them separately.

### 1. SAVINGS BANKS.

In the year 1887 the Board instructed the Finance Committee "to supervise and report upon the working of Penny Banks in Board Schools." The Committee thereupon made a careful inquiry as to what was being done in the schools for the encouragement of thrift, and it appeared that banks had been established in 129 of the then existing 1,075 departments. It was also found that there was a desire on the part of many of the teachers to facilitate the carrying out of any system of banks which the Board might see their way to introduce. Finally, in December, 1887, the Board decided that Penny Savings Banks should be established, wherever practicable, in the boys' and girls' departments of the schools, and they laid down a series of regulations for their conduct. These regulations, which received the approval of the Post Office authorities and of the National Debt Commissioners, provided that each scholar depositor should be furnished with a book in which the head teacher should enter the amounts of the deposits, which were to be made in cash, and that the teacher and another person (usually a Manager) should act as co-trustees and keep an ordinary account with the Post Office Savings Bank for the purpose of investing the deposits. The interest received on the trustees' account was to be apportioned amongst the scholars' accounts according to the amounts deposited. The Board also arranged to send officers to audit periodically the accounts of the banks, but at the same time it was clearly laid down that the Board were under no pecuniary liability in regard to the funds. The Managers of 24 of the 129 banks then in operation at once brought their banks under these regulations, the remainder continuing as before. In the year 1891 the number under the Board's regulations had increased to 56, and the abolition of school fees in that year appeared to have a favourable effect on the establishment of banks, for in 1892 the number reached 112, just double that of 1891.

In 1894 it was decided that whenever the balance in the hands of the two co-trustees of a bank reached the sum of £100, the Accountant of the Board should, for additional security, be appointed a third co-trustee. In 1899, a difficulty arose with regard to one of the banks which had not been brought under the Board's regulations. In this case the bank was carried on by the teachers of a school on their own responsibility, and the difficulty led to the Board deciding that all such banks should be at once placed under their regulations, thus providing, amongst other things, for the periodical examination of the accounts by officers of the Board. This decision did not affect all the banks outside the Board's regulations, but only those which were being managed solely by teachers. In the same year the Board also amended their regulations with a view to providing for the deposit of money by means of stamps as well as by cash, the latter having until then been the only system. The two systems, however, were not to be combined in one bank, for, although a bank might be conducted under either system, the one chosen was to be adhered to exclusively. This condition was laid down by the Post Office authorities, as they were apprehensive that confusion might arise in the accounts if the two systems were worked together.

In 1903, except for a few banks in schools in Southwark, managed entirely by the Women's University Settlement, all the banks in operation were under the Board's

z 2

regulations; those which were originally outside those regulations having gradually applied to come under them.

The following Table shows the increase year by year in the number of banks under the Board's system, and their financial progress:—

| Year. | No. of Banks. | No. of Depositors on Books. | Balance at beginning of Year. | Amount Deposited, including Interest, &c., during Year. | Amount Withdrawn during Year. | Balance at end of Year. |
|---|---|---|---|---|---|---|
| 1 | 2 | 3 | 4 | 5 | 6 | 7 |
| | | | £ s. d. | £ s d. | £ s. d. | £ s. d. |
| 1889 | 24 | 2,448 | — | 504 19 7 | 305 11 1 | 199 8 6 |
| 1890 | 38 | 4,856 | 199 8 6 | 1,560 3 2 | 1,329 10 6 | 430 1 2 |
| 1891 | 56 | 8,436 | 430 1 2 | 2,479 9 2¼ | 2,181 4 3½ | 728 6 0¾ |
| 1892 | 112 | 16,684 | 728 6 0¾ | 5,336 5 5¼ | 4,420 15 3¼ | 1,643 16 2¾ |
| 1893 | 129 | 19,953 | 1,643 16 2¾ | 7,112 19 7¼ | 6,527 13 6¾ | 2,229 2 3¼ |
| 1894 | 145 | 24,471 | 2,229 2 3¼ | 8,634 12 10¼ | 7,976 0 2½ | 2,887 14 11 |
| 1895 | 166 | 29,530 | 2,887 14 11 | 11,050 12 6 | 10,293 13 3¼ | 3,644 14 1¾ |
| 1896 | 187 | 33,572 | 3,644 14 1¾ | 14,024 6 9¾ | 13,300 0 3¾ | 4,369 0 7¾ |
| 1897 | 205 | 37,827 | 4,369 0 7¾ | 15,808 10 0½ | 14,923 6 6½ | 5,254 4 1¾ |
| 1898 | 231 | 41,879 | 5,254 4 1¾ | 17,600 3 9¼ | 16,692 14 6¾ | 6,161 13 4¼ |
| 1899 | 271 | 49,098 | 6,161 13 4¼ | 21,983 17 4½ | 20,907 13 5½ | 7,237 17 3¼ |
| 1900 | 319 | 56,981 | 7,237 17 3¼ | 26,063 1 1½ | 24,843 19 4½ | 8,456 19 0¼ |
| *1901 | 340 | 59,578 | 8,456 19 0¼ | 22,671 3 8¾ | 16,776 11 6¼ | 14,351 11 2¾ |
| 1902 | 376 | 65,744 | 14,351 11 2¾ | 30,697 12 8 | 29,344 19 4¾ | 15,704 4 6 |
| 1903 | 390 | 68,790 | 15,704 4 6 | 33,354 15 8½ | 32,920 18 2 | 16,138 2 0¼ |
| — | — | — | — | 218,882 13 6 | 202,744 11 6¼ | — |

* Nine months only. Up to and including 1900 the period is one year ending on December 31st; for 1901 it is the nine months ending on September 30th, 1901; and thereafter it is the year ending on September 30th.

The average number of depositors in each bank was 102 in the year 1889, and it had risen to 176 in 1903. The balance in hand at the end of the year (see column 7) increased from year to year without an exception during the whole period, and at September 30th, 1903, it amounted to over £16,000. In 1903 there were nearly 1,100 Senior departments in the schools, and the 390 banks in operation were therefore more than one-third of the possible number, seeing that there might be a bank in each department. Applications for the establishment of new banks are still being received, and it is anticipated that the number will rapidly increase during the next few years. The above figures point to a steadily growing interest in the work on the part of teachers and Managers, and this has been regarded by the Board with much satisfaction. With the teachers, as with the Managers, the work is entirely of a voluntary character and does not form part of their regular school duties. It is probable that in many cases the scholars save for temporary purposes only, such as clothing, holidays, entertainments, and the like, and even this is satisfactory as it denotes thrift, if only in a limited way; but it is reasonable to assume that a proportion of the money deposited represents savings which are intended to be permanent, or to be ultimately used for technical and other education after leaving the Elementary school.

## 2. Store for Books, Apparatus, and Stationery.

In the beginning of the year 1873 the Board entered into a contract with a firm for the supply of books, stationery, and small apparatus to their schools, the terms being that books should be supplied at a discount of 30 per cent. and all other articles at certain net prices which were agreed upon. In June, 1874, this arrangement was reconsidered, and the Board determined to establish a Store of their own. The grounds for this conclusion were—(1) that the system would be more economical, partly because the Board would be able to enter into direct negotiations with the various publishers and manufacturers, and so obtain the goods on better terms, and partly because they would escape the payment of profit to an intermediate agent; (2) that the goods would be supplied with greater expedition to the schools, being always in stock in the Store and ready for delivery; and (3) that the Board would be able more satisfactorily to check the quality of the goods.

A Store was accordingly established, and up to 1884 it was administered by a Sub-Committee under the control of the School Management Committee; the duties of the Sub-Committee including the choice or selection of the various kinds of articles to be used in the schools, as well as their purchase and supply to the schools; but in that year the work was transferred to a Standing Committee, known as the Store Committee. The duties of the Store Committee were subsequently limited to the purchase of goods and their supply to the schools, the remainder of the work being re-transferred to the School Management Committee. In the latter part of 1891, in connection with a general re-arrangment of Committees, the Board resolved that the duties hitherto carried out by the Store Committee should be transferred to the Finance Committee. The latter Committee subsequently appointed a Sub-Committee, known as the Store and Supply Sub-Committee, to whom they delegated most of the work, on the understanding that the Sub-Committee should report to the Committee every fortnight in regard to such matters as contracts, staff, &c. The administration of the Store has been continued under these conditions, without alteration, since the beginning of 1892.

Originally the business of the Store was carried on in an old building at the rear of the Head Offices of the Board, but in course of time it became apparent that this building was unsuitable and too small for the work, and in 1890 the Board determined to erect a new building. A site was ultimately acquired at Bowling Green-lane, Clerkenwell, and, after some delay, the new building was completed and the Store was transferred to it in 1896. A few years later, in 1901, the great increase in the quantity and variety of the goods supplied to the schools owing to the increase in the number of schools and to the development of various subjects of instruction and the introduction of new subjects, rendered it necessary to make some addition to the premises, and the Board secured the lease of an adjacent building. This has been used chiefly for storing and dealing with surplus and waste stock returned from the schools, thus leaving the main building free for the accommodation of new stock.

The work of the Store, so far as it can be gauged by the financial results, has practically doubled during the last ten years. In 1892-3 the stock in hand represented about £14,000, whilst in 1902-3 it had reached over £26,000; and in the latter year the total value of the goods issued to the schools was about £101,000, as compared with £53,000 in the former year. The expenditure for administering the store and carrying on the work nearly doubled also, having risen from £6,400 in 1892-3 to £12,500 in 1902-3. The two statements set out below show the figures for 1902-3 in detail. They afford some idea of the volume of the business transacted by the Store; but to appreciate more fully the work involved, it must be remembered that the variety of the goods is enormous, and that many kinds have to be supplied in large quantities. They range over the whole field of requirement for every subject taught by the Board, and the mere enumeration of these subjects would form a list of considerable length.

### COST OF THE GOODS, THEIR DISTRIBUTION, &c.

| | £ s. d. | £ s. d. | | £ s. d. | £ s. d. |
|---|---|---|---|---|---|
| Stock in hand March 25th, 1902 ... ... | | 23,554 17 6 | Goods supplied to Schools— Books, Apparatus and Stationery... | 83,886 7 4 | |
| Goods purchased ... | 98,335 10 0 | | School Libraries ... | 1,722 19 11 | |
| *Less* Discounts ... | 1,837 9 5 | | Needlework Materials | 5,397 10 8 | |
| | 96,498 0 7 | | „ Implements | 4,143 16 4 | |
| *Less* Waste Paper, &c., sold ... ... | 607 11 3 | | | | 95,150 14 3 |
| | | 95,890 9 4 | Clothing and Stores for Industrial Schools | ... ... | 414 12 1 |
| Stationery for Offices of the Board, &c. ... ... | | 3 145 7 9 | Clothing & Stores for Residential Schools.. | ... ... | 574 19 9 |
| | | 122,590 14 7 | Sundries—Goods supplied to Offices of the Board ... | 649 12 6 | |
| *Less* Stock in hand March 25th, 1903... ... ... | | 26,201 13 0 | Carriage of sundry parcels and forms | 338 9 9 | |
| | | 96 389 1 7 | Forms supplied to Sundry Schools in connection with Bye-laws Dept. ... | 329 9 8 | |
| *Balance*, being difference between the Cost of Goods and the Amount charged to the Schools ... ... | | 424 10 5 | Furniture Warehouse ... ... | 1 10 9 | |
| | | | Sundry Sales ... | 701 10 11 | |
| | | | | | 2,020 13 7 |
| | | | Stationery for Offices of the Board, &c. | ... ... | 3,145 7 9 |
| | | | | | 101,306 7 5 |
| | | | *Less* Old Books and Apparatus returned, and Waste Paper ... | 3,619 2 6 | |
| | | | Needlework, &c., returned ... | 873 12 11 | |
| | | | | | 4 492 15 5 |
| | | 96,813 12 0 | | | 96,813 12 0 |

COST OF ADMINISTRATION, &c.—1902-3.

|  | £ | £ | s. | d. |
|---|---|---|---|---|
| Office Stationery and Packing Materials ... ... | — | 360 | 19 | 1 |
| Carriage of Goods ... ... ... ... ... | 1,942 16 10 |  |  |  |
| *Less* Carriage of Sundry Parcels from and to Schools for the Offices of the Board ... ... ... | 338 9 9 |  |  |  |
|  |  | 1,604 | 7 | 1 |
| Cartage of Trade Refuse ... ... ... | — | 11 | 10 | 6 |
| Salaries and Wages ... ... ... ... ... | — | 9,342 | 2 | 0 |
| Rent, Rates and Taxes ... ... ... ... | — | 327 | 11 | 5 |
| Insurance ... ... ... ... ... | — | 85 | 17 | 6 |
| Repairs and Cleaning ... ... ... ... | — | 206 | 11 | 5 |
| Fuel, Light and Water ... ... ... ... | — | 278 | 3 | 5 |
| Printing, Advertising and Stationery ... ... ... | — | 76 | 6 | 5 |
| Postage ... ... ... ... ... | ... | 157 | 10 | 0 |
| Sundry Petty Cash Payments ... ... ... | — | 74 | 12 | 0 |
| Furniture ... ... ... ... ... ... | — | 22 | 13 | 3 |
|  |  | 12,548 | 4 | 1 |
| Interest on Average Capital employed (estimated at £5,000 at £3 per cent.) ... ... ... ... | — | 150 | 0 | 0 |
| Rent : Interest on half the amount borrowed for the premises of the Store ... ... ... ... | — | 882 | 0 | 0 |
|  |  | 13,580 | 4 | 1 |

### 3. INSURANCE FUND.

In 1873 the Board decided to insure their permanent school buildings, and all school buildings leased or hired for several years, in insurance offices to the extent of two-thirds of their value, and the furniture, books and apparatus, at the rate of 12s. for each child accommodated. This latter sum was under the average value of the furniture, &c , but it was considered necessary to allow a margin for deterioration. This arrangement was in force until 1878.

In 1878 the formation of the Board's Insurance Fund was commenced. From that year up to 1885 the furniture, &c., was insured in insurance offices, as before, at the rate of 12s. per head : but the school buildings were insured for only one-third of their value, and the difference between the premiums paid and those which would have been paid under the arrangement of 1873 was annually set aside to form the nucleus of an independent insurance fund.

In 1885, when the Fund amounted to a little over £5,000, the Board, in order to admit of larger sums being transferred to it, decided that no further insurances should be effected in insurance offices, except in cases where the Finance Committee considered it advisable to do so in consequence of some special risk arising from the character of the adjoining property, &c., and that a sum approximating to the amount which would have been paid for insurance—viz., 1s. 6d. per cent. on two-thirds of the value of the buildings, and on 12s. per head for the furniture, &c.—should be invested annually on account of the Insurance Fund.

In 1893, when the Fund amounted to about £30,000, the Board came to the conclusion that this sum, together with the interest of about £1,000 per annum derivable from it, would be sufficient to cover all normal risks, and they decided that after the year 1894 no further payments should be made into the Fund, except the interest accruing from it; further, that all cases of special risk should be insured in insurance offices as hitherto. All property not insured specially was thus to be automatically insured in the Board's Fund.

In 1895 the Board approved a scheme for the extension of the Fund so as to cover the risk of possible loss arising from the explosion of any of the numerous boilers in the schools in connection with heating apparatus, &c. At that time the Fund amounted to about £32,000, and it was arranged that annual amounts should be paid into it, in respect of the boilers, until the Fund, as combined for both fire and boiler explosion insurance, reached the sum of £40,000, including interest. The first annual payment into the fund on account of the boilers was made in 1897, and amounted to £282, being based on the rates usually charged by boiler insurance companies.

Up to 1896 none of the above arrangements applied to temporary or hired buildings, which were all insured in insurance offices; but in that year the Board decided that the iron buildings provided for serving as Temporary schools, Manual Training centres, &c., should be placed upon the Fund, and that, with a view to the additional risk, an annual payment should be made into the Fund in respect of the iron buildings equal to 4s. per cent. on two-thirds of the value of the buildings and of the furniture, &c.

In 1901 the Board again made a change in the scheme of the Fund. By this time it amounted to about £37,000, but only the interest, and comparatively small annual sums for the boilers and iron buildings, were being paid into it, and it was thought advisable to accelerate the rate of accretion and also to aim at securing a Fund of a larger amount than the £40,000 contemplated in 1895. The annual payments of 1s. 6d. per cent. on the buildings and their contents, which were discontinued in 1894, were accordingly revived, and were not to cease until the Fund had accumulated "to an amount exceeding eight years' payments calculated on the current values," after which, and so long as it exceeded the "eight years' payments," it was to be augmented only by the interest accruing from it.

At March 25th, 1903, the Fund amounted to about £53,500, with an annual income from investments of about £1,500. Approximately, the "current values" of the buildings and contents are now over 9½ millions, and the annual payment on this amount is about £7,250, and "eight years' payments" would be about £58,000.

There can be no doubt that the institution of this Fund has led to a great saving of money. It has been in existence for about twenty years, and it may safely be estimated that the average annual amount which would have been paid for ordinary insurance premiums during that period would have been at least £4,000, for at the present time it would exceed £7,000. Taking this low average of £4,000 a year for twenty years, the aggregate premiums would have amounted to £80,000; whereas, during the twenty years the payments out of the Fund in consequence of loss and damage by fire have amounted to only £4,750.

The head offices of the Board, the books and apparatus, the furniture stores, and the Board's Industrial schools and Residential schools have always been, and are still, insured in insurance offices, as they are considered to be special risks.

### 4. ASSESSMENTS TO LOCAL RATES.

The Board have suffered from the tendency of the local assessment authorities to impose excessive assessments on the schools, and they have taken every opportunity of objecting to these assessments, not only by appearing before Assessment Committees, but also on various occasions before the Assessment Sessions, and once in the Court of Queen's Bench. For some years the assessment authorities had no fixed principle in common for deciding the ratable values of the schools, and, as many assessments were, in the judgment of the Board, unreasonably high, in 1885, by which time the payments for rates had reached a large amount, they appealed to the Assessment Sessions in certain cases in the hope that some equitable basis of calculation might be laid down. Generally, the decision of the Court was that the Board were to be considered "hypothetical tenants"; that the cost of the land and buildings was to be taken into account, and that $3\frac{1}{2}$ per cent. on the former and $4\frac{1}{2}$ per cent. on the latter were fair percentages for ascertaining the "ratable value." It was held that these percentages approximated to the interest, or return on his outlay, which an individual might obtain in the market by way of rent for the schools; but the inclusion of the Board amongst the "hypothetical tenants" was hardly compatible with this theory. Any person, or any body other than the Board would find great difficulty in putting a Board School to profitable use, except, perhaps, on such low terms as to rent as would enable them to recoup themselves for a large outlay in adapting the building to their needs; and, therefore, if the schools were in the market, the Board would be able to hire them at low rents, probably much below the figures obtained by the above percentages. The schools, in fact, have been assessed at amounts equivalent to rents which only the Board, and no one else, would be willing to give, and the "higgling of the market," the usual test of value, has been ignored. The Board have since brought other cases before the Courts, without, however, being able to induce them to seriously re-open the question of the principle or basis of assessment; nevertheless, some of the assessments have been reduced, and these decisions have no doubt had a good effect on the various assessment authorities and have brought about savings in the Board's expenditure for rates which have considerably exceeded the cost of the appeals.

In 1885, the Board instructed their officers in the Accountant's Department who are entrusted with the rating and assessment work to claim in future that the basis of assessment should be 4 per cent. on the value of the land and 5 per cent. on the value of the buildings for the "gross value," which calculation produces a lower assessment than that of the 1885 decision, for, although the percentages are higher, the resulting "gross value" has to be reduced by one-sixth for the "ratable value." It will be observed that the percentages are on the "value" of the land and buildings, not the "cost" as hitherto. It had become clear to the Board that the "cost" basis was unjust to them in nearly all cases, and often led, indeed, to absurd results. In acquiring land, they must purchase any properties standing upon it, and buy out leasehold, trade, and other interests, and the outlay may thus be far beyond the value as vacant land. These buildings and interests are all destroyed to make way for the school, but under the "cost" principle they were taken into account in the assessment as though they were in existence, and the Board were paying rates on them as well as on the school which had taken their place. A similar injustice was suffered in connection with the buildings. The Board's published accounts show a total expenditure on each building, and this amount was invariably taken as the "cost." But in the course of years much work is necessarily done to a building which is in the nature of replacement, and where enlargements or additions are made a portion of the existing building has frequently to be pulled down and rebuilt; and, all this expenditure being included in the accounts, the total is ultimately swollen by such items to an amount out of all proportion to the actual value of the building. A careful investigation was accordingly made in the Accountant's Department into the expenditure on each building, and all which did not add to the value was eliminated. All the assessment authorities were induced to adopt this principle, and at a conference, convened by the London County Council, which was held in 1899, they formally affirmed it.

The Board were represented at this conference, and they submitted a statement of their views on the assessment of public buildings in general and Board Schools in particular. They showed that the percentages which might properly be employed for assessing private properties were excessive when applied to public properties, and, from a careful consideration of all the circumstances connected with the latter, they argued that their "ratable value" would be fairly and adequately represented by 3 per cent. on the value of the land and buildings. This percentage was based to some extent on the fact that the Board borrowed money at about that rate for their land and buildings, and that the interest roughly represented rent. This 3 per cent. principle was subsequently brought before the Courts, but they declined to adopt it. The Board, however, still held the opinion that 3 per cent. was reasonable and fair, and they were confirmed in this view by a Return which was published by the London County Council, which, after showing the actual assessments of the properties held by public authorities in London, compared them with assessments estimated on the 3 per cent. basis. Amongst these properties, of course, were the Board Schools, but these had been separated, and the result brought into prominence the fact that of all the various classes of public buildings in London the Board Schools were the most highly rated. The aggregate "ratable value" of the public buildings other than Board Schools is £240,000, which, the Board were surprised to find, is considerably under 3 per cent. on capital value, for on that basis it would have to be increased to £280,000; on the other hand, the aggregate "ratable value" of the Board Schools is £360,000, whereas on the 3 per cent. basis it would be only £280,000, or about the same figure as the other properties. Shortly, the aggregate "ratable value" of the Board Schools has been fixed at £80,000 above the 3 per cent. basis, whilst that of other public properties is £40,000 below. For the public buildings other than Schools these assessments represent 2·64 per cent. on capital value, whilst for the Board Schools they are 3·90 per cent. These figures speak for themselves, and they justify the Board's contention that their Schools should not be assessed at higher rates than 3 per cent. on the value of the land and buildings for "ratable value."

## 5. SUPERANNUATION.

In 1886 the Board formulated a scheme of superannuation for all their servants, including teachers. The funds were to be provided by a deduction of 2 per cent. from salaries, and the superannuation allowances were to be on the Civil Service scale—*i.e.* one sixtieth of the final salary for each year of service up to a maximum of forty-sixtieths. The deductions were to be kept and invested as a distinct Fund, but this was not to affect the liability of the Board to make good the allowances. It was necessary for the Board to obtain powers from Parliament to give effect to the scheme, and in 1887 a Bill was introduced into the House of Commons; but owing to the pressure of public business, it did not reach a second reading. In March, 1888, the Board, in anticipation of Parliamentary powers, put the scheme into force, in the case of officers other than teachers absolutely, but only tentatively as regards the latter, as their 2 per cent. contributions were to be returned in 1893 if in the meantime Parliamentary sanction had not been obtained. In the course of the next five years fifty officers were superannuated on the "sixtieths" scale, but no teachers were superannuated because of the above arrangement. In the meantime a Bill was introduced into Parliament in each session up to 1891, and dropped in consequence of the state of public business, with the exception of the last, which was "read" a second time and committed to a Select Committee. Subsequently, the House of Commons instructed the Select Committee also "to consider the whole question of the superannuation of elementary school Teachers in England and Wales." No action was taken in that year, but the Select Committee was revived in the following year (1892) and unanimously recommended the establishment of a State-assisted scheme for teachers. Finally, on the motion of Sir Richard Temple, the Chairman of the Committee, the House affirmed that it was desirable that a State-assisted scheme of superannuation for elementary school teachers should be established at an early date. Another Bill, on somewhat different lines to those previously introduced, and limiting the Board's contributions to amounts equal to the deductions from salaries, was introduced into Parliament in 1892, and was read a second time, but finally dropped on the dissolution of Parliament. The next year, 1893, was that in which the teachers were to be repaid their contributions if Parliamentary powers had not been obtained. The Board, therefore, formulated a scheme which came into force on March 25th, 1893, and provided for refunding the contributions, with interest, of those teachers who desired to withdraw, and the continuance of the remainder in the Fund together with the officers: for the reduction of future superannuation allowances to such amounts as an Actuary certified the Fund would afford, and for the formation of a Superannuation Committee, consisting of representatives of the Board and of the members of the Fund, to assist the Board in the administration of the Fund, At this time the Fund amounted to nearly £105,000, with a membership of about 1 100 officers and 7,500 teachers. A large majority of the latter, about 5,800, withdrew from the Fund, and were repaid their contributions, with interest, amounting to over £60,000. Now that the Fund was to be self-supporting, the first business of the Superannuation Committee was to arrange for a valuation by an actuary. He advised that for the present the Fund could only afford to pay superannuation allowances at the rate of 13·4 per cent., or less than one-seventh, of the "sixtieths" scale ; and this rate was in force for three years.

The members of the Fund were not satisfied with the scheme of 1893, which carried with it the reduction of allowances from the "sixtieths" scale to less than one-seventh of that scale, and they desired that the Board should support the Local Authorities Officers' Superannuation Bill, which was being promoted by the Municipal Officers' Association. The object of that Bill was to extend the Poor Law Officers' Superannuation Act of 1896 which gives allowances on practically the "sixtieths" scale, to the officers of other local authorities, including School Boards, but not to the teaching staffs of the latter. In compliance with this desire, the Board, in 1897, petitioned Parliament in favour of the Bill, and also asked for an amendment whereby teachers under school boards would be brought under it ; but the Bill was dropped in consequence of the state of public business. The question of superannuation for Elementary school teachers, both in Board and Voluntary schools, was, however, in the course of being settled in another manner. Following on the affirmation by the House of Commons, in 1892, of the desirability of a Government scheme of superannuation for all Elementary school teachers, a committee of officials of the Treasury and the Education Department had been appointed by Government to draft the scheme, and finally, in 1898, Parliament passed the Act [1] under which all Elementary school teachers are now superannuated.

At the end of 1896 the Fund was again valued, and the Actuary reported that the assets had so far improved that the rate of superannuation allowance might be raised from 13·4 to 17·5 per cent.—*i.e.* to about one-sixth of the "sixtieths" scale. The higher rate was accordingly put into force, for existing allowances as well as new ones. Whilst this scheme of 1893 was in operation no further valuation was made, as it became evident, on the passing of the Teachers' Act in 1898, that the whole question of super-annuation would have to be reconsidered and placed on a different footing. Under that Act all future teachers were compelled to contribute to the Government Fund, and existing teachers were given the option of doing so or not. The Board at once decided to discontinue bringing new teachers under their own Fund, so as to obviate the hardship of having to pay to two Funds ; but the difficulty remained in regard to teachers already in the Board's Fund, most of whom had joined the Government Fund, and were anxious to withdraw from the former. The Board were convinced that the only reasonable

[1] 61 & 62 Vict., c. 57.

course was to repay the contributions of the majority who desired to withdraw (about 4,200 out of 4,400), and allow the minority to remain in the Fund; and they proposed to adopt this course. Legal action was then taken by a few teachers and others who objected to changes in the Fund, but ultimately all opposition was withdrawn, and the majority were repaid their contributions. In the meantime the Board had obtained the authority of Parliament for such repayment, and also for administering the balance of the Teachers' Fund (the original Fund having by this time been divided as between officers and teachers) for the benefit of those teachers, numbering about 200, who remained in it, this authority forming part of the Act of 1902 which is referred to in the next paragraph. The Board have now, therefore, ceased to have any concern with the Superannuation of their teachers, except this small remnant for whom the Teachers' Fund will be continued so long as there are any members in it.

When it was seen that the Government Fund would supersede the Board's Fund so far as the teachers were concerned, the question arose as to the position of the officers in the Fund. Hitherto it had been one Fund for all, but the new circumstances made it advisable to divide the Fund as between officers and teachers, so that each class might be treated in a manner suitable to it. At March 25th, 1900, the Fund was accordingly divided equitably between the two classes, the division being made by the actuary who valued the Fund in 1896. The Board had in the meantime decided to promote a Bill in Parliament for obtaining power to pay to the officers, out of the School Fund, annuities equal to the superannuation allowances payable from the Officers' Superannuation Fund; in fact, to double the allowances. This Bill was introduced into the House of Commons early in 1902, and it became law in June of the same year. The main purpose of the Act[1] was to reconstitute the Officers' Fund and to put it on a legal and permanent basis. Practically all the officers of the Board came under the Fund, and each had to contribute to it to the extent of 2 per cent. of his salary or wages. The Fund was administered by the Board through a Committee consisting of four representatives appointed by the Board and four elected by the Officers, the expenses of administration being borne by the School Fund. Speaking generally, an officer is entitled to retire from the service and claim his Superannuation allowance after reaching the age of sixty years, and the Board may require him to retire on reaching sixty-five years. He is also entitled to an allowance before sixty years of age in the event of his being disabled by permanent infirmity of mind or body. The full scale of allowance is one-sixtieth of the final salary for each year of service (not less than 10 years, however, nor more than 40, being taken into account) but this is only laid down as a maximum which is not to be exceeded, the actual rate being limited to such proportion of the full scale as the Fund will afford, as ascertained every three years by an actuary. The first actuarial investigation was made at December 31st, 1902, when the rate was fixed at 21 per cent., or a little over one-fifth, of the full scale, and this rate will be in force for three years, at the end of which period the Fund will be again valued with a view to

---

[1] 2 Edw. 7, c. 36.

fixing the rate for the subsequent three years. This is the allowance from the Superannuation Fund; but the Board were empowered by the Act to contribute in every case an equal allowance from the School Fund, subject to the proviso that if at any time the Superannuation Fund should be found to afford more than one-half of the full scale, the Board's allowance must then be only of such amount as might be necessary to bring the combined allowances up to the full scale. The present rate of allowance from the Superannuation Fund being 21 per cent. of the full scale, it follows that even with the Board's equal contribution the combined allowances amount to only 42 per cent., or considerably less than one-half, of that scale. It is hoped that the Fund will in time give better results than this when the senior officers pass out of it, who receive a superannuation allowance calculated on their whole service, though during that part which preceded 1888 they paid no contribution to the Fund.

The following statements show the financial progress of the Officers' Fund and the Teachers' Fund since March 25th, 1900, when the two Funds were formed by the division of the original Fund; and further particulars are given with reference to the annuitants on, and membership of each Fund :—

OFFICERS' FUND, MARCH 26TH, 1900—MARCH 25TH, 1903.

| | £ s. d. | £ s. d. | | | £ s d |
|---|---|---|---|---|---|
| Amount allocated to Fund at Division on March 25th, 1900 ... | 39,179 4 0 | | Superannuation allowances ... | | 3,651 18 1 |
| | | | Sundry expenses ... ... | | 262 8 6 |
| Less depreciation in value of investments ... ... | 4,180 17 5 | | Balance at March 25th, 1903 ... | | 47,401 13 1 |
| | | 34,998 6 7 | | | |
| Two per cent. deductions from salaries ... ... ... | 12,271 8 0 | | | | |
| Dividends and interest ... | 3,805 2 0 | | | | |
| Contributions by Board under Act | 241 3 1 | | | | |
| | | £51,315 19 8 | | | £51,315 19 8 |

.At March 25th, 1903, eighteen of the officers superannuated before March 25th, 1893, on the full "sixtieths" scale, were still receiving allowances, amounting to £604 18s. 6d. per annum, and 70 of those superannuated since the latter date, on the reduced scale, were receiving allowances amounting to £604 12s. 8d. per annum, being a total of 88 officers receiving allowances amounting to £1,209 11s. 2d. per annum.

At December 31st, 1902, when the first triennial valuation of the Fund was made in accordance with the provisions of the Board's Superannuation Act, there were 2,168 contributors to the Fund, of whom 1,755 were males (with an average age of 40 years) and 413 were females (with an average age of a little over 33 years).

TEACHERS' FUND, MARCH 26TH, 1900—MARCH 25TH, 1903.

| | £ | s. | d. | £ | s. | d. | | | £ | s. | d. |
|---|---|---|---|---|---|---|---|---|---|---|---|
| Amount allocated to Fund at Division on March 25th, 1900 | 108,881 | 8 | 6 | | | | Deductions returned to contributors | 87,493 | 11 | 9 |
| | | | | | | | Superannuation allowances... ... | 2,897 | 5 | 7 |
| | | | | | | | Sundry expenses ... ... ... | 930 | 0 | 3 |
| Less depreciation in value of investments ... ... | 11,783 | 6 | 4 | | | | Balance at March 25th, 1903 ... | 34,385 | 16 | 4 |
| | | | | 97,098 | 2 | 2 | | | | |
| Two per cent. deductions from salaries ... ... ... ... | | | | 20,261 | 17 | 1 | | | | |
| Dividends and interest ... ... | | | | 8,346 | 14 | 8 | | | | |
| | | | | £125,706 | 13 | 11 | | £125,706 | 13 | 11 |

At March 25th, 1903, eighty-four of the teachers superannuated since March 25th, 1893, on the reduced scale, were receiving allowances amounting to £1,267 14s. per annum.

At September 29th, 1902, when the first valuation of the Fund was made, there were 188 contributors, of whom 71 were males (with an average age of 56 years) and 117 were females (with an average age of 53 years).

# INDEX